THE LIFE OF
PETER TOSH
STEPPIN' RAZOR

THE LIFE OF
PETER TOSH
STEPPIN' RAZOR

JOHN MASOURI

OMNIBUS PRESS

London / New York / Paris / Sydney / Copenhagen / Berlin / Madrid / Tokyo

Exclusive Distributors
Music Sales Limited,
14/15 Berners Street,
London, W1T 3LJ.

Music Sales Corporation
180 Madison Avenue, 24th Floor,
New York,
NY 10016,
USA.

Macmillan Distribution Services,
56 Parkwest Drive
Derrimut, Vic 3030,
Australia.

Every effort has been made to trace the copyright holders of the photographs in this book but one or
two were unreachable. We would be grateful if the photographers concerned would contact us.

Typeset by Phoenix Photosetting, Chatham, Kent
Printed in the EU

A catalogue record for this book is available from the British Library.

Visit Omnibus Press on the web at www.omnibuspress.com

CONTENTS

Foreword by Roger Steffens

It's late August 1981 in sizzling Los Angeles. Peter Tosh is in the smoky upstairs dressing room of the Roxy on Sunset Boulevard, between shows. The small room is crowded wall-to-wall with his band and backup singers and a few fans, myself included. He is in a disputatious mood, engaged in a fierce monologue concerning Haile Selassie's famous address to the League of Nations in June of 1936. For some reason, he has chosen me, the only white person in the room, to deliver his "livatribe" to.

"Dem never tell the true history of what took place," he insisted. "When HIM come to speak, dem try to keep His Majesty out of the hall, lock up all the doors. Then suddenly – Poof! – Selassie I appear before them and alla dem bloodclaat diplo-fuckin-mats pull out their guns and fire at him and all the bullets bounce off him until all their guns empty. Then one by one His Majesty fix them with his stare and they drop dead when they meet his eyes. Every one of them bloodclaat – DEAD!!"

As some cautious laughter began to stir the shocked listeners, Tosh jammed a forefinger deeply into my chest, almost into my shoulder blades, roaring, "This a no joke business I man a-tell you. This is HISTORY!"

Daring to speak, albeit in a soft non-confrontational tone, I said, "Well, Peter, it seems to me that after a couple of days don't you think they would have been missed by the other members of their delegations and word would have leaked out somehow. I've never seen reports of dead bodies carried out of the League of Nations."

"This is the truth, it really happen!" he insisted. You can't dispute that!"

Feeling retreat to be the only appropriate response in light of such venomous heat, I held my thoughts as he turned to other vexatious thoughts, leaving me to wonder about his sanity. His set thereafter was a thunder-rebel display of political engagement and righteous indignation, featuring compositions of his like 'The Poor Man Feel It', 'I'm the Toughest', 'Legalize I', his ganja anthem that was banned forever from airplay in Jamaica, and, inevitably, 'Get Up Stand Up', co-authored with his former partner Bob Marley, which brought the enraptured crowd to their feet, screaming for more.

By this time, he had become known throughout much of the world through his connection as the first artist signed by the Rolling Stones for their own record label. However, relations with the Stones had deteriorated at that point, and he was convinced there was a conspiracy to keep reggae, and his music in particular, off the American airwaves. His reputation as the successor to Bob Marley, who had died three months earlier, was clear to most critics, although Tosh, unbidden, gratuitously denied that he was the new King of Reggae. "There's nothing new about me!" he harrumphed.

In a life bedeviled by injuries, beatings and harsh criticisms, there were also moments of tremendous triumph and high praise. A fierce critic of what he called the Babylonian Shit-stem, he would ironically, 25 years after his passing, be awarded that system's highest honor, Jamaica's Order of Merit. He aroused controversy wherever he travelled, and bowed to no man. In many parts of Africa today he is held in higher esteem than Bob Marley. But the details of his life have never been researched with such depth, nor any biography of his extraordinary life made, until John Masouri's groundbreaking work herein. It is, unquestionably, the most anticipated book in the reggae world, about a unique life that has resisted the best efforts of many other writers to essay it.

A longtime observer, particularly of the British reggae scene, the amiable Masouri has already written what I feel is the very best book (of over 400 already published) on the Wailers' music, *Wailing Blues: the Story of Bob Marley's Wailers*, which is essentially the history of the band's rhythm section, Carlton and Aston "Family Man" Barrett. With that major work, ten years in the making, under his belt, he was primed to take on the first in-depth look at the inflammable Bush Doctor himself, Peter Tosh.

The process has taken four years of devotion to Tosh's slippery history. In *Steppin' Razor – The Life Of Peter Tosh* he has had to sift through mounds of contradictory theories, rumours, myths and legends. We learn previously unknown details of Peter's relationship to Rita Anderson in the months before she became Marley's wife. The gates to Coxsone Dodd's essential Studio One are opened, and we discover the process that groomed the group for a successful career. When Marley left for most of 1966 to join his mother in America, Tosh began to truly come into his own with a series of singles featuring his own compositions that proved, to him, that "no Wailer is indispensible". He would make the Wailers' first Selassie-oriented record, 'Rasta Shook Them Up', following Selassie's tumultuous visit to the island in April of 1966.

Details of his gradual radicalism include a wild tale of Tosh's stealing a bus and driving it through the showroom window of a big downtown store, during the Walter Rodney riots. He leaped from the bus to help loot it to the ground, among the first of his many encounters with Jamaica's vicious police and army forces. His actions were proof positive that he didn't just talk the talk, but walked, and suffered the consequences thereof, the walk.

A surprise comes from John's revelation of Peter's description of why he shortened his slave-master name of McIntosh, which I won't spoil here. It is a delightful and important indication of his masterful deconstruction of language, with which he would rail against "the Crime Minister who shit in the House of Represent-a-t'ief" and his manager whom he called his "damager". Even the Queen of England was an object of his wrathful humour, dubbed "Queen 'Ere-lies-a-bitch".

Among the important first-hand accounts of living and working with Peter is that of guitarist Al Anderson, the talented New Jersey native who joined Marley for his debut solo set, *Natty Dread*, then left to become part of Tosh's first touring band, led by Sly and Robbie. Anderson reveals Peter's generosity to his band mates as opposed to Marley's parsimony. Apparent to him was Tosh's interest in otherworldly affairs, as revealed in his 1976 single, 'Vampire'. Tosh was convinced of the existence of "duppies" – ghosts and vindictive evil spirits. Masouri reveals the derivation of the term, another intimate detail that makes this book so rich. Eventually, these beliefs, coupled with vivid hallucinations, would infect his sanity, and the author does not shy away from confronting these unpleasant facts of Peter's gradual disintegration.

Later, he judiciously unravels the various theories for the shooting that left four wounded and three dead, including the Bush Doctor himself. In a riveting minute-by-minute account, Masouri reconstructs the event and its aftermath, outlining all the rumours and weighing their veracity. He is unflinching in his conclusions. His masterwork then ends with an affirmative appraisal of Tosh's ongoing legacy and the value of his achievements, solidifying, at last, Winston Hubert McIntosh's place in the pantheon.

Roger Steffens, 2012

PART I

RASTA SHOOK THEM UP

Chapter 1

Didn't It Rain

"I didn't start playing the blues, ever," T. Bone Walker once said. "That was in me before I was born, and I been playing and living the blues ever since. That's the way you got to play them."

When Peter Tosh lived in Westmoreland, back in the fifties, the parish had a tough reputation. In 1938, sugar workers set fire to fields and refused to work until they got better pay and conditions. News of their anger and frustration spread like wildfire, triggering island-wide strikes. Union leader Alexander Bustamante emerged as a people's hero, was jailed for his beliefs and then formed the Jamaica Labour Party in 1943. Jamaica's first elections took place a year later, shortly before Peter was born. The Labour Party duly won by a landslide – Bustamante having outflanked his cousin Norman Manley, who headed the rival People's National Party, or PNP.

Within just 20 years, Jamaicans will have voting rights and a new constitution, as well as independence from Britain. The politicians played their part except two of the country's most valuable exports – reggae music and Rastafari – won't have originated with them, but with the same, poor black underclass that had forced change in the first place. Their struggle will provide a central narrative of Peter Tosh's music once he's found his own voice and freed himself of a religious upbringing that had its roots in colonialism, as well as Christian tradition.

Retracing his steps entails a trip to Savanna La Mar, just 20 miles from Negril. Unlike its more fashionable neighbour, "Sav La Mar" has less obvious charms. The *Rough Guide* describes how "a profusion of low-lying concrete keeps the air still, making it hot and uncomfortable" and it's true. Whereas Kingston is vibrant, Savanna La Mar has an air of weariness. Remnants of colonial grandeur are silent witnesses to wealthier and more influential times, at least for some. Norman Square, on the corner of Great George Street and Rose Street, represents the final flowering of the planter class, as does the Court House with its ornate pillars. Next to it is the Cast Iron Fountain, imprisoned in an octagonal, gilded cage flanked by arches, each bearing a carved pelican. A brace of accompanying signs warn users to 'keep the pavements dry', although it's difficult to imagine the stuttering trickle of tepid water causing much of a disturbance.

The main thoroughfare is Great George Street, which stretches from the northern outskirts of the town, all the way down to the quayside. That's where you'll find the Westmoreland Parish Church – an imposing building with stained-glass windows and a fountain out front. Traditionally, its congregation would be drawn from the town's middle classes; women wearing starched petticoats and intricate lace, squired by local worthies in British style dress, despite the baking heat. American and Japanese cars and trucks have now taken the place of mules and carts but Savanna La Mar still has weekly markets, where voices strain to be heard amidst the constant clamour. Traders with handcarts laden with farm produce still push their way through the crowds, bantering with bevies of women wearing gaily coloured headscarves. Those food shopping may find mangos, oranges, star apples, breadfruit, ackee, beans, peas, okra, cashews, cabbages, sweet potatoes, cassava or arrowroot, depending what's in season. Livestock cries out and tables groan under the weight of mullet, wahoo, snook, bull shark and the curiously named burro grunt; also tilapia, which they call St. Peter's fish.

Markets are the same the world over, and it's just the minor details that change. There's always the odd skirmish or commotion, and fifties Jamaica was no exception. Walk through the market place in Peter's time, and you'd see people struggling with barrels, sacks or bales of cloth. Middle-class women would buy ornaments made from cut glass or china, whilst others settled for a pair of "sand platters" – wooden sandals for walking on the beach. Today's stallholders sell gaudily coloured string vests and x-rated dancehall outfits; bootleg CDs, Rasta knitwear and the usual tourist stuff, most of which is imported. Their predecessors were more self-sufficient, and traded bags of coffee and cocoa for calico, shoes, crockery, pots, pans and spoons – items they couldn't grow at home or trade with a neighbour. In other respects, life has continued along the same slow-moving path. Women in headscarves carrying baskets still rest themselves on wooden benches, sharing gossip and comparing prices. Some carry bunches of daisies, chrysanthemums, hibiscus, lilies or Sweet Williams, the colours looking radiant against their brown and black skin. Once Baptists would have gathered on the street corner, preaching against smoking, dancing and drinking – pursuits cherished by those trying to shake off a week's worth of toil. The rum bars probably won't have changed much, except they would have had their share of World War II veterans in Tosh's day. Like their American counterparts, these men had lain their lives on the line for democracy, and yet met with the same old prejudices back home. Some chose to dull reality with over-proof rum, having repeat conversations with men either tired and spent, or maybe younger and blinded by ambition born of giddy half-truths. Their womenfolk might have had a "Chinese Bump" where the hair is softened with juice from a cactus, and then rolled on top of their heads and skewered with hairpins. Those were frugal times, and yet music from the jukebox flowed through their bodies as they whirled in faded dresses and bright smiles.

Their gaiety masked a local music scene in transition. The big bands had started to break up, and some of the more talented local musicians had already left for Britain or America. Others headed for the north coast where clubs and hotel bars reverberated to the sounds of Trinidadian calypso and Jamaican mento. Favourite artists included Count Lasher, Lord Fly, Count Sticky and Hubert Porter, whose 'Ten Penny Nail' kept Jamaican audiences smiling for months. This was the music Peter Tosh heard as he reached his teens – songs like Lord Composer's 'Hill & Gully Ride,' Harold Richardson's 'Healing In The Balm Yard,' Lord Messam's 'Linstead Market' and Monty Reynolds' 'This Long Time Gal A Never See You'. Lyrically, these songs often poked fun at people's everyday lives and some even wove political commentary into the mix, thereby laying the foundation for seventies roots music. It was music people could relate to, and gave the impression of being for *them*.

As an indication of calypso's popularity, Harry Belafonte, who spent part of his childhood in Jamaica, had the first million selling LP with a collection of calypso songs. This was in 1956, when Peter Tosh was 12 and dockside labourers really did load bananas onto ships in the cool of evening, singing as they worked. Belafonte tells of this in 'Day O (The Banana Boat Song)' and could have easily been describing Savanna La Mar back in the early fifties, when buses with no doors and wooden poles to support the roof would trundle down Great George Street, ferrying passengers from the centre of town to the quayside. Some 60 years later and two familiar landmarks are still visible from there: a rundown pier and the Old Fort, which was started in the eighteenth century but never finished. The outer wall has mostly fallen into the sea now, but people still swim in the harbour and go out to sea in fishing boats.

Typically candid, the *Rough Guide* dismisses Savanna La Mar as "rather soulless" and advises tourists to head five miles out of town to Petersfield, where a dazzling blue mineral pond lies like a castaway jewel among endless cane fields. It's a breathtakingly beautiful place even at twilight, when fruit bats stream from nearby caves and crickets strike up their evening chorus. Blue Hole Garden is another local beauty spot, where you'll find a deep, natural pool surrounded by gardens, waterfalls and sprays of white trumpet flowers.

Real-life pirate of the Caribbean Henry Morgan set sail for Panama not far from there, in 1670. He left from Bluefields, which is a few miles east of Savanna La Mar along the A2, a road that follows the coastline southwards and is framed first by green mountains and then sheer limestone cliffs as the landscape gives way to swamplands known as the Great Morass. The houses in Bluefields are scattered around a gently curved bay with white sand beaches and palm trees. Pelican Hole, an estuary haven for seabirds, isn't too far away and nor are the ruins of a Spanish settlement called Oristan, dating from the sixteenth century.

The next village is Belmont, where a hand-painted sign welcomes visitors to the Peter Tosh Memorial Garden – entrance fee US $5, or $300 Jamaican. Peter's mother, Alvera Coke (nee Morris), still lives in an adjoining house just yards from the busy highway, across from the ocean. Increasingly frail and elderly, she offers a courteous, if occasionally bemused, reception to the succession of foreigners who stop by. There's an unmistakable sadness in her eyes. Also, the surroundings are disappointing given that a projected museum/library remains unfinished, and the various CDs, T-shirts, posters and recordings on sale can't even begin to properly represent her son's achievements.

Peter's tomb is housed in a white, oblong building with a roof that juts over the front like the peak of a baseball cap. It has red, green and gold "V" shaped stripes on all sides, and neatly kept borders lined with white gravel chips. These same ribbon-like designs then reappear on the interior walls, where they criss-cross the tomb itself and meet either side of a mural facing the entrance. The lines "In Loving Memory Of Peter Tosh", framed by ganja leaves, form its centrepiece, and "Jah Is My Keeper" is painted above that in large, uneven letters, adorned by bolts of lightning. There's a cartoon-like image of him wearing wrap-around shades and smoking his pipe in one corner, and the words "Legalise It" emblazoned in the other. Inside, sunlight is refracted through arched stained-glass windows whose bold colours and naïve patterns give Peter's sepulchre the look of a child's bedroom, rather than the final resting place of Jamaica's most radical superstar. The place has been smartened up since 2001, when the Tosh estate was awarded a settlement (believed to be in the region of US $2 million) over rights to the name "Tuff Gong" – the label Peter had formed with Bob Marley and Bunny Livingston more than 40 years earlier. Everything's now more inviting than it was and happily, there's been no attempt to dilute Tosh's message during the facelift. "Legalize Marijuana" still stares boldly from a nearby fence, whilst another has a portrait of Peter wearing his trademark black beret, a spliff dangling insouciantly from his mouth.

Peter spent the formative years of his life in this sleepy corner of western Jamaica, which might appear like paradise to those who live and work in over-populated cities, but is still a backwater of sorts. The ocean twinkles invitingly, rivers and streams are plentiful and the surrounding countryside is undeniably lush and fertile. It's a land where immediacy and the sense of a dark, foreboding history exist side by side, as if superimposed upon one another in transparent layers. The sites of former plantations – Orchard Great House for example – nestle uneasily next to flimsy shacks housing the descendants of those left broken and bereft in the wake of slavery – people who'd been sold into servitude and robbed of everything that had defined who they were, whether family, land, language, traditions, religious beliefs or self-worth. It was the plantation owners, not their former slaves, who'd

7

been compensated after Emancipation. In the hundred or so years that followed many black people were forced to return to the plantations at starvation wages, this time as labourers and with no political rights. In the words of Rachel Manley, "Their freedom proved to be as much myth as reality." As a consequence, Jamaica inherited "a seemingly permanent underclass which lived in poverty and had no voice".

Peter's passport lists his birthplace as Church Lincoln, which is in the Grange Hill district, less than 10 miles inland from Savanna La Mar. There's a cluster of other hamlets nearby, including Mint, Top Lincoln and King's Valley. The Morris family were farmers, and led a hard but decent life based on Christian values. We can rest assured they regarded a good reputation as vital currency. In Church Lincoln, no scandal can go undetected for long as Alvera knew only too well. Her name is supposedly German by the way but its similarity to the Spanish "Elvira" is unmistakable. I'm told it means "foreign", but perhaps "unfortunate" would suit her better.

Most stories of unwanted pregnancy centre upon love-struck youngsters. This one differs in that Alvera was 26 when she gave birth. She'd met Peter's father, James McIntosh, whilst working in Saxham, just a mile or so away from where Lee "Scratch" Perry was born. Although in a different parish, Saxham is no appreciable distance from Grange Hill, and Alvera was there for only five months before returning home for the birth. She named her child Winston Hubert McIntosh. This may have been to appease her family, since she and McIntosh never married or set up home together. On Peter's birth certificate, Alvera's occupation is listed as "Labourer", whilst the space for his father's details is left blank. McIntosh did come to look for Alvera before she gave birth, but wouldn't see her again for another decade. He kept busy in the meantime though – the randy McIntosh would have 13 other children, and Peter never knew any of them.

"My father was a bad boy, a rascal," he told the authors of *Reggae Routes*. "That's what him do for a living. He just go around and have a million and one children! Me never come on the earth under no wedlock. Me is what them call illegitimate, that mean say me is a criminal, bomba rassclaat! That's why me go write a song called 'Illegitimate Children'. It took me years to find out I was one…"

He was born on October 19, 1944. According to astrologer Jill M. Phillips, "the intensity that characterises those born on October 19 marks them as unlike any other Libra. These broad-minded individuals find fulfilment through both the worldly and spiritual sides of their nature. They have strong, yet flexible opinions. They are curious about life, have a fierce love for learning, and are able to transcend their limitations. Though extremely focused, and can withstand setbacks and disappointments.

"October 19th natives are often the centre of attention within their family. Their sunny personality makes them lovable and although they have no trouble making friends, they often find themselves in controversial situations."

All will be revealed in time to come. Back in 1944, it was wartime and Jamaica, like every other British colony, had rallied to the Allied cause. US forces landed in the Philippines that very same day. The naval battle that followed effectively put paid to the Japanese threat in the Pacific, although not before nature intervened. Hurricane Havana, with winds in excess of 160 mph, was headed for Jamaica even as Alvera went into labour. It struck Savanna La Mar on October 20 and whilst the winds may have slowed a little by then, the damage it caused was severe. Several US Navy ships were capsized and well over a hundred aircraft were wrecked or blown overboard from aircraft carriers, causing 800 deaths. In the words of Admiral Nimitz, the typhoon's impact "represented a more crippling blow to the Third Fleet than it might be expected to suffer in anything less than a major action".

The war would end just a year later. After the horror came relief as people began to piece their lives back together, or were forced into trying something new. Alvera too would make a fresh start on what's been described as "a substantial piece of land" owned by her father, where Peter is now buried. In the absence of any support from McIntosh her family had provided her with somewhere to live, although the rest would be up to her. Her sense of failure and guilt must have been all consuming at times. "Mama Tosh", who moved to Belmont when Peter was three, never had any other children and you can understand why.

Music Times reports she left Grange Hill because, "I was having a hard time supporting myself and the child. I always had to support myself and Peter without a father so I always had a job." Peter will later tell *Reggae Routes* his mother couldn't look after him because she was "out slaving".

"I have no mother here, I have a *bearer*," he sneered. "Jah is my mother and Jah is my father. My earthly parents don't know my potential or my divine qualities. They weren't taught how to diagnose or be aware of such things. They were looking at skin complexion and because me born so rassclaat black, she know me was a curse according to the shit-stem them times there. From I born, me learn say, 'If you're brown you can stick around; if you're white then you perfectly alright and if you black, stay back.'"

Subsistence farming was hard, but then so was the weather at times. Westmoreland was hit by further tropical storms that year, and the next two years after that. This was nothing new, as there'd already been three major hurricanes in Savanna La Mar's history. The first arrived in 1748, just 20 years after it was founded, when it was almost swept out to sea. The second struck in 1780 and left fishing boats hanging from the trees, whilst the third occurred in 1912 and deposited a schooner in the main street. Such vengeful acts of nature, seen through a prism of Biblical and African folklore, can take on profound significance for people having to live in the midst of them. Peter would later incorporate the sound of thunder and lightning in his records, and it's not hard to imagine what inspired it.

It seems he was a reasonably happy child. Despite recalling how she'd leave him to cry as an infant ("Let him sing," she'd say) his mother says he was always drawing and listening to songs on the radio. Asked when she first realised Peter had a talent for music, Alvera said Peter was only about two years old when he first started to sing.

"Any song he heard on the radio or at church he would sing over," she told *Music Times*, proudly. "He could catch the words so easily. People always wanted to hear him sing, but in those days he would be singing Christian songs." The first song she recalls him singing was an old spiritual. "Roll away, roll away every burden of my heart. Roll away…" She says Peter would accompany himself on a "sardine pan guitar", and that older people would encourage him by giving money.

"In those days a penny was like a pound, and so by saving the half pennies and pennies and putting them together, I could buy me a shirt or a pants or even a suit of clothes," he would later tell radio presenter Habte Selassie. "That was the beginning of me realising my potential, and whatever ability for music I had in me."

His first instrument was rudimentary at best. Back then sardine cans were A5 size and maybe an inch thick – just the right shape for a makeshift guitar body if you're already hallucinating notes pouring out of it. All it needed then was a piece of wood for the neck and strings made out of fishing line held taut by nails. The chances of keeping it in tune and achieving any real mastery on it were practically zero, but making his first guitar (with help from his grandfather perhaps) must have been a proud moment. It showed hunger too, because it was desire, rather than curiosity that compelled him towards the magic world of sound and its infinite possibilities.

An Indian man who lived up the road from Alvera then took Peter's musical education one step further.

"My mother and father didn't know anything about instruments," Peter would later tell Timothy White. "Me just see a man in the country play guitar one time and say, 'My, the man play that guitar nice.' It attract me so much I just sat there, taking it in for about half the day and when him done – he was playing one tune for that whole half day – he had hypnotised me so much that my eyes extracted everything he had done with his fingers. I picked up the guitar and played the tune he had just played, without him showing me a thing. And when he asked me who'd taught me I tell him it was him!"

Two months before his sixth birthday, Hurricane Charlie happened. It was the worst tropical storm in 70 years and caused extensive damage. Port Royal was destroyed for the third time in its history as the death toll neared 200 and families lost everything they had. Crops were destroyed and fruit trees uprooted, which in turn made food hard to come by. Amidst the devastation, a new chapter opened in Peter's life.

"I used to go to work and leave Peter with his grandfather in the daytime but then after a while he got a job, so I had to find someone else to help me with him," Alvera explains. "My aunt in Savanna La Mar, Loretta Campbell, decided to help and so Peter started to live with her. He went to school during the week and on weekends he came home."

Euriah and Loretta Campbell lived in a street made of red earth that was mostly hot and dusty, but stuck to everything after it had rained. Men and women would walk barefoot to save their shoes, which they knotted over their shoulders. By Jamaican standards it was almost suburban although there was no sidewalk, only clumps of rich foliage dotted among the houses. Nevertheless, it was a decent neighbourhood back in the fifties, before zinc fencing appeared and the area became rundown. The Campbells were already helping raise a young niece but had a spare bed and could offer

Peter more stability than at home. At least he'd get a decent education staying with them. Bluefields School had been typical of those found in country villages with its single classroom, wooden benches and worn-out blackboard. Resources were limited, books were scarce and a tap outside provided the only form of refreshment. Facilities were less basic in town, and the teachers better qualified. Peter would attend the Savanna La Mar Infants and Primary Schools and they're still there at 50 Rose Street – the two schools being situated next door to each other. Then as now, they are government run and so unaffiliated to any religious organisation. The Campbells were however, and took Peter to church almost every evening and twice on a Sunday.

The Pentecostal Church in Bluefields had consisted of little more than a rudimentary altar and floor space, whereas the one in Savanna La Mar had a piano. It's almost a cliché to read of singers being raised in the church and yet there's no denying its influence on so many musically inclined youngsters. A religious upbringing shapes a person's thoughts, gets inside their minds and affects them for the rest of their lives. Peter will famously rail against his, even as it informed his character. The good news is he got to learn a lot more about music's power to transform people from an early age, and the lessons would never leave him.

The cornerstone of the Pentecostal Church – apart from acceptance of Christ's teachings as written in the Bible – is the importance of being born again. Followers have to be baptised in the Holy Spirit and can't be saved otherwise, since good works or penance can't suffice on their own. The key to the Pentecostal faith can be found in the Book Of Acts, Chapter 2, which describes what happened at a Jewish festival in Galilee.

"And when the day of Pentecost was fully come, they were all with one accord in one place. And suddenly there came a sound from heaven as of a rushing mighty wind, and it filled the house where they were sitting. And there appeared unto them cloven tongues like as of fire, and it sat upon each of them. And they were all filled with the Holy Ghost and began to speak with other tongues, as the Spirit gave them utterance. And those dwelling at Jerusalem were Jews, devout men, out of every nation under heaven. Now when this was noised abroad, the multitudes came together and were confounded because every man that heard them speak in his own language. And they were all amazed and marvelled, saying one to another, 'Behold, are not all these which speak Galileans?'

"Others, mocking, said, 'these men are full of new wine.' But Peter, standing up with the 11, lifted up his voice, and said unto them, 'Ye men of Judaea, and all ye that dwell at Jerusalem, be this known unto you, and hearken to my words: For these are not drunken, as ye suppose, seeing it is but the third hour of the day and that which was spoken by the prophet Joel. And it shall come to pass in the last days saith God, I will pour out of my Spirit upon all flesh: and your sons and your daughters shall prophesy, and your young men shall see visions, and your old men shall dream dreams. And on my servants and on my handmaidens I will pour out in those days of my Spirit; and they shall prophesy. And I will show wonders in heaven above and signs in the earth beneath, blood and fire and vapours of smoke. The sun shall be turned into darkness, and the moon into blood before the great and notable day of the Lord come. And it shall come to pass, that whosoever shall call on the name of the Lord shall be saved."

Those wondering how Hubert Winston came to be known as "Peter" need only reflect upon his family's religious beliefs. Dr. Samuel C. Gipp discusses these references to Peter in a well-known Bible commentary.

"Here Peter lives up to his true personality," he writes. "When others are silent, Peter speaks up! Peter was always quick to say exactly what he thought, even if what was on his mind was not always correct. Time and again Peter speaks first and thinks later. Peter may have to answer for his actions, but he certainly seemed to have made up for his error by quickly speaking up for Christ later. Those Christians who judge Peter harshly for his denial of Christ one time, will have to answer for their own multitude of denials through silence."

Outlawed by his blackness and illegitimacy, Peter was prevented from self-pity by childhood innocence and the Campbells' disciplined routines. His horizons had expanded since the move to Savanna La Mar, but he still looked forward to seeing family and friends back in Belmont most weekends. One trip home would prove especially memorable.

"I will never forget that when I was seven years old, the Devil tried to blind me with barbed wire," he recalled on the Red X tapes. He'd heard his mother calling and ran towards her, not noticing the barbed wire fence until it was too late. The barbs were at face height and missed his retinas by a fraction but when Peter wiped the blood from his face, both eyelids were so torn he could see right through them. We can assume a doctor or even local midwife applied stitches, and he was forced to wear a bandage over his eyes for several days. It's also possible he was treated with a poultice of herbs, to draw out any infection and ease the stinging pain. Peter would retain trust in natural healing practices for the rest of his life, and suffered no obvious, long-term effects from the injuries he suffered as a child.

His mother had a shop by this time – in reality just a lean-to by the roadside, from where she'd sell whatever fruit and vegetables were in season. Peter loved drawing and would sit in there at weekends, sketching the people who passed by. Alvera delighted in his creativity but will later refer to him as "troublesome", because he was always touching things. Whenever she cautioned him, he'd say, "Mama, hear me say, me name Tosh, so me must touch it."

Years later, when Roger Steffens asked him how he got the name Peter Tosh, he replied that Peter was his pet name and as a youth growing up, his friends would call him "McIntouch". "Well, I don't like to be mocked, so I just take the MacIn off from there," he explained. Peter's size – he was tall even as a child – undoubtedly prompted some teasing as well, although he rarely lacked company. He and his best friend Kingsley Daley, whom Peter called "K.D", would go fishing, climb trees and trap mongooses. Even as a grown man, Peter would call K.D. from Kingston, wanting to know if he'd seen any mongooses. Finches, pigeons and woodpeckers were plentiful and the pair used to stalk them by hiding in trees with branches tucked into their clothes, for camouflage. Once in position, they wouldn't be able to move or breathe a word until an unwary bird drew near, then they'd kill it with their slingshots, light a fire and eat their fill. Often, they'd take a line down to the beach hoping to catch that evening's supper, or visit rivers and streams where clingfish would lie in wait under the waterfalls. Either that or they'd go exploring in the fields, where sugar cane of all hues, from green to black, towered above them. Farming in the area was still not mechanised and so neighbours helped one another, especially during planting and harvest time when the larger farms would employ additional workers. You could hear them singing from afar as they chopped cane with their machetes, just as they'd done for generations – first as slaves, and then hired labourers or small-time farmers. Donkeys would be tethered nearby, weighed down with hampers holding water containers. The stalks were then transported to the mills for crushing, and the juice boiled to make sugar. It was hard work, but life in the countryside could also be idyllic. Villagers wove baskets out of bamboo or made mats from banana leaves, and there was no shortage of cabinetmakers, tinsmiths, shoemakers, potters or rope makers.

As Peter sat in his mother's store, he'd see the local women stroll past with goods balanced on their heads, or watch as a sporadic procession of ducks, geese, chicken, goats and dogs wandered listlessly in search of food or shade. Lunch might be boiled plantains or yam and a little fish, served with a drink made from bitter oranges and sugar. Lizards would dart along the walls, making short, rapid movements before freezing motionless or basking in the hot sun. Ram goat roses, white azaleas and mammy trees with their crimson fruit provided splashes of local colour, as did plum roses and rose apples. White winged doves fluttered among the outbuildings, and scorpions scurried in the shadows. It was a world mercifully free of "globalisation", where chain stores simply didn't exist. Since Jamaica was an island it relied on imported electrical goods and there were few phones or televisions. The postal service was hit-and-miss too, just like the water and electricity supplies – providing you were connected to begin with, and most people weren't. Instead, they cooked over fires, divined for water with forked sticks and made do with candlelight. Some even grew a little marijuana in their back yards, which they'd boil up and drink as a tonic. Westmoreland is famous for its herb, thanks to the many indentured Indian workers who came to Jamaica. Some brought seeds with them and it was these "Indie Royals" as they were known, who taught Jamaicans how to cultivate it.

Emancipation Day celebrations fell in August, when people treated themselves to a well-earned day off and towns and villages hosted donkey races, sports, food stalls, merry-go-rounds and maypole dancing, as well as concerts by local mento musicians. Vendors laden with guineps, tamarind and other fruit walked through the crowds, whilst others sold foxtail grass (for stuffing mattresses) or brooms made from dried coconut fibre. Ragged children in bare feet played hide and seek or ring games like Drop The Handkerchief, hoping they'd be treated to cups of shaved ice mixed with syrup called "snowballs". "Bruckins" – derived from "bragging" – was also popular. This was a game of one-upmanship, of Creole origin and accompanied by exaggerated movements. We'll see echoes of it in how Tosh brandishes a sword or Ethiopian cross on stage nearly 30 years later.

Despite the rural setting, consumerism was already on its way. Little girls craved dolls, although the only ones they saw were pink with blue

15

eyes and maybe blonde hair. Toys were expensive and hard to come by, so children would have to improvise with whatever came to hand – usually wood, clothes and nails. Boys played cricket of course, inspired by the West Indies team, which was one of the few areas where Jamaica's unwritten colour bar didn't apply.

When Peter was eight, Jamaica's athletes won gold and silver at the Olympic Games held in Helsinki, even breaking two world records. This was a cause for great celebration. A year later, Britain's newly crowned Queen Elizabeth II stopped off in Jamaica on her way to Australia. It was the first time a reigning English monarch had visited the island, and vast crowds turned out to cheer her. Soon afterwards, in 1954, there was an island-wide outbreak of poliomyelitis, which afflicted over 800 people. Some Rastafarians believed the Queen's visit had brought bad luck but such misgivings were soon swept aside as Jamaica celebrated 300 years of British rule.

Tercentenary activities went on for the entire year. The most popular was a road show featuring sports and music that travelled throughout the different parishes, Westmoreland included. Kingston hosted an Industrial Fair during September and then just a few months later, Norman Manley's PNP won the general election. One of his first tasks was to welcome HRH Princess Margaret, who visited Jamaica during February. Deference to Britain was still very evident, especially in country districts where it wasn't uncommon to see portraits of the Queen and Prince Philip hanging on people's walls. A lot of Jamaican boys were named after Winston Churchill, including Peter Tosh.

When he was 10, Alvera took him to meet his father, who still lived in Hanover. Peter will later claim McIntosh gave Alvera "a few shillings and several oranges" at this meeting. It's the only time Peter will see him, and yet it's doubtful the experience unsettled him too much. His uncle and grandfather still served as primary male role models and he was being kept busy at school and church in any case, where he sang in junior choir and at concerts. Alvera recalls aunt Loretta telling her that Peter had sang in front of 100 people or more outside the courthouse one day, whilst his teachers had urged them to send him for proper music lessons after he'd shown promise at the piano.

Years later, Habte Selassie asked Peter how he got started in music. "It's the other way round, because music happened to me," he explained.

"I was born with music inside of me and that was the first flower that bloomed on my tree but I was the highest key in my school, and also the lowest key, seen? That means I was very important in music and any time it was taking place at school... Any activities, like concerts and all of those things and I am not involved, then you knew something was missing, because in those times, when I was 12 and 13, I sang like a girl. My voice was the highest pitch until I was 16, 17 and even now I can still do them, but in falsetto.

"I was the only one in my family to be musically inclined and my mother loved that," he continued. "It encouraged my grand aunt to find me a music teacher, because it was quite obvious music was in me. When I was about 12, 13, I went to my first music tutor which was a lady called Mrs. Scott. She was my music teacher for about a year, and after about six months I was playing fifths and B-sharp and all of these kinds of things. I was playing classical music, and from she first taught me it's like I was magnetic towards it, and learning so easily. In those times you didn't look at the keyboard, you look in the book, because Mrs. Scott, she was a very aggressive woman when it comes to that. You have to look in the book and your fingers have to be like eyes, seen? But reading and writing is the greatest thing in music. I can't play the music I used to when I was 13, because I played by notes back then and now I play by ear. I feel out the chords and make lots of mistakes but I remember how it was, and it was one of the most beautiful times in my life... I used to go to my music lesson three times a week, so I would get like maybe four or six hours' worth of lessons altogether but when I leave that lady's place, it was impossible for me to play a piano unless I sneaked in the church. You had to practise to get good at it but I never had access to a piano and if I'd have had that, oh man, the music that would be coming out of me now would be incredible..."

In 1983, Peter told Mel Cheplowitz he'd studied "practical piano forte music" for six months aged 13 and reached the fifth grade. He can be forgiven for feeing disenchanted after his formal training ended. The lack of a piano led him to concentrate on guitar, except he'd continue to play piano whenever he got the chance, like at Christmas time when the school would organise singing, dancing and poetry recitals. Some of the older students would act out scenes from Shakespeare and Peter's school had a decent choir too, featuring a certain Hubert McIntosh. Hymns like

'No More Auction Block For Me', 'Rock Of Ages', 'Swing Low Sweet Chariot' and 'Coming Through The Rye' were among his favourites. These songs dated from slavery days, but had lost none of their relevance. It was singing in choirs that had introduced Peter to the joys of harmonies and Christmas was always a special time of year, even though gifts might only consist of food, a hand-me-down dress or pair of second-hand shoes. There was little chance of having a traditional Yuletide in any case, with temperatures in the nineties.

Jamaican schoolchildren would see pictures of snow in books, but never experience it. The nearest they came was during the rainy season, when hailstones sometimes fell from the sky and children would gather up the frozen pellets and make drinks from them by adding sugar or lemon. Out in the countryside, villagers marked Christmas by painting tree trunks white and welcoming the Jonkonnu – groups of street performers whose songs, theatrics and arresting costume designs were rooted in traditional Ashanti rites from Ghana. The Jonkonnu would surface on Christmas Eve, and stick around for about two weeks. Rowdy crowds followed them as they leapt and pranced, acting out ancient rituals whilst playing bamboo flutes and drums.

When Peter was 13, a heavy earthquake shook almost the entire island, causing extensive damage. There was also a serious rail accident in Kendal, not far from where his parents had met. The train was on its return journey from Montego Bay to Kingston when it derailed, killing 200 people and injuring many more. In the aftermath, they were numerous sightings of people killed in the disaster. These ghostly figures are called "duppies" in Jamaica and fuelled by local superstition, are considered very real indeed. Members of Peter's family still living in nearby Grange Hill would have helped to pull bodies out of the wreckage and tend to survivors, so we can be sure this event had a significant impact.

As always, there were divisions between the inner lives of Jamaican country people with their beliefs in African-derived folklore, and what children were taught in school. Jamaica's education system followed the colonial model, and so history and geography lessons rarely touched upon anything controversial. At no point were pupils told that Africa was the cradle of civilisation, or how Jamaica's original inhabitants had been killed or died out during what Rachel Manley describes as the island's "brief and humiliating past". Peter would discover all this later, and view much of his early education as part-propaganda, part-betrayal. Not that he was much of a rebel at the time. By all accounts, he enjoyed school and made friends easily, despite his busy schedule allowing little opportunity for relaxation. Church activities still took up a lot of his attention and it was there, among the swaying adults and joyous exclamations to God, where his musical education continued to bear fruit.

In some ways he remained resistant to the Pentecostal faith. He told Roger Steffens there'd been many attempts to have him baptised for instance, but that he'd always refused. "Yeah man, physical resistance and spiritual resistance!" he purred. "I go to church because my parents go to church, and I believe the things they were doing at the time were right because they were the ones growing up in righteousness, and their life was supposed to be an example, seen? I was living in belief, not knowing, except the concept instilled within me was to do things that were right, and I never think I should hurt a man. That's the way I was born and raised, and that's the way I grow and feel within myself. I don't think I should harm anything that has life and I'll have nothing to do with what is wrong, but at the same time I didn't know right from wrong at that time, because there was no one to teach me."

He'll grow increasingly disdainful about his church upbringing in future, complaining that he was taught God had made man in His own image – which according to the only pictures he'd seen of Jesus meant Caucasian.

"I was taught that Jesus the Son of God was a white man," he sneered, "and hearing black people singing, 'Lord wash me, and I will be whiter than snow' made me sick. They would always teach me about the Devil, Satan and hell – the teachings of the Christians…"

The music was something else though, and still the soaring harmonies filled his soul with joy. Anthony Heilbut talks of gospel as having "constructed a world complete unto itself". He mentions its distinctive language, special rhythms and complex sense of ritual and decorum. "Gospel has its own very superior aesthetic standards," he writes. "The audience's musical sophistication is remarkable; it's nothing rare to see thousands of people roaring their approval for the subtlest change in tune, time or harmony. But the most universal approval comes for honesty of emotion. Church people understand spirit, "soul" if you will, better than anyone."

Before emancipation, the slaves' only opportunity to express themselves openly came when singing hymns. Black singers tend to flatten and slur notes, and invest them with more feeling. They also found little difficulty identifying with the themes of salvation and deliverance found in so many of the old-time spirituals. Whilst he'd later reject its religious framework, the influence of gospel singing on Peter's career would last a lifetime and this, together with his popularity at school, helped instil plenty of confidence in his own abilities.

"He used to sing higher than the radio!" his mother recalls, affectionately. "I'd say 'Oh stop the noise, too much noise', and he'd say, 'Alright, when you hear me sing on the radio, then you can turn it off.'"

Jamaica didn't have its own radio station until 1959. Before then many Jamaicans would tune in American stations like WINZ or WCKY, broadcast from Miami. The sounds of New Orleans and America's Deep South flooded into Jamaican homes via inexpensive, battery-driven transistor radios, which had now become commonplace. The alternative was a British cable system named Redifusion, operated from a wall-mounted box and that introduced Caribbean audiences to crooners such as Frank Sinatra, Nat King Cole and Bing Crosby. Whilst such singers would prove influential, it was the American rhythm and blues artists and doo-wop groups that captured the attention of most Jamaican teenagers. By the time Peter started at Manning's High School his favourites included Billy Ward & The Dominos, Sam Cooke, Little Anthony & The Imperials, Ricky Nelson, Fats Domino, The Platters, Lloyd Price, Clyde McPhatter, Jackie Wilson, Dion & The Belmonts and Ray Charles. Even Marty Robbins... The outpouring of music from across the Gulf of Mexico was intoxicating, and it was augmented by jazz, country and western, British pop and whatever else was happening in Cuba and Latin America, as well as other parts of the Caribbean.

His head swimming with youthful exuberance, Peter was convinced that he had a contribution to make – if not as a balladeer, then in a group. He was now growing increasingly distracted. Inevitably his schoolwork began to suffer, and relations with his family became strained. He left school earlier than expected but couldn't decide on a trade, despite pressure from those close to him. He was beginning to feel as if he'd outgrown Savanna La Mar and its surrounds, and to crave new experiences. The catalyst would arrive right on cue, and Peter could scarcely believe his ears after hearing some of the earliest Jamaican hits by Higgs & Wilson, Theophilus Beckford, Laurel Aitken and others, which combined elements of calypso, rhythm and blues and doo wop, yet sounded so fresh and new. There was no mistaking the American influences in these records, but there was something else too – an expression that could have only been created right there in Jamaica, and that spoke directly to his collective subconscious. Kingston was clearly the place to be and fortunately for Peter, members of his family were prepared to help him.

His mother told *Music Times* that Peter was 17 when leaving for Kingston. "He said he would like to learn welding and I had an aunt in Kingston, Mary Tomlinson, who agreed to find a place for him, which she did. We were very poor, so I knew I couldn't afford to send him to medical school or law school or anything like that. That's why I didn't mind that he took up singing. I thought it was a good idea to learn welding too, but it was his decision to make, then once he got to Kingston he changed his mind about that. He said he couldn't sit in one place all day long, so that's when he started to direct all his attention to music."

Alvera would have undoubtedly preferred her son to sing "Christian songs about the Lord and Saviour" rather than secular music but such considerations were far from her mind as she bade him farewell. K.D was supposed to go too but when he failed to show up for the third time, Peter left without him.

"Why did you leave Westmoreland?" asked Steffens, years later.

"To learn."

"What did you take to Kingston when you left?"

"Well, all I took was my little grip, and some food to eat on the way, and myself and Jah in my heart," replied Peter.

"When he was going to Kingston I tell him I don't approve because he's not saved," Alvera would later confide to Fikisha Cumbo.

"How you know I'm not saved Mama?" Peter had replied. "I *am* saved and I'm going."

"He only said that so he could go to town," reflected his mother, sadly, "but I knew he was lying."

There are four main roads out of Savanna La Mar. One leads west to Negril, another to Grange Hill and Lucea, and a third to Petersfield. The fourth heads east, hugging the coastline to Black River and eventually Kingston. After Black River the road bends inland, and skirts round a succession of villages with names like Speculation, Lovely Point and Pepper. As Peter's bus neared Mandeville, the landscape changed to grassy pastures reminiscent of English farmland. It continued like that through Clarendon until they reached the market town of May Pen and then Old Harbour, where ships still docked, awaiting cargos of fresh produce. The next stop was Spanish Town, just 15 miles from Kingston, where the government buildings and churches would remind him of Savanna La Mar in their ornate, but faded splendour. Soon, his bus will enter Kingston and pull up near Coronation Market in the bustling downtown area. His journey had covered less than 150 miles, yet lasted six hours. The food he'd brought with him was long gone and he was tired, despite tremors of excitement welling below the surface. The coming months would test his resolve like nothing he'd ever experienced before except, flush with youthful innocence, he felt ready for the challenge and smiled broadly as aunt Mary walked over to greet him.

Chapter 2

No Sympathy

Peter spent three months in Denham Town, living with his aunt. Years later, he would describe it as "a new page, totally different from what I grew up with". Denham Town is in West Kingston, shares its borders with Jones Town and Trench Town, and has an unenviable reputation for violence that persists to this day. Death is an ever-present reminder – across the Spanish Town Road is May Pen cemetery, where many an outlaw lies at rest.

Whilst he may have been staying with family, acceptance from the local community was another matter. New arrivals, especially from the country, are invariably given a hard time. Remember Jimmy Cliff in *The Harder They Come*, on his first day in town? No sooner does he step off the bus than he's robbed of everything he's got. Peter may have been confident; but adjusting to life in West Kingston wouldn't be easy.

Burning Spear, who journeyed to Kingston from St. Ann's at the start of his career, says country people lead calmer lives. "They tend to live like one, together," he says. "People were there for each other, but then when you go to Kingston, it wasn't like that. It's like they don't care about anyone else and nothing surprises them. It was totally different, so it was really hard for you to leave the country and live in the city. It may take you some time before you can accept that way of life and to settle down because people in the country have more time to digest things, and to think and learn about them. You can get to know about yourself more because you have the time, but city people aren't like that."

Alvera knew this, which is why she'd been concerned for Peter's safety. Her brother and his family also lived in West Kingston, and she'd heard enough stories to fuel her fears. Real and ever-present dangers lay in wait for the unwary and her son could be headstrong, so it was easy to imagine him getting into trouble. Whilst Peter did try his hand at welding, he hated being cooped up all day and soon left. He still hadn't decided what to do for a living when leaving Aunt Mary's and going to stay at his uncle's house in Trench Town, at 19 West Road. Alvera's brother was a cabinetmaker but the family also made syrup, which they sold to retail outlets in Kingston. As cottage industries go it was successful enough, and Rita Marley's father was rumoured to have worked for them at one point.

The Morris family had seven children between them – five boys and two girls. Peter's favourite was six-year old Pauline, who they called "Offie" since her middle name was Ophelia. At 17 Peter was oldest of the youngsters, and closest in age to the two boys from his aunt's previous marriage. Housing in Trench Town once meant lean-to shacks, but Peter's new home was purpose-built. The rooms were small though, and must have felt cramped given the number of people living there. Pauline remembers Peter babysitting her and the younger ones, and being caring towards them. As Alvera's only son he was welcomed into the family and behaved well in return, but his restlessness was only too evident. Peter's uncle had grown up in Belmont and felt sympathy for his lanky nephew, who was never happier than when singing along to the radio and strumming a guitar.

Trench Town was alive with music. Sound systems like Sir Coxsone's Downbeat and V Rocket would set up on the corner of Fifth Street and Central Road most Friday and Saturday evenings and they'd still be there playing music as dawn broke. That's where Peter heard Higgs & Wilson's 'Manny Oh', Alton & Eddy's 'Muriel', Jackie Edwards' 'Tell Me Darling' and the Blues Busters' 'Donna' – records that had marked the birth of the local recording industry, and made every other youngster on the island want to be a singer. Crowds of people spilled onto the streets where they'd laugh and remonstrate with each other, or buy roast corn, ripe bananas and oranges from the vendors who thronged the sidewalk. A sense of camaraderie filled the air but then this was 1962, and political rivalry had yet to make its presence felt. On weekday evenings, people congregated by the bridge and met with friends, or practised singing. Locals called this spot "corner", and were quick to extend Peter an invitation.

"We treated each other like family," recalled Beverley Kelso. "Everybody walk from one yard to the next and everybody know each other's name. After school, you'd go home and do your chores. You have to clean and wash up dishes, do the housework and go to the store. After that now you'd take a shower, get fresh and you'd come out in the street. Everybody would play something. Boys and girls would play football and cricket; some play marbles and girls would be jumping the rope... This was in-between say six and eight o'clock because children had school in the morning so when it got dark, they'd stop playing and get called in. There was no television back then. Some people had Redifusion and would listen to Ranny Williams on RJR. His show was at 10 on a weekday night. We'd all listen to his show sat round the radio and if a family didn't have a radio, they'd go and visit people who did. The street would be quiet and then after the show was over, everybody would go to bed..."

At its southern extremity, Trench Town began at First Street. Its two main thoroughfares were Central Road and West Road, which went past the Clock Circle all the way up to Thirteenth Street and an area known as Ghost Town. Nearby was the Ambassador Theatre, where young hopefuls auditioned for Vere Johns' 'Opportunity Hour'. This was Jamaica's number one talent show and other heats were held at the Majestic, just two blocks away on Maxfield Avenue. A walk in the other direction, down the Spanish Town Road, led to downtown Kingston, close to the waterfront. That's where Peter discovered Orange Street, also known as "Beat Street", which hosted a profusion of record and liquor stores, clubs, rum bars and whorehouses. The main action however revolved around places like Chocomo Lawn, the Jubilee Tile Gardens and Forresters' Hall, at the corner of Charles Street and Love Lane. These outdoor dancehalls were jam-packed most weekends thanks to a steady diet of "jump blues" by American artists such as Fats Domino, Louis Jordan and Smiley Lewis, who'd headline at the Carib or Regal Theatres on their occasional visits to Kingston.

As a Trench Town youth, naïve to the city and lacking funds, Peter didn't get to visit downtown too often. Most of his musical education came from hearing records closer to home, in local dances or on the radio. That's how he came under the spell of acts like Eric "Monty" Morris, the Jiving Juniors and Mellow Larks, whose 'Time To Pray' topped the JBC charts for several weeks that summer. As well as learning the words

25

to certain songs, Peter practised guitar every chance he got and began sketching out songs of his own, since the inspiration was already welling up inside him. In years to come he'd tell Habte Selassie that Trench Town "was where the music was at and it was there I was supposed to be, because it helped to bring out what was inside of me. Because the more I hear people sing, the more I sing, and the more I hear music, the more I sing."

There was some government housing opposite his uncle's place. Peter would often stop by there in the evenings, and join in with the reasoning sessions that invariably started up once a pot of food went on the fire. Several families lived in this communal block and mingled in a central recreation area ringed by kitchens, bathrooms and toilets. Ras Cardo, who knew Peter during those early years, testifies to the fact life was hard in these tenement yards.

"Besides the usual domestic inconveniences of not having your own toilet, bathroom or kitchen facilities in your rooms, there were the additional problems of people not getting along with each other," he writes in *Reggae Jamaica*. "Some people in the same yard were rival tenants always looking for a chance to hurt the other person. People had to live vigilantly, always sleeping with one eye open. Many people will not be able to comprehend what it feels like to be living or merely existing in such conditions from day to day, and around some people who may be at war with you or some member of your family. It was scary to say the least and there was no electricity. Most people used kerosene lamps to pierce the veil of darkness that descended at nights and others would use flashlights. It was a constant happening where a fight that began on one street would end up in a chase on another street and in another yard."

Such experiences taught Peter just how easily people can become victims. He saw some die because of carelessness whereas others lost their lives amidst howls of rage and frustration. As the pressure got to them, it made some people kinky, crazy, angry and lost to themselves.

Soon after his arrival, a Trench Town woman killed her husband and cut up his body into tiny pieces. They named her "Chicken Back" after that. Ghetto humour could be cruel, but it was never far from the truth. Anyone living in such circumstances quickly developed a hard exterior by necessity. It didn't pay to show your feelings too openly and yet somehow Peter would retain his sense of humour, despite the growing realisation that poverty and crime were interlinked, and the system did nothing to alleviate people's struggles. Jobs were hard to come by, especially for anyone with a Trench Town address. Somehow, the majority of people living there survived by honest means but because they managed to exist on so little, they were often suspected of being criminals – an assumption that still holds true today. Trench Town people had to be resourceful, since few options were available to them. Some turned to woodcarving, whilst others made ironing boards, tea strainers and other household items, which they'd sell in the markets. The less fortunate might gather up scrap iron or bits of copper, or scrape a meagre living from returning glass bottles to the liquor stores.

Peter's adventures with K. D. now belonged to a different world. City life was more eventful in every way and especially in August, when Jamaica gained independence from Britain. The opening ceremony took place at the National Stadium where a capacity crowd watched a massive firework display, and then fought back their emotions as a choir sang the new national anthem. All over Jamaica, streets were lined with flags and bunting, and the rejoicing went on for days. People developed a thirst for anything that reflected Jamaican identity, whether it was music, sport, art or even the local "patois". Derrick Morgan dominated the charts with songs like 'Forward March' and there was no escaping Lord Creator's 'Independent Jamaica', even if he was from Trinidad.

It was at this point that, at the corner of West Road and Third Street, Peter met with two other young neighbourhood singers. One was a skinny, half-caste youth named Robert Nesta Marley, who people called "Robbie" but we'll refer to as "Bob", just to avoid confusion. The other was his friend and step-brother Neville O'Riley Livingston, otherwise known as "Bunny". Peter was a little older than them, and radiated confidence. Bunny remembers him singing 'Go Tell It On The Mountain' and 'Sinner Man' with characteristic swagger during that first meeting, yet his new friends were more experienced and Bob had even made one or two records. Like Peter, Bob had been raised in the countryside (in St. Ann's) and grown up fatherless. The nearest he'd got was his grandfather Omeriah Malcolm, who was a noted disciplinarian. Bob's father was a white man he'd scarcely met, who'd toured the island inspecting government property and married Bob's mother when she was just 16. Their union hadn't lasted and by the time Captain Norval Marley died in 1957, Bob could barely remember what he looked like. Interestingly, old-timers like

Bunny Lee swear that Bob's real father was a light-skinned Jamaican from St. Elizabeth who worked as an usher at the Ambassador Theatre, but who then disappeared after being pushed aside by Bob's mother.

Bob was 11 when his mother met Bunny's father, Thaddeus, who was a builder. He'd provided a welcome degree of security, and the two boys quickly became inseparable. Both shared a love of music. Bunny was two years younger, but already playing "stick drums" and also a primitive guitar he'd made from a sardine tin, just like the one Peter had started out with. His two new friends lived in a government yard on Second Street. Bob had left school at 15 and worked for a while as a welder until an accident almost blinded him. He'd become even more determined to make a career out of music after this, and would enter local talent competitions singing a song called 'Fancy Curls' which he'd written himself. Other times he'd go hang out at Back O'Wall, where the Rasta camps were. That's where other young hopefuls like Ken Boothe would hang out. Almost a year before meeting Peter and just days before his seventeenth birthday, Bob recorded a couple of songs for Leslie Kong – a Chinese Jamaican who ran an ice cream parlour with his brothers, and wanted to expand into the local record business. Bob's first excursion into a studio resulted in 'Judge Not', which Kong issued under the name of Robert Marley, backed with 'Do You Still Love Me'. By the time Kong issued 'One Cup Of Coffee' he'd changed Marley's name to "Bobby Martell" yet it made no difference, and the song still flopped. Kong invited him onto shows in Clarendon and Montego Bay, headlined by Derrick Morgan. The crowd booed when he sang 'One Cup Of Coffee', but then cheered as he started into 'Judge Not'. It had proved a valuable lesson – one he was determined to learn from.

Peter listened keenly. Instinctively, he measured himself against these two youths and knew he could match them given the opportunity. He wanted success so badly it began to haunt him, and he thought of little else after that initial meeting. Soon, Peter would visit Bob and Bunny at the house on Second Street, where they'd gather round a Phillips radio the size of a suitcase and tune into WINZ, broadcast live and direct from Miami, and catch up on all the latest doo-wop, rock'n'roll and rhythm and blues records. Whilst Joe Higgs would help to polish their raw talent, this is where the three friends' understanding of harmonising began. Bunny and Peter's voices dovetailed right from the start so they let Bob sing lead vocals, and his voice was more expressive in any case. By now, Peter was working for a dry cleaner called Mr. Tibbs on Fourth Street. It didn't satisfy him, but meant he could at least give his uncle and aunt a little money each week. Bunny says Peter was a real character, who still couldn't stop from touching everything, and especially girls! He was always playing practical jokes on friends and neighbours, and was full of humour.

Every day that Peter wasn't working or had finished his shift at the dry cleaners, Bob and Bunny would pass by the Morrises' and call for him before heading for one of their favourite rehearsal spots. They might go and visit Joe Higgs or Bob's friend Vincent "Tatta" Ford, who lived on First Street. Other times they'd pass by Alton Ellis' yard on Fifth Street, or meet up with friends like Junior, Sabu and Tabby, who lived in another tenement block just up the road from there. Once settled somewhere, the group would work on songs and practise harmonies until long after dark. Peter's guitar playing provided rhythm and key for these early rehearsals although he didn't have his own instrument at this juncture, which made his determination to play even more salutary. Joe Higgs lent him one occasionally; Bob then stole a battered acoustic guitar from a local night club which the group would share, although Peter got most use out of it. That guitar was damaged after they'd raced each other down the street, collided and ended up in a tangled heap of legs, arms and splintered wood. Peter had to hobble around for the next few days, after his ankle swelled to the size of a breadfruit. Their next guitar came from a Rastaman named Deacon, and it was a beauty. They'd attach a pick-up to it in due course as their fortunes improved, but success was still a long way off.

Joe Higgs, who was a hard taskmaster, continued to play a major role in the group's development. The loose aggregate of young hopefuls attending his ghetto classroom included Garth Dennis and his sister Joan, Barrington Sayles and Junior Braithwaite, who they called "Bratty'. Joe would think up names for the group like "the Teenagers" and even "the Roosters", but none stuck until Bob opened his Bible at Jeremiah chapter 9, verse 19, and read, "For a voice of wailing is heard out of Zion…" Legend has it they chose the name Wailers because they "started out crying", and it would be hard to argue otherwise.

The year 1963 was now drawing to a close, and it was a momentous time – topped by news of US President John Kennedy's assassination in November. Dr Martin Luther King had led 250,000 marchers to Washington in August and stood on the steps of the Lincoln Memorial declaring, "I have a dream..." A month later Hurricane Flora ripped through the Caribbean, leaving thousands homeless. It was as if triumph and tragedy were locked in each other's embrace but then something unexpected happened the following March, when Millie Small became the island's first-ever international pop star with 'My Boy Lollipop' – a cover of Barbie Gaye's American rhythm and blues hit that raced up the UK charts, peaking at number two. Millie's vocals were irrepressibly naïve, but the song's insistent rhythm put Jamaica's new ska beat on the map, and did wonders for the local record industry.

Peter and the others – including Junior Braithwaite – were now rehearsing harder than ever. Under Higgs' direction they'd not only learnt about harmonies, but intonation, timing and phrasing... Everything they needed to start their professional careers. Unfortunately Higgs and Bob then fell out and the two of them weren't speaking by the time the Wailers auditioned for Coxsone, whose new studio was just a 20-minute walk away, near Calvary Cemetery.

Coxsone had earned his nickname after expressing admiration for an English cricketer. Things like that happen in Jamaica. One day you make a harmless remark and then before you know it, everyone in the community is calling you something different. Coxsone's real name was Clement Dodd and whilst he didn't sing or play an instrument, he possessed an unrivalled ear for music. His popularity as a DJ was founded on the rhythm and blues records he'd bought in America, with wages earned from farm work, but the turning point came after he started to record one-off acetates for his sound system and then realised their sales potential. That had been five years earlier. By the time he'd settled into his new premises at 13 Brentford Road (which he called "Studio One") he was producing hits with Delroy Wilson – a schoolboy singer from Trench Town, who the Wailers knew and respected, and was a real inspiration to them.

It was a neighbour of Bob and Bunny's, Alvin "Seeco" Patterson, who'd recommended they go and audition for Coxsone. He and Bob had written a song called 'Simmer Down' after Bob's mother had voiced objections about the Wailers' lifestyle, since none of them seemed interested in regular work. All they wanted to do was sing but she warned that tough times lay ahead ("the battle would get hotter") and it wasn't good to rush into things since "sweet goat run him belly" (i.e., they get diarrhoea from eating unripe shoots.)

Seeco and Bunny's accounts of the audition differ significantly but it's clear that Coxsone didn't care too much for the Wailers' covers of doo-wop and gospel songs and only got excited after hearing 'Simmer Down', which Bob had dismissed as a novelty tune. Coxsone however, was listening out for hits, not Sunday morning reveries, and it wasn't until Peter began strumming the chords to 'Simmer Down' that his ears pricked up. They'd barely got to the second verse when he signalled for them to stop and offered to record it. Bunny says they went back the next day, but Coxsone told Roger Steffens they didn't return to Studio One until a few weeks later, after further rehearsals.

The group took on another member before that first recording session, so maybe it didn't take place the following day after all. The newcomer was a 15-year-old girl named Beverley Kelso, who lived on Fifth Street and sang at a local youth club. She was shy, but added something different to the group's make-up, and 'Simmer Down' sounded better than ever. The Wailers were now a quintet, and ready for a date with destiny.

Chapter 3

Climb The Ladder

The audition had been a real eye-opener for Peter. It was the first time he'd been anywhere near a studio, and he couldn't wait to go back and make a record.

"That first morning we were rocking and singing as we go," Beverley recalled. "Bob would be pushing Bunny, and Bunny would be pushing Bob and Peter... They'd be laughing and teasing one another. They used to say a lot of funny things. I'd crack up to hear the things that came out of their mouths. In those times nobody ever smoke, and Junior and I were the two little short ones. We'd stay in the back, talking to one another whilst Bob, Bunny and Peter would carry on with their antics. Peter was always clowning around and when you're with them, you don't want to leave them for a minute! But we walk to Studio One and it was quick. The studio was by the burial ground and there was this track where you could walk all the way from Jones Town to Brentford Road. We take the short cut and end up on that little dirt road where Rita Marley used to live, right by Calvary Cemetery."

That first session is thought to have taken place on July 6, 1964. Members of the Skatalites gradually filled the studio, taking little notice of the youngsters. Peter watched as the musicians set up their instruments. This was what he'd dreamt of, and now it was happening, right before his eyes. They recorded 'Simmer Down' in just two takes and everything went down onto the one-track tape at the same time – voices and instruments, including the drums and horn section. Bunny claims they recorded five songs that day, whereas Beverley only remembers them singing the one.

Coxsone knew that 'Simmer Down' was a hit, and lost no time getting test pressings over to the radio stations.

"It was like Trench Town light up when 'Simmer Down' come out because everybody love that song!" Beverley exclaims. "Everybody turn up their radios full blast and they play it like six times! This is on RJR. They say, 'This is brand new from the Wailers' and I remember screaming with delight as it played."

Peter was showering when 'Simmer Down' drifted over the airwaves and still had soap in his ears after running outside to hear it better. The smile on his face would last for days. This is what they'd been working towards, and the feeling was better than he'd ever imagined.

'Simmer Down' was a smash hit in the period leading up to Christmas 1964 and the message in it had relevance too, since rival gangs now began to roam West Kingston. Trench Town elders called these youths "rude boys", and thought the Wailers had it just about right.

Beverley didn't remember how the second session went or what they recorded but 'Mr. Talkative' and 'Climb The Ladder' are leading candidates and the energy levels on those records are again off the hook. What exuberance! The only group that could match the Wailers for sheer excitement was Toots & the Maytals, who were also members of Coxsone's stable.

The Wailers would become regulars at Studio One, and go there most days to rehearse or record. If Coxsone liked one of their songs, he'd make a test pressing and play it on his sound system to see how the crowds reacted. If they loved it, he'd keep it as an exclusive for a while, and then press it on a vinyl 45 when demand was at its height. This was record promotion Jamaican style and it worked, since he could sell upwards of 20,000 copies if the song was a hit.

Coxsone had unashamedly modelled Studio One on Motown and, like Berry Gordy, wanted to groom acts capable of writing and performing hits to a high standard. He even borrowed Motown's slogan "The Young Sound Of America" and changed it to "The Sound Of Young Jamaica" but it was his wide-ranging choice of material that differentiated him from other producers. Over the years he'd record pop, Latin, jazz, folk, blues, gospel and soul, as well as every Caribbean genre. Next to his office was a recreation room where staff could listen to records and pick out songs.

Maybe they'd discover one they wanted to cover, or that would give them ideas to write something of their own. Coxsone's record collection would greatly assist the Wailers' musical education, but it was the opportunity to try out things for themselves, and to learn from more experienced musicians that would arm them with more practical skills.

Coxsone appointed Roland Alphonso to tutor the Wailers during their first few months at Studio One. He and Beverley Kelso had been neighbours in Jones Town, and everyone liked the kindly saxophonist. He helped them with songwriting and also taught them the value of teamwork, since there was always someone who needed harmonies. Alumni often refer to Studio One as a university, and that's certainly where the Wailers learnt their craft. Over the next two years they'd feature on songs by a dozen or so different artists, beginning with calypso singer Lord Bryner. Jackie Opel, who'd arrived from Barbados two years earlier and attained near instant stardom on the back of hits like 'Push Wood' and 'Cry Me A River', often called them for sessions. They also liked Delroy Wilson a good deal, and contributed harmonies to 'I Want Justice' soon after arriving at Studio One.

During the early days, Peter happily contributed guitar or keyboards to other artists' records when asked, and liked the feeling of sharing in a grand, musical adventure. The first time he'd played guitar on a session was during the recording of the Wailers' 'I Am Going Home'. That was another milestone and a satisfying one, although no sooner had he heard the playback then he was figuring out how to make his instrument sound better.

When they weren't in the studio, he and the others would be out in the yard round the back, eating roast ackee and breadfruit or joking around with some of the other artists and musicians. Bob and Bunny will later gain a reputation for being withdrawn but not so Peter. The closest he came was during the recording of 'Your Love'. Peter was supposed to sing baritone, but couldn't manage it and so was replaced by Joe Higgs, who was now back in the fold. Inwardly, Peter smarted at this indignity, but decided to keep his feelings under wraps for the sake of the group. He'd get his chance to shine on two original songs recorded that autumn, the calypso-tinged 'Maga Dog' and a rollicking 'Hootenanny', on which trumpeter Johnny "Dizzy" Moore and Roland Alphonso trade phrases. 'Hootenanny' was Peter's first lead vocal with the Wailers, and credited to Peter Touch & the Wailers when released on 45. It was yet another proud moment, and put a spring in his step. Peter's musical influences differed slightly from those of the others. He was steeped in mento from his time in Westmoreland, and definitely had more of a feeling for folk and country material. Bunny recalls that Peter would often take up his guitar and imitate Johnny Cash, and have them all falling about with laughter as he launched into songs like 'Ghost Riders In The Sky', complete with yodels. In Bunny's own words, Peter "was pure laughter" and "pure jokes", and Coxsone agreed.

"In the early days, Peter Tosh was very jovial," he told Leroy Jodie Pierson and Roger Steffens. "He would do things to make you laugh. Even as a youth, he was always respectful to me. He was very inspiring and hardworking. He had that country flavour from the early stages. He was from the outskirts, and they have a deeper mento flavour to their melody than whoever was in the city dealing with universal songs like 'That Doggie In The Window', Louis Jordan or whatever."

Such influences strongly inform 'Maga Dog', which Peter delivers with gusto. It's almost pure calypso, set to a driving Skatalites rhythm. The chorus is borrowed from an old-time saying whilst the storyline warns against feeling sympathy for skinny, i.e., "maga" dogs (or their human equivalents), since they're liable to turn round and bite you. Such sentiments would come back to haunt him in future but he's still only 20 years old, and intent on enjoying life to the full.

On their days off the Wailers might head for the strip of beach next to the refinery on Kingston's waterfront, where they'd exercise, swim and race each other. Peter was fastest, and once he got ahead there was no catching him. He'd recently become interested in martial arts and was always getting the others to rush him, so he could show off the moves he'd learnt from a book he carried around. The only way to beat him was to close in on him, pin his arms to his sides and bowl him over, which is something they rarely managed to do. Seeco often joined in their games of football and cricket, but Peter's height made him seem ungainly at times, and he'd often sit games out.

Joe Higgs was another friend they saw a good deal of, despite the occasional falling out. He'd accompany them to the studio and help them out with harmonies, often in the company of a girlfriend. Peter plays guitar and is back singing baritone on 'Habits', which features Junior on lead vocals. The Wailers' line-up is still fluid at this stage, just like their repertoire. It's as if they're drinking in all the musical experience they can, although the group's identity will ultimately suffer because of it. Peter's next single will be 'Amen' – a gospel roustabout he'd lifted from the new Impressions album. That's his rhythm guitar powering the rhythm, and Bob joining him in some high-spirited call and response. Junior wasn't there when the Wailers recorded two former Blues Busters hits – 'Donna' and 'Wings Of A Dove' – and the blues staple 'Nobody Knows'. At least 'Dance With Me' was an original, even if rather lacklustre. Bob sings lead vocals on all four but Peter dominates the harmonies, and Beverley shares the spotlight on 'Wings Of A Dove'.

It's not yet Christmas, and the Wailers are treading water – either that or they're trying out different styles and seeing what sticks. 'Go Jimmy Go', and a cover of Dion & the Belmonts' 'Teenager In Love' (with Peter singing falsetto) hardly did them justice as was the case with the Skatalites, who were in otherwise irresistible form on hits like 'Ball Of Fire', 'El Pussy Cat' and 'Guns Of Navarone'. Alas, their success will be short-lived after Don Drummond murders his girlfriend and is committed to a mental hospital, where he'll eventually die. Drummond was their talisman, and had recently been named among the world's top five trombonists by jazz star George Shearing but there were other outstanding talents to hand, and Peter was determined to learn as much as he could from them. Ernest Ranglin, who'd arranged Millie's 'My Boy Lollipop', was Jamaica's most accomplished jazz guitarist, and Peter marvelled at the older man's dexterity whenever he stopped by Studio One. That's his rippling guitar work on 'It Hurts To Be Alone', Junior's finest track with the Wailers and also his swansong, since he'll soon leave for America.

Coxsone hadn't considered them ready, and so the Wailers hadn't given any stage performances yet. Their first will take place at the Palace Theatre over the Christmas holidays. 'It Hurts To Be Alone' was doing well on the charts, and anticipation was running high. The boys all wore matching dark suits that Peter had pressed himself. He called these suits "shiners", because of the sheen of the fabric. Underneath, they wore black shirts decorated with gold spots the size of a half-crown, whilst Beverley squeezed into a white crinoline dress that her mother had made for her. Their hearts were racing as they ran out in front of the packed house but then just as they started their act, there was a power cut and the theatre was plunged into darkness. It wasn't the Wailers' fault but the crowd threw bottles at them, sending splinters of glass flying about the stage. About

10 minutes later and the power came back on. That was the cue for Bob and Peter to return from the wings, flapping their arms like demented chickens. Beverley wanted to laugh so much she could hardly sing, but then there was another blackout and this angered the crowd even more. Skirmishes broke out between disgruntled patrons and the police, and the Wailers returned to Trench Town feeling disconsolate.

Peter and Bob both wrote songs about what had happened. Peter sang one called 'Jumbie Jamboree' ("jumbie" means ghost or "duppy" in Jamaican patois) whilst Bob refers to the flying bottles on 'Hooligans' and in chastising the troublemakers, lets people know that he's no anarchist. The Wailers' next gig was in Montego Bay and that was a disaster too, because there was no PA system. Again they faced an abusive crowd, despite Bob's best efforts at pacifying them. There were a few unhappy faces during the long drive back to Kingston. Beverley had worn a new stage outfit she'd had specially made. She told the others that Coxsone had paid for the material, and let her keep the change. This went down badly with Peter and Junior, who were upset at not having any money. Dissension began to worm its way into the Wailers' ranks since they had records on the charts, and yet none of them had anything to show for it. Beverley told Roger Steffens that she doesn't remember ever getting royalties or weekly payments and yet, years later, Peter will tell author Sebastian Clarke that Coxsone paid the Wailers £15 or £20 for every side they recorded, plus £3 a week and money towards stage clothes. This doesn't sound *too* bad, although Coxsone clearly didn't appreciate it when people asked him for money.

"Dodd used to give his artists mint balls and a bus fare if they demanded money," reported Clarke. "He was also violent in his response to verbal or threatened violence. Tosh states that Jimmy Radway, who worked for Dodd, once asked him to play the organ on somebody's tune. Tosh refused and went with Bunny to sit in the studio yard. When Dodd returned he asked them to leave, but Tosh said it was his blood, sweat and tears that had built the studio. An argument ensued in which Peter and Bunny abused him and goaded Dodd to go for the gun he always carried around with him, but he called the police instead..."

Soon they'll be falling out with Seeco too, who'd been urging Bob to demand a bigger share of the Wailers' income, such as it was. Junior had complained to Coxsone about this, who saw him and Peter as troublemakers. Bob came away feeling embarrassed and didn't speak to Seeco for weeks afterwards.

"I don't know if Bob got paid or get money every week. All I know is that I didn't get any and I know that Peter didn't get any," Beverley continued. "If Bob get any money, then only Bunny know about it because Peter would get upset and say that Bunny and Bob are brothers and so they're keeping it in the family. After Junior left, Peter used to complain to me and he was not happy because I didn't have anything to say. I would listen, but then the day after he'd complain, they would all be back together. But I didn't see anybody get paid and I never heard Coxsone say, 'This is for you and this is for you.' I didn't know anything about that."

Bunny Wailer disputes this. "Wailers were brothers," he told Roger Steffens. "Wailers would never go about their business without worrying what's happening to a next man. No, the Wailers didn't live so. If Peter head hurt him or anybody had an accident, then every man would be heading for where he was. We shared everything we had. If I knew that Peter didn't have any money and I came into some, then I go look for him. That's how Wailers lived."

With Junior gone and Beverley contributing little, the Wailers reverted to being a trio, at least for a time. They'll also become disenchanted and kept their own counsel, even at Studio One.

"From as far back as the sixties, the Wailers were feared as much as they were admired," says Bob Andy. "They were a very strict bunch of guys, and always had screw faces. They would keep anyone away from them with just a look. They didn't accommodate anyone. People liked and admired them but were sort of scared of those looks, which protected them from any kind of intrusion or invasion of their privacy. They would mix because they were brethren, but they also had a very elitist attitude."

They weren't like this with everyone. In the spring of 1965, Peter met a young singer from Port Antonio called Leonard Dillon, who performed under the name "Jack Sparrow". Peter played guitar as his new friend auditioned for the other Wailers, and Bob and Bunny took him to him straightaway. His song 'Ice Water', recorded for Coxsone, features the Wailers' harmonies. Dillon will later form the Ethiopians with Stephen Taylor and write the prophetic 'Everything Crash'.

Coxsone thought Junior was a better singer than Bob, and felt disappointed after "Bratty" left to join his family in Chicago, where he hoped to become a doctor. If he'd harboured doubts about the Wailers' future, then they were soon dashed away by 'Love And Affection' – a joyous romp with catchy chorus that could be heard blaring out of every jukebox that summer. Peter's baritone is now distinctive as his lead voice and he sings falsetto too, remember.

He and Bob's friendship will soon be tested like never before. On their way to Brentford Road the group often walked along Greenwich Park Road, where they'd see a teenage girl stood outside No. 18A with an infant daughter in her arms.

Bob and Bunny would call her "the black gal", and laugh at her. Not so Beverley, who discovered the girl's name was Rita Anderson, and she had a group called the Soulettes who wanted to record a song. That's how Rita, her cousin Constantine Walker (whom they called "Dream") and friend Marlene Gifford joined Studio One. Beverley recommended them, and jokes about Rita's skin colour soon ceased. Some accounts would have us believe that Peter was with Rita before Bob stole her away from him, but Beverley remembers it differently.

"To be honest, Peter and Rita didn't hook up. I know that one point, Peter watching Rita, and Bob was watching Rita. It was like the two of them were at war, seeing which one of them was going to get Rita. She wasn't "that black gal" any more and I was watching them but there was a problem I think, going around. Peter force himself on her against Rita's will. How the studio make up, we could walk through the studio and there was a little side room. We all would go into that side room to rest and relax. Anyone could go in there to meditate or whatever else you want to do. One day Peter was in there and I see that Rita went in too because I was there looking at what Siddy (engineer Sidney Bucknor) was doing and said that I felt a bit tired, and that I was going to go and sit down. When I was going inside I saw that Rita's back was turned towards me and Peter was forcing himself on her. I could see that was something wrong because Peter and Rita weren't together, and they weren't even friends. It was like he wanted sex with her and she was pushing him off and I could see that he was feeling her up and so when Peter see me, I just take my time, back out and come out smiling. Bunny was there, looking at me. He wanted to go inside but I wouldn't let him, because I didn't want him to see what I'd just seen. Bunny realised something was going on but until this day I never tell anybody what I saw, because they would say Rita was playing for that and that wasn't fair. Even though Bunny didn't get to go in, it's like he realised what was happening and maybe he said something to Peter about what a foolish thing it was but I don't think Bob hear about it, because otherwise he and Rita wouldn't have got close. Things break down now, and Bob get with Rita... This happened around the same time. Peter and Bob were both after Rita, but Peter try and get there first by forcing himself on her but as far as I could see, nothing ever came of it because she play into Bob and then everyone know they are together."

Coxsone placed the Soulettes under Bob's direction and he proved a hard taskmaster, even whilst succumbing to Rita's charms. Bunny, meanwhile, was dating Marlene who everyone called "Precious". Peter began to feel left out. Junior had left and he was still smarting to see Bob with Rita. If what Beverley says is true, then he's guilty of attempted rape. Was he trying to spite Bob, or just maddened by Rita's earthy sensuality? Also, did race come into play? Rita was black, and Bob half-white. What if, in Peter's mind, she'd chosen white over black, and it was a racial slight he was reacting to?

Beverley returned for 'Lonesome Feelings' and was joined by Cherry Green, who'd been part of the scene round Joe Higgs' place. Coxsone had enrolled a new band and the Wailers sound re-energised. 'Lonesome Feelings' was a hit and so too Joe Higgs' 'There's A Reward', recorded at the same session. Cherry then left and never sang with the Wailers again.

"Those were the amateur days and maybe some people couldn't keep up to the standard of what music is supposed to be," Peter said to Fikisha Cumbo. "Because when you're born you start creep, and then you walk and then you become conscious and you start to see what's going on. Well after we start music, we just creep, more creeping and some of the creepers maybe couldn't walk or never intend to walk, so we have to creep-walk away leave them, or they creep away leave us and the group eventually work down to three. Maybe it's a financial disposition we had to go through and they couldn't cope with it. Every man had financial responsibilities, but some people can't really cope without money for a couple of days or weeks or any amount of time. Well we were determined to do it without money, and we were fooled that way."

Chapter 4

The Toughest

In late summer 1965 Coxsone returned from a trip to London having signed a distribution deal with Island Records. This was the label – owned by a white Jamaican called Chris Blackwell – that had catapulted Millie to stardom. The UK market for West Indian music (known as "Blue Beat") had now grown considerably and offered fresh opportunities for producers like Coxsone, who spent Island's advance on a two-track Ampex tape recorder.

He got back to find the Wailers still reeling from the Impressions' recent visit to Jamaica. Maybe that's what infused songs like 'One Love', 'Do You Feel The Same Way Too' and 'The Jerk' with such joie de vivre. The 'jerk' was America's latest dance craze, as immortalised in hits by the Larks, Contours, Miracles and Capitols. The Wailers wanted to show they were hip too, even if they were from the islands – a fact they cheerfully acknowledge on the calypso classic 'Shame And Scandal'. Peter sings lead on a song that's laced with humour, and has a delightful twist in its tail. The storyline revolves around a young man whose father tells him he can't marry his girlfriend, because she might be his sister. His mother says not to worry though, because that's not his real father after all! Peter's a natural at singing this kind of material but must have winced when Coxsone suggested they do a cover of 'What's New Pussycat'. You'd assume a song like that – then a UK hit for Tom Jones – would be an affront to the Wailers' integrity, but they did it anyway.

In late autumn, they recorded 'Rude Boy (Gone A Jail)', which borrows from the Impressions' 'Keep On Moving', and stirs in a little Jamaican folklore for good measure. By Christmas it was a smash hit, reaching number four on the charts and inspiring a dance called the 'Rude Boy Ska'. Eager to try out his new two-track facilities which allowed him to re-use the same backing tracks, Coxsone persuaded Peter and Bunny to sing harmonies on 'Pussy Galore' – an alternative cut of 'Rude Boy' that's rife with sexual innuendo. The artist, Lee Perry, was known as "Chicken Scratch" after a record he'd made about the dance craze. He was Coxsone's right-hand man and would fill in wherever needed, helping out with the sound system, auditioning new acts and doing odd jobs around the studio. He couldn't really sing, but just made the occasional novelty tune. He had character though, and the Wailers liked him enough to sing on another of his records, 'Hand To Hand' aka 'Man To Man'.

It was at this point the Skatalites finally succumbed to internal strife and went their separate ways. Tenor sax player Tommy McCook left to lead the Supersonics over at Treasure Isle, but Jackie Mittoo and Roland Alphonso stayed with Coxsone to head a new band called the Soul Brothers. It's them playing behind the Wailers on 'I'm Still Waiting', which went Top 20 in January 1966 backed with 'Ska Jerk' – a cover of Junior Walker & the All-Stars' 'Shotgun' that sounded a little dated even then.

In November, Peter had lent his baritone to Delroy Wilson's 'Jerk All Night' and a couple of numbers by the Soulettes. He'd helped out on these songs in between recording a handful of new tracks with Bob and Bunny, including 'Good, Good Rudie' aka 'Jailhouse'. Finally, the Wailers have nailed their colours to the mast and identified themselves with rude boy culture. "Rudies" had become confused with hardened criminals whereas they were the punks of their day – surly and aggressive at times, but with no real agenda stoking their dissatisfaction. Whilst the Wailers had sympathy with them – and even *looked* like rude boys in their tight pants with flannels dangling from the back pockets – it's as well to remember they weren't about to get distracted from their musical ambitions. They defended the rudies because they shared their frustrations, and sided with them against police brutality. The lyrics of 'Jailhouse' warn that after "batons get shorter, rudie gets taller" but most daring of all is the line, "We're gonna rule this land, right now. You can't fight against prediction..."

42

Music like this made Peter feel proud. Songs written about what was happening around them had a sense of purpose, and could make a difference to people's lives. No wonder he bridled when Coxsone suggested they cover 'White Christmas'. Peter thought this was pushing the Wailers' credibility too far. He railed and cursed, forcing Bob to compromise by singing, "I'm dreaming of a white Christmas, *not* like the ones I used to know". Bob clearly had fewer scruples since he and Coxsone made further gospel records together, including a cut of Prof. Alex Bradford's 'He'll Wash You Whiter Than Snow'. We can imagine what Peter thought about that one. He and Bunny are nowhere within earshot and don't reappear until 'Another Dance' – another Impressions cover, but featuring Bunny on lead for a change.

Bob and Bunny will record a couple of tunes on their own around this time. Peter had fallen out with Coxsone after helping himself to some records. He felt that he was entitled to them, but Coxsone thought differently and after the pair almost came to blows, Peter was banned from the premises for a while. It was the same old complaint, over and over. The Wailers still weren't getting enough money, and yet they were more popular than ever. Admittedly 'Another Dance' hadn't done too well yet it still scraped into the Top 20, even without a great deal of interest from Coxsone.

Peter was no long happy with the Wailers' musical direction. He considered it a backward step singing covers (the Moonglows' 'Ten Commandments Of Love' for example) and was chafing at Coxsone's conservative outlook, as well as his meanness. He wanted the Wailers to make their mark with original material that *stood* for something, and that people could relate to. This will take time, and the group weren't exactly short of ideas in the meantime. Their last hit of 1965 was 'I'm Gonna Put It On', which flew into the Top 5 and mixes gospel with a proud declaration of independence, thanks to the line "I rule my destiny..." Bob's attention will then begin to stray after his mother invites him to join her in America. She and Thaddeus had settled in Wilmington, in the state of Delaware, and had written to say that work was plentiful there. Bob was tempted since the Wailers wanted to try and produce their own records, which cost money. He and the others knew there was little chance of them getting ahead in Jamaica but then just as he planned his next move, Rita announced she was pregnant.

Bob confided in Beverley and confessed he didn't know what to do. She suggested he talk to Mr. Dodd, who recommended they get married. The service took place on February 10. Coxsone made the arrangements and may have even paid for it, but invitations were scant.

"Peter and Bunny didn't know about it, and I didn't know that," says Beverley. "It was a Saturday afternoon and Peter come to me saying, 'How come you never tell me that Bob and Rita get married? You didn't tell me anything,' so I tell him I didn't go to the wedding... I was invited but I was sick so I didn't make it but I was there in the evening and Peter start on me. I told him I didn't know why he hadn't been told about it and then the next thing I see Bunny come saying how Bob and Rita get married and he didn't know about it. I say, 'But you and Bob are brothers, so why did he never invite you?'"

The marriage must have been arranged quite hastily, because Rita's not visibly pregnant in the wedding photo. Bob's new bride has claimed he left for Delaware the day after the wedding, although Beverley disputes this.

"He didn't leave for a while, because they opened that record shop," she told Roger Steffens. "That was before he left for America, right in front of Rita's house. They build a little board shop but I didn't go up there regular because I didn't like what I was seeing. It was their lifestyle. This Rasta business started with Rita's brother. He used to go to the university and he never comb his hair. He used to preach to them, telling them things about Babylon and whatever. The preaching come from out of Rita's house, I remember that clearly and they start smoking now, more and more. They start saying 'Rastafari' and making wild talk. Bob start to grow his hair, Peter start and Bunny not combing his hair any more either... They pass their spliff to me and I back away from it, because I didn't want no part of that."

Marijuana (which Rastafarians called "herb") was illegal in Jamaica and yet Peter found it aided his meditation, stirred his imagination and soothed his frustrations. It helped put a smile on his face and a warm glow in his heart, so what was there to fear? It was a plant that grew naturally and wasn't at all harmful like alcohol and tobacco, which were freely available yet enslaved people. Peter surmised the authorities were lying, and believed the Rastas when they said smoking herb opened a path to the divine. It was a holy sacrament, and he'll defend his right to smoke it with great conviction from now on. Unfortunately for him, Trench Town was a happy hunting ground for police looking to secure a reputation for themselves, so woe betide anyone caught smoking a chalice when the "blue seam" burst into someone's yard, hoping to add to their night's tally. Most of these officers weren't local, but were from neighbouring stations. No one from outside really cared what the police got up to in places like Trench Town, and these officers knew it. That's why people congregated on street corners, because they could see in several directions at once. There were no walls in Trench Town, only wire fences, so there was nothing to stop the police driving up West Road and standing upright in their Jeeps, watching what people were up to 50 yards away.

The Wailers were now firmly identified as Trench Town artists who'd sided with the rude boys – a perception that won them no favours from radio DJs or society people. Conversely, they were heroes to ghetto people and even lack of airplay couldn't prevent 'It Hurts To Be Alone', 'Rude Boy', 'Jailhouse' and 'I'm Gonna Put It On' from dominating the RJR charts as 1965 drew to a close.

Before Bob left, the Wailers gave a farewell performance so they could raise money towards his trip. It had been a while since they'd performed, and they made sure they were ready this time. In developing their stage act they'd taken their cue from American stars like James Brown and Jackie Wilson, whose dynamic routines packed as much excitement as their songs. Beverley didn't sing with them, and wasn't missed. The show raised £12 towards Bob's trip, but then descended into chaos after gangs of youths stormed the entrance and battled with police outside.

After the show, Bob left for the US where he'll stay for the next six or seven months. Coxsone apparently paid for his ticket and expressed concern that the Wailers wouldn't last without him. Bob assured him that Peter and Bunny were talented enough to keep the group going, although even he must have harboured reservations. Peter and Bunny still hadn't forgiven him for marrying Rita on the quiet, and felt that he'd betrayed them. They may also have suspected Rita got pregnant on purpose, which meant that Bob had been duped. Since his and Rita's first child won't be born for another 18 months either she miscarried, or she wasn't pregnant at all. Whatever the truth of that situation, the trust between band members was definitely beginning to fray.

Bob had originally wanted Bunny to go with him to Delaware. This invitation wasn't extended to Peter, who didn't want to leave Jamaica in any case. Bunny chose to stay, and drew closer to Peter during Bob's absence. Despite Coxsone's qualms both were determined to keep the hits coming, and prove themselves as lead singers. Their first move was to recruit Dream, who'd since changed his name to "Vision" after a Rastaman from Trench Town told him that, "old man get dream, young man see vision". He and Peter harmonised well together behind Bunny, who'll handle most lead vocals from now on. The Wailers were booked to perform at a local theatre shortly after Bob left, and the new line-up went down a storm.

Peter told Roger Steffens: "I remember one time we were performing at the Ward Theatre and from we start sing, boy! Is just some kind of money come up on stage, poof! Drop beside me and some half a crown lick me head and all them things, by the hundreds! I stop sing and pick up two pockets full, but before I come off the stage it was all begged out. Every man in the audience come beg it back until me have just the one two-and-six pence left in me hand, out of two pocket full of money! Yeah man, those things amusing still, cos me just laugh but me have some fantastic experiences on stage…"

One of the first songs they recorded without Bob was 'Sinner Man' – a traditional song popularised by Nina Simone that Peter will later rewrite as 'Downpressor Man'. He'd been singing it a number of years already, although Bunny is curiously allowed to overshadow him. Just to compound the error, Coxsone credited the 45 to "Bob Marley and the Wailers", despite Bob having nothing to do with it. Was this a deliberate ploy to fool people into thinking Bob was still there? Peter thought so, especially when their next release, a Cuban-flavoured ditty called 'Guajira Ska', was credited to the "Soul Brothers". No matter, his spirits will be well and truly lifted the following month when Emperor Haile Selassie I of Ethiopia pays a state visit to Jamaica – an event Bunny has likened to "the second coming".

Indeed, April 21, 1966 will forever be etched into Jamaican history after thousands of Rastamen poured into Kingston and made their way to the airport to greet His Majesty, who was escorted from the plane by Trench Town's very own Mortimo Planno – a Rasta leader who'd travelled to Ethiopia and met with the Emperor several years previously, as part of a government fact-finding mission.

This spectacle angered the authorities, who'd been powerless to prevent it. Rastafarians were still scorned in most parts of Jamaica, and yet they'd all but hijacked this important occasion. As if that wasn't enough, the Emperor had also requested to meet with Rastafarian elders during his visit and so at some of the official functions, Jamaica's ruling elite duly interacted with Rastafarians for the very first time. Typically, Bunny, Peter and Vision had missed the Emperor's arrival, since they'd spent the best part of the day waiting on payment from Coxsone, who kept them hanging around for hours and then paid them a pittance. Their mutterings of discontent had continued all the way down West Road as they joined the revellers, who filled the streets everywhere they looked.

Seizing the moment, Peter went back to Studio One a few days later and cut 'Rasta Shook Them Up' with the Gay Lads singing harmonies. It's the first song he'll record without any of the other Wailers and the first by any of the group – Marley included – that mentions Rastafari. Peter even recites a few words in the ancient language of Ethiopia during the introduction, which is another first. He'd picked up the odd phrase of Amharic in the Rasta camps, and it's to Coxsone's credit that Peter's original vision was left intact. 'Rasta Shook Them Up' is a celebration, pure and simple, but it's also a declaration of allegiance, which carried a certain element of risk at the time.

Peter, Bunny, Rita and Vision all thirsted for more knowledge about Selassie and the Rastafarian faith. One of the people they visited was Bongo Donald, who lived near Rita on Greenwich Park Road. Bongo Donald and other Rasta elders would reason with them and read from books on African history, as well as the Bible. Peter now felt empowered like never before. He was learning about his own history, and a once proud lineage that had been shattered by the heartless brutality of the slave trade. It was a history – headed by ancient royalty – he wished to reclaim, and 'Rasta Shook Them Up' was only the start.

Within just a few weeks he went back into the studio with the Soul Vendors and recorded 'The Toughest' – a song born out of frustration, since Coxsone had suggested Peter sing James and Bobby Purify's 'I'm Your Puppet', but the lanky Wailer was having none of it. Whilst Coxsone has claimed he co-wrote it and that it's really a sound-system boast, Peter invests it with an altogether different meaning. Again issued under the name "Peter Touch", 'The Toughest' will become his biggest hit to date and help define him in terms of his musical personality. "Anything you can do, I can do it better, I'm the toughest," he declares, before

47

noticeably distancing himself from the rudies' lawlessness with the line, "Stop from doing wrongs, change your foolish plans". Most telling of all, he then points out that "You come with your bitterness, but I just use my skill".

Peter, like the other Wailers, rejected the violence and negativity associated with rude boys. Instead, they sought ways of expressing the social conscience that accompanied their growing immersion in Rastafari. The music had begun to change in any case. Soul music, rather than rhythm and blues, had become a dominant influence and local musicians – following the example of Trinidadian guitarist Lynn Taitt – responded by slowing down the beat and placing more emphasis on melody and arrangements. The result was rocksteady, as typified by hits like Hopeton Lewis' 'Take It Easy', Alton Ellis' 'Do Rocksteady' and Delroy Wilson's 'Dancing Mood'.

The Wailers' first rocksteady hit was 'Let Him Go', written about a rude boy who's been wrongly imprisoned. It also exposes a society that discriminates against people because they're poor and can't get work. Bunny sings lead on that one, in addition to 'Who Feels It Knows It' and the haunting 'Sunday Morning'. Songs like these, together with Bob Andy's 'I've Got To Go Back Home', are among Studio One's finest rocksteady sides except there was no stopping Duke Reid over at Treasure Isle, who dominated that era with hits by Alton Ellis, Phyllis Dillon, the Paragons, Techniques and Melodians, among others.

Coxsone was losing out to his fiercest rival, although it wasn't for lack of trying. Peter sang harmonies on Ken Boothe's 'The Train Is Coming', another of that summer's biggest hits, while Rita joined Bunny and Peter on 'Rock To The Rock' and 'Making Love', another engaging slice of rocksteady romance. Listening to her and Peter carousing like this, it's easy to forget that he'd tried forcing himself on Rita less than a year earlier. Oh to have been a fly on the wall, and seen the dynamics between them in the studio that day!

Peter will sing lead on a spate of tunes before Bob returns to Jamaica. That's him crooning 'When The Well Runs Dry', which owes more than a little to Otis Redding's 'You Don't Miss Your Water'. The Wailers also covered two songs by the Temptations, 'Baby, Baby I Need You' and 'Don't Look Back', during this period. In years to come, Peter will revisit 'Don't Look Back' in the company of Mick Jagger. This early version strays little from the Temptations' original but it's interesting to note that Peter was attempting to incorporate rock into his repertoire even as far back as 1966. 'Can't You See' marked a radical departure for the Wailers, and would have graced any Rolling Stones album from that era. Ten years hence and Marley will be lauded for his ability to connect with rock audiences, yet it was Peter who took the first steps down that path.

Rock music was now in the ascendancy, fuelled by the emergence of a counterculture defined by longhaired hippies preaching love and freedom, and also growing disenchantment with America's involvement in the Vietnam War. Music was no longer viewed as entertainment alone, but as a vehicle for protest and rebellion – a change of emphasis that accurately mirrored Peter's own ambitions, and made him even more determined to write songs that mattered. In July, Kingston was again beset by looting and demonstrations after the authorities razed Back O'Wall – a shantytown community that had sprung up on a stretch of Kingston's waterfront. Most of the inhabitants were Rastafarians, who lived in makeshift shelters built of cardboard and driftwood. The destruction of their camps was seen as revenge for the embarrassment they'd caused during Emperor Haile Selassie I's visit but the fallout would create widespread hardship, as Kingston's ghetto communities swelled with refugees. Once the land had been cleared, the JLP used it to build housing for their supporters, who they began arming to secure territorial advantage. The rude boys thus came under the sway of political benefactors, and became even more emboldened as a result. A state of emergency was declared in October and curfews imposed in West Kingston, where the majority of incidents had flared up.

As 1966 drew to a close, Coxsone released two further Wailers tracks. 'Dancing Shoes' was delightful, but it was 'I Stand Predominant' that confirmed the group's spiritual awakening with its use of "I and I" – a combination of higher and personal self that's central to Rastafarian belief. Peter and Bunny will embrace Rastafari wholeheartedly and it will remain their inspiration and guiding light for the rest of their lives, yet they were also intent on taking heed of what protest singers like Bob Dylan were doing, by infusing pop songs with social commentary. Bob was already a huge Dylan fan and had even changed his name from "Robbie" in deference to the American. The last batch of songs Peter, Bunny and Vision recorded before his return to Jamaica included two Dylan numbers

– 'Blowing In The Wind' and 'Like A Rolling Stone'. Bunny changed the lyrics slightly on the latter, whilst tapes of 'Blowing In The Wind' have never surfaced. Bunny will also make changes to the El Tempos' 'My Dream Island' and re-title it 'Dreamland'. It's beautifully evocative and yet won't be released for more than two decades, by which time Bunny will have re-recorded it at least twice.

Coxsone had found Peter and Bunny hard going compared to Bob. They were confrontational at times – usually over money – and had remained resolutely suspicious of his motives. More than two years after first joining Studio One, they viewed him as a robber who enticed his victims with dreams and music and then exploited them financially. Both felt betrayed by him even though Coxsone had nurtured their careers, and made it possible for them to accrue professional skills. He'd turned their youthful fantasies into reality, exposed them to a wealth of new ideas and provided them with a musical education. In his own mind he didn't owe the Wailers anything and so he understandably bristled at Peter and Bunny's behaviour, which he deplored. Bunny was especially confrontational. He was vehement when reminding Coxsone of all the records they'd sold, and demanding money for royalties. If it wasn't for the Wailers' strong following in Trench Town Coxsone would have boxed him down for sure, but he was fearful of repercussions. Everything then came to a head one day after another shouting match, when Bunny whipped out his ratchet knife, held it to Coxsone's stomach and told him he was leaving, never to return. Peter wasn't there, and yet automatically fell in line with his friend. The Wailers' stay at Studio One was now over, but at least Peter and Bunny had proven themselves capable of making hit records without Bob. That was significant, and it'll do Peter's confidence a world of good in future.

"During that period when Bob was absent from the group, the members who stood their ground proved that we were the Wailers with or without Bob," Bunny recalls. "Those recordings are there to show that no member of the Wailers was indispensable. Every one of us was fully clad, and ready and able to deliver themselves so that the group became the Wailers, no matter what. Looking back, it's good to know that we'd grown into each other in such a way so that if one member's missing, you don't even feel it."

Chapter 5

Stepping Razor

Coxsone tried to persuade Bob to record for him after he got back, either with Peter and Bunny or without them. If Bob was tempted he didn't show it, but remained loyal to the others and readjusted to life back in Jamaica as best as he could. Rita had either lost the baby or never been pregnant in the first place, but at least they were able to make a fresh start. Bob had saved a little from his factory job and Coxsone came up with money in lieu of royalties, which was a surprise. There was definitely enough to book a studio, pay a few musicians and get a record out, although Bob suggested they hire Studio One, which didn't go down too well.

It was November when Peter and Bunny reluctantly went back there to record two of Bob's new songs. 'Freedom Time' reflected what was happening in black America. Also known as 'Get Ready', it was inspired by gospel and the Civil Rights movement, whereas 'Bend Down Low' was real saucy. Peter liked the message in 'Freedom Time'. Impregnated with black history, it showed how far the Wailers had come. Like the Beatles, the Wailers were making the transition from pop group to cultural figureheads. They'd outgrown Coxsone in both the cultural and creative sense, and were a different entity from the group he'd auditioned two years earlier.

On his return, Bob was taken aback by the others' appearance. Rita had written to him, telling him how much they'd been influenced by the Emperor's visit but it was still a surprise to see they'd started to grow dreadlocks. Bob himself had grown out his hair so he looked like one of the hippies they'd been hearing about. He'd listened to a lot of rock and soul music in Wilmington, and could appreciate what artists like Dylan and the Beatles were doing. The soul influences went deeper of course, and the name of the Wailers' first label reflected this. Wail 'N Soul 'M started out as "Wail And Soul Them" after Bob remarked that he and Rita's marriage had marked a coming together of the Wailers and Soulettes. Bunny then shortened the name to "Wail 'N Soul 'M" and designed the logo, which depicted three clasped hands. The Wailers were now in business for themselves and whilst money would be hard to come by, none of them doubted they had what it took to be successful.

The three Wailers would balance boxes of records on their handlebars as they wove down the busy Kingston streets on their bicycles, delivering them to retail outlets all over the city. Peter delighted in boasting of how good their new record was, and then watching people's faces after they'd put it on the turntable and the opening bars of 'Freedom Time' rang out. Rita did her share too, by manning the lean-to store outside of her aunt's house in Greenwich Park Road. Most days she'd be sat there under a sign proudly declaring "Wail 'N Soul 'M", selling records by the Wailers and newer producers like Bunny Lee, Joe Gibbs and Lee Perry, who'd just left Coxsone under acrimonious circumstances.

Trench Town was now divided, and people had to be careful about making rash utterances. Ghetto communities continued to be carved up along political lines, and rivalries often threatened to spill over into violence. Peter was still living on West Road, straining to curb his frustration. For whatever reason, he chose to voice a tune for Prince Buster that will appall Bunny when he first hears it almost 20 years later. He'll be upset on three accounts – the title ('Simpleton'), name of the band (Crackers) and poor quality of the song itself. Buster had wanted to record the Wailers but didn't get on too well with Mortimo Planno, who'll exert considerable influence over them as they venture deeper into the Rastafarian faith. Buster was one of Jamaica's best-known artists and ran a popular sound system called Voice Of The People. He'd been the first producer to take Rastafarian drummers into the studio, after recruiting Count Ossie to play on the Folkes Brothers' 'Oh Carolina', and was generally fearless. He'd challenged Duke Reid and Coxsone when they ruled the Kingston dancehalls, fought them physically, forged his own sound by putting his faith in the creativity of local musicians and then struck a deal with Emile Shallit's Blue Beat label in the UK that guaranteed him widespread distribution. A former boxer, he was friends with Sam Cooke, Malcolm X and Muhammad Ali, who bought him a Cadillac and had it shipped to Jamaica. Buster's popularity wouldn't last but he was a major personality in every sense. He was also one of Peter's earliest mentors, and an important one. When Ali was stripped of his world title for refusing the US draft, every black man took note. Ali was not only a great boxer, but also a beacon for black nationhood. He'd allied supreme confidence in his own ability with wonderful humour, and then swore allegiance to Elijah Muhammad's Nation Of Islam.

Peter was 22 and his heart beat with pride after hearing Buster's stories about Ali. Men like these didn't sit around and wait for the white man to give them anything. Just like James Brown, they were saying, "Open the door and I'll get it for myself". The way they explained it, racial pride wasn't a sin but a virtue. It signified both strength and cause for celebration. Even in Jamaica, people heard the phrase "Black Power" a lot more now. It was the summer of 1967 and the hippy revolution was in full swing although there was a feeling that these white kids weren't rebelling out of necessity, but from a desire to shock their parents. People living in Trench Town were more in tune with the riots happening in New Jersey, after white cops killed a black protestor. To their way of thinking, James Brown wasn't just referring to physical exertions on 'Cold Sweat', but the clamminess felt after scenting revolution in the air.

The Wailers respected Planno and became regular visitors at his yard on Fifth Street, where Rastafarians would gather to talk, read their Bibles, cook food and smoke herb. That's where Peter heard news of what was happening in black communities worldwide, including Africa. Trench Town had no libraries or bookstores but Planno's Friday night meetings acted as a forum where people from far and wide pooled knowledge. Speakers often included teachers and university lecturers, and not just Rastafarian elders. Peter's love of Africa took root in this fertile soil and he'd listen intently as people told of travels to Ethiopia and elsewhere. Above all he learnt about colonialism and the systematic rape of his ancestral lands. The realisation of what had been lost during 400 years of slavery now hit home with considerable force.

Planno's trips to Kingston's red light district and his greed for money will eventually tarnish his relations with the Wailers, but he acted as their manager for about a year and produced their most devout tune yet – a Rastafarian anthem called 'Selassie Is The Chapel' they'd modelled on Sonny Til & The Orioles' 'Crying In The Chapel'. Bunny wasn't there the day Peter, guitar in hand, sat down with Bob and two Rasta drummers and cut 'Selassie Is The Chapel'. He was first to see through Planno, and would visit their friend Tartar instead. One night police stormed the yard, and ordered everyone to lie face down whilst they searched for marijuana. They didn't have to look far. Tartar was arrested for possession, whilst Bunny was charged with "being in the vicinity". Shearer's government had imposed a mandatory 18-month jail sentence for possession of herb, and there was little chance of them avoiding prison.

The three Wailers left for St. Ann's shortly afterwards, to rethink their direction and take stock. Accompanied by Vision and Rita, they went to Nine Miles where Bob's family lived when he was a child. His grandfather had since died and left a plot of land, which Bob and others now planned to cultivate. Rita was heavily pregnant with her and Bob's first child, daughter Cedella, who will be born in two months' time. Peter's girlfriend Shirley, Bunny's sister who had been around the group since she was a young girl, was also about to give birth to their son Andrew, born on June 19. Peter won't stay with her, but then he was hardly the monogamous type.

"Peter had lots of girlfriends," says his cousin Pauline. "Three of them got pregnant for him at the same time but Steve was his first child. I remember his mother coming to the house in West Road when I was a kid. I think she just used to live up the road. She was the only one of Peter's girlfriends my mother and father would allow into the house, but other girls would come and stand outside the gate sometimes. Dave, who they called Horace, was born around the same time but I remember Peter used to argue with his mother and chase her from the gate, telling her to stay away – then when she was pregnant he tried to deny it. He was really lovey-dovey with Steve's mother though. She was Chinese Jamaican, and may well have been his first love. Peter was very magnetic back then. He was this tall, good-looking young man and the way he walked, it was as if he was so free..."

He'd have few opportunities to meet girls in Nine Miles unless it was at the nearby springs. Peter liked going there at dawn and bathing in the early morning light, before working on the farm. In truth, his enthusiasm for ploughing or planting was strictly limited. Most of all he liked it in the evenings, once he'd picked up his guitar and the Wailers began to sing and work on new material. Peter left for Kingston before the others. He either got bored, wanted to be with Shirley or had business to attend to – your choice.

The group had cut several tunes before heading for St. Ann's. They'd wanted to record as much material as they could with Bunny, who was due for sentencing. 'Mellow Mood', 'Nice Time', 'Hypocrites' and 'Thank You Lord' came out of one session; 'Bus Dem Shut' and 'Stir Up' another. Bob was writing some great songs and Peter told him so. They'll put the Wailers back on top, and with a brand new label as well. It was around this same time they recorded 'Lyrical Satyrical', which allowed Peter to show off his guitar skills, and 'This Train', featuring Bunny on lead vocals. By the time 'Nice Time' goes Top 10 that autumn, he'll be languishing in Kingston's General Penitentiary, where he'll spend the next two months before serving a year's hard labour on a prison farm.

Bob felt the loss of Bunny keenly, and would get frustrated when trying out new songs since the harmonies never sounded right. His mood lightened when 'Bus Dem Shut' and 'Stir It Up' charted but he and Peter were also feeling the pressures of raising young families. Peter, aged just 23, was father to at least two sons, if not three, and it took time to collect money from record sales.

As Christmas approached, American singer Johnny Nash came to Jamaica and performed on a televised charity show called Nuggets For The Needy. Nash was billed as "America's First Negro Teen Idol" and had starred in a film called *Take A Giant Step* that had been partially filmed in Jamaica. He was a fine singer, but considered a little too mainstream until recording 'Let's Move And Groove Together' in 1965. That song was co-produced by his manager, Jamaican born entrepreneur Danny Sims. He and Nash were friends with Ken Khouri, owner of Federal Records, who found them a house to rent in the hills above Kingston. Shortly afterwards, Johnny Nash met Bob at a Rasta gathering held to commemorate Ethiopian Christmas. Jamaican DJ Neville Willoughby had taken Johnny there, and made the introductions. Bob told him about the Wailers, and was invited to the house in Russell Heights. He, Peter, Rita and Mortimo Planno went up there and after upsetting the domestic help – who refused to serve dreadlocks – ran through some songs and chatted about their hopes for the future. The canny Sims saw Marley as a rough diamond, and was immediately impressed by his songwriting. Whilst Nash was a fine singer, he needed help with lyrics, a commodity Bob and Peter had in abundance, even if Sims did think it needed refining. The initial handful of songs they recorded for him and Nash were all written by cohorts of Sims, and clearly aimed at the American market.

The Wailers were now effectively a trio of Bob, Peter and Rita. This line-up recorded 'Pound Get A Blow', which Peter wrote about the fears surrounding Jamaica's decision to switch currencies. Poor people were convinced they'd lose out and Peter tapped into their mood with grim certainty. "Prepare for starvation," he told them. He'd written 'Funeral,' with Bunny, and Coxsone's ears must have picked up at hearing the lines, "What a big disgrace, the way you rob up the place. Robbing everything you can find..." Bunny claims that another of Peter's compositions, 'Hammer', was also recorded at those sessions. The new label was doing well and to ensure airplay, they bought a 15-minute slot on RJR called Wail 'N Soul 'M Time. The Wailers were leaving nothing to chance, as Peter prepared for another career-defining hit.

Joe Higgs had written 'Stepping Razor' for the 1967 Festival Song Competition but then abandoned it after the entry panel said it would encourage rude boys. Peter will later claim the publishing to 'Stepping Razor', despite the give-away line "don't watch my size I'm dangerous". He was well over six feet tall and a karate expert, so why would anyone need convincing that he's dangerous? Whereas Joe was just five foot four. 'Stepping Razor' will reinforce the image of Tosh as a swashbuckling rebel you'd better not mess with. All of Jamaica heard it, and the name on the label read "Peter Tosh & The Wailers".

Peter's identity is growing more distinct and his emergence will coincide with the rise of black consciousness. He'd first heard the phrase "Black Power" at one of Planno's Friday night sessions. There'd been a shift in attitude within the ranks of young black people, and many were no longer willing to accept second-class citizenship or be denied their rights – the riots that spread like brushfire through American cities a year or so earlier had proven that. Those feelings of frustration and powerlessness, exacerbated by opposition to the Vietnam War, could no longer be contained and there were parallels with the liberation struggle in Africa as well. The more Peter learnt about what was happening in Africa – and especially countries like South Africa and Rhodesia – the more he felt consumed by injustice.

The March 12 edition of the *Gleaner* reported how "police with riot equipment stood by yesterday at the British High Commission office on Duke Street, where slogan-carrying demonstrators staged an hour long demonstration against the recent hanging of Africans in Rhodesia by the illegal Ian Smith regime.

"At one point a demonstrator emptied a dustbin in front of the Commissioner's office and shortly afterwards the British High Commissioner was supplied with a police escort on the way to his car parked in front of the building. Led by recording artist Prince Buster, who joined the demonstration shortly after it had begun about mid-day, the protestors carried slogans denouncing the British and Rhodesian governments and calling for retaliation. Some of the slogans read, 'Queen signature ignored – Parliament say no because it would be against the white', 'The British Is A Germs' and 'Who have eyes let him see'."

That same day, two men were arrested by Denham Town police officers and charged with obstructing traffic in the Spanish Town Road. They were named as Winston McIntosh, aged 23 of 19 West Road, Kingston 12, and Gladstone Edman, 20, of 18 Fifth Street, Kingston 12.

"Both men were charged after they refused to obey police instructions to move on," continued the report. "The police say that a group of people was moving along the Spanish Town Road protesting against the hanging of Africans in Rhodesia. It was approaching peak hour and when the police tried to disperse the crowd some of them refused, holding up traffic on Spanish Town Road. McIntosh and Edman were then arrested and charged with obstructing traffic."

Prince Buster later posted bail for Peter (for it was he) and Edman, who'd become inflamed after hearing about the three black prisoners who'd been put to death in Rhodesia. They'd been hanged at the behest of Ian Smith, whose breakaway regime had unilaterally declared independence from Britain and established white minority rule. Smith had been copying South Africa's methods, confining blacks to townships and stifling political opposition. His rogue administration hanged the three men in open defiance of British authority and despite a royal reprieve from the Queen. Two of the accused had murdered a white farmer and the other a local chief, but Britain had removed the death penalty at home and throughout the colonies. The hangings were therefore illegal and had prompted fears of impending genocide against blacks in Rhodesia. British Prime Minister

Harold Wilson described Smith's regime as "essentially evil" but said he was powerless to stop them. There were more than 100 other prisoners on death row in Rhodesia, and eight of them awaited hanging. The United Nations had already imposed sanctions, but dozens of countries (including Jamaica) now called upon them to use force if necessary to prevent further executions.

The situation had made Peter's head spin. A white, racist regime was killing black people and yet the British government refused to act. The protestors wanted to send a message by bringing Kingston to a standstill, and Peter's cousin Carlton remembers the incident well.

"Peter, Bob and Mortimo Planno had planned to demonstrate in the street outside of Denham Town police station but Bob and Planno didn't turn up and so Peter went without them," he says. "He ended up going to jail for lying down in the street and blocking the traffic but Peter was always watching the news, and following what was happening in South Africa and other places. He was always strongly interested in those things, and anything affecting the unfortunate. Peter would give his life for them."

The incident marked the beginning of Peter's radicalism, and it won't be the last time he sees the inside of a prison cell. As if taunted by songs like 'The Toughest' and 'Stepping Razor', Kingston's police will continue to single him out for harsh treatment, and Peter's blatant disregard for local ganja laws won't help matters. In future, he'll think of other ways in getting his message across but the demonstrations did have some effect. Less than two weeks after he and his friends had manned the barricades, Miriam Makeba sent a message to Jamaican Prime Minister Hugh Shearer, saying, "Your understanding and sympathetic gesture concerning black martyrs killed in Rhodesia will be deeply appreciated by freedom loving black people the world over."

A month later and Dr. Martin Luther King slumped to the floor of a hotel balcony after being felled by an assassin's bullet. His death will trigger yet more riots in more than 100 American cities. President Johnson called out the National Guard and Bob's take on the situation, 'I'm Hurting Inside', brought tears to the eyes. There was no going back, although he and Peter's rebel spirit now took a different form from when they were championing the rude boys. For evidence take a listen to 'Fire Fire', and Peter's introduction is priceless by the way. "Will you kindly reduce the temperature on me sir? It's too hot down here," he asks in his best British style accent. The rest of the song is revolutionary to the core. It asks for no quarter and gives none. "Babylon's burning, they have no water," Peter purrs, with barely disguised pleasure. 'Fire Fire' is up there with the Rolling Stones' 'Street Fighting Man' or the Beatles' 'Revolution'. It's no fluke either, because Peter recorded 'Them Have Fi Get A Beatin'' around the same time and maybe even at the same session, since Jackie Jackson – who's magnificent – plays bass on both. As is his wont, Peter will later re-record 'Them Have Fi Get A Beatin'' but it's hard to beat the original as he urges the righteous to seize the time and drive out wrongdoers. There's nothing racist about his polemics. What he's against is "Babylon" – the system people use to oppress others, and that prevents Jah's will.

Bob's far more cautious than Peter, but is still in outstanding form. 'Don't Rock My Boat' is the best of his recent songs and with Nash and Sims now back on the island, expectations are running high. Nash will record his breakthrough reggae hit 'Hold Me Tight' that summer, using a mix of Caribbean and American musicians. From the minute his honeyed vocals meshed with Jamaica's rocksteady sound, Nash's career was transformed. He and Sims owned a label with arranger Arthur Jenkins called JAD, formed out of their initials. Right from the start, they were intent on making records for the US and European markets, and not Jamaica. Bob and Peter understood this, and signed songwriting deals that would pay them a small retainer – enough to stave off starvation and help fund their own productions. Throughout the rest of 1968, JAD will record literally dozens of tracks with the Wailers at the house in Russell Heights. Jimmy Norman and Al Pyfrom, both long-time associates of Johnny Nash, will write a fair few of them, whilst Bob contributes 'Bend Down Low', 'Nice Time' and 'Mellow Mood', among others. Peter's selection includes 'Hammer' and a new song, 'Love,' that will find its way onto Johnny's next album (also called 'Hold Me Tight'). This LP will become a bestseller that autumn, and Peter's chest must have swelled with pride to see his name in the credits. Not only that, but Johnny Nash had chosen to cover one of his songs before any of Bob's – a fact that's scarcely been acknowledged outside of Peter's own circle of admirers.

Chapter 6

Arise Black Man

In late August, Peter, Bob and Rita were rewarded with a trip to New York. Danny Sims wanted them to gain experience of how things worked in America and meet with some industry people he knew. Such an invitation proved he was convinced of the Wailers' talent – not just Bob's, but also Peter's. In an interview with Roger Steffens, he insisted the latter's contribution to Johnny Nash's success shouldn't be underestimated.

"Peter had his own agenda, but he was with us ninety percent of the time. We used his guitar on practically every track we did. He held us together; he held our rhythm together. Along with Paul Khouri, Peter was the teacher for that rocksteady sound. Peter directed us, and we spun off Peter Tosh. I never worked with a guy I liked working with more than him. He was always with us, always! I saw him as the Rock of Gibraltar with that rhythm."

It was Peter's first trip outside of Jamaica and the affluence he saw around him when strolling down Fifth Avenue, where Danny lived, must have been overwhelming. Years later he'll tell his cousin Carlton "there's nothing new about New York" and rechristen it "Old York", although he'd got used to the place by then. As he'd arrived during that first trip, television news reports centred on the aftermath of rioting at the annual Democrats convention and the murder of several black militants in Cleveland. He could have been excused for thinking he'd entered a war zone, yet there was no denying the Big Apple's charms. Sims' apartment faced Central Park and it was but a short walk from there to West 65th Street and Impact Sound studios, where he and Nash's productions were given their final polish. Richard Alderson, who'd worked with Dylan, Nina Simone and Harry Belafonte, was resident engineer. Belafonte owned shares in Impact Sound and was now a prominent spokesperson on black issues, in addition to his roles as singer and film star. He'd marched with Dr. Martin Luther King and campaigned in Mississippi. He was also an acquaintance of Danny's, who inducted Peter into the highly charged atmosphere of New York race relations. Whilst there's no evidence of it, Peter may well have met with prominent black activists on that trip. He certainly learnt a great deal more about the struggles faced by African-Americans in areas like Harlem, where Sims was sure to have taken him.

No less importantly, he was also introduced to songwriter Jimmy Norman, who worked closely with Nash and Sims. Jimmy couldn't recall Peter visiting his Bronx apartment during the autumn of 1968, but Bob and Rita certainly did. The two of them spent the evening round the piano with Jimmy and his wife, Dorothy Hughes, singing and exchanging ideas. Jimmy's songwriting partner, Al Pyfrom, was also there. He and Norman were stalwarts of the Broadway scene, yet still admired the outpouring of soul and rock music heard on radio stations all over the city. It was an era when Aretha Franklin, James Brown, Jimi Hendrix, Sly & The Family Stone, the Beatles and Rolling Stones were in their heyday, and pop music was giving voice to more pressing concerns than stealing a kiss or winning over the girl next door. To most New Yorkers, Caribbean music was outmoded. They thought it meant the kind of calypso ditties Harry Belafonte had popularised almost a decade earlier, and few knew anything about rocksteady. With the success of 'Hold Me Tight' this was about to change, and Sims and Nash remained convinced that more hits would come with a little additional expertise.

"I was asked to go to Jamaica to work with Bob and the Wailers, so for the next six or seven months Bob, Peter Tosh, Rita and I wrote and recorded music," Norman will tell Marco Virgona. "Some of theirs, and some of mine. We recorded maybe 40 of my songs altogether."

He and Arthur Jenkins left for Jamaica within days of Peter's return from New York. Meanwhile Johnny and Danny flew to London, where 'Hold Me Tight' was rapidly climbing the charts and will soon peak at number four. Jimmy Norman loved the rocksteady sound, although he and Jenkins weren't all that impressed with Federal, where most of the JAD material had been recorded to date. In the months ahead they'll book the studio above Randy's record store at 17 North Parade, right in the heart of downtown Kingston. Randy's was owned by Vincent Chin – a Chinese Jamaican record producer who'd started making hits prior to Independence, most notably with Lord Creator. Vincent and his wife, Pat, were well respected by Kingston's music fraternity, and Peter and Bob will retain strong links with them for years to come. When not recording, they'll work on songs with Jimmy and Al at the house in Russell Heights. During this period the Wailers recorded 'Fallin' In And Out Of Love', 'What Goes Around Comes Around', 'Splish For My Splash' and 'Stranger On The Shore' – most of which had been written for Johnny Nash and Lloyd Price. Ironically, the best song they recorded was 'Soul Rebel', which features Jimmy's deep baritone and yet had been written by Bob, who casts himself in the role of "soul adventurer".

Jimmy would spend seven months in Jamaica altogether and loved every minute. He says he got on better with Peter than Bob, or at least initially.

"Peter and I talked more and he showed me around a bit," he told me. "He was my main communicator for the first few weeks I was in Jamaica. When I first went there, the three of us would just hang out together. I'd go to clubs with them and see people dancing, and I was amazed at how everybody's heads would be going up and down at the same time, doing the rocksteady. That really threw me!

"Peter was a better musician than Bob, and certainly as a guitarist. He and I used to write music every day, either in the studio or sat out in Danny's garden but one of the first things I wrote after I'd got there was this song 'Soon Come'. I remember everyone saying this phrase "soon come" and so that's what grabbed me, because it wasn't anything I was used to. Peter later stole it and put his name on it. Well he changed some of the lyrics and then made out it was his, which is the same thing because whilst the lyrics are slightly different, the melody and everything else is identical. In the end I just left Peter's name on it, but I later recorded the Coasters on it as well."

Peter and the others will discover that Jimmy was quite a character, and eager to try out new experiences. By the time I spoke with him he was old and frail and living in a New York nursing home, yet he still relished the memory of having visited Planno and sampled his first-ever chillum, loaded with high-grade marijuana.

"Peter and Bob were always smoking ganja but they never had any cigarette papers so they'd walk round with a pocketful of this thin, brown paper we used to buy patties in. That's what they'd roll their spliffs with, or at least when they weren't smoking the chillum because oh man, that wasn't funny! I thought everybody smoked too much down there. For three dollars you could buy so much herb it wouldn't fit on the table. It was stupid. They'd load up a chillum, say their prayers and then go through this ritual..."

Jimmy's induction into the Rastafarian lifestyle was naturally skin deep. Whilst he saw evidence of poverty, there was still a vast difference between his reality and that of a sufferer forced to live in one of Kingston's shantytowns. Life on the streets was getting harder, and Prime Minister Hugh Shearer's government was growing increasingly fearful of insurgency. Black Power was viewed as a destabilising force and revolutionary literature banned, even as independent publications – some of them linked to pro-African organisations like the Ethiopian World Federation and United African Congress – began to proliferate. Influential black figures such as Stokeley Carmichael and H. Rap Brown were told they couldn't enter Jamaica and yet one of them was already there, teaching and lecturing right under their noses. This was Dr. Walter Rodney, a Guyanese lecturer based at the University of the West Indies. His main subject was African history, but it was Black Power that filled his talks as well as his classrooms. In mid-October he left for Montreal where he attended the Congress of Black Writers. Prime Minister Shearer saw his opportunity and issued an exclusion order that prevented Rodney from re-entering Jamaica, despite his family living there. The following day Black Power was headline news as American athletes Tommie Smith and John Carlos, who won gold and bronze in the 200 metres at the Mexico Olympics, stepped up to the podium sporting Civil Rights badges and raised their black-gloved fists in a Black Power salute. It was a gesture that sent shock waves reverberating around the world. Fresh lines of engagement had been drawn, and panic set in.

When his students heard what had happened to Rodney they began demonstrating at the university gates. They were soon confronted by baton-wielding police, who fired tear gas at them. Rodney's teachings had meant a great deal to them. They saw him as a symbol of resistance who stood up for what he believed in. His own political education had started early, from accompanying his father on rallies organised by the labour movement in Guyana. He then visited Cuba in the aftermath of their revolution and moved to Kingston, where he graduated in History from the University of the West Indies before taking up a teaching post in Tanzania. By the time he returned to Jamaica in January 1968 his focus wasn't just on teaching African history, but raising black consciousness. This is what had compelled him to take his message into the union halls and Rasta camps, where crowds gathered to hear him talk outside of university hours. Peter had listened carefully as Rodney warned against confusing Black Power with racial supremacy and defined it as "a call to black peoples to throw off white domination and resume the handling of their own destinies". According to him, Black Power meant a break with imperialism, which is historically founded on white racism. He wanted to see the black masses rise up and overthrow their oppressors, and criticised the harsh sentences for possession of marijuana. He then told of a new law regarding 'suspicion', which meant the police could stop and search whosoever they saw fit – i.e., poor blacks living in ghetto communities like Trench Town. He reminded them of the discrimination they faced because of their skin colour and claimed the police were "agents of social oppression". This was music to Peter's ears. He liked how Rodney championed Jamaica's black underclass, and railed against the bourgeoisie who'd assumed control after Independence but then continued with the same elitist philosophy as the British. Peter knew instinctively why the government wanted to silence Rodney. It was because he spoke the truth, and was beginning to open people's eyes to what lay behind the country's growing inequalities.

As news of the students' protest spread, full-scale riots broke out in other parts of Kingston, where buildings were torched and shops looted in an orgy of lawlessness. The streets soon became littered with the charred, overturned shells of cars and buses. Peter had already tasted jail for standing up for what he believed in, but as soon as word reached Trench Town that people were rioting in the corporate area, Peter felt he *had* to be part of it. It was a people's uprising and now the authorities must take notice – the burning buildings, trails of broken glass and upturned cars saw to that. Smoke filled the air over downtown Kingston and in the heat of the struggle, Peter wasn't found wanting.

Ralph Emerson once described heroism as "a military attitude of the soul". He noted that heroes are not without faults; they can be stubborn and not necessarily given to reflection. This seems to sum up Peter pretty well.

"Peter really was that kind of a person," concurs Bunny. "It's not like he portrayed an image. Peter was a revolutionary. Peter was arrogant, outspoken and him no really worry about if him head a go cut off after him make certain statements. When him do certain things, him no think about that. He wasn't an actor. He really was that kind of a person and everything he stood for from an early age, he was really serious about. He was very conscious of Africa from an early stage. He was conscious about self-defence too, and was the kind of person that would speak out for people who don't have that kind of a voice, or don't have the ability, don't have the strength and don't have the will. He would take it upon himself to do things, like even in the Rodney incident when he took a bus packed with people, and drive it in a store. And people would go out and loot that store and he would drive it to Trench Town without even thinking that he's doing any harm, but just participating in whatever is the reaction of the people. He's the kind of person who always wanted to stamp out isms and schisms and he would make it known he feels that way, whatever the circumstances. And afterwards, he's not worried about that..."

We can just imagine his exhilaration as he sent that mini-bus through a storefront, shattering windows and doors in a rush of hot-blooded destruction. After his passengers had grabbed what they could, he drove them back to Trench Town where he received a hero's welcome. That felt good. That felt *very* good, and action really did speak louder than words.

The riots would last all day and well into the evening. Next morning, it was as if Kingston had been under siege. Three people were said to have died, and over £1 million worth of property had been damaged or destroyed. Peter's celebratory mood will last until his 24th birthday, on October 19. That's when he discovered the store they'd looted belonged to someone with strong connections to Joe Williams; a police officer feared throughout West Kingston and whom Bunny calls "the baddest man in the world".

Bob wasn't involved in the riots because Rita was just a day away from giving birth to their son David, now better known as "Ziggy". Peter, on the other hand, will have to disappear for a few weeks until the storm has blown over, leaving Shirley and baby Andrew to fend for themselves. Joe Williams went after him, just as everyone in Trench Town knew he would. Williams was a patriarch who everyone called "Massa Joe" or "Papa Joe", and his approach to police work wasn't all that different from a Western style sheriff's. The police would drive around Kingston's ghettos and use informants to tell them who'd been involved in the riots. That's how Williams learnt that Peter had been caught up in the demonstration. He got to know everything that happened in Trench Town sooner or later, and knew only too well that Peter wasn't into crime or violence. It's just that life in the ghetto was getting harder and youths like him, grown disillusioned with the system, were now prepared to take risks in making their voices heard.

Peter was duly summonsed to the police station but refused to go. This would prove a major mistake. "Joe Williams was the rudest of the rude boys. All rude boys answer to Papa Joe," explains Bunny. "He wouldn't go out and get people, he'd *send* for them, and don't let him wait on you neither."

When Williams and his men passed through a ghetto neighbourhood like Trench Town they'd drive real slow, so they could take everything in. And they drove Jeeps with no doors, so they could leap out and have some sufferer pinned up against a wall and robbed of his spliff within seconds. It was intimidating and meant to be. You may think only the guilty are going to run or react in that situation but that's not true. Youths would tremble in fear as Papa Joe's Jeep pulled up beside them. Next thing they knew, he'd be asking them what they're doing there and where they lived.

"If by chance he doesn't believe them, then he'd order them in the back of the Jeep and take them there, and wake up whoever's inside. Don't even bother lying to the man," says Bunny. One day Williams saw Peter on the street and tried to catch him but Peter spun him off-balance and sprinted away, leaving the rest of the policemen sat in the back of the Jeep, too dumbfounded to give chase until it was too late. Fortunately, Massa Joe wasn't trigger happy like others on the force and so wouldn't kill people without due cause. His methods were different. He'd sneak up behind some rude boy as they were in bed making love to their girlfriend and push his gun butt into the back of their head, ordering them to finish before yanking them out the door. No doubt about it, Joe Williams was a dangerous adversary, and he'd have Peter in his sights from now on.

Bunny states that most of Peter's scrapes with the police happened outside of the Wailers, after he'd left the group. He says his friend just couldn't help himself – that he'd stand up for his rights and treat the police with disdain when a little bit of diplomacy might have worked wonders. Most police officers want deference and shouting at them was just asking for trouble. In Jamaican vernacular, "Peter nah bow". His altercations with the police would grow in frequency and get more brutal. He was now a marked man, and with powerful enemies.

"Hear me now, Peter was a very arrogant person," says Bunny. "Don't violate Peter's rights, don't try to intimidate Peter, don't treat him like you want to make him squint or succumb to your type of intimidation. Peter is not that type of guy. Peter was a soldier and wasn't the kind of guy to be pitied. Don't feel sorry for him because even if he were brought down, he'd still say something to make you laugh and twist some words around, comically. And if he's wounded, then he'll still try and walk..."

In a bid to stay out of Massa Joe's clutches, Peter went back to Westmoreland. That's where American photographer Chuck Krall met him for the first time. Krall was with the US Peace Corps, and stationed in a little fishing village called White River. He says Peter was performing with a beauty pageant, singing and playing guitar during the intervals. The Wailers' musical anchorman was in exile but instead of hiding, he'd joined a travelling fair.

"He was very much into African politics," says Krall. "He'd talk about the colours used on African flags, and the different kind of clothes people would wear. I was with Peter in the countryside somewhere and as we wandered around, he pointed towards these guys who looked like Southern blacks and said they were from Africa; that you could tell by their undergarments, which you could see peeping out from their clothes. He was right too, because we went over to talk with them and they confirmed what he'd said.

"He was also well versed in the Old Testament and Shakespeare. I'd met fishermen who were barely literate, yet they'd recite lengthy passages of the Bible and Shakespeare. When you think about it, patois is like seventeenth century English but there'd be productions of Shakespeare in small towns throughout Jamaica at that time and they were surprisingly popular, so that's probably where it started for him."

Peter's troubadour alter ego will soon get bored and hanker for Kingston's bright lights. The music was calling, and he had to go back there.

"He was always willing to listen to music from across the spectrum," Chuck recalls. "He used to listen to certain country artists a lot, especially Jim Reeves. It was interesting how Jamaican people's tastes would change depending on where they were from, and what the radio reception was like. There wasn't much coming from Cuba but the best radio station was WGBF, which came out of Miami. There was a woman who came on late at night called Trish Robins and she was probably the person responsible for introducing rock music to Jamaica. It was an FM station with a free-form format and so she'd play a lot of album tracks. He and I both spent a lot of time listening to that station and I think her show was a massive influence on Peter's guitar playing."

It was an era when rock guitarists were allowed a lot of freedom to express themselves. Peter will have heard Jimi Hendrix, Carlos Santana and Eric Clapton, as well as some of the blues masters who'd managed to cross over to rock audiences. Trish Robins' show must have been a lifeline for him.

At this juncture, his recent trip to Manhattan seemed a long way off. There was little to do in Westmoreland, and he longed to be back in the studio or at the house in Russell Heights, where Bob and Rita were. Nash and Sims returned in November, and Johnny headlined a show called Smashville '68 at the Carib Theatre. 'Hold Me Tight' had helped put Jamaican music on the map, and the crowd knew it. Johnny also sang at a few fundraisers in the lead-up to Christmas, including the annual Nuggets For The Needy and Edward Seaga's Grand Christmas Charity Ball, starring Curtis Mayfield and the Impressions. The National Arena was full to capacity that night, but we presume Peter wasn't there.

As New Year approached, Bob and Rita moved the Wailers' shop to No. 100 Orange Street. Across the road was Beverley's ice cream parlour, owned by Leslie Kong, who'd produced Bob's first-ever recordings. Beverley Kelso says that Bob and Rita's marriage was on the rocks at this point due to his affair with Pat Williams, who'd just become pregnant by him. Rita wanted to divorce him, but Beverley persuaded her not to for the sake of their children, even though she despaired of Bob's behaviour. She then distanced herself from him and Rita after Pat almost blinded her during a tussle on the sidewalk.

It wasn't until after the New Year that Peter ventured back into Kingston and rejoined Bob and Rita at further sessions in Russell Heights.

Johnny Nash's latest hit was 'You Got Soul', which had gone Top 10 in England. In-between promotional visits to Europe, Johnny booked time at Federal, where he was joined by Richard Alderson and a handful of American session musicians. According to Richard, their party had been stopped and questioned by customs officials when arriving at Kingston airport. Shearer's government believed that Rastafarians, fired up by Dr. Rodney's Black Power rhetoric, were plotting a revolution. Some of Nash's entourage were mistaken for black militants, and were questioned for hours – especially the guy with an Afro and copy of *Muhammad Speaks* in his briefcase.

After their release, they were followed back to Russell Heights, arrested and then taken off for yet more questioning. It had been 10 years since the Cuban revolution, and Shearer wanted to make sure that didn't happen in Jamaica. Nash and Sims couldn't be trusted, and nor could their friends because trumpeter Hugh Masekela was also given a hard time after accepting Sims' invitation to visit Jamaica in February. His grilling was so zealous, he wondered if he hadn't landed in his native South Africa! He and Miriam Makeba had now separated but both were under surveillance by the FBI.

Hugh doesn't mention Peter in his autobiography, although he added trumpet to 'Love', which Peter wrote and sang. They also must have smoked a lot of herb together since Masekela talks fondly of staring out the window, stoned out of his mind on five-star ganja. Masekela may have liked herb, but had serious credibility. Just the previous year, he'd performed at the Monterey Pop Festival on the same bill as Jimi Hendrix and Otis Redding. He was a classically trained musician, and like his former wife, a figurehead of black South Africa's struggle against apartheid. Peter couldn't fail to learn from a man like this, who defied stereotypes and wasn't afraid to speak the truth. Hugh was also proudly African, and determined to keep his country's black musical tradition alive, even in exile. He'll get his reward too. Shortly before visiting Jamaica he'd travelled to Zambia and discovered 'Grazin' In The Grass' – an instrumental that'll roar to the top of the US charts and bring him international renown, just as 'Pata Pata' had done for his ex-wife a few months earlier.

Michael Manley also had an effect on Peter. He was the son of former PNP Prime Minister Norman Manley and in years to come he'll seize the initiative from Shearer's party and establish the PNP as the voice of the majority black population. The younger Manley vowed to stem the growing divide between Jamaica's rich and poor, and aroused interest from Rastafarians by being photographed with a "rod of correction" that he claimed Emperor Haile Selassie I had given him. Shearer was now cast as "Pharaoh" whilst Manley would be called "Joshua" after the leader of the Israelites.

It was at this point that Bunny was freed from jail and met with members of Johnny Nash's circle for the first time. Richard Alderson says Bunny was deeply suspicious of Danny Sims and didn't really take to any of the foreigners who were now part of Bob and Peter's lives. He'll remain on the fringes of that scene, confirming Jimmy Norman's description of him as "a loner" and even "a gangster". It's easy to understand why he might feel left out. Only weeks earlier, he was doing hard labour on a prison farm with only the occasional cricket match to look forward to. None of the other Wailers had written to him and whilst Bob had been to see him once, there'd been no sign of Peter. Bunny was unprepared for Nash and Sims and their flash retinue. A lot had happened in his absence, and it'll take time for him to adjust.

Chapter 7

Go Tell It On The Mountain

Bunny's first recording after his release was 'Tread Oh'. Peter took several Rasta brethren in the studio with him that day – Ras Michael, who played repeater drum, Skatalites bassist Lloyd Brevett and singer Joe Sarkey. Their presence turned the session into a Rastafarian cleansing ritual. Peter – who played keyboards on 'Tread Oh' – was now a regular visitor to Ras Michael's place down by the waterfront, which was popular with a younger crowd. Ras Michael believed in the healing powers of music and his yard often filled with people playing drums and different instruments.

The Wailers' relationship with Planno was over by then. It had deteriorated after they'd agreed to play a benefit show, but then caught him charging admission. They refused to go on and Planno was forced to refund the angry patrons, causing him shame. Bob then left for Nine Miles but Planno was determined to teach him a lesson and sent some thugs after him. Bob's neighbours ran them off and so Planno transferred his attention to Peter, who was strolling through Trench Town one day and found himself surrounded by youths brandishing sticks. Drawing on his karate skills, Peter seized the ringleader and gave him a good beating. The rest of the gang swiftly backed away and he wasn't troubled again. Problem solved. Planno's last act was to try and burn down Aunt Viola's house in Ghost Town, where Bob and Rita still lived. A local gang called the Vikings intervened and won the day, leaving Bob feeling indebted to them. Planno will leave the Wailers alone after this, and smoulder impotently on the sidelines.

With Bunny's release, the group's full vocal sound was now restored. Soon he'll take part in his first JAD sessions with the Wailers and whilst the results aren't exceptional, it served as a welcome exercise for him. Bunny sang lead on 'Treat You Right', while Peter's 'The World Is Changing' is typically forthright and warns that mankind is headed for destruction. It sets the tone for what will become a Peter Tosh trademark – a haughty attitude based on the fact that he has all the answers! The beat's now changed from rocksteady to reggae – a choppy, syncopated groove built around an organ shuffle and rhythm guitar. Peter felt at home with it straightaway, but then he was one of its architects.

It will be his last session for JAD, and it sounds like he enjoyed himself. That's him playing melodica on 'Milkshake And Potato Chips' and 'It Hurts To Be Alone', plus he plays harmonica on Rita's 'Lonely Girl'. Three months earlier, JAD had shifted their operations to Randy's Studio 17, above the family record store in North Parade. It had four tracks, just like Federal, and the makings of a great sound.

"The studio had opened in 1968," says Vincent's son Clive, who was just 16 at the time. "At first, just the family used it, but then Danny Sims and Johnny Nash's company came. That was all because of the engineer who was working there at the time, Bill Garnett. He was the one who'd custom-built the board for us, so he brought Johnny Nash, Arthur Jenkins and Danny Sims up to Randy's. That's how it all got started with Johnny Nash's crew.

"I remember them well. It was very unusual to see a black American dressed in this funny-looking shirt they call dashiki and the platform sandals they used to wear. Also the bell-bottom pants and their hair in Afros with beads around their necks. I was fascinated by how they spoke and the way they did things. They booked the studio for three-and-a half months and might call in any time, whether it was 12 noon or 12 midnight. That's when they'd usually come, then they'd work right through the night."

Clive recalls Lloyd Price, Quincy Jones and Cissy Houston passing through Randy's during JAD sessions. This was celebrity stuff and Peter – still in his early twenties – was right in the middle of it.

"The sound they got hadn't been done before and I think that's what propelled the influx of foreign musicians and artists coming to Jamaica,"

Clive explains. "They wanted to capture that sound, because everyone started looking towards Jamaica after that. We were doing something new, but that scene around JAD was the first eye-opener like that in Jamaica. We all learned something from it. When those guys recorded horns it wasn't the usual thing, because they'd sometimes use French horns. Arthur Jenkins would write out the scores, Boris Gardiner did the conducting and Peter Ashbourne was involved as well. All the leading musicians you can think of would be there, like Harry Butler."

Peter was already a noted rhythm guitarist, but you can't be around musicians like those and not improve. The Wailers had more studio craft now, and a better understanding of the music business. They disagreed with Lloyd Price when he said reggae couldn't cross over without the involvement of American singers like him and Johnny Nash but Price had a point. Nash had just sealed his second consecutive Top 10 UK hit with 'Cupid', and Trojan Records were about to smother Jamaican tracks in strings. Bob's friend Desmond Dekker was the exception with his rude boy look, topped by a revolutionary's beret. 'Israelites', produced by Leslie Kong, was a number one in England and selling well in America, despite Dekker's sufferers' lyrics. This was heartening. The doors may be opening for acts like them, and they had to be ready. In the meantime Peter was back playing sessions at Randy's.

"Peter Touch was the first Wailer I ran into during the late sixties," says Aston "Family Man" Barrett, the future Wailer then playing bass with the Hippy Boys. "I used to see him walking around with his box guitar and melodica on Orange Street near this place called Idlers Rest, which was right by Randy's on North Parade. This was long before they even build the studio upstairs. He would pass through there and I would hail him up but it was Reggie (Hippy Boys' guitarist Alva Lewis) who first introduced me to him. Peter knew we were musicians and so he asked if we could bring him in on sessions. He said he could play guitar and piano and I remember Reggie saying if we get any recording, then he can join us. I say, 'But I thought you were a singer?' so him say 'Yeah I sing, but I can play music too.' He was kind of versatile that way and so we'd take him on sessions with us sometimes but he was more like a comedian to me really, walking around making jokes and with this Black Power fist hanging round his neck. But he was always very revolutionary, even from early."

As well as carving Black Power pendants, Peter used to make Afro combs and sell them in the Wailers' shop. He was resourceful, as well as creative, and the timing was right. Nash's entourage may have turned heads a year ago, but Jamaican people had caught on fast and it was no longer unusual to see women wearing head wraps, or youths with Afros strolling through North Parade in bell-bottom trousers and beads. Bunny's girlfriend Jean Watt had a tailors' shop downtown where customers could choose from yards of brightly coloured African style fabric. Bunny divided his time between there and the Wailers' record store on Orange Street. Whilst there was plenty of stimulus all around, the group wasn't doing much recording and money was scarce. Dave Barker recalls seeing them perform on a stage show around this time, and getting booed off because they'd turned Rasta. By now the professional routines they'd mastered at Studio One were long gone, and audiences weren't sure they liked their more natural style of presentation. The Wailers decided to regroup, and withdrew from live appearances for a while. Peter, as already mentioned, was busy elsewhere.

"We did quite a lot of tracks with Peter at Randy's during 1969, not only vocal tracks, but also instrumentals," recalls Clive Chin. "There was never any ambition to do an album with him. The whole purpose of those recordings was just to get the studio up and running but we had great times together. Peter was the only one of the Wailers you could work with easily, and he was one of our in-house musicians. He would be there from when we open in the morning, at nine o'clock, up until closing time around six or seven in the evening. He'd bring his guitar and if he had tunes to record, then he'd sit there at the turntable and work them out. The man played at least six different instruments, including keyboards, guitar and bass. He also blew melodica, because he knew all the chords from playing keyboards. I've even seen him sat at the drums but he was always innovative in whatever he did.

"He spent the first year with us after Randy's opened and played on a lot of our productions between 1968-69. He used to take care of auditions for my father as well. Singers have to find the right key, so if you could play an instrument and particularly a piano or guitar, you would hold that position. My father gave Peter the job when guys like B. B. Seaton, Winston Samuels, Beanie and Fred Locks, who sang as the Lyrics, and Joe White were there...."

"I remember that Peter would go upstairs and he'd be there the whole day doing auditions, playing on tracks or doing back-up vocals. He'd be there from Monday to Saturday and sometimes on Sundays as well. He was very close to my father – closer than any of the other Wailers. My father used to drop him home in Trench Town because Peter never used to drive them times. He used to take the bus and so my father would drop him home in the evening time, late. He'd turn round to me and say 'don't come out of the car. You stay in the car,' and then he'd take Peter through this zinc fence..."

Vincent, who most people called "Randy", was unusual in that he was friendly to Rastafarians and respected their culture. Musicians even saw him at the Rasta camps from time to time. Peter felt relaxed around him. He liked the family atmosphere, and the wages came in handy too.

"Randy's had a different vibe to what you'd find at Dynamics and Federal, or even Studio One and Treasure Isle," continues Clive. "It had a very warm and friendly atmosphere. There was nothing hostile about it. You never felt like you had to be on your best behaviour, or think about anything else other than making music. The musicians could carry their little smoke and their drinks and food up there and feel comfortable. We'd ask them to take out their empty bottles and stuff like that, but they respected my father and treated him well.

"I remember one Friday evening when police raided this group of musicians on the corner and arrested about eight of them for having some weed. Gregory Isaacs and Big Youth were there but my father went to Central police station and bailed out every one of them, and they loved him for that..."

Vincent paid his musicians promptly and sponsored radio slots on JBC and RJR, which drove up sales. He and his wife "Miss Pat" manned a full-scale operation that dealt with every aspect of the record industry, and they nurtured Kingston's newer generation of producers in the process.

"That way they could make a life for themselves and that's how come we became so popular, because we were right in the heart of Kingston," recalls Miss Pat. "It was a meeting place, and you could always get a back-up singer or a musician right there on the corner of North Parade and Chancery Lane. That was a fun time. It was really easy for them to create their music, and then they'd be all excited with the idea of getting it pressed and then putting it on the turntable and getting the reaction of the public. This was around the time they were filming *The Harder They Come*. Perry Henzell had these big film cameras set up on the sidewalk for days and we couldn't sell a thing because everybody was so excited!"

"Being downtown was a real experience," recalls Junior Dan, another of Randy's regular session players. "There wasn't much money so sometimes you'd go round the market stalls and maybe just buy a slice of pudding if you couldn't afford anything else. As a musician, you had to live with the people. You're not some big star. You're just somebody downtown. That's how it was."

"None of us had any money in those days," agrees Bunny Lee. "We just do it for the fun of it, and so you could just buy a little food and clothes. We used to look after one another. It was one love, really."

In July 1969, the topic on everyone's lips was the moon landing. Crowds gathered in yards with televisions to watch grainy, black and white footage of Neil Armstrong taking that first "giant leap for mankind". To say that Peter was transfixed is an understatement. He made a tune about it called 'Apollo 11' that's so technical he must have taken in every detail, and from lift-off to "splashing down in the Atlantic".

"Countdown begins in five seconds," he announces on the intro, which contains a sample of the actual broadcast. He then describes heading for the moon "at 15,000 miles per second" as a tenor sax careers behind him. Peter played organ on 'Harris Wheel', on the flipside of Derrick Morgan's 'Moon Hop', around the same time. A fast paced instrumental, it's not that impressive but then Peter had to cope with a Hammond tuned to C-sharp, instead of C.

Derrick Morgan recorded 'Man Pon Moon' that summer, and Peter sings a little like him at times. He plays rock guitar on that track – perhaps remembering those evenings with Chuck Krall spent listening to Trish Robins. He'll record plenty of organ instrumentals at Randy's, and some featuring melodica. This was a child's instrument, easy to play and relatively inexpensive. Most Kingston music stores sold them and they could be carried around easily. Peter soon mastered it, as you'd expect. He couldn't whistle though.

'Whistling Jane' will be credited to Jackie Mittoo, who plays organ, and is a cut to Alton Ellis' 'What Does It Take (To Win Your Love)'. It's a real oddity unlike 'You Can't Fool Me Again', which Peter delivers with righteous anger. A litany of accusations levelled at church and state, it's marred by an amateurish rhythm and organ playing.

'Earth's Rightful Ruler', which refers to Emperor Haile Selassie I, is better by far. U Roy was already popular with local dancehall audiences since he was the MC with King Tubby's sound system. The hits that will seal his reputation, voiced over classic rocksteady rhythms, were still some way off but this is a livewire performance and groundbreaking in its way.

It wasn't the first track featuring an MC that Peter played on – Count Matchuki's 'Stick Up' has that honour – but more than 40 years later 'Earth's Rightful Ruler' is still compelling. Peter's introduction, voiced in Amharic, was originally recorded over a rhythm featuring Ras Michael and his Rasta drummers, the Sons Of Negus. After a minute or so this rhythm fades, and then another starts as U Roy takes over. This second rhythm is a slowed-down cut of the Reggae Boys' 'Selassie', which keyboard player Glen Adams swears was his production, despite Lee "Scratch" Perry having claimed the credit for that and 'Earth's Rightful Ruler'.

The voices on 'Selassie' deliver their message like a hammer blow. "Selassie, ah go burn them with fire. It's hot, it's hot, but we not gonna die…" 'Selassie' and 'Earth's Rightful Ruler' are anchored in the frenetic rhythms of early reggae, and show just how quickly the music can change.

It was the Hippy Boys who played on it – the same group Lee Perry called the Upsetters, and whose hit list included Smith's 'Everybody Needs Love' and Stranger Cole's 'Bangarang'. Anchored by the Barrett brothers' rhythm section, the Hippy Boys were the hottest young band in Jamaica. Peter had played with them already, and knew their qualities. In fact the chemistry felt right from the very first rehearsal.

"The Wailers had a little store with one entrance on Orange Street and another on North Parade," says Clive Chin. "It was in this alleyway near where my father had a rum bar and that's where they used to rehearse when they first got together with Fams and Carly – right behind my father's place."

Family Man and his younger brother Carlton, who played drums, recorded two tracks during that first session with the Wailers. One was a cover of Junior Walker's 'Hold On To This Feeling', the other a loose interpretation of James Brown's 'Say It Loud I'm Black And Proud' which they'd renamed 'Black Progress'. Both were recorded at Randy's, with 'Hold On To That Feeling' proving they hadn't given up hopes of a crossover hit yet. It's good, but nothing like as explosive as 'Black Progress'.

"We've been down too long," Bob cries. "We got to stop living on our knees and start living on our feet." He's rapping on it, not toasting like a reggae MC would but 'Black Progress' is invigorating from start to finish, and the Wailers' tightly knit harmonies are a marvel.

Stokely Carmichael had called James Brown "the most dangerous man in America", while LeRoi Jones described him as "our No. 1 black poet". He was assuredly the world's biggest soul star, toured in a private jet with "Out Of Sight" emblazoned on the side and had a political streak too, after headlining benefit shows for Carmichael's radical student organisation, the SNCC, even whilst endorsing Dr. Martin Luther King and Democrat Hubert Humphrey.

"I was interested in humanity, in what would bring people together," Brown told Cynthia Rose. "What has always interested me is helping people learn to survive."

The decision to entertain US troops in Vietnam and a few ill-advised political alliances then led to him being heavily criticised by black militants. Brown had countered with 'Say It Loud (I'm Black And I'm Proud)' – a song he described as "a wake-up call, a rallying cry; a statement of *pride*."

Peter and Bob had heard 'Say It Loud' when they were in New York. It was even on the *Billboard* charts. They'd never forget the thrill of hearing such a joyous celebration of blackness on crossover radio. All three Wailers loved and respected Brown, as did the Barrett brothers. In the late sixties, the Godfather's brand of raw, seriously funky soul could be heard blasting from record stores all over Kingston. His messages were simply put and struck a chord with Jamaica's poor, who identified with Brown's common touch and gospel roots. His sound was influential too. Peter's version of O. C. Smith's 'Little Green Apples', recorded for Randy's Impact label, was probably inspired by James Brown's cut.

Peter recorded a number of other organ instrumentals around this same time, including 'Selassie Serenade', 'The Return Of Alcapone', 'Sun Valley', 'Crimson Pirate', 'Moon Dust' and 'Green Duck', which were issued as singles on a variety of different labels in the UK. Some are definitely Bunny Lee productions, but his playing is perfunctory. Peter's no keyboard king like Jackie Mittoo, and here's the evidence.

"I released quite a few Peter Touch instrumentals but didn't credit him by name, since I didn't want to mash up the group," Lee explains. "It's just that Peter had to earn a living. He used to hang out at Randy's and my shop. He was a very talented musician as well as a gifted singer. It's just that anything Peter Touch could sing, Derrick Morgan could do it too and Derrick Morgan not only brought me in the business, he's also my brother-in-law..."

Whilst 'Earth's Rightful Ruler' and 'You Can't Fool Me Again' didn't chart or get any airplay, they compare favourably with certain Wailers songs recorded around the same time. 'Trouble On The Road Again' will be one of the last releases on Wail 'N Soul 'M, and features what Family Man calls "scrub guitar". He says Peter's rhythmic style of playing was derived from country and western, although there are traces of soul, funk and rock in it too.

Bob sang 'Comma Comma' at that same session and whilst it's good, Johnny Nash will have the hit with it. For proof of the Wailers' own commercial ambitions, search out their cover of the Archies' 'Sugar Sugar', which Clive Chin describes as "that bubblegum song". Was this a last, desperate fling of the dice? Or had Vincent Chin fallen into the same trap as Coxsone, and imagined they could shed their political and religious objectives without so much as a backward glance? The song was banal whilst the Archies themselves weren't even a real band, just session musicians personified by cartoon characters. Peter sings lead on a cover of the Box Tops' 'The Letter', which goes some way towards restoring dignity but the Wailers seemed to have lost their way. They even auditioned for Lloyd Daley's Matador label around this time but were turned down as his wife considered them "too unruly, too ghetto".

Shortly afterwards they'll record a few sides for Federal engineer Ted Pouder, who invited them to cut new versions of 'Thank You Lord' and 'This Train'. Also a song Peter wrote called 'Wisdom' – sung by Bob on this occasion – and that Peter will later re-title 'Fools Die'. None of these tracks were hits, or caused much of a ripple. The Wailers were at an impasse and so Bob went to see Leslie Kong, whose stable of artists (apart from Desmond Dekker) included Toots and the Maytals, the Pioneers and Jimmy Cliff, whose protest song 'Vietnam' was about to climb the UK charts. Three brothers – Leslie, Pots and Cecil – ran the Beverley's label. Leslie was frail and wore sunglasses, even indoors. He had a reputation, like Vincent Chin, for treating his artists and musicians well, and they gave him plenty of hits in return. Bob and Bunny had known him for years, but Peter took to him soon enough. The Wailers agreed to record an album for him, for which they were paid a decent advance. Recording then took place throughout May 1970, after intensive rehearsals. There were good feelings all round. Kong booked time at Dynamic Sound and recruited his usual musicians. The majority of them were familiar faces, and it took no time at all to lay a dozen or so rhythm tracks. The voices were then added later. Peter was the one who showed the other musicians what chords to play – Gladstone Anderson would then work out the arrangements on piano. The other band members included Winston Wright (organ), Jackie Jackson (bass) and Hux Brown, who played guitar.

"The Wailers, they were cool guys man," says Hux. "The serious one was Peter, because Peter was the musician out the three of them. He understood music more than Bob or Bunny because he was a good guitarist himself, and so he was more talkative. He'd give us directions and say things like, 'No man, give us a bit more of this or that, or let me hear you try this…' The other guys, they were just singers really. You'd never hear Bob or Bunny say, 'put in more organ there, or play the bass this way.' That was just as well, because we didn't have time for no inquest! You had to work quickly and if a man had nothing to contribute, then it's better him say nothing and just go along with whatever's happening."

Kong was wise enough to leave such decisions to the musicians. He stayed out of their way and kept things simple. The Wailers had played him their songs; he'd liked them and booked the studio. Gladstone Anderson oversaw the sessions, and the next day he and the other musicians called in at the ice-cream parlour to collect their cheques. That's how it worked.

The first single was 'Soul Shakedown Party', which Kong licensed to Trojan in the UK. It's the Wailers' strongest recording in ages – hugely infectious, and with wonderful harmonies. It sounds as if it was specially tailored for the UK market, although it failed to chart there. No matter. It sent out a message that the Wailers were back and sounding better than ever. Their second single for Beverley's will be 'Stop That Train' – one of four songs to feature Peter's lead vocals. It's arguably his best song to date – one written by someone who's learnt their craft, and senses their time draws near. Again, he expresses solidarity with Jamaica's ghetto people. "Some living big, but most are living small. They can't even find no food at all…" The song's framework makes familiar use of a train analogy, but other lines reveal a more reflective individual than heard previously. "All my life I've been a lonely man, teaching people who don't understand,"

Peter laments. "Even though I try my best, I still can't find no happiness." He's assumed the role of someone who works hard for the common good, yet receives scant reward or appreciation for his efforts. Such sentiments will resurface throughout his career, and give rise to a great deal of anger and frustration at times.

Peter had been singing the American Civil Rights anthem 'Go Tell It On The Mountain' for years, and it shows. Johnny Nash had covered it on his latest album *Prince Of Peace*, and may have been following his example. Jimmy Norman's 'Soon Come' is tailor-made for Peter as well, even if it is written about a girl. "I don't like hanging round or to be pushed around," he tells her, with no pretence at romance. He then revisits his rock track 'Can't You See', which is now much improved for having been cut in a reggae style. Years later, Bunny will heed the lines, "You break my heart and shatter my brain. If you have a conscience, ain't that a shame?" and reflect on the destructive nature of Peter's last relationship.

The rest of the album belonged to Bob, who'd written 'Cheer Up' in a bid to restore the band's spirits. 'Soul Captives', 'Back Out' and 'Caution' are good too, especially the latter. "Black soul is black as jet. Caution, the road is hot," he warns the black nation. "Said you got to do better than that... Don't want to see you on the ground, brothers."

The Wailers' sound was now reborn. It was the first of their albums to be conceived as such, and not just compiled from assorted singles. It was progressive and they were now headed in a positive direction, except no crossover hit came out of it and then Kong spoilt everything by calling the album *Best Of The Wailers*, which implied they wouldn't surpass it. This angered Bunny, who told Kong it would be the last Wailers music he'd ever hear, since their best was still ahead of them. Rumours that Bunny possessed mystical powers grew rapidly after Kong died of heart failure, soon after the album was released.

At least they now had renewed confidence, as well as a little money in their pockets. Peter's thoughts now drifted back in the direction of his solo career, starting with a re-recording of 'Sinner Man' called 'Oppressor Man'. Cut at Randy's with the Hippy Boys, it's credited as a Wailers production, despite Bob and Bunny's absence. He'll issue it on the Trans Am label, and the loping rhythm is beautifully understated. Peter's made the song his own, and 'Oppressor Man' offers clear indication that he's ready to go it alone should he wish.

That won't happen for a while yet. There was still magic in the Wailers' sound, and it pained him they hadn't achieved their breakthrough yet. No disrespect intended, but if the Upsetters and Desmond Dekker could do it, then why not the Wailers? They now ached with ambition, and were fiercely competitive. That June, Nicky Thomas' 'Love Of The Common People' went Top 10 in the UK and will stay on the charts for three months. Thomas was a part-time singer they called "Nigel". The rest of the time he was a gardener and odd job man. The Wailers had tried their utmost to cross over and to see someone like him having all that success was more than Peter could bear.

"Peter was a very radical type of person and he don't take no bullshit," says deejay pioneer Dennis Alcapone. "Peter was a man of his own and he go with whatever he believe. He was a very strong character but out of all the Wailers he was the one I really did like most. He was a nice person and quite generous really but I can remember one incident when me, him and Keith Hudson were standing outside of Randy's talking and Nicky Thomas came running up to us with a newspaper in his hand saying, 'Look at this. Me have a tune in the British charts.' Peter was a bit upset and said, 'Move yuh bloodclaat! It a pure big man yuh a talk to.' Nicky Thomas said something about how the Wailers never get a tune on the British charts yet so Peter and Keith, they curse him and chase him away but the next thing we know, he's on a plane to England to promote 'Love Of The Common People'.

"At that time I was recording for Coxsone and never knew that people abroad would be listening to my tunes. I was just grateful at hearing my songs on the radio and felt happy for that because it make you more popular in your area, and it was a joy if you could buy two hot Guinness at night-time. A little was just enough for those of us trying to make a living from the music. But it was just the love of it kept us going sometimes."

Chapter 8

Fussing And Fighting

Lee "Scratch" Perry was now a regular visitor to Randy's. Most of his productions were instrumentals featuring the Upsetters. Once 'Return Of Django' had rocketed into the Top 5, Perry had taken them to England the previous November but then left the band members stranded in London without tickets or money. They'd had to play one or two sessions to raise their airfares and felt humiliated. Meanwhile Perry treated himself to a Jaguar and had it shipped back to Jamaica. It wasn't the first time they'd been caught napping. Moonlighting as the Harry J All-Stars, the same band had played on 'Liquidator', which spent five months on the UK charts and earned a fortune for insurance salesman Harry Johnson. There was money to be made from the music business but it was unscrupulous entrepreneurs profiting from it, not musicians.

Perry had a shop at 36 Charles Street, where he masterminded the flood of novelty records that secured his early reputation. Most revolved around themes such as spaghetti westerns, doctors and horror films. During the afternoons, he'd oversee rehearsals in a room at the back of his shop, opposite a bar called the Green Door. That's where the Wailers went to see him in August. Bunny Lee had suggested they work together but Bob had said, "Who, Chicken Scratch?" The Wailers didn't take him all that seriously, although he'd earned Peter's respect since collaborating on 'Earth's Rightful Ruler'. Scratch was a few years older than them and more experienced. He knew their potential, whilst the Wailers were looking to offset recording costs. The idea was to split everything down the middle; the productions would be shared, and Perry would then take care of promotion and distribution. Crucially, nothing was put in writing.

Perry booked Dynamic for their first session together. This resulted in 'Try Me' and another James Brown cover, 'I Guess I'll Have To Cry, Cry, Cry', aka 'My Cup'. Soon afterwards they cut 'Small Axe', written about Coxsone, Duke Reid and Federal, who'd formed an alliance called "the Big Three". Jamaicans often leave the "H" out of words, and it was Peter who'd suggested the line "If you are a big tree, let me tell you, we are a small axe. Ready to cut you down..." Infused with Biblical references 'Small Axe' is an underdog's cry of intent, and a determined one.

With Randy's booked and anticipation running high, they'll start laying down tracks in September. They'd rehearsed the songs over and over by then, knew exactly what they were doing and left nothing to chance. Peter and Bunny were in exceptional form. The way they weave harmonies is breathtaking at times, and especially on tracks like 'Reaction' and 'Soul Rebel.' The latter is incendiary – nothing like the JAD version – because The Upsetters too were firing on all cylinders. They sensed where the Wailers were headed and were ready for anything. Even when they played cover versions, they'd still try something different, like when they combined elements of 'Rude Boy" and the Temptations' 'Cloud Nine' on 'Rebel's Hop'.

The Wailers' output from 1970/71 is widely celebrated. Perry has claimed that he co-wrote much of the material but Bunny fiercely disputes this and says the pint-sized producer had "no principles". Others pay tribute to his inventiveness and the ability to communicate with musicians, despite not playing any instruments. Whatever the truth of this relationship it was a creative period for everyone including Peter, who continued to practise every chance he got.

"One evening Peter picked up this acoustic guitar and started playing some really soulful American riffs," says Dave Barker, whose 'Prisoner Of Love' was a big hit during that summer. "I sat there watching his fingers moving up and down the strings and he made that guitar talk! He just sat there playing the blues and neither of us said anything because Peter could also be very quiet at times. But I couldn't believe what I was hearing, because he played some notes and phrases you never hear in Jamaican music, I tell you..."

Bob had gone to see relatives of his father in the hope of borrowing money before the Wailers teamed with Scratch. After they turned him down he wrote 'Corner Stone' with the line "The stone that the builder refuse will always be the head cornerstone." Whilst Perry may have made suggestions here and there, this was a Wailers project without apology. They'd lived these songs and were adamant in making music on their own terms, free of artifice and concessions.

The new album will be called *Soul Rebels*, and prove a compelling mix of soul, Black Power and Rastafarian influences. Scratch licensed it to Trojan in the UK, who put a black girl on the cover with bare breasts, wearing combat fatigues and cradling a rifle. They hadn't realised Rastafarians would find the image distasteful, and this wasn't their only mistake since the credits stated "All songs written by Bob Marley". Just put yourself in Peter's kung fu slippers for a minute, then imagine what he must have felt after contributing songs like '400 Years' and 'No Sympathy'. The latter is desolate, as if wrapped in sadness. It mourns the absence of friends when you need them, whereas '400 Years' is a stinging indictment of colonial rule and will become a mainstay of Peter's stage act for years to come.

If Trojan were hoping the Wailers would emulate the success of Jimmy Cliff or Desmond Dekker they'd be disappointed. Whilst *Soul Rebels* sold within the core market, it barely caused a ripple beyond it – possibly because the songs were too dark and inward looking. It's fair to say that British skinheads eager to do the "moon stomp" weren't too impressed, but the Wailers will keep on working with Scratch regardless. They liked the sound they were getting, as it was real and authentic. It had depth to it, and was something new for Jamaica.

Around Christmas time, the Upsetters unleashed 'Clint Eastwood' – an instrumental Family Man says was the first-ever dub track. Scratch hadn't paid them and so they'd left him temporarily. In their absence, he recruited a different band to play on 'Duppy Conqueror,' but Bob didn't like the rhythm and persuaded the Upsetters to return. Once the magic was restored 'Duppy Conqueror' became a smash hit in Jamaica. The Wailers now seemed revitalised. They were a group at the height of their powers, and supernatural forces beware! Bunny and Peter switch harmonies on 'Fussing And Fighting', which arose after further disagreements over money. Members of the Wailers and Upsetters were beginning to tire of Scratch's sharp business practices. The new material was good though.

'Long, Long Winter' was an Impressions song and Peter's second attempt at 'Sinner Man' was much improved. Did we mention that he exuded confidence? One day Dave Barker looked on in amazement as Peter rolled a spliff during a live recording – lit it, took an enormous lungful, then nonchalantly strolled up to the mic and delivered a harmony right on cue. Coolness personified.

'Keep On Moving' is another of Bob's outlaw songs, and Bunny and Peter both get short cameo appearances. Peter portrays himself as a fugitive and sings, "I've got two boys and woman. They're going to suffer now." In fact he's got at least three sons, and definitely more than one woman! Peter may have been a ladies' man, yet he's no romantic. In the lyrics of 'Brand New Second-hand', he strips bare some girl who's been acting innocent. He calls her "a disgrace", and is pitiless in his condemnation of her. He clearly doesn't like lies or pretence, and isn't afraid to let her know just what he thinks of her.

"Peter is another good writer. He writes how he feels," Perry told *Reggae Routes*. "Any time Peter writes a tune, he writes it for a reason. He doesn't do it because he wants to sing a song. He does it because it means something to him or he's saying something about somebody or something. He doesn't do things for a quick price. He does it because he wants to send a message."

How he let Bob steal a march on him and write the Wailers' first ever herb tune is a mystery, given his passion for smoking it. 'Kaya' (a slang name for marijuana) will be the band's first release of 1971 and the message is beautifully understated. In fact 'Kaya' could easily be mistaken for a love song if you weren't listening all that carefully. The dub cut's far more obvious, with a pastiche of Cheech & Chong, reggae style, on the intro as their herb dealer knocks on the door and Peter asks, 'A who that sah?'

The Wailers' sessions for Lee Perry will continue until around Easter. 'African Herbsman', which they adapted from Richie Havens' 'Indian Rope Man', will prove another highlight. The real-life African herbsman was a soldier friend of Peter's who'd served in Angola. Some afternoons he'd pull up outside of Scratch's shop in his Jeep, then regale them with tales of how powerful the herb was over there. He said it was so strong, the rebel fighters believed it made them invisible. Peter, who was already fascinated by natural medicine, loved hearing these stories.

It was a joyful time for him. 'Duppy Conqueror' had put the group back into contention, and he was writing decent songs. The music too, was flowing like lava. Scratch was running his own sessions and whenever they overlapped, Peter gladly helped out where needed. The same night Bunny re-recorded 'Dreamland', Peter played guitar and melodica on a couple of Junior Byles' songs, including 'A Place Called Africa'. All three Wailers then lent harmonies to Little Roy's 'Don't Cross The Nation'.

"Peter was one of Jamaica's greatest guitarists and he was militant, but he was my best friend out of the Wailers," says Little Roy. "I could feel the love coming from him because he liked this song I did called 'Earth' where I'm singing, "The earth is the Lord's and the fullness thereof. The greenest herb tree and the brownest collie weed." He had a record shop in Westmoreland and would buy records to sell up there. He used to say to me, 'Roy, you should bring me some of those tunes where you're singing about the brownest collie weed.' He was a fun guy. He and Bob Marley were the stars of the Wailers. I can't differentiate between them really."

Peter plays melodica on two of the Wailers' final tracks for Perry, 'Memphis' and 'Sun Is Shining'. Bob wrote the latter and it's sublime, but it also marks Peter's finest-ever performance on that instrument. 'Sun Is Shining' will be the Wailers' first single on their new Tuff Gong label, once the group are back fending for themselves. Scratch had promoted a handful of shows for them over the holiday period, including a packed night at the Sombrero on Molynes Road. Beverley Kelso joined them on stage and said it was the best show they ever did. Their relationship with Scratch then swiftly deteriorated after they discovered he owed Randy's money for studio time, and hadn't admitted it. This would embarrass them in front of Vincent Chin, whom they respected. Subtle as ever, Bunny marched into Randy's and demanded that engineer Errol Thompson, whom everyone called "E. T", hand over the tapes.

"I was there when that incident happened," says Clive Chin. "Money was owing on the session and Bunny Wailer wanted to use brute force to get what he wanted but Errol stood up to him. He said he wasn't going to give up the tape and told Bunny he had to pay for it. That's when Bunny started with all kind of bad mouth business. My father didn't pay him any mind though. He insisted that Bunny wasn't getting the tape and it's still there at Randy's to this day, because Bunny went and recorded the song over somewhere else. Bunny is a very hot-tempered guy. Out of all of the Wailers he had a difficult temperament and I believe that held them back in certain ways..."

Bunny gave Perry a beating one Friday night at the Sombrero, after the producer told them he was only prepared to pay a small royalty on record sales, rather than 50 percent as promised. Bunny had immediately attacked him, scattering the patrons and knocking over several tables. A day or so later, the Wailers walked into Scratch's shop demanding an explanation. Perry smiled as he gestured towards a burly man stood behind the counter. This was his new bodyguard and the sight of him enraged Bunny, who let fly at Perry, punched him in the face and then held his ratchet blade against the startled bodyguard's neck, who was now desperately wishing he was someplace else. Eventually – and mainly because of Bob and Peter's intervention – Scratch agreed to meet with them later in the week, when they could go through the paperwork together.

On their return, Scratch acted very nervous. Peter noticed a phial of yellow liquid on his desk and true to his name ("Touch"), picked it up. Scratch immediately got irate, which aroused Peter's curiosity even more. He unscrewed the cap to take a sniff and realised it was acid. Perry had it there for protection and must have been horrified as Bunny seized hold of him and threatened to pour it over his head. Finally, once everything had quietened down, Scratch showed them some paperwork and that's when they discovered that Rita had been collecting records from Randy's and selling them, but then pocketing the money for herself.

This episode left Bob embarrassed and the other two Wailers glowering with resentment. All that hard work and they had nothing to show for it because Randy's kept records of any transactions and Rita's signature was all over them. Bob was mortally ashamed, but felt Scratch had been exonerated. Not so Bunny and Peter. They'll view Rita with increasingly jaundiced eyes in future, and never work with Perry again. According to Bunny, Scratch had spent lots of money on "whoredom and foolishness", and the licensing deals he made with Trojan weren't anything to shout about either. He'd called the Wailers' follow-up album *Soul Revolution* and issued it on his own Maroon label in Jamaica before handing it over to Trojan and then releasing the instrumental tracks as *Soul Revolution Part II*. The Wailers had no say in any of this, and they regretted ever getting involved with him. Just to make things worse, the cover design was again amateurish. Glen Adams had photographed the Wailers posing as Black Panthers in Lee Perry's garden, and pretending to fire toy guns. The photos really weren't all that convincing, although Peter's a model of revolutionary chic in his red beret and striped poncho.

Adams will soon migrate to the States while Bob is rewarded with an invitation to Sweden, where Johnny Nash is due to star in a film. JAD had agreed to provide songs for the soundtrack, and Bob was only too happy to leave Jamaica behind. Peter was left with far fewer options, and walked away nursing his anger and frustration. Bob had tried to defend Rita and swore to pay the money back, yet there was now a rift between him and the others. At least Peter could raise a little extra money by playing sessions, which is how he spent the rest of that summer. One of his first stops was Treasure Isle, where his friend Lloyd "Tin Leg" Adams was resident drummer. U Roy's breakthrough a year earlier had given Duke Reid's label a lift and there were still plenty of hits coming from the wooden studio on Bond Street. Phyllis Dillon's 'One Life To Live', Ken Parker's 'Help Me Make It Through The Night' and the Melodians' 'Everybody Bawling' were all recorded there throughout 1971, and Peter may well have played on some of them. It was at Treasure Isle where he met a young keyboard player named Earl "Wya" Lindo, who'd call in after school to play sessions and cut the occasional instrumental. Wya admired how Peter lived his life with such freedom and sense of purpose. You'd imagine that Peter would clash with the Duke, who was a burly ex-policeman and fond of firing shots into the ceiling whenever he got annoyed. In fact the opposite was true, and they'll remain on good terms until Reid's death in 1975.

Joe Gibbs was another matter entirely. He and Peter agreed to work on productions for a 50–50 split, just like the deal with Perry. Peter badly needed the feeling of being his own man but wanted to concentrate on the music and not business. He was content to leave that to others, providing they were fair. The first track he recorded for Gibbs was a remake of 'Maga Dog' – a track that'll sell a reputed 75,000 copies on its way to the number one slot. Everyone was delighted with its success but then Peter knew it was a good song the first time round, when he'd recorded it for Coxsone.

In Jamaican parlance, a "maga dog" is one of those malnourished curs that roam the Kingston streets. Try and pet them and they'll bite you, although there's no mistaking the fact that Peter's talking about a person – someone who's taken his kindness for weakness. Joe Gibbs will claim that

Rita and her friend Judy Mowatt sang harmonies on 'Maga Dog', although bearing in mind Peter's grievances with Rita, that's hardly likely. This new version is slower than the original – which was raucous energy all the way – and set to a sinuous reggae groove. Peter himself plays guitar, piano and organ, and his vocals are a lot more distinct. It's a fine effort, but then Peter's brief tenure with Gibbs was studded with them. 'Black Dignity' is a righteous chant, and decorated with Peter's staccato organ. Not for the first time, it finds him speaking in Amharic. He's urging black people to wake up from their "slumbering mentality", and this will be a central theme of Peter's work for years to come. He alludes to it again on 'Arise Blackman', which shares similarities with 'Awake Rasta' – a song Scratch had introduced to Peter.

So far things weren't going too badly with Gibbs, who trusted Peter's instincts whilst venturing a few suggestions of his own. Following Perry's example on 'All In One', he persuaded Peter to record 'Rudie's Medley', which starts off with covers of Desmond Dekker's '007 Shanty Town' and 'Rude Boy Train'. Peter sings all the different voices, even imitating Dekker's distinctive quaver which he pulls off quite magnificently. You'd never guess it was him until the track segues into 'The Toughest' and the line "anything you can do, I can do better. I'm the toughest" hits home. Several years earlier, Prince Buster had recorded a courtroom drama called 'Judge Dread', where he'd sentenced rude boys in a mock trial. Peter will use the same concept on 'Here Comes The Judge' except it won't be rude boys in the dock, but historical figures such as Christopher Columbus, Sir Francis Drake, Henry Morgan and Alexander ("so-called") The Great, who've been brought to trial for "robbing and raping Africa, stealing black people out of Africa" and killing over 50 million of them "without a cause". This in addition to brainwashing them, teaching them to hate themselves and "holding them captive for more than 400 years".

Although comical in places, 'Here Comes The Judge' is a history lesson and political statement rolled into one. Peter's humour often carried a sting in its tail and that's nowhere more evident than here – especially since all of the prisoners are sentenced to death by hanging, and by their tongues instead of their necks!

The revolutionary within Peter burns brightly at this point. Fuelled by his avid reading about black history and politics, he's driven by a feeling of retribution. Black people in Jamaica are in the majority, and yet too many are forced to live in squalor, with no recourse to the jobs and opportunities middle-class Jamaicans take for granted. 'Them Ha Fi Get A Beatin' dates from this period, and is one of Peter's better protest songs. "Don't you wait 'til your back is against the wall," he warns his audience. "Just one step to progress and I know Jah will help you all." As elections approached, 'Them Ha Fi Get A Beatin' followed 'Maga Dog' into the charts. Joe Gibbs was delighted, except Bunny Lee claims that Peter did all the work and was soon complaining at being paid in dribs and drabs, or "$50 here and $100 there until it added up to £1,500". Peter will later tell Fikisha Cumbo he only got money out of Gibbs after threatening him with violence, saying, "Me not a boxer and all that fuckery, and me didn't want to go to jail for murder." Two months later, the producer will offer him $500 to record a solo album and Peter will rudely decline, cursing Gibbs for his lack of respect.

Clive Chin, who was present during some of their sessions, says that Joe Gibbs was more of a businessman than record producer. "There are two distinct types of producers," he begins. "There are the ones who go in and explain what they want, and come out with something that's unique. Then there are the ones who just give a musician the go-ahead to produce something, and then pay for the session afterwards. I consider these people to be associate producers, because real producers don't just pay for a session, then sit back and listen to the tapes after the musicians have left – they make things happen. At the same time, we should remember that these talented artists and musicians weren't household names at the time. They were people who were striving, who played from their hearts and their souls and they were more than happy to do music with you without a contract."

Peter would soon tire of his arrangement with Gibbs. He and Bunny were busy in any case, moving the Wailers' shop to new premises at 127 King Street. Helped by a friend called Jack Wise, they decorated the walls with record sleeves and posters; then released a second single on Tuff Gong called 'Send Me That Love', which was a waltz, and featured Peter on xylophone – no kidding. Bob returned in June, just as Peter was again warring with Joe Gibbs, who'd taken the rhythm of 'Maga Dog' and issued several different cuts to it, giving them names like 'Skanky Dog', 'Mangy Dog', 'Boney Dog', 'Hot Dog' and 'Bull Dog'. This infuriated Peter, who felt he hadn't been properly compensated for 'Maga Dog' in the first place.

With vengeance in mind he headed for Randy's and recorded a new song, conceived in a similar style to 'Maga Dog' but with Bob on guitar and singing harmonies. Peter called it 'Once Bitten' and warns, "I don't want to hear a word you say – step back with your lies." He then took the same rhythm and voiced 'Dog Teeth', with spoken lyrics straight to Gibbs' head. "No dog who bite me will ever bite me again,' he promises, before reminding himself that, "If you lie with dog, you must rise with flea."

Chapter 9

Rod Of Correction

During Bob's absence, Peter and Bunny decided to form their own labels, separate from Tuff Gong. Bunny came up with two names – "Solomonic", which he kept for himself, and "Intelligent Diplomat", which Peter chose and shortened to "Intel Diplo".

"Selassie say we have to live as intelligent diplomats among men, so you have to be wiser than the serpent and more harmless than the dove. That's how you survive," said Bunny by way of explanation. He then sat down and drew designs for each of them. Intel Diplo would have a five-pointed star with one eye, whereas Solomonic had a six-pointed star with two eyes. Peter rushed the artwork to the printers and 'Dog Teeth' became the debut Intel release on his new label. Copies were proudly displayed at the Wailers' shop on King Street and Peter enjoyed hanging out there. Musician friends were always stopping by to say hello and Keith Hudson rented the office upstairs, which made life interesting. Alas, there'll soon be further tensions within the Wailers to worry about since shortly before Bob's return, Rita had told Peter that Bob was planning to make off with the group's money. Bunny advised him to forget what she'd said but Peter had to say something and told Bob he'd had a vision, so it wouldn't sound like an accusation. Bob wasn't fooled by this and rounded on Peter, causing him to feel shame at having let a woman's gossip get the better of him.

The gulf between Peter's aspirations and his day-to-day reality weighed heavily. Despite all the Wailers had achieved he and Bob were still living in Trench Town, where conditions continued to wear them down. Only recently, Peter had been forced to jump a fence in Saboo's yard on First Street during a police raid. Whilst he escaped unhurt his guitar was damaged in the scramble, causing him to curse the fact that God-fearing people like himself were still being persecuted – just for smoking a little herb and playing music. He was growing impatient to leave, but didn't have enough money to rent somewhere better. Ironically, it wasn't until they'd celebrated Trench Town in song that things started to improve. "One good thing about music, when it hits you feel no pain," sang Bob on 'Trench Town Rock' – an anthem for the downtrodden that not only roared with defiance, but exulted in their lowly status. What a turnaround! This track and one called 'Screw Face' will transform the band's fortunes as 1971 drew to a close.

'Trench Town Rock' was a number one hit in Jamaica. U Roy then voiced 'Kingston 12 Shuffle' over the same rhythm, with Peter playing melodica. That was a hit too, whilst 'Craven Choke Puppy' was written about Lee Perry and tells of a dog gorging itself, only to splutter and choke. Scratch's disloyalty still rankled, but Bob was now writing hits like there was no tomorrow. Whereas 'Trench Town Rock' celebrated ghetto life, 'Concrete Jungle' dwelled on the other side of the coin. "Darkness has covered my life, and turned my day into night," he laments. "No chains around my feet, but I'm not free. I am bound here in captivity." His other songs included an early version of 'Catch A Fire' (on which Peter chants in Amharic), 'Guava Jelly', 'Redder Than Red' and 'Lick Samba'. Also two songs – 'Satisfy My Soul Jah Jah' and 'Satisfy My Soul Babe' – that shared the same rhythm track but dealt with differing subject matter. Most impressive of all was 'Lively Up Yourself', which could make even the lowliest sufferer feel 10 feet tall. Bob had learnt to really connect with people in his songs. He didn't chide them like Peter sometimes did, but let them know he shared their concerns. He was a communicator who wrote memorable, inclusive songs, and audiences will love him for it.

Jamaicans would go to the polling booths in early 1972. The PNP, led by Michael Manley, had adopted Delroy Wilson's 'Better Must Come' as its theme song and the phrase would be scrawled on walls throughout Western Kingston, where many were desperate to believe it. All three Wailers leaned towards the PNP, especially Peter. Like his father, Manley had expressed sympathies with the Rastafarians, and he also had a black girlfriend – JBC newsreader Beverley Anderson, whom he'll marry the following summer. She knew of his playboy reputation, but says he wasn't interested in money. "He cared for his music, car, his clothes and his art. That's it."

Manley was a jazz fan. It was Beverley who introduced him to local delicacies such as stew peas and reggae music. She remembers the Wailers hanging out under a tree in the JBC yard "singing and playing their music, hoping for an opportunity to appear on television", she wrote in her autobiography. "Later, at PNP headquarters, I reasoned with Peter Tosh for a while almost daily. "There was much anger and deep hurt in him. I have never met anyone so ready to both implode and explode."

The Wailers joined Manley on the campaign trail in November, performing with "the Caravan Of Stars", which later became known as the "PNP Musical Bandwagon". Alton Ellis and Max Romeo were among the other acts. The charismatic Manley was star turn however, well armed with slogans such as "Giving Power To The People" and "A Government Of Truth".

By the time the PNP win the election on February 29, Bob will be in London with Johnny Nash and won't return home for nearly three months. Whilst details are unclear, it's thought the Wailers met up in New York over the holiday period, after Trench Town MP Anthony Spaulding had arranged a handful of club appearances for them. They'll play at least three shows in the US, beginning with a date in the Bronx on New Year's Eve. Everything went well until the final show, at a club in Brooklyn. Halfway through their performance a local roughneck began firing into the ceiling, causing people to panic and the gig to be cancelled.

After the election, Spaulding will become Jamaica's new Housing Minister and proved indispensable to Bob and Peter as they prepared to leave Trench Town. Both shared the belief that Manley's victory heralded a better future for Jamaica. Whilst the rich complained about having to pay more tax, Manley's reforms encompassed work schemes for the unskilled, land reforms, the introduction of a minimum wage, improvements to basic schools, new day-care centres and equal pay for women. He also chose non-alignment from either the US or Russia which endeared him to Castro, although Manley was never a Communist.

Peter celebrated Manley's victory with 'Lion' and 'Here Comes The Sun', which he recorded at Randy's with his friend Lloyd "Gitsy" Willis and the Barrett brothers. Family Man was on leave after taking a job on a cruise ship, playing to tourists as they sailed between Jamaica, Cuba and Haiti. He was happy to be back in the studio, and gave a broad smile upon hearing 'Lion' for the first time. "Lion" was street slang – a greeting between Rastafarians. The term was a symbol of brotherhood although its popularity soon spread and before long every street kid was using it, whether they were Rasta or not. This was a new development. Rastafarians had traditionally kept a low profile for fear of persecution but now youths sporting dreadlocks were aggressively begging off people or indulging in criminality with no thoughts of observing Rasta precepts. Certain artists targeted in this way felt intimidated, but not Peter. "I only hear your words, yet I don't see works," he sneers before putting them in their place with the lines "Locks on your head, talking about you're dread. And you believe that is all."

"There are lots of guys wearing dreadlocks who are one million miles away from Rasta. They are like night to day," says Peter on the intro. "And I know the consciousness of Rasta is *righteousness*." 'Here Comes The Sun' is the Beatles' song, and Peter may well have identified with its writer George Harrison. Both men toiled in the shadows of greater talents, and had grown tired of being their group's poor relation. Peter's version isn't all that remarkable, although the song's sentiments will prove prophetic before the year is out.

First, the Wailers had a break-in at their shop to contend with. Thieves stole an amplifier, turntable and stampers for two songs that Coxsone will later issue on 45. Peter had suspected he might be involved, yet Tuff Gong will continue to flourish. In late January, Bob had left Sweden for London. Trojan and Pama Records were now distributing the Wailers' music in England, and there was strong support at grassroots level. Suitably encouraged, Bunny joined Peter in launching a solo career, debuting with 'Bide Up', 'Arab's Oil Weapon' and 'Pass It On'. Another of Family Man's protégés, a bass player called Robbie Shakespeare, helped out on that session. Peter, who played guitar, was impressed. The youth had potential, and was roots as they come.

Bob got back in late summer, excited about the possibility of a deal with CBS and forthcoming UK tour dates with Johnny Nash, who'd had a hit with 'Stir It Up' in April. It was Bob's first real success as a songwriter, and the connection with Nash – who was now billed as "King Of Reggae"

– could do him and the other Wailers no harm at all. First they had to get their affairs in order and so Bob recruited his friend, footballer Allan "Skill" Cole, to act as their manager. He'd played in Brazil, home of the current world champions, and was looking to extend his connections with the local music industry. Bob admired his soccer skills, and trusted that Cole had the necessary business acumen. Peter wasn't so sure but like Bunny, hoped for the best.

The Wailers' party left for London during mid–August, amidst bomb scares and union unrest, and was taken to Sims' apartment at 3 Cromarty Villas on Queensborough Terrace, just off the Bayswater Road. Nash and Sims liked company (especially of the female variety), and the flat soon became overcrowded. Peter, Bunny and the Barrett brothers duly moved to a nearby hotel, although they'd spend hardly any time there. The Wailers saw a lot of Delroy Washington on this trip, and relied on him to show them around. He and Peter were like family. Peter had been friends with two of Delroy's uncles back in Savanna La Mar, and taken the youngster to school on the handlebars of his bicycle some mornings. Delroy also had an aunt who was a neighbour of Peter's in Trench Town.

In readiness for the tour, the band rehearsed at Condor Music in Kingston-upon-Thames. Condor was several miles out of London and the Wailers had no car, which meant they had to use public transport to get there at first. Johnny Nash and his band rehearsed in the big room, while the Wailers were allocated a smaller space across the hall, where they were joined by two members of West London reggae band the Cimarons – Locksley Gichie (on guitar) and Carl Levy (keyboards). Eager to invest his music with authenticity, Nash drafted some of the Wailers' party to play on tracks from his *I Can See Clearly Now* album. There were still no signs of a tour, although the Wailers did play club dates in Bristol, Willesden High Road and at Peckham's Bouncing Ball, where they met promoter Brent Clarke. Sims hired him as a publicist and assigned him to look after the Wailers. One of his first tasks was to find them suitable accommodation, and he chose a small, three bedroomed house in Neasden.

"The first person I met from the Wailers was Peter," says Brinsley Forde, future lead singer with Aswad. "I was acting at that time, and working at my local greengrocers to make some extra money. I was out in the front, putting tissue paper under the apples and I remember turning to the right and seeing this giant walking down the street, wearing a beret and with a black fist hanging round his neck. He walked towards me and I found myself blurting out, 'You're Peter Tosh!' It was like seeing this apparition walk out the mist. It turned out they were staying at the Circle, which was just around the corner from the main street in Neasden."

Brinsley says Peter was a solitary figure who didn't like socialising all that much, although he'd occasionally join in when the others started jamming. Bunny was withdrawn too, and fiercely committed to the Rasta cause. He had a reputation for being argumentative, and was fastidious about the food and hygiene. Peter shared a room with him, and decorated it with a poster of Che Guevera. Both missed Jamaica though. England was getting colder by the day and Delroy Washington says there was an intimidating atmosphere around the group, who didn't suffer fools gladly. One local hanger-on, keen to impress, arranged for a friend in Jamaica to post a consignment of herb to the house. Badly wrapped and smelling to high heaven, it was intercepted and everyone in the house arrested, including Peter and Bunny. They were eventually released without charge, but this episode did nothing to improve their mood.

Needless to say, those tour dates never materialised. Sims hadn't bothered to sort out work permits and it became apparent he was only really interested in Johnny Nash's career, and maybe getting Bob signed to CBS. They did play a couple of gigs in Brixton and Croydon and maybe one in Portsmouth, but had to stay under the radar for the most part. The fact is that few people knew of them outside of Caribbean enclaves in London and elsewhere. They had no crossover hits or mainstream exposure to their name and the one time they did support Nash they blew him off stage, which didn't go down too well with him or Sims. Esther Anderson will claim she first thought of it, but the Wailers were already wearing red, green and gold, and opening their set with 'Rastaman Chant', complete with nyahbinghi drumming. No recordings exist of these shows, but Family Man confirms they played songs like 'Screwface', 'Trench Town Rock', 'Lively Up Yourself' and 'Duppy Conqueror'.

During rehearsals, they tried out new material that'll end up on the *Slave Drover* album. Bob liked Gichie's style of playing, which had a blues feel. It especially suited 'Concrete Jungle' but the Cimarons' guitarist gives credit to Peter for holding down that essential reggae beat.

"I learnt how to play wah wah guitar from Peter; that rhythm style with the brisk movement," he says. "Peter had been playing it a long time. He was a good musician and very laid-back as a person. He didn't talk too much and was very quiet. He was more of a reader and a thinker than a conversationalist but he was a nice guy when you got talking with him."

It was now late September. In two months' time 'I Can See Clearly Now' will top the US *Billboard* charts, and advance promotion proved crucial. Nash and Sims promptly left for America and not for the first time, the Barrett brothers will be stranded in London without any means of getting home. In years to come Peter will describe Nash and Danny Sims as "black pirates" and mourn the fact he'd received only $350 in royalties from Sims' publishing company, Cayman Music. It was at this point that Brent Clarke went to see Chris Blackwell at Island Records, and explained the Wailers' predicament. As well as reminding him of the songs Marley had written for Nash and the Wailers' run of Jamaican hits, he played Blackwell tapes of the demos they'd made for CBS. Blackwell was intrigued, and arranged to meet with them at Island's studios in Ladbroke Grove. Blackwell was impressed with their charisma from the moment Bob, Bunny and Peter walked through the door. During their discussion, he said he'd paid Coxsone thousands of pounds for UK sales of their Studio One sides, which didn't best please them. Either the wily Coxsone had been short-changing them, or Blackwell was smarter than they realised.

Brent Clarke negotiated a two-album deal on the Wailers' behalf. Blackwell agreed to pay them £8,000 per album, with the band retaining the rights to release them in the Caribbean. Clarke received £1,000 in commission and the remaining £7,000 was paid into Byron Lee's bank account in Jamaica. Lee owned Dynamic Sound studios, and could therefore deduct recording expenses at source. Clarke then loaned the band £750 towards their tickets home but failed in getting them to sign a management contract and never did get his money back. There's gratitude for you, except he wasn't the only one with money problems. Soon after the Wailers' return, they found that a good deal of their savings had disappeared. Skill had used the money to pay off gambling debts, and this latest blow hit them hard. Peter seethed with indignation. Not for the first time, someone around Bob had stopped the group in its tracks. He and Rita moved out to Bull Bay shortly afterwards, near where Bunny and Jean Watt lived, and Peter wouldn't stay in Trench Town too long either. Thanks to Tony Spaulding's intervention, he'd been offered government housing in Bridgeport, in Greater Portmore. This was on a peninsula midway between Kingston and Spanish Town, not far from Ras Michael's Rasta camp. It was out of the city, and yet within easy driving distance of Central Kingston. Peter had a car now – a white Oldsmobile no less – and was often seen careering round Kingston in it, with girlfriend Yvonne Whittingham by his side. He and Bob always claimed they were apolitical but living in Jamaica, everyone needed allegiances.

Work on the new album began in October, but at Randy's and not Dynamic. "Allan Cole was managing Bob at the time and I remember him coming around, booking the studio and paying the session fees," remembers Clive Chin. "Bob didn't want anything to do with the financial end of it. That's why he had Allan. He entrusted him with their affairs as a friend, and also a member of the Twelve Tribes."

Bob had won out and kept Skill on board. Then again, Peter and Bunny wanted no part of the bookwork either, and prayed for a just outcome. There was now real unity between the Wailers and the two Barrett brothers, musically speaking. All shared a common purpose, which was to make an album that would redefine reggae music and put the Wailers on the world map. They certainly had the songs, and the facilities weren't lacking either. Their sessions at Dynamic were spread over two days and took place in Studio B, where Eric Donaldson had voiced 'Cherry Oh Baby' and the Rolling Stones were about to record *Goat's Head Soup*. Both days went smoothly since they'd been rehearsing the same songs for months already. 'Concrete Jungle' was among the tracks they finished first, together with 'Midnight Ravers' and 'Kinky Reggae', which Bob had written after witnessing Nash and Sims' exploits with groupies. 'No More Trouble' and 'Slave Driver' were sufferers' tracks of immense power and persuasion, but just as onlookers thought the band had got *too* militant, Bob pulled out a handful of love songs, including 'Rock It Babe', which Island later renamed 'Baby, Baby We've Got A Date'. These won't get highlighted so much. In fact two of them won't even be included on the album, since Island thought the Wailers' rebel image would be more appealing to rock fans (and they were right).

Other musicians came and went during the sessions. Bob's old friend Seeco played some percussion, and Winston Wright and Bernard "Touter" Harvey shared organ duties. Touter had been playing in the Youth Professionals with Robbie Shakespeare and was another of Family Man's protégés. None of these musicians, like drummer Sparrow Martin and members of Inner Circle, will be mentioned in the album credits.

100

"We backed the Wailers many times as youths," recalls Inner Circle's Roger Lewis, whose group had also supported them on Manley's campaign tour. "One day Peter Touch drive to our house in Chelsea Avenue and ask us to come and play with them. He came into the yard with a spliff in the corner of his mouth, as always, and say to us, 'Right now, I want the fat boys to come down and play some music for we as Wailers.' I remember we played on 'Stir It Up' and maybe one or two other tracks. I played lead guitar and my brother played bass but some of the other man them couldn't come because they were still at school."

Bob had made a demo recording of 'Stir It Up' for Johnny Nash, but this version's much better. Dynamic's eight-track board and cleaner sound quickly won the band over since they also breathed new life into 'Small Axe' and 'Duppy Conqueror' during those sessions, as well as three of Peter's compositions – 'No Sympathy', 'Stop That Train' and '400 Years'. The improved facilities had made a world of difference, and confidence was running high as Bob boarded a flight to London with the master tapes.

Chris Blackwell listened intently to the playback, but thought the album lacked something. Bob mentioned how he liked rock guitar, which is how American guitarist Wayne Perkins got involved. He knew nothing about reggae, but plugged in his sustain pedal and gave it his best shot. His playing on 'Concrete Jungle' especially will draw in hippy audiences like bees to honey. Johnny Nash's keyboard player, John "Rabbit" Bundrick, then overdubbed synthesizer, clavinet and organ, to somewhat lesser effect. The album now sounded utterly unique. There was nothing in rock music like it, and nothing in reggae either. It "catch a fire" as they say in Jamaica, and so that's what Island decided to call it.

Peter and Bunny waited expectantly back in Kingston but first Bob had to go and resolve contractual matters with Danny Sims, who was in New York. Whilst he was there Bob befriended a young filmmaker called Lee Jaffe, and met actress Esther Anderson. Blackwell invited them to Jamaica and so they arrived in Kingston during early February.

"I went to Island House on Hope Road and there was this tall fellow in the yard. He was very handsome and someone said it was Peter Tosh," says Esther. "I went up to him and said hello and asked him if he was coming with us, because we were about to go round the islands on this plane Chris had chartered and visit Trinidad for Carnival. He said he didn't want to get mixed up with 'no Babylonians' and I was very disappointed, but then Bob said he would come and everything happened from there."

Esther was light-skinned and born in a Jamaican country parish, like Bob. In the early sixties she left for England to pursue an acting career and after helping Chris Blackwell launch Island Records, dated Marlon Brando. Shortly before meeting Bob she'd starred in Sidney Poitier's film *A Warm December*. Poitier had helped politicise her, and opened her eyes to issues of race and black consciousness. She and Bob would become romantically involved during that trip to Trinidad, and even wrote a song together.

"We wrote the lyrics to 'Get Up Stand Up' on the flight back to Jamaica in about 20 minutes," Esther explains. "It was based on something that happened to us in Haiti. Bob was really pissed off when we wrote that song. We were very close then, and I remember the plane dipped and sent us sprawling to the ground. Bob said the reason the plane didn't crash was because he was on it – that the Rastafarian god had saved us and I believed him!"

Bob would still visit Rita and the children over in Bull Bay, but now spent a lot of time with Esther at Island House – a detached residence with outbuildings that served as Island Records' HQ in Kingston, and was just yards from the Prime Minister's official residence. Soon the Wailers will use it for rehearsals, in readiness for their first UK tour.

Chapter 10

Mark Of The Beast

When Peter met Yvonne Whittingham his whole life changed. She was not only attractive but had a keen interest in black history and social affairs, and cherished the same ideals as he did. The two quickly became inseparable and moved to Bridgeport, situated midway between Spanish Town and Kingston, and a relatively short drive from both. People say it was a lower middle-class area but Peter was out of the ghetto at last, and feeling generally pleased with himself. From where the couple now lived, they could stroll through West Bay to the beach, where fishermen mended their nets and sold fish straight off the boat. It was the beginning of a new era; Peter was in love and the Wailers had a record deal. Nothing in his solo career had given him the same thrill as singing with Bob and Bunny, yet he also had his own future to think about.

Whilst Bob was away Peter recruited Family Man and drummer Lloyd "Tin Legs" Adams for a session at Treasure Isle. Two songs were laid that day including 'No Mercy', featuring Bunny on conga drums.

"Look wha' Babylon a do," Peter wails. "He gives I a basket to carry water. He beat us up, kick us down and put us in jail." In little over three minutes he roundly condemns police brutality, calls for the legalisation of marijuana and then exposes the inequality that has been allowed to go unchecked since independence. "The rich man has it all, but the poor man got none," he tells us. "Them have no mercy, none at all." The melody does borrow a little something from his friend Leonard Dillon's

'The Selah', the Ethiopians' hit from the year previously, but the melody is probably derived from a spiritual in any case.

The other track Peter recorded during that session was 'Can't Blame The Youth', which proclaimed his revolutionary stance for all to see. Any time people resist the system they're met with violence and oppression. It's the same the world over but as a post-colonial nation, Jamaica has its own set of problems and youths fired by black consciousness were angry at hearing the same old lies. Peter will be their spokesman. As a child, he was taught that Christopher Columbus, Marco Polo and even celebrated pirates like John Hawkins were "very great men", despite having spent most of their time "robbing, raping, kidnapping and killing". 'Can't Blame The Youth' is a scathing indictment of the Jamaican educational system, as well as the British model that preceded it. Peter knew that Jamaica would never achieve real independence until it shed every last vestige of its colonial past. To his mind, that also meant embracing a black man's philosophy, meaning Rastafari. Peter cemented his solidarity with Jamaica's ghetto poor on this record, and not for the first time invests his music with a calypso feel. You can imagine Harry Belafonte singing 'Can't Fool The Youth' and that's a compliment, not an insult. He then quotes from Luke Chapter 10 in the final verse. "What was hidden from the wise and prudent, is now revealed to the babes and suckling," he warns, as the lop-sided rhythm reaches its finale and his vocals fade into the distance.

Carly Barrett is back on the drum stool for 'Mark Of The Beast'. Noel "Scully" Simms again plays conga drums, just as he did on 'Can't Blame The Youth' and Peter's lyrics continue down the same outspoken path. "I see the mark of the beast on their ugly faces. I see them congregating in evil places," he begins, before accusing the police of framing him for ganja. "What have I done to be incriminated / humiliated / convicted?" he demands of his tormentors.

Peter referred to 'Mark Of The Beast' as "a historical song. [It] was written the first time I was brutalised by the police, seen?" he'll tell Roger Steffens. "That night, it was about 10 o'clock. I came from the country with some fresh sensimilla... This was in 1972. I was inside my house, testing out this good herb and it was very exotic, seen? It start to create inspiration and the inspiration that came up, I suppose it was a prophetic inspiration. I was seeing between the lines into the future, which was to manifest in the next 15 minutes. I was sat writing at my table, and it happen because there was some people keeping a party inside of the yard where I live. People were outside dancing but I was inside making music, totally locked off. It's like I couldn't even hear what was going on, even though it was a party. So I was there tapping on my table, creating the rhythm and singing, 'I see the mark of the beast on their ugly faces. I see them congregating in evil places. Me know them a wicked.' Well I didn't even reach a second verse. I heard a shot fire and say, 'Wha' that?' My woman, she went outside to look and say it was the police. Seconds later, I saw people running right out the house and through my apartment. So I was there, in permanent communication with the inspiration and here's a guy coming inside... He came through my door, see I with my spliff and say, 'Wha' that?' Him say, 'A ganja yuh have.' Him say 'ganja' and me say, 'ganja is a bird in a Australia.' He don't know that. Him say, 'Is wha' that?' Me say herb, him say make him see it. I give it to him, he smelled it and say, 'a ganja man.' Well, he's a guy in plain clothes and could be a robber, seen? He look ordinary, like he's just coming out the rum bar, and I'm well high, I take my spliff from him and start to push it out in my hand, into my pants' waist. So he went outside to call him friends and say one criminal inside here. There were about six of them. Two of them came inside to get me. After they'd dragged me outside, two held onto this hand and two held onto the other hand. And the one who was leader for that execution squad took a gun out of his waist and started to punch me in the abdominal, with a loaded .38, seen? When he get tired he use his fist, same place, then he call for a rifle and take it from his friend. Meanwhile they're holding me like Jesus on the cross, seen? He slammed the rifle into my ribs, dislocating my lower vertebrae. He give back the rifle, went behind my house, and took a piece of stick that catch the clothesline... He break off the bottom, which is the biggest part and come back whilst they're holding me and boof! To my forehead and that needed seven stitches, so I was prophetically looking into the future, and it happened."

His injuries will heal but leave permanent scars, both physically and otherwise. Three years previously he would have got an 18-month jail sentence, despite the violence used against him. Peter wouldn't have been able to tour behind *Catch A Fire*, which would have been catastrophic for him and the group. Yet there's no evidence of him being charged for possession, or of the police being reprimanded for using excessive force.

"Police look 'pon Rasta with no form of respect," he told Jeff Cathrow. "Not only in Jamaica, but universal. From you have dreadlocks you are being ignored in the society, seen? Because people always judge the book by its cover."

He'll later tell Fikisha Cumbo that 'Mark Of The Beast' can be attuned to what he was dealing with "physically, spiritually and mentally".

"I was thinking about the administration, and how them guys as black people call themselves police and administer to the poor. They humiliate them, take them unto death and then him just go back and drink whisky and laugh. Him just take it for a joke, 'cause I've been faced with those kinds of torture many times, knowing how I live in society not to offend or to be subversive and yet being offended by society; it a total aggravation that.

"I've seen how the police can just shoot a man or put a gun or a knife in his hand and say, 'Well, him draw fi it,' and then it's accepted in society. Yet it's an innocent man, because dead men tell no tales and all their administration is towards the poorer class of people in the ghetto. Only people in the ghetto feel the pains when the rich commit their crimes and so it go from the days of Columbus, Marco Polo, Henry Morgan and Francis Drake..."

Asked if he felt like retaliating, Peter replies that, "Yuh can't go out there, give him one lick and just leave him, because otherwise you end up in jail. That is what the devil wants you to do. The devil don't love people who make second thought, he love all the people who just make one thought and move. But you have to think twice in everything you do because it's the devil run this bloodclaat place; this hell we live in, and the devil have him agents all around you..."

Whilst marijuana remained illegal, Peter would be an easy target for the police since he steadfastly refused to acknowledge any attempt to criminalise it, and reserved the right to smoke it wherever he pleased. As far as he was concerned it was a natural plant that grew wild for the benefit of mankind, and no attempt at controlling it could ever be justified. Compromise was out of the question. The authorities were wrong and that was final.

His defence of marijuana was fuelled by a sense of injustice, but Peter loved attacking middle-class sensibilities in other ways too. Few invested swear words with such potency or humour, and "bloodclaat" is one of the most offensive in the Jamaican vernacular. Put simply, it means "blood cloth" or sanitary towel. Rastafarians don't allow menstruating women in their presence and so using this term – or the equally abusive "bombaclaat"

– had real shock value. (Interestingly, Esther Anderson claims Peter was squeamish about blood, and had insisted Yvonne try and stop menstruating.)

"Peter was magnificent," reflects Lee Jaffe. "He was a tremendously powerful presence and everything about him was just perfect physically but I felt every word out of his mouth was totally thought out, and totally precise. There were no random things coming out of Peter's mouth because it was all scripted, but in a very poetic way. You felt like he must have just spent all of his time thinking up this stuff, and then phrases just appeared fluently, as if watching a movie. And he didn't need a second take. He was really prepared with his lines all the time."

Lee rapidly became caught up in Jamaica's spell and Rasta culture. He'd been on his way to Chile but decided to stay on the island and share in the Wailers' adventure. A young, white American hippy overflowing with creative ideas and steeped in rock and the blues was now in their midst, and Peter welcomed him without reservation. "I felt that he was accepting of my presence and he treated me with openness and respect," Lee continues. "I think he trusted Bob's instincts about me, which led him to be very open-minded towards me. I think he felt that my being so close to Bob meant that there must be a real purpose for me being there."

Esther Anderson had also become transfixed by Rastafarianism, and was first to use it as a marketing tool. As well as taking photos of the Wailers she filmed them rehearsing at Island House and bathing at Cane River Falls. Nearly 40 years later she'll make a documentary based on that flickering black and white footage, in which the camaraderie is self-evident. None of the group lived in Trench Town any more and since moving out to Bull Bay, Bunny had written some beautiful new songs including 'Hallelujah Time', 'The Oppressed Song' and 'Reincarnated Souls', which Island had earmarked as the title of the Wailers' next album. It was an idyllic time, falling midway between the satisfaction of having delivered *Catch A Fire* and anticipation surrounding their first overseas tour. This was the band members' opportunity to write and rehearse, especially after Blackwell encouraged them to try out Harry J's new studio in nearby Roosevelt Avenue.

Peter's contributions would be slim, but quality. The only new composition was 'One Foundation', which underlined his folk roots whilst sporting hippy-friendly lyrics about social harmony. It's not a blockbuster like '400 Years' or 'No Sympathy' but has a pastoral feel; similar to the songs Bunny was writing.

"When I first encountered Peter's work, I was absolutely knocked out by his lyrics," Esther recalls. "I loved his songs as much as I loved Bob's. Having been brought up on the American Civil Rights movement, I loved songs like '400 Years'. I knew how much of an impact influential people like Angela Davis and Dr. Martin Luther King had on us as young people growing up and so to hear a voice like that coming out of Jamaica was incredible. His lyrics were extraordinary, but then so was the music. I thought it was fantastic but then I was Jamaican just like them. I'd been to the same government schools and all of us had been through similar experiences where our families were concerned.

"I knew that Peter was estranged from his father, just like Bob and myself. That's where this myth came from, that Chris Blackwell was some sort of father figure to Bob, but it was nothing of the sort. Bob used to say some very personal things about his father and how he'd abandoned his mother, but Peter never said too much about any of that. He never talked about his family or his own circumstances. What he talked about most was the condition of black people and what could change things around for them. He would be the one making that kind of discourse all the time. You could sense the influence that religion had on his life, but then his relatives were the normal kind of Jamaicans who used to go to church every Sunday. I got the feeling he'd abided with the rules at first, but then as he grew up and began questioning how these people were living, he just found it so hard to take because he couldn't deny the truth, and he questioned it much more than anyone else I spoke to at that time."

Following the expiry of his contract with JAD, Peter signed his song publishing over to a young American called Don Williams, who worked with Shelter Records' Denny Cordell in Los Angeles and was visiting Kingston partly on business, and partly because of his love of reggae music. The deal will put a little money in Peter's pocket as thoughts then turned to the band's UK tour dates, due to commence in a month's time. Earl "Wya" Lindo, who Peter knew from Treasure Isle, was hired to play keyboards. He was a member of Now Generation, and a top quality musician. Bob played decent rhythm guitar and so the band was now complete, with Family Man and Carly providing its rhythmic anchor as usual.

Catch A Fire was released on April 13, just two weeks before the Wailers were due to open their UK tour. That well-publicised 'Zippo' lighter sleeve made it stand out but then Island advertised *Catch A Fire* in all three leading British music weeklies, which was a first for any reggae release. It signified something new and different for Jamaican music, and couldn't have been timed better since it arrived on the coat tails of *The Harder They Come*, the cult Jamaican movie that gave overseas audiences their first taste of Rastafarians and life in Kingston's shantytowns. It was a taste that will quickly lead to hunger, and enshrine the Wailers as the ultimate roots reggae trio.

That first tour will be fraught with tensions. Peter and Bunny were suspicious of Chris Blackwell, and Bunny almost didn't make the plane after some mishap with his drums. The Wailers party felt the cold immediately they arrived, and wrapped themselves in winter clothes for their photo shoot with Esther on the Thames Embankment. Peter looks the friendliest but it should have been Bob, who'd left the band's cramped accommodation and was comfortably installed in Esther's Chelsea apartment.

In those days bands travelled huddled in the back of Ford Transit vans, not luxury tour buses. The Wailers had no roadies, which meant they had to hump their own gear in and out of venues. Did I also mention the food was bad, and the reception at guesthouses often hostile? Bunny did, frequently. Peter was a lot less vocal, but still didn't enjoy being on the road. After a short stint in northern England the Wailers returned to the Bouncing Ball in South London. Soon after they arrived, Peter put his feet up on the table and refused to move them. The club owner wasn't best pleased, and Peter's surly defiance would continue to be a source of embarrassment all evening.

"He and Bob were very different people and how they worked together I'll never know," says Don Williams. "I saw them out on the road together a little bit and there really wasn't a lot of personal interplay between them. They were very different personalities. Peter was much more of a tough guy. I never saw Bob get aggressive, but Peter could be very aggressive. Family Man was a gentle soul, as was Bunny but Peter didn't have that – he had a much harder edge to him."

On May 1 they recorded two sessions for the BBC. The first was a radio special hosted by John Peel – the hippies' radio DJ of choice, who paid a price for his support for reggae music. "Those audiences who clutched him to their collective bosom in the late sixties and early seventies often reacted with depressing hostility and snobbishness whenever he played something other than rock," said Peel's widow, Sheila Ravenscroft. "His inclusion of

Jamaican music so exercised racist elements that he received the occasional death threat. He kept one postmarked Walsall. The correspondent, clearly a newcomer to hate mail, began 'Dear John' before getting down to some serious threatening. There was also the time when a box of turds arrived for John in the morning post from another listener outraged that his ears had been besmirched by black music."

That same day they filmed their *Old Grey Whistle Test* appearance. It'll be the Wailers' first time on British television, and seriously challenge most viewers' perception of reggae music. The vision of them singing 'Stir It Up' and 'Concrete Jungle' is now forever etched on Britain's musical DNA but if the band were at all nervous about making their overseas television debut, no-one was showing it. Bob's soulful lead will steal the show, but Peter looks super-cool in his shades and Rasta bobble hat. His presence adds a touch of rock'n'roll menace to the Wailers' line-up, whilst Bunny exudes spiritual intensity.

It'll be three weeks before they can return to sunnier climes. The next round of gigs will be at universities, playing to mainly white audiences. Island's promotion campaign was bearing fruit, but it'll be their four consecutive nights at London's Speakeasy that makes even rock royalty sit up and take notice. That John Peel *Top Gear* session was broadcast on May 15, which is when they opened at the Speakeasy. Located in the West End and a favourite hang-out of rock stars, promoters and influential media folk, not to mention pretty girls hopeful of an introduction to same, the Speakeasy was packed for the Wailers, their reputation having preceded them and drawn a curious crowd. It was unusual, if not unique, for the Speakeasy to have booked the same act four nights running and this, coupled with Island's knack of picking winners, added to the anticipation. Mick and Bianca Jagger, who'd hired a reggae band to play at their wedding, attended one night. Other celebrity guests included Eric Clapton, Jeff Beck and members of the Who, yet the shows were nearly cancelled after Bunny refused to play or re-enter the venue. On walking downstairs to the basement stage area, the group had been confronted by the sight of a life-size vampire, sat upright in a coffin. It was there to promote *The Rocky Horror Show*, but Bunny had immediately fled back up the steps and ranted about Rastafarian attitudes towards the dead. Eventually, he'll be reminded that the Wailers were "duppy conquerors" and their mission was far too important to be derailed so lightly. He'll be back, hunched over his conga drums, by show time as the Wailers open their set with 'Rastaman Chant'.

'Rastaman Chant' had been the last track they'd recorded before leaving Jamaica. Essentially, it's an invocation. The original melody goes way back in time, and was appropriated by Rastafarians for their religious chanting. The Wailers weren't to know, but it would be their last ever recording as a vocal trio. It's also the perfect synthesis of Rastafarian worship and reggae music, and achingly beautiful.

Opening with it served to prepare people's minds for what they were about to receive. It was a cleansing mechanism, akin to saying grace before eating. Peter will refer to it as "sacred" in a discussion with Fikisha Cumbo, and then aim a telling swipe at organised religion. "When you go to a church, the pastor says, 'We will now stand and sing hymn number such and such from page such and such,' and them stand and sing it to the devil, so why can't we sing something to the Almighty?" he asked her.

Perversely, 'Rastaman Chant' will close and not open their follow-up album for Island, *Burnin'*, 'Reincarnated Souls' having been shelved. The majority of tracks were finished, although some needed overdubs and so the Wailers booked time at Island's studio in Basing Street. It was there, during their residency at the Speakeasy, where the Wailers re-recorded the backing vocals on 'Reincarnated Souls' and completed 'I Shot The Sheriff', which Esther Anderson claims she co-wrote with Bob. Clive Chin believes her, "because Bob was the kind of guy who wanted to leave his imprint in everything".

Esther also co-wrote 'Get Up Stand Up', which the band recorded at Basing Street but didn't finish to their satisfaction. Peter will later invest it with an altogether different dynamic once Bob invites him to add an extra verse or two. He and Esther had now become good friends and would talk about music, art and politics for hours at a time, either at the Wailers' lodgings or her Chelsea flat. Both were searchers after truth, and determined to find answers. Esther lent Peter copies of Franz Fanon's *Wretched Of The Earth* and *Black Skin, Black Masks* – books he devoured avidly, and that fuelled many subsequent discussions about race.

"Peter was quite articulate for someone of his education and background," she confirms. "People could understand what he was talking about and that is why I gave him those Franz Fanon books. I was always having those kinds of conversations with Peter. When he came here on that first tour, we used to go upstairs and I'd sit on his bed and talk to him about all those things for ages and that was unusual, because he never allowed a woman to sit there normally. My friendship with Peter went way beyond what I had with Bob because there was nothing sexual between us, and that meant we could really talk. He was very hyperactive. He had a hundred million things to tell you and was coming out with things all the time. At that time I was always buying books for Bob on African literature or poetry and he used quite a few lines from them in his songs, like how the rain doesn't just fall on one man's house alone, but it was Peter who showed most interest in subjects like that really. I wanted to encourage every one of them but I didn't have that kind of relationship with Bunny – maybe because I didn't check him as any great musician. By then I'd got to know the Rolling Stones, the Beatles and the Who, as well as everyone signed to Island. Peter was skilled on the guitar so that was always going to draw me towards him, much more than someone who just tapped on some drums without really knowing how to play them. Because I didn't see Bunny as being a proper musician at all."

After shows in Fulham (at the Greyhound pub), Northampton and Leicester the band performed at the Paris Theatre in Central London on May 24. This show was recorded by the BBC and broadcast as part of the network's *In Concert* series. Producer Jeff Griffin told a reporter from *Distant Drums* that he went into the Wailers' dressing room just before show time and could barely see for great clouds of ganja smoke! Further engagements in Exmouth, Bristol and Hertfordshire followed before they played to a full house at Birmingham's Top Rank Suite. The tour will end a day later at the Coach House in Southampton, amidst growing acrimony.

Bunny had continued to complain throughout, especially since the incident at the Speakeasy. Family Man says his face had worn "a permanent screw", and Bunny's negative attitude also troubled Chris Blackwell, who'd sunk time and money into organising a series of US dates beginning in mid-July. During a meeting with the Wailers after the tour had finished, Blackwell told the band they'd be playing "freak clubs" in the US. He meant rock venues but Bunny immediately over-reacted and the meeting broke up in disarray. His refusal to compromise will effectively end his membership of the Wailers because as Bob will later point out to Jamaican broadcaster Dermot Hussey, if someone sings on the records but then refuses to promote them, "them nah defend nutten".

Chapter 11

Talkin' Blues

Shortly after their return, they asked Joe Higgs to fill in for Bunny. He'd tutored the group since the outset, written one of Peter's biggest hits ('Stepping Razor') and was now living at Island House – factors that made his appointment a formality. His harmony singing was faultless and he played conga drums reasonably well but Bunny's departure couldn't be papered over so easily.

The US tour was scheduled to last until late August. Peter had demanded that Yvonne accompany him and Bob agreed, just to keep the peace. Her presence will allow Peter to distance himself from the others, although the opening shows at Paul's Mall in Boston were congenial enough. Most days they'd work on new songs whilst smoking some strong Colombian herb a friend had brought them. In the mornings Peter would practise his martial arts in the car park, which must have startled a few unwary passers-by! A television series called *Kung Fu* starring David Carradine was very popular at the time, but it was Bruce Lee who Peter admired most. Against all odds, Lee had inspired an international kung fu craze and even attracted Hollywood backers for his breakthrough film, *Enter The Dragon*. Just three weeks previously, he'd collapsed in Hong Kong and been diagnosed with cerebral edema. Few suspected it at the time, but he'd be dead within days of the Wailers leaving Boston and heading for New York, where Max's Kansas City awaited them.

Lee Jaffe had convinced the owner to book the Wailers for four nights from July 19–22 inclusive. They'd be supporting Bruce Springsteen, Columbia

Records' current poster boy, who was already being touted as the next Bob Dylan. The headline act couldn't be better, and the venue – on Park Avenue South, off Union Square – was perfect. The Velvet Underground's Doug Yule once said that "walking into Max's the first time was like walking into the bar scene in *Star Wars*; a slow pan across alien beings engaged in unfathomable activity." During the late sixties, Warhol and his entourage would hold court in the backroom from midnight. The waitresses called it "Siberia" since the inmates were always so stoned, they'd never tip. In 1973 it was a different crowd, but old habits died hard. Max's wasn't just a rock venue. Waylon Jennings and Willie Nelson both performed there that year, but no one had seen or heard anything like the Wailers before. Every night they'd play three half-hour sets, then pile into taxicabs back to the Chelsea Hotel on West 23rd Street. Most of the rooms there had kitchens, which meant the band could cook their own food. Peter and Yvonne often ate alone, and sometimes stayed behind to watch Springsteen before rejoining the others. Peter liked the honesty in Springsteen's songs, and also the soul in his voice when he sang about life back in New Jersey.

In late July he and Bob headed for A&R Recording studios on Horatio Street and put the finishing touches to 'Get Up Stand Up'. Peter had written another couple of verses, and they'll transform the song into a tour-de-force. On the first attempt he sang "We're sick and tired of this bullshit game, dying and going to heaven in Jesus' name. We know and we understand that Jah is a living man." Bob told him he mustn't say "bullshit" and so Peter changed it to "ism and schisms" instead. It's a term that derives from the Rastafarians' mistrust of all forms of authority. Isms, being exclusive, are naturally divisive and therefore lead to schisms. This is why many Rastas consider it an insult to refer to their way of life as "Rastafarianism". "Bullshit game" wasn't so eloquent, but got the message across just as well. Like John Lennon, Peter wasn't afraid of being confrontational and if he snorted with derision at being censored, well Bob deserved it.

"When I heard the lyrics they'd added to 'Get Up Stand Up' that last verse about 'die and go to heaven in Jesus' name', that is definitely Peter's voice," says Esther Anderson. "Bob certainly didn't come up with those lines when I was with him. Peter had been through experiences to make him think like that and he used to talk like that anyway. He totally saw through the whole thing where religion was concerned because I remember him mentioning that line from the church, how the Lord would wash people 'whiter than snow'. He used to say, 'How can I be washed whiter than snow when I'm a black man? That means I'm never going to be clean or good.' He realised it was just lies.

"All of us were coming out of colonial Jamaica and just as we began to realise that something was amiss, Black Power came to the island and Dr. Martin Luther King and the whole Civil Rights movement happened... At last, we had some people we could look up to. We started listening to Angela Davis and the Black Panthers, and certain Jamaicans began waking up. It stands to reason that disenfranchised people like the Rastafarians would look to any kind of liberated voices and things quickly grew from there. At the same time the hippy movement came about; people were smoking dope and saying to hell with the "shit-stem", as Peter called it but then Miami is so close and so we were fed everything from America – not just music, but everything else that was going on as well. Bob used to say, 'Watch those colonial black people, because they're the ones who'll keep you down' and he was talking about those in England, as well as Jamaica. He knew that just because England wasn't in charge any more, it didn't necessarily change people's thoughts. The main thing that united Caribbean people was the Rastafarian movement but instead of preaching peace and love, it had this reactionary spirit behind it. It preached liberation, and it urged people to speak up for themselves."

The Wailers had been booked to play 17 dates with Sly & The Family Stone, but were sacked from the tour after just four. They hadn't gone down well with the sophisticated black audiences that flocked to see psychedelic soul's reigning bad boy. Joe Higgs admitted that people hadn't been able to understand what they were singing about; didn't understand the music and weren't impressed with the Wailers' scruffy-looking presentation. Next thing they knew, the band members were out on the street with their luggage and watching Sly's tour bus disappear without them. That was in Las Vegas but they were soon whisked off to San Francisco, where a local promoter had agreed to book two shows at short notice. That's where Peter was reunited with an old acquaintance – former Peace Corps worker Chuck Krall, who'd become a freelance rock photographer.

"I was living in San Francisco at the time and had a call from Chris Blackwell saying the Wailers were coming to town and Island needed someone who could understand patois and help the band out," Chuck explains. "The first day they arrived I walked in the kitchen where they were staying and Yvonne had just handed me some melon when Peter appeared. I offered him a piece out of politeness and he just stood there and finished it in front of me. I thought he would take a bite and hand it back but no, he ate it all! It felt like some kind of test but I must have passed because Peter later invited me to his room and handed me a 45 called 'Can't Blame The Youth'. As I stood there looking at it he said, 'You don't remember me, do you?' Then I remembered that when I was in Jamaica with the Peace Corps I'd gone to a town called May Pen, to an event sponsored by the Jamaica Youth Organisation. Byron Lee & The Dragonaires played some music, and the Prime Minister gave a speech. Peter was there too, and he'd danced with Miss Jamaica. This was in 1968, and that was the year I also met Bob Marley and Joe Higgs for the first time. They were standing outside this jerk place in Kingston and we got talking. They wanted to know what my beard represented, and why I didn't eat pork...

"Peter didn't become a brother until later. I remember he was always wearing this floppy woollen hat. I'd make fun of him about that but Peter didn't take any nonsense. He was a pretty imposing guy and he was not the sort of person to let things pass, especially if someone used a racial slur. He was quite strict on that level. African–Americans often looked down on Jamaicans with scorn, even more than whites. It was as if the Jamaicans weren't as good as them. This was especially true in the late sixties and early seventies but Peter wasn't having any of it..."

Chuck says Yvonne was "the Angela Davis type", and well versed in Black Panther literature. She and Peter make a handsome couple, as Chuck's photographs verify. Those two shows will take place at the Matrix – a rock and student hangout on Broadway – on October 19 and 20. The opening night coincided with Peter's 29th birthday and attendances were good, but then local station KSAN-FM had been playing their music all summer. KSAN-FM invited them to record a radio session that same month, at the Record Plant in Sausalito. Their set list revolved around *Catch A Fire* as you'd expect, but with additional songs like 'Get Up Stand Up'. Peter makes a point of singing "bullshit games" when his turn comes. Island may call the shots in the studio, but he's not about to be tamed on stage.

The Wailers proved so popular with San Francisco audiences that they were invited back to the Matrix on October 29 and 30. In the interim period they travelled to Los Angeles and recorded a show in front of three movie cameras and about a dozen onlookers at the Capitol Records Tower in Hollywood. Shelter Records had recently launched a film production company called Shelter Vision, and had ambitions of entering the music video business. Filming took place on October 24 and when clips finally leaked out many years later, the first thing we saw was Peter sitting on the floor, and keeping time on a bass drum at least two feet across. Only he could transmit a feeling of reverence wearing sunglasses and a shapeless, yellow woollen hat with bits dangling from it. He sings lead on 'Can't Blame The Youth' and 'Stop That Train', and is magnificent. That Capitol Records Tower performance is among the highlights of their debut US tour, although they enjoyed playing to packed houses during those two remaining Matrix shows.

On their return home, Joe Higgs quit the band. The tensions within the Wailers had made him unhappy, and life on the road didn't suit. Bob and Peter intended to replace him, and hoped Bunny would rejoin. He didn't of course, not even after hearing the Wailers had "mashed down Sly Stone". The group will get two weeks' break before returning to England for another tour. Once back in Jamaica, Peter felt the need to re-launch his solo career and get some songs on the radio. With this in mind, he'll press up three further singles on Intel Diplo before the year's out. Pick of the bunch is 'What You Gonna Do' and Peter's musical roots, steeped in calypso, are all over it. It's a finely wrought story, written about the consequences of a police raid, and that's Robbie Shakespeare on bass.

'Burial' is a re-working of 'Funeral' with Bunny on backing vocals and percussion, whilst 'Foundation' is the same track that'll appear on *Burnin'*. Island had released the Wailers' follow-up album on their opening night at the Matrix, but Peter didn't see a copy until they got back to Jamaica. When he did, he was livid. Esther Anderson's photographs filled the inner sleeve, and he was absent from most of them. He took it badly; the paranoia that afflicts every herb smoker reared its head and Peter became convinced he was being sidelined. Bob's single-minded vision for the Wailers didn't seem to include him, or brook any argument. He didn't feel as if he had any say in the Wailers any more, and that Bob was in cahoots with Chris Blackwell. Peter still enjoyed playing with Family Man and Carly though. They had the one-drop sound he liked and after touring with them, he could appreciate their qualities even more.

The maiden name of the Barrett brothers' mother was Marshall, and singer Larry Marshall was their cousin. He'd started out way back in 1962 before settling at Studio One and cutting hits like 'Mean Girl' and 'Nanny Goat'. Just as the Wailers had done, Larry tired of Coxsone's penny-pinching ways and began producing his own records. 'I Admire You' had proved an instant success and he was now looking to record a follow-up. Peter accompanied Family Man and Carly to Randy's when they laid the rhythm to 'She Is My Woman' and joined in on guitar. The track's quite rudimentary but Peter's choppy chords knit the whole thing together and he'd been pleased to help out an old friend. Peter also lent a hand on a couple of other sessions before leaving for England. That's his melodica floating over a cut of John Holt's 'It May Sound Silly' for Spanish Town producer Harry Mudie. The orchestration made 'Well Bred' (the name Mudie gave it) Peter's most sophisticated record to date – not that there was ever any deliberate intention to play sessions again. They just happened as a result of him being in the studio with friends, or working on his own material.

In early November, the Wailers flew to London and played a benefit show for Ethiopian Famine Relief at the Sundown Theatre in Edmonton. MC Dennis Bovell introduced them as "Bob Marley and the Wailers" which must have angered Peter as they walked on stage. With no percussion or third harmony, it was a rockier performance than seen previously. Bob even looked like a rock star in his unruly Afro and satin jacket. Peter stays calm and assured throughout. He finds the groove and stays there, and doesn't mug to the crowd like Bob does. When he steps up to sing 'Stop That Train', his vocals are strong and distinct. If Peter lacked stage presence in the past, then he has plenty of it now. Watch him spit his lines on 'Get Up Stand Up' and you realise he means every word. Bob, who loses the thread momentarily, appears lightweight by comparison.

"At Edmonton we had a really good rig, and they had a terrible one, so we didn't try and talk to them," recalls Dennis Bovell, whose band headlined. "People were saying, 'Oh, Matumbi were fantastic,' so we laid low. We didn't go anywhere near them, because they'd been suffering from feedback and stuff. They didn't have a technical person who knew their requirements. They were using guys who were accustomed to rock bands, and all the levels on stage were wrong as well. They were coming over as being really loud and it wasn't about being that, it was about being mellow."

The next leg of their UK tour was due to start imminently, but the first five dates had to be cancelled after Peter fell ill with bronchitis. It was snowing when the Wailers finally got the *Burnin'* tour underway,

Legalise it, and I will advertise it…" PETER SIMON

The Wailers, Studio One publicity photo, 1964.
MICHAEL OCHS ARCHIVE

Bunny, Bob, Peter and Rita, Kingston, 1968. ASTLEY CHIN

JAD label rehearsal, Russell Heights, Kingston, 1968. ASTLEY CHIN

Peter in militant mood, recruiting soldiers for Jah army. LEE JAFFE

Playing a Rasta drum with the Wailers, 1973. CHUCK KRALL

The Wailers during their first US tour, San Francisco 1973. Peter and Yvonne are at the far right. CHUCK KRALL

Peter and girlfriend Yvonne Whittingham in San Francisco, 1973. CHUCK KRALL

Bob and Peter perform together for the last time at the Starlite Bowl in Burbank, California, July 1978. CHUCK KRALL

Peter with Freddie the parrot, 1975. FIKISHA CUMBO

Peter in a marijuana field during the *Legalise It* photo shoot, 1976.

Bob, Mick Jagger and Peter photographed backstage at the Palladium, New York, June 1978. MICHAEL PUTLAND/GETTY IMAGES

Mick Jagger and Peter rehearsing 'Don't Look Back', *Saturday Night Live*, New York, December 1978. PETER SIMON

Peter backstage at the Palladium in New York, during the Rolling Stones' *Some Girls* tour, June 1978.
MICHAEL PUTLAND/GETTY IMAGES

Peter with ganja pipe, in more innocent times. Note the early attempts at tour merchandise, circa 1976.

at Blackpool Locarno on November 22. The following night they played Leeds Polytechnic, to a rapturous reception. It's my favourite of the Wailers' live recordings with Peter, whose wah-wah playing is fiery throughout. In fact he's so feisty that he'll solo when he feels like it, even if it means halting Bob in his tracks (as on 'Slave Driver').

Dates in Liverpool and Doncaster followed before they drove back to London for another radio show hosted by John Peel. They played just a handful of numbers this time, including 'Can't Blame The Youth' and 'Get Up Stand Up'. The recording won't be broadcast until Christmas Day by which time the Wailers will be back in Jamaica, and the group in disarray. They'd been booked to play further London shows but the remaining dozen or so tour dates were cancelled. Island let slip to the music press that the Wailers hadn't liked the cold, but the dissatisfaction afflicting the camp was by no means confined to the weather.

"I went with them when they played some of those gigs," said Delroy Washington. "They weren't welcomed with open arms because I remember we were at one of those places – possibly Northampton – when this guy threw something at Peter from the balcony and Peter took after him like you wouldn't believe! One minute he's playing music, and then he's put his guitar down nice and neatly and gone off to find this guy and fight with him. I had to be telling him he couldn't be doing stuff like that. It's laughable on one level, but that was something that really happened. Peter would get upset with people behaving stupidly. You're not talking about heavy patience where Peter was concerned..."

Peter's main source of unhappiness wasn't the music or audiences, but Chris Blackwell. Bob had made poor business decisions in the past, and Peter just couldn't shake off the feeling that the Wailers were being exploited.

"A lot of entertainers and especially the Rastas were very suspicious of Blackwell," says one well-known reggae sideman. "It wasn't unique to Peter or Bunny; it was common among the entire reggae community, because even those who were involved with him had been quite skeptical beforehand. He was the white man who'd come to take everything they'd earned and that way of looking at someone is hard to turn around. People used to say, 'Watch the white man!' Even Bob, because he'd keep Chris Blackwell at a distance before getting to know him better."

Peter claimed that Blackwell told them it would take five years to establish the group, despite the fact that he and Bob had already acquired years of hard-won experience by then. They were ready for success, and had earned the right. If Blackwell disagreed, that meant he was trying to fool them. Also, the band had faced hardships on the road, which Peter considered unacceptable.

"We go a England and stay about two days before the tour start or maybe three," he told Carl Gayle. "When it start now we hear that we have to wake up early in the morning because we go a Birmingham, or some place about 800 miles away and we drive there in a van, and sit down on our batty for five, six, seven hours. Me no like that kind of treatment there and we nah get nuh food either. Before we even get to look about some drink or a little water we hear there's no time and then we reach the scene late, due to traffic jam. We're supposed to rest up, tune up our instruments, eat some food and them things there, but sometimes we have to go onstage in the clothes we've been wearing all day and this went on for days..."

After deriding the tour as "a whole pack of bullshit", he told Gayle he was paid just £100 in expenses, which seems a desperately poor return for so much effort.

"After waiting several months to get some funds we were confronted with a pile of papers so high, telling us that we owed Island Records £42,000 as tour expenses," wrote Sebastian Clarke in his book *Jah Music*. "And yet before we made the tour there was an agreement that Island Records would cover all the expenses. On a subsequent visit to Jamaica, Blackwell had talks with Tosh who became infuriated, left and returned with a machete to confront Blackwell who left immediately."

The sight of Peter waving a cutlass in his face was all Blackwell needed, and he'll steer well clear of him in future. As a Jamaican he knew just how volatile such situations could become, and wasn't prepared to take any unnecessary chances. Peter believed Bob had betrayed the Wailers by siding with Chris Blackwell, and it happened because Bob was half-white. The old saying was, "If you're white, you're alright. If you're brown stay around but if you're black, stay back." Well that's what it had come to. It felt like he and Bunny were too black for the group now they were at the threshold of success, despite having worked long and hard in building the Wailers' reputation. Bob had sold them out right at the point where they were supposed to stand firm, although Peter felt it was time to strike out on his own in any case. "I did not come on earth to be a background singer," he told *Behind The Music*, except now he'll have to prove it.

120

PART II
DON'T LOOK BACK

Chapter 12

There's One In Every Crowd

In January 1974, Rastafarians from all over Jamaica celebrated Ethiopian Christmas by attending a grounation in Clarendon. It was this nyahbinghi that inspired 'Distant Drums', a reverential, yet mournful instrumental produced by Family Man, who'd caught the vibes and called a session at Randy's. All three Wailers turned up that night. Peter and Bob played repeater drums and Bunny the funde as they invoked holy communication on the trio's very own 'Last Post', since they'd never record together again.

Peter and Bunny will remain regular visitors to Island House, at least for a while. Soon they'll be gathered round the radio, craning their necks to hear Muhammad Ali's return bout with Joe Frazier. Ali won the fight on points; the referee was accused of cheating but all of Jamaica knew that Frazier just wasn't the same after losing to George Foreman, in Kingston. The island had mysterious powers, as well as its share of troubles. On April Fool's Day, Michael Manley announced the opening of a "Gun Court", housed in a Kingston prison camp, and promised indefinite detention with hard labour for anyone caught with a firearm. Opposition MPs objected yet Manley's support hardly wavered, since most people hoped it would mean less tyranny on the streets.

Phrases like "Heavy Manners" and "Black Redemption" now appeared on walls in PNP areas, even as news broke that Marvin Gaye was coming to town. Promoter Stephen Hill booked the Wailers to play both shows – one at the Carib Theatre on May 28, and the other three days later at the National Arena. Like most Jamaicans he still viewed the Wailers as a trio, even whilst acknowledging Bob's higher profile. The latter was canny enough to release his latest single, 'Rebel Music (3 O'Clock Roadblock)', during the build-up to Gaye's arrival, and it was an immediate hit on both stations.

The first show was a fundraiser for a new Sports Complex in Trench Town. Marcia Griffiths opened the show accompanied by Rita and fellow singer Judy Mowatt – friends now better known as the I Threes. They'll switch to harmonies after the Wailers appear, and Bob leads the group into 'Burnin' And Lootin'' and 'Slave Driver'. The audience was fired by the Wailers' rebellious, Rastafarian rhetoric, yet this wasn't a reunion. Like Lee Jaffe, who plays harmonica on 'Rebel Music', Peter and Bunny were Bob's guests, even if Peter does upstage him on 'Get Up Stand Up'. Gaye came out swinging to a tumultuous welcome and especially at the National Arena, where he performed with an orchestra. This wasn't gutbucket soul but a sophisticated production showcasing songs from Gaye's bestselling *What's Going On*. Young girls screamed as he delivered his trademark love songs, whilst lines like "this ain't living, bills goin' sky high" resonated with those in the cheap seats. The Wailers couldn't match him and they knew it. Bob therefore took notice after being approached by Gaye's Jamaican-born aide Don Taylor, who offered his management services. His appointment will distance Bob from Peter and Bunny yet further. They didn't have a manager or record company, whereas Bob will sign a new contract with Island, keep the Barrett brothers onside and transform Island House into a launch pad for continued success. Family Man turned one of the back rooms into a makeshift studio so they could make demo recordings and then helped move the Wailers' record store onto the premises. In the meantime Bob toured the island with Esther, searching for somewhere they could build a love nest. Eventually they found the perfect spot in Little Bay, just up the coast from where Peter was born. He and the Barretts would visit them there from time to time and so too Lee Jaffe, who says that Bob and Peter treated him "like family".

"No one knew who they were at that time but I knew what was happening and there was no other place in the world I wanted to be at that time," he reflects. "I've carried those memories with me for the rest of my life. I was there for three years and I never had any money during the whole time I was down there. I lived with no money. I mean I was a communist anyway, and full of this revolutionary ardour. I was just happy being part of the revolution. I didn't even have any clothes. I used to wear all of Bob's clothes because we were both the same size. Rita would make sure they got cleaned, then after a while I grew these dreadlocks and had a beard...'"

Bob was now receiving royalties from Johnny Nash's covers of his songs but Peter was struggling to get by on very little, and couldn't afford studio time. The sessions he'd played on – chiefly for Ras Michael, on the *Nyahbinghi* album – had occurred because of friendship, and weren't paid assignments. The little money he did receive barely covered essentials. It was at this point that Lee Jaffe came to the rescue.

"Sitting on his porch in 1974, Peter handed me a corn trash spliff, lit it and played me his acoustic guitar, performing unrecorded songs that were to become Tosh's anthems, 'Legalise It' and 'Equal Rights'. It was an unforgettable experience," he told Roger Steffens. "I knew instantly that these were great songs – ones that people needed to hear. The question was, 'How could we make it happen?' We didn't have any money and so I asked Bob Marley if he could help. Soon after that we began recording rhythm tracks at Duke Reid's Treasure Isle studio. Duke was the kind of guy you didn't want to mess with. He was a larger than life character – six foot three, 350 pounds and carried a six shooter shoved into his waistband. There were even bullet holes in the ceiling from when Reid went haywire after he thought some of his artists were singing out of tune. To complete the scene, we took Peter's long-time friends Family Man and Carlton Barrett along with Al Anderson and Tyrone Downie, who'd all been working with Bob."

Tyrone Downie was another of Family Man's talented protégés, and a young keyboard player of some renown although Al Anderson wouldn't arrive in Jamaica for another few months. If Bob minded Peter borrowing his musicians, he showed no sign of it. In fact Lee Jaffe claims he was "extremely encouraging", and wouldn't have lent Peter the money otherwise.

The songs recorded during those first few sessions were a mix of old and new. Crucially, there was no sign of 'Legalise It' or 'Equal Rights'. Jaffe played harmonica on 'Whatcha Gonna Do', which is another of Peter's storytelling songs – one that's again drenched in mento influences. First we'd told about a man arrested on ganja charges, leaving his wife and children without means of support. We're then told about another woman whose son is arrested for illegal possession of a firearm, which as

125

we've already heard, means "indefinite detention". Manley's reforms may be well intended, but can the police be trusted? Peter's airing his views on Jamaica's unjust legal system, and writing the kind of songs that'll make him a hero to the poor. Bunny sings harmonies on 'Til Your Well Runs Dry' – a Southern style reggae / soul / blues hybrid he co-wrote with Peter about a man who's asked to put his grievances aside in order to save his relationship. Lee Jaffe plays harmonica on that one, whilst Bob co-wrote 'Why Must I Cry' – a romantic ballad and quite unlike any of Peter's compositions. It's hard to imagine the Stepping Razor singing a line like "I'll never fall in love again", yet he delivers it well enough. Despite their problems, there's an undeniable spirit of co-operation between the three Wailers. 'Burial' is a re-working of 'Funeral', which they'd written during their stay in the countryside, and Peter remakes it in his own, uncompromising image. Did he intend it as a comment on the end of the Wailers we ask ourselves? And are the lines "What a big disgrace. You rob everything you can find," aimed at Chris Blackwell? "I ain't got no time to waste on you. I'm a living man, I've got work to do," Peter announces, with barely veiled contempt. "You're taking people's business on your head. Might as well you be dead..."

Other sessions will yield a prototype 'Ketchy Shuby' (inspired by a children's game) and revised versions of 'No Sympathy' and 'Brand New Second-Hand'.

In time, Peter will overdub drums and guitar parts on certain of these tracks. Duke Reid will have died by then and his studio fallen into disuse. Street gangs were already terrorising the Bond Street area and saw no reason to spare singers and musicians the indignity of being robbed.

"When Duke was there, they didn't bother anyone too much even though it was always a dangerous neighbourhood," says Junior Dan. "You might have a problem getting to and from the studio, but you wouldn't be bothered inside there. That never started to happen until Duke fell ill and the place closed down soon after. They couldn't rent it out to anybody, and the area round there became a ghost town. Everyone stayed inside, just looking out..."

Lee Jaffe accompanied Bob and Family Man to San Francisco for sessions with Taj Mahal that summer. They visited Shelter Records in Los Angeles and then journeyed to the label's studio in Tulsa, Oklahoma, which is where Lee met with members of Leon Russell's band – most notably bass player

Carl Radle, who doubled as Eric Clapton's bandleader. Radle, drummer Jamie Oldaker and organist Dick Sims had travelled to Miami that April, and played on Clapton's *461 Ocean Boulevard*. This was the album that included the guitarist's cut of 'I Shot The Sheriff' – a song that'll be perched at number one on the US singles chart by November. Opinion is divided on how Clapton got to hear it. Some claim rhythm guitarist George Terry played him a cassette of *Burnin'* whilst others say it was Bee Gees' percussionist Joe Lala, who'd just returned from Jamaica on vacation. There's also a strong possibility that Shelter's Denny Cordell or Don Williams introduced it to Carl Radle – a man Jamie Oldaker says "always had cassettes with him, full of different types of music. Carl was fond of experimenting, and we'd never know what he was going to come out with next."

Lee Jaffe was the closest Peter had to a manager at the time. He initiated talks with Radle about him producing an album with Peter for RSO, who'd also signed Clapton. The idea appealed to the hard-drinking Okie, who would meet Peter soon enough. The success of 'I Shot The Sheriff' persuaded Clapton to record his next album in Jamaica, once producer Tom Dowd had suggested he "tap the source". He and his entourage arrived there during late August, just as news of Richard Nixon's resignation filled the airwaves. After resting in Ocho Rios for a week or so they relocated to the Terra Nova hotel in Kingston and prepared for sessions at Dynamic, where the Rolling Stones had recorded 18 months earlier.

"Eric Clapton came down and wanted Peter to play so they got in touch with me and I took Peter to the Terra Nova and introduced them," recalls Lee. "Eric had ran away with his best friend's wife, right? He brought her to Jamaica and they were so fucked up, him and Patti Harrison, they were rolling around on the floor. We thought, 'What the fuck? We can never sign with these guys. This is not going to happen.' It was horrible. He was rolling around on the floor with his best friend's wife and he couldn't even stand up to shake Peter's hand, so we thought, 'damn...'"

Patti was still married to Beatle George Harrison yet Clapton had won her fairly, after a fashion. He'd also kicked heroin, assembled a great band and discovered his singing voice, but in all honesty, he was still a mess. After quitting heroin he'd been left with a serious drink habit yet his playing remained unaffected, and was typically exquisite. At Eric's bequest, Don Williams finally brought he and Peter together, and Tosh will be in the studio with him every day after that.

"The thing is I'm not too sure if Peter knew who Eric was!" exclaims drummer Jamie Oldaker. "It was Peter who was pretty famous in Jamaica – far more so than this white guy playing guitar. I know that Eric's fame certainly wasn't an issue when we were down there.

"He was just into playing reggae back then. He was taking us into new territory as musicians but then Eric was always soaking up different influences. We had this open-minded approach to music, fuelled by a lot of alcohol and drugs except there was also a lot of creativity going on and we were all quite innocent in certain ways."

461 Ocean Boulevard – described by Anthony De Curtis as "Clapton's great comeback album" – will be number one on the US album charts by the year's end. It was a remarkable feat for an artist who'd been off the scene for some time, but recording the follow-up wouldn't be easy.

"Tom Dowd got us down there for *There's One In Every Crowd*, which was almost 50-50 reggae stuff and Marcel Levy songs," Clapton wrote in his autobiography. "When we got down there, people were just wandering in and out of the studio lighting up these massive, trumpet joints. After a while I didn't know who was in the studio and who wasn't, there was so much smoke in the room. And Peter was *weird*. He would be sitting in a chair asleep, like he was comatose and then someone would count it off and he'd wake up and play with that weird kind of wah wah reggae chop, then at the end of the take he'd just nod out again! He didn't seem to know what the tune was or it didn't matter but then we'd get him to sing. He sang the pilot vocal to 'Burial' and also to 'Whatcha Gonna Do' and I literally couldn't understand a word. It was hard enough when those guys talked because you'd have to ask, 'Could you say that again slowly please?' but when they sang, everything disappeared. I had to have it translated by someone and I still don't know if I sang the right words on that!"

Eric's delivery – especially on 'Whatcha Gonna Do' – borders on parody in places. Mick Jagger could often get away with this sort of thing when singing country or reggae but not Clapton, who sounds decidedly uncomfortable. His cut of 'Burial' isn't convincing either and nor 'Don't Blame Me' – a song co-written with George Terry in the style of 'I Shot The Sheriff', but that lacks Marley's dramatic sense. Peter also recorded demo versions of 'Can't Blame The Youth', 'Mark Of The Beast' and 'No Mercy' during these sessions, except there's no evidence to suggest that Clapton was interested in covering them. The guitarist will soon abandon his search for another hit reggae track and refocus his energies on more familiar blues and rock material, but at least Peter made an impression in other respects.

"I remember him telling me that Jamaica was a little island owned by white folks and he was right, because I could see a lot of rich white folks running around whilst the majority of black people looked poor as anything and couldn't even feed their families," says Oldaker, who'll tour with Clapton in the weeks ahead. Lee Jaffe had hoped that Peter might join them as the support act, but this never materialised. Carl Radle was still interested in producing him though, and promised to stay in touch.

A few weeks later and Island released Bob's first solo album, *Natty Dread*, credited to "Bob Marley And The Wailers". Peter and Bunny felt rightfully aggrieved by this since Bob had no right to the name "Wailers", which now referred to his backing musicians. Bunny was so upset he adopted the name "Bunny Wailer" in retaliation. As he entered his 30th year Peter reflected on how everything he'd worked for had been taken from him – the money he'd earned during the Wailers' stints with Coxsone and Lee Perry, and now the group's legacy. His mood was hardly improved by the news that two friends from Studio One were racking up chart hits over in England: Ken Boothe with 'Everything I Own' and 'Crying Over You', and John Holt with a smooth rendition of Kris Kristofferson's 'Help Me Make It Through The Night'. Even Trojan helped turn the knife in his back by repackaging *Soul Rebels* as *Rasta Revolution*. Peter felt like he was on the ropes, just like Muhammad Ali as he soaked up punishment from George Foreman during the 'Rumble In The Jungle' – a world heavyweight bout held in Kinshasa, Zaire during October. A month later and Clapton's cut of 'I Shot The Sheriff' would be sat atop the US singles charts. Endorsement by a major rock star meant a lot, but it was Bob and not Peter getting the accolades. This was irritating. Bob hadn't even met Clapton, whilst Peter had spent days in the studio with him and could yet end up on the same label! In the meantime others were outstripping him, and taking reggae music international. Even Stevie Wonder, whose 'Boogie On Reggae Woman' went top three in the US, two months before the Jackson 5 arrived on the island.

The Jacksons will play at the National Stadium on Saturday March 8, and the Wailers were again offered a support slot. All three will participate, although there was little doubt whose gig it was. The morning of the show, scores of Jamaican teenage girls gathered outside the Sheraton Hotel, eager for a glimpse of the Jacksons. When the brothers emerged, dressed for a basketball game against a team of Kingston's high school students in the National Arena, the girls all charged forward, causing the group to race back inside. Excitement over the Jacksons was at fever pitch and so to avoid crowd trouble, it was decided they and not the Wailers would open the show. Some 15,000 Jamaican teenagers charged with adrenalin leapt to their feet as the Jacksons ran on stage, and Michael led them on hits like 'I Want You Back' and 'Dancing Machine'. Each brother wore a different coloured outfit, with Michael resplendent in pink. Their fans screamed right through the performance, and only a fraction of them stayed to see the Wailers.

"The new line-up of Bob Marley and the Wailers was previewed at a Jackson Five concert in Kingston early that year," crowed *Distant Drums*. "The crowd were enthralled as Bob, centre stage, performed his mystical dance steps, living the music. To his side were the I Threes, adorned with red, gold and green gowns and head dresses."

The reality was slightly less rosy since proceedings had started an hour and a half late, and were then stopped twice because of crowd disturbances. The Wailers performed well, but the show was far from being a success. Peter was dressed as if for a martial arts contest, apart from the woolly Rasta hat perched on his head. Ever-present "darkers" concealed any hint of emotion, even after he'd stepped up to the mic and launched into 'Mark Of The Beast', which is as defiant an act of provocation as you could wish for. The Jamaican police hated how this Rasta youth from Trench Town was challenging their authority, and Peter was already a target to many in the force. The Jackson family arranged to visit Island House the following day. Lee Jaffe took photos of them relaxing with Bob, Bunny and Family Man, but Peter is conspicuous by his absence. Either he hadn't been invited, or he had better things to do than hang out with visiting superstars. Talking of which, the following month saw the release of Eric Clapton's new album *There's One In Every Crowd* and none of Peter's songs were on it, or his guitar licks. To his mind, this was yet another example of the humiliation he constantly had to endure. Apart from anything else, the revenue from having written songs on it would have proven handy, and it'll be scant consolation that the album receives a lukewarm welcome from critics, and sells poorly.

Peter's next brush with an overseas artist wasn't planned, and arrived sooner than expected. Martha Velez lived in Woodstock and sang backing vocals for Van Morrison. She was signed to Sire Records and had recorded in a blues-rock vein before becoming enamoured of reggae after listening to Johnny Nash. Martha expressed an interest in working with Bob to Sire's Seymour Stein, who'd arranged a meeting in New York back in April. Bob came away from it having agreed to produce her next album, although it will be Family Man who does most of the hard work. On her first trip to Kingston, Martha recorded two tracks with Bob and Lee Perry. She then returned a short while later for sessions at Harry J's, which is where she'll record original songs like 'Wild Bird', as well as versions of 'Get Up Stand Up' and 'Bend Down Low'. Peter's contributions don't exactly leap out at you but he's there's in the background, filling in on rhythm guitar.

Whilst she was unfamiliar with the Jamaican lifestyle, Martha told Marco Virgona that she viewed her time there as "a very enlightening experience".

"Previously, making albums had to do with getting musicians and going in and working," she pointed out. "But in Jamaica it meant that a group of people were not only making music but there was a complete philosophy that guided their lives. It meant more to them than anything. If what they were doing did not coincide with their religious beliefs then they would not deal with it. That was mind-boggling."

She talks about how "the pace, the logic and inner rhythms" were decided "by a higher spiritual belief", and admits to being overwhelmed by this at first. "It was a testing ground," she continued, "because I had to take time out to understand. There weren't any short cuts. We had to talk about what the songs would mean in light of the bigger picture. That's a wonderful conversation to have but to do it in a recording situation, I had to shift gears completely and cool out. It was an awakening for me."

This wasn't the only change. Martha's voice now betrayed the influence of Judy Mowatt, who was another regular visitor to Island House. A few days before her album sessions were due to start, Martha's party headed for a resort in Negril called Sea Grapes. Peter and Yvonne joined them there, and also stopped by Bob and Esther's place in Little Bay before returning to Spanish Town. Negril was a sleepy fishing village back then and had few amenities – not even a reliable electricity or telephone service, although by way of compensation, it did have seven miles of white sand beaches! Rick's Café had just opened, and the locals were used to seeing foreign hippies soaking up the laid-back atmosphere. American guitarist Eric Gale had been introduced to this idyllic beauty spot by Dickie Jobson and was so taken by it, he chose to call his next album *Negril*. He was living in Jamaica by this point, and knew exactly which musicians to call for the sessions. Peter and Family Man joined him at Harry J's, and came out all smiles after a good night's work.

Identifying *Negril* as "an instrumental album written, arranged and produced in Jamaica", UK publication *Black Music* described Gale's playing as "sensitive, subtle and graceful". His album's actually a delightful hybrid of reggae, nyahbinghi, soul and jazz, with just a touch of calypso added for good measure. Peter's most telling contribution is the scything wah wah that underpins Gale's lead guitar on 'I Shot The Sheriff'. Further traces of him are less distinct and yet according to Family Man, just sitting in on these sessions proved quite a learning experience.

As Gale himself acknowledged on tracks like 'Rasta', reggae music was changing, and it was Rasta philosophy that was driving it. Just over a year previously, Dr. Vernon Carrington, aka "Prophet Gad", had launched a new Rastafarian organisation called the Twelve Tribes of Israel that extended a welcome to Rastafarians of all races, even Jamaica's brown-skinned intellectuals. Not everyone welcomed such innovations however (including Peter), and the Twelve Tribes' emergence led Rastafarians of different houses to redefine their faith. Bunny responded in a musical way, by writing songs intended to outline Rastafarian principles and the movement's history. 'Rasta Man' and 'Armagideon' were among the first tracks to result from such soul-searching. Throughout the rest of that summer, he'll book time at Aquarius studios by Halfway Tree and record his first solo album, *Blackheart Man*, a term often used to frighten people. Rastas were still seen as criminals by sectors of Jamaican society and so Bunny wanted to turn such misconceptions around and present Rastafari in a more positive light, which is something he'll achieve in outstanding fashion. He too re-recorded tracks he'd sung with the Wailers – namely 'Reincarnated Souls', 'This Train' and 'The Oppressed Song'. Peter was at the studio with him most days, contributing guitar, melodica and keyboards as required. Tyrone Downie played organ, whilst Robbie Shakespeare joined them on bass after a stint in the Youth Professionals.

Bunny had signed to Island during a cagey rendezvous with Chris Blackwell at the Wyndham Hotel, and received a reputed US $45,000 advance, which he spent on a Jeep and 140 acres of farm land in St. Thomas. Suspicious as ever, he'd demanded to be paid in cash, and then carried the money around in a grip for weeks until finding the right plot. He and Jean Watt had been squatting on some government land in Bull Bay prior to this, not far from where Judy lived with Skill Cole and Rita had chosen to build a house for her and Bob. It was a tight scene but then when Bunny was about to record, Skill told him he'd have to pay for the other Wailers to sing on his tracks, including Judy and Rita. Not surprisingly, Bunny refused his offer and sang all the harmonies himself. He and Peter now felt more divorced than ever from Marley's circle, and were determined to make it on their own terms. Released in 1976, just as reggae broke big in the US, *Blackheart Man* will prove Bunny's pièce de résistance, whereas Peter's own debut album was still some way distant.

The tracks he'd recorded to date weren't bad, but they could hardly stand comparison with Bob and Bunny's recent efforts. It was make or break time for him and yet unlike the others, Peter had no record deal and was forced to borrow money for studio time. This caused resentment, and put him in a dangerous mood.

The words "radical" and "controversial" don't even begin to describe 'Legalise It', which he again recorded with help from the Barrett brothers. Peter's views on marijuana were well known, except he'd never aired them so openly before. "Legalise it, and I will advertise it," he promises, before explaining how it's not just musicians like himself who smoke it, but doctors, nurses, lawyers and even judges. First he exposes hypocrisy within Jamaica's legal system, and then shows up the medical profession by expounding herb's healing powers. This isn't the rambling of a red-eyed sufferer, but an articulate attack on policies he's vehemently opposed to. Yet the way he sings 'Legalise It' is curiously understated. It's the message that's in your face, not the performance, and which continues to resonate 40 years later.

Peter also recorded 'Igziabeher' that day, which is Amharic for "Let God be praised" (and the reason this track is also known as 'Let Jah Be Praised'). Deeply reverential, 'Igziabeher' is Tosh's contribution to the debate about Rastafari, and a worthy companion to tracks from Bunny's *Blackheart Man*. This is what a song of praise sounds like that's been shaped by life in a Kingston ghetto. Peter's intoning scripture over sepulchral chords, and that's Al Anderson wailing away on lead guitar. Bob had recruited him during a recent trip to London, whilst putting finishing touches to *Natty Dread*. Peter admired the young American's bluesy playing on 'No Woman No Cry', and had made him feel welcome after arriving in Jamaica. Al also overdubbed guitar on 'Brand New Second-Hand', 'Burial' and 'Why Must I Cry' at this same session, which again took place at Treasure Isle.

Lee and Peter now had an album's worth of material in the can, and yet some of the tracks still lacked polish. Resourceful as ever, Jaffe flew to Miami where he met up with an old college friend called Robbie Yuckman, who was a big-time smuggler. Lee played him a cassette of the unfinished recordings and asked if he'd fund some additional recording time. Robbie took one listen to 'Legalise It' and said they were trying to put him out of business! He liked what he heard though, invited them to stay at his house in Coconut Grove and booked studio time at Criteria, where Eric Clapton had recorded 'I Shot The Sheriff'.

"Criteria was like the hippest place to record in America," Lee told me. "That's when we met this hippy guy with hair way down below his waist called Albhy Galuten, who had one of the first synthesizers. He was a white guy right? He was in college but then dropped out because his goal was to play on these R&B records, so he went to Criteria in Miami and just hung out until he got established. He added synthesizer to 'Igziabeher' and 'Ketchy Shuby'."

Albhy had worked at Ardent Records in Memphis as a 17 year old, in 1965. That's where he met a lot of the musicians who would end up recording at Criteria like Duane Allman, whom he played with on Derek & The Dominoes' 'Layla'. Albhy had taken a study break at Berklee College in Boston before rejoining his old friends in Miami during 1971. Atlantic Records used to block book rooms at Criteria for their artists, sometimes for a whole year. There was always some big-name singer on the premises, and it wasn't unusual to see record executives such as Ahmet Ertegun and Jerry Wexler put their heads round the door, taking in a studio playback or voicing session. Atlantic had discovered that if you record a band in their hometown, they're likely to be distracted and spend more time going to parties or hanging out with their girlfriends than making hit records. Atlantic's solution was to take them to Miami, put them up in a nice hotel overlooking the beach and let them swim or sunbathe in the mornings before leaving for the studio, where a feeling of camaraderie prevailed. It was easy to pool ideas in such a relaxed

134

environment and there was plenty of interaction between Studios A and B, which is where Peter was based. When he got there he discovered that it was engineer Alex Sadkin who'd introduced Albhy to reggae music, and he in turn had played Eric Clapton the *Burnin'* album, with 'I Shot The Sheriff' on it. Mystery solved!

It was a mutual friend named Seth Schneider who then introduced Lee to Albhy, who'd found his niche and describes himself as the "go-to synthesizer player in Miami" during that period.

"Peter and I weren't exactly kindred spirits," he admits. "We didn't share the same background and I hadn't been to Jamaica by then. All we had in common was a love of Otis Redding and Southern soul. That's where the roots of the music come from but I didn't know too much about reggae, and Peter didn't really know what he wanted from me either. To be fair, I don't think anybody involved with reggae would have known what to do with a synthesizer at that time, although he may have suggested sound effects. There were two main kinds of synthesizer players back then – those who played an ARP 2600 like myself, and those who played a Mini-Moog. The Mini-Moog guys tended to be soloists, whereas I did a lot of work for people who couldn't afford to hire musicians, but wanted orchestration on their tracks.

"My memory is of Peter mostly sat at the back of the control room and watching, whilst occasionally smiling and grooving to the music. Basically, they just played me a bunch of tracks and said, 'take a pass at this'. It wasn't as if they had anything planned. Peter just said 'try something and see what happens' so I did and what you hear on the record, that's what happened after I began improvising."

'Ketchy Shuby' now rides a bubbling stew of reggae drum and bass whereas 'Igziabeher' recasts Peter as Moses on the mountaintop, invoking "lightning, earthquake, brimstone and fire" and with a soundtrack to match.

"To some people, having played on 'Legalise It' is my best credit," says Albhy, whose client list includes Kenny Rogers, Dolly Parton, Diana Ross and the Bee Gees (who sang on nine number one hits under his direction.) "Having produced *Saturday Night Fever* is nothing to them. I remember I was in St. Croix and met some local musicians who knew nothing of Eric Clapton or the Bee Gees but when I said I'd worked on 'Legalise It' they went wild! To these people, that was the absolute pinnacle of my career."

Chapter 13

Legalise It

By mid-1975, Joe Cocker's reputation was in the doldrums. A year earlier, the British-born singer had performed at the Roxy in Los Angeles and drunkenly stumbled through his set, causing Diana Ross to leave in floods of tears. Subsequent shows weren't all that well received and neither was his next album *Jamaica Say You Will*, which couldn't even scrape into the Top 40 on its release in April. Although crippled by alcoholism, Cocker was still an artist of immense talent and conviction, especially when singing his trademark, gospel-drenched blues and soul.

What persuaded him to leave his rented house in Paradise Cove, Malibu for Jamaica isn't clear. Maybe he had fond memories of the place, because he'd holidayed there five years earlier before embarking on the infamous 'Mad Dogs & Englishmen' tour. What's more likely is that his manager Reg Lock – who was an old friend of Denny Cordell's – heard reports about Eric Clapton's trip down there and thought a change of surroundings might revive Joe's spirits. The resulting album, produced by Joe's former soundman Rob Fraboni, will contain two Bob Dylan covers, one of them, 'The Man In Me', featuring Peter, Tyrone Downie and the Barrett brothers. Joe had arrived in Kingston with members of Stuff including Cornell Dupree, Richard Tee and drummer Steve Gadd, who grew fearful of leaving the hotel after someone accosted him on his first day in Kingston. Sessions took place at Dynamic, although 'The Man In Me' was recorded at Randy's. British band Matumbi had already recorded a reggae version but Cocker's take on it is delightful, and built around Peter's characteristic rhythmic chop.

"Cornell Dupree was there that night," recalls Clive Chin. "He watched Peter play rhythm guitar and was astonished by what he'd heard – so much so that he went up to Peter afterwards and shook his hand. He'd been stood there next to me saying, 'Damn, that guy's good!'"

"Joe was an alcoholic at the time," adds Lee Jaffe. "He was so nervous about meeting the Wailers that he started drinking in the morning although the session wasn't until seven o'clock that night and of course Peter and the other band members were late. By the time they arrived around 8.30, Joe had passed out so he never met them..."

Clive's account differs slightly, since he remembers Joe standing upright when the band arrived and whilst he can't be certain, he suspects Peter had a hand in what happened next. "We set up a mic for Joe Cocker to do a rough vocal and bwoy I tell you, the man was so charged that night, when I looked round to see why he wasn't singing he was stretched out on the floor. Someone had built him a spliff and knocked him out! He was out cold!"

A&M boss Jerry Moss didn't like the album, and Joe would later accuse him of deliberately failing to promote it. Called *Stingray*, it reached only number 70 in the US album charts and yet it's weathered the ravages of time remarkably well. 'The Man In Me' may have even been a surprise chart hit if A&M had released it as a single – Cocker having returned to voice it a day or two later. Peter now had few expectations where big-name rock artists were concerned yet the link with Shelter Records still represented his best hope of wider exposure, especially after he was invited to record in Tulsa, where Carl Radle awaited.

On May 20, the *Gleaner* announced "Peter Tosh to finish first album in US". He was reported as leaving for Oklahoma a day earlier "to put the finishing touches to his first album *Legalise It*, named after his current hit single." He's described as a "prolific protest writer who writes lyrics in the hope that they will eventually lead to the downfall of Africa's minority governments."

"My music fights against Ian Smith and my way of thinking is that you can't tell a man love when he is hungry," Peter said. "I am fighting for the freedom of Africa." He then describes one of the tracks on this album, 'Igziabeher,' as "being full of the sort of sound effects that will make man beware." Typically forthright, he calls Chris Blackwell a "pirate. Island

Records were the first to violate the contract we had. People think we have money but I don't even have a home."

He claims the Wailers didn't earn "a cent" off *Burnin'* and *Catch A Fire* but states his willingness to sign with another foreign company, providing they're not "pirates and downpressors who only want to help themselves". He then goes on to say that the Wailers "will sing as a group but we will not record as a group for Island Records. Not for Chris Blackwell, because Bob will find out one day that they are just using him."

"We had a deal on the table from RSO Records, which was owned by Robert Stigwood," explains Lee Jaffe. "They flew us out to Oklahoma and we recorded with Clapton's band. It was actually Carl Radle who organised it and from a business standpoint, it looked really attractive but when I got back to Jamaica and we listened to the recordings, they sounded really good but... I remember having long discussions with Peter and Yvonne about it and we decided that for Peter's first solo album, it needed to be Jamaican so that was the end of the deal and the Eric Clapton tour. It was a tough decision to make but I didn't want to be the one responsible for Peter making this record with a bunch of white guys from Tulsa. *Natty Dread* had just come out and that was the first Wailers album that had made any money. It had sold something like 100,000 copies in the US. It wasn't huge but it proved the Wailers had a healthy fanbase outside of Jamaica and I wanted Peter to reach that fanbase as well."

The trip was organised by Carl Radle's manager Ricky Hill, who greeted Peter and Jaffe on their arrival. Lee had accompanied Bob and Family Man there several months earlier, and was already familiar with the terrain – especially the Shelter studio, which was another converted church, just like Basing Street. That's where Peter will spend most of his time according to drummer Jamie Oldaker, who says Peter didn't go looking for company at all from what he can remember.

"Eric Clapton was signed to RSO and I think that was the whole idea, to get Peter connected with them as well," says Jamie. "The thing is, Peter spent more time sat in a chair smoking joints than he did playing music. The amount he smoked was unbelievable! He'd build these huge spliffs and sit there for hours getting absolutely hammered. We'd all be amazed, wondering what was going on. We'd be there ready to play and he'd be sat there staring at the floor. He was a decent musician though. I think Rick Durban was the other guitar player, and Walt Richman played on some tracks as well. We were just a bunch of kids really, and Peter was sat there trying to explain to us how reggae was played. We tried our best to please him and I'm not sure we did a great job at doing that but I do know he kept some of the stuff because I can hear it on the *Legalise It* record. The basic, underlying rhythm tracks on most of that album were definitely recorded by us in Tulsa but then all of a sudden and quite mysteriously, everything went sideways. Peter went back to Jamaica and the tapes disappeared, because I've no idea what happened to the masters. I suspect Peter and Lee Jaffe approached CBS with them but legally they had no right to put those tracks out since they hadn't paid for either the musicians or the recording. And they definitely used some of it because if you took some of those tracks apart, you'd find my drums and tambourine parts on there. Peter just overdubbed stuff on them when he got back, or at least that's what Carl told me. I don't exactly know what happened but I got the impression he didn't like working with a bunch of white guys."

"Them white guys there, them don't know reggae," Peter will later confess to Fikisha Cumbo. "Me tell them how to play, but them still don't play it black so me just have to wait 'til me come to Jamaica. Me take off what them play and put on black 'pon it..."

"We knew it was good, but it wasn't something we felt should be on Peter's first solo album," Lee will later tell Roger Steffens. "I decided to borrow a bit more money from a friend in Miami and we flew to Jamaica. Santa Davis and Robbie Shakespeare would replace the drums and bass, whilst American guitarist Donald Kinsey ended up playing lead guitar on several tracks. Kinsey became a permanent member of Tosh's band. It was only after six months and with the help of Gary Kurfirst that we got the album onto Columbia Records."

Lee Jaffe left to go on tour with Bob Marley in June, which slowed things down a little. New manager Don Taylor's influence was already being felt. Bob now travelled with his own road crew – including a Jamaican cook – and was really getting his act together, unlike Peter. One of his closest allies at this juncture was Tommy Cowan, a former singer with rocksteady group the Jamaicans who'd worked as a sales manager for Dynamic before forming Talent Corporation and opening an office-cum-distribution centre at 1c Oxford Road in Central Kingston. Up until now, Peter had placed the administration of his Intel Diplo label in the hands of a character called "Biggs". Although fond of gambling, Biggs had a decent job and so Peter had trusted him until discovering that funds had gone astray. In retaliation, he "repossessed" Biggs' car – a bright yellow, custom-made Volkswagen with a Lincoln Continental back and Mercedes Benz front – for a while, before investing in a VW "Bug" of his own.

Vivien Goldman describes Talent Corporation as a place "where musical legends regularly dropped by for juices and banana bread under the straw-shaded outdoor tables". Tommy managed Inner Circle, and had his own label called Top Ranking. He'd launched Talent Corporation only recently, and christened his new venture with an album called *Rass Claat Dub*. Peter heartily approved, and became a regular visitor from when it first opened. He'd been friends with Inner Circle's Lewis brothers for several years already and still played the occasional session with them, most notably on Jacob Miller's 'Forward Jah Jah Children'. Cowan will produce Israel Vibration's first two albums and also played an important role in Ras Michael's career. Peter played guitar on Ras Michael's first three albums and also his best-known song, 'None A Jah Jah Children', which bears more than a passing resemblance to 'No Woman No Cry'. No matter, and Peter had the utmost respect for Ras Michael's nyahbinghi drumming and chanting. He admired its purity, and loved how the sound of Rastafari had begun to redefine reggae music in ways few could have imagined only a short time previously. Yet for Peter this wasn't enough, and he wanted to seize the time and drive his message home more forcefully. Knowing it would be a bestseller, Tommy Cowan agreed to distribute 'Legalise It' on 7", but the scale of the controversy even took him by surprise.

"Now that was a very bold move," observes Nambo Robinson, "because the Jamaican authorities didn't like ganja and they were very disturbed by what Peter was saying on that record. Except people didn't need encouragement. What they needed was to see it decriminalised! They were making criminals out of users, and that was the point. I mean Jamaican youths didn't need anyone telling them to smoke ganja. We all did, and that was our choice."

"Peter wanted to make a statement," adds Lee Jaffe. "He was a revolutionary. He was determined to change the social structure left over from colonial rule and for him, herb was key to a spiritual and political awakening."

Whilst the two never met, Peter shared common ground with John Sinclair, former leader of the White Panther Party who'd recently been freed from a US jail after initially being sentenced to 10 years' imprisonment for giving two spliffs to an undercover agent. John Lennon and the Black Panther Bobby Seale had been among his most vocal supporters.

"Marijuana puts you in a whole different state of being," he's quoted as saying in *Guitar Army*. "The effect it has is as a radicalising agent, simply because it's illegal to get high in this society. Its effect on people's consciousness is to make us really aware of the artificial barriers that have been erected inside our heads to keep us apart, so the power structure can keep us in line. Weed helps put people back in touch with their senses. It helps people to feel more, and in a social order that's successfully dehumanised and desensitised people that's really a subversive function. Industrial society demands a very serious attitude from the people who are caught up in it. It demands subservience to the "owners" and the machine itself – it demands allegiance to the concept of efficiency and control, and it severely limits the possibilities for life and consciousness among its people. Instead of deadening people's consciousness, marijuana helps bring people back to life and expands their awareness of the world."

Sinclair goes on to describe marijuana as "a revolutionary force", and says that smoking it became a political act from the moment it was made illegal. Those who fight against such decisions become "enemies of the state" and if Peter isn't considered one of those already, he soon will be.

"Peter was the element of extremism in terms of what one really stands for," Joe Higgs once remarked. "He was like the oak tree; he's firm but then again the extremism of his being vulnerable to the wind. You kill an Indian but you respect his determination. A lot of us are there for a purpose and Peter had his. I didn't always agree with him, but I respect his opinion."

On July 25, 1975, Tommy Cowan took out a small box ad in the *Daily Gleaner* informing readers that Peter Tosh's new single, 'Legalise It', "was available at all leading record shops in Jamaica". Nothing unusual there you might say, except both radio stations banned the song and tried to suppress it. Peter's reaction was swift, bold and decisive. He'd fling the ban right back in their faces and if his message offended them, then he'd shout it longer and louder than ever.

Two weeks later, on August 12, Cowan took out a much larger advertisement quoting the song's lyrics – in full. The *Gleaner* had preferred to take the money and sit on the fence, whilst hoping to sell a few more copies. It did, and with an ad that was unashamedly provocative. Three days later the *Gleaner* reported that, "'Legalise It,' the latest single by Wailers guitarist/vocalist Peter Tosh, has been taken off the air on the recommendation of the Jamaica Broadcasting Authority. This has led to a series of protests in recording circles by Peter, his distributor in the island, Tommy Cowan, and several of his fans, including fellow Wailer Bunny Livingston."

The article goes on to say that, "The first time the public heard the tune, which calls for the legalisation of ganja, was on the ill-fated Jackson Five show several months ago, when Peter introduced the tune as his latest composition." 'Legalise It' was described as having done well "on radio and in discotheques until the ban was introduced a couple of weeks ago."

Tommy Cowan made the point that "if a radio station with 25 years of experience sees fit to play the tune regularly, I don't see how a body of less experienced people sees fit to ban it from airplay." Peter was typically more direct. "It has to be some form of victimisation because the tune is not subversive. It is not fighting the government," he said, choosing to ignore the fact that Jamaican law prohibited marijuana's use. A spokesman for the Broadcasting Authority told the *Gleaner* they'd been "very concerned about that particular record. We had a meeting at Jamaica House, and later a meeting with the radio stations after receiving complaints from several persons. It is a criminal offence in Jamaica to smoke ganja yet the tune goes on to say that even the judges and the lawyers smoke it." He added that the Authority was an advisory body to the government and could only recommend that the tune be banned, but warned that breach of the law by the radio stations "would lead to prosecution".

A spokesman for RJR confirmed that the Authority had requested that airplay of 'Legalise It' be discontinued, and they were told that if the station continued to play the song it would be breaching the law. Peter later admitted to Fikisha Cumbo that he asked Michael Manley to intercede on his behalf in getting the ban lifted, and had promised him 60 copies of his forthcoming album in return. Only Peter Tosh could approach the Prime Minister with this kind of proposal and expect a positive outcome! Except Manley will eventually meet with leading Rastafarians and reggae artists, including Peter – not in a bid to secure money or influence, but to determine how his reforms were being received at grass-roots level. Jamaica's charismatic leader had initiated national literacy programmes, workers' co-operatives and land lease projects in a bid to close the gap between rich and poor. In his view, capitalism gave rise to race, colour and class oppression, and he was hell-bent on transforming Jamaica into a more egalitarian society. "Socialism is love," he'd declared, to general approval from Peter's circle of friends. That said, Edward Seaga was now leader of the JLP and Manley faced stiff opposition – especially after Seaga called for fresh elections on the basis that people backing the PNP in 1972 hadn't been told they'd be voting for the "alien ideology of socialism".

On a recent trip to Cuba, where he'd been awarded that country's highest honour, Manley had told Castro he would "walk to the mountain top" with him. Manley admired Castro, but not unreservedly. He admired how Castro had made strides in improving standards of literacy and health care, and wanted the same for Jamaica. Manley dreamt of implementing reforms in agriculture, education, science, health, tourism, housing, shipping and the training of security forces, and whilst most would flounder, this led to an influx of skilled Cuban workers. As far as America and the JLP were concerned, Jamaica was now playing host to revolutionaries, and the middle classes didn't like it one bit. Notorious for its right-wing views, the *Gleaner* started to stir up trouble, aided by a sharp deterioration in the economy caused by the price of oil quadrupling within just 12 months. Many of Manley's socialist programmes began to unravel due to lack of funding, and scores of business people left the island – hastened by Manley's declaration that, "we have five flights a day to Miami".

A few weeks later, news arrived that Emperor Haile Selassie had died of respiratory failure after a prostate operation on August 27, 1975. Many believed he'd been assassinated yet to Rastafarians, it was unthinkable that God could die. After all, if Selassie I was the Messiah, surely that meant he had everlasting life? Bob ended any confusion with the song 'Jah Live', recorded at Harry J's with Lee "Scratch" Perry. It's one of the most powerful and moving affirmations ever set to music. Within the next couple of weeks, he'll go into Joe Gibbs' studio and record 'War', adapted from a speech Selassie gave to the United Nations in 1963 and which began, "Until the philosophy which holds one race superior to another is finally and permanently discredited…"

"You remember the time they say HIM die? I was in Jamaica, and coming to America," Peter explained to Roger Steffens. "Bunny drove me to the airport. When I reach the airport I heard lots of excitement, all the heathens gather saying 'a God has died' and all kinds of little fucked up propaganda. Sometime I feel like thumping a guy in the mouth for telling me them fuckery there, seen? But when I check it, I see it's just his ignorancy and he's lost in fantasy. The spirit say to me, 'You must not travel today,' and so I just cancel my flight and went back home because I was aggrieved over the public mischief and the propaganda, seen? I didn't go nowhere for three days, then I rebooked my ticket and went to America. I came to New York, went to my hotel and relaxed. I was meditating, thinking of what was happening in Jamaica, down in the Valley of Jehosphat, and thinking something strange was going on."

Lee Jaffe had now fallen out with Bob and left the *Natty Dread* tour. Things had come to a head after they'd performed at an open-air concert in New York's Central Park. Lee was annoyed that he and Esther Anderson hadn't been listed among the credits on *Natty Dread*, despite both of them having contributed to several of the songs. It wasn't so much the money that had upset him, but the principle, because whatever happened to the spirit of one love? Rather than get drawn into legal battles Lee turned his attention towards Peter once more, and redoubled his attempts to find him a record deal.

"I had a couple of things happening. Atlantic Records had an A&R guy named Jerry Greenberg who wanted to sign us and there was another label interested as well called Bearsville, owned by Bob Dylan's manager, Albert Grossman. The studio they had was state-of-the-art. I went up there with Peter and there was all this Woodstock mystique about the place, which we liked..."

Woodstock is two hours north of New York, in the Catskill Mountains. It's overlooked by Overlook Mountain, because what better name for it? According to Barney Hoskyns, the view from there is "extraordinarily beautiful. Thick with maple and pine trees, surrounded by lakes and the huge Ashokan reservoir..." By the time Lee and Peter arrived there, it had been an artists' colony for over 70 years. It was a place, according to Sally Grossman, where "you got visions". There was something in the mountain air; a natural mystique perhaps, that had cast its spell over a fraternity of rock musicians headed by Bob Dylan, the Band, Van Morrison, Jimi Hendrix and Paul Butterfield. Dylan wrote most of the songs on *Another Side Of Bob Dylan* and *Bringing It All Back Home* in an upstairs room at the Café Expresso on Tinker Street, just yards from where Hendrix had rehearsed before headlining the Woodstock Festival. The area had a glorious past, but was still a haven for musicians. Just a few months before Peter got there, Muddy Waters was awarded the keys to the city after recording his Grammy-winning *Woodstock Album* at Bearsville. That's the kind of place it was. Woodstock's musical community knew where the roots came from, and wasn't at all shy about honouring them.

Back in Jamaica, "roots" meant artists like Johnny Clarke, Jacob Miller, Big Youth and the Mighty Diamonds, whose recent singles – and especially 'Right Time' – had taken the male vocal trio format to exciting new heights. Meanwhile, Bob's live cut of 'No Woman No Cry' – recorded during his last tour – went Top 30 in the UK. It was the first overseas chart success by any of the Wailers, and helped cultivate a feeling of optimism among Kingston's musical elite. Peter felt hopeful of the Bearsville deal, and 'Legalise It' had reaffirmed his status in Jamaica. The timing of another Wailers reunion – this time supporting Stevie Wonder at the National Stadium on October 4 – therefore couldn't have been better.

The day before rehearsals began, all thoughts were on the "Thrilla In Manila" – the third world heavyweight bout between Muhammad Ali and Joe Frazier, which was screened live at the National Arena. Thousands jammed in the venue that evening, craning up at the huge screen and watching for signs of tension between the two fighters. Prior to the fight Ali had accused Frazier of being "an Uncle Tom", and waved a toy gorilla in his face. His actions would cause divided opinion among the Wailers' entourage, and lead to some heated exchanges. Everyone in the camp loved Ali but most were willing Frazier on by the end, when the increasingly brutal fight was stopped in Ali's favour.

As on previous occasions, rehearsals took place at Island House, which Bob was negotiating to buy from Chris Blackwell. (It'll become known as "56 Hope Road" once the deal goes through.) Outside in the unlit yard, people stood around the parked cars, reasoning whilst smoking their spliffs or drinking a juice. Inside it was almost as dark, and the still night air thick with ganja smoke. Rehearsals generally lasted until midnight, when Peter and Bunny would take off in different directions – Bunny towards the east, and Peter heading west for the Spanish Town Road.

The Stevie Wonder concert was being advertised as "the Dream Show" although the National Stadium wasn't full, possibly due to high ticket prices. Harold Melvin and the Blue Notes didn't perform as advertised and there were long delays in setting up the equipment, which the crowd acknowledged with spells of slow handclapping. The security was such that the Wailers could only reach the stage by making their way through the audience. Bob and Peter clutched their guitars, and were flanked by a large group of Rastas who then surged into the VIP section situated near the front of the stage, paying no heed to the police barricades. Resentment towards the Wailers deepened as a result of incidents like this and yet Peter – dressed for the occasion in a white martial arts suit – seemed to revel in such confrontations. During the opening 'Rastaman Chant' he had an unlit spliff in his hand, but didn't light it. After a medley of early Wailers hits, Bunny then took the mic for 'Battering Down Sentence'. This is when the show started to get serious, and Peter's outlaw persona was allowed free reign. After 'Mark Of The Beast' and 'Can't Blame The Youth' he launched into 'Legalise It', a song he introduced with the words "Well this is the tune that an unauthorised authority banned from the radio station, but I know they can't ban it right here." Cheers rang out around the auditorium, and also when he sang the line, "Judges smoke it. Even the lawyer too." By then, he'd lit his spliff and was waving it in the air so everyone could see it, just feet away from where police officers were standing. Such defiance even took Bob and Bunny aback, since the latter says that Peter had never burned a spliff on stage with the Wailers before. "Sometimes he'd get even we nervous because of his attitude of dealing with herb as if it was cigarette, like tobacco," Bunny reflects. "He said the freedom he should have, is like the freedom a man should have to smoke a cigarette that would kill him later on, or the priest that burns his frankincense and myrrh…"

That was the moment where Peter's solo career as a performer really took off, and it was at the very point where he, Bob and Bunny played their last show together, although none of them realised this at the time. Three days later, on October 7, Peter undertook a number of interviews at Talent Corporation. The first was with *High Times* magazine, but his most revealing remarks were reserved for New York journalist Fikisha Cumbo. After telling her that he prefers message music – "I don't like, 'I love you darling' and all this love you 'til the star blue or 'til I climb the highest mountain and all them bumbaclaat and all that crap" – he elaborated on his feelings about the Dream Concert.

"Although you see me out there singing, I was only singing because it was my duty," he began. "I wasn't singing with the right feeling because

I was getting a fight. That's why you see me singing in my gi (martial arts outfit) and num chucks. There was spiritual irritation and musical irritation... The way it spiritually affect you, it's almost physical. If more people were there it would have been nicer but I wasn't singing with the right spirit, so it seems as if I wasn't paying too much attention to the reaction of the crowd."

When asked about his affiliations with record companies, Peter replied that several companies were interested including Atlantic, EMI and Buddha, and that the *Legalise It* album was already finished. He's scathing about the record industry in Jamaica and claims that 90 percent of the musicians in Jamaica have no practical or theoretical training, but rely on pure inspiration. "They are just inspired musically; go to bed and get inspiration and get a rhythm and say 'I have an idea.' Most people who play right now, some of them just come to the studio and hang around and learn how to play a piano or an organ and become professional. I see that many times, because many of them pass through my hands."

He then claims his music is a gift from the Creator, and that he doesn't believe in anything – he *knows*. "I am successful where inspiration is concerned. I get that daily and from Him I'm getting inspiration, that is all the success I need," he told Fikisha. "I've never been financially successful. I don't know when I will be and I don't care neither, so long as I can find somewhere to lay my head, food to eat and my family is taken care of – not to barely survive, but to live." He then admits to having "a whole nation of children, about 50".

Shortly afterwards, he'll inform *Black Music*'s Carl Gayle that he lives in "a rented apartment" and "driving a battered Volkswagen". After denying rumours that the Wailers broke up because he and Bunny didn't want to tour, he says after two years they still haven't been properly compensated by Island and that only "just the other day" did they receive "a likkle monkey bread, some likkle fuck up kind of sum". Peter's reputed to have been paid $6,000 in royalties around this time, and therefore had enough to pay back Bob the money he owed him. Bob instructed him to give it to the Twelve Tribes but Peter refused, calling them "the Twelve Bribes". He also tried to make off with an amplifier from the rehearsal room at 56 Hope Road but was stopped from doing so by Bob, who said it "belonged to the Wailers". Consumed by anger and shame, Peter stormed from the premises, vowing never to return.

"From a spiritual point of view, I don't like it," he told Fikisha, speaking of the scene at 56 Hope Road. "I have facts why I don't like it, and I don't think I'll be going back there neither. Me not getting with Bob again, and me not singing with him no more. It's a whole heap of t'ings that aren't right before man and the Almighty and I can't deal with it."

Peter compared his struggle with that of rebel forces in Rhodesia and Angola. Black people in those places are "fighting for the freedom of black people so if it don't come about by free will, it have to come by force will because for 400 years we have been working for bucky master. That's what you call a slave driver in Jamaica."

This wasn't the pronouncement of a peace-loving Rastaman, like the ones Bunny portrayed in his new songs, but that of a revolutionary – someone who believes in getting their freedom "by any means necessary", to quote Malcolm X. On Tuesday November 11, the MPLA seized control in Angola. It should have been an occasion for celebration but that night Peter and Yvonne were involved in a near fatal accident at Six Miles on the Spanish Town Road. Peter had arranged to go in the studio with Bunny and was taking Yvonne home before returning to Kingston. Some reports suggest she then decided to go somewhere else and so Peter did a U-turn, forgetting or failing to notice they were on a one-way street. A car coming the other way then struck them almost instanteously, badly damaging the passenger side where Yvonne was seated. Peter's soul mate will spend the next few months in a coma, then die without ever regaining consciousness.

"A guy came down a one-way at zoom speed, and I was driving about 25 miles an hour," Peter will later inform a Washington radio DJ. "I saw death and destruction coming down the way and said, 'Wait. It's death that,' swerved to the left and death swerved to the left too. I swerved back to the right, and death did the same thing too, but because of my spiritual preparation to expect the unexpected, all I did was just watch what was going to happen. I was in a state of spiritual awareness, seen? Well, the guy crashed into her side. I was driving this Volkswagen but all those things are still spiritually motivated 'cause you have evil spiritual motivation, and righteous spiritual motivation, seen?"

He'll be left disfigured and scarred in the aftermath, both physically and mentally. He also broke several ribs, some of which had already been broken in skirmishes with the police. Bunny and Bob went to look for him at the hospital and encountered a young policeman they'd seen play in goal for a local football team. Unfortunately, he wasn't at all helpful. Bunny thinks this is because policemen were taught to discriminate against Rastas and scorn songs like 'Natty Dread', which celebrated Rasta culture. The Kingston force reportedly used mops for target practice at that time, and certainly felt no sympathy for Peter Tosh. The young police officer started to curse Bob, who said something back to him. Next thing they knew, Bob was arrested whilst being called "a dirty little Rasta boy" and dragged off to the station amidst taunts of "Just because your name is Bob Marley..." Bunny then invoked Rastafari, which brought more police in their direction. He was knelt in the street at this point, calling upon Jah and getting frightened stares from the churchgoers spilling out of a nearby church, since it was a Sunday morning. After he finally got to see Peter, he got dressed and they left together. Peter was in considerable pain, but managed to get to the entrance just as Bob drew up outside. He'd been set free soon after arriving at the station, where one or two policemen had recognised him and told their over-zealous colleagues to leave him alone.

Peter was devastated by what had happened. Guilt over Yvonne's death weighed heavily upon his heart, and he missed her more than he ever thought possible. Friends are unanimous in calling Yvonne (whose name was sometimes spelt "Evonne", after Australian tennis player Evonne Goolagong) "the love of his life", and claim they were clearly devoted to one another.

"Yvonne had a real raspy voice," says Al Anderson. "She was one of these women men love to talk to because she was more just some little girl. She had straight hair, light skin and green eyes... She was really pretty and Peter loved her to the bone! Whenever I went to Peter's yard, he'd give me a fistful of the best herb so I'd sit there now, getting red, and Yvonne would bring me some Irish moss to drink, and some rahted rice and peas and fish. At this time, Peter wasn't touring. He and Bunny weren't so close, and he and Bob didn't move with each other. It was just Peter and Yvonne. The next thing I know, Peter is showing me how his car had got mashed up. He's saying, 'Man, I crash the vehicle and Yvonne is dead.' He was crying his eyes out man, because she was the nicest girl for him. He was always holding her hand, and they'd be kissing and hugging, can you imagine? Those two really loved one another. At first, Yvonne's parents weren't too happy about her being with the crazy Peter Tosh, but they got to love him because he became such a central part of her life..."

Lee Jaffe describes Yvonne as being "super intelligent, and super knowledgeable about music... She'd be reading all the time. She was a real intellectual. Peter really looked to her for advice about which songs to record – all through the *Legalise It* album and up to the day she died. That was a real turning point for Peter, and he was a different person after that.

"In a sense, he was guilty of homicide because he was a reckless driver, all the time. He drove way out of control, and way too fast. Peter killed her and he blamed himself for her death. She was in a coma for six months before she died and every day I'd drive him to the hospital. He got stitched up right after the accident but his jaw was broken and he wouldn't get it fixed. His face was crooked after that, and he was left badly scarred but never seemed to care. He'd want to go to this place in St. Thomas called Bath, where they had these hot mineral springs so I took him there often, and that's the only thing he'd want to do. That accident was a terrible tragedy for him. I know for sure it affected Peter's relationships with people, because he had such great opportunities after that and completely blew it. Peter was not the same person after she died. That was a really tough time for him. He became increasingly more bitter and paranoid. And increasingly more difficult."

Ras Karbi was a close friend of Peter's and continued to visit him at his home near Spanish Town. He confirms there were changes in his demeanour, and hints that Peter was beginning to feel cursed.

"I'd go there often because I was living nearby," he says. "One day I went there and was told this dread had visited the day before, and been smoking in the bathroom. There'd been a gas leak and there was an explosion that blew off the door, fatally injuring the dread and the mango tree outside died as well. That's when I realised there was something wrong around Peter and that he had bad karma. I really liked him a lot though. He'd be there writing songs and singing them into his tape machine but then his mum would visit and say, 'Peter. Why don't you cut off all that hair and come a church? You were brought up a Christian and now you've fallen under the spell of Rasta. God doesn't love that!' I was shocked to see that, but after the accident he became very quiet and withdrawn. He was very sullen."

Yvonne died in early February, when the life support machine was switched off. Remaining faithful to the lyrics of 'Burial', Peter didn't attend her funeral. He'll later admit to another journalist that an experience like that "can ruin people's minds" and drive them mad but you have to get over them, "otherwise you're going to be counting stars in the middle of the day".

"He was always moaning about his first love, the one who die in the car crash," says Haile Makkel, who would often go running with Peter. "That was the love of Peter's life and he never get over her because every time we talk, he'd mention her. His favourite car was that VW but then when it kill Yvonne, he call it 'the vampire wagon'. He'd say how these ghosts were always trying to get him, and that they'd been trying to get him since he was young. That's why he buy a Hillman Hunter because he become the Hunter now, and he's hunting vampires!"

Chapter 14

Word, Sound & Power

Everything inside of him felt smashed. His body and heart hurt worse than any pain he'd yet experienced. He'd been betrayed by friends, exploited by record companies and was now mourning the death of his soul mate. Some would curse their luck, but Peter believed supernatural entities were out to get him. Gripped by thoughts of spiritual warfare and feeling broken inside, he somehow wrested enough strength to reinvent himself. The Wailers' mission, forged in the searing heat of Trench Town's mean streets, would now intensify. Lee Jaffe remembers that, "Peter's anger became focussed on social and political issues. He took it upon himself to be the spokesman for all oppressed people."

In the weeks leading up to Yvonne's death, the JLP and CIA conspired to spread rumours that Manley's government was preparing for a Communist style takeover. Propaganda then escalated to systematic destabilisation when sections of Jones Town and Trench Town went up in flames and hundreds were left homeless, just as the IMF and World Bank held a conference in Kingston. As Beverly Manley later observed, "crime was being used to strike fear into the hearts of people in the hope that the government would seem out of control and thus lose its legitimacy."

The situation had arisen after the US asked Manley to withdraw support for Cuba's intervention in Angola. Manley refused, reiterating how Jamaica had been the first to break off relations with the apartheid regime and back the ANC. The US withdrew aid and investment in retaliation, but

Manley stood his ground. Thereafter, Jamaica will teeter on the brink of civil war as a result of America's refusal to have another Communist state on its doorstep. Gangs armed by the CIA were now roaming Kingston, prompting Manley to announce that anyone possessing a firearm would face life imprisonment. There was tension in the air and everyone felt it, no matter which side they were on. Peter watched for signs, just like many other Rastafarians. Judgment time approached, but then came news of Robbie Yuckman's murder.

"Robbie was murdered in Coconut Grove by this crazy guy that worked for him, and who organised this rip-off from a warehouse they had," explains Lee Jaffe. "I never liked this guy but what happened was, Robbie had this warehouse and only a few people knew about it. This guy organised for these people to come and rob the place whilst he was there. The idea was that he'd be tied up with the rest of them, so he wouldn't attract suspicion… Robbie used to work with the Cubans, who in turned worked with the Colombians. The Colombians would bring in maybe 20 or 30 thousand dollars' worth of herb in tankers or big fishing trawlers, and the Cubans would go and bring it ashore in these really fast boats. Robbie was one of the people they'd give it to, and he'd then distribute it on the mainland. This guy I'm talking about would drive the stuff to New York but after the rip-off, Robbie asked the people working for him to take lie detector tests and he got scared. One day Robbie opened his door to find this guy standing there with a gun that had a silencer attached. He shot Robbie and then when Robbie's girlfriend came downstairs to see what was going on he shot her as well, so it was a high profile case because she was an editor with the *Miami Herald*. Some time went by and the guy's girlfriend went to the police and turned state's evidence, got immunity, and testified against him. She'd broken up with him but got back in touch, told him she wanted to get back together and then set him up but before the trial began, she and the guy got back together and she acted like she was crazy on the witness stand, so the guy got off. There was a lot of talk among Robbie's friends about how they were going to kill him but the guy was in a car accident involving this brand-new Corvette he'd got from ripping off Robbie, and he was crippled…"

Lee had lost an old friend, and Peter his main financier. Fortunately there were other irons in the fire, and they did have an album almost finished.

"I had offers from both Atlantic and Bearsville but Peter was still signed to Island as part of the Wailers and needed a release," says Lee. "Chris

Blackwell wasn't returning my calls and this carried on for a few months. Finally, I got a call from Chris, told him what was happening and he said, 'Well, I really think Peter should be on a major record label and I have a guy I think could help.' That was Gary Kurfirst. I was in New York and we drove up to this little town north of New York on the Hudson River. It was a rainy, grey, foggy day and we drove up this driveway that was like half a mile long to this giant English style manor house overlooking the Hudson. We knock on the door and this guy comes out who was only a couple of years older than me, in his early twenties. I remember Chris saying to him, 'The music business is good, hey?' When he was 16 years old, Gary had rented this warehouse on Long Island that held maybe 3,000 people. He was getting all these major groups to play there, and he had this local band as the opening act, which was Mountain. They started getting a large following and after he got them signed Gary became this prodigy at Columbia, because everyone thought he was a child genius. He got us the deal with Columbia. I remember he got all these Columbia big wigs to travel down to Jamaica, and I booked them into the Stony Hill Hotel. It's a little run-down now but there was only one phone in the lobby, so all these guys were fighting over the phone the whole time. It was really funny."

Lester Bangs was in Jamaica at the same time, and documented his experiences in *Creem* magazine. "I have a revealing conversation with a New York music biz veteran who used to manage Mountain," he wrote. "Now he manages one of the top reggae acts in the world, one who records out in the USA and he is down here trying to sign Peter Tosh, one of Bob Marley's ex-Wailers and writer-singer of the currently big, banned Jamaican hit 'Legalise It'. My New York vet laughs and says, 'This is the only fucking place I know where the rooster crows while I'm eating lunch. It's the only place I've been where you can buy a 14-karat gold bracelet for 10 bucks off a guy in the hotel parking lot and when you look inside, "karat" is misspelled. I've been here a fucking week, waiting for one tape from Peter Tosh.'

'Why don't you just go get it from him?'

'He never got around to making a copy yet.'

'You mean he has it? Then why don't you borrow it from him and make a copy yourself?'

'Well you see, when you go to the studios, the engineers may or may not be there and if they are there, they may or may not get around to doing this or that..."

Bangs did get a glimpse of Peter, and describes how dressed in "a navy blue tracksuit and militant black beret, Peter Tosh would yell as he practised high flying karate kicks in the car park". He also mentions how Bunny would occasionally turn up in his new Range Rover, which he'd bought with the advance for 'Blackheart Man'. Lee Jaffe explains that the reason Chris Blackwell had been so helpful in getting Peter a deal is because he knew that if Peter was on a major label and getting similar levels of promotion as Marley, then it could only be good for the entire reggae genre. He also believed in his talent, despite Peter's behaviour towards him. The question remains why, since the Wailers' original two-album deal had now expired, Peter should need a release from Island. It could only be that Blackwell had agreed to sign Peter, but then one side changed their mind. According to Roger Steffens, Peter sent copies of the *Legalise It* album to Columbia, EMI and Island, but only Blackwell received it. Island even printed a label for *Legalise It* but never scheduled it for release. "The tape ended up in the garbage, where someone with a keen eye rescued it for posterity," wrote Steffens. Maybe Chris Blackwell decided that Peter was too troublesome, or the deal might prove complicated given the situation with Carl Radle. Peter will sign with Columbia in any case except any dispute with Shelter or RSO still had to be resolved beforehand.

"Just before he was to have his first album, *Legalise It*, released by Columbia Records some complications developed," says Herbie Miller, who'll become Peter's manager in due course. "Peter had been funded by an interest in Texas (actually Tulsa) to do the recording who later placed a claim on the master tapes. This frightened Columbia Records executives and threw the deal in jeopardy. Tosh meanwhile, had just lost his woman, Yvonne, in a car accident. I visited him at his home with papers informing us that the conflict had been settled and stating that the Texans had relinquished their claim.

"In the company of his late friend Barry Maurice, I found Peter lying under his dining room table in the darkness. He would not communicate with us so we waited around, since the matter was of utmost importance. When he finally emerged Peter explained that only his body was lying there, that he was in flight with Yvonne and that they were in Texas dealing with the pirates who were trying to derail his career, and who had agreed to back off. In effect, Tosh delivered to Barry and I the message that we arrived with, before we even disclosed why we were there."

If Columbia hadn't yet realised what kind of character they'd signed, they soon would. By the spring of 1976 Herbie had entered into partnership with Ozzie Brown, who managed Taj Mahal. He rang Fikisha Cumbo, asking if she could go and stand bail for Peter since their lawyer was out of town. Peter had flown into New York from Jamaica and been arrested for having a spliff so Fikisha went to the courthouse in Queen's and found him calmly awaiting his fate, dressed like a martial arts instructor and with a red, gold and green tam in his hand. Once freed and rested – the herb tasted especially sweet that day – he'll head for Columbia's studios on East 30th Street. This is where Miles Davis had recorded *Kind Of Blue*, and Bob Dylan voiced 'Like A Rolling Stone'. It had history and like most studios Peter used overseas, was a converted church. There was a spiritual energy there, and sessions went surprisingly well – especially after he and Lee Jaffe had flown in Jamaican engineer Karl Pitterson, who'd just mixed Bunny's *Blackheart Man* album.

"He had a sound that was so fresh, so new, I just had to get him to work with Peter," says Lee. "I knew that Karl was a genius, even at that early stage. He had a great ear and he was very opinionated. Sometimes I didn't agree with him but I always listened to what he suggested and reasoned with him. It wasn't like he was stubborn. He was easy to work with and I always valued his opinion because most of the time he was right."

Peter's vocals sound sharper and more prominent on many of the tracks. It's not that there was anything wrong with the original Jamaican mixes but the overall sound is brighter, and Columbia must have been delighted with the results – especially on tracks like 'Igziabeher' and 'No Sympathy'. In addition to his A&R duties, Gary Kurfirst also managed an all-black blues-rock trio called White Lightnin', which he'd signed to Island. Their lead guitarist was Donald Kinsey, son of blues singer Big Daddy Kinsey. After touring and recording with Albert King from the age of 18 Donald was steeped in the blues, although he'd become fascinated by reggae after hearing the Wailers' Island releases. He met Bob first, at an Island press launch in New York, the day after Marley had played the Beacon Theatre. This was during the first week of May.

"About a week later, Peter Tosh was also in New York working on his first solo album," says Donald Kinsey. "Lee Jaffe was representing him so he invited me over to his apartment to introduce me. Peter was cooking when I went in but I met him, sat down and listened to some of the tracks he'd been doing and man, he just instantly invited me down to the studio.

They were going in the studio about six or seven that night and that was the *Legalise It* album."

Within minutes of Donald plugging in his '57 Gibson Les Paul, Peter knew they'd made the right choice. Whilst his contributions to 'Brand New Second-hand' are comparatively restrained, Donald's playing on 'No Sympathy' and 'Till Your Well Runs Dry' has that blues feel Peter likes so much.

"Musically, I wasn't playing heavy, but more mellow kind of textures," he told a Dutch journalist. "I had to discipline myself. In reggae they do a lot of doubling on the bass-line and there are so many different methods they use for doing that but the skank... oh man! The skank is that chikka, chikka sound; the scratchy rhythm and Peter Tosh is the godfather of that. Give that guy a wah wah and put a pick in his hand and that's just gone! He was the ultimate."

Donald joined Bob's Wailers soon after this session. He'll play on Bob's *Rastaman Vibration* album and then tour with him but just before they left, Bob received word from Lee Jaffe, who'd returned to Kingston and been jailed for possession of marijuana. Bob bailed him out, and they put all grievances behind them. Lee was now free to finalise arrangements for *Legalise It*. Gary Kurfirst had signed Peter to a two-album deal with Columbia, but rights for the rest of the world were still undecided. These will eventually go to Virgin Records, owned by entrepreneur Richard Branson.

Mick Brown, writing in *Richard Branson: The Inside Story*, says Branson went on an exploratory trip to Jamaica with his lawyer and friend Charles Levison, who'd worked for Chris Blackwell and knew the Caribbean well.

"Branson's principal target was Peter Tosh, who had sung with Bob Marley in the Wailers. Tosh had a reputation for being difficult. According to local rumour, he had once threatened Chris Blackwell with a machete and the fact that Tosh had probably planted the rumour himself did nothing to diminish his fearful aspect. He treated Richard Branson with imperious disdain; twice inviting him to his home and being pointedly out on both occasions, then declining to share his torpedo-sized spliffs when a meeting was at last arranged. He did however, sign for Virgin and his first solo album *Legalise It* was released in 1976."

Branson's upper middle-class bonhomie wouldn't have gone down too well with Peter, who suspected Virgin's approach was more about money than any real affiliation with his music. (Branson's contraceptive advice centre, HELP, wouldn't have been too popular with a Rasta like Peter either.) Virgin had struck gold with Mike Oldfield's *Tubular Bells*, and released albums with U Roy and the Mighty Diamonds before signing *Legalise It*. Its London office – in Vernon Yard – was a hippy hangout, and staff and visitors openly smoked ganja in the A&R department. One former staff member recalls that Richard Branson "was never a music person and had little contact with the day to day running of the label". After recent events, that's hardly surprising. The previous September Virgin had agreed to distribute a small reggae label called Atra Records, owned by Sebastian and Brent Clarke. Their contract will soon be terminated. One morning in March 1976, Branson woke up to find three men stood by his bed. They knocked him around for a bit and dragged him downstairs whilst demanding £5,000 in cash, as they believed Virgin had been cheating them. The case didn't reach court until 18 months later, when the Clarke brothers, together with Dennis Bartholomew, were charged with blackmail and assault with intent to rob, although these charges were later dropped.

Virgin tried to sign the Rolling Stones and other major rock acts during this period, but were turned down. Branson's label was still viewed as an eccentric choice – one that had little clout within the industry. It was reggae and punk that afforded it the opportunity to try something different and gain credibility at a time when other labels were still unsure of whether these genres would sell or not. Virgin's gamble would pay off handsomely as it built up a reggae catalogue to rival that of Island's.

Island had released Bob's *Rastaman Vibration* album in late April, a week into his US tour. The cover was mock sackcloth, even down to the actual texture. The surface was ideal for cleaning and preparing herb on, Bob noted. True to form, Peter and Lee Jaffe resolved to go one better. The cover of Peter's forthcoming LP will be gloriously controversial because there's Peter, sat smoking his hookah pipe in a ganja field. It was every stoner's dream, and Peter Tosh was living it. Cue Al Anderson, who asked, 'Who's hipper than Peter Tosh?'

Lee Jaffe took the photos in Blue Fields, near where Peter's mother lived.

"I was going for the most radical thing," he says. "I wasn't going to soften his image and that's why I think Peter enjoyed working with me. I was there to further the cause of revolution and Rasta and to fight racism and change the social structure of the world.

"In America, people had never seen herb fields before. I was a big pot smoker and I didn't know what a herb field looked like either. Bob had taken me to one near Nine Miles. We'd gone hiking to a herb field, walking up and down these mountains and I remember looking down and seeing this valley glowing… I just couldn't believe it. It was unreal, so when Peter and I were discussing the album cover, I suggested we go shoot there. I borrowed this Hasselblad from somebody and then delivered the best six pictures to Columbia, but they lost them. Peter went crazy and I flipped out. Fortunately I had more so the one that made the cover was my seventh choice!"

The gatefold sleeve will have great photos of Al Anderson, looking super cool in his shades, black leather jacket and *Natty Dread* T-shirt. Family Man owlishly sucks on a chalice whilst cradling an acoustic guitar; Tyrone Downie and Robbie Shakespeare both hold spliffs and Peter stands in a field, arms outstretched as if presenting a winning entry in the Chelsea Flower Show, except he's dressed in a tracksuit with a towel slung over his shoulder and has that same felt hat perched on his head. This transcends mere artwork. It's a *statement*.

Despite his Columbia deal, Peter was at liberty to continue releasing singles in Jamaica on his own Intel Diplo label. At the end of July, Jamaican paper *The Week End Star* ran an advertisement announcing "And now… Talent Corp. presents for general release – the latest masterstroke from the great Peter Tosh – 'Ketchy Shuby'. Available at all record shops." Peter's depicted looking very red-eyed. Small dreadlocks poke from under the brim of his felt hat and is that a long-stemmed ganja pipe resting on his shoulder?

'Ketchy Shuby' is a countrified 'Bend Down Low', and full of innuendo. (In Jamaica, "ketchy shuby" is a game like cricket, but without formal rules.) The actual record had been a long time coming, but sounds all the better for Carlton "Santa" Davis' overdubs. Bunny told Peter he should have Santa as his drummer when he puts a band together and with *Legalise It* due for release, Peter will have to deal with that soon enough.

There would be no surprises on the album, which contains just nine tracks. Sebastian Clarke will describe as "a markedly uneven work" but the half-page advertisements that appeared in US music publications that

August begged to differ. "Pure Jamaican. Pure Peter Tosh," they declared. "Peter Tosh is one of the original Wailers, and perhaps the purest; maybe that's why he's the most revered musician playing in Jamaica today. And why *Legalise It* was the most eagerly awaited album of this year in Jamaica. His songs ('Stop That Train' and 'Get Up Stand Up', among others) make no concession to supposed American or European tastes. So if you like any of the reggae music you've been hearing lately, you're ready for the next step."

Chris Blackwell had demonstrated the importance of marketing (with that famous "Zippo" sleeve), as well as radio and media exposure in getting rock fans to connect with reggae. He'd spent comparatively large amounts advertising *Catch A Fire* in the mainstream music weeklies, and Peter now hoped that Columbia would follow suit. It wasn't as if this black, outspoken, six-foot-four Jamaican protest singer had an image problem, or couldn't easily be marketed. He was rebel incarnate and whilst that fiery Rasta agenda may prove off-putting to some, a little religion hadn't hurt the likes of Elvis or Johnny Cash. Peter had known exactly what he was doing that day in Westmoreland, sat in front of Lee Jaffe's camera. It was Ivan Martin from *The Harder They Come* revisited. Remember the scene where Jimmy Cliff's in the photographer's studio, striking poses with pistols still warm from a shootout with the police? The difference being that Peter wasn't celebrating criminality, but flaunting God-given rights he believed no one could deny him. Rock and country music had its share of outlaws, but Keith Richards and Willie Nelson had nothing on Peter Tosh. Columbia needed to be bold and grasp the nettle. Its latest signing epitomised the spirit of rock'n'roll, whilst spearheading an exciting new genre. Needless to say he also had plenty to talk about, as members of the US media would soon find out.

"I went to interview Peter in New York and he was fantastic. He was so charismatic," recalls Vivien Goldman. "He was charm personified, even when we argued. He was less arrogant than he became later. A lot of good things were happening for him..."

Peter clearly agreed, since he told WHRW radio presenter Murray Elias that, "I like the way things work out, irrespective of the humiliation, because after humiliation is power and majesty, and every day I get the inspiration to write some exclusive tunes the world will have to listen to and I don't mean just black people, but everyone who is oppressed."

Murray interviewed him on July 8, at the Island offices in New York. Island press officer Charlie Comer, an old friend of Chris Blackwell's, was looking after Peter at the time. Asked if he still considered himself a Wailer, Peter replied, "Yes man. I was and is and will forever be a Wailer." After praising "other brothers that have a message in their music" like Harold Melvin & the Blue Notes, Richie Havens and the O' Jays, he outlines the distinction between influence and inspiration. "No roots music can be influenced," he says imperiously. "It can only be inspired. It has to be an in-born concept. Roots music is something that *springs* from out of you, from *way* down!"

Murray informs him that 'Legalise It' is now banned on WNEW in New York, which compels Peter to retort that "the more they ban this tune, the more people are going to want to hear it... And I talk on behalf of ALL those who smoke herb. It is for their rights and their protection from police hostility, because it's not me alone who has been brutalised by them."

He's then asked whether Michael Manley will overturn the banning of 'Legalise It' in Jamaica.

"Well, 'im love the message, that's one thing I know of him," Peter replies. "That is one Prime Minister what I respect. 'Im open the eyes of the people, who are always being taught inferiority about Africa. Them teach we that Africa is the dark, desolate continent, and how pure cannibal come from there. Those are the things they teach me in school; that the black man was born in sin and all that bullshit but Michael Manley come and break down all of that, seen? Michael Manley is the FIRST Prime Minister from the days of colonialism to stand up for a revolutionary movement in Africa, which is the MPLA and me love those things, because irrespective of what people want to say, that's no fake. It's serious business man."

Manley had declared a state of emergency in June and wouldn't lift it until November. Kingston's ghetto areas had turned into war zones, and those who knew where all the guns came from weren't saying. Trench Town was already a very different place from when Peter lived there. Jungle and Rema were divided along political lines, with most of the fighting taking place at the borders of Seventh and Ninth Streets. Certain roads were blocked off, and residents lived in fear from security forces and local gunmen alike, since both were fond of rape. Murders were commonplace, and met by a wall of silence by overcrowded families living in housing

161

schemes named after revolutionary hot spots like Angola, Zimbabwe, Mozambique, Mexico and Havana. The jails too were straining at the seams. Best name for a temporary prison? "No Man's Land" – where rival gang members were often forced to share a cell.

August found Peter sat in the New York office of *Roots News*, smoking an "S"-shaped pipe stuffed with herb. Evol Graham is present at this meeting. He was art director for Tropical Soundtracks, a Jamaican label affiliated to Michael Manley that had folded a year beforehand. Leroy Mattis was also known as Leroy Mabrak. He'd brought Count Ossie's Rastafarian drummers to the US in 1972 to play at the premiere of *The Harder They Come*. Peter felt at ease with them, and complained he had little money. "Right now I can't even buy a piano or do certain progressive things I would like to do," he laments, before promptly changing the subject. "We have been brainwashed and mis-educated and given European values and way of life," he stated. "Our traditional culture was heavily suppressed... They have removed the chains from off our feet and hands and have placed them on our minds, so there are many things we have to unlearn in order to be free."

He made the cover of *Black Music* in September. A headline poses the question "Peter Tosh – Reggae's Next Giant?" Inside is the interview with Carl Gayle conducted the previous October at Talent Corporation. Peter's wearing a *Legalise It* T-shirt, and has that trusty ganja pipe hanging out of his mouth. Gayle describes Peter as "tall, slim, bold, youthful, open-minded, frank, determined, nonchalant and tongue-in-cheek".

That same month, UK music weekly *NME* printed a letter announcing the launch of a campaign called Rock Against Racism – an organisation inspired by Eric Clapton's racist outburst on stage in Birmingham, supporting Enoch Powell's view that England had too many immigrants. "Come on Eric, own up; half your music's black. You're rock music's biggest colonialist," the writer goads, before asking, "Who shot the sheriff Eric? It sure as hell wasn't you."

Once he'd returned to Jamaica, Peter formed a band in readiness for his first solo tour dates. Inspired by Rasta terminology, he called it Word, Sound & Power. Robbie Shakespeare was the first recruit and since Santa was touring with Jimmy Cliff, he quickly recommended Sly Dunbar.

"I put that band together," says Lee Jaffe. "I used to tell Peter that if he had Family Man and Carly as his rhythm section then what happens if Bob's touring at the same time? It would cause problems between him and

Bob so we had to get him a band of his own. Sly and Robbie were based at Channel One at the time and played on the majority of Jamaica's top 20. In those days, 10 Jamaican dollars was worth 10 US and they'd get paid 10 dollars a song. They'd start playing in the morning and not finish until late at night so they were making real money! I'd go see them at Channel One every single day whilst trying to persuade them to come on tour. It was a hard case to make because I was only offering to pay them 200 dollars a week..."

They relented because Bob was breaking big, and Sly and Robbie figured they had a chance to do the same thing for Peter. Lee told Roger Steffens: "That band was amazing, just incredible – Al Anderson, Donald Kinsey, Wya Lindo on keyboards, plus Sly and Robbie. They were the hottest band anywhere on earth at that time!"

Peter had originally wanted Tyrone Downie to join them but he decided to stay with Bob. That left the door open for Errol "Tarzan" Nelson. He'll share keyboard duties with Wya Lindo, who'd recently returned from San Francisco. He and Peter were old friends, so that was an easy call. Lead guitarist Al Anderson describes Wya as "king of the shuffle, and one of the baddest Jamaicans who ever touch an organ. The man is a dominant figure. He's not subordinate ever!"

Al had quit the Wailers after threats on Marley's life went unheeded. JLP gunmen had approached him in Epiphany's nightclub one night, giving him a message for Bob. The JLP wanted him to withdraw from the Smile Jamaica concert, which the PNP had promoted as if part of Manley's re-election campaign.

"Tell them I'm turning the other cheek," said Bob, after Al had passed him the message.

"Bob was a gangster, and I didn't like that about him," recalls Al. "I liked the Jah thing about Bob, which he showed during the day but at night, when Frowser, Tek Life and those boys used to come up to Hope Road, it was over. I remember sitting with him one time and Bob was saying, 'Oh, that one's wanted for murder.' I said, 'How can you surround yourself with these guys?' He would always say, 'This is Jamaica and you don't understand,' but I just couldn't live with it because of my insecurities. I was too worried about preserving my life and getting what I needed to survive because Bob would just give me money when he felt like it or I asked him and it took nerve to do that, I tell you!

"Peter Tosh took care of me 10 times better than Bob Marley did. That's because Peter gave me royalties, and he gave me respect. He smoked good weed, but Bob would just smoke bush weed and talk fuckery. Well Peter wasn't into that. He was a rebel music man and when I joined his band he advanced me and gave me a place to stay. Bob Marley never did any of these things and yet Peter hardly had any money at that time."

Word, Sound & Power made their debut at the Jamaica Arts Awards, held in the National Arena. They then assembled for rehearsals at the Golden Strand Hotel in Miami during mid-October. Herbie Miller and Ozzie Brown were now part of Peter's management team but Columbia still took the precaution of appointing two of its staff as tour manager and accountant. Karl Pitterson was sound engineer and Peter had recruited Biggs to prepare his food and run errands. Everywhere they stopped, Biggs would shop for health foods and fresh vegetables to cook on his portable stove or blend in his food processor. According to Herbie Miller, there was friction between the Columbia guys and the Jamaican contingent. Late rehearsals and copious ganja intake didn't help the situation any. Road manager Ted Cammann even doubted the tour would get off the ground at one stage.

"We loved reggae music and were fans of the Wailers so working for Peter was an honour, but they were from a different culture and it was hard for me to understand at first," he told Miller. "It was a little overwhelming. It took a few days to definitely settle in. There were a couple of individuals who were kind of difficult because that was a part of their personalities, but it was an interesting and fun group. It made being on the road very enjoyable."

Their main modes of transport on that first tour were two station wagons, and occasionally the train. The tour started in Florida and whilst Peter will claim there were 20,000 people at the Miami show, this may have been an exaggeration. The highlight of the tour would be two sold out nights at the Beacon Theatre on October 16 and 17. New York was papered with black and white posters of the *Legalise It* cover in the two weeks prior to those shows, creating keen interest.

"It was incredible," says Lee Jaffe. "Can you imagine, a big poster of a guy with dreadlocks in a marijuana field, smoking a pipe full of herb? Nobody had ever seen anything like that before. I did a really good job!"

It would be Lee's last involvement with Peter as he was fired after these shows. After denying the rumours that Peter hung him upside down from a light fitting in his hotel room, he says it was Herbie Miller and Ozzie Brown who turned Peter against him. "They told Peter a lot of lies about me, but they didn't know me at all," he says. "They were just trying to get a job. They had nothing behind them. They had zero. They had Columbia because Peter was signed to them, but that was all my doing."

Two days after the final Beacon Theatre performance, Peter celebrated his 32nd birthday in a New York hotel room with Herbie Miller, Ozzie Brown and his wife, Muna, Wya, *Soul Magazine* reporter Fikisha Cumbo, photographer John Bright and "a few white people". Peter wore his Sun Of Reggae T-shirt and puffed contently on his ganja pipe as Biggs served Irish Moss and offered everyone fresh fruit and sugar cane. We're talking about a time when vegetarianism and herbal remedies were looked upon with suspicion. Not that Peter cared. He didn't travel anywhere without his assortment of potions.

"When on tour, Tosh purchased charms and amulets from African shops," Miller recalls. "One such purchase at the Nyahbinghi African Shop in New York was a pair of lion's testicles that were supposed to ensure protection. He also had aerosol canisters to spray his car engine, home and body to guard against evil. I experienced first-hand Tosh's belief in their usefulness as well. On our first American tour in 1976 we were sharing adjoining rooms with access to the same bathroom. I had no deodorant and asked if I could use his. He said, 'Yes, it's on the counter.' After checking out all the bathroom sprays, ointments, tubes, bottles and so on, I hollered out that I saw no deodorant. He insisted it was there and proceeded to enter, producing from the counter an aerosol canister decorated with black cats, snakes and a turbaned, genie type of character, handed it to me and left. After taking a good look and contemplating the situation I sprayed the canister in the air and shouted a hale and hearty thank you."

Miller says Peter would burn incense in hotel rooms, on the tour bus and backstage areas to cleanse them of undesirable spirits. He'd also spray his guitar with various potions, offer incantations in Amharic and "use expletives as positive sound vibrations to dispel evil spirits, duppies and vampires". He and Miller grew close on this tour. Peter admired his friend's knowledge of world affairs and Herbie may have even replaced Yvonne in this respect. Sly thinks Peter may have met with Angela Davis and filmed a video special for Harry Belafonte whilst touring behind *Legalise It*. Belafonte's activist spirit was undimmed, as confirmed by his recent outburst on US television. "It is my personal feeling that plantations exist all over America," he'd told the nation. "If you walk into South Central Los Angeles, Watts or Over-the-Rhine in Cincinnati, you'll find people who live lives that are as degrading as anything that slavery had ever produced."

The tour ended in Boston, where Peter's entourage met with a frosty reception. They'd travelled there by train, and were tired. The hotel manager said the rooms were already booked, but was finally prevailed upon to let the band members up to their rooms. One of the staff later admitted that he'd been told to turn them away, as the manager didn't want a group of blacks staying there. Just to make things worse, two of the party had stones thrown at them after they'd wandered down a nearby street looking for somewhere to eat. The atmosphere was tense and intimidating and the band members felt threatened, which was a shame, as everyone wanted to finish the tour on a high.

Typically, Peter didn't show any signs of fear at all, not even after several police officers gathered by the hotel doors. As the party milled about in the lobby, fearful of the outcome, Peter looked towards the entrance and began to sing out loud. "I see the mark of the beast on their ugly faces. I see them congregating in evil places…"

As we've already noted, the man was fearless and also reckless. Ras Karbi witnessed another example of this, and on that same tour during late 1976.

"One day I said to him, 'Peter, what are you going to do with your money?' Because he'd just been signed by Columbia at the time and he said, 'I'm going to arm the African freedom-fighters.' I said, 'Peter, listen to me. Never say that to anybody, because when you go on tour reporters are going to be asking you that question.'

"Some time later he did a show for African Liberation Day at Howard University and the MC was Stokeley Carmichael. I was living in Boston and so I went to the show and after it had finished, I saw Peter on the bus being interviewed. I never heard the question but I heard the answer. 'I'm going to arm the African freedom-fighters' he said and I thought, 'Holy shit…'"

Robbie Shakespeare often sat in on interviews with Peter during the *Legalise It* tour, and would sometimes request journalists edit out part of the conversation if Peter strayed into dangerous territory. "Sometimes Peter would say things I didn't think should be said, and especially when he'd kick out against Bob," Robbie explains. "After he and Bob went their separate ways it left him kind of bitter. I used to tell him not to get caught up in thinking about the Wailers any more because he's a frontperson now."

Their show at the Sanders Theatre was recorded, and is the perfect synthesis of roots reggae and blues – one capable of appeasing white, American youngsters reluctant to stray too far from a rock framework. US hippies and Jamaican artists like Peter had a certain amount in common. Both sets of people were longhaired rebels who liked playing guitars, smoking weed and making out with girls, and the fact that Peter's two guitarists were both American did his cause no harm at all. For proof, just listen to live versions of 'No Sympathy' or 'Steppin' Razor'. Peter also played a fair amount of guitar on the *Legalise It* tour. That scything wah wah formed an integral part of the band's sound, but occasionally detracted from his performance. Because whilst he was visually arresting and a powerful singer, Peter still seemed a little uncertain at times. It's as if he felt awkward in the spotlight, although he'll put this right on subsequent tours. The highlights of this one won't necessarily revolve around his own actions but the kinetic storm created by Word, Sound & Power, and especially during extended drums and bass workouts. In Sly Dunbar's own words, this is where he and Robbie Shakespeare really meshed together, and "found their pocket".

"At the same time we were touring, the Channel One sound was breaking out and taking over Jamaican music," Sly explains. "It was a revolutionary sound for reggae and gave Peter's shows something different. We'd often dub the songs when we were on tour with him. In fact we were probably the first group to ever play live drums and bass to American audiences, and people were amazed when they heard us do it..."

Back in Jamaica, Bob was squiring beauty queen Cindy Breakspeare and finalising plans for the Smile Jamaica concert, due to take place on December 5. Manley promptly chose December 15 for a general election, which made it look as if Bob was endorsing him. This is what angered JLP gunmen, who felt aggrieved that he hadn't paid them any mind after sending word with Al Anderson. Bob's response was to go in the studio and cut 'Smile Jamaica' – a feel-good song that stayed in the charts for months, and which the PNP shamelessly co-opted for its campaign.

Donald Kinsey has talked about how various band members "were getting shaky" before the show. "Everybody's getting upset and thinking this is going to be dangerous," he told one journalist, although Bob tried to assure him otherwise. On December 3, two days before the show, he and the Wailers were rehearsing at 56 Hope Road when gunmen appeared at the door and fired indiscriminately. Bullets started to spray around the room, injuring Bob, Don Taylor and band assistant Louis Griffiths, who was shot in the back. Only a few months previously, the Jamaican media had proclaimed Marley "reggae's first superstar" and yet now he'd almost been assassinated.

Somewhat improbably, the show went ahead. In a magnificent display of theatricality, Bob showed the audience his wounds at the end of his set and then left for Nassau, prior to a lengthy spell of exile in London. Donald Kinsey also left Jamaica after the gig and went back to Chicago. No one ever offered him an explanation of what had happened, although most commentators assume JLP enforcers ordered the hit. Ten days later, Manley won the election by some distance. Even Seaga admitted that "never before in the history of Jamaica had the people spoken so loudly and so clearly". Cracks will soon appear however, since Manley had recently cut a deal with the IMF and this will later contribute towards his downfall as graffiti began to appear all over Kingston proclaiming, 'It's Manley's fault".

Chapter 15

Equal Rights

During his stay in New York the previous August, Peter had told *Roots News* that his next album – which he'd already called *Equal Rights* – was going to be "a killer, and even heavier than *Legalise It*". He'll deliver on his promise with a set Herbie Miller describes as the singer's "grand narrative, his tour de force. To me, Peter Tosh's accomplishment here ranks alongside the best works of that same period by Marvin Gaye, Stevie Wonder and Curtis Mayfield. *Equal Rights* is a masterpiece on any level you take it – a superbly innovative document in the development of reggae."

Peter told Fikisha Cumbo that his new songs were about "colonialism, imperialism, exploitation and victimisation, here, there and everywhere. The first album is relating to the legalisation of herb and this second one to equal rights, meaning universal justice," he explained. "Legalisation of herb is only part of the justice that man is supposed to get, but equal rights is *all* of man's rights, seen?"

The title track is both profound and revolutionary. Peter has been likened to a musical Che Guevara on occasion, and the comparison's deserved for once.

"Everyone is crying out for peace, no one is crying out for justice. I don't want no peace. I need equal rights, and justice," he sings by way of an opener. He's not asking for what doesn't belong to him. He just wants his rightful share, and the fact that he doesn't have it means someone else has it instead. 'Everybody's talking about crime,' he continues, but 'tell me, who are the criminals?'

"I remember hearing Peter sing 'Equal Rights' and thinking to myself, 'This is the answer. It's not just about peace, because how can I be at peace with someone whilst they're still stealing things that belong to me?'" asks Nambo Robinson. "These people, they're from a privileged background and that's why people are reluctant to call them names sometimes, but a thief is a thief, right?"

As 'Equal Rights' draws to a close, Peter starts ad-libbing. He mentions the liberation struggles happening in Palestine, Angola, Botswana, Zimbabwe and most telling of all, "right here in Jamaica…"

By early 1977, the island was in meltdown. CIA agents masqueraded as foreign businessmen, and the destabilisation of Manley's government was now tantamount to regime change. Supermarket shelves were empty, and essential items rationed. It wasn't just ghetto people who were suffering. Jamaicans in general faced hard times, and Peter was determined to lend his voice to the struggle but first there were certain hurdles to overcome. Herbie Miller says that booking studio time was made problematic by "power cuts, public roadblocks, curfews, military operations and outbreaks of violence". It had become impossible to travel freely throughout Kingston, and their studios of choice – including Joe Gibbs and Dynamic – were in areas that were most badly affected. Eventually it was decided they'd record the majority of tracks at Randy's, where improvements had been made since Peter's last visit.

"We had a two-inch Ampex machine with a 16-track recording head by then," says Clive Chin. "We never really got to use it to the fullness though because when I left Jamaica in April 1977, that machine was only a year old. Peter just laid the basic rhythm tracks there. It was between himself, Robbie Shakespeare, Sly Dunbar and a couple of keyboard players."

In fact Carly Barrett played drums on a handful of tracks, before he left to join Bob in London. 'I Am That I Am' is largely autobiographical, and a fertile mix of personal assertion and idealism. "I'm not in this world to live up to your expectations, neither are you here to live up to mine," Peter announces in the first verse, before warning listeners not to underestimate his ability or belittle his authority. "It's time you recognised my quality," he tells them. Carly's rim-shots can be heard ricocheting throughout 'Jah

Guide', which is a testament to Peter's Rastafarian faith and finds him borrowing from the 23rd Psalm. Again, it's voiced with absolute certainty but it's 'African' that will change a lot of black people's thinking.

Many years earlier, Marcus Garvey had made a similar clarion call. "All black people across the globe, in America and in Africa are part of a single race, a single culture and have to be proud of the colour of their skin," he said. "All of Africa must be independent and united. Africa for the Africans!"

Like Garvey, Peter was an advocate of black pride and 'African' ranks alongside James Brown's 'Say It Loud I'm Black And I'm Proud' in terms of its cultural impact. "No matter where you come from. As long as you're a black man, you're an African," he states. "No matter your nationality. You have got the identity of a black man..."

Encouraging people of the Diaspora to embrace their cultural heritage was one thing, but few artists of any genre risked supporting the African liberation movement so openly as Peter did on 'Apartheid'. Most believed they'd lose work and popularity by aligning themselves with revolutionaries – this in an era when the American and British governments still viewed Nelson Mandela as a terrorist. Peter wasn't just bold in writing songs like 'Apartheid', 'Equal Rights' and 'African', he was *proud*.

"The ANC and SWAPO were the two main movements to liberate southern Africa – Zimbabwe, Namibia and South Africa," said Herbie Miller. "The theme of this whole record was to do with that particular struggle. Peter had a deep interest in the struggles of the African people."

Only a year earlier, the United Nations had declared 1976 "the International Year Against Apartheid". The black townships in the southwest of Johannesburg, collectively known as "Soweto", had intensified their efforts to rise up against the apartheid regime. It had been 16 years since the Sharpeville massacre, and nothing had changed.

"When Peter first sang about apartheid a lot of people in Jamaica didn't really know too much about the situation in South Africa," notes his cousin Pauline Morris, who remembers how Peter had joined protests and demonstrated outside the British Embassy when he was a teenager. "He was a rebel with a cause and that's why Peter had a negative relationship with the police in Jamaica. They all knew who he was and dubbed him a troublemaker but he'd studied what was going on in South Africa and took it personally."

Pauline goes on to say that Peter "was 100 percent misunderstood by the Jamaican media. They took him too lightly," she says. "I don't think they were too sophisticated about what was going on at all."

Whilst Peter's outspoken views made him a hero to Jamaica's poorer classes, his blatant disregard for authority meant he remained a target for the police, who'd often stop and confront him, especially in public places. It was as if they wanted to shame or embarrass him, to teach him a lesson, yet Peter did little to protect himself, despite the recent attempt on Bob's life. 'Jah Guide' indeed...

In such volatile times warriors didn't run, but *stood firm*. Robbie Shakespeare lived in McGregor Gully, a feared PNP stronghold and ghetto neighbourhood over in East Kingston. Every day they were recording 'Equal Rights' he got in his battered Triumph and drove to the studio where in addition to playing bass, he served as creative director.

"I was looking for a sound for each song, doing things to match Peter's concept and philosophy," he told Herbie Miller. "I wanted my sound to reflect the artist and his energy. And it shouldn't sound like anything I had done for anyone else."

Whilst the basic rhythms were all recorded at Randy's, the overdubs were split between Dynamic, Joe Gibbs and Aquarius, depending on availability. Herbie was co-producer and says most of the sessions at Randy's were fun although Peter would get upset if the musicians were late, which didn't happen too often. They worked hard too. Each session would last seven or eight hours, yielding an average of two tracks a day. Sly and Robbie were the driving force, and always thinking ahead. They saw how Bob Marley's sound was defined by his backing musicians – now firmly established as "the Wailers" – and wanted to give Peter his own distinctive style. With Family Man at the helm, the Wailers epitomised roots reggae music whereas Sly and Robbie were more inventive, and so steered Peter away from becoming too predictable. Ultimately, both bands wanted to make mainstream hits whilst retaining a Jamaican feel. This was a tall order but Sly and Robbie were young and ambitious, and eager for a challenge.

The new album will be a progression from *Legalise It*, but then Peter had grown since those fractured sessions of two years earlier. He'd overcome his grief for Yvonne, and the Columbia deal gave him the opportunity to show what he could do although, contrary as ever, Peter arrived at Randy's armed with nothing more than incomplete ideas.

"He had sketches, titles and outlines contained in a book with unfinished material," says Herbie. "It frustrated Robbie and all of us that he would come to the session with just a sketch. We figured that if he had written it all out, we could have just done it but what he got was that spontaneity that comes with creating right there. I don't know if he wanted that consciously, but that's what he got, plus Peter was in touch with things that we are only just understanding, like his interest in otherworldly stuff; the power of the ones who have gone before us, the communications that you can have with them. You realise now how advanced he was in embracing our culture at its deepest root."

The track that best illustrates this is 'Vampire', which opens with spooky howls and is a holy crusade by any other name. By "vampire" he means anyone "with a bloody meditation" and who fights against righteousness. He's commenting on the fact that Rastafarians like himself are engaged in spiritual warfare, yet were still viewed as bringing shame on their families, because of their faith. "They only drink up the old wine," sings Peter. "Have no room for the new wine."

"Peter was not afraid of anyone or anything," writes Ras Cardo. "He knew the consequences quite well. The enemy was after him and time was also his enemy. He described the enemy in many ways, the 'shit-stem' (system), vampire, hypocrites and evil forces existing in high and low places. He was not referring to what we in Jamaica call 'duppy' (ghost.) He meant evil spirits as it is written in the Bible, especially in the book of Ephesians 6:12."

Except Peter had supernatural visions too. "Returning from the country one afternoon, Tosh crashed his car into a bridge," says Herbie Miller. "On every occasion that he'd had an accident, he was convinced that either a duppy or a vampire caused it. On this occasion his story was that 'a blood sucking vampire tek the steering outa mi hand. Yes I, the bredda just grab the steering wheel and crash the car inna the bridge.'"

Anyone who smokes as much herb as Peter Tosh can be forgiven the occasional lapse of reason but his world was populated with spirits, and he made no attempt to hide the fact. Such preoccupations will lead him down dark and dangerous pathways in future, but were still within manageable bounds during the making of *Equal Rights*. As usual, he'd set aside a portion of studio time for brushing up some old songs. He liked how Word, Sound & Power played them on stage and in rehearsal, and relished taking his road band into the studio for new versions of 'Downpressor Man', '400 Years', 'Steppin' Razor', 'Mark Of The Beast', 'Ketchy Shuby' and 'Can't Blame The Youth'. The majority of these tracks sound rejuvenated in Sly and Robbie's hands, just like Peter's solo cut of 'Get Up Stand Up' – a song he now transforms into a personal triumph. There's an echo of Bob Dylan's 'Ballad Of A Thin Man' in how Peter delivers the coup de grace, and to a preacher no less. "You a duppy, and you don't know what life is really worth," he sneers. According to Herbie Miller, this early version of 'Get Up Stand Up' contained the line, "don't be no nigger now". Such terminology was highly controversial back in 1977, more than a decade before the first stirrings of gangster rap. A Columbia executive will later request that it's taken out, but there's no doubting Peter's commitment! Bunny dropped by to sing some harmonies and will soon record his own version of 'Get Up Stand Up', but Peter has now possessed the song completely. It's become his, just like 'Steppin' Razor', which Joe Higgs had penned 10 years earlier.

"On 'Steppin' Razor' Peter wanted me to play one-drop and not my newer style, the straight four," Sly told Herbie Miller. "But 'Steppin' Razor' was a militant song so I couldn't start with a one-drop, because that would sound timid. I was influenced by the music of Motown and Stax, so I played something on the hi-hat that sounded like the intro to 'Shaft', then Peter put on his wah wah guitar..."

Al Anderson's playing on that track is beautifully understated, and yet he still gets to cut loose for a few bars. His contributions lend an international dimension to the music whereas Peter was consumed by thoughts of vengeance, and kept harking back to past indignities. "If they only knew how dangerous I am," he'd say to an engineer. "Blood and fire fi dem!"

"There were two sides to Peter," says Clive Chin. "If you knew him, you could get a lot of laughs out of him but there was another side to him as well, because if he was really angry or annoyed about something, then he could be very dangerous to be around..."

Fikisha Cumbo knew him well, and visited him during the summer of 1977 at his home in Renfield Drive, over in Ensom City. His house is made of green stucco, and has a red, gold and green gate. He has a puppy, and there's a large birdcage in the back yard full of turtle doves. He told her that he'd personally caught all of these birds except for Freddie the parrot, who lived freely in the yard and would fly to Peter whenever he held out his arm. There's another birdcage in the house, next to a giant speaker box with exposed tweeters. Fikisha duly takes note and reports that, "Birds and music appear to be the two things Peter Tosh loves the most." He told her about his obsession with flying and how the elder Rastamen once knew how to fly, but had lost the art. There's a large portrait of Emperor Haile Selassie I hanging on the wall of his sitting room and he doesn't have a telephone yet, as they aren't all that easily available in Jamaica – something that's worth bearing in mind when tales emerge of him failing to keep appointments, or going AWOL.

He takes Fikisha for a ride in his green Hillman Hunter – an English make that's covered in stickers depicting a lion, and flags belonging to Zimbabwe, Ethiopia and other African countries. Marley is in exile, and Peter is the most prominent Rasta artist left on the island. People call out as they're driving along, and then crowd round him whenever he stops anywhere, eager to hear him talk and catch a glimpse of that famed rebel spirit, although most are left charmed by his warmth and humour. After buying fruit in Coronation Market they head for Greenwich Farm, where he chooses their evening meal from a barrel of live catch at the water's edge. Fikisha isn't a girlfriend remember, but a journalist. She lists Peter's attributes as "speedy, wild, free, early riser, businessman, organic juicer, health food maker, roots man, rebel, bird man, bird-rapping, junky kitchen, pipe smoking, quiet, friendly, smiling, pensive, rambunctious, brutalised, karate loving, and his little bit of 'egocentricity'."

One of his closest associates is Wya Lindo, who plays organ on the new album. Fikisha describes him as "a cross between a real intellectual and a space cadet" with his "Bowery bum look and strange way of living". His lifestyle is said to be "that of a sufferer, a man who lives in the hills in a primitive mode, eschewing all modern conveniences such as electricity, showers, hair combs, shoes and the like. In his house there are no floors, in a true sense 'cold ground is his bed and rock stones are his pillows'."

He and Peter are one-off characters. Neither seems capable of distinguishing between vision and reality at times, yet both are capable of sharp insight. 'Babylon Queendom' was already featuring in Peter's stage act. It's summoning the glories of an ancient African monarchy, and addressed to a colonial power that has accrued great wealth from slavery, but now faces imminent destruction. "Babylon, your queendom is falling," he chants somewhat gleefully, before calling for reparations. "Give me back me land, my language and my culture..."

"The Queen of England and all the people who represent the colonial powers still owe it to the African people of the western hemisphere to right those wrongs, after they put us through that very inhuman experience," Bunny Wailer explains, referring to slavery. He'd just released *Protest* – the eagerly awaited follow-up to *Blackheart Man*, and an album that promptly divided opinion as to the wisdom of stirring a little disco into the reggae mix. Peter defends Bunny by saying that it's his brother's way of "getting to the people. It's psychological penetration," he remarks, somewhat unconvincingly.

Fikisha is told the new album will include '400 Years', 'Jahman In A Jamdown', 'You Can't Blame The Youth' and 'Mark Of The Beast', although none will make the final cut. Whereas 'Steppin' Razor' and 'Get Up Stand Up' take these songs to new heights, '400 Years' can't compare with the Upsetter version. The most surprising omission is 'Hammer', which is another of his outlaw songs. Also known as 'Hammer Dem Dung' (Hammer Them Down), it casts him in the role of wanted man – the victim of colonialism and persecution. Peter will later release it as a single on Intel Diplo, backed with the latest cut of 'You Can't Blame The Youth', and it blared from transistor radios for weeks that summer as Peter lived up to his bad boy reputation. "They keep on holding me and they won't let go. Gimme your hammer, make me hammer them down. They keep on fighting me, and all of them got to go..."

Final mixing took place at Criteria, where Peter had enjoyed working a year or so earlier, and could meet up with one or two friendly faces. Not only did Criteria afford better facilities, it was just an hour's flight away and brought respite from the increasingly unstable situation in Kingston. Karl Pitterson, who'd made his name mixing *Blackheart Man*, accompanied Peter to Miami. It's been reported that Criteria's in-house engineers looked down on him but Karl told Roger Steffens that everybody was amazed by what he did. "They'd never heard their studio sound like that before," he crowed, "and they began to see a wider capability of their place with the frequencies that were happening."

Karl helped choose the songs and running order, and expressed reservations about leaving off 'Vampire' and 'Jammin' In A Jamdown' – not that anyone else noticed. *Equal Rights* was released in the UK on April 1, accompanied by a press release that termed it "roots music of incomparable sophistication, and politics of certain truth". The publicity shot depicted Peter in a peaked cap and sunglasses, and with an "S"-shaped ganja pipe hanging out of his mouth. He'd wanted a revolutionary look for the cover and could have no complaints about the Warhol-like series of profile shots of himself wearing a Che Guevera beret and wraparound shades, and looking serious as your life.

As soon as he received finished copies, Peter requested an appointment with Michael Manley, which was promptly granted. When the police stopped his car at the gate of the Prime Minister's official residence Peter pulled out his ganja stash, placed it on the dashboard and asked, 'Is this what you're looking for?' A superintendant was called, who phoned for clearance and then reluctantly waved him through. Manley greeted Peter warmly and was handed a signed copy of *Equal Rights* bearing the legend, "from one living hero to another".

Chris May, writing in *Black Music*, made *Equal Rights* Album Of The Month, awarded it a maximum five stars and called it "an infinitely superior release to the disappointing *Legalise It*," and an "inspiring, politically activating breakthrough in radical Rastafari." Peter is said to be "dealing with deeper, more fundamental issues," whilst 'Apartheid' is described as "a declaration of war on South Africa's doomed fascist regime. Tosh pulls no punches here – 'You're illegal,' he tells Vorster and his thugs. 'You cross the border and murder women and children and we are going to fight you 'til you collapse.'"

Jamaica's *Weekend Star* will later reflect on how people had questioned whether Peter and Bunny could make it on their own "after spending so much time in the shadow of Bob's charismatic personality". They refer to *Blackheart Man*, released the previous summer, as that year's best reggae album and say that *Equal Rights* "far outstrips" Peter's debut. "It is an extremely powerful musical collection containing some of the hardest-hitting, most revolutionary lyrics produced anywhere for a long time," they continue. "Peter has never been known for subtlety. His method is direct, unrestrained, straightforward, blunt and hard-hitting. On *Equal Rights* he is at his best, spitting out the searing lyrics with a moving intensity, though appearing almost contemptuous and even detached at times."

Rather than promoting the album with a tour, it's decided that Peter will do a series of radio and press engagements instead, before going back out on the road with a band. His first interviews were due to take place in

New York during April, but had to be delayed after an incident involving Clive Chin, who happened to catch the same plane as Peter.

"I was walking down the aisle, looking for my seat when I hear someone say, 'Clive!' When I look around I saw Peter sitting there by himself and he said, 'Come and sit with me man' so I sat down and he began telling me how he was going up to New York to promote this album *Equal Rights*. Everything was nice, the plane took off and just as we're flying over Cuba, Peter draw out him pipe, takes two big pull off it and the whole cabin is nothing but smoke! I start to say, 'Peter...' and him snap back, 'Wha' 'appen? You want a draw?' Me say, 'No man, you're alright,' but then when we reach Kennedy airport the police were waiting for us and I'd never had such drama in my life until that evening. Oh man, they made sure we were put away, I tell you! We were in jail all that night because we nah get no bail until Saturday and then when we go before the judge, Peter cuss him out and says how he's the Minister for Ganja and herb should be legalised. I couldn't believe it. At one point the judge lean over to the clerk of the court and say, 'What is he saying?' The clerk told him that Peter must be a mad man or talking in Arabic but that was my first time coming to America, and on American Airlines as well... As a matter of fact President Carter had just got into office and he was very lenient towards marijuana, otherwise we'd have been deported immediately!"

Once freed, Peter appeared completely unfazed by the incident, and it certainly wasn't going to cramp his style any. Pauline Morris says that Peter took everything in his stride and was clearly at ease during most of these engagements, despite meeting with incomprehension some of the time. Writing in the liner notes of *I Am That I Am*, she describes "his playful banter", and him "strumming soft chords on a summer evening with an omnipresent spliff held loosely between his lips.

"Peter was seldom without his guitar," she continues. "He brought it along on radio interviews and kept it in constant reach whenever people came to visit." We're told that his playing "formed a musical bed to casual conversations" and that's certainly true of his appearance on a Chicago station where the interviewer has so little to say, you fear that he's been left catatonic by breathing in Peter's ganja smoke. In-between espousing the merits of wealth redistribution, Peter chides him for leaving "dead air" and plays some beautiful acoustic versions of tracks from the new album, together with old favourites like 'Stop That Train' and 'Can't You See'. Hearing these songs stripped bare is to appreciate the strength of his writing skills. He's also an excellent guitarist and enjoys playing around with the rhythms, as well as the language since at one point he informs his hapless host that "marijuana is a girl from Cuba" and "ganja is a bird in Australia".

His next appearance will be in Eugene, where he sings an impromptu composition called 'I'm Getting Disgusted, Don't Wanna Get Busted' which he dedicates (or rather "livicates") to "all the intellectual herb smokers in Oregon". He also plays an adaptation of Richie Havens' 'Handsome Johnny' that day. Has it really been six years since the Wailers adapted Havens' 'Indian Rope Man' we wonder?

Radio presenter Chris Mays had driven cross-country from Toledo to reach Eugene, which is halfway between San Francisco and Seattle. Local station KZEL-FM was tucked away in a trailer park, in a former laundromat. Chris was due on air from seven until midnight, and couldn't believe her eyes when Tosh arrived with an entourage of maybe 20 people and a kilo of high-grade Jamaican herb. No sooner had they settled when Peter began rolling a giant-sized spliff, which he smoked throughout their interview.

"Once he began to speak, it was clear I had totally lost control of the situation," writes Mays. "He preached the religion of ganja eloquently, poetically, in stream-of-consciousness thought patterns that rambled from one thing to the next. He spoke of the history of marijuana in his culture and his people's history. He spoke of it as religion and occasionally stopped long enough to toke and play a song."

In her own words, Chris managed "little more than a few stunned giggles" in response, and listened back to the tapes with more than a degree of embarrassment, yet still describes Peter as one of the most fascinating people she'd had the honour of meeting.

His mini-promotional tour ended in Miami. Soon, Bob will threaten to steal Peter's thunder with his latest album, *Exodus*, and news of a triumphant European tour. Marley and the Wailers had been based in London since the assassination attempt back in December. Songs like 'Jamming', 'Waiting In Vain' and 'Three Little Birds' will become mainstays of FM radio in years to come, but it was deeper nuggets like 'Natural Mystic' and 'Heathen' that alerted the faithful. Bob will have four crossover hits in a row over the next seven or eight months, beginning with 'Exodus' itself – a UK Top 20 hit in June, and which marries Biblical scripture with joyous expectancy. "We're the generation. Tell me why. Trod through great tribulation…" *Rolling Stone* had just voted Bob "Performer Of The Year", whilst the *New York Times* had dubbed him "the Third World's first superstar".

Buoyed by Marley's success, Island had signed a roster of new reggae acts, including Burning Spear, the Heptones, Toots & The Maytals, Max Romeo and Third World, and the number of 7″ singles pressed in Jamaica had reached record levels. Culture's 'Two Sevens Clash' was the year's defining anthem and there was widespread absenteeism throughout the island on July 7, when all the sevens clashed and Biblical prophecy hung thick in the air. Recent Dennis Brown hits included 'Here I Come', 'Milk And Honey' and 'Wolf And Leopards', whilst Channel One's Joseph Hoo Kim, Bunny Lee (now so prolific he'd been renamed "Striker"), Lee "Scratch" Perry, Niney The Observer and Joe Gibbs were among the top producers. Errol "ET" Thompson was resident engineer at Joe Gibbs, and his exploits at the mixing board – especially on 'African Dub, Chapter 3' – granted him dub-master status alongside the likes of King Tubby and Prince Jammy, who'd been busy recording the debut album by Black Uhuru whilst Peter was away, and with the Stepping Razor's own band. Was this reggae's best-ever year? Many people believe so but if not, then it was certainly one of them.

Thanks to Island and Virgin's advertising revenue, the British rock press finally began to take reggae seriously. All the major music weeklies ran features and reviews, especially after reggae received public endorsements by punk celebrities such as Johnny Rotten and Paul Simonon. 1977 marked the Queen's Silver Jubilee but there was little cause for celebration in a country reeling from rising unemployment, racial tension and conflicts with the IRA. That summer, the Sex Pistols' 'God Save The Queen' was banned and still got to number one, although not officially. For a short time it felt like the establishment was rocking, and scores of angry, disillusioned people living in Britain's inner cities had found their voice. Clashes between far right and far left groups became commonplace as the unlikely alliance between punk and reggae continued to grow. It wasn't just Britain's black population who knew what it was like to have no money and face police harassment, because most punks knew about that too. Lee "Scratch" Perry and Bob Marley's 'Punky Reggae Party' was no accident, and the Clash's 'London's Burning' wasn't all that far removed from a Jamaican style assault on Babylon in truth. It's just that Rasta artists believed music must also have a spiritual purpose, and this was a major difference between punks and the reggae fraternity. Their common enemy was the system, but most reggae and punk fans didn't like disco either. Donna Summer's 'I Feel Love' risked censor because of its orgasmic lyrics, and its soulless, but insistent rhythm could be heard everywhere that summer. Even Frank Sinatra and Ethel Merman would be voicing disco records by the year's end, after the *Saturday Night Fever* film and soundtrack struck home. Disco was all about escapism, and Peter hated it with a vengeance.

During rehearsals for his next tour, he's approached by a German film crew who are making a documentary called *Auf Den Sporen Des Reggae*. After dismissing ASCAP and PRS as "pirates", he claims that what passes for reggae is often "nothing more than just drum and bass, or maybe a piano. And yet my music might have 20 instruments, and all playing a different line."

The tour starts in Los Angeles during July and will stretch into December. Just before he leaves, one of the Jamaican newspapers prints a report claiming that Peter will be starring in a movie "as a karate expert, destroying a villain to the beat of his tune 'Steppin' Razor'." Needless to say this never materialised, but then the tour almost didn't happen either.

"Peter didn't like touring," says Robbie Shakespeare. "If Herbie and I sat down and told him, 'Peter, we're going to leave next week', he'd go to Westmoreland and hide! We wouldn't be able to find him so we'd have to send a friend of his to go looking for him. He was hard to deal with in the early days. He'd cuss and quarrel all the way but then once we'd got started, he'd learn to enjoy it. It's just that he knew he wouldn't be able to get the herb or the food he wanted, and that would put him off."

"Other people might relish travelling the world and seeing new places but guys like Peter felt like fish out of water," says David Barham, who helped promote some of his earliest tours. "I think they felt alien. They'd try to create a cocoon around themselves with their own customs and their own food and friends so they wouldn't have to deal with the outside world too much. Peter learned to deal with it after a while but for the most part, guys like him tried to stay within their own small circles. They didn't like being on the road so there were no big parties or anything like that. It was a hardship for them so they were always trying to make it as comfortable and as familiar as they could, and that's how they handled it."

David had worked for a company called Concerts East that promoted stadium shows. His boss then bought an interest in a Long Island club called My Father's Place, owned by a larger-than-life character called Michael "Eppy" Epstein. Concerts East put David in to run it, and he and Eppy then formed a separate company to promote reggae music. They managed Burning Spear for a while and started bringing reggae acts to the US on a regular basis, booking tours on special cut-price tickets that allowed stopovers along the East coast, all the way from Florida to Canada. This is how the *Equal Rights* tour got off the ground.

Before he and Barham got established, Eppy would contact promoters who booked reggae bands to play venues in Brooklyn or the Bronx, and then arrange for these same acts to play at My Father's Place on a Monday night, where they'd attract a very different kind of audience. Small numbers of Afro-Caribbean fans might journey out to Roslyn, but for the most part it was young white kids who crowded through the front doors to see Kingston's finest. These fans might be bold enough to venture into black areas to visit specialist reggae stores during the day, but most wouldn't dare attend club nights or shows in those places. Eppy's club was the first venue in the New York area where white people felt comfortable watching reggae acts, and the industry was quick to take note. Record labels were pouring money into radio promotions at the time. They'd give everything away free – stickers, badges, posters and T-shirts etc – except for the actual records. They'd also buy up tickets to shows so that radio presenters like Eppy – who had the only formatted reggae show on US radio at the time – could offer them as competition prizes. Most FM stations played album orientated rock. The most popular was WNEW-FM, which carried a live broadcast from the Bottom Line each week. Eppy followed suit on local station WLIR, except his broadcasts were from My Father's Place, including some recorded at his Monday Roots sessions.

Eppy loved reggae, which sat well with his hedonistic, hippy vibe. Despite having been described as "a fat, ugly Jewish guy who wouldn't have got laid in 100 years were it not for the fact he owned a club", he was a popular figure and hosted some notorious parties back at his house, where there were legendary scenes involving a hot tub. Looking back, it's as if he and members of the Rolling Stones were on some kind of collision course, although he couldn't have imagined it at the time.

"There was more and more reggae coming out on different record labels," he begins. "Marley had just released *Exodus* and he and Peter were both touring... It was right at that point when Jane Rose, who worked for the Stones, phoned me and said she had a problem. She said Keith Richards and Ronnie Wood wanted to come out to Long Island and see Gregory Isaacs, and she was worried about sending them out there. I told her it was no big deal but she yelled back, 'You don't understand. They're *Rolling Stones*.' I didn't give a shit about the Rolling Stones because I was a reggae fan but she started talking about how they'd need two bottles of rum and all this other stuff, like security. Anyhow Keith and Ronnie came to the club, and we had these guys sat round the table with them who looked like they were Gestapo. They were horrible, and they created this negative zone that was so fucking sad. Keith came up to me and said, 'Can't you get rid of these guys?' I said, 'Yes thank God, but make sure Jane doesn't find out.' He told me not to worry and started chuckling to himself, so I guess that's when he first took a liking to My Father's Place.

"In fact Keith liked the Monday nights so much he rented this big house in Old Brookville, and he'd come out to the club regularly after that. Everybody got used to seeing him and Ronnie, but remember, no one was going to bother them on Monday nights because reggae people aren't like that. Sometimes they'd dance with a girl or whatever, and then other times they'd totally take over. I remember how Culture stopped playing once after Keith and Ronnie walked on stage. He didn't know who they were!"

Eppy had billed Gregory Isaacs as "the Frank Sinatra of reggae" that night, and still insists that Gregory would have been the Rolling Stones' first signing had they not run into him at a bad time, since he barely acknowledged them. The Stones were searching for someone with authenticity, someone who could match their own rebel image and repeat the same kind of international success as Bob Marley. It was but a short step from Gregory Isaacs to Peter Tosh, and the seed was planted right there in Roslyn, at My Father's Place.

"I'd like to think we helped get Peter the Rolling Stones deal," says David Barham. "Keith Richard's son Marlon lived within five miles of the club. Every year he went to a nearby summer camp and Keith's father lived out there too so Keith would come out to stay and naturally gravitated towards the Monday night reggae sessions. A lot of the stars would hang out there and Keith wouldn't hesitate to get on stage and sit in with an act like the Mighty Diamonds. It was all done in the spirit of fun so I think the Rolling Stones connected with reggae very strongly during that time period."

They still hadn't met Peter by this stage, or seen him perform. That would have to wait a little longer. Whilst it's hard to pinpoint exact dates and venues, Peter's 1977 tour appears to have been a success. He certainly made an impression on Garry Steckles, who reviewed one of his shows for *Caribbean Week*.

"It's a late fall day in Toronto and Massey Hall, a university theatre, is packed for Peter Tosh's first concert in that city," he writes. "The atmosphere is expectant and this being a reggae concert, the air is heavy with smoke. Suddenly, an anonymous voice on the public address system announces that smoking of any kind is forbidden in Massey Hall, that the hall's smoke detectors are wired to the fire department and that if one of them goes off, the hall will be cleared and the concert will be cancelled. It's greeted by a chorus of boos, but everyone puts out whatever he or she is smoking. A few minutes later, Tosh's band Word, Sound & Power comes on stage and launches into the opening number. Then Tosh strides out, majestically, and there's a buzz in the crowd as they realise he's holding an enormous marijuana spliff in one hand. Tosh walks up to the microphone, glances up to the ceiling and notices a smoke detector. He puffs casually on it then slowly and deliberately, exhales an enormous cloud of smoke in the direction of the detector. Everyone waits, tensely, to see if it's going to go off. It doesn't. The crowd cheers, and Tosh starts the concert with 'Legalise It'."

Chapter 16

Peace Treaty

In January 1978, five JLP gunmen from an area known as Southside were shot dead in "the Green Bay Massacre". They and several others had been lured to a firing range by government security forces before being slaughtered. There will be no inquest, and no arrests. Jamaica's political infighting was getting out of hand, and even some ghetto warlords thought so. After rival enforcers Claudie Massop and Aston "Bucky" Marshall were forced to share a jail cell and discovered how much they had in common – not least a distrust for their political handlers – they declared a truce. It was their idea to put on a free Peace Concert that would raise funds for youth development projects and also serve as a homecoming for Bob Marley, who'd been in exile for over a year.

In early February, they flew to London and met with Bob, who'd just been diagnosed with melanoma cancer. Ignoring his doctors' advice, he agreed to appear at the euphemistically named One Love Peace Concert and plans quickly fell into place from there. It would be held at the National Stadium on April 22, 12 years to the day since Emperor Haile Selassie I had arrived in Kingston. Vivien Goldman tells how Claudie Massop went to see Peter and asked him to perform. "'What kind of concert is it?' Peter asked him. 'A peace concert,' Claudie explained. Peter looked at him and said, 'Claudie, the only peace you're going to get in this country is six by six.' 'What do you mean by that?' he asked. Laconically, Peter replied, 'Six foot six is called rest in peace.'"

As the Peace Treaty committee had arrived in London, Richard Branson was headed in the other direction. Lightning Records had just had a number one hit with Althea & Donna's 'Uptown Top Ranking' and he didn't want to be outmanoeuvred. Reggae was going mainstream and if his new Frontline label was to capitalise on this, he needed to act quickly. Existing titles by artists like U Roy were selling like hot cakes, and there was plentiful talent in Jamaica hoping for a record deal. Branson will sign around 20 acts after landing in Kingston on February 3, including Gregory Isaacs, Big Youth, Tapper Zukie and Prince Far I.

Johnny Rotten, who'd just quit the Sex Pistols, travelled with the Virgin delegation, as did DJ/filmmaker Don Letts. Branson spent most of the trip trying (unsuccessfully) to persuade Rotten to rejoin the Pistols, but the main objective was to keep him out of the media spotlight. In July 1977, Rotten had appeared on Tommy Vance's Capital Radio show and showed impeccable taste by playing reggae 45s by Culture, Dr. Alimantado and Augustus Pablo, among others. He and Don Letts were regular visitors to reggae strongholds like the Four Aces in Dalston, and their championing of Jamaican music would have a persuasive effect upon London's rock press, who'd long grown accustomed to deriding reggae before Johnny Rotten made it fashionable.

"John Rotten didn't actually mean a lot to people in Jamaica," says Don Letts. "All they knew was that he was a white man with a number one record and that was enough. Richard had booked an entire floor of the Sheraton Hotel for myself, John, Ken Berry and whoever else was there and essentially what happened was, we were encamped there for a month whilst jungle drums were beating and telling the locals, 'White man with money at the Sheraton – come!'"

Vivien Goldman, who'd accompanied them on the trip, describes the Sheraton Hotel as a "somewhat offensive institution, a bland crate of a skyscraper" and "the last bastion of American imperialism". It's the same New Kingston hotel featured in *The Harder They Come*, where Jimmy Cliff rides around the grounds in a gleaming white convertible, but the Sheraton wasn't at all luxurious by western standards. The ground floor escalator didn't work, the carpet was worn and there were cracks in the wooden balconies. Guests and their visitors would sit at round white tables by the pool, under a big Sheraton 'S' logo whose reflection could be seen in the water. Potted plants were dotted here and there, whilst the poolside bar hosted a stream of onlookers, attracted like moths to a flame by the promise of big money signings to Virgin's new reggae label. "It got so that you felt like you were wading through your singles collection every time you went to get a glass of water," Vivien later wrote in *Sounds*.

The Virgin party stayed at the Sheraton for a month. Legend has it that Ken Berry typed out standard record contracts on the hotel typewriter and paid the artists their advances from a suitcase of cash. Branson was keen to make such payments in Jamaican dollars, as the local currency was very weak at the time. He rarely ventured outside the hotel grounds but his fellow travellers did, despite the volatile surroundings.

"There was all of this political violence going on, which is one of the reasons we spent a lot of time at the hotel," recalls Don. "I remember seeing the Gun Court and you know why Manley painted it red? He told the people 'red is dread'. Jamaica *was* dread around that time. I remember when we arrived at the airport, we were going to hire a car and the man was saying, 'Don't get a green or a red car, because if you drive the wrong colour car in the wrong part of town, you're a dead man.'

"Another time we went with Vivien Goldman to interview Peter Tosh who was a serious brethren, let's put it that way. All these photographers turned up and he told them they could only take one picture. 'Just one bloodclaat picture,' he said. He then made John and I sit in the car outside, in searing heat with no air conditioning. He said John was a pagan or something like that and 'heathen man can't come inside'."

Peter had heard reports about goings-on at the Sheraton, and must have enjoyed turning the screw on these wide-eyed foreigners who seemed so out of place in his own environment. "Peter was very tall and imposing and he always had his sunglasses on," says David Barham. "You could never really tell if he was joking or not. He always kept you a little off-centre and most times it would be a put-on although I did see where he was menacing for real on one or two occasions. That usually happened when he thought someone was trying to take advantage of him. Then he'd get extremely upset but acting menacing was a PR exercise for Peter. He knew he would get attention for that and he played it to the hilt."

As well as intimidating punk icons, Peter delighted in winding up local police officers, despite the obvious dangers. "One day Peter was driving down Three Miles, heading towards Spanish Town and he ran into a roadblock," recalls his cousin Carlton. "This policeman stopped him and asked to see his driving licence, saying his name is Inspector Roach. Peter asked if he was really called Inspector Roach, the man say yes and so Peter look him right in the eye and say, 'Stop right there. I'm going for my spray gun.' Inspector Roach gets real angry now, yelling, 'Get that man!' But another policeman say, 'Don't you know him? That's Peter Tosh and he's a real comedian.'"

After some deliberation, Peter agreed to perform at the One Love Peace Concert but first he'd appear at a three-day festival in Trelawny, hosted by his friends from My Father's Place. The Island Music Festival was a prelude to Reggae Sunsplash in that it was designed to bring people to Jamaica for a reggae music event. It was held at the White Sands Hotel from Friday February 24 and continued until the Sunday, with Peter Tosh as the headline act. Culture and Burning Spear topped the bill on the Friday, and Big Youth on the Saturday. Somewhat unusually, the festival was organised in conjunction with the Jamaican government, who recognised its usefulness in attracting tourism.

"That was the show where Woody and Keith saw Peter Tosh for the first time," says Eppy. "They went to Jamaica just to see Peter. Gregory had met with them but only had one thing on his mind, which was the white powder. That's when Woody told me their second choice was Peter Tosh, and could I introduce them? I called Peter and the conversation went like this... 'Peter, the Rolling Stones want to produce a record with you' and he said, 'I man don't need no Rolling Stone. I don't play rock'n'roll. I'm a reggae artist.' I couldn't believe he didn't know or care about the Rolling Stones. I mean how can you *not* know who the Rolling Stones are? Peter was smart, but he wasn't what you'd call educated."

Peter and Herbie Miller met with Rolling Stones Records' label manager Earl McGrath during February for informal discussions. Both parties seemed pleased with how it went and so Keith and Woody decided they'd attend Eppy's festival, where they could speak with Peter and see him perform.

"We had horrible, horrible weather over that weekend," says Eppy. "It was the most ridiculous thing I ever did in my whole life. The road was out and people couldn't get to it from Kingston. How it came about, there was a place called Chela Bay in Boscobel owned by two rich people from Atlanta. I guess they were ganja smugglers but they'd bought this bed and breakfast place right next to the Playboy Hotel. It was a hotel for young rich kids who smoked pot. There were only 30 rooms but it had a pool and little piece of beach. They turned their restaurant into a venue called the Roots Club and they'd invite bands to come and play. I saw the Mighty

Diamonds there and fell in love with the whole thing. That was around 1974, then on my second trip to Chela Bay I came up with the idea of doing a staff and friends' all-inclusive trip to Jamaica. This friend Ronnie Wagner, who everyone called Jumbo Jet, owned a travel agency and had been taking people down to Jamaica for three years. He'd organise a trip for himself and a bunch of people every winter. We'd all just get crazy. We'd get naked and smoke dope, but then I suggested we should put on a reggae festival in Jamaica. We decided to call it the Island Music Concert and hold it in Trelawny, which is close to Montego Bay and had none of the negativity associated with Kingston. The logo was this lion's head and a microphone, and the T-shirts went down better than the concert!"

"Man, that was a show!" exclaims Carlton. "Peter lost all his instruments that day because here comes the wind and the rain, and the man was there singing even though the microphone was electrifying him. When he tried putting it next to his mouth he was getting shocked and after they finished the show, Keith Sterling's keyboards were damaged and most of the other instruments didn't work properly again either. All these people were stood in the rain, holding umbrellas as the lightning and thunder broke out. Peter wasn't bothered by any of that. It's like it inspired him and gave him a powerful vibe. All of the musicians wanted to leave but Peter stand firm and give it everything man!"

It was one hell of an audition, and judging by the grins on the faces of Keith Richards and Ronnie Wood, he'd passed with flying colours. The day after the show, he met with Peter Simon in the hotel restaurant. Simon's photographs had illustrated Stephen Davis' recent book, *Reggae Bloodlines*, and he was known to be a major reggae fan. Peter was in reasonably good spirits, despite having to wait so long for some fresh goat's milk he'd ordered from a nearby farm. After some prompting, he admits to having met with Rolling Stones representatives, and confirms they'd discussed a record deal, and even prospective tour dates with the Stones.

Peter told Simon that whilst he's happy to work with Bunny – who'd planned to join him on stage in Trelawny, but didn't make it because of bad road conditions – he had no intention of working with Bob. Rumours that the three of them were planning a reunion in support of the peace treaty are clearly unfounded. Choosing to stay on safe ground, Simon remarks how there's a lot more social and political content in Peter's music than in Bob Marley's latest songs.

"Well, it has to be because I am he who went through grave tribulation," Peter snaps. "Bob Marley hasn't been through what I've been through. I've been totally humiliated and brutalised by the shit-stem…"

He goes on to suggest that Bob gets preferential treatment because he's light-skinned and then denies harbouring any resentment towards white people, since he "loves the man who loves himself". Somewhat optimistically, he predicts that marijuana will be legalised "within a couple of weeks" and announces that he's even written a song especially for the occasion, called 'Bush Doctor'. The only discordant note came after Peter said he hoped Rolling Stones Records weren't "going to be afraid of the music like Columbia was". Herbie Miller and Ozzie Brown quickly persuaded him from saying any more, and the moment passed. Warren Smith, who assisted with the promotion of the Island Music Festival, describes Miller as "very hands-on" and "a unique Jamaican. He was educated and confident. I would say that he was a better manager than anyone else out of Jamaica although it wasn't the usual artist/manager relationship. He and Peter weren't tight on a personal level. It was more of a business relationship for them, because Peter never let him get too close. Herbie loved jazz and was well versed in black history but he never got involved with the production."

"Herbie Miller was one of these guys I could never figure out," counters Eppy. "He had this colonial Jamaican mentality, and acted as if he was above everyone else. I guess he felt like he had to compensate or something. Herbie would come into my room, pick out like 50 jazz records and ask if he could have them – the implication being that if I wanted to book Peter in future, then I'd better hand them over. He was always putting himself on a high horse, like he was aristocracy or something, yet the Stones had wanted to sign Peter anyway and Herbie had nothing whatsoever to do with it, because Keith and Ronnie were behind the whole thing."

Despite Keith and Ronnie's enthusiasm, there could be no final decision without Mick Jagger's approval and since Peter was due to perform at the One Love Peace Concert in a few weeks' time, Jagger arranged to attend. There was now a sense of renewed urgency in the camp. Fresh possibilities lay ahead, which is maybe why rehearsals featured a few new faces. Male vocal trio the Tamlins were recruited to sing harmonies; Uziah "Sticky" Thompson played percussion whilst Keith Sterling and Robbie Lyn doubled up on keyboards – Keith having taken over from Tarzan on piano, and Robbie playing organ and synthesizer. Guitarist Mikey Chung had filled in for Al Anderson at the Trelawny show and he'll keep his place in the band, despite Al's return. Mikey will also back Jacob Miller at the Peace Concert before joining Peter on a permanent basis. He and his brother Geoffrey were well-respected Kingston session players, and Geoffrey was also a talented producer/recording engineer. They and Robbie Lyn had played in Now Generation – a band renowned for its sophisticated arrangements and that had backed Peter on the Joe Gibbs hits 'Maga Dog' and 'Them Haffi Get A Beaten'.

"I'd just left the In Crowd," says Robbie Lyn. "I was just at home, freelancing around the studios and Herbie Miller lived pretty near to me. We never really spoke a lot but we knew each other casually and then one day he just turned up at my gate and asked if I'd be interested in playing with Peter Tosh. I had no problems with that because I'd backed him before on a few shows.

"He wasn't really touring when I'd first worked with him. He'd just been doing one or two shows in Bermuda and different places in Jamaica, like Montego Bay. I remember a trip to Trinidad that was a total fiasco because the police were determined to frame him, from even before we got there. As soon as we arrived we saw newspaper headlines about how the Police Commissioner was going to get Peter, because he was so outspoken about ganja. We checked into the hotel, which was this little, off-road place and some guys who lived nearby were telling us that the police had been surveying the area and there'd been plainclothes people hanging around there too. The night before we left the police came to the hotel at four o'clock in the morning and next thing we knew, one of the roadies and Peter had been taken to jail because the police had found this and that, but it had all been organised beforehand. Peter only had a few herb seeds on him but by the time he went to court, the police had come up with a whole big bag of evidence..."

Robbie had played with Peter in Trelawny and if he'd been at all worried when Tosh pulled out his ganja pipe during 'Legalise It' then he didn't show it. He knew to always expect the unexpected when Peter was around, but even he was surprised when Lee Perry and Bob Marley called round and asked if he was free to play on a session. He recorded two songs with them that day, 'Blackman Redemption' and 'Rastaman Live Up'. Bob was currently riding high on the UK album charts with *Kaya*, and attended a private showing of Theo Bafaloukos' new film *Rockers* that same

191

evening – a ghetto take on Robin Hood with a large cast of local reggae stars, including Robbie Shakespeare.

Next day it was the Peace Concert, and the streets outside the National Stadium still teemed with people long after the festivities began. Island press officer Charlie Comer accompanied Mick Jagger to the show. He'd first met the Wailers in 1973 and liked Peter a lot. He enjoyed Peter's sense of humour, and how he played around with language. More importantly, he respected how Peter *always* spoke the truth. Charlie and Mick were stood at the side of the stage and so had a ringside view of Peter's performance. It was the first time Jagger had seen him in action, and he was impressed. Since this was a Peace Concert and designed to quell political rivalries, the leaders of both parties attended. Prime Minister Michael Manley was sat in the second row to the right of the stage, whilst Opposition leader Edward Seaga was in the same row, but way down to the left. Both kept poker faces and didn't give anything away. Many doubted the peace treaty would last and the atmosphere was strained in the backstage areas, as police, army, gang leaders and musicians congregated uneasily. "It was like being in a war zone," said Family Man. It would be Marley's first performance in Jamaica since the assassination attempt of 16 months earlier, and tensions were running high. Inside the stadium it was a different story as 20,000 people cheered and danced to the sounds of Dennis Brown, Big Youth, Culture, Althea & Donna, Dillinger, U Roy and the Mighty Diamonds, but it was Jacob Miller who provided the earliest star turn. Halfway through his act, he invited rival gang leaders to join him on stage and a couple of minutes later they shuffled into view, looking awkward for once. No matter how reluctant it was a display of unity, and the Concert gained momentum from there. Cheekily, Jacob seized a policeman's helmet whilst singing his latest hit, 'Peace Treaty Special'. He even brandished a spliff at one point, whilst racing around in his battered old "water boots" – his roly-poly belly bouncing off the top of his khaki shorts.

"Jacob Miller had everybody laughing. He was the funniest thing they ever see," recalls Al Anderson. "The One Love Peace Concert was all about him and Peter, because Peter Tosh came and *destroyed* it."

First came the cleanser. A brooding 'Igziabeher' and then '400 Years', with Peter decrying the "same old imperialistic, colonial mentality". He's addressing the politicians sat in front of him, and you can see and hear the sap rising in his voice. During the intro to 'Burial' he can resist no longer.

"Four hundred years and the same plantation business," he announces. "Black inferiority and white brown superiority rule this little black country for a long time." Each syllable is spat out with disgust, as if the subject's distasteful to him. The crowd are excited now; Peter's in defiant mood and the band's on fire, driven by Sly and Robbie's livewire rhythms. After warning that "peace is the diploma you get in the cemetery", he calls for black people to cast Lucifer "into utter darkness and bring love and justice to black people once more.

"Because learn this, white men teach us that we must die to go to heaven. Why?" he asks. "So they can come to Jamaica and take away everything... and inherit the bloodclaat earth. And we are gone to where? To heaven, gone to drink milk and honey. 'Cause we are what? Fools."

You can hear voices shouting – not at Peter, but in support of his comments. His anger is stirring up sections of the crowd, and their reaction is energising him. He tells of Jamaica's past, and how Columbus came with a cross round his neck "to trick black people".

"Look how bloodclaat long we are here waiting for Jesus," he roars. "All the war in the earth and Jesus can't do a thing about it... It's you and I have to come together with love. Heartical love and respect for each other. Because them little fuckery there (is) done with. And learn this now. We can't make the little pirates come here and rob up the resources of the country and have poor people here box shit out of hog's mouth. Them things there have to stop."

Peter has now crossed the line between performance and politics. He's delivering the most incendiary speech in reggae history, and yet he's banned the camera team from filming him. "Talking about pirates... You have some little pirates now who just come from America with their cameras and their TV business to go and do what?" he asks. "Get rich off a you and I...

"Hey you! Just turn off those things, do you hear me?" he yells. "Just go somewhere else with it. Leave here with it." The lights are blinding him, and he wants to see who he's talking to. Once his vision's restored, he lashes out at the colonial mentality that still rules Jamaica, and reminds the gathering how there's nothing to buy in the shops, not even basic amenities like oil and soap. After addressing Michael Manley "personally" and as someone he regards as "a friend", Peter unleashes another key issue that's bothering him. He wants the two leaders to legalise herb and let it play a role in strengthening the Jamaican economy, since there are "thousands of acres of land lay idle out there where we could plant herb". Instead, herb smokers are branded criminals and face persecution, despite most of them – and especially Rastafarians – being law-abiding citizens. Peter says he's never resorted to theft or crime, even though having "been through the lowest degradation of humiliation, incrimination and brutality". After noting how Jamaica's jails are full of sufferers, he says the system is "laid down to belittle the poor" and orders the government to end police brutality, which must have gone down a treat with the scores of police in and outside of the stadium. He then dedicates the next song "to those who get humiliated for a draw of herb", which is the cue for the band to start playing 'Legalise It' and for him to light his spliff.

It's one of those classic rock'n'roll moments, except Peter isn't being filmed of course. We don't get to see if there's a smile flickering at the corners of his mouth, or he's wearing a mask of grim determination as he picks up his guitar and delivers another withering burst of wah wah. The rest of the band lay out whilst he and Sly improvise in tandem. The rhythm's getting faster and more insistent now. It's a warrior's heartbeat, which then erupts into a magnificent, 10-minute version of 'Get Up Stand Up'. "Preacher man don't tell me bullshit," snarls Peter, who brings his heart-stopping performance to an end by ad-libbing lines like "we ain't gonna bow to no imperialism". What a dramatic finale.

"The historic Peace Concert. You'll never forget this one," predicts the MC, who calls Peter "the son of reggae". The only thing remaining was for Bob to steal all the plaudits by bringing Manley and Seaga up on stage, joining their hands above his head as he chants, "Jah, Rastafari". It was riveting, and yet Peter had also left an indelible mark on the day's events.

"Bob smoked a chalice before he took the stage and he was red," says Al Anderson. "You can hear it in his voice. The only thing he did was join the politicians' hands and it looked great. Anybody who could get Manley and Seaga up on stage like that was a star and Bob took all the headlines for it but he never really performed. Peter and Jacob Miller, they *wrecked* the place!

"Robbie and I were looking at each other when Peter made that speech. We expected Seaga's boys to rush the stage, y' know? We just thought to ourselves, 'Oh no, here goes the boss,' but then we start laughing because Peter was so comical with it. Listen to the crowd's response; the man was Richard Pryor man! He was funny and direct; he spoke like a leader. He spoke to the politicians and he spoke to the people. That's the man!"

"The politicians who were at that show, they just had to sit there and take it because what could they do?" asks singer Pam Hall. "He only said those things as a result of them breaking promises, so although it was seen as him being disrespectful, that's what a lot of us had been thinking. He was talking the truth and we could all recognise that, but most of us would have never dared do that. That's what made him so powerful, y' know? Him nah ease up man!"

"Peter's performance, according to almost everyone who was there, dwarfed Bob's," says Roger Steffens. "Facing an audience lined with army personnel, police, government officials and 200 international journalists, Tosh lashed out at the political leaders about racism, classism, police brutality and economic policies as the citizenry cheered him on. This was a public confrontation with authority in which Peter left no doubt about where he stood and his belief that the police were doing the work of the devil in his country."

"The truth has been branded outlawed and illegal," Peter told the crowd. "It is dangerous to have the truth in your possession. You can be found guilty and sentenced to death. I've been found guilty many times for having the truth in my possession. Condemned by the devil and sentenced to eternal judgment in Hell among his people."

He'll later tell a radio presenter in Boston "The reason why I had to do that, I found myself doing spiritual work in the midst of corruption because this peace business was just a lot of destruction to kill more people. More people die since the peace treaty was signed until now. I did not intend to come there, but it was for the people's benefit, because that's what was told to me; that the concert will be beneficial to the poor people in the ghetto, seen? I made a speech because there was the Minister For Opposition and the Prime Minister and members of Parliament so that was the right time to say what I did as a representative of the people, 'cause irrespective of what men want to see, I live within the shit-stem. I've become a victim of the shit-stem too many times and I've been brutalised by the police; not because I am a criminal or I'm doing subversive things within society, but because they know I speak the truth and the truth is destructive to the functioning of corruption, seen? And they don't like that, but what else can I do? Jah say after all these humiliations, there will be honour, power and majesty, so when I get those things from the Almighty who create thunder, lightning and make the earth quake, I want to see the man who will stop me from doing my Father's work."

195

Beres Hammond had been on stage earlier, singing his number one hit 'One Step Ahead'. As Peter launched into his speech, Beres wondered how it was all going to end. "You didn't know whether there was going to be a stampede or what when Peter was on stage, and because of the words coming out of his mouth. Fireworks man! After he left, you could almost cut the tension in the air, it was so thick, but it cooled after a while and then Bob came on stage, got some politicians to hold hands and that just sealed it off. But everybody was talking about Peter's performance after the show, because it was really on the edge."

"It was scary being a white person out in that crowd, let me tell you," remembers Elizabeth Barraclough. "When Peter started into his speech, it really began to rouse people. If it hadn't have been for a few older women standing nearby, I dread to think what may have happened. It was very frightening. It was one of those moments in your life that you never forget. I remember thinking, 'Whatever happened to peace and one love?'"

If Peter had been hoping for an insurrection it didn't happen. The audience had gone there for the music and to enjoy themselves, and Jamaica's downtrodden couldn't have afforded tickets in any case. There's scant footage of Peter in action that night, for reasons explained earlier. He'd ordered the cameras to be turned off as he gave one of the most memorable concerts of his career. That's typical of the man. He'd been astute enough to protect his rights, but failed to ensure that his message would reach a greater number of people. Ashante Infantry, writing in *The Toronto Star*, described Peter's appearance at the One Love Peace Concert as the "most impassioned of his career" before pointing out that because of legal wrangling, audio recordings won't become available until 2000 "and this diminished his legacy".

Filmmaker Theo Bafaloukos is more sympathetic, and asks the question, "When Peter Tosh made some remarks about foreigners entering the island posing as tourists and filming everything in sight to take back to America and other places to sell for big dollars, why did the people in Jamaica not see the truth and logic of his reasoning? Instead they try to label Peter as insane and to make the world believe that he was angry at Bob for Marley's so-called success."

"Peter Tosh had a lot of wisdom and common sense," adds Ras Cardo. "They could not fool him in any way and steal his materials. Many did not like him for this. He was just too smart for them to handle."

"Peter was very strong," agrees film director Howard Johnson. "His character was flawed but powerful. He must have been so paranoid after he made that speech at the Peace Concert because he'd made some powerful enemies and they were out to kill him. He'd done the most heroic thing we'd ever seen from any singer or musician in Jamaica. To say what he did, and with the country's leaders sat there and listening, that was a death sentence. I remember thinking, 'My God, he's a dead man.' He should have left the island, because it was obvious they were going to try and kill him."

Charlie Comer had feared for Mick Jagger's safety at one point, but Jagger wasn't at all concerned. Peter was the real deal, a charismatic outlaw type who wasn't afraid to stand up for what he believed in. He was dangerous, outspoken, controversial and talented. He was also the perfect fit for the Stones' label. The authenticity that Jagger craved and occasionally mocked surged through Peter Tosh like an electric current, and Mick liked him as a character as well. He had a good sense of humour, wasn't at all overawed by the Stones and had a fantastic set of musicians. Signing him wasn't even an option, but a *necessity*.

In an interview conducted shortly after the Peace Concert, Peter spoke admiringly of Keith Richards who he says, "really loves and respects the music. The Rolling Stones are completely different (from other labels.) They're musicians," he points out. "They've been playing for the same time as me and they've also shared many of the same problems – especially police victimisation. I know they have feelings inside of them for our music."

Whilst respecting this viewpoint, Earl McGrath adds further insight into how Peter ended up on Rolling Stones Records. "I had a friend at Columbia (Mike Pilot) who said they were pushing Peter off the label because certain people didn't like him so I said Peter should come and see me because I would like to speak to him and his management. They came over and he said he'd like to make records with us, I went down to Jamaica with Mick and we signed him up, but the reason I signed Peter was because Keith was in a bad state. He wasn't interested in anything and I thought if we can get Peter's thing up and running, then he'd get interested because he was such a big reggae fan and that's just what happened. Keith got involved and felt stimulated by it, and it was something he and Mick could share. Peter Tosh helped keep the Rolling Stones together at that time, frankly."

Back in early 1977, Keith had been busted for possession of heroin in Toronto and was in danger of serving a lengthy jail sentence – a possibility made more likely every time he missed a court date. He was due to face trial in October and to say everyone in the Stones' camp was worried is an understatement. They'd launched their own label as long ago as 1970 after signing a distribution deal with Atlantic. "We want to release the odd blues record and Charlie Watts wants to do some jazz," said Jagger at the time. "What we're not interested in is bubble gum music."

Jimi Hendrix was their primary target back then but such ambitions soon fell by the wayside. After rancorous disputes with their management, they were forced to become tax exiles. The Stones were in financial difficulties until January 1977, when EMI paid them a million dollar advance and promised to back independent productions. Neither party could have wished for a better start. The Stones' latest album, *Some Girls*, will become the band's all-time bestseller and no sooner had Keith's sentence been announced – he was told to play a free show for the Canadian Institute Of The Blind – than news of a US tour swiftly followed. Against the wishes of Atlantic's chief executive Ahmet Ertegun, Peter was offered a support slot once the tour started in June.

First he'd need to recruit a new guitarist because Al Anderson had just jumped ship and rejoined Bob in readiness for a forthcoming US tour, scheduled to begin in less than two weeks' time.

"Peter Tosh was great," he said, "but by then he'd got a manager named Herbie Miller. Peter was in a bad position financially after he'd left the Wailers and because he was wanting to go out on his own as a solo artist, he needed money to record and so went to Herbie Miller, who had this reputation as a bad guy. You don't borrow money from somebody like that and then make him your manager. Herbie Miller became powerful when he started working with Peter, so he decided to crush all of us little people who Peter felt close to. The Rolling Stones weren't exactly the greatest people to be around either, since they had their problems too. I mean Keith and Mick don't get along at times and I really didn't want to be around that, so I just backed out. Bob asked me if I was happy working with Peter or did I want to come back into the band and I told him yes. I was looking forward to playing with him again."

On May 6, an announcement was made to the press. "Fellow Jamaican artist and former member of the Wailers, Peter Tosh, has signed with Rolling Stones Records in America. Tosh, originally with CBS (and Virgin in Britain) is widely rumoured to be touring with the Rolling Stones in the near future."

It transpires that Bill Wyman had wanted to sign Eddy Grant instead of Peter, but Mick and Keith overruled him. He and the rest of the Stones had been listening to Jamaican music for years. Charlie Watts' brother-in-law used to keep him supplied with all the latest "Blue Beat" records back in the early sixties whilst Mick and Bianca had hired a reggae band to play at their wedding. That was in 1970. Two years later and Keith was driving them all mad by playing tapes of *The Harder They Come* on the tour bus every night. That was around the time they recorded *Goats Head Soup* in Kingston, back in 1972.

"Jamaica, the music island!" Keith once exclaimed. "Jamaica's a wonderful place, kind of free and easy. I'd been there on and off in the sixties, but only for a visit. After *Goats Head Soup* I've lived there whenever I can. I have family there – villagers welcome me with open arms. They like music and they like musicians and as long as you don't get your head chopped off with a machete, you're all right! I think there's a certain power of influence that comes up from the roots in Jamaica. It kept me there – I didn't leave."

The Stones' party had stayed at the Terra Nova whilst recording *Goat's Head Soup*. Keith's next stop had been a rented villa called Casa Joya, overlooking Mammee Bay. He then bought Point Of View from UK singer Tommy Steele – a house near Steer Town on Jamaica's north coast that had orchards, an Olympic grade swimming pool and large courtyard. From then on, it won't be hard to spot the reggae influence in the Stones' music, whether they're covering Eric Donaldson's 'Cherry Oh Baby' or writing originals like 'Hey Negrita', which has an obvious reggae feel and came from Ronnie Wood's love of the genre.

"All of us, independently and together, were into reggae," Ronnie wrote in his autobiography. "It was also a mood of the time. I listened to quite a bit with Eric Clapton – I used to hang out with him in that period. In the 1970s Keith and I would go to the clubs and we'd take along our own reggae music. For instance, we'd go up to the DJ and ask him to put our music on so that everyone would be dancing to Toots & the Maytals or something. We would do that at every club and get our favourite music played, and we'd be rocking. It was like having a massive party everywhere we went in the world – New York, London, Germany and all across Europe."

Chapter 17

Bush Doctor

Once he'd signed on the dotted line, Peter booked sessions at Dynamic in early May. That's where the majority of his next album was recorded, and it'll take reggae music to another level. The arrival of Geoffrey Chung, his brother Mikey and Robbie Lyn had given the band a different feel and outlook. It was now tighter, better organised and even more creative.

"That's when the Peter Touch sound expanded so much more," says Sly Dunbar. "Myself, Robbie, Mikey and Peter would be in the studio together, playing music and working out songs. We were trying to take Peter in the direction we thought Jamaican music should be headed. That meant taking him into the American market place and making an album that could be played alongside those by Stevie Wonder, Earth, Wind & Fire or Curtis Mayfield... Geoffrey Chung was a great musician himself. He understood where we were trying to go, and he played a very important part in getting that sound down on tape. That's the main reason why we went to Dynamic, because Geoffrey was there and he brought a more international sound to reggae."

"Peter was searching for his identity at the time and so Mikey Chung was given the role of innovating certain elements within his music," confirms Robbie Lyn, who played piano, organ, Fender Rhodes and clavinet at those sessions. "That gave Peter's music a slightly different sound, and it came from listening to music from all different sources."

"I was attending the Jamaica School Of Music at the time, studying composition and we were always buying and listening to records," says

Mikey. "We wanted to open our minds to what was new so we listened to *everything*. Geoffrey, even more than I, had a real liking for rock music and that's how we got to hear Jimi Hendrix, Santana and a lot of those seventies groups. Being a musician, you want to compete at the same level as them. You don't want to just sit there and think, 'Oh well, this is Jamaica and so we'll just play our normal kind of rhythm.' We'd listen to singers like Aretha Franklin and Donny Hathaway and take note of who was playing on the records. That's how we came to know of Eric Gale, Cornell Dupree, Chuck Rainey and Richard Tee. We knew those people and had studied how they got a particular sound. Geoffrey and I had been to America, and we knew how things worked."

The album they laid at Dynamic would be called *Bush Doctor* after a new song Peter had written. Jamaica was still buzzing after his performance at the Peace Concert, and that fiery speech calling for an end to ganja laws. *Bush Doctor* isn't another call-to-arms like *Legalise It*, but celebrates herb being legalised with such certainty, you'd swear Manley had agreed to it already. Peter appoints himself Minister For Herb and announces an end to police brutality and "disrespect for humanity".

"There'll be no need to smoke and hide when you're taking a legal ride," he promises, over an insidious reggae groove that manages to sound busy and laid-back at the very same time. The job description of "Bush Doctor" is two-fold incidentally, because he's also a healer.

"You have two kinds of doctor," he told Bruno Blum. "You have a bush doctor and a drugs doctor. The drugs doctor is the one from the hospital, who give you injection and insulin and all them kind of things they put inside of you. He gets the natural ingredient then laces it with chemicals and drugs to make it defective so that he can achieve some more money. You're a patient and that drugs doctor's asking you what's wrong, but a bush doctor doesn't do that. He knows what's wrong, seen? So that's the difference. A bush doctor makes all his medicines from bush, seen? I have some medicine that's made from herb; one spoonful and it'll cure any kind of bronchial infection. Yes I. It can cure asthma, bronchitis or any form. It's pure herbal extract, undiluted, with no water, seen? The water come from the herb and then you mix it with honey."

His argument's now a familiar one. Herb has many useful and healing properties, whereas cigarettes are addictive and sold openly. It's hard to imagine any Rolling Stones-affiliated release opening with a health warning, read from a cigarette packet, but *Bush Doctor* does. "Warning. The Surgeon General warns that cigarette smoking is dangerous, hazardous to your health. Does that mean anything to you?" Peter asks. (I think we can rest assured he didn't care that most foreign reggae fans mixed their herb with tobacco, and couldn't afford to smoke it "ital".)

He relishes the role of educator, offering wise counsel to the masses. It's this single-minded determination to spread the truth which some take for arrogance, and occasionally for good reason. 'Moses – The Prophet' is a history lesson. It isn't just a tribute to Marcus Garvey, Jamaica's first national hero, but other prominent ancients. "Do you remember Moses? The man nah dead..." Peter's list includes names like Elijah, Jeremiah, Marcus (Garvey) and even Satan. The production's first-rate, although that beautiful flute will be added later.

'Stand Firm' will resonate with a generation of Jamaicans raised by God-fearing Christian families (not unlike Peter's own) who've turned their backs on the church and searched for spiritual fulfilment in Rastafari or elsewhere. "Jacket and tie come tell me say. If you want to be saved son, you've got to go in your grave son. Well that is bullshit I say," sings Peter, confident in the knowledge that he's just shocked most of Jamaica. The phrase "jacket and tie" is shorthand for authority of course, and he shows no mercy to the clergy either. He calls the priest taking confession "another pirate" and declares the necessity of loving Jesus Christ as "fantasy. A whole pack of ignorancy I say. All you've got to do is live clean, and let your works be seen."

'Pick Myself Up' was recorded at Joe Gibbs, and the birdsong on the intro isn't the only clue to a well-loved hobby. "Sitting in the morning sun and watching all the birds passing by. Oh how sweet they sing and oh how much I wish I could fly..."

Peter claimed he wrote it for Rastafarian brethren who "reach a little way down the road and find out there is a lot of tribulation, so they get weak and stumble by the wayside". He's speaking for people wondering where their next meal's coming from, and offering hope to the downtrodden. The message is simple – don't give up hope. More than 30 years later, in his inauguration speech, Barack Obama will tell Americans "We've got to pick ourselves up, and start all over again..." ("I knew that I'd heard those words before!" Sly would exclaim.)

"Peter would come up with songs very, very quick," says Robbie Shakespeare. "He'd come up with them just like that. You could give him a topic and he'd finish a song off in no time. He might come into the studio with just half a song and from when we find the rhythm, he's ready..."

"Peter would often turn up with very little worked out," Mikey Chung concurs. "He was a great believer in spontaneity and that's how the magic came, because he wrote most of those hit songs in the studio and then voiced them straightaway. A lot of those vocals were done on the first take. Sometimes I saw him sing the lyrics perfectly and if the engineer didn't get it, then Peter would refuse to do it again. That's because he knew that he'd get nowhere near it, no matter how many times he tried, and you'd really have to work to get him to do it again. That's why he liked working with Karl Pitterson because when Karl was at the board, he was always recording. Sometimes you'd say, 'OK, ready,' and he'd say, 'Ready? We've finished that already!' He'd seen the magic happen and captured it before you'd even noticed and Geoffrey was very much like that as well. Something invariably happens on the first take that you can't get again. Nobody knows why it should be like that but that's what often happens. The magic comes and it's a powerful thing. Well Peter really believed in all that."

As usual, he chose to update some older material, and there'll be three such tracks on his new album. 'Soon Come' is now in a different league from the Beverley's version. Jimmy Norman's lyrics still fit Peter like a glove, although he won't get credited on the album or 2002 reissue. There's no mistaking who wrote 'The Toughest' though. This was Peter's first signature tune, recorded with the Wailers at Studio One, and it's a great choice. Sly's playing a Pocomania-style rhythm he'll adopt for Black Uhuru's 'Youths Of Eglington', and there was a different sax break on it originally. An instrumental cut of this rhythm – called 'Tough Rock Soft Stones' and featuring duelling saxophones – will later surface as a bonus track although the title will prove disingenuous, since none of the Rolling Stones are on it.

'Them Haffi Get A Beaten' is the other reconstruction, and Joe Gibbs wouldn't recognise it with its unhurried, yet soulful vocals. "Tell me how long the good has to suffer for the bad," Peter demands, with just a slight trace of weariness. Best of the outtakes is 'Lesson In My Life', which he'll re-record another time. After a harmonica fanfare, he intones the kind of lyrics that have biographers' pulses racing. "I've learnt a lesson in my life," he drawls, before warning "always be careful of mankind. They make promises today, but tomorrow change their mind... Always be careful of your friends. Money can make friendship end. For a single pound, they will carry you down."

Leaving prophecy aside, and despite the verses bearing the bitter taste of experience, the hook's full of optimism. Peter is stating that he's a progressive, truthful, genuine and determined person, who loves people with the same outlook. Critics will accuse him of being holier than thou, yet this almost qualifies as a confessional where Peter Tosh is concerned. Midway through the sessions, Mick Jagger and Earl McGrath arrived to see how their new signing was getting on, but Peter clearly didn't need company.

"When Mick and I were in Jamaica and they were recording *Bush Doctor*, Peter Tosh completely ignored both of us," says Earl. "Mick said he was going to join in because this song 'Get Up Stand Up' was playing and when he started to sing, 'Get up, stand up. Stand up for the whites' everyone laughed except Peter Tosh!"

Peter's focus was on work, not accommodating rock stars, even if they were paying the bills. The new album represented his biggest challenge and he had a lot to do before June 10, which is when the Stones' tour was due to start. It was Earl McGrath's idea for them to rehearse at Bearsville in upstate New York, where they'll have some privacy and yet still be within relatively easy reach of Manhattan. In-between rehearsals, Peter can finish his album there and prepare for life in the spotlight. He's about to discover that being around the world's biggest rock band is like joining a circus, since there's always some controversy doing the rounds, whether about drugs, fallings-out, court cases or marital problems. A few days after Mick Jagger arrived at Bearsville with Texan model Jerry Hall on his arm, lawyers acting on behalf of his wife served him with divorce papers. Bianca Jagger was filing on the grounds of irreconcilable differences, just two days after their seventh wedding anniversary. Her attorney will claim a $12.5 million settlement plus $13,400 a month living allowance. Earlier in 1978, a Los Angeles court had ordered Jagger to pay $1,500 a month for the upkeep of his nine-year old daughter, Karis, with Marsha Hunt. Another old flame of Mick's, model Chrissie Shrimpton, had threatened to publish love letters in the *News Of The World* before being persuaded to back down. Keith Richards meanwhile, was still officially living with Anita Pallenberg but had started a relationship with Swedish model Lilly Wenglass Green. He was going through a heroin cure involving electro-acupuncture, which helped bring relief from withdrawal symptoms. Eric Clapton had used it when coming off heroin, but the treatment was by no means infallible. The Stones had also invited censor by making a disco record – 'Miss You' having been released on May 19 – and whilst it'll immediately strike a chord with club-goers, many of the band's rock fans weren't so sure.

Peter and his entourage will arrive on May 27 and stay until June 8. He'd been there before – with Lee Jaffe, to discuss a possible deal with Albert Grossman – and knew his way around to a certain extent, although he'd barely leave the studio complex for the majority of his stay. Albert owned at least around 30 acres of land in and around Bearsville as well as several houses, two studios and a restaurant. The principal studio was on Speare Road, which was the main road through town. There were two studios in fact, A and B, although the largest one wasn't operational at the time, except for rehearsals. Most people rehearsed in the barn at Turtle Creek, which had a better ambience. Turtle Creek had a big house next to it and there were also three or four others in the immediate vicinity where band members could stay. In addition there was an apartment above Studio A, which is where Mick and Jerry Hall stayed.

Back in 1978, regular visitors included Todd Rundgren, Foghat, Paul Butterfield, Bobby Charles and Elizabeth Barraclough, whose debut album would be released in June. Elizabeth was living with Albert and Sally Grossman at the time, and had witnessed Peter's riotous performance at the One Love Peace Concert in Kingston. She'd feared for her safety that day and had no interest in searching him out, or the Rolling Stones for that matter.

"Albert had this big black dog called Skipper that had killed another dog and was the subject of a court order," she recalls. "It hadn't been off the chain in seven or eight years but I'd started taking him on walks that summer. Skipper and I emerged from the woods right next to the studio and this security car came racing up; two big, burly guards leapt out and started yelling questions at me. Skipper jumped on the car and they just rolled up the windows so damned quick! They demanded to know who I was but I said, 'No, who are you?' They said they were security and I said, 'Hell no. *He's* security.'"

Peter's entourage included percussionist Larry McDonald, who'd been a mentor of Herbie's for many years. Larry says Peter "liked the way I constructed my combustibles", which is some compliment. Donald Kinsey had now replaced Al Anderson and as he entered the grounds he saw Mick exercising in the yard and Keith stood under a tree, playing his acoustic guitar but with pulse monitors attached to each of his arms. "Man, I got to stay on top of the beat," Keith informed him, neglecting to mention they were part of his heroin cure.

John Holbrook remembers that the Stones started off rehearsing at Turtle Creek, but then found it wasn't big enough and so relocated to Studio A. "The Stones got themselves situated there and then Peter Tosh arrived and set himself up in Studio B," he says. "That was the only functional studio at that point. It was just the band and myself and my two assistants at first. Mick and Keith would wander in and out. Theoretically they were producing the project but they weren't all that engaged with it. They'd just stick their head round the door and say, 'All right lads?' We'd say, 'Fine,' and that was it. It was Sly & Robbie who did most of the hard work. They really took the reins and were the most hands-on. Peter would just be sat at the back of the control room, barely visible in this huge cloud of smoke. He'd be puffing away on these gigantic spliffs all day long, and then occasionally I'd hear these deep rumblings coming from where he was sat."

"The whole reggae aesthetic was a little bit foreign to us, meaning the Woodstock crew, to be honest with you. The band came that first day and kept wanting to hear more bass. We had these big, professional Westlake monitors but they kept saying there wasn't enough bass. We were wondering what to do and then someone suggested we use speakers from a PA system so we got these massive speakers that had sub-bass and managed to get them in front of the console, between the board and front window. It pumped out massive amounts of bass and Peter and his musicians started to feel a bit more comfortable after that. The actual bass tone was very important to them. Robbie Shakespeare would have the settings on his bass and amplifier turned up full and then we'd be listening in the control room to even more bass! It was a great learning experience for me and it was fascinating to see how all the polyrhythmic elements fitted together.

"The weird thing is, I don't recall Peter ever getting on the mike and singing anything else but the song he did with Mick. Maybe he did briefly but all I remember him doing was smoking huge amounts of pot. Sly and Robbie weren't like that. There was no messing about where they were concerned. They really were the best reggae musicians in the world at that point.

"The other thing I remember was that everyone spoke in patois and I'd get paranoid sometimes because I'd often be the only white guy in the room and I wouldn't understand a word they said! I'd just catch the occasional word like "bumbaclaat" and think, 'What the hell are they talking about?' I could never penetrate the patois. I still don't know what "bumbaclaat" means. You can see why Chris Blackwell had such a leg up on everyone else, because he was the only person who knew what they were talking about!"

It wasn't just the language John and other Bearsville regulars had problems with, but the culture. They weren't used to seeing people smoke such copious amounts of ganja in the name of religion, and they'd certainly never heard a gospel song like 'Creation' before which starts off with Peter intoning, "In the beginning was the word" amidst Biblical thunder and lightning. Waves crash against the shoreline and seabirds emit their mournful cries before he croons, "Jah is my keeper, so whom shall I fear?"

Peter originally called this track 'Night Sounds,' although 'Creation' suits it better. It's hymn-like, and rife with scriptural references lifted from the opening verse of St. John's gospel, the first line of Genesis, Revelation Chapter 19, verse 6 and even the Book of Psalms. In an interview with John Swenson he claims to have written it in his mother's yard, surrounded by the sounds of nature.

"I woke up in the morning and I went into the bushes where the birds were singing their song. It was about five thirty, six o'clock and I just taped the birds. Then I went down to the brook where the water was flowing down the hillside, and taped the sound of that. I went by the seaside and taped the sea flowing in on the edge of the shore and combined them together. That's how I created the idea called 'Creation', and it was very beautiful."

"He'd recorded those nature sounds on a cassette and that's all he had when he came into the studio," confirms Robbie Shakespeare. "This was whilst we were at Bearsville. We knew we had this song to finish but he wanted someone who could play harp on it. I remember they come bring him this little instrument they call an Autoharp and he was cussing like hell, asking if that was the only harp they could find and yet by the next morning, Peter came out and he was playing that little harp like a professional. He learnt it real quick."

Elizabeth Barraclough was originally asked to play Autoharp on 'Creation' but she suggested they contact folk singer Happy Traum, who lived locally and was a skilled instrumentalist. Happy claims that it was him and not Peter who played on 'Creation', although he wasn't credited. Weeks after the session, someone from Rolling Stones Records rang him to say that if they admitted he'd played on the album, it would prove they'd violated some government rule or other.

"The first thing I should mention was that there was a real buzz about the place," he recalls. "People had been saying the Rolling Stones were in town and how there'd been sightings of Mick and Keith, but nobody seemed to know for sure. Then suddenly there was all of this security around the studio. The two small dirt roads leading to Studio A were blocked off, which meant nobody could get up or down, and this caused quite a stir around town. We knew something was happening but even though I'd spent a lot of time at the studio, working on records and other stuff, I had no expectation of being invited up there to meet the Stones. Then I got a call from one of the engineers who said, 'Maybe you can help us, because there are some guys recording up here who want to recreate the sound of a harp.' He didn't know exactly what they wanted so I suggested they use an Autoharp. My daughter had one I'd bought her at a flea market. It was pretty out of tune and probably worth about 30 dollars but I said I'd take it up there personally because my ears had pricked up immediately once he'd said it was for Peter Tosh, and that Mick Jagger was producing the record.

"I walked into the studio and Peter was there with Robbie Shakespeare and a couple of other guys who were sat around smoking joints. There was an unbelievable amount of pot in the place but Peter and I sat down together, just the two of us, and I start teaching him how to hold it, press the buttons and strum but after about five minutes of that he said, 'No man. You play it.' We had to wait around for a while before they were ready to record, people kept handing me joints and before I knew it, my head was swimming and it felt like I'd entered another world! I still hadn't heard the song at this point. Finally they played the track, I'm listening to it and Peter Tosh is stood in the control room, watching me through the window whilst I'm strumming this thing, trying to find the right places to come in or the right chords... A few minutes later the track finished and they said, 'OK man, that was great. Thank you.' I said, 'Wait. I haven't done it yet,' but Peter said, 'No man, we have what we want.'

"I went back there a couple of times after that, got to see the Rolling Stones rehearse and witnessed a lot of what went on behind the scenes. There were a lot of drugs being consumed. It was pretty heavy although I never saw any of the reggae guys do any of that. They stuck to smoking their pot, whereas the Stones were definitely into other stuff. It was fascinating seeing that contrast between the reggae and rock'n'roll lifestyles."

One day Keith turned up in the studio flourishing a big bottle of pharmaceutical cocaine, prised off the lid and poured a great pile of it on the desk saying, 'This should keep you going.' John Holbrook, who'd never seen that much cocaine before, recalls that Peter and his crew weren't too impressed and in fact took a dim view of it. "Yet it was an amazing moment, seeing this mound of sparkling cocaine sitting there."

Keith plays lead on 'Bush Doctor' and 'Stand Firm'. His taut, bluesy contributions have been criticised and whilst they're not the best guitar licks on the album, his presence will at least command people's attention and boost sales. It'll be Mick Jagger's contribution that works best, and provides Peter with the biggest single of his career.

"Mick and Keith gave Peter a lot of freedom to do whatever he thought was necessary but we didn't go overboard with it," says Sly Dunbar. "There was no ego between any of us, nothing like that and so one day we were sat around, thinking of a song for Peter and Mick to do together. That's when someone mentioned 'Don't Look Back', because Peter had already done a version of it at Studio One. We all thought it was a good song to do and just went for it."

"Well I am the one who asked Mick to do a song with him," says Robbie Shakespeare. "I don't remember who suggested the song though."

Jagger told *Old Grey Whistle Test* presenter Jo Whiley that it was Peter's idea to do 'Don't Look Back', which makes sense as he'd often reworked songs from his own back catalogue. The Stones were keen Temptations' fans as well of course, and had recently covered another of the group's songs, 'Just My Imagination', on their latest album.

"I thought Peter and Mick's duet worked pretty good, even if it was more poppy than what most reggae fans were used to," remarks John Holbrook. "When they said Mick was going to come in and do his vocal, I remember setting up these two Harman 87 mikes side-by-side and then seeing Peter and Mick reacting to each other as they sang together live. That was really something. They were dancing around and joshing each other. All of that happened spontaneously and it was great. We did two or three takes but it was pretty much one take with just a couple of lines patched in here and there."

Peter starts things off; Jagger joins him for the chorus, and then takes the second verse. He's mugging his way through it, and he and Peter begin ad libbing even before the fade out. "How far you been walking?" asks Peter. "A hundred miles," retorts Jagger. "You still got far to walk man," admonishes Peter, who then admits to feeling tired, but says he'll still keep walking. Jagger typically has the last word. "I'm walking bare foot," he says. Would he have been that loose on a Rolling Stones recording? Maybe, and it's a great record anyway with its familiar melodies, loping rhythm and irresistible drum patterns.

The Stones would play old blues and rock'n'roll songs during rehearsals and there were jam sessions most evenings, although we're reliably informed that these rarely involved Peter or any of his band members. Sly and Robbie don't ever recall jamming with the Stones, although Donald Kinsey says they all had fun together, blending styles and influences. He also mentions that whilst Peter's style of playing was folk-orientated, he had a Delta roots feeling when playing the blues. One jam session that did take place happened at Jack DeJohnette's house. He lived nearby, and invited some of Peter's musicians over one day. Alas, this summit meeting between jazz and reggae masters was never recorded, but he wasn't the only one to be impressed by Sly Dunbar's drumming. On June 1, Charlie Watts and Ronnie Wood had taken the helicopter shuttle back to New York, where they celebrated Woody's birthday at the Plaza Hotel with John Lennon and Yoko Ono. Whilst they were in Manhattan, Charlie had some badges made up with "Sly Dunbar Fan Club" printed on them and took great delight in handing them out to people.

It'll be Robbie Shakespeare's turn to shine next, when he arranges additional horns and backing vocals for some of the tracks. These sessions took place at the Atlantic studios in New York, at the corner of Broadway and 60th Street, where Talking Heads and Chaka Khan had recently worked on bestselling albums. Luther Francois (soprano sax), Randy Brecker (trumpet), Lou Marini (tenor sax and flute) and Barry Rogers (trombone) were brought in for the occasion, and this same horn section will later overdub tracks that Word, Sound & Power record with Manu Dibango in Jamaica. Following Marley's example, Peter also decided to recruit some female backing singers, and beamed with satisfaction after Gwen Guthrie, Yvonne Lewis and Brenda White showed what they could do. The 27-year-old Guthrie had sung backing vocals for Aretha Franklin and Cameo, in addition to penning hits for Ben E. King and Sister Sledge.

"There was this woman in New York whose husband used to be a jazz drummer and she was the one who got the girls together for us," says Robbie. "I was there in the studio, balancing the vocal tracks and getting it to sound just right... From time to time I would separate the voices and listen to who was singing what so we'd know which one to pitch up and when I got to Gwen's voice she sounded like an angel, I tell you. I remember saying to that lady, 'What's the name of that girl? She's really something!'"

Gwen will later relocate to Jamaica and record her own hits with Sly & Robbie, but not everyone agreed with such enhancements at the time. "I thought they'd filled up the tracks a little too much in places," admits John Holbrook. "I thought the raw tracks sounded really good, because I wasn't too fond of all those back-up vocals and the horns. To me, it didn't need dressing up like that. If you'd heard the basic tracks, they would have been fine. Where they messed up was in the post-production, because there was too much sweetening in my view, but maybe they were trying too hard to cross him over to a different audience..."

Once they'd returned to Bearsville, the race was on to mix the album and have it finished before the tour started. In order to achieve this Peter sent for Karl Pitterson, who immediately got to work with Sly and Robbie.

"We did that album in three days and nights, not sleeping at all," says Robbie Shakespeare. "Mick and Keith were rehearsing in the studio next door and didn't interfere with us at all, even at that stage. I don't remember them ever making any suggestions. They just left us to do our own thing and trusted us to get it right, except every now and then they'd stop by and take a listen."

Donald Kinsey recalled how Karl Pitterson, "was really pushing it to the limit. He had a very creative mind and he loved the challenge. I've seen him in there trying to figure something out and a certain look would come over him, like he was a madman but Karl had a magic with music, I tell you. The house is gonna get rocked!"

After Bearsville, Peter left for New York and SIR (Studio Instrument Rentals) in midtown Manhattan for what Donald has described as "dress rehearsals". The Stones were there and he says there was plenty of cocaine about, although no one from Peter's group expressed any interest in it. They were more concerned with the whereabouts of a Jamaican keyboard player called Bernard "Touter" Harvey, who'd played with Bob Marley before joining Inner Circle and travelling up to Bearsville with the Stones' party. Several weeks earlier, the Stones had decided to incorporate a little reggae into their show and recruited Touter to provide Jamaican style organ shuffles. Mick had seen him perform with Jacob Miller at the One Love Peace Concert, and liked how he played. Unfortunately things hadn't worked out as expected and so the Stones were forced to send for a replacement.

"The day after the Peace Concert Mick Jagger came to me and said, 'Touter, I'd like you to come play with us.' He'd chosen me to replace the great Billy Preston, but how could I fill those shoes?" Touter asks. "I went up to Woodstock with them and tried my best but then Mick said he didn't think it was going to work out the way they wanted it to, so Ian McLagan came and finished the tour instead."

McLagan, formerly of the Faces and Small Faces, had known the Stones for years. He'd even played on the *Some Girls* album, which the Stones recorded in Paris. Ron Wood and Keith Richards had rung him from Bearsville, saying they needed a keyboard player and would he like to tour with them? He left two days later, on June 6. After little more than a day's rehearsal and even less sleep, McLagan then boarded a plane for Florida where the Stones' tour was due to begin in two days' time. Writing in his autobiography, he said Keith would pump reggae out of his Nakamichi beat box. "He loved to play cassettes loud, and he played reggae with extra bass so that it boomed because as he told me in his best Rasta voice, 'That's how they play it down in Trench Town man...'"

Chapter 18

Some Girls

*S*ome Girls was released on June 9, just as the Stones completed a final day's rehearsal at the Civic Centre in Lakeland, Florida. They're billed as "The Great Southeast Stoned Out Wrestling Champions" but everyone – including Peter Corriston, designer of the *Some Girls* sleeve – knew their real identities. Corriston had depicted each band member in drag, and included brief biographies to match. Mick Jagger is transformed into "probably the most successful woman in radio" whilst Charlie Watts becomes a "beautiful and talented showgirl, model and actress..." Peter was handed a copy of their new album and there were the Stones pictured alongside Marilyn Monroe, Lucille Ball and Jayne Mansfield, plastered with lipstick and wearing women's wigs.

You can draw your own conclusions as to what he was thinking, stood with the LP in his hands and surrounded by people fired by thoughts of another drawn-out, hedonistic rampage across America. Rumour has it Peter didn't like the fact that Luther Vandross – who sang on a lot of New York sessions during that era – was gay, and so wouldn't let him in the studio. Homosexuality was against the law in Jamaica, but Peter's fortunate the US media didn't think to make it an issue.

'Miss You' is now a disco anthem, despite the presence of rock guitars and a Parisian busker on harmonica. WBLS refused to play it after accusing the Stones of racism, even though 'Miss You' wasn't at fault. Atlantic had wanted Jagger to change the lyrics of the song 'Some Girls' because of the lines "black girls just want to get fucked all night. I don't have that much jam" but Jagger and the other Stones weren't for turning. By the time the Reverend Jesse Jackson called for the album to be banned it had already sold four million copies and few people took any notice – not least the band and their record company.

Earl McGrath issued the following statement: "It never occurred to us that our parody of certain stereotypical attitudes would be taken seriously by anyone... No insult was intended, and if any was taken we apologise." The Stones weren't out of the woods yet though. Most of the living women stars depicted on the sleeve threatened to sue and the inner sleeve had to be replaced.

Once the tour started, Ian McLagan became a regular visitor to Keith's room after shows. "Keith's room was a party room because he liked people around him and to listen to music and get nicely toasted," he wrote in *All The Rage*. "It was my non-stop rock and roll university. We'd listen, play and talk for hours about the music. It was an ongoing education to me, and there was something to learn from each of the Stones. They had forgotten more about the music they loved than most people ever learn."

McLagan describes being around them as "like having the British Museum of Popular Music reference library at your fingertips", except Keith's love of reggae provided another piece of the jigsaw puzzle, and an invaluable learning experience.

"He'd play songs by Gregory Isaacs, Jacob Miller and a load of other stuff designed to get inside my head and heart," Ian continues. "It was all so new and it took a while to appreciate the depth of this music, but all I had to do was to pick up on the rhythms and get comfortable with them. Charlie loved the drumming and was a great help explaining the technical side of the way they played the bass drum and snare drum ass backwards. 'It's backwards rock and roll basically, if you think about it.' I was amazed. Keith showed me how the left and right hand bounce off each other on the keyboards, called skanking, which is the groove that pulls and pushes the beat, or as Keith puts it, 'Like a lion walking in the jungle, padding from side to side, real slow'."

By the time Peter joined the tour, the Stones had played other warm-up shows in Atlanta, Washington DC and Passaic, New Jersey, where Keith Richards showed his disdain for the mostly music industry crowd by "rearing back and giving us the finger with both hands". Promoter Bill

Graham, tour manager Peter Rudge and Jim Callaghan, who worked as the Stones' head of security, had quite a task ahead of them, and the tour was still only a few days' old.

Throughout the next seven weeks, second billing will be shared between Peter, Santana, Patti Smith, Foreigner, Journey, Southside Johnny and the Asbury Jukes, Van Halen, the Doobie Brothers and Etta James, who'll one day record her own cut of 'Miss You'. Peter played dates of his own in-between supporting the Stones, but nothing could have prepared him for the events of June 17, when he performed in front of a 90,000 strong crowd at the John F Kennedy Stadium in Philadelphia. The photo on the back of *Bush Doctor* may have been taken there and it's a huge audience for a country boy from Westmoreland, who once dreamt of appearing at the Ambassador Theatre in Trench Town.

"That was the first time we saw such huge crowds," recalls Sly Dunbar. "We also performed on the same bill as Santana and Journey. We were opening for all of them, so we really got a chance to study their performances and get a grasp on this whole concept of rock'n'roll."

"That was an experience man, I tell you!" said Donald Kinsey, to Dutch journalist Jas Obrecht. "It was the first time I'd been in a situation on that level. After we came on, we got a few apples up there on the stage, and a few cans... This happened for about 10, 15 minutes. Mick Jagger eventually came out on the stage and made a statement, which was really nice. He said that we were invited on this tour as his guests and told the people to just cool out, to sit back and get into the music, then we struck into 'Don't Look Back'. That tour there really exposed reggae to a wider audience."

"Mick would come out and introduce Peter because some of the people would get restless," admits Sly. "He made people realise it wasn't just another band that was playing. The Rolling Stones had a connection with us, and things started working out much better between ourselves and the audience after that."

Considering that most people at these shows weren't reggae fans, and their exposure to it may have been limited to reaching for the radio dial as Boney M's 'Brown Girl In The Ring' or 'Rivers Of Babylon' invaded the airwaves, Peter wouldn't go down too badly overall. Mick would only come out and join him every now and then, although he and Keith would often watch from the wings. During that first show Peter had deflected a bottle from hitting Sly, then looked out at the crowd and yelled, 'What the bombaclaat are you doing?' Apparently, the whole place went quiet, although this seems unlikely. What's more certain is that Sly and Robbie had to go back to the drawing board after that show. That's when they realised how important the out-front engineer was because on subsequent tours they'll demand stage monitors and a sound engineer, and make sure to soundcheck as much as they could. What evolved was the sound out front, and their level of performance. They and Peter had to put more energy into what they were doing, and develop a proper stage act.

"After that first show we did with the Stones, I felt shame, shame, shame, shame," admits Robbie. "We'd set up in a little corner, thinking how we'd play in just an ordinary club and it was this huge, massive stage. I tell you, when I step out there and see the crowd my knees start giving way on me. I was shaking and shivering all over and after that I went to find Mick and I ask him some questions about how it works. He explained to me that you have to be an actor. You have to be acting and to be saying the words like you're expressing real emotion. The next time we went on stage now, it was a totally different thing. I remember after that show I was like gasping for breath; that's how much I'd been working. From beginning to end I was running up and down, trying to make a difference. Touring with the Stones was one of the greatest learning experiences for me as a musician and we carried it over to Black Uhuru and other things but trust me, we learn a lot from that tour with them."

"The audiences really weren't all that receptive to him, but then it's hard to open for the Stones," says Warren Smith, who attended several of the shows on that tour. "Everybody is just waiting for them, and in those days reggae was still quite novel. I wouldn't say he went over that well but then he got his name out there, so it had definite value in that sense. The thing is, you can't be a club band and then go on a big concert stage and pull it off. It's too different but that's what Peter did and so they kind of got lost in some ways. Mick is the master. He knows how to pose and strut. He knows how to do all those things except you wouldn't get Peter doing any of that. In fact he hardly talked to the audience at all, but then it's really shocking to get up before 50,000 people with a live microphone. I never saw Peter show any sign of stage fright though. He was usually pretty confident but boy, did he smoke a lot of ganja! I don't think he was as bad as some of them, going out on stage completely stoned but he smoked high-grade stuff, and that definitely holds you back a bit. It'll dry out your mouth and restrict your vocal chords, and it must make you a little more nervous..."

On June 19 the Rolling Stones played the Palladium in New York City, in front of a celebrity crowd that included Bob Marley, Paul and Linda McCartney, Warren Beatty and Diane Keaton. In a month's time Bob will be on the front cover of *Rolling Stone*, and the proud recipient of a Third World Peace Medal presented to him at the Waldorf Astoria on behalf of "five hundred million Africans". Peter was pleased to see him and they arranged to meet up again in California, later in the month. Michael Putland took a photo of them backstage at the Palladium with Mick Jagger, who joined Peter on stage for 'Don't Look Back' and strutted like a rooster in his black felt hat. Earlier that day, Peter had been shopping at a bike shop on Ninth Street and bought several different types, including a unicycle.

"What's unknown by most is that Peter Tosh had a grand sense of humour," says Herbie Miller. "He was young at heart and as funny as any stand-up comedian, and also spent quite some time purchasing toys and gadgets associated with youth culture and activities for his own use. So, skateboards, roller skates, slingshots, electric motorcars, unicycles and layback cycles were most precious and guarded. He also loved pets and kept fishes, a variety of rabbits, guinea pigs, hamsters and birds. I once had to talk Peter out of returning from a European tour with a pet chimpanzee; for me, it was a monumental achievement since it was virtually impossible to talk him out of some things, including 'beating the gate' with the hamsters from a previous tour."

When he wasn't shopping, reasoning and smoking giant spliffs, Peter relaxed by listening to soul and gospel music, and reading from a large book about Emperor Haile Selassie I that showed His Majesty playing with lions. He and the band have now found their feet and begun to enjoy the experience. They feel more at ease when opening for the Stones in Hampton and Myrtle Beach, where Mick joins him for 'Don't Look Back'. There's a good spirit among the Stones party, which most folks attribute to Ronnie Wood. Their concert at the Rupp Arena in Lexington on June 29 is one of their better ones, despite a fan getting shot outside the venue and two others falling through a plate glass window in a dispute over tickets. If Peter feels any sympathy, then you wouldn't know it. Just before launching into 'Get Up Stand Up' he points at whoever's still sitting down and yells, "No sick people are allowed in here. Rise up!" Donald Kinsey plays a storm on that one, as he does throughout the entire tour. His lengthy solo has real bite, and is perfect for this crowd. Soon, he'll be back on home territory. During the first week of July, the Stones swing through the Great Lakes region, playing mostly stadium concerts in Cleveland, Buffalo, Detroit and Chicago. Peter headlined several shows of his own along the way, including one memorable night at My Father's Place. That's when Eppy realised what an impact the Stones' association was having on Peter's career.

"At the ticket outlets, they were crossing out "Peter Tosh" and writing "the Rolling Stones". I even found a kid trying to get in through the air conditioning duct! I was afraid he was going to get killed and thank God it didn't rain because there were a thousand people queuing outside the door. It was ridiculous but most of them had no idea who Peter Tosh was. They thought "Peter Tosh" was code for the Rolling Stones. I remember trying to put this kid straight about that. He'd been waiting outside the club since 10 in the morning. He had one of those tickets with Peter's name crossed out on it and was convinced the Rolling Stones were playing that night. I asked him how he knew that and he said there'd been clues in the local newspaper but I never did get to the bottom of what he was talking about."

The Reverend Hahnemann was at My Father's Place that night, and later interviewed Peter for a now defunct music magazine. The article was never published, although his notes survived.

"Amateur cub reporter that I was, the only tape recorder I could come up with was my sister's toy one. It's now a pretty funny scene to me (although I felt like an idiot at the time) as I remember Peter and other Rastas cursing at the ridiculous little 'bombaclaat' machine as we tried to listen to tapes of his music. Even worse, I only brought one 60 minute tape, and since I was with Peter for almost seven hours, Jah only knows what great stuff is lost forever and my memory is not much help here, since from the minute I arrived Peter shared spliff after spliff of what I thought at first was hash, but was actually just naturally super-resinous buds of the finest mountain-grown Jamaican ganja. How I drove Peter around on various errands that day I'll never know."

He describes Peter as having "a strong, military-like bearing accented by starched and pressed, fatigue-like clothing", but says the spit and polished image "disappeared the moment he took off his shades. He had no whites of his eyes, only reds. No exaggeration.

"When I saw them live, in front of a capacity crowd at My Father's Place on Long Island, he and his band were so good it spooked me and shook me," he continued. "I'm not new to reggae but damned if I wasn't ready to have my entire conception of the music destroyed and rebuilt in a single night."

Peter's voice was said to be, 'deep and resonant as a cave, saturated with urgency, admonishing us to either pick up on the vision or go away. No in-betweens tonight. Finally, as the band charges into the international anthem 'Get Up Stand Up', Peter breaks loose himself, high-stepping it around the drum kit like some mad Chinese hillbilly, his wide grin nothing less than a crack in time."

The Reverend's interview with Peter took place two days later, at a small motel on the outskirts of Westport, Connecticut. He's playing a club there that evening and then driving all night to open for the Stones the next afternoon at Soldier's Field in Chicago. Peter's band wasn't always allowed to soundcheck when opening for the Stones but just once in a while, something interesting might happen. One of Peter's road crew told the Reverend, "You should hear Mick Jagger sing with our band. I heard them do a version of 'Miss You' that Mick's people had to break my hands to get the tape out of my hands, seriously. It was as good as anything the Stones have ever done, and it was our band's first time on the song."

The Reverend also makes reference to Peter leaving Columbia. "In the almost non-existent bidding war that followed (the word 'uncooperative' travels fast in corporate America), Rolling Stones Records came out top. And judging by the piss poor conditions Peter and his band are enduring this summer, the Stones didn't part with even one dollar they didn't have to. The motel room is exactly twice the size of the bed. I've heard of cheap motels, but never one without TV or air-conditioning."

Later on, he says that, "like Keith Richards, Peter Tosh seems to have earned himself a place on the Interpol blacklist. In June he was arrested again for marijuana, this time by New York cops. While in their custody, during the course of one night, he was moved seven times to seven different jails. To many it seems a naked attempt to isolate Peter and make him give up the struggle."

Peter wasn't the only one facing difficulties with the police. Keith's ex Anita Pallenberg had taken up residence in Westchester, upstate New

York. On July 20 a 17-year-old boy was found dead of gunshot wounds in her bed. He'd been shot in the head with a stolen and unregistered .38 revolver. Five months later, Anita was cleared of any involvement in his death but her relationship with Keith was effectively over.

That night Peter played the first of two consecutive nights at the Starwood Club in West Hollywood. This first show sold out immediately. The Stones had a night off, and despite the Stones' press agent trying to quell talk of Jagger and possibly Richards' involvement, there were many in the audience that night who were convinced one of them would appear. Atlantic Records' press office denied the rumours and yet in truth, there were signs that the Stones might show. The Starwood management had hired more than a hundred extra security people, had issued all their employees with laminated name badges, issued dated backstage passes and rented walkie-talkies. At least six officers from the local fire department scurried about, taking photos of overcrowded balconies and uniformed motorcycle police cordoned off a three-block area. A Channel 2 news team waited expectantly outside and whispers went around, promising the imminent arrival of Aerosmith, Joe Cocker, Rod Stewart and the Governor of California, Jerry Brown. Robbie Shakespeare recalls that things got "a little explosive" that night. Chris Blackwell was there – he's even rumoured to have signed Sly and Robbie to Island that same night – but the Stones never showed up. It was their day off, and they'd spent it jamming on a stew of rock'n'roll, blues and country in their suite at the Fairmont Hotel in Dallas.

Between shows, Peter hosted further skirmishes with the rock press at the Tropicana Hotel near Sunset Strip – a place that's popular with musicians, but a trifle seedy. Fred Rath's article for *NME* will bear the headline "Tosh And The Mission", and tell of "faded, crumbling portals". He describes it as "almost Tom Waits' territory, except all the street life that hustles in and out of the steamy café at the front is too busy noticing itself to be that down to earth.

"Backstage in the hotel, Peter Tosh holds court with a succession of American journalists trying to find another ambassador for reggae apart from Bob Marley. Some of them don't even know what reggae is – such is the lack of exposure it gets here. Marley is staying in more salubrious quarters. Tosh, who was working on the Rolling Stones tour, has no heralded announcement of his presence and no clustering fans at the door. He is unperturbed.

"The aroma of Rasta cooking and herbs is unchallenged by the air conditioning unit in his room, which has been turned off. There is so much activity in there we go out and sit at a table by the pool to talk about his daunting task in America. Marley might have broken down the gates of Babylon, but there's an awful lot of resistance left inside."

"Reggae has always had to struggle for acceptance," Peter informs him. "We've gone through years of that and it has not stopped reggae from getting better and for more people to appreciate it."

Strumming his guitar, Peter talks about the business interests that control the media and dictate what's promoted on US radio and television. He bemoans such unfair advantage, yet disregards the fact "that he drew an ultra-full house on each night at the Starwood on the strength of a possible Stones' sit in".

When asked about the Stones, he mentions "uncountable blessings... Even though they come to see somebody else, they accepted the music, so everything was positive when they left. It's like who they came there to see, they did see that person. That's the power of the music. All these people who came to see the Rolling Stones didn't go away unsatisfied. I am always aware of any situation that I come on, and I am always ready for adjustment. That's a part of psychology."

A reporter from *Slash* magazine also caught up with Peter whilst he was staying at the Tropicana.

"Some Rasta musicians were meticulously washing bag loads of fruit in the kitchen. Peter sat on a stool with an acoustic guitar on his lap, his unicycle laid on the floor beside him. 'Please don't light that cigarette here sir. Surgeon General warns that cigarette smoking is dangerous.'" He tells the reporter that the smoke disturbs his third eye visibility. "I find it very nice with the Stones," says Peter a little later in the conversation. "I find that we can do some progressive business because of their respect and their love for the music."

Peter tells the journalist he's off to see Bob Marley, who's playing at the Starlite Amphitheatre in Burbank that night. He, Mick Jagger and Diana Ross were backstage, and Peter joins Bob on stage for a rousing duet on 'Get Up, Stand Up'. "The Pope felt that one!" Bob exclaims, as the pair triumphantly slapped hands afterwards. Pope Paul VI, who was rumoured to be ill, would die within two weeks of this concert. His replacement Pope John Paul I then also died, just 33 days later. Since Rastafarians regard the Pope as the Anti-Christ, this will be an occasion for rejoicing. The presence of celebrities backstage was an indication of how fashionable reggae had become. Peter was moving in high society rock circles but this was of little interest to Bob, who turned down Jagger's offer of sitting in with them that night. Brenda Smiley from *American Bandstand* was there but since no reggae act ever appeared on that programme, we assume she wasn't impressed.

"I was there when the Wailers played at the Burbank Amphitheatre," says photographer Chuck Krall. "Peter just marched onto the stage during their set and took the microphone away from Bob Marley. That's around the time he was riding round on his unicycle. Like a lot of great songwriters he got more involved with the lyrics than the performance. He believed that unless you could reach out to the audience and engage them with your lyrics then the words didn't mean anything. Most Americans didn't understand the words anyway and so Peter got into more of a rock'n'roll thing. He could really get rocking whereas Marley had a hard time in America. That's because most of the people who came out were white college kids who could relate to reggae because it was about smoking pot. That seemed to really bother Bob, because there were hardly ever African Americans at his concerts. Peter was different. He was a great advocate for Jamaica and I always loved him for that. He was very proud of who and what he was and yet Bob had something of an identity crisis due to him being half-white. The fact that he was elevated into becoming a spokesperson for the Rastafari movement gave him problems too, but Peter never got involved with that. He was a very strong character, plus he was so big and healthy.

"He went over the top at times and he did it with such grace and style that people didn't quite know how to handle him. The police certainly didn't. It wasn't as if he was some kind of radical, but he did push the envelope. For instance he smoked immense amounts of marijuana. A tremendous amount! Marley always mixed it with tobacco – usually Craven A – but not Peter. What was all the more amazing is that he couldn't travel with it, so he was reliant on connecting with local people who'd get it for him. I had this policy that I never photographed anyone with dope of any kind but Peter told me that he didn't care and it made no difference, since everybody knew he smoked pot."

The Stones' tour ended with two nights at the Anaheim Stadium in California. Peter will later claim to have played in front of 200,000 people over these two shows and whilst the capacity was just a third of that, it's still a lot of people. The final show coincided with Mick Jagger's 35th birthday, and there was a festival atmosphere backstage. At the after-show party Mick gave Donald Kinsey his shirt and jacket in exchange for the guitarist's beret, which had a clown badge pinned to it. Everyone left happy, and even Peter looked as if he was enjoying himself. The tour had grossed millions of dollars, but generated a lot of negative coverage. Ed Kociela, reviewing the closing date in the *Herald Examiner*, described Mick Jagger as "a parody". He says the Stones "laboriously trudged through their two-hour performance. It was an embarrassment. You can't trust the Stones any longer. They have lost that most important and vital trait – consistency. The importance of the group is gone. Only rarely did Jagger flash the charm and sing with passion. It just wasn't happening on the stage. It was Richards, who must go on trial later this month in Canada for drug charges, who was trying to drive the band."

According to one report, "Whilst the tour was commercially successful, it was dogged by drunken, sloppy performances. Tour photographer Lynn Goldsmith later compared it to Bruce Springsteen's 1978 tour, which she had also covered. 'With Bruce it was no drugs, no drinking, long soundchecks and long shows. With the Stones it was no soundcheck, lots of parties and running off stage as quickly as possible to catch the private plane.'" Not everyone agreed with this assessment, as the *Some Girls* tour had heralded a return to basics. The set was less showy, and the Stones played plenty of older numbers like 'Tumbling Dice' and 'Street Fighting Man', in addition to showcasing songs from the new album.

There were no plans for a European leg of the *Some Girls* tour and so Peter bade farewell to the Stones and headed back to Jamaica for a well-earned rest. After arriving at Kingston airport, he walked outside and found his car blocked by another vehicle. When he asked the driver to move it, the man pulled out a gun, aimed it at his head and said he was a Detective Superintendant with the Kingston police force. He told Peter that he'd wanted to kill him ever since hearing his outburst at the One Love Peace Concert, and to tread carefully. He then put away the gun and drove away.

A few days later, journalist Arthur Kitchin visited Peter at the singer's home in Renfield Drive. His article will appear in the *Weekly Gleaner* on September 18. After informing readers that Peter's just completed a six week tour with the Rolling Stones, "performing in places where reggae had been previously unknown", he says the high point was performing at the JFK Stadium in Philadelphia, "watched by a live audience of 120,000".

"Like most artistes of his class, Peter Tosh is highly articulate, expressing his thoughts with the same degree of ease and clarity that he plays his guitar," he writes. He then warns that Peter's normal speech "is punctuated liberally by expletives or what are more commonly described as 'bad' or 'five shilling' words.

'Bad words is my language,' argues Peter, who claims they help dispel 'any evil vibrations which may be present.' He talks about warding off the Devil and says, 'I don't deal with fear. My struggle is for justice. It's 400 years I'm here. Some were brought and some were sent. I was sent for the fulfilment of the revelation.' As if in direct confirmation of Peter's words, the sounds of a nearby thunderstorm reverberate inside his small, but cosy Ensom City home, and flashes of lightning briefly illuminate the somewhat gloomy interior. Several acquaintances are present, including Peter's woman, a quiet and unassuming brown-eyed beauty whose demure exterior strongly contrasts with her mate's volatile and often explosive personality. Neatly dressed in a red T-shirt and navy blue tracksuit bottom with red, green and gold stripes on the sides, cuffs tucked into black socks worn inside black, ballet type lounge shoes Peter stretches out his six-foot frame on the furry living room carpet and inhales deeply from a small spliff containing some of the best ganja available."

We're told that Peter finds it difficult to find suitable food when on tour sometimes, and has to live for "weeks at a time on just cornmeal, mint tea and honey". After two hours, Kitchin gets up to stretch his legs and takes in more details about the room he's in. "A large piano stands near the front door and in one corner between a speaker box and a lounge chair, his black and red coloured guitar rests on its stand. Pictures, plaques and newspaper clippings adorn the walls. Multi-coloured tropical fish swim in a small glass tank and a single blue and white parakeet swings contently inside his cage. Several kinds of fresh fruit – mangoes, pineapples, naseberries, pawpaws and sweetsops picked from a tree in the garden rest inside a large glass bowl placed in the centre of a wooden table on one side of the room. The smell of ganja is overpowered by the scent of burning incense, frankincense and myrrh."

Peter says he's not a millionaire – "That's another type of lie they spread to try and kill you" – but spends his money on musical instruments, which then end up costing him twice as much as they're worth once he's paid to get them through customs. In summing up, Kitchin describes Peter as an "accomplished, yet humble musical prodigy", who smiles gently and wishes him safe travel before lingering by the piano and playing and singing a few bars of Dylan's 'Like A Rolling Stone'. "What would I do without music?" he asks, as Kitchin steps outside into the bright Jamaican sunshine.

Chapter 19

When The Whip Comes Down

Retribution wasn't long in coming. Around 10 in the evening of September 11, Peter was stood outside Aquarius studios near Halfway Tree, waiting for his musicians to arrive. They were about to rehearse for a forthcoming European tour but Sly & Robbie had been delayed.

"I was standing at the studio doors with what we call a spliff tail in Jamaica," Peter told Bruno Blum. "I had it in my fingers, leaning against a car and was thinking of the arrangements of the music because I was rehearsing for this tour, seen? I was thinking of which songs I was going to sing, and who we were going to use for background harmonies… I was waiting for Sly and Robbie and whilst I was there I felt something touch me and then when I look I see a guy in plainclothes with my spliff tail in his hand. He said nothing. He was just standing there looking at me, so I took it from him and said, 'What happen?' And he took it back the same way. I say to myself, 'What kind of guy is this who come and take away my bloodclaat spliff in that kind of way?' He then says that me and him must go down so. I say, 'down so?' From the mere fact that he mentioned 'down so' makes me feel that he must be a cop because 'down so' means lock up. That's my interpretation, so I just blow it away right before him and say, 'So is it this you want to carry me down so for?' He grabbed at the paper, but all the contents were blown out, seen? I stood there still and he tore off my shirt and my trousers down to my waist. He try everything physical but because he's just another weak guy and don't eat good food and think constructively,

226

I just eased him off so he pulls out a gun and juk it my face and then says I must come with him. I say, 'No you can't do that bloodclaat.' He start to point up his gun in my face like that but me just ease him off and he walk up the street to look for his friends. He saw one of his friends passing and said to him, 'Come help me carry this criminal down so.' Well I don't like being called a criminal, seen? The next guy run come with his aggression and I say, 'Don't do that bloodclaat. What's the matter with you?' He pull out his gun and start with the same fuckery, but their aggression couldn't even shake me, seen? One throw a blow and strike me in the mouth so I punch him down, because that is my defence. Well after they find out they couldn't manage me they went out into the street looking for assistance and I was just standing there, because I didn't intend to run. I am not a criminal. I was waiting there and a police car arrived, a police came with his uniform and said to me, 'What happen Peter?' I tell him these two guys trying to humiliate me and incriminate me illegally and unlawfully and I don't appreciate that. He said to me, 'Let's walk down the road,' so I just walk with him, intelligently and voluntarily down to the station…

"I went down there to explain the situation and how the circumstances were created and I saw a bundle of guys, about eight to 10 guys sitting inside the station. Well I just went there to explain how the shit-stem doesn't respect Rasta, seen? They first have to find out if you're big in society and have a bag of money before they respect you as a Rastaman, seen? Well, I just walk in there humble to explain what's happening and the corporal for the station, he look at the guy bleeding and said to him, 'What's wrong with you man?' He then turned to the corporal and said I mashed him down. The corporal, he sent out his boy and that's the way I treat him. He come back all bloodied and I come in there well smooth, seen? Well they chuck me in a corner and whilst I was in that corner, every one of them grab all different kinds of weapons of destruction and said, 'Kill him.' I was using my hands like this to keep off the blows, because all the blows were made for my head, seen? Well I got so many blows in my head that one of my hands couldn't take any more and it broke, but even when the hand was broken, it was still getting beaten by batons and things. They beat me for approximately an hour and I find out their intention was to kill me, seen? I know the only way I have to stop them is to play dead and just lie there, but they damage my liver and my lungs. They break my hand…

"My head, it was bleeding badly also. They throw water on my head and tell me I must get up, but I just lie down the same way and play dead but after a minute now I got up, I stood there and wipe off the blood 'cause there was blood all over the station, seen? They said, 'Carry him go lock him up' seen? 'Lock him up in the dumb cell.' A dumb cell is a place without air hole, seen? That's where they were taking me to but some of the prisoners saw the humiliation and thought it was one of the world's biggest criminals who'd been captured, seen? When they realised that it was me they were surprised because they have never seen a criminal or a gunman get so much beating. They say, 'No, you cannot put that man in the dumb cell. Put him in my cell,' seen? It was after midnight by then but the prisoners took care of me 'til about three o'clock, because no doctor came to see me. My lawyer came and then three lorries of soldiers and police took me to the hospital, seen? Like it's the biggest criminal being captured in Jamaica. Many soldiers were there and they all knew I got that because of my militancy in the society and what I stand for, seen? Because there was a Peace Concert in Jamaica and I made certain speeches to government leaders and the Prime Minister, and they didn't like it."

Robbie Lyn and trombone player Ronald "Nambo" Robinson followed Peter to the station and were shocked at the brutality of what they saw. "Peter had been in a sedate mood, just being easy-going," remembers Robbie. "He had a little spliff in his hand and he wasn't even out on the road because there was an incline towards the entrance and he was just standing there, a little out of the way. We were just waiting on a few people to arrive but Halfway Tree is a busy place and so there's always something happening except I believe that incident was predesigned. I don't know if the police knew Peter was going to be there or whether one of them spotted him and sent out the alarm but we saw a couple of them strategically position themselves just before they approached him. I think it was a vendetta they had because of what Peter said at the Peace Concert. It hadn't gone down too well with a lot of the police, and that was their way of responding. Peter never had a chance, let's put it that way. He tried to resist for a while. He'd do certain martial arts movements but he wasn't trained. It was just for show more than anything because it didn't work. Before long they subdued him, bossed him around for a while and then they drove him off to the police station. That's where they really did a job on him. Nambo and I went there and saw they had him inside. We could hear them beating him and him bawling like a baby. At one point he tried to jump through the window when the pain was too much, it was terrible. He had no chance and that went on for a long time. After a while Bob Marley came down to the station and he would have had considerable influence at the time but it made no difference. A lot of well-known people in the entertainment business came there but the police had their agenda for what they were going to do with Peter and they did it because he got a broken skull, and they broke bones in his hand… He couldn't do anything in terms of business for a while. It was a horrific experience. I felt helpless, because I couldn't do anything…"

"Peter was properly beaten," adds Nambo. "He was black and blue from the blows they rained on him, it almost brought tears to my eyes. I just couldn't understand why they wanted to treat him like that, but I think it was because he wouldn't surrender to them. He kept on speaking and the comments he was making, they were feisty, y' know? But he was beaten indiscriminately and by people of rank too, because I remember seeing officers there, possibly up to the rank of superintendant. I kept expecting them to say, 'No, this isn't right,' but no, nothing like that. They were teaching him a lesson, I tell you. We knew about police brutality but none of us had seen anything like that before.

"When this superintendant realised they had an audience, he ordered some other officers to clear us away from the station, but it too late by then. They'd almost killed a man for using abusive language, because that was all Peter was doing really. It was a serious injustice, but people like him and Fela Kuti, they're not looking out for their safety. They'll just speak and get hurt and then speak again. It's normal for people like them to keep standing up for what they believe is right, and that really furthered my respect for Peter, because doing something like that takes great courage."

Bunny Lee claims the police told Peter's friends that he was dead when they rang the station. Peter later told John Swenson that, "What happened to me *is* death. No mystery about that, it is death because when one's central nervous system is damaged it is either insanity or death. And my central nerve system has been beaten and exposed out of my head. I could touch and feel it. Every time I would touch it, it would make my entire temple tremble and that is death. These photographers came and took a picture of my head and when I look at that, it looks like a dead man."

Peter claims he had 48 stitches that night, other reports state 20. The fact is, he'll never fully regain his health after this incident. He'll complain of frequent headaches, and his behaviour will grow more and more erratic as the pains increase. More than 30 years earlier, jazz pianist Bud Powell was badly beaten by police in Philadelphia. "His head was so damaged he ended in Bellevue; his sickness started right there," said jazz writer Geoffrey Haydon. "Before the injury Powell was childlike and highly strung, but afterwards he was pursued by demons. The blows to the head did not abort his creative brilliance – his full artistic flowering was yet to come – but it condemned him to a life of mental torment."

Alvera came and stayed with Peter for a while after his beating. "Poor Mama's one son," she said, with tears in her eyes. It was in the hospital that Peter learnt he'd been charged with using indecent language, assaulting a police officer and resisting arrest. When the case reaches court he'll get another look at police constables Raymond Melbourne and Edward Watson, who testified that Peter had been smoking "a ganja cigar", and then used abusive language whilst preventing them from detaining him. Watson said he had gone to assist Melbourne after being summoned for help and that Peter had thrown several punches at him, one of which caused an injury to his right eyebrow.

Peter's attorney, Howard Hamilton, told *The Gleaner* there'd been "evasiveness, contradiction and downright lies throughout the Crown's case". He said the defence wasn't disputing the fact that Watson got an injury, but that it had been sustained as a result of Peter deflecting a blow meant for him. In passing sentence the magistrate said there was no doubt in his mind that the blow was "well directed". He called it "an unfortunate incident" and added that people should have some regard for policemen. Peter was offered a fine of $120, or two months imprisonment. On entering the witness stand he'd refused to take the oath unless he could say "Almighty *Jah*," instead of "Almighty God". "I don't know God," he told the judge who might have appeared even-handed were it not for the fact that he did nothing to condemn the levels of violence used by the police, let alone recommend any kind of inquiry.

On October 7 the Rolling Stones appeared on the popular American television show *Saturday Night Live*. That same day, *NME* carried a picture of Tosh with a bruised face and his arm in a sling under the heading "Tosh Brutalised".

"Reggae star Peter Tosh sustained a fractured arm and severe head injuries resulting in over 20 stitches in the wound last Tuesday following an incident in Kingston, Jamaica," the article declared. "Despite the intervention of his old friend and former associate Bob Marley, who turned up at the prison where Tosh was being held and made an impassioned plea for his release, the 33-year-old musician remained in the police cells overnight. The following morning, handcuffed and under heavy guard, Tosh was taken to the prison hospital where he received treatment for his arm and head injuries. He was later released on bail after being charged with possessing ganja and resisting arrest. Despite the seriousness of his injuries Tosh's manager was adamant that Tosh was even more determined to play his concerts in Britain in November."

Rolling Stones Records had just released simultaneous 12″ and 7″ versions of 'Don't Look Back' in the UK, with 'Soon Come' on the flipside. The 12″ had extended versions of each song, but there was no mention of Mick Jagger anywhere to be seen – only that famous Rolling Stones tongue logo. Both releases came in picture sleeves with a photo of Peter alone, smiling and rolling a spliff. The previous week, Third World had entered the UK Top 10 with a cover of the O'Jays' 'Now That We've Found Love' that'll stay on the charts for over two months. There was every expectation that 'Don't Look Back' would do the same, even though Peter wasn't available to promote it. It finally entered the UK Top 50 on October 21, but won't go any higher than number 43. This was a major disappointment. If Peter couldn't make the Top 40 with a single featuring Mick Jagger, then something was wrong. Executives at his record company started to realise that Peter Tosh was no Bob Marley, and he'd be a lot harder to market than first thought.

Their main worry was still the court case hanging over Keith Richards' head, after he'd been arrested in Canada for possession of heroin and cocaine. His trial date was October 23, and took place at the New Court House in Toronto. The prosecution dropped the cocaine charge, and Keith pleaded not guilty to heroin trafficking but guilty to heroin possession. The Crown accepted the plea, and *Saturday Night Live* producer Lorne Michaels testified on the significance of the Rolling Stones, and the guitarist's role with them. The following day Keith was sentenced to a year's probation and told that he'd have to continue with his heroin addiction treatment. He was also required to give a benefit performance for the Canadian National Institute for the Blind – a stipulation inspired by a blind teenage fan who'd followed the band all over the US. That same day Mick Jagger was interviewed for BBC2's *The Old Grey Whistle Test* and calmly announced that he'd be leaving "for the jungles of Jamaica" on Wednesday, to film a video with Peter Tosh. When asked about 'Don't Look Back' he says the Stones thought they were just going to be putting a record out with Peter, but then found themselves in the same studio complex. Jagger, looking studious in glasses, then rejected the suggestion that Peter was a protégé of his by saying, "He needs no introduction. He's not like a young kid. In fact he's older than me!"

The video of 'Don't Look Back' was filmed at Strawberry Hill – a resort in the Blue Mountains owned by Chris Blackwell, where Jagger had stayed whilst attending the One Love Peace Concert. They'd originally planned to film it weeks earlier, but been forced to postpone it while Peter recovered from his injuries. Filming was scheduled to last three days, between October 26 and 29, but was completed far quicker. Mick and Peter were well used to each other by now, and yet Peter occasionally looks uncomfortable as Jagger mugs to the camera and acts a little camp. Whilst the vocals were cut live, the rest of it was pre-recorded. Peter's not really playing his guitar (note the Ethiopia sticker) and when the sax comes in there's no one to mime the solo – only Sly & Robbie, Robbie Lyn, Keith Sterling and Mikey Chung grooving, just like on the record. Peter and the band posed for Island photographer Adrian Boot afterwards and appear so laid-back, you'd hardly suspect they'd been playing host to rock royalty.

The video was supposed to kick-start the single and send 'Don't Look Back' racing back up the US and UK charts, although any hopes of it emulating 'Miss You' or even the Stones' latest single, 'Beast Of Burden', will soon evaporate. It was the likes of Chic, Donna Summer, Foreigner and John Travolta & Olivia Newton-John who dominated the US charts that winter, whilst British pop fans preferred the quasi-reggae sound of Boney M and 10cc, who'd entered the charts with 'Rasputin' and 'Dreadlock Holiday' respectively.

On November 3, the *Bush Doctor* album is released. Generally speaking, the reviews weren't that favourable although *Creem* journalist Richard Riegel described it "one of the best albums of 1978 and 1979" and then reminds readers how Peter is "on American radio at last, thanks to Jagger's duet with him on a spirited remake of the Temptations' 'Don't Look

Back'." Riegel asks if the Stones' involvement is necessary in convincing people of how important an artist Peter is, and can't seem to make up his mind. On one hand, "Reggae is still a tenuous commodity in the States, even after 10 years of being just on the verge of happening here." On the other, Peter has clearly been blessed "with enough creative integrity to keep on making superb albums, with or without the patronage of Babylon and its superstars". After discussing and praising the songs Riegel asks, "Is Peter Tosh, with all his kidding/not kidding about marijuana legislation and Rasta Diaspora, really our long-lost 50s' hipster existential Negro, decked out in dreadlocks for the New Age?"

He certainly thinks so, but others weren't so sure. Within two weeks of release, *Bush Doctor* made headlines for entirely different reasons. A news report dated November 15 carried the headline "Ganja Smell Causing Problem For A Record".

"Boots, one of Britain's biggest record retailers, is refusing to sell a top reggae record because the cover has a sticker with a smell similar to cannabis," it proclaimed. "The sticker on the cover of *Bush Doctor* by Jamaican artist Peter Tosh reads "Scratch And Sniff" and "Don't Look Back". When scratched it gives off a smell similar to that of the drug. A spokesman for the record company EMI said the label, manufactured in Florida, did not contain cannabis but a herbal medicine widely used in Jamaica. Boots have sent back hundreds of advance copies. The EMI spokesman said the record was still on sale in other shops in Britain or other countries."

In fact it smelled like patchouli, and no self-respecting reggae fan would dream of shopping for records in Boots anyway, which was a chemist's grown into a department store, and had a music section that rarely strayed from mainstream tastes.

"That was my idea," sleeve designer Neville Garrick later admitted to Roger Steffens. "The picture had been picked out so I hand painted green herbs and suggested that we add a sticker that you could scratch and smell herb. I guess it became kind of controversial."

In fact Peter got off lightly, because the original marketing idea was even more tasteless according to Earl McGrath. "I remember this advert I made for *Bush Doctor* which said, 'the Bush Doctor is not a gynaecologist. It's a new record on Rolling Stones albums and tapes,' but they wouldn't print it anywhere."

The European leg of the *Bush Doctor* tour finally got underway in late November, with dates in Hamburg and Stockholm serving to raise the curtain on a sold-out night at Amsterdam's Paradiso. Earlier in the day, Peter had shared a radio interview with Mick Jagger, who was in Holland promoting the Stones' latest single 'Shattered'. There were high expectations of Mick joining him on stage that night, but this never happened. Backstage, Peter met a guy who said all his family had been killed in a plane crash. As the sole survivor, he'd thought long and hard about committing suicide until passing by a record shop one day and hearing 'Pick Myself Up'. Since buying a copy of *Bush Doctor*, he'd played it over and over and swore to Peter that it had helped save his life.

Next up was the UK, where they'll perform in Manchester and Cardiff before heading for London and playing two nights at the Rainbow Theatre, on December 6 and 7. *Melody Maker* reported that Peter's British dates had been arranged and cancelled twice whilst recovering from his injuries. Momentum had been lost, although fans still feverishly speculated whether Mick and Keith might join him at some of these concerts. "Mick did say that he plans to be back in London in a couple of weeks," said Stones press agent Keith Altham. "I am sure that if he was in town he would go along and appear on stage with Peter. The London gigs seem the obvious ones but there are no definite plans for the Stones' involvement, but if Mick or Keith are in London, well it seems most likely they will get up on stage."

That should have sold a few extra tickets, except Peter packed considerable drawing power of his own, especially in London. News of his performance at the One Love Peace Concert and subsequent beating had been all over the reggae grapevine for weeks. He was the music's most fearless revolutionary, and had Jamaica's hottest rhythm section backing him. Jagger's possible involvement therefore meant little, especially once Matumbi had been named as Peter's support band. Matumbi were signed to Harvest, which was a fellow EMI subsidiary. They'd recently played most of the same venues supporting Ian Dury & The Blockheads, and were well respected by British reggae fans. Peter remembered them from his last London show with the Wailers, at the Sundown Theatre in Edmonton, and was pleased to see bandleader Dennis Bovell once more.

"We shared the same bus, and so all travelled up and down the motorways together," says Dennis. "I remember once, it was near Christmas and there was a pile-up on the other side of the road. This was here in England and as we passed by Robbie Shakespeare was trying to find a news channel, so we could find out what had happened. As he turned the dial on came this religious song and Peter went mad. He started shouting to get that 'bumbaclaat song off the radio!' It was a typically religious Christmas song, the kind he must have sung as a kid in Jamaica, and that's probably why he didn't want to hear it any more. I was sat there thinking, 'It's only a Christmas carol Peter, so come on, lighten up…'

"A couple of days later and he fell out with the Tamlins. Peter started complaining they were getting too flash, so he disciplined them. They'd started the tour standing near the front of the stage but finished it right at the back. Peter said they were *backing* vocalists, and so they had to be at the back, serious! Keith Sterling said to me once, 'I want to resign but I daren't…'"

"Let's hear it for the hardest working reggae band in the world – Word, Sound & Power," announced the MC at the Apollo Theatre in Manchester. This wasn't the loose-limbed outfit of *Legalise It*, but a finely honed rhythm machine that had found its métier playing to stadium crowds, and played with more power than any other reggae band, including the Wailers. Sly Dunbar works overtime, driving the band forward and peppering certain songs with bursts of Syn drum. He and Robbie's extended jam on 'Burial' takes the breath away. As they roar into '400 Years', light ricochets off the handcuffs dangling from Peter's wrist – an accessory he says, 'symbolised slavery continuously, four hundred years of the same philosophy'."

The following night they played at the Sophia Gardens in Cardiff. It was then back to London for those dates at the Rainbow Theatre in Finsbury Park. Peter and the band rehearsed at Manticore studios in West London. That's where *Black Echoes'* Jon Futrell found him. In his opinion, *Bush Doctor* lacks "the uninhibited, youthful defiance and musical prowess" of Peter's first two albums. He says it's an album that "falls short of what's expected from the man who has twice been badly beaten at the hands of the Jamaican police and who is alleged to have run rampant with a knife through the press office of a certain record company, but it is important as a fusion of two diverse musical cultures."

After referring to the Rainbow concerts as "disastrous", he writes that "observers attribute Tosh's current bleached reggae to the Stones, and a misguided attempt to broaden his appeal."

Not everyone agreed with him. Peter played Bradford's St. George's Hall during that same tour watched by Emma Ruth, whose review appeared in *NME* during mid-December. "The Peter Tosh backlash *doesn't* start here," she began. "It was a filthy night – what's sometimes called a 'pea-souper', and yet still the crowd turned out." Whilst she thinks Peter "lacks the ebullient charisma of Marley, in a way he's more magical. Thoroughly mesmerised, the audience let the music wash over them whilst Tosh moved around as if in a trance or stood immobile, letting the dreadlocks swing. Sometimes his delicate elfin grace made him appear aloof, but it was unintentional. Tosh's approach was so casual that one could have overlooked his brilliant, understated rhythm guitar playing."

Dennis Bovell says that Matumbi's lead singer almost didn't make it to the next gig after hurting himself at the Rainbow. "Yeah, he fell in the orchestra pit but he got back up and soldiered on, then went straight to hospital afterwards. He'd jumped in there for effect but couldn't see a damn thing because he was wearing sunglasses. Peter used to wear these dark glasses, and so Bevan started wearing them too. They both used to wear these blinkered ones that had bits at the side. We thought it was a singers' thing!"

Two days after the tour finished, *Melody Maker* printed an article by Vivien Goldman entitled 'The Bush Doctor's Dilemma'. Several days earlier she'd interviewed Peter in the back of a car driven by Dr. Alimantado, who sped them through the streets of London to the Holiday Inn at Swiss Cottage, where Peter was looking forward to some well-earned rest. He and the band had only arrived in the country that same morning, and everyone found the soundcheck tiring.

"The exiled dreads stood shivering miserably round the stage wearing gloves, scarves and an assortment of the peaked caps that are de rigueur these days – the bigger the cap's crown, the mightier the length of the locks beneath," she wrote. Goldman has a copy of the new album, and informs Peter that the Glimmer Twins credited with production of *Bush Doctor* are in fact Mick and Keith. "Two little batty bombaclaat," snarls Peter, who insists that he and Robbie Shakespeare are the real producers. It's the first sign of a rift developing between him and the Stones, despite them being listed as *executive* producers – a term for (usually absentee) parties, often used to credit those who fund a recording and a cursory title at best. Truthful as ever, he confesses that it was his choice to record 'Don't Look Back', and admits he'd done it to generate airplay and get more exposure. Vivien then applies the coup-de-grace, for him "finally achieving international success on the backs of a white rock band".

Herein lies the dilemma Vivien refers to. Peter wants and demands success but only on his own terms, without making the kind of compromises that Bob Marley seems to take in his stride. Either Peter can't write love songs such as 'Stir It Up' and 'Is This Love' or doesn't want to, since the closest he comes to romance is when idealising over his African heritage. On the rare occasion he has written about girls, he's dismissed them as "brand–new second-hand". Rather than making people happy, Peter wants to wake them from their mental slumbers and face reality, which is a less enticing prospect. He's also intent on spreading the gospel of Rastafari, which Jon Futrell once called "the chief culprit for reggae's inability to cross over". Peter knows he has to entertain, but it's the message he values most. Unlike Marley, who crafts his songs with subtlety, Peter's style is very direct. As a result, his music is unlikely to appeal to anyone who didn't share his beliefs. Vivien Goldman however, begged to differ.

"I firmly believe that Peter would already have been the respected, international spokesman – and star – he deserves to be *if* he was white. Peter is one of reggae's major artists – and yet can only be successful by drastically diluting his message, issuing a song that's totally removed from what he wants to sing. It's especially sad that it's this particular reggae musician whose integrity has been brought sharply into question since Peter, above all, was reggae's fierce and noble warrior. Now he's lurched to fame on the shoulders of the dissolute, decadent, reactionary capitalists of rock & roll."

Peter didn't see it that way. He didn't have the same budget whilst making those first two albums for Columbia, and these new 24-track recordings are so much better produced. He's worked hard making music to attract bigger audiences, and just delivered what he regards as the best album of his career. Yet people are complaining, and accusing him of having sold out when all he's done is broaden his musical palette and raised standards. He hadn't expected this, and in quieter moments must have reflected on whether he'd allowed Sly and Robbie and the rest of the band too much influence.

"People are just there to criticise and deteriorate your self-confidence," he snaps at Bruno Blum. "And to try and show you that you're going on a different level, which you know you are not…"

"Peter was always having to explain that his music wasn't just plain and simple," notes Robbie Lyn. "It's like these critics want the music to remain the same forever because when Bob and Peter branched off, people said they were selling out and losing their roots. They couldn't see the bigger picture because if you want to capture the international market, then you have to start doing things a little differently. If not, then your music can get clichéd after a while. You can make the songs and the words different, but if you're not trying out new sounds then your music's going to start sounding the same, and after a while you can't tell one track from another.

"That's why he made it known to us that he wanted to have counter melodies and all sorts of different instruments in his music. I remember that on *Bush Doctor*, we spent a great deal of effort in complementing his songs, and trying to create some form of identity for him..."

In his interview with Blum, Peter admits that he's also being criticised for singing with a white man, even though he and other black people "live in a white man's world". According to him, white people control "approximately 98 percent" of media outlets and record companies. "You can find a few black ones, but you have to search and they are still white owned same way because of the oppressive system, seen? So to get across and to deal with music you have to deal with white people, irrespective of what them want to say."

Peter's skirting around sensitive issues here, and he'll face accusations of bigotry once his views on women become more widely publicised. Vivien Goldman went so far as to liken his sexist attitudes to those of a Sicilian farmer "who locks his pregnant, unmarried daughter up in a pig pen for the rest of her life" – this after a meeting with Peter in a Kingston car park back in 1976, when he informed her that if she was menstruating, then she should keep her distance.

"Do you think that equal rights are for women, as well as men?" Bruno Blum asked him. "Equal rights is universal, for man or woman," Peter replied, before alienating his female fans in droves by claiming that, "A woman was created for comfort of a man, seen? A woman cannot carry a bag of sugar weighing two hundred pounds. A man can do that, seen? There are many things. A woman must not put on a man's apparel, seen? A woman during her cycles, she have a period which comes around every month and during that time she must be isolated and kept alone for that period of time for spiritual purposes, because she distorts the communication between the Father and the Son during that period. A man must not sleep with his woman whilst she stays that way. Babylon or western philosophy tells you that is all right but the Rastaman says no, and the Rastaman's culture is the traditional black culture, seen?"

Bunny Wailer had once thrown Vivien out of a recording session for wearing shorts. She called their philosophy "hideously retrogressive" and yet Bunny was currently working with Marcia Griffiths, who was the most prominent of Jamaica's female singers. He and Peter were still close, and the two friends saw a lot of one another when time allowed.

"The spirits and the musical concepts within us still communicate heavily 'cause we've been singing harmony together for a long period of time and we still have that spiritual link," Peter told Bruno Blum. "Every time we meet with each other, we have that feeling to do something musical together.

"The other day Bunny recorded a song for Marcia Griffiths called 'Tribulation'. He wrote the song and produced it. Well I came inside the shop and I was listening to the way she was expressing the tribulation and just imagined the harmony that should be sung around it. I say to Bunny, 'Boy, that song reach down inside of me.' I tell him what harmony he should use and he said, 'Just listen keenly,' and the same harmony I was trying to show him was already there! Right now Bunny has an instrumental released in Jamaica that I blow melodica on called 'Anti-Apartheid,' and it's dangerous, I tell you..."

Other future projects didn't work out quite so well. Dennis Bovell was scheduled to remix one of Peter's tracks once the UK tour finished, but this never happened. "When we last met in London, he was staying at No. 1 Harrington Gardens in Mayfair," he recalls. "I went there to take him some herb and then waited for my moment to whip my hat off, because I'd just cut my dreadlocks off. After I'd done that he just looked at me like he'd seen a ghost, and then carried on talking to the other people in the room like I wasn't there! After about five minutes of that, I thought, 'Oh well. Time to leave' and I never saw or heard from him again. The record company were saying to me, 'What have you done to Peter man?' Because we'd planned for me to do some mixing for him, but he definitely didn't want me any more. Eventually he sent me a message via the record company saying there were some things a man should never do, and cutting off his dreadlocks was one of them."

Chapter 20

Mystic Man

It's December 16, 1978 and Peter is at the offices of Rolling Stones Records at 75 Rockefeller Plaza in Manhattan. Mark Mehler of *Circus Weekly* says Tosh was tired after several previous interviews and especially one with "an arch feminist, who tearfully objected to Tosh's Jamaican brand of chauvinism".

"My lifestyle can *never* change, no matter how much money I make," he told Mehler. "I'll get more aggressive against imperialism, that's the only change. More aggressive against the system, because the system's only set up to victimise, exploit, kill, brutalise and do everything that's degrading..."

Earl McGrath ran the Stones' office. This is a man said to be "having the party of his life. I don't think he was sitting in his office planning the future for that record company," one insider said. "He was too busy entertaining. That's how I recall him because the office was a mad house. I heard this story how Johnny Winter fell asleep in the Rolling Stones' office with a lit cigarette in his hand and almost burnt the place down. It was a bit of a scene."

Peter had learnt to turn a blind eye to the Rolling Stones' excesses, or so it seemed. His only rock'n'roll vices, if you can call them that, were a liking for the ladies and smoking herb, which he considered a holy sacrament. He didn't trash hotel rooms, gamble or get raving drunk or stoned, and he didn't care for debauchery either. Yet he still had charisma.

"Peter was a star, no question," says David Barham. "He cultivated this aura of danger around him but it was all to do with his personality. He really engaged with his audience and whilst he could be abrasive at times, that was his big, black scary alter ego, come to unleash hellfire and brimstone down on non-believers. I think he played up to that a bit. He'd spout his rhetoric in a very prophetic, almost preacher-like manner and it was very theatrical, which was great. To my way of thinking that was all part of his show and I never felt he was entirely serious."

Later that same evening he'll appear on *Saturday Night Live*, which was filmed less than half a block from the Rolling Stones' office, in Rockefeller Plaza. He's booked to perform two songs – one of them 'Don't Look Back', featuring surprise guest Mick Jagger. In commercial terms, Peter had now reached the mountaintop. *Saturday Night Live* had been on air for three years and attracted huge ratings for its fast-moving blend of comedy and variety acts. Elliott Gould, Dan Aykroyd, Bill Murray and John Belushi, who delighted in parodying well-known American figures, were among the cast. Belushi and Aykroyd will later reinvent themselves as the Blues Brothers. Mick Jagger had met them in Los Angeles, where they were partying hard with Ronnie Wood. Shortly afterwards the Rolling Stones were invited on *Saturday Night Live*, then Peter's name entered the frame. Eppy was in Jamaica working on Max Edwards' 'Rockers Arena' when he got a call from Jane Rose. Eppy sometimes referred acts to *Saturday Night Live* if someone cancelled and she was lobbying for him to recommend Peter.

"I called the booking agent and he said, 'But Eppy, Peter doesn't mean anything to people outside of New York. Maybe in Boston or LA but most Americans don't know what reggae is. It's premature and it doesn't make any sense to put Peter on but if you had Mick Jagger singing with him, then maybe I could pull it off.'

"I went back to Jane and she said, 'That's not happening in our lifetime!' Anyway so there I was in Jamaica working on this great record, Jane calls back and says there's been a cancellation and Mick has said OK. She says 'You've got Freddie Silverman's seats' – he was the guy who ran NBC at that time – and to drop what I was doing because Mick and Keith wanted me to be there. I got the first flight back to New York and met up with Dennis McNamara, who drove us to NBC. Once they close the doors you don't get in because it's recorded live. They'd already started but I said, 'but I have Freddie Silverman's seat!' They made checks and got us into this show that I loved so much.

"Backstage the booking agent sits me at his desk, opens a drawer and there's a gold razor and gold cocaine spoons. Here I am holding court in his office and having the time of my life. Peter never touched cocaine though, ever. I know that. I saw people use it in front of him and he'd never join in."

It's less than two weeks from Christmas and festivities are already underway. Peter walked into Studio 8H flanked by Mick Jagger, Keith Richards and some Rasta brethren. After a few introductions – his fellow guests included comedians Bob Elliott and Ray Goulding – he stood quietly observing the frantic costume changes, each one more surreal than the last.

"*Saturday Night Live* happened twice every Saturday night," Mikey Chung explains. "The first show was a rehearsal, and then the second show went out live. It was fascinating watching them do all those sketches and routines in-between doing the set changes. All that happens right before your eyes. It was amazing to see how everything was timed to the nearest second, like a military operation."

Stephen Davis, writing in *Reggae International*, witnessed a "super esoteric" dressing-room conversation between Peter and the two Rolling Stones about gospel singing in Jamaican churches. "Jagger speaks of wandering incognito around them, learning how to sing really high. Tosh very regal and totally lacking in nerves, Mick loose and at home, straddling Rasta reasoning and the vibes of the ultra-centre of the '70s media zeitgeist backrooms of *Saturday Night Live*.

"The two madly different music masters eventually stroll out to the studio floor for the dress rehearsal where they do the Temptations' 'Don't Look Back' with great energy and humour. Mick jogging before he goes on, Peter slowly toking from his epic pipe, emitting an aura of 'this is what the modern prophet should be doing'. Mick looks a little grey before he hits the raised stage for the real show but by the time of the midnight live performance, he is shining, funny and ready to rip and reggae. Tosh, as usual, is philosophical and unnerved."

Mick Jagger, resplendent in a white suit that night, had strolled on stage unannounced. There'd been no pressure on him beforehand, and he and Peter give a wonderfully relaxed performance. Peter's lack of nerves is extraordinary when you consider that it's his first major television appearance and millions are watching. It wasn't like back in Jamaica, where the one television station operated from 6 p.m. until midnight, and the term "ratings" had a very different meaning. Mikey Chung says that Peter never suffered from stage fright, and wouldn't have shown it even if he had.

The second tune he played that night was 'Bush Doctor'. Looking directly into the camera, a red, gold and green scarf knotted nonchalantly around his neck, he tells the huge television audience that cigarette smoking is dangerous and then sings, "Legalise marijuana..." It's probably the only pro-marijuana song to ever receive coast-to-coast television coverage in the US and more than 30 years later, you still don't see or hear anything like it on mainstream television. Every time it plays on YouTube, you half expect someone to shout "Cut!" and the screen to go blank. And to think that Peter Tosh is accused of having sold out! Suffice to say the band's in great form, and that's Gwen Guthrie singing gospel-fired harmonies alongside two other black, female backing singers.

"That was where Peter went overboard and started to breakout," says Sly Dunbar. "Peter Touch got into the homes of a lot of Americans when he did that show, and especially because Mick was there as well."

Two weeks after appearing on *Saturday Night Live*, Peter performed 'Don't Look Back' (without Mick) on a German television show called *Rock Pop*, filmed in Munich. What a contrast. Peter and the whole band were miming, and with a largely uncomprehending audience sat in a semi-circle just a few feet away. This time they do have somebody miming tenor sax, and it's Al Anderson! Bob wasn't touring at the time and there was no animosity between his and Peter's musicians, even if they didn't play sessions together.

Once back in Jamaica, Peter became intent on recharging his system. He ran a lot, bathed in sea and rivers, and revelled in the Jamaican countryside. Being close to nature was a return to the source, aided by meditation. He was now eating good food, drinking root tonics and smoking the best herb. His favourites were sensimelia, lambs bread, goat shit and a special variety he called "short-day herb" with little bumps on the stick. "And each of those can blow your head off," he would say. "Herb is anti-fungus, anti-virus, antidote and anti-bacterial. You would never think something has so many antis in it. It is dangerously dangerous to diseases."

His home parish of Westmoreland was famous for the quality of its herb. Peter had retained close links with the area, and took a keen interest in community projects. He'd occasionally visit local schools and colleges and talk to the students, who'd look on in amazement as he rode his unicycle. He'd also grown closer to the Ethiopian Orthodox Church, where he'll be baptised Wolde Semayat – an Amharic term for "Son Of Thunder". What a perfect name for Peter Tosh!

Spiritual regeneration thereby went hand-in-hand with the physical. Once restored, his thoughts turned in the direction of a follow-up album, which he and Geoffrey Chung will co-produce at Dynamic. Peter had been disappointed with the reaction to *Bush Doctor* in Jamaica. The local radio stations weren't really behind it and the title track was banned in any case.

"A lot of people in Jamaica used to talk about they never heard his music on the radio," says Sly, "but the radio DJs there didn't really care about the music. Some of them came into it after working in the background. They played no part in the development of the music and they didn't know where it was coming from."

Lack of support at home only made reggae figureheads like Marley and Tosh more determined to prove their critics wrong. Peter wasn't going to be bullied into returning to a more basic style of production or playing the same style of music he was making three or four years ago, when he was still finding his feet. Since then he'd grown a great deal both musically and otherwise, and wanted to move the music forwards, not backwards.

"What do you say to those critics who say that *Bush Doctor* was too commercial?" a radio presenter once asked him. "Them people are idiots man," Peter had answered. "They are very fanatic in their thinking and talking, but them don't know nothing about music. They only hear music and accuse."

He makes the point that most of his critics smoke herb and therefore live with the very real possibility of getting busted. Yet they couldn't support a song like 'Bush Doctor', which defends their interests. "I also have a song like 'Stand Firm' which says, 'Live clean and let your works be seen. Stand firm or go feed worm', and yet them still say that's commercial, seen? But I am not here to please them because the more critics you get, is the more progress you make. So let more critics come 'cause every time they criticise me I get more inspiration, progressively."

He'll start as he always did – by noting down a few lyrics, booking some studio time, calling a session and then seeing if they can rouse a little magic.

"Peter might play guitar and sing us the songs whilst I accompanied him on electric piano and from there, everything can happen," recalls Mikey Chung. "Robbie, Sly, Peter and myself would work on songs together and then cut the basic tracks. Sometimes Peter wouldn't have all the lyrics so we'd have to establish verse, chorus and so on first, before we could finish them. From there now, Robbie Lyn would come in and play piano, and we'd start overdubbing from there. We'd add rhythm and lead guitar and the horns..."

That's how he arrived at tracks like 'Mystic Man', which is unmistakably autobiographical, and will become the title track of his new album. "I man don't drink no champagne," he sings. "No, I don't. And I man don't sniff cocaine..." The list quickly grows to include morphine ("dangerous"), heroin, fried chicken, frankfurters ("garbage"), hamburgers and soda. He doesn't "play fools' games on Saturday" or "congregate on a Sunday". He's a mystic man; a man of the past who's living in the present and "stepping in the future".

"That song come from being around the Rolling Stones," says his cousin Carlton. "That's why him have to sing that song. He had to let them know who he is, if they didn't know already. You see Peter he didn't play around; the man stand firm at *all times*. He didn't care who you are, but nothing's going to get in the way of his principles. That's the kind of man he was. He was a loving man, and he was clean. He never got corrupted in nothing. He wasn't a drugs seller; he wasn't into drinking alcohol or smoking tobacco. All this man do is smoke his herbs and that's what he couldn't understand, because why couldn't he just smoke his herbs in peace?"

Peter wanted freedom to smoke herb everywhere, including Buckingham Palace, home to British royalty and symbolic heart of the Babylonian empire. His latest ganja anthem, 'Buk-In-Hamm Palace' (note the deliberate misspelling), is the musical equivalent of storming the Bastille. It clocks in at over eight minutes, and the dub version on the 12″ will be longer. It opens with Peter testifying to music's healing properties, but then here comes the anarchy. "Light up your spliff. Light your chalice," he chants. "We go a smoke it in a Buckingham Palace. Lend me a paper. Lend me some fire. Make me chase 'way vampire..." Some interesting stuff happens five minutes in, when Peter scats over chicken scratch guitar. "This is true emancipation, come to set my people free," he enthuses. The

Latin percussion will be overdubbed later but this is brilliant, exciting and funky music, blessed with a great arrangement, and classy harmonies and horns.

"I got a lot of cussing for suggesting songs like 'Buk-In-Hamm Palace', trust me!" says Robbie Shakespeare, whose bass line betrays mastery of disco pyrotechnics. "If any of his friends tell him 'Peter, you start playing funky,' he'd always tell them it was my fault. He'd say, 'bwoy, Robbie is the one behind that.' He'd start to cuss me but if someone said the song was very good, then he'd say it was him! He and I were friends so we had it as a joke, y' know? But he trusted us and the musical knowledge was there. When you're hungry and pushing ahead, and you find an avenue where you can experiment, then you make use of that, right? Because that was the time we start to use a lot of synthesizer and two or three guitars playing mostly rock or blues, because we feel that fit in good with the reggae. I got cussing for that too but it work out well in the end."

Robbie Shakespeare and Mikey Chung – who'll be credited with "invaluable assistance in the production of this album" – had a lot of say in the kind of music he was making, but Peter had the final word. As well as success, he wanted his music to make a difference and trying to homogenise such ambition with mainstream American tastes was never going to be easy.

His musicians weren't so encumbered. They were still busy making their reputations and listening to contemporary music by the likes of Kool & The Gang, Brass Construction and Barry White. Sly Dunbar loved the Philly International sound and was eager to incorporate elements of it into reggae. Third World's cover of the O' Jays' 'Now That We've Found Love' had just been a massive hit, and their follow-up single 'Cool Meditation' will stay on the British charts for over two months. This was the acceptable face of reggae, but it was also extending the music's reach and taking it international. Sly liked how Third World used African influences in their music, as on 'Lagos Jump'. He'd recently returned from a trip to Senegal feeling energised by the rhythms he'd heard there, and such influences were bound to surface in his own work.

"We were experimenting, because I'd just made a record of my own called *Sly, Wicked And Slick*," he explains. "There was this song on it called 'Rasta Fiesta', and we were listening to it and said, 'Let's make a beat like this for Peter.' The very next thing we did after that was 'Buk-In-Hamm Palace' because if you listen to it, it has that same groove. Robbie and I

Peter learnt to ride his unicycle by pedaling up and down hotel corridors. PETER SIMON

Peter demonstrating his unicycle skills in Kingston, 1978. ADRIAN BOOT/URBANIMAGE.TV

'Don't Look Back' video shoot with Mick Jagger, Strawberry Hill, Jamaica late 1978. ADRIAN BOOT/URBANIMAGE.TV

Peter with Word, Sound & Power, Strawberry Hill, Jamaica late 1978. Left to right: Mikey Chung, Robbie Lyn, Peter, Keith Sterling, Sly Dunbar and Robbie Shakespeare. ADRIAN BOOT/URBANIMAGE.TV

TOSH
BRUTALISED

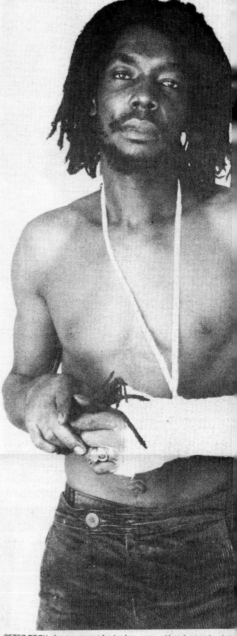

EX-WAILER Peter Tosh was arrested and held overnight by Jamaican police last Tuesday. In the process he sustained a broken arm and severe head wounds which later received over twenty stitches.

Despite his injuries, Tosh — now emerging as one of the leading international figures of Jamaican music — will still be visiting the UK in late October for a series of dates to coincide with the release of his new album and single on Rolling Stones Records.

The arrest came last Tuesday outside the Kingston studios where he was rehearsing with his band, Sound And Power. Tosh — who is a karate expert — had stepped outside for a break when he was apprehended by a policeman for allegedly smoking a spliff.

During the arrest the policeman drew his gun. A struggle apparently ensued, during which the policeman's gun was knocked to the ground. More police arrived and Tosh was taken into custody.

At this point he was not apparently suffering from any injuries.

Despite the intervention of his old friend and former associate Bob Marley, who turned up at the prison where Tosh was being held and made an impassioned plea for his release, the 33-year-old musician remained in the police cells overnight. The following morning, handcuffed and under heavy guard, Tosh was taken to the prison hospital, where he received treatment for his arm and head injuries. He was later released on bail after being charged with possessing ganja and resisting arrest.

A leading Jamaican lawyer has now been appointed to defend Tosh against the charges, and he has already made several counter-charges against the police.

This is not the first time that Peter Tosh has brushed with the notoriously vindictive Jamaican police. In early '75, shortly after his split with The Wailers (formed in the early '60s by Marley, Tosh and Bunny 'Wailer' Livingstone), Tosh was arrested outside his home — again on a ganja rap — and later received hospital treatment for rib and internal injuries. Tosh later told *Black Music* scribe Carl Gayle that he had been beaten with rifle butts and handcuffed to a stretcher for several hours before being allowed medical care.

Shortly afterwards he released "Mark Of The Beast", an anti-police song.

Tosh's dispute with the Jamaican police is not confined to these two arrests. He had long been a critic of the force, and in particular of its apparently selective and often vicious application of the island's ganja laws (despite the widespread and much publicised practice of smoking the 'erb it is still illegal). From the outset his songs have been passionate, vitriolic and militant, as titles like "I'm The Toughest" (his first solo disc from '66), and "Get Up Stand Up" (co-written with Marley), readily testify. His 1976 ganja paean "Legalise It" became a rallying cry both in Jamaica and elsewhere, and also saw Tosh's elevation as self-styled 'Minister Of Herb', since when he has often defied arrest by smoking 'erb openly. As a Rastafarian, Tosh regards the weed as a God-given sacrament.

Beside his skill in karate, he often carries a bolas — a weapon resembling two blackjacks joined by a short length of rope.

But undoubtedly the uneasy relations between the police and the international star were stretched tauter than ever after his appearance at the Kingston 'Peace Festival' in April this year. Attended by 200 international press, and several thousand Jamaicans, the concert was held to celebrate the 'peace' between rival polical gangs in the ghettos of Kingston, and to raise funds for the emergent Peace Movement. Bob Marley topped the bill; both Prime Minister Michael Manley and opposition leader Edward Seaga were present and later joined hands onstage with Marley.

Peter Tosh had his own ideas on what the peace concert was about, however, and besides playing the

TOSH displays stitches.

PETER TOSH after treatment for broken arm and head wounds, clutc[...] dreadlocks snipped off for stitches.

night's outstanding set, delivered an obscenity-studded denouncement of the ganja laws and the way the police and army "brutalise the poor people for an ickle draw of 'erb". A dread smoking a blazing chalice appeared below the stage, while Tosh himself lit up a giant spliff before the Prime Minister and the delighted crowd, and senior police and army officials glowered powerless.

Whatever else, last week's in[...] is unlikely to subdue the righteo[...] of Peter Tosh, who is said to be [...] intent than ever on making a si[...] impression during his forthcom[...] European tour.

NEIL SPENCER

THRILLS

NME feature on his beating at the hands of the Kingston police after returning to Jamaica from the Some Girls *tour, October 1978.* NME

Receiving an award in Brooklyn, 1979. CHUCK PULIN

Peter with the Tamlins, who sang backing vocals on many of his hit records and world tours. RON GALELLA/WIREIMAGE

Peter and Bunny in total harmony. The two former Wailers would remain friends until shortly before Peter's death.
ADRIAN BOOT/URBANIMAGE.TV

Peter and Keith Richards. Their friendship would finally fragment in 1981, after a dispute involving Keith's house near Ocho Rios, on Jamaica's North Coast ADRIAN BOOT/URBANIMAGE.TV

Peter and Marlene Brown in 1982. ADRIAN BOOT/URBANIMAGE.TV

In concert with Word, Sound & Power. Note bassist Robbie Shakespeare's confident stance. GEORGE CHIN/ICONICPIX

Bunny and Peter reasoning in Kingston.
KIM GOTTLIEB-WALKER · LENSWOMAN.COM

Dick Wingate, music industry executive visits Peter in
Kingston around the time of Equal Rights.
KIM GOTTLIEB-WALKER · LENSWOMAN.COM

The Bush Doctor in repose. LEE JAFFE

took it to him. He was playing it in his room and start jumping around to it, grooving on it and then he start to sing a few lines on it like, 'Light up my spliff, light up my chalice,' and I thought, 'Yeah, this is good!' Robbie asked Mikey Chung to come up with some arrangements so we could put some horns on it, just to make it sound different and even up until now, there's still no other recording like it in Jamaica."

Peter and his band wanted to take reggae into areas where it had never gone before. They wanted to do something with it so that musicians from outside of Jamaica would feel inspired to play it, and want to learn more about it. That's what Sly and Robbie's predecessors had done with ska and rocksteady and they were just as keen to push the boundaries, and let the world know how versatile, irresistible and powerful reggae was. They wanted to establish reggae as being equal to jazz, blues or soul and added to Peter's missionary zeal, there could be no stopping them.

Whilst he still referred to one-drop reggae as "heart music", Peter listened to many different types of music, including country, rock, soul and jazz-funk. He had no liking for disco though, which he called "pure bullshit. People gazing in fantasy looking to find reality; it's the devil's music." As we've discovered already, Peter loved playing around with language, and in a New York hotel suite one time he expounded on the letter "D", which he said stood for "devil, disco, demon, dangerous, deception, dagger, depression, disruptive, deprive…"

Disco was played in all the clubs, and was the music of the day. The Stones knew this, which is why 'Miss You' had proved so successful. Peter could therefore hardly be blamed for trying something similar. By the end of 1978, *Saturday Night Fever* had become the bestselling album in history, with sales of over 30 million. The Bee Gees won five Grammys on the strength of material like 'Staying Alive' as disco went mainstream, and it took on a glamorous allure. *Time* magazine called it "a Cinderella world of self-stardom" even as nightclubs proliferated and DJs replaced bar bands. Maligned by the music press (so what's new?), disco had continued to attract large audiences in the US, and its popularity spanned racial and generational divides. American viewers were treated to television specials on the New York club Studio 54 and disco group Village People whilst some radio stations were so smitten they changed formats.

Peter's new music wasn't disco, but a hybrid of funk and reggae. Had he wanted to compete with Donna Summer or the Bee Gees, he would have contacted his old friend Albhy Galuten, the synthesizer player from Criteria who produced *Saturday Night Fever*. Peter was just keeping abreast of the times that's all, and with a strain of contemporary black music that deserves a great deal of credit.

He was now writing freely, and the notes he'd scribbled in various notebooks were giving birth to some serious songs. 'The Day The Dollar Die' documents the spiralling cost of living until "dollar see that, have heart attack and die..." His vision of financial meltdown sounds more like 35 years later, and Babylon's demise guarantees a happy ending. "It's going to be nice. No more corruption," he croons, joyously. "People will respect each other" and best of all, "I won't need a pocket..." Because when the currency fails the people will be free to trade, and by honest means.

'Crystal Ball' is a companion piece, and just as good. Peter's asking the leaders what they see when they look ahead. From his viewpoint, he sees Biblical Armageddon – a grim vista of wars, rivers of blood, injustice and inequality. The vision is stark but the music is irresistible, and his use of "inna the shitty" for city bold and amusing. The track that's least like reggae is 'Can't You See' which he's recorded twice before, for Coxsone and Leslie Kong. It's now the perfect synthesis of reggae and rock and not least because of the howling lead guitar solos, since Peter's even singing in a rock style. This is what Sly means by "he was singing so raw" back then. You can hear it on live shows from around this time. His voice is earthier, and he finally does the song justice.

Sly and Robbie hardly let the grass grow beneath their feet in between anchoring 'Mystic Man' sessions. They'd saved as much of their money as possible whilst on the road and invested it in studio time. In a short time, their Taxi label will be storming the reggae market with hits by Junior Delgado, Dennis Brown, the Wailing Souls, Tamlins, Jimmy Riley and Gregory Isaacs, who gave them their first number one hit with 'Soon Forward'. After touring with the Stones, Sly and Robbie had searched for something that would give their music a lift, and make it sound more powerful when played live. Sly started using an open snare – which he then overdubbed with a Syn Drum – and Robbie played with even more attack than usual. Such changes made the music sound more militant, and Black Uhuru came along at exactly the right time. Sly and Robbie had played on the group's first album for Prince Jammy, and invited them to record for Taxi. Peter was fond of them too, and liked what they stood for. They were rebels like himself; fighting against the system with righteousness and reggae music. Lead singer Michael Rose says he learned a lot by watching Peter record.

"I get enough inspiration from Peter, trust me," he concurs, "because the man was *militant*! And we find nothing like that round here right now."

In early January, Sly and Robbie were at Channel One studios on Maxfield Avenue, working on several new Black Uhuru recordings. Sly then had the idea of inviting Keith Richards to join them.

"Keith was in Jamaica and so I rang him and said we were doing a session and did he want to come and play? He said, 'Yeah, no problem,' so we invited him down to Channel One and what he played that day, it was like a *rocket!*"

That's Keith getting lowdown and nasty on 'Shine Eye Gal' – a reggae tour-de-force that's steeped in ghetto reality, and with a rhythm to match. "I'm drawn to reggae because there's nothing happening in black American music," Richards told Victor Bockris. "They're going through the disco phase. It's very popular and no wonder people are drawn to it. Reggae took off because there are more Jamaicans in Britain and America than there are in Jamaica! Bob Marley has created an international status for reggae and now Africa will be a big market for the music too. Trouble is, I don't know if roots reggae is what people want to hear from me. When I've got an album's worth of material in front of me, then I'll think about releasing it. I've got Robbie Shakespeare on bass, Sly Dunbar on drums, and Robert Lyn on piano. I've been going to Jamaica for over 10 years now..."

U Roy played Black Uhuru's 'Guess Who's Coming To Dinner', 'Abortion', 'General Penitentiary' and 'Shine Eye Gal' on exclusive dub-plates for almost a year before they were released. His sound system was called Sturgav, and people would tear down the fence to get closer to that thundering reggae drum and bass. The excitement would soon reach the ears of Island's Chris Blackwell and also Virgin, who'll win the race for Uhuru's *Showcase* album. After his adventures at Channel One Keith left for Compass Point studios in Nassau, where the Stones will resume work on their next album, *Emotional Rescue*. Much to engineer Chris Kimsey's surprise, they recorded a reggae song called 'Jah No Dead...'

The influence clearly worked both ways, although not in everything. As usual, Peter was spending time reading his Bible. His social and cultural concerns are well known, but spiritual objectives were important too and there's at least one gospel reggae track on each of his albums. He's in familiar victim mode on 'Jah Say No', but then ends the song bathed in glorious conviction. It's a song of pride and dignity, whilst 'Recruiting Soldiers' opens with a greeting in Amharic and is a close relative of Marley's 'Jah Live' in that it refutes news of Emperor Haile Selassie I's death and is a rallying cry for the Rasta cause. Peter comments how Marcus Garvey is now a National Hero and revered, but from what he can see, "If he was here right now, he'd go to jail same way..."

Barbara Charone, Keith Richards' first biographer, interviewed Peter before leaving for Nassau. Her article will appear in *Creem* magazine during March, and it opens with a ringing endorsement from Richards who says, "If anyone can bring reggae music to the rest of the world, especially America, then Peter's the one to do it along with Bob Marley. After all, we were second to the Beatles. You need a door opener and then you need the serious stuff. I'm not saying Marley isn't serious. It's just that Peter has chosen his scene, his band and his music very carefully. And he's done an amazing job of putting it all together."

In Barbara's opinion, Peter has no need of exploiting his connections with Bob Marley or the Rolling Stones, despite poor sales figures. "His first two albums released on CBS, *Legalise It* and *Equal Rights*, did not sell well, despite critical acclaim," she reports.

She's taken by his personality though, and credits him with having "a friendly smile, lots of nervous energy and enough confidence to make him a star", as well as "a unique individualism that is most attractive". When asked about the beating he received just a few months earlier, Peter says he's been left with a hefty medical bill, as well as scars and recurring headaches.

"The oppression that I live, that's what I sing," he tells her. "I can't get up as an international singer and sing about love when the police brutalise me. No man, that is madness. People do that and it worries me, but do I look like a madman?"

Hardly surprising then, that Barbara calls Jamaica "a bizarre cross section of the beautiful and the damned", and a place "where graffiti on the walls proclaims 'The Poor Can't Take It No More'".

On the evening of February 4, JLP enforcer and Peace Treaty organiser Claudie Massop died in a hail of bullets at the corner of Industrial Terrace and Marcus Garvey Drive. He was executed by a detachment of special police who'd ambushed him as he returned home from a football game. He and two companions were ordered to get out of the car with their hands in the air. A search was made of the vehicle, and a revolver found in the trunk. An officer showed this gun to a man sat in the back of an unmarked car across the road, who then gave the order to kill. There were entry wounds in Massop's armpits, which indicates he was defenceless when the shots were fired. None of the three men were wanted by the police and yet no questions were asked, but everyone knew that Claudie's talk of peace had distorted the political balance, and that he and Aston 'Bucky' Marshall – another of the Peace Concert organisers, who'll be murdered in New York the following March – had to be taken out. The Peace Treaty was no more, just as Peter had predicted.

The world already felt like a more dangerous place. In December Vietnam had invaded Kampuchea and now the Chinese were making inroads into North Vietnam. Two weeks earlier, the Shah of Iran had been driven into exile by Shi'ite Muslims. At times, it felt like these really were the "Last Days" as prophesised in the Bible. Peter will tap into the zeitgeist once again on 'Rumours Of War' – firstly by pleading for divine intervention, and then with talk of "war in the Lebanon, Pakistan, Namibia, Soweto, Johannesburg, South Africa...".

'Fight On' was written in support of African freedom fighters, and is a song of equal importance to Marley's 'Africa Unite' or 'Zimbabwe'. To Peter's way of thinking, black liberation has to start with the restoration of Africa and an end to colonialism. "We need majority rule," he thunders, and it's a call that will be heard all over the African continent in due course.

Peter was in America by the time he heard about Claudie Massop's murder. He and the band were preparing to play several nights at the Roxy Theatre in Los Angeles after warm up concerts in Huntington Beach and San Diego. A typical set list would now include '400 Years', 'Steppin' Razor', 'Pick Myself Up', 'African', 'Burial', 'Soon Come', 'I'm The Toughest', 'Bush Doctor', 'Don't Look Back', 'Get Up Stand Up' and 'Legalise It'. There were few variations and yet Peter wasn't too regimented, since the band members still had a fair amount of freedom. Those Roxy dates took place on February 5, 6 and 7. Britt Ekland arrived one night dressed in a luminous, purple sheath that was so tight it looked as if it had been sprayed on. She was Rod Stewart's girlfriend but this meant little to Peter, who wasn't all that interested in celebrities or celebrity.

Ken Tucker, writing in the *Herald Examiner*, described him as "an imposing figure. From his thick, splayed dreadlocks to his Army surplus boots and the kung fu togs in-between. All this was undercut by a witty, debonair touch – a pair of handcuffs dangled from Tosh's left wrist". Tucker points out that Peter has worn cuffs "in all seriousness, and they were applied by real police". He correctly identifies that his music is "meant to excoriate the social ills that plague many of Tosh's brethren, from unduly harsh sentences for marijuana possession to a more endemic, systematic oppression meted out to all Third World inhabitants". The music's described as "long, sustained grooves that carry the lilt of American soul music and R & B, along with the kineticism of African melodies". He calls it "folk-trance music that leaves one not numbed, but quite the opposite – in a state of heightened awareness". Peter would have loved that.

After a short trip to San Francisco, he played two consecutive nights at the Old Waldorf, playing two sets a night. Jeff Cathrow, writing in *Reggae Report*, describes the crowd as "sometimes rude and unappreciative. Unfortunately, the audiences at the four sold-out in advance shows consisted primarily of Rolling Stones fans who had come hoping to see Mick Jagger and Keith Richards appear with Tosh," he writes, under a headline proclaiming "Tosh Mashes San Francisco". The Stones never showed, naturally. The review praises Tosh's "hard yet soul-soothing reggae" and states: "Sly Dunbar held a tight rein on things with the power bank of drums he controlled, glancing left and right under his 'Prince Valiant' dreadlocks." Robbie is described as "possessed by the relentless throbbing of his bass. Robbie stomped, ran and lurched, resembling a dreadlocked King Kong warding off evil Babylonian captors". (Did *Reggae Report* really print that?) "His bass was so powerful it could be felt throughout the Old Waldorf, and to further complement the heavy vibrations came the stinging lead guitar work of Donald Kinsey. Kinsey's solos were as outrageous as his snakeskin and velvet jacket, and only the roots reggae purists in the audience later denounced his rock-orientated style.

"Tosh failed to encore the second show, as the crowd became too concerned with their Quaaludes, cocaine and the whereabouts of Mick Jagger. Cries of 'Bring on the Stones' were heard, and as Peter Tosh left the stage, he gave the audience a sneering glance..."

Cathrow ventured backstage after the show, where Peter was railing about the Jones Town massacre in which 900 members of a religious cult committed mass suicide. "And WHO is being found guilty for that?" he barked. "Who is responsible for that? No one knows... Jah know! We are living in a tense age, seen? And the whole world is preparing for war."

The Friday shows were noticeably better. Fewer people expected the Stones to show, and many more reggae fans were in attendance. Next stop was the Catalyst Club, which Matty Zorn described as, "Santa Cruz's number one Babylonian boogie spot". These West Coast crowds suited Peter. Hippies liked reggae's trance-like rhythms and spiritual, revolutionary message, and recognised its affinity with the stoned, new age consciousness promoted by bands like the Grateful Dead. Alas, Peter's music was sometimes viewed as a mite too sophisticated. Local newspaper *Good Times* claimed he "adds a lot of gloss to this essentially simple and soulful music" – an observation that Peter countered by saying he's "only putting reggae where it's supposed to be". The article ends by looking forward to his Catalyst show, "which will be a sign of what to expect from the wedding of reggae and the music industry."

In fact it was a sell-out. "The air was filled with approving raised fists, and Peter Tosh was nearly obscured by sweet smoke. The ex-Wailer later produced a cigar-sized, handmade cigarette and shared the wealth by dropping it into the sea of waiting hands."

He got a similar reaction in Colorado, where he performed on February 13. Under the headline "Tosh In Concert: Kingston With Touch Of Vegas", local journalist Michael Ross reported that "reggae star Peter Tosh returned to Boulder on Tuesday night for two sold-out performances at the Boulder Theatre that verified Tosh is a showman in the best – and unfortunately the worst – sense of the word. With his big nine-piece band, this most prominent alumnus of Bob Marley & The Wailers may yet inherit the title of 'James Brown of reggae'. Like Brown, Tosh's is an energetic live performance that carries the same intensity in a stadium as it does in a posh theatre downtown. Tosh gave the overflowing crowds just what they came for – solid sets of Jamaica's national music presented with a refreshing flair and punch."

Ross takes exception to the MC "in a garish satin jacket coaxing applause from the audience" and the selling of merchandise in the lobby. He also claims that Peter's Tuesday night performance "was almost too smooth, too slick a presentation for a reggae show", whatever that may mean. It's a parallel to what Muddy Waters experienced after the great bluesman had taken his electric band to England back in the early sixties. British audiences had expected to see him wearing overalls and singing plantation songs – not dressed in fine suits and delivering gritty commentaries on Chicago's mean streets.

Two shows at the Dallas Palladium on February 15 went without incident and also a date at Ole Man River's in Avondale, which prompted local journalist Bunny Matthews to fantasise what might happen if Peter turned up unannounced at the ranch style home of America's Mr. Average.

"Peter Tosh, conditioned by daily preparations of THC, dressed in a Mexican serape bearing the Ethiopian national colours, blue jeans and green and yellow Nikes and with spliff of potent herb dangling from his mouth, walks past the station wagon with imitation wood trim parked on the cement driveway and flips off his tam exposing a whole head of prolific dreadlocks, which he swings about like an unleashed nest of black vipers. Peter takes a toke and then, sweet as Tupelo honey, offers the usual Rastafarian greeting, 'Peace and Love'. Mr. Average succumbs to cardiac arrest and collapses on his monogrammed doormat. Thus is dread..."

He plays the Capri Ballroom in Atlanta on February 22 and sings a magnificent, slower version of 'Downpressor Man'. It's interesting to note how certain of his songs continue to evolve. Some are self-contained time capsules, whereas others are definitely more organic. Next stop is Madison (Headliners on the 25th) and Minneapolis (Thumpers on the 26th). Peter then gets to spend a week in New York, most of which is taken up by putting finishing touches to the *Mystic Man* album at Sound Mixers, and with Geoffrey Chung sat alongside him. Since he was pleased with what they'd done on *Bush Doctor*, Peter called for the same group of seasoned New York session musicians as last time. Gwen Guthrie, Yvonne Lewis and Brenda White again sing harmonies, and they're joined in the studio by George Young (alto sax), Lou Marini (tenor sax), Howard Johnson (baritone sax), Mike Lawrence (trumpet) and Barry Rogers (trombone). Ed Walsh adds layers of Oberheim synthesizer, Ed Elizalde plays lead guitar on 'Can't You See' and Sammy Figueroa plays congas on 'Mystic Man' and 'Buk-In-Hamm Palace'.

"We used those guys because we'd seen their names on records," says Mikey Chung, who arranged the horns with help from Clive Hunt. "They were top of the line, and sometimes Peter's management wasn't so enthusiastic because they cost more. It was the same thing with the background singers, but it worked. People thought we were getting too Americanised or whatever but we knew what we wanted and we got it. We were real perfectionists when it came to that."

Sammy Figueroa and Barry Rogers had recently played on Chic's 'Le Freak' – a disco anthem that sold six million copies. Knowing his opinion of such things, we assume they didn't mention this to Peter! What's important to remember here is that no one was forcing him to compromise, or interfering with his creative process. We should also note that Rolling Stones Records was backing him all the way, and granting him the means to show what he could do.

His next show will be at the Convocation Hall in Toronto on March 4. Peter played two shows there, an early and late show. A review duly appeared in the *Globe And Mail* dated Monday March 5. Paul McGrath describes him as "the most respected musician–poet–preacher in reggae, more so than his former collaborator Bob Marley because he has stayed angrier longer and has shied away from pop phrasing". McGrath goes on to say, "He was commanding on his stage as Martin Luther King was in his pulpit, and the feeling of staring the entire black race in the face was as present there as it was at the Washington Memorial when Dr. King explained his dream." The reviewer also talks about Peter's "messianic message" and "the infectious, sinewy rhythms".

"The problem with smoke in the hall (where a strict no smoking rule is in force at all times) didn't escalate until Tosh sang 'Legalise It' for his encore," he continues. "At this point the joints started to fire and the security guards started to look very nervous but none of them were willing to tangle with a hall full of Rastas pursuing the dictates of their conscience..."

The following night Peter played My Father's Place out in Long Island and was given a royal welcome by Eppy and other old friends before travelling to Philadelphia and performing at a packed Walnut Street Theatre. Flyers had stated that Peter would be accompanied by "a VERY special guest" but this turned out to be local band Exuma, not Mick Jagger as many thought.

"There were isolated shrieks of 'We want Jagger' from the crowd but they were shouted down almost immediately by Tosh devotees, and the whining ceased," wrote one reviewer, who accuses a local newspaper of calling Peter "a Jagger imitator", and dismissing reggae records as "all sounding the same".

That night's biggest cheers were reserved for 'Bush Doctor', and "Peter certainly seemed to enjoy himself, strutting back and forth across the stage with a spliff the size of an Optimo, teasing the front rows and singing with a power and range not detectable on vinyl."

This same reviewer mentions how "the Bush Doctor is now working out of New York". In fact he's not living there yet, although he is looking around for an apartment. On March 7 and 8 he played the Bottom Line on West Fourth Street. The Bottom Line had fewer tables than Max's but Bill Graham acknowledged it had become as important as the Fillmore East in helping to develop an artist's career. The Mighty Diamonds and Toots & the Maytals had passed through back in 1976 but few, if any, other reggae acts had been there since. It mainly hosted rock, pop and new wave acts as well as record company launch parties and showcase events. The early shows were especially popular with music industry types, who could eat there if they were lucky enough to find a seat, or join the hundred or so people allowed to stand between the tables if not.

Murray Elias, who worked there in the late seventies, calls it "the right venue at the right time. Record companies liked it, and VIPs felt comfortable there. The sound quality was awesome, and so was the live mix. Bands were treated great as well..."

Peter was now one of the hottest draws in New York. The seven dollar tickets sold out fast, despite his March 3 show being broadcast on WNEW FM. He's travelling to and from these gigs in a black limousine, and cuts quite a dash as he arrives outside the Bottom Line. Patricia O'Haire, writing in the *New York Daily News*, said the club was populated with the "usual mix of fans, media types, record company people and hangers-on, sitting closer-than-this and waiting almost anxiously for the entertainment to begin." She describes people milling around the entrance on West Fourth and across Mercer Street. "The backstage was crowded too – the communal dressing room was smoky and packed with musicians tuning instruments, drinking tea or rum, chattering, getting stage clothes, smiling and without the usual tension and nervousness associated with performers about to go on-stage.

"In the middle of the room, at the eye of the storm, was a tall, slim, graceful looking man named Peter Tosh, calmly peeling and eating an orange. He's dressed in black, satin type trousers tucked into knee-high boots and yellow kimono style jacket with sleeves that stop just short of a manacle dangling from his right wrist.

"On his first solo tour here, Tosh brought along a bag of interesting songs but his performing style hadn't quite pulled together," she remarks. "At that time he seemed to be working with his body only; his mind seemed to be off somewhere else and the two weren't connecting – and they weren't connecting with the audience either, not like now. This time, electricity sparkles like a Con Ed generator. Backed by a solid band with three back-up singers, he weaves a powerful path from the slower, easier paced numbers which open his show to the strong, biting and bitter statements that bring the audience to its feet, cheering."

Robert Palmer reviewed Peter's first night at the Bottom Line for the *New York Times*. He says that Tosh "brought the tightest, most powerful reggae that has yet played in the United States into the Bottom Line on Wednesday."

He calls Peter's current tour "the most extensive yet attempted by a Jamaican reggae artist. But not even Keith Richards' presence at the second show of the evening detracted from the impression Mr. Tosh and his band made on their own terms. They were simply overwhelming."

Like Patricia O'Haire, Palmer notes how Peter was "a somewhat indifferent performer" during his initial appearances in New York, but has since "become really exceptional". And he makes special mention of Sly and Robbie, describing them as "one of the very best rhythm sections in all of popular music" before remarking how Wednesday night's shows "were of the highest quality all the way round. One came away feeling that if any Jamaican star is going to explode in the United States, it will surely be Mr. Tosh."

You can tell why Peter liked New York. Audiences there were more progressive, and accepted how he was attempting to move the reggae genre forward. His shows at the Bottom Line were the talk of the town, prompting Peter to inform a radio presenter in Bethesda that reggae music is "breaking down all the barriers that have been put up, seen? Within a few months, it will be all over. Yes, that's the power of reggae music. Millions of people are going to buy it, and reggae will be the music but it takes more than that to convince them. They've got to hear good music on the record and see a good act on the stage."

He played two shows at My Father's Place on March 15 and 16. The first was broadcast on WLIR, and Eppy will later release it on his own label. "Just to straighten one thing out," he insists, "Mick Jagger *never* played my club." The following night Peter was back at the Bottom Line, and this time he will have company. Word had spread of his sensational appearance 10 days earlier and since Mick and Keith were both in New York, people knew there was every chance one or two Rolling Stones might be at these return dates. Murray Elias remembers the build-up to those shows, and tells of a man called "Bush Doctor Steve" whom he describes as "the Stones' Dr. Feel Good".

"He'd given himself that name because he was such a big Peter Tosh fan," says Murray. "He's the guy who laid on the refreshments for the Stones the night they descended on the Bottom Line. He procured some opium and before the first intermission he escorted Mick and Keith to the VIP lounge, which was essentially a freight elevator. It was a space where you could get a little bit of privacy to do drugs or whatever so everybody piled in there – Bush Doctor Steve, myself, Mick and Keith and a supervisor whose girlfriend worked for Keith as his nanny up in Westchester. Everyone had this tenuous link to each other so we were all gathered in this freight elevator doing copious amounts of opium. It was as if we were playing musical chairs, taking it in turns to snort this stuff and it was happening at a frantic pace. You zap a line and then move but the party ended abruptly when someone dropped this clear bottle of opium, which broke the second it hit the floor. It was quite a moment. Everybody was so messed up and high that no one knew how to react until a voice rang out, yelling, 'No-o-o-o!!!' I remember seeing Mick and Keith snatching at thin air, just before it smashed on the ground..."

The Bottom Line was so packed that night Jagger couldn't reach the stage and had to be passed over the heads of the crowd. As he and Peter launched into 'Don't Look Back', even the industry heads looked happy. "It was right at the moment in time," says Murray, who never doubted the Stones' interest in furthering Peter's career.

There'll be no credit for "the Glimmer Twins" this time since Mick and Keith weren't involved with the new album as producers or performers. Peter was very much on his own this time, but had every confidence in what he was doing. Mind you, members of the Rolling Stones will be busy elsewhere in any case. Keith Richards and Ronnie Wood had formed the New Barbarians, just for the fun of being on the road and playing together. At the end of April, this merry band will support the Stones at two benefit concerts at the Civic Auditorium in Ontario, as agreed at Keith's sentencing. In a declaration to the Canadian court authorities, Keith will announce that he's "grimly determined" to change his life and abstain from any drug use. "I can truthfully say that the prospect of my ever using drugs again in the future is totally alien to my thinking," he said.

Whilst Keith turned Barbarian, Mick Jagger battled with Bianca over divorce proceedings and then flew to London for Eric Clapton and Patti Harrison's wedding. Peter knew the happy couple of course, but wasn't invited and therefore missed out on a jam session involving several Beatles, the whole of Cream, Elton John, Rod Stewart and half the Who. That same month Rolling Stones Records took out a full-page advertisement in *New Musical Express* announcing Peter's new album, *Mystic Man*, and a series of UK tour dates, ending with two further nights at the Rainbow.

"*Mystic Man* picks up where *Bush Doctor* left off as Tosh's unique musical vision continues to develop and expand," it promised. Co-producers Word, Sound & Power are said to reside at the core of the music, and there's "a five-piece horn section which is featured prominently on the LP, giving a whole new dimension to Tosh's music". Tucked away in the bottom left-hand corner is the slogan "Don't let disco get you down, keep listening to reggae sounds."

Annie Leibovitz took the album cover shot, which shows Peter's head in profile with his face cupped in his hands, which are held as if in prayer. We can't see his face as his dreadlocks are pulled forward, obscuring his eyes and nose. His right hand is scarred and a simple gold chain rests on his bare chest. On the back is a photo of him riding his unicycle, smiling and looking happy against a city landscape. (Note the rude boy style flannel sticking out of his jeans' pocket.) It's a decent sleeve and great record except Lester Bangs will soon spoil the party by reflecting on how "in retrospect, it's beginning to look as if there were some sound reasons why the great reggae invasion never quite caught on in the States.

"On the most basic level, perhaps the rhythm itself, so hypnotic to fans, seemed too lazy and lopsided to most American. Then too, the Jah Rastafari-Marcus Garvey-Old Testament stuff in the lyrics soon became as big a formula as anything going, while the average listener hadn't the slightest idea what these guys were babbling about."

He claims that "last year Peter changed from apocalyptic militancy to tinsel MOR about as pallid as Bob Marley's. *Mystic Man* is an improvement over *Bush Doctor*, though you're not quite sure whether it's because the music has a bit more force or you're just desperate for *any* decent reggae.

"I'm very happy that Tosh doesn't eat fried chicken, hot dogs ('garbage') and hamburgers or drink 'pink, blue, yellow, green soda,'" he continues, "yet you still have to wonder about a reggae record whose hottest cut is a bald-faced shot at the disco market. 'Buk-In-Hamm Palace' sets up an irresistible groove – not unlike Marley's 'Exodus' (or at one point, the Jacksons' 'Get It Together') – that'll lift and drive you for almost nine minutes." Bangs ends his review by comparing *Mystic Man* to Culture's *Two Sevens Clash* and Dr. Alimantado's *Best Dressed Chicken*. "Next to them," he says, "Peter Tosh is whitewashed."

Chapter 21

Lessons In My Life

The rest of 1979 will fly past in a haze of controversy, awards, artistic triumphs and romantic highs. First Peter needed to replace Donald Kinsey, who'd left to tour with his own band. Auditions were held at SIR studios in New York where they recruited a young African-American guitarist named Daryl Thompson, son of jazz tenor sax star Eli "Lucky" Thompson.

"I was playing with a rock band in New York and got a call from someone who knew Teresa Del Paso. She was Peter's business manager at the time," Daryl explains. "This friend asked me if I'd ever heard of Peter Tosh and I said no, I hadn't. I was aware of Bob Marley, because I'd seen him on *Don Kirshner's Rock Concert*. I remember thinking, 'Who's this guy with the funny hair singing an Eric Clapton song?' That's how ignorant I was and then when he started into the second song, I couldn't tell the difference! The beat just sounded the same to me but I was coming from the Jimi Hendrix, Jeff Beck and Eric Clapton school, and that was the only exposure I'd had to reggae by that point.

"In the end, I decided to go and audition for kicks. Peter didn't actually do much. He just sat in the back with these dark glasses on and never spoke to me. I remember he was sat between two beautiful women and had a great big spliff in his hand. I'd never seen a spliff before so all of that was quite new to me, and then after a while all I could see was a cloud of smoke coming from the back of the room... It was Sly, Robbie and Mikey

Chung who ran the audition. They said they'd auditioned about 30 other people but they liked me and asked if I wanted to join. The thing is, I could barely understand a word anyone was saying! At one stage I thought someone had hemorrhaged because every other word was "bloodclaat" so I asked them for twice as much money as I was making with the other group, thinking they would turn me down and I could get out of there without too much fuss. I was amazed when they said, 'Sure, no problem.' I thought, 'Well this is simple economics, and I can't turn it down now...'"

Daryl had been playing guitar since the age of six. As a teenager, he'd studied with jazz masters Chuck Wayne and Pat Martino yet his heart was in rock music, especially after hearing Jimi Hendrix for the first time, back in the late sixties. Hendrix and John McLaughlin will remain primary influences. Jamaican music had never entered the equation but then Peter wasn't interested in replacing Donald Kinsey with a reggae guitarist, but another rock or blues player.

The following evening, Daryl met up with the other band members at a hotel in Queen's, where they'd stay overnight in readiness for an early morning flight from LaGuardia Airport. "We were headed for Holland," he says. "Peter's sitting in first class and I'm about four or five rows behind him. I'm sat there thinking, 'Here I am on the plane with him, and we haven't even been introduced yet' but then soon as the plane takes off, Peter pulls a gigantic spliff out of his pocket and lights it up – in first class! The stewardesses were running around looking at each other like they didn't know what to do... I'm now saying to myself, 'Oh what a mistake I just made. I've joined this band and the second we get off this plane the cops are going to arrest us...' I felt like I was in such deep shit. I was 23 years old and did not want to go to jail. Finally one brave stewardess walks over and taps Peter on the shoulder saying, 'I'm sorry sir, but you can't do that here.' I'm wondering what's going to happen but Peter looks up at her, smiles and says, 'No problem,' then puts the spliff out and tucks it right back in his pocket!

"I was convinced we'd be arrested the minute we landed and yet we got to Holland and there was no problem at all, which was such a relief. That's when I discovered we'd be playing the Pink Pop Festival, in front of 80,000 people. We were on the same bill as Dire Straits, Rush, Average White Band and the Police, who were fairly unknown at the time. Peter was presented with a gold record whilst we were there and Mick Jagger flew in for the day. Can you imagine? This was my first show with Peter Tosh and here's Mick Jagger flying in to sing with us... Actually that show was a fiasco for me personally because I didn't really know the music that well. Also, I'd hung around to watch all the other bands and we were the last act to play so I was exhausted by the time we actually got on stage."

The Pink Pop Festival was a three-day event held at Landgraaf over the Pentecostal weekend. Peter played on Whit Monday, June 4, and despite Daryl's reservations it was another pulsating performance. People were still dancing and waving their arms in the air long after the rain began to pour down. Hunched out of sight behind the amplifiers, members of the Police looked on amazed at their counterparts in Word, Sound & Power, especially once Mick Jagger had bounded on stage. This show will mark the last time he and Peter sing 'Don't Look Back' together, just hours after they'd received their gold discs. Jagger had been flown in by helicopter for the ceremony, but will leave in very different circumstances.

"As we were leaving the venue, hundreds of people gathered around the bus and started rocking it back and forth," says Daryl. "The crowd was pushing this woman and her child right up against the bus. The child was crying and she was screaming for help so I told the driver to open the door and let her on the bus, otherwise her little boy, who was maybe seven or eight years old, was going to suffocate. The driver didn't want to do it at first, because Mick Jagger was sat with us and he'd said not to let anyone else on. Finally, we drive off and Mick Jagger says to the child, 'Do you know who I am?' He was so full of himself, and acted like the kid should be grateful that we let him on the bus. The thing is, this kid had nearly been crushed to death and so he looks up at Jagger and said, 'No, and I don't care.' I was on the floor! I had tears in my eyes, I was laughing so much. Jagger was such an asshole and the boy put him right in his place!"

Peter made a typically unruffled appearance on Dutch TV show *Top Pop* before sampling the delights of Amsterdam, where cannabis cafes will one day be named in his honour. That night's show at the Paradiso put everyone in good spirits although Peter's mood will soon alter for the worse once he encounters British journalist Adrian Thrills, who interviews him for *NME*. His article, printed on June 16, anticipates Tosh's forthcoming London shows and is headlined "Promoting Jah By Monocycle".

After arriving in Paris, Thrills went to meet Peter during a soundcheck at the Pavilion de Paris, one of the bigger venues on the present tour.

"When he is not bellowing 'one, two, one, two' – or with a little more conviction, 'JAH RASTAFARI!' into one of the mics on-stage, Tosh is whizzing around the arena on his chrome-plated monocycle, spliff in hand looking more like an escapee from the adjacent Big Top," writes Thrills, who observes there's "not even the hint of a bicycle clip at the bottom of his immaculately pressed denim flares".

Their interview would last just 10 minutes. Thrills notes how Peter's demeanour was one of "slightly stubborn disinterest" and that, "Trying to put even mild criticism to Peter Tosh is like talking to a brick wall whilst sucking a mouthful of gobstoppers." He describes him as "pompous" for refusing to concede that his earlier work was better than *Bush Doctor*, which Thrills claims was "greeted with an almost universal panning". To his mind, Tosh's current work "lacks soul and toughness", an accusation Peter naturally refutes.

"But now the music is more perfect," he argues. "It is more beautiful. It is more properly decorated than it was because in those days there was no synthesizers and clavinets and them bloodclaat t'ings! It takes more instruments to make reggae acceptable to the ears of people, and the best is yet to come man..."

Thrills is unconvinced, and he doesn't care for that night's concert either. "Despite the grace afforded by the backing trio the Tamlins and the best rhythm section in the world, his live show is a letdown," he writes. "Tosh is forsaking much of his militancy and spontaneity for the new Holy trinity of compromise, accessibility and bland musical sophistication. Particularly disappointing in his current set is the bias towards orthodox rock guitar breaks and keyboard soloing, and the horrendously excessive use of synthesized disco percussion. They're unnecessary concessions to commercialism. Maybe it has them skanking in Strasbourg, but I doubt whether British audiences preoccupied with authenticity are going to be swept off their feet."

He goes on to describe Daryl's guitar solo on 'Burial' as "dreadful" and the new songs "increasingly grandiose and cumbersome". We should pinch ourselves here and remember this is a show where Sly and Robbie pull out all the stops, and engage in extended, duelling dub workouts that fair take the breath away with their power and rhythmic intensity. Robbie Shakespeare admits that Peter didn't always appreciate this part of the show, as it took away attention from him. Much to his chagrin, Sly and Robbie got several encores that night in Paris, causing Peter – who was otherwise resplendent in a red and purple kaftan – to simmer with resentment on the sidelines. His jealousy will sow seeds of discord among the band members and yet Sly and Robbie were fast becoming stars in their own right and, in truth, he was fortunate to have them. Alas, Peter remained convinced that he'd been wronged and as a result, there was a pall hanging over their trip to the UK, which he'd scarcely been looking forward to in any case. On Monday June 18 they played at the Civic Hall in Wolverhampton. Martin Culverwell, writing in *Melody Maker*, began his review with the line, "Peter Tosh has fallen".

He went on to write: "Aiming for some kind of crossover audience (more American rock than disco) he has lost his militant black following and not gained any other. The huge, quarter full Civic Hall echoed Tosh's failure and the problem facing reggae."

Culverwell claims reggae's stagnation "is a direct product of the religious attitude of its bands and artists". Where Peter's music is concerned, he says "The rebel soul has gone and what's left is a mish-mash of hard rock (lead guitar, two organs and the decorative arrangements), funk (the drumming) and reggae (the bass and rhythm guitar.) Reggae's greatest musicians plod through Americanised, sanitised versions of some of its best songs – 'Get Up Stand Up', '400 Years', 'Legalise It', 'Steppin' Razor' and so on." He paints a picture of Peter, dressed in a yellow and black karate suit, placing one foot on a monitor with head in hands, "looking bored through another howling Funkadelic guitar solo. The police needn't have bothered hanging around outside," sneered Culverwell. "Peter Tosh won't stir up any trouble."

In that same issue, Simon Frith reviews *Mystic Man* and opens by saying he almost didn't make it through the title track due to how the "excruciating" backing vocals bring out Peter's "worst aspect – his dumbness". Later, Frith correctly identifies that Peter is "making a new sort of black music. His sound has as much to do with funk and disco as with reggae. It is generous, easy, unthreatening and urgent but he's kept his Rasta hopes and Jamaican dreams, and his words are still militant, righteous, committed. The result is an angry album that doesn't sound angry at all." Frith also points out how the majority of white audiences "share none of Rasta's political, religious or racial concerns. The only common element is drugs, and even this is dubious.

"Tosh doesn't come over slick," he concedes. "His religious themes retain their hymnbook openness." He describes it as "an enjoyable album, filled with incidental pleasures... but it is enjoyable like most other popular albums, as background music for dancing, talking, eating."

The English rock press was always hard on him. Admittedly, most journalists didn't take to his lecturing or haughty tone, which is fair enough. Except they knew little about his music and couldn't relate to the lyrics either, yet still felt no shame in being so disdainful. Unfortunately reggae had long been an easy target in the UK, ever since a Radio DJ had snapped a record on air and thrown it into a waste-bin, calling it "garbage". That was back in the late sixties and there was still an undercurrent of racism in how reggae was viewed by the (largely white) British media. You could sense it as they snickered about Peter's prodigious ganja use and then dismissed much of what he talked about, especially if it had anything to do with Rastafari. Maybe they were scared of his uncompromising blackness, and sought to emasculate him with words – even taunting him with the accusation that he wasn't black enough. It was therefore ironic that most black reggae fans seemed to respect Peter highly and not just for his views, but also for having the courage to speak up for what he believed in. It was white reggae followers who proved more judgmental, and erected barriers of supposed authenticity that black artists crossed at their peril. Peter's crime was that he wanted his songs to reach a wider audience and to grow as an artist. After years of struggle, he was simply making the most of whatever opportunities came his way. Retaining his integrity was never in doubt, and yet it's a subject his white inquisitors just can't let go of.

After shows at Manchester's Apollo Theatre and the Top Rank Suite in Cardiff, it was back to London where he was booked to play two nights at the Rainbow Theatre, beginning June 21. The atmosphere around the camp had now picked up a little. Most of the band members had friends in the capital, and places like Harlesden, Brixton, Tottenham and Ladbroke Grove were havens for visiting Jamaican musicians thanks to their bustling networks of clubs, sound systems, record shops, studios and record labels. Daryl Thompson was now more settled, and known to everyone in the group as "Foreigner". He was also receiving quite an education. Mikey Chung taught him how to cook Chinese food and play "the reggae chop" on rhythm guitar, whilst Sly Dunbar became his reggae grandmaster and introduced him to a world of music he never knew existed. Only the process of familiarising himself with Jamaican culture was left to trial and error, and it led to some inevitable consequences.

"They had their own cultish ways about them," he says. "It was a closed society in truth and the longer I was amongst them, the easier it got but I always felt like an outsider. It's not like they, meaning Jamaican people, try to exclude you, but there were certain things I could never understand, and certain words that just left me nonplussed. Everything about them was different – the music, the food, the jokes and the way they talked... everything! One thing I found out was they don't really appreciate it when you try and speak like them and that was something I had to learn. I was trying to use patois when I was first with them but they kept laughing at me so I made a point of always speaking in my own dialect after that. I learnt to just be myself basically."

Outside the Rainbow, crowds spilled over into the road amidst the usual clamour that accompanied big-name reggae events. Queues snaked down the Seven Sisters Road both nights and London's Rastafarian community came out in force, belying reports that Peter had lost the support of his core audience. There was a sparkle to his performance that first night, and from the minute he strode on stage in an African-style fringed top, with a determined glint in his eye. At one point he stalks across the stage, taking long, angular steps that make him look like a rare species of crane. It's a different Peter Tosh from the one who'd made his London debut just 10 months earlier, when he'd struggled with a misfiring PA system. Sebastian Clarke, brother of former Danny Sims' PR man Brent Clarke, witnessed both shows, but clearly wasn't impressed by this latest visit.

"Unfortunately for Tosh, his performance has degenerated into soppiness and if I were him I'd be writhing in agony over the music he's currently playing," he wrote. After describing how "the music is so overwhelmingly rock / pop and so loud that it is difficult to understand what Tosh himself is singing about," Clarke says that, "Tosh as a performer held an image of rebel defiance, though it's one of contempt for his audience. He goes through his routine like a man bereft of feeling or the need to communicate. He treats the audience like they should be grateful for him being there and then announced that the critics in the audience know they will never see another band like Word, Sound & Power, even in the 29th century."

Clarke concedes that Sly & Robbie are "the most devastating drums and bass combination", but accuses Robbie of playing "pop dribble" and says the band are "not given the space to showcase their ability because of Tosh's one-dimensional music. Even the experience of the Sly & Robbie rhythmic display was now deleted from the show. In Paris, Sly & Robbie had three encores so it was taken out. The MC here tried to work the audience up to chant, 'Mystic Man', but the words couldn't emerge, but still Tosh made his obligatory encore with the audience staring him dead in the face. I am sorry Mr. Mystic Man, but you ain't mystic at all…"

Others disagree, despite some of the band members referring to Peter – out of earshot, naturally – as "Mistake Man". (This was reciprocal, since Peter had taken to calling Sly and Robbie "Slime and Rob Me".) After London came a gig in Sweden and then a barnstorming appearance at the Roskilde Festival in Denmark on June 29. Daryl Thompson bought Peter a handsome-looking pipe that day, and had just presented it to him when the boss started reciting scripture.

"He was sitting in the front of the bus and suddenly started muttering stuff. He kept saying, 'My Father has to purify this place before we can pass through' and wouldn't let the driver start the engine. He was adamant the place had to be purified before we could leave and so we're just sat there looking at each other, wondering what he was on about and then out of a clear blue sky, rain fell on the bus *and only on the bus*. We could see across to the other side of the street and it was absolutely dry but the rain came down on the bus for just a few minutes and it was the strangest thing I'd ever seen. We really believed Peter *was* a mystic man at that point, because the rain came from out of nowhere."

They'll return to Europe in a couple of weeks but first it's back home to Jamaica and a headlining slot at Reggae Sunsplash II, which took place between July 3 and 7 at Jarrett Park in Montego Bay. Bob Marley, Burning Spear and Third World are the other main attractions. Apart from showcasing an array of Jamaica's musical talent, Reggae Sunsplash also provided a welcome boost for the island's tourist industry, which tended to fall away during the summer months. It was unusual for a reggae event headlined by Rasta artists to gain support from leading businesses and local authorities in Jamaica but a turning point had been reached. Reggae music was now a commodity and, somewhat inevitably, will increasingly leave its ghetto roots behind. Peter will eventually rail against the Reggae Sunsplash organisers (who were middle-class Jamaicans), and accuse them of exploiting the music for profit. Yet he was in relaxed mood on the day of the show, after agreeing to be filmed for US television at the soundcheck.

"Music is psychology, seen? And if the music does not penetrate the heart, the soul, the mind and the body, then you aren't going to feel it," he tells the bewildered reporter. Later that night, dressed in familiar martial arts gear, he'll become transformed into a musical preacher – a rebel priest fired by truth, who's come to free the people. It's illusionary of course, but then so is most great art. It helps too that the Reggae Sunsplash crowd is full of believers, who cheer every time he raises his staff aloft and then launches into hits like 'Legalise It' and 'Get Up Stand Up', which retain a frisson of danger. The 20,000 revellers have come to see Jamaica's most controversial reggae star and won't leave disappointed. Midway through 'Buk-In-Hamm Palace', Peter pauses to light his new pipe and with a smile flickering around his lips, takes a deep draw and blows clouds of ganja smoke into the still night air. The applause is tumultuous and despite the large number of tourists present, there's no sign of this audience missing Mick Jagger or complaining about a change in musical direction. Naturally enough, Peter and the rest of the band always enjoyed playing in Jamaica, although Daryl Thompson wasn't quite so keen.

"The reason for that was that a lot of those concerts would have like 15 reggae acts on the same bill and after about the third band, I was bored to tears," he confesses. "It was so repetitive and everybody would copy one another. Also, a lot of it was quite pretentious. You could see through it. Some people were authentic and genuinely believed in Rastafarianism, but to others it was just a ploy, similar to what happened with the hippies in the late sixties.

"I loved being in Jamaica though. Peter would always make sure I was in a nice, safe spot and it was fun in the daytime. I loved the juices, eating the fish and being at the beach and all that but the shows in Jamaica always started very, very late. Whereas shows in Europe and America usually started around eight o'clock, the shows in Jamaica wouldn't start until midnight and the headliner wouldn't go on until five in the morning!"

For Peter, this sojourn back home offered a welcome respite from touring. He liked nothing more than hanging out with his Rasta brethren, soaking up the sunshine and smoking some potent strain of local herb, but he also had a few domestic difficulties to overcome. He'd installed one girlfriend called Grace in Keith Richards' house on the North coast, but needed to find somewhere else for Melody Cunningham, whom he'd met whilst touring with the Stones.

"I was at the show in Boston when Melody first came backstage and sat besides Peter," recalls Ras Karbi. "I remember she had these extension braids that some people could mistake for dreadlocks and she was wearing make-up too. She had everything you'd imagine Peter wouldn't like, but she was kind of cute at the same time. Peter was desperate for a woman at that time in his life. He had this song he was always singing that went, 'All my life, I've been a lonely man...'"

Whilst this wasn't entirely true, he was smitten enough to propose marriage to Melody and will eventually find her a house in Sterling Castle, within easy driving distance of central Kingston. Melody – who he called "Rhythm" – will bear Peter two children, a girl named Niambe and his youngest son, Jawara, who'll later record as Tosh 1. It had been four years since Yvonne had died but if Peter craved marital security, then he had a strange way of showing it. Apart from Grace and Melody he was still seeing a girl called Rose, and close associates all mention Nabi, who had a young child for him.

In actual fact he was spending more time on the road than raising a family allowed, and it was hard for him to leave the island sometimes. Touring tended to get him down for a variety of reasons. Most performers can't wait to get back in front of a live audience and feed off all that energy. They want to see people enjoying themselves but this wasn't enough for Peter, who confused concert halls with the pulpit or classroom at times, especially when looking out at the crowd and seeing mainly white, inebriated youngsters with little grasp of what he was about. We've already established that he didn't much care for the food or cold when touring overseas, and finding decent herb was always a problem – added to which he was still feeling the effects of cumulative beatings and whiplash sustained in a series of car accidents.

"Before a tour was undertaken, Tosh would often pay a visit to his 'bush doctor' who he sometimes called 'mi four eye man' – returning with vials of oils, charms and medicine," recalls Herbie Miller. "His four-eye man advised when he should or would travel. Many times the rest of the band would be on their way to the airport when an announcement directed to Peter was broadcast on national radio, since none of us knew where he was. Bassist Robbie Shakespeare eventually stopped showing up to the airport unless Peter was already there. Later Robbie and others refused to travel on the same flights with Peter because he attracted stricter customs and immigration interrogation and had to explain every bottle, vial, root, bush, balm and ointment in his possession. Furthermore they felt uncomfortable flying in his company because he had such disdain for Christianity. It was difficult to travel with anyone who opposed the Christian concept of God and Jesus as vehemently as Peter did. 'The only Jesus I know is the S.S. Jesus, a slave ship,' he would say."

Just a few days later, on July 12, he'll appear on an Italian television programme called *Strix* with Ilona Staller, now better known as the porn star "La Cicciolina". This wasn't quite the mismatch it seems. Twelve months earlier, the 28-year-old Hungarian – who'd made her reputation with a radio show called *Do You Want To Sleep With Me?* – had been the first woman to bare her breasts on live Italian television. Like Peter she was no stranger to controversy, although she'd yet to make porn films and had recently stood for election on behalf of Italy's first-ever Green party, La Lista del Sole, campaigning on an anti-nuclear and pro-human rights ticket. Staler was also a staunch vegetarian and defended her position with great passion, which elicited murmurs of approval from the tall Rastaman sat next to her.

After that night's show in Bologna, Sly Dunbar discovered that one of his most treasured possessions had been stolen – a pair of custom-built drumsticks given to him by Charlie Watts that were irreplaceable. Later the next day the tour bus arrived in Montreux and pulled up outside the Casino, which had been rebuilt since being destroyed in a fire several years earlier. The band's concert there on July 16, in a small town situated on the shore of Lake Geneva and framed by mountains, will prove a milestone in Peter Tosh's career. Dennis Brown and Steel Pulse were on the same bill, but it was the Mystic Man who closed the show and took all the accolades. If he was at all overawed by the thought of jazz giants like Ella Fitzgerald and Nina Simone having trodden the same boards, then you'd never know it as he sauntered onto the stage with a towel slung over his shoulder for the opening '400 Years'. It was a mainly middle-class, white crowd as you'd expect in such an affluent corner of Europe, except no one could accuse them of lacking enthusiasm. Roars of applause greeted old favourites like 'Bush Doctor' and whilst they were initially thrown a little by the funk/reggae fusion that is 'The Day The Dollar Died' ("taken from our new album"), they rapidly adjusted.

This current edition of Word, Sound & Power was now firing on all cylinders, and had the raw, visceral energy of a rock band thanks to Sly and Robbie's rhythmic drive and Daryl Thompson's pyrotechnics on lead guitar. Leaving aside the spliff that he'd been brandishing in the air for all to see, Peter listened intently as Daryl unleashed a blistering solo on 'Burial'. His pleasure was all too evident, prompting the guitarist to later remark that "Peter was very generous. He allowed you your time in the spotlight and whenever I was soloing he'd look as if he was enjoying it. He'd close his eyes and would have this wonderful smile on his face. I never saw him frown when I played and he never told me my solos were too long or don't do this or that. In fact he never gave me any directions at all. I was doing a lot of theatrics back then, playing with my teeth and behind my head. I'd roll around on the ground and stuff like that. It was the same clown routine that guitar players like Chuck Berry and Jimi Hendrix did but he just said to do whatever felt right. There was never any restriction. He always allowed me the freedom to be myself."

Midway through the show, Peter strapped on his guitar and played fast, unaccompanied wah wah guitar before leading the band into a Jamaican reel featuring Keith Sterling on bass. "This is the only music that has light, love and reality," Peter suddenly announced. "It makes all the funky get kinky." During a break in 'Buk-In-Hamm Palace' most of the band members took up percussion instruments including the Tamlins and Mikey Chung, whose wispy beard and beret gave him the appearance of a Chinese revolutionary (which is why everyone called him "Mao"). Whereas the Wailers had rarely strayed from nyahbinghi style drumming whenever immersing themselves in pure rhythm, Word, Sound & Power's approach could easily rival that of Fela Kuti's Africa 70, Santana or even Sly & the Family Stone. It's a fabulous show and the crowd knew it.

"After Peter left the stage the people kept stamping on the floor," recalls Nambo Robinson, who played with Dennis Brown that night. "They were chanting, 'Reggae, reggae, reggae…' They just wouldn't stop stamping their feet and calling out for more. They must have done that for like half an hour and they wouldn't leave so the promoters had no choice and asked all of the bands to go back out on stage together, which we did. The music was so powerful at that time. It was beautiful, and I've yet to see that kind of thing happen again."

Ten days later, Peter was a guest at Mick Jagger's birthday party in New York. It was there he met singer Carly Simon, who was part owner of the Tin Roof Club in Martha's Vineyard, where he'll play in just over a week's time. Talk within Jagger's circle of friends centred on Anita Pallenberg, who faced a manslaughter investigation. A fortnight earlier, whilst the Stones were in Paris, her 17-year-old lover had killed himself with one of Keith's guns during a game of Russian roulette. Anita will eventually be cleared of any involvement in the youth's death, but the house in Westchester was now shrouded in sorrow and darkness. Being around the Stones could hardly compare with life in Trench Town, yet both paths were fraught with danger.

Peter's next show was on Friday August 10, at the Theatre St. Denis in Montreal. He travelled by plane, while the band and road crew followed in a tour bus. Shortly before crossing into Canada, one of the crew members got left behind after they'd stopped at a service station. After hitching a ride he finally caught up with the bus 30 miles away, at a border crossing. Peter meanwhile had problems of his own, as reported in *Caribbean Week*.

"I'm waiting to pick Peter up at Dorval airport on a flight from New York," writes Gary Steckles. "Publicist Charlie Comer emerges from Customs and Immigration and he's got a problem. The immigration people are being difficult, and although Tosh has the necessary work permit they want more evidence that he's coming into Canada for a legitimate purpose. And Tosh, an immensely proud man, is standing imperiously awaiting developments. He isn't begging to get into any country. I dash back into the parking lot and find a poster in my car advertising the concert. It has a large, unmistakable picture of Tosh on it. We show it to the immigration officer, who looks at the picture, looks at Tosh, and waves him through.

"Driving into Montreal, Tosh tells me he's hungry. 'I can't get no good food on this tour. It's hamburger this and Kentucky that,' he says. We drive to a tiny Jamaican food store and his eyes light up at the sight of crisply fried fish with peppers and onions and vegetable patties. Finally, a happy Peter Tosh is delivered to his hotel."

The theatre holds just over 2,000 people and is packed to the rafters. It's Peter's second appearance there and he's feeling even more militant than usual. "I'm afraid he's going to give another speech," said a worried Charlie Comer, who'd accompanied Mick Jagger to the One Love Peace Concert. Less than an hour earlier, the theatre management had called out the city's riot squad after ticketless fans threatened to charge the entrance.

The atmosphere was still tense, and Comer didn't want Peter causing further problems.

"As predicted, Tosh strode on stage, sang his opening number and went straight into his speech, which went on and on and on," Steckles continues. "What Tosh didn't realise was that his rhetoric was wasted on about half the crowd. Most French Canadians speak excellent English, but they couldn't handle the singer's broad Jamaican dialect. For the best part of an hour they just sat looking baffled, wondering what on earth was going on.

"The next day, he stops traffic in Montreal riding up and down the main street on his unicycle as part of a Comer-inspired publicity stunt. That night, at the sold out St. Denis, he puts on a show that local critics describe as one of the best pop concerts ever seen in Montreal. Word, Sound & Power are in such a groove they don't want to call it quits, and Sly Dunbar and Robbie Shakespeare are on stage, trading dub patterns on drums and bass fully 20 minutes after Tosh has finished his final encore."

A reviewer in the following day's *Montreal Star* announces how "the Bush Doctor cured anything and everything that ailed the overflowing crowd – with music that rearranged the senses, touched the soul and kept the feet moving.

"By the time the tour culminates with Tosh headlining the revived Monterey Pop Festival on September 8, the Mystic Man will be recognised as the most important popular performer to emerge in this decade," the paper predicts. "Most superlatives would understate last night's event. Tosh cast a spell over the audience and held it spellbound for a good two hours.

"He is an explosive performer. His voice, honey-toned, soulful and exquisitely restrained, is a beguiling and accomplished instrument... and it speaks the truth." He's said to roam the stage "with the grace and agility of a panther", whilst Sly & Robbie are described as "the best rhythm section in reggae. With guitarist Daryl Thompson aboard, Word, Sound & Power is a monster band capable of destroying any audience, anywhere."

The reviewer goes on to say that it was "the most satisfying and entertaining musical experience since a young and hungry Bruce Springsteen stormed Place des Arts a few years ago", then talks about "a celebration of the spirit. Best of all, it was a chance to hear music so inspired and deeply felt that it has the power to change the way we think and live. It's been a long time since that has happened in the pop-rock world."

Steckles had helped book the next two concerts on the tour – an outdoor show in Ottawa and a date at Toronto's Ontario Place Forum on August 14 – and went along to see how they turned out.

"The mood in Ottawa was perfect. The concert was being held in a lovely wooded area, and the promoters had put on a spectacular barbecue for the band, with lots of fish and chicken. The crowd was good, and Peter was in great form. He'd led the band in an impromptu singalong of Rasta chants a couple of hours before and now he was working up a serious head of steam with 'Buk-In-Hamm Palace.'

"As usual, about half an hour into the show he took off his tam and shook out his locks with the crowd roaring approval. He hung the tam on an unused microphone as he strode around the stage and when his back was turned, a souvenir-hunting fan scurried up to the stage and grabbed the tam. That's when Flash got into the act. Flash was Peter's bodyguard on tour – a six-foot plus dread from Boston, and that was the only name I ever knew him by. He was crouched, as usual, behind a huge speaker at the side of the stage, ready to dash to Peter's defence in the event of any trouble. He quickly realised the fan was only a souvenir-hunter and no kind of threat to Peter but he didn't want to give up the tam. Before anyone knew he was even moving, Flash reached the fan in three or four strides, threw him over his shoulder without breaking stride and kept going to the far side of the stage. There he gently put the fan down, retrieved the tam, sent the chastened culprit back into the crowd and resumed his watch from behind another speaker.

"The next day we're in Toronto and the government-run entertainment complex on the city's waterfront is about to experience its first reggae concert. The Ontario Place Forum, where the big shows are held, has been packed since noon. Concerts there are subsidised and the price is cheap but seating is on a first come, first served basis so thousands of ardent Tosh fans had been camping out for hours to make sure they got a good view.

"About 10 minutes before the show, Ontario Place staff started to carry seats out onto the huge circular stage which is surrounded by the crowd and revolves slowly during a performance. The seats were for VIPs, among them as I recall tennis star Bjorn Borg and Jamaica's High Commissioner in Canada, but the crowd didn't appreciate the special attention they were getting. Booing started and it was getting louder. Peter and the band were

Steppin' Razor: The Life of Peter Tosh

due on stage in a few minutes and publicist Comer – who didn't want his number one client to be greeted by boos, and was worried what Tosh's reaction to them would be – was getting agitated.

"I was standing beside him at the front of the tunnel that leads from backstage out into the Forum itself when the brainwave hit him. 'You go out and draw their fire,' he said, pushing me into the arena before I had a chance to protest. The crowd assumed I was the first VIP about to take my special seat while they'd been waiting there all afternoon. The booing mounted, then the missiles started coming in my direction. Nothing too serious – a few oranges and apples, a couple of bottles... I dodged and ducked for a minute or two; the boos finally giving way to laughter as the crowd tired of the sport. Then the real VIPs were ushered on stage, with virtually no crowd reaction and a couple of minutes later the concert started.

"One of my lingering memories of Tosh occurred at the end of that show," he reflects. "I was in the tunnel, waiting to leave and Peter was winding up his performance as he often did, by leaving the stage but continuing to sing. He was standing about a foot away from me, eyes closed and it dawned on me that by the end of a performance, he was absolutely, totally in his own world. Virtually in a trance, with no idea of who or what might be around him. 'Babylon, your Queendom is falling,' he sang, eyes shut, with the crowd outside roaring for him to return. And he believed it."

Herbie Miller has talked about Tosh's performances "attaining a ritual state of trance-like intensity", and how "certain songs could go for 20 to 30 minutes, ending in total rapture." Peter's fast approaching the height of his powers, and his vision is certainly more far-reaching than when he first started out as a solo act. At that last show, Peter had walked out on stage wearing a long-sleeved, striped, ankle-length hooded robe and keffiyeh or Arab headdress, which was held in place by a circlet of rope and made him look as if he'd just stepped from a page in the Old Testament. He'd dressed like that in solidarity with the Palestinians, who continued to suffer under Israeli rule. Peter was now making use of symbolism and not just to get noticed, but to also focus people's attention on the issues he cared about, including events in the Middle East.

On Friday August 17, he headlined a concert in New York's Central Park that according to *News World* reporter Linda Solomon, "attracted the biggest crowd in the history of the Dr. Pepper–Schaeffer Festivals, which New York police estimated was 30,000 strong.

"The weather was clement for a change and the crowd, an almost equal mix of blacks and whites, was feeling no pain. There was if anything a festive temper in the air, and an ample cloud of herbal smoke made more accessible by the numerous hawkers who lined the pathways to both press and general ticket entrances to Wollman Rink.

"Earlier in the week Tosh had enticed 20,000 people to the Ontario Place in Toronto, where more than half sat outdoors in the rain to watch the shows. He is a giant of an entertainer, a man with a plan and a voice instead of a gun or machete. He is a commanding presence. Dressed in a colourful variation of a dashiki, flowing black trousers gathered at the ankles and more gold jewellery than even Sammy Davis Jnr wears, he strides the stage, microphone in hand and alternatively stares off into space or peruses the vast audience for eyeball contact. He has a lot of energy for a vegetarian but Mystic Men don't eat garbage or drink soda. They do 'step into the future' though he says, and he makes the Rastas' dreams seem viable."

Robbie Shakespeare is hailed as "the spearhead of a superb rhythm section", whilst Sly Dunbar's drumming is said to "surpass the requirements of reggae". Even the Tamlins are championed as "reggae's equivalent to the Jordanaires of Nashville". Solomon ends her review by describing how Peter "cavorts like a grim genie" and "takes dramatically long drags from his ever-present spliff, which had its own ashtray planted atop a microphone stand. If reggae is the music of black kings just like Tosh says it is, then he is its leading ambassador."

Two surprises awaited Peter as he prepared to leave Central Park that day. First he discovered that John Lennon and Yoko Ono – who lived in the Dakota Building, facing Central Park – had been watching him from the wings, and then came a joyous family reunion.

"I'd heard on the radio that Peter would be performing at Central Park but didn't know how to get in touch with him," explains his cousin Pauline, who'd grown up with Peter in Trench Town. "I must have been around 18, and the last time I'd seen Peter was maybe five or six years ago. I had no tickets and didn't know how to get there but I was determined to see him. I couldn't get in to see the show, but saw a limousine round the back and thought, 'That's what he's going to leave in' so when the show was almost over, I went and stood near where it was parked. Right after that, Peter appeared and I called out to him. Remember that I'm an adult by now and I wasn't sure whether he'd recognise me but when he caught sight of me he said, 'Offie?' My middle name is Ophelia and everyone in the family had called me 'Offie' when I was small. We started reaching out to each other through the fencing but then all of a sudden this security guard knocked my hand out of the way. I guess he thought I was a fan or something so Peter got angry and said to him, 'What is it with you?' He told me he was staying at the Howard Johnson and to call him there so I went to see him the next day and that's where our relationship restarted.

"I remember the first time I went to the hotel, this journalist lit up a cigarette, which was totally forbidden around Peter. He had some words with the guy, went into the bathroom and came back out with some kind of spray, like an air freshener, and started spraying it all around the room. I wasn't used to anything like that because he not only sprayed the room, but also the guy. It was unbelievable! That's when I started seeing this other side of Peter, because he was so different to how most people thought of him.

"When he was out in public, you saw the militant side of Peter but behind closed doors with family and friends, we'd see a more humorous and loving side of him. He was such a storyteller. He always had something to tell you and you'd never get bored being around him. Even though Peter was a cousin, he was more like a brother to me really. I have five brothers and there was a time when I actually thought he *was* my brother. That's when we were living in Trench Town, at my parents' house on West Road. In fact I still remember how he used to babysit me sometimes..."

Two days after performing in Central Park he appeared on *Rockers TV* – a weekly reggae show filmed in New York City and hosted by Earl Chin, whom Peter had met in Los Angeles. Cradling his acoustic guitar, Peter talks about the importance of a healthy diet but then admits to eating cornmeal porridge "maybe four times a day", with just the hint of a wry smile. He seems relaxed around Chin, who's an amiable Rastafarian and clearly a fan of the music. So few Rasta people were involved with the media back in the late Seventies, and yet there were several organisations in New York struggling to get their voices heard, including the Caribbean People's Alliance. This group will pay Peter Tosh the greatest tribute of his career. At a presentation on the steps of Borough Hall in Brooklyn they announced that August 23 would be "Peter Tosh Day", and paraded him around the borough's Caribbean communities as if he was a prize fighter or returning war hero. As ever, Peter drew sizable crowds at every stopping place. His own black people were finally honouring him, and pride welled in his chest at the sight of so many excited faces. Two days later, on the Saturday evening, he headlined a programme called Peace, Love And Unity, again promoted by the Caribbean People's Alliance. "The Mystic Man Comes To Brooklyn" screamed the flyer. "The protest music of Peter Tosh starkly dramatises the imperilled position of black people under Western domination," it reads. "In these times of economic genocide and racist bigotry it is righteously fitting for Peter Tosh to perform in Brooklyn, the place of abode for the third largest urban concentration of black people in America. Hail the man. Power to the masses!"

The concert took place in the gymnasium of a private art college called the Pratt Institute on Willoughby Avenue. The organisers had hoped to raise funds for various community projects but hadn't anticipated having to carpet the floor with rolls of thick paper to prevent it from getting damaged. This had led to further expense and whilst there was a good turnout, the proceeds will ultimately disappoint. The show opened with a set by local reggae band Monyaka. Gwen Guthrie was on next, followed by a slide show devoted to the struggles in South Africa. Peter was billed as "African Reggae Master Rastaman" and gave a shortened, but no less compelling version of his current stage act. Soon, the *New York Daily News* will print an article announcing that Peter's been invited to address the United Nations on the subject of apartheid. This address was scheduled to take place on September 23, the day after he's participated in a No Nukes concert at Madison Square Garden, headlined by Bruce Springsteen. The report describes Peter having "mushroomed into an international force" since being exposed by the Rolling Stones, who are credited with "opening up the rest of the world's eyes and ears to one of music's strongest entities.

"Tosh has captured the imagination and spirit of the people. Last week for example, he was given a proclamation on the steps of Borough Hall that August 23 was "Peter Tosh Day" in Brooklyn. Only hours earlier, Tosh had visited two restoration centres in Bedford-Stuyvesant where he was given 'the key to the black community'. Tosh didn't end it there. Two days later, he performed at the Pratt Institute under the auspices of the Rastafarians.

"'Thanks for coming to Brooklyn,' shouted one teenage well-wisher. 'Stevie Wonder doesn't come, Marvin Gaye doesn't come here and neither do the O'Jays.' Tosh flashed a smile and proceeded to play before 4,000 people who were enraptured by the soul and sensibility of the music from his new *Mystic Man* LP. The authenticity of his style and feelings could be verified by the reaction of his audience: they cheered and cheered him into the night."

This is a majority black audience, remember, with very different ideas of what constitutes authenticity. They knew Peter's worth, as teacher, revolutionary and minstrel. Powerful black voices like his merited respect and not just from a young audience, but elders raised on Richie Havens, Gil Scott Heron and the Last Poets. These are the people he'll meet on his trips round Brooklyn. Most are focused on building or saving communities, and so to be honoured in that way – even if Peter didn't actually address the United Nations in the end – was a significant achievement.

The concert at Brooklyn's Pratt Institute had barely stopped ringing in their ears when WLIR broadcast Peter's show at the Calderone Auditorium in Hempstead from a month earlier, when the band had again excelled on 'Buk-In-Hamm Palace'. Four days later and Peter's expected at the Second Annual Tribal Stomp, Pot Luck Picnic And Dance in Monterrey, where he'll meet up with old friends Soul Syndicate and Donald Kinsey, and headline over Joe Ely, the Chambers Brothers, Nick Gravenites, Maria Muldaur and the Clash. It was the first date of the Clash's US tour and as journalist Pat Gilbert will recall, "It was as if wartime Hollywood's influence had been absorbed, filtered through the London post-war experience, given a punk/rude boy twist and blasted back to the US." Lee Perry had produced the band's version of 'Police And Thieves' but hopefully they didn't make the same mistake as Dennis Bovell and praise him within Peter's earshot.

"Peter gave me a lecture one time," Dennis explains. "He spent the next half an hour telling me what an unscrupulous character Lee 'Scratch' Perry was, and to never mention the man's name in his presence ever again. He said, 'Don't you ever call that person great, because he's a *vampire!*'"

When Peter arrived that afternoon, he saw 500 people milling about on a derelict-looking fairground site that was big enough to hold 20 times more. The promoters had wanted to re-enact the Monterrey Pop Festival of 1967, which had starred Jimi Hendrix, the Who, Janis Joplin and Otis

Redding at the height of flower power. Even the poster artwork sought to relive that era whilst the MC was Wavy Gravy, of Woodstock fame. The promoters were good on nostalgia, but what they lacked was finance, organisational skills and most important of all, paying customers. Angered by the poor turnout, members of a certain UK band sliced the upholstery with knives, causing $10,000 worth of damage. There were also thieves about, as Peter found out to his cost. Earlier that day, Jamaican conga player Larry McDonald had steered him in the direction of some high-grade marijuana, which then went missing.

"He was hoarding it in his hotel room but the bag disappeared so he called the police. He actually called the police!" exclaims Larry, as if he still can't quite believe it. "They said to him, 'Mr. Tosh, what has been stolen?' He say, 'them t'ief me t'ing,' and still the police keep questioning him about what's been taken. By this time a crowd was gathering and then his manager shows up who says to me, 'Larry, what's happening?' I say, 'Well, they take the stuff out of Peter's room at the hotel, and he's reported it.' He start to clutch at his head then goes up to the policeman and says, 'Officer, I'm so sorry. This has all been a terrible mistake, there was some jewellery went missing but we've found it and Peter was misinformed. I'm so very sorry.' Peter was certainly a character. Oh man, was he a character!"

Peter was still upset about the show in Monterrey several days later, after arriving in the city he calls "Hellay". Los Angeles is home to reggae historian Roger Steffens, who accompanied Peter to Hank Holmes' apartment in Fairfax where Tosh was shown more than 20 records issued in his own name that he never knew existed, and for which he hadn't received "a cent". After acknowledging the Monterrey crowd was smaller than expected he says some local comedian had overstayed his welcome, making everyone else late, and that he wasn't informed about a 10 o'clock curfew until 10 minutes beforehand, just as he went on stage! The show sounds like a disaster but once it's off his chest, Peter's interview with Steffens throws up several interesting titbits, including the news that he's reading a book called *History Of The Italian Massacres In Ethiopia*, which outlines the atrocities of 1934–37.

"When I read that book it brought tears to my eyes," Peter admits. "Terrible, terrible... Any man found with a picture of His Imperial Majesty had his head chopped off! You can see these photos of Italian soldiers with the heads of Rastas in their hands, boasting and posing... They sent a dozen heads in baskets to show off to their families. Plenty of people don't know these things."

When people tell you stories about African warriors who can disable a lion with one karate chop and of man-eating trees that walk up to people, catch them in its branches and carry them inside the trunk, leaving no trace, it's tempting to dismiss them as being childish, or at least "child-like". Peter's imagination has that same quality at times, only it's rooted in the vision of a glorious and mysterious African past, which lends his fantasies just a little more weight.

An account of Hank and Roger's meeting with Peter will appear in the December 1979 edition of *Reggae News*. After declaring a liking for the Commodores, Teddy Pendergrass and the Isley Brothers, he says there's "about two albums' worth of unreleased material" in Columbia's vaults, and that he's written a song for a possible Wailers reunion called 'Here We Are Together Again'. Since any coming together of Peter, Bob and Bunny would create massive interest, this is some scoop. Unfortunately little else will happen with this project for some time, and Bob won't be involved in any case.

By mid-September Peter was back in New York, spending time with Pauline and thinking he should get a place in the city. That's where his record company was based and he liked the New York studios, as well as the markets and juice bars. He had plenty of friends there too, including Jamaican expats like Glen Adams and Glen Brown but more importantly, he now had close family to hand.

A one-night stand at the Bottom Line – without Jagger – on September 13 didn't prove anything like so memorable as last time, although it served as a handy warm-up gig for Peter's visit to Madison Square Garden the following week, where he participated in the MUSE Concerts for a Non-Nuclear Future. The Garden was booked for four consecutive nights between September 19 and 22, when Peter joined Bruce Springsteen, Tom Petty, Jackson Browne, James Taylor, Carly Simon, Ry Cooder, Bonnie Raitt and Gil Scott Heron in registering his concerns over nuclear energy.

It was an accident at a plant on Three Mile Island, near Harrisburg back in March that had underlined the dangers of nuclear power. 140,000 people were evacuated amidst fears of radiation, just as Columbia Pictures released a film starring Jane Fonda called *The China Syndrome*, with a storyline about a meltdown at a nuclear power plant. Two months later more than 65,000 anti-nuclear protestors marched on the Capitol to hear celebrities and politicians warning of further dangers from nuclear accidents. These people were out to save the planet, apart from the ones dressed as mushrooms and singing, "Two, four, six, eight. We don't want to radiate..."

Shortly afterwards, Graham Nash and Jackson Browne organised a series of benefit shows throughout southern California, culminating in a sold-out concert at the Hollywood Bowl on behalf of MUSE (Musicians United for Safe Energy). The New York event that followed is also known as "the No Nuke Show". Tosh was the only reggae artist invited to take part, which is indicative of how well he was regarded within the music industry at that time. With tickets priced at $18.50, this was a different kind of show for Peter, who supported Bruce Springsteen on the closing night. It was September 22, and many New Yorkers were celebrating Rosh Hashanah, the Jewish New Year. You can imagine the reaction as Peter strode purposefully on stage, wearing the same Arab robe and headdress he'd premiered in Canada. Forthright as ever, he was declaring his solidarity with the Palestinians, who were viewed as terrorists by many Americans, not least the US government.

Peter won't feature on the double album *No Nukes*, despite having been listed on Elektra Records' press release. All four shows were filmed, but he won't appear in the documentary either. This may be due to his controversial support for Palestine except he's waving a spliff around during most of his set, and takes hearty pulls on it in full view of the cameras. It wasn't one of his best performances in truth, despite the occasion. The following day, another 200,000 people gathered in New York's Battery Park. "Either we turn off the TV and climb out of our shells and take a look at hell," warned James Taylor, "or we will fail ultimately. Biblically, it will be Armageddon."

Anti-nuclear protests will eventually force the closure of a dozen or so reactors and Peter won't abandon the cause either, but make even stronger statements in future. In the meantime, his past appeared to be catching up with him. That November in London, Theo Bafaloukos' film *Rockers* will attract rave reviews after screenings at the Ace in Brixton and Screen On The Green in Islington. Since 'Steppin' Razor' figures prominently on the soundtrack, Virgin decided – without Peter's consent or involvement – to issue it on 7″, backed with 'Legalise It'. Reviewing it for *NME*, Charles Shaar Murray snottily announced they were the only Peter Tosh tracks he needed, and called their release "a ploy calculated to irritate Tosh, EMI and Rolling Stones Records. Now let's hope Tosh is too stoned to go round to Virgin and duff 'em all up..."

There was slim chance of that, and Peter had other worries regarding the Stones in any case, after hearing they'd been courting fellow Jamaican singer Max Romeo. First they invited this potential rival to Electric Lady Studios and got him to sing on a track from their next album, and now the grapevine was awash with rumours that Max may sign to their label. Peter may not have always shown it, but he enjoyed his exclusive relationship with the Stones. They, on the other hand, just loved the music and were indulging their taste for it.

"There was something about reggae that struck a serious chord for us," explains Ronnie Wood. "The fundamental ital rhythm was a mutual love of ours, and it weaved into the foundation of our musical creativity the same way blues did. A load of great reggae bands suddenly appeared on the scene, like the Slickers, the Heptones, Max Romeo and Pluto Shervington. In those days Keith and I would take our own reggae records to clubs and tell the disc jockeys they had to play them if they didn't want to risk being on the end of Keith's ratchet. We were only trying to cheer the place up..."

A couple of months after jamming with Bob and the Wailers at a show in California, Ronnie and his girlfriend Jo Howard were in the Caribbean, holidaying on the island of St. Martin. Soon after arriving they'll be arrested for possession of cocaine and jailed for five days, before being deported to America. Somewhere in the Jamaican countryside, his pipe stuffed with high-grade, Peter Tosh wasn't thinking of musical brotherhood, but where this partnership was headed.

Chapter 22

Oh Bumbo Klaat

Chris Hinze was a Dutch flute player in his early forties searching for musical adventure. To call him "classically trained" is an understatement. In the late Sixties, after graduating from the Royal Conservatory in The Hague he won a scholarship to Berklee College Of Music in Boston. By the time he fell under the spell of reggae he'd composed symphonic works and travelled extensively, recording with local musicians in Indonesia, India and Japan.

Reggae's hazy rhythms prompted a trip to Kingston in early 1980, where he met Mikey Chung. Luck was on his side, since there was no better guide to the local music scene. A friendship developed between the two musicians; Chris had a deal with CBS that would cover the costs of recording an album and so he arranged to return several weeks later, armed with fresh compositions.

"The first night I arrived, I went to take a walk but the people at the hotel said not to because Kingston was so dangerous," he says. "I went out anyway and you could literally feel the tension... They warned me never to go out like that again on my own, and so I stayed close to the musicians after that."

He describes Mikey Chung as "the key man who set up everything. He was the one who brought in the other guys and tuned the instruments. He was the intellectual of the group and very important in terms of getting the sound we wanted."

Mikey booked Aquarius Studio in Half Way Tree, where they could run through some ideas before doing the actual recording. Sly and Robbie were there and also Sticky Thompson, whose percussion playing was now Zen-like in its devastating simplicity.

"We all loved making music so much," says Mikey. "In those times we were free to do what we wanted. We were free to create. We didn't have anyone around us saying, 'you can't do that' or 'you must do this'. The music was allowed to flow back then. We could try different things and experiment."

Which is not to say they were unprofessional in any way. "No, because the musicians were very disciplined," says Chris. "The only person who turned up 24 hours later than arranged was Peter Tosh which was OK because I was very happy that he wanted to do it. The talks I had with him were very positive. He was a thinker and philosopher, and I was so pleased that he'd turned up. He was very cool and relaxed. Everything was nice; we were almost ready for the recording and then what happened? There was a power cut! Luckily we were ahead of schedule and I had time to spare but the power cut just went on and on... It was unbelievable, because then I had only one day left to record before leaving."

Chris lived in New York, and so found working at Aquarius something of a challenge. The facilities weren't exactly state-of-the-art and he remembers that whenever they listened back to anything, it was always so *loud*. "There was this leakage that came from nowhere, and getting a clean recording was difficult," he sighs, and yet the rhythm tracks are faultless. Chris gave them names like 'East Kingston', 'Walking Alone In Hellshire Bay' and 'Bamboo Reggae', which suits their pastoral nature. The majority were instrumentals since Peter's vocals appear infrequently, and are sketchy at best. 'Puss And Dog' only has a couple of lines, whilst 'Silver And Gold' borrows from the hymn 'Roll Away', which he used to sing in choir practice. Some people claim Peter wrote a song about Bob Marley at this session that was so unpleasant the musicians refused to play it, yet Chris Hinze refutes this. His next step was to take Mikey Chung to New York, where they overdubbed several of the tracks at Electric Lady studios. Most of Chris' flute parts were recorded there, and they're exquisite. The album will initially be released as *Word, Sound And Power* in honour of the band members, although it's now better known as *Kings Of Reggae*.

In late February, Peter joined a cultural mission to Grenada led by Prime Minister Michael Manley. At least 20 entertainers were involved, including the Theatre Group for National Liberation. This "Festival of the Revolution" would last for two weeks and marked the first anniversary of the People's Revolutionary Government seizing control of the country. Like Jamaica, Grenada now had close ties with Cuba and was flirting with Communism, although Peter wasn't. In the presence of Michael Manley, he responded to the Grenadian Prime Minister's greeting of "Welcome comrade" by retorting "I man don't come red. I come black."

Whilst he and Manley were in Grenada, Bob Marley and Jacob Miller travelled to Brazil, where Chris Blackwell arranged to book a series of South American concerts. No sooner had they returned to Jamaica than Jacob was killed in a car accident, on March 23. Reports of his death vary. Some claim he died from a burst blood vessel and that's what had caused his car to spin out of control and hit a lamppost. Less charitable folks said he'd been opening a can of food and lost concentration, but then came mutterings that Jacob had been freebasing cocaine up at Strawberry Hill, and this is what caused him to haemorrhage. His death proved a tragedy for the music, and not only family, friends and well wishers. Thousands paid tribute as the singer's body lay in state at the National Arena, and then watched in hushed silence, punctuated only by sobs as a priest from the Ethiopian Orthodox Church officiated at his funeral.

A week after Jacob's passing, the *Gleaner* announced two concerts – "Youth Consciousness Parts 1 and 2, featuring superstar Peter Tosh" – to take place over Easter at the Ranny Williams Entertainment Centre in Kingston.

"Tosh, in his first appearance since the historic One Love Concert at the National Stadium, will be accompanied by Word Sound and Power featuring Sly and Robbie," it declared. This wasn't strictly true, as Peter had played at last year's Reggae Sunsplash, but no matter. Second on the bill was Black Uhuru, now described as "one of the hottest groups on the Jamaica scene" whilst the Tamlins and UK dub poet Linton Kwesi Johnson, who was making his debut on the island, served as show openers. The first concert was held on Saturday April 5 amidst fairly opulent surroundings since the Ranny Williams Centre sat in the grounds of Jamaica House, which is the Prime Minister's official residence. It's a large venue, but has little or no atmosphere when half-full. Radio DJ Winston Williams was master of ceremonies, and even his regular plugs hadn't shifted the unsold tickets in Record Village, or at Music Fair stores in Kingston Arcade and Little Premier Plaza. Youth Consciousness Part 2 took place two days later, on Easter Monday. The beachside venue at Fort Clarence made a better fit, as did the afternoon start and reduced admission for children. Alas, the turnout still failed to match Peter's expectations and he'll be disappointed by the outcome. He'd taken a risk in staging these concerts, and can only be applauded for having done so. Idealistic as ever, he'd hoped to raise revenue for community projects and right a few wrongs resulting from the Peace Concert. He also wanted to play for Kingston audiences again, rather than at tourist events on the north coast. Needless to say he'll learn from the experience, and do things differently next time.

Dr. D. K. Duncan, the General Secretary of the PNP, attended Saturday's night show. As he arrived at the Ranny Williams Centre, a young police constable said he couldn't park in a certain area. A scuffle broke out, and the policeman was pushed to the ground and sworn at. "Boy, don't you know who I am?" bellowed Duncan, who'll later write to Jamaica's Police Commissioner claiming he'd been dealt with unfairly, and denying any assault had taken place. To his undying shame the letter ended with "Yours in the struggle", which must have raised a sneer or two.

Bob Marley must have laughed at that one. He was currently involved in a nation's real-life struggle over in Zimbabwe, which celebrated Independence in April. He and the Wailers would play directly after the Union Jack came down and Zimbabwe's new flag – bearing Rasta colours – fluttered over the stadium. Peter's former bandmate had a knack for such historic moments although an earlier African trip in January had backfired after Bob and the Wailers had travelled to Gabon as guests of President Bongo, but then ended up playing at his daughter's birthday party. During their stay, Don Taylor was found to have cheated the band out of some money and was then fired after getting a severe beating. Taylor also managed Jimmy Cliff, who'd been in Gabon with Marley and would soon be performing in Soweto to 65,000 people – most of them poor blacks, as whites needed a permit to attend. Jimmy was the first reggae artist to defy the cultural boycott and visit South Africa whilst avoiding the hated "honorary white" status, despite *The Harder They Come* having been banned by the apartheid regime. Peter was now more determined than ever to visit Africa himself, and regretted how music and politics had grown so intertwined. It's no exaggeration to say that people were risking their lives listening to his records – his albums were banned in South Africa – and yet he was being told that he couldn't go there and sing for them, which didn't seem right.

Reggae's popularity had continued to spread at rapid pace. The *Gleaner* acknowledged as much in its April 30 issue by announcing that, "In its twelve-year history, reggae has got its foot in the door of international music and in what can be seen as a make-or-break situation, it is now set to explode in the Far East. Reggae has had number one songs in Britain, France, Switzerland and even Germany, but has failed in its bid to make any lasting impression on the charts in the USA, despite the fact that stars such as Bob Marley and the Wailers, Peter Tosh and Burning Spear have had numerous successful US tours."

Sadly, these artists' records still weren't being played in Jamaica either, as Basil Wilson explains.

"Peter's conflict was that he could not get his songs to be played locally. The last interview that I did with him, he was quite astonished by the difficulty he was having in getting any of his music played in Jamaica. His music got much more airplay in Europe and other places, but look at the music and examine its class significance. Reggae music was the music of the poor, of the working class and the wretched of the earth, whereas Jamaica's radio stations were controlled by the middle class and so there was a tremendous reluctance to give the music exposure, and grant it legitimacy."

Peter wasn't the only singer to highlight Jamaica's social problems, or to warn against the political violence that continued to tear communities apart. As Manley's current term of office drew to a close, tensions increased on both sides. Areas like Jungle and Tivoli Gardens had turned into war zones, and few families escaped tragedy. On May 20, 153 female inmates perished in a fire at the Eventide Rest Home. The cause of the blaze was never officially determined, although many believed it was arson. Gunmen had entered the premises several times, threatening to kill the staff because of their political affiliations, but no one imagined they'd burn it down – not with so many helpless elderly women inside. The incident sparked island-wide condemnation, prompting Michael Manley to declare May 26, 1980 – when the victims were buried in a mass grave inside the National Heroes Park – a national day of mourning.

Jamaica was in crisis, its moral compass creaking under the strain. Fear and uncertainty stalked the land and yet others led very different lives. After the Stones' latest album was released in June, Keith Richards gave an interview to *Oui* magazine under the heading, "Keith Richards: The Thorniest Stone". The guitarist's been up for days and the reason for that becomes immediately obvious when he takes out "a glass phial of a glittery substance that sparkles", which is almost certainly pharmaceutical cocaine. He pours some out onto a copy of Michael Thelwell's novel *The Harder They Come* and snorts it right in front of the journalist, despite protests from his PA. He talks openly about his drug use, and is gloriously unrepentant. The conversation then turns towards Rolling Stones Records. Keith enjoys having his own record label as it "enables us to sign other acts, music that we enjoy". He's then asked if Peter's still on the label. "Oh yeah, the guy's selling more records than anybody else. It's almost unbelievable. Can *not* believe it," he drawls, with obvious sarcasm.

'Is Tosh hard to work with?' the journalist asks.

"He's all right. You gotta know how to handle him," Keith replies.

'How do you handle him?'

"Well, if I have to handle him, I just grab hold of his collar and he knows what I mean by that. Yeah, he knows that he's fucking up. It's happened to me enough times after all."

The disenchantment with Peter is palpable despite Keith's coke-fuelled bravado, yet he's full of admiration for his Rastafarian neighbours on Jamaica's north coast, where Point Of View is undergoing repairs. "The house is being rebuilt and they haven't got the old roof off yet," he explains. "The whole place is being rewired, because I need better electricity for decent sounds. I can *relax* there. There are about 20 Rastas around the place and they look after me more than I could possibly wish for, the state I'm usually in. Nice people. The best..."

Here's a man who loves Jamaica, respects Rastafarians and spends "hundreds of dollars a week" on new releases at a record store in the Bronx. It's little wonder he and Peter took to each other yet there's no love lost between them now and just to rub it in, Keith says the Stones have signed Max Romeo, whom he describes as "a great singer – one of my favourites".

He and Mick turned up on *Rockers TV* next, which implied they were serious in reaching out to the reggae audience except there was no

290

mention of Peter Tosh, which is strange considering he's signed to their label. Instead, Earl Chin asked them about Bob Marley. 'Could You Be Loved' had recently gone Top 5 in the UK, and will stay on the charts all summer. It was reggae mixed with funk, and Bob had also received his share of criticism. After acknowledging how Marley is being "pushed so hard", Jagger insisted that a degree of compromise is necessary.

"You can't be touring America and expect to be exactly the same person as you were when you were living in Trench Town," he says, which may be a reference to Peter – the choice is yours. Keith remains subdued but then jokes that the Stones will only perform in Jamaica "when we get good enough", knowing only too well that most Jamaicans couldn't afford a ticket. He lists Jacob Miller, Dillinger, Big Youth and Black Uhuru among his favourite artists (spot the deliberate omission), but Peter doesn't care. He's just written a song about the perils of friendship, and the lyrics allow no room for compromise. "They will come with great pretence, to gain your confidence," he begins. "They will look right in your eyes, and tell you the wickedest lies. Make you promises, that never accomplishes... They'll take you round the bend and fry you in the end." This song will be called 'That's What They Will Do' and if anyone tells you Peter didn't write it about the Stones, they're lying.

On Wednesday, July 2, he'll return to the Ranny Williams Centre and headline the opening night of Reggae Sunsplash 3. Jamaica's annual showcase was bigger than ever this year after uprooting from Montego Bay and moving to Kingston. Festivities will be spread over four days and it's an all-star line-up featuring Sugar Minott, the Mighty Diamonds, Beres Hammond, Culture, Barrington Levy, Michigan & Smiley, Burning Spear and Dennis Brown. Not for the first time, Black Uhuru and the Tamlins open for Peter, who gave another unforgettable performance. He and the band had to leave for Europe the next day and so no one got much sleep, since they hadn't gone on stage until well past midnight. Sly Dunbar suggests it's one of the best shows they ever did, which makes it even more of a pity that Peter should feel so ripped off by the organisers, who he claims "are going to jail".

Sly and Robbie were now top-flight producers, as well as Jamaica's foremost rhythm section. When they're not out on the road with Peter they're at Channel One studios, churning out hits with the likes of General Echo, the Wailing Souls, Yellowman, Dennis Brown and Jimmy Riley, which could then be heard blaring from every rum bar and sound system for miles. Peter suspected they had divided loyalties, and wanted a band that was exclusive to him. Bob had proved the wisdom of this by keeping the Barrett brothers on retainer yet that wasn't an option where Sly and Robbie were concerned – not just because of the costs involved, but since they had ambitions of their own. When they asked if Black Uhuru could support Peter on this next tour Herbie Miller turned them down, saying they'd already booked an opening act. He and Peter were driving identical BMWs by this time and had the look – and instincts – of a confirmed double act. As Sly and Robbie reached Vienna they discovered there was no opening act, and wouldn't be for the rest of the tour. The writing was on the wall from that moment onwards, but the European leg of the *Mystic Man* tour still yielded its share of good humour.

"One day we were all on the bus and Peter brought out these crackers," says Daryl Thompson. "He's a Rasta so he took his finger and was rubbing the salt off them. I look over at Shakespeare who's sat next to me and ask him if Peter knows that crackers are cooked in lard. Robbie shook his head and I was getting ready to tell Peter this and was halfway out my seat when Robbie grabbed me by the seat of my pants, pulled me back and said, 'Don't tell him a word!' We sat right there and watched Peter eat these crackers and every time he reached for one, he'd carefully rub the salt off it. He did that with the whole packet and Robbie and I were cracked up laughing. Finally when he finishes off the packet, Robbie stands up and says, 'Hey Peter. How were the pork biscuits?' Peter said there was no pork in them so we tell him to read the box and of course he sees that they're cooked in lard and gets real upset. That tickled us no end, and we never let him forget it. There was this constant banter going back and forth, and the guy could be a lot of fun at times."

The second week of July they played at a different Italian city nearly every night before landing in Rome on the 13th. The Tamlins' Carlton Smith told Roger Steffens there were 20,000 people at the concert.

"The police came on stage and asked us to tone it down," he said. "It was like the Pope and the people in Vatican City couldn't take the vibrations that were up there! When we finished the show there was this young lady who the chief of police took back stage. He said, 'Peter, this young lady would like to touch you.' Peter say 'Yeah man, make her touch me man,' and when this young lady touch Peter, it was like she got electrocuted. She faint right away, like people get epilepsy. She started to sweat and froth..."

Daryl Thompson remembers overheating at one of these shows, and being amazed by Peter's reaction. "We were playing outdoors and the sun was beating down. I had no shirt on. I'd had to take it off because it was so wet and when I got to my solo I was so hot, I felt weak and was on the brink of fainting... I fell onto my knees and then I rolled onto my back and lay flat down on the stage playing the solo. I was afraid that I would faint and fall and break my guitar. I'd instinctively figured that I couldn't fall if I'm lying on the floor so I stayed there until I finished my solo. By this time the audience was going crazy. Peter told the audience that, 'When you play reggae music the way it's supposed to be played, that's how you're supposed to feel.' He was stood there pointing at me lying on the ground and smiling. I thought he was going to get angry with me but I honestly couldn't stand up any longer. I was afraid that I was going to pass out..."

Their next stop was Brazil, where they played at Il Festival Internacional De Jazz in Sao Paulo during late July. Peter arrived for the press conference wearing wrap-around shades and a red beret, and with an African talking drum slung across his shoulder. Talk about cool. The guy had charisma, and Al Anderson's words again spring to mind. "Who's more hip than Peter Tosh?" he once asked. "The guy was hip man..." The show at the Palacio das Convencoes do Anhembi was filmed and one of the cameras follows Peter on his journey to the stage door, imperious in his Arab robe and headdress, and with those impenetrable shades offering no clue as to his mood. People press against the walls and draw back respectfully as he passes. No one dares talk to him and Peter doesn't stop or look round but marches straight ahead. He walks right through this crowd of hangers-on and into the spotlight, where he receives rapturous applause. It's another great show. The musicians have plenty of room to spread out and Daryl takes full advantage, playing guitar behind his head and with his teeth like Hendrix, then falling to his knees during 'Bush Doctor', his face contorted with blues pain. The crowd loves it. There's none of the elitism Peter's encountered in other places, and no expectations of Mick Jagger joining him. Everyone's happy by the end of the show except Daryl Thompson, who's teased mercilessly for having had braids put in his hair, and walking around in a Rasta hat. Robbie Shakespeare will call him "Jah D" after this incident, which I guess made a change from "Foreigner".

In one of the more bizarre episodes from his career, Peter made a cameo appearance – as himself – in a popular television series called *Aqua Viva* (*Water Life*) whilst in Brazil. He turns up at a party given by Stella, who looks like Dame Edna Everage with her red hair and huge glasses. She greets him excitedly and within just a minute or two, he's sat on the couch singing 'Don't Look Back' and playing guitar as the other guests gather round, clapping delightedly. It's a rare example of Peter Tosh relaxing in front of the cameras, and appearing wholly at ease with his surroundings. He and his party flew to Rio after Sao Paulo, where Herbie Miller recalls him entertaining visitors in his hotel room on the 26th floor.

"Dermot Hussey and I were part of that group as Tosh explained his philosophy, including the ability to fly. To clear the air of the herb smoke that enveloped us all, Peter politely opened the window overlooking Ipanema beach while he resolutely argued his conviction. It seemed to some that at the moment he opened the window, he was about to prove the point of his argument and take flight. As a caution, Dermot and I quietly took up positions at the window just in case he was about to demonstrate the ability to fly. Needless to say he was smoking some good herb and we were not about to stand by and watch..."

Daryl Thompson has a keen interest in alternative healing and new age philosophies, and would often talk with Peter about such things. "Sometimes he'd knock at my door at four in the morning and tell me about his dreams, then ask me to interpret them for him," he recalls. "He would dream that he'd gone to see his dead grandmother and he'd be flying in the air, but then when he woke in the morning, he couldn't do it. He was convinced we all had the ability to fly at one time but we'd forgotten it, so I'd try and explain to him about the astral body and the dream body, and how it shouldn't be confused with the physical body..."

Peter was supposed to leave for Canada soon after returning from Latin America, but the authorities there had imposed a temporary ban on rock concerts after incidents of crowd trouble and his shows were postponed. He was in Jamaica during early August, when Hurricane Allen sent 40-foot high waves sweeping over the eastern shoreline, killing eight people and causing extensive damage. This hurricane was later renamed Andrew, the same as Peter's 12-year old-son with Bunny's sister. Peter would take him to Westmoreland, where they sampled the delights of Jamaican country living. He and the boy went fishing together, and would often sing oldies by Stevie Wonder, Ray Charles and Kenny Rogers late into the evenings. Peter also encouraged his son to study piano. "From the start it was inside me to sing and play instruments," says Andrew. "From that point forward, I knew that my heartbeat was music and one day it would just be music out of my mouth, and writing and singing my own songs."

Andrew will one day embark on a musical career of his own, centred on his father's work. His first record will be a version of 'Can't Blame The Youth' but for the time being he's attending school in Duhaney Park, practising the unicycle and feeling very proud of his famous dad. No one's making the claim that Peter was a model father, but the love he had for his children was undeniable. Being around family kept his mind from dwelling on problems relating to record companies, band members, critics, booking agents and promoters – also old friends, since Bob Marley had collapsed whilst jogging in Central Park, and then managed just one more concert before being told that he had cancer of the lungs and stomach, and a malignant brain tumour. As Bob underwent chemotherapy treatment his dreadlocks fell out, leaving him all but unrecognisable. Whether Peter would have acknowledged him is a moot point.

"Peter definitely seemed to harbour some residual resentments towards certain people," says Daryl Thompson. "I know that his feelings were hurt by something that had gone down with Bob Marley and Chris Blackwell, who he would always refer to as 'Chris Whitewell'. He also had something against Bob Marley because he, Bob and Bunny had been the Wailers, and then all of a sudden it was Bob Marley and the Wailers. It was like he and Bunny had become an afterthought and the same kind of thing happened with the Rolling Stones. I think he felt cheated by them in some way but I noticed he carried quite a few grievances like that. He was quite close-mouthed about them though. He wouldn't openly say that he hated these people but you could feel it. Like we would never play any of Bob Marley's music on the tour bus or anything like that. You were either in the one camp or the other and that was it."

It was election time in Jamaica and the run-in was already the bloodiest in the island's history, since almost 900 people had died in skirmishes between the two parties. Election day was October 30 and marked by a series of incidents. Manley's motorcade was fired on in May Pen and a PNP candidate killed in Gordon Town. Seven people were then shot and killed on National Heroes Day in Kingston, and two children died when JLP and PNP factions clashed in St. Elizabeth. Even battle-hardened Jamaicans felt their country was teetering on the brink after a PNP minister was seen firing a weapon on national television. Gunfire had disrupted a rally in Spanish Town and the killings never stopped, even after the polling stations closed. By the following afternoon, it was discovered the JLP had swept to power in a landslide, leaving the PNP in serious disarray. The people had spoken, and they'd grown tired of going without essentials like food, soap and petrol. They wanted change and for Manley and his supporters, the dream of social democracy was over.

In a final speech, Manley admitted that his decision to stand by Cuba and other Third World countries had not been popular with the United States, and this had hastened his downfall. "Maybe what I did wrong was to challenge the power of the western economic structure... And for this I will remain unrepentant and unreconstructed," he thundered. Within days of the election, Edward Seaga was sworn in as Jamaica's Prime Minister and after expelling the Cuban Ambassador, severed all ties with Castro. Soon, the shelves in local shops will fill once more, as America helps out with food supplies. The recovery will alleviate some of the suffering but little else changed. The political levers swapped hands and there was an exodus of gang members from the losing side yet what Peter referred to as "the shit-stem" remained intact, and those with vested interests wanted it to stay like that. He'd been thinking back to the Peace Concert, and what had gone wrong. The truce hadn't worked because the people involved hadn't been sincere, but that wasn't the only reason. Two years later and it looked like a set-up, intended to lure supporters of both sides into the open. These people had then become targets and in the words of drummer Santa Davis, "deep-rooted things happened that people just couldn't forget.

"It was just for the moment," he told Roger Steffens, "and Peter see through that a long time. It was just to get people more relaxed so you can deal with them. Because you can't deal with a lion when he's enraged – yuh haffe give him some kind of sedative fe cool him down. Well the Peace Treaty was a sedative, to calm people down for a bit."

That's what Peter will call another new song he's just written – 'Peace Treaty'. There's grim humour in the way he renames Kingston "Killsome City" but it's the observation that "all those who sign that peace treaty is now resting in peace in the cemetery" that resonates most. If it had come out sooner 'Peace Treaty' would have created more of a stir, but it won't be included on his next album for some reason – maybe because the topic's too localised. Shame, because there's a line in it where he claims that Babylon wants him dead for telling the truth and whilst it may sound like a cliché, you'd better believe it.

The lyrics in his notebooks – some of them mere fragments – were now multiplying at a steady rate. November 2 marked the 50th anniversary of Emperor Haile Selassie I's coronation, and there were celebrations all over Jamaica. For a committed Rastaman like Peter this meant joining the brethren in prayer, chanting and meditation. It was brotherhood but also communion, since the heart couldn't help but grow closer to Jah at these grounations. 'Rastafari Is' came out of this experience. Peter always included at least one Rastafarian song of praise on his albums and this is a rockier version with keening lead guitar, tight harmonies and grumbling bass-line.

Two days after the Rasta celebrations, Bob was baptised Berhane Selassie in the Ethiopian Orthodox Church and then flown out to a clinic in Bavaria, where he was put under the care of cancer specialist Dr. Josef Issels. Island Records denied there was anything seriously wrong with him apart from "exhaustion", but there was a dimming of the light and you could feel it. Ronald Reagan won the US elections that month and then on December 8 John Lennon was murdered in New York, just a couple of blocks from where Peter will soon buy an apartment.

Earl McGrath had now resigned as President of Rolling Stones Records, and this will entail a change of label for Peter, as the former executive explains. "The last Stones release I worked on was *Emotional Rescue* and by the time that came out we'd sold eight million records," he states proudly. "Mick's gone on record as saying that when I joined Rolling Stones Records it became a proper business. I don't know whether that's a compliment or not but I quit working for the Stones after the second Peter Tosh record. One of the main reasons I quit working for them was because I had a 50-50 deal on anything I brought to the label, which was Peter Tosh and Jim Carroll. That meant the Stones only got 10 percent each and they became seriously grumpy so I said, 'Look, you keep Peter Tosh and I'll keep Jim Carroll.' They said OK and that was it.

"The only record of Peter's that made any money was 'Don't Look Back'. The *Bush Doctor* album sold quite well but that's only because Mick and Keith were on it. His appearances on the tour were very successful though. Keith would come on stage sometimes, and then Mick would get up and they'd do their song together. I found that thrilling but I never saw Peter on stage when he wasn't being derogatory about something. The rest of the band members were very sweet but not Peter. He never looked happy during any situation I shared with him and he wasn't a particularly pleasant individual to deal with. He was never interested in money or anything like that but he just wasn't interested in being friendly."

Peter's next album won't be released on Rolling Stones Records, but EMI. The Stones' logo will be there, but the sentiment won't. Peter's relationship with the world's greatest rock band is on shaky ground, although his appetite for making music remains undiminished. Towards the end of January, he booked studio time at Dynamic with Geoffrey Chung. The majority of tracks on *Wanted Dread & Alive* will result from these sessions and they were recorded with the same musicians he'd taken on the road.

"We were trying to get a group sound on that album," says Mikey Chung. "Instead of building up the sound with lots of overdubs, we were trying to bring out what we really sounded like as a band."

Daryl Thompson didn't even know they'd be recording until the day before. That was on January 18, 1981. Twenty hours later and he was strapping on his guitar and trying to figure out what key Peter was in. "There was no preparation at all," he says. "Peter just came in, played the songs to us on his guitar, everybody found their spot and we built the tracks from there. There wasn't too much planning, and he never told anyone what to play. Sly and Robbie would come up with the rhythm; Mikey Chung would work the harmony parts and then show them to the keyboard players. Peter didn't have too much to do with any of it, except for the background vocals. There were certain things he wanted from the backing singers I guess, coming from the Wailers and Impressions, but he was very self-effacing. He wasn't like an iron-fisted dictator or anything like that. It was an organic process, and he trusted us to do what we were there for."

Sticky Thompson and Noel "Scully" Simms on percussion, a Jamaican flautist and a trio of horns players called Rass Brass will be the only non-salaried musicians used on this album, giving it more of a Jamaican feel. There were further sessions on January 20, 21, 28 and 29, and also February 2 that yielded 14 or 15 tracks, some of them cut in a contemporary dancehall style. Peter's not making rockers or funky reggae any more, but reflecting what's happening out on the streets. 'Coming In Hot' could be mistaken for a gunman tune on first hearing. "I just clean up my nozzle, load the barrel... Firing some musical shot." It's drawing from the same well of inspiration as 'The Toughest', except it was actually written about a fever that confined him to bed for three days.

"Stepping into 1981, I was 104 degrees," Peter told Roger Steffens. "And I mean hot, hot, hot... Even my eyeballs were hot. Next day it went higher and the whole a me catch a fire. I couldn't take it no longer."

As he lay there, his body consumed by fever, Peter imagined reggae music as a virus, coursing through his bloodstream and spreading from his head to his toes. The doctor fears the worst, and tells him he has reggaemylitis. "Is it contagious?" Peter asks. "Is it outrageous? Is it vicious, or is it dangerous?" Alas, the doctor says it's incurable, and there's no relief.

"Peter was more intelligent than most of his fellow entertainers and he had a real grasp of language too," attests Nambo Robinson. "He'd twist words around except he always knew about them from a dictionary point of view, and I don't think a lot of people understood that about him. I paid attention to him and little by little, found he actually knew what he was saying. He could tell you where these words came from, whether they were originally from Italian or whatever, even if he then changed them round to mean something else. He was a genius at things like that..."

'Reggaemylitis' was an instant hit – not on 45, but with everyone sharing an emotional bond to the music. It made people smile and proved that Peter had been listening, because the swaggering rhythm wasn't all that different from the beat coming out of Channel One and Joe Gibbs. It was just produced to a higher standard that's all. 'Wanted Dread & Alive' is another of his outlaw tunes, and an obvious choice as the title track. There's a hint of 'Keep On Moving' in the line "I've been accused of a shooting, which Jah knows I would never do". He's on the run – hunted by "evil forces", and "with nowhere to hide". His life and freedom are at stake. It's good versus evil, which justifies him owning two guns for self-protection, even though he's innocent. It's a comic book Western, and skilfully executed. Listening to this track, it's fascinating how some reggae music manages to sound so happy, in contrast to what the lyrics are dealing with. People couldn't help but dance to Peter's misfortune although it slows to a shuffle on 'Cold Blood', which revives another Jamaican staple

– the musical courtroom drama. Not for the first time, he's stood in the dock after being held on ganja charges and although unspoken, there's so much personal history in this song. "Every time I see Babylon (the police) my blood runs cold... Ten degrees. Below zero," he sings and with good reason, since "the Grudge" (meaning judge!) finds him guilty "for an exhibit they could not find".

'Rok With Me' is a remake of a track the Wailers recorded for Johnny Nash and Danny Sims called 'Rock Sweet Rock'. Unusually for Peter it's a love song, and unabashedly romantic. "You're the sweetest rocker in town. I love to see you go round," he croons to the object of his affections. It's his 'Stir It Up,' sang over an irresistible wheel and turn style groove. Peter will later release it on his own Intel Diplo label, after EMI failed to recognise its potential. He also recorded updates of 'Maga Dog' and 'Stop That Train' at these sessions, although they'll be held over for the next album. Both versions are well-nigh definitive. 'Maga Dog' features some additional lyrics (about an illicit visit to an obeah man), and is now completely transformed from its calypso origins, whilst 'Stop That Train' rides an unstoppable groove, with Daryl sounding like George Harrison circa 'All Things Must Pass'. In Nambo Robinson's own words the horns "cut like razors" on these tracks, thanks to Geoffrey Chung.

"He made our horns sound like Memphis!" he exclaims. "I don't know what he was doing to really bring that sound out, but he was a genius. He was one of the main engineers responsible for establishing us but then Geoffrey had the advantage of working closely with Clive Hunt, who did some serious arrangements as well. We all learnt a lot from him."

Bob Marley had used Rass Brass on 'Survival' and would have taken them on tour had they not chosen to stay with Dennis Brown, who gave them their first break on 'Visions'. The members included Dean Fraser (alto and soprano sax), Ronald "Nambo" Robinson (trombone) and Junior "Chico" Chin, who usually played trumpet with them, but was replaced by David Madden on the *Wanted Dread & Alive* sessions. Peter liked these young horns players. They reminded him of the Skatalites, and they were well trained thanks to bandleader Alfred "Babe" O'Brien and the National Volunteers programme.

"Peter was a kind person, speaking from experience, and quite generous because that was another way of him showing appreciation," says Nambo. "He never paid what was called standard; he paid what he thought you deserved and left you with the feeling he would have given you more if he could. That was quite satisfying but I think he saw himself on the same level as us, as a fellow musician really. Peter was different in that respect, and he'd give us plenty of freedom as well – not to go off at a tangent, but to express ourselves. Yeah man, that was a joy and then as we left he'd say, 'Keep in touch. I want you for the next session.'"

Every album contains a surprise or two and *Wanted Dread & Alive* is no exception. 'Fools Die' is a successor to 'Creation', sung magnificently over just flute and electric piano. It's simple, but delicate – beautiful and yet strong. Also known as 'Lips Of The Righteous', this semi-classical opus forms a parallel with Bob Marley's 'Redemption Song', especially when Peter proclaims, "We've got to build a better nation. Clean up Jah creation or there will be no future for you and me." This message isn't just addressed to world leaders or politicians, but everyone who can make a difference, i.e. all of us. He again champions the poor in this song, which the Wailers had originally recorded for Ted Pouder back in 1970 as 'Wisdom'.

Those years of struggle when he, Bob and Bunny almost starved trying to keep the group together now seemed far away, except for the mental scars they'd left behind. Bob is still in the clinic in Bavaria and unbeknown to all, will never see Jamaica again. Whilst other band members kept a bedside vigil, Family Man stayed on at 56 Hope Road with a gun in his waist, ensuring that thieves didn't take advantage of Bob's absence. He sat in with Peter one day in late January and lent dancing bass to 'The Poor Man Feel It', which is a litany of everyday hardships for Jamaica's under-privileged. "We've got to find a solution to this pollution (meaning corruption)," he insists, "because only the poor man a feel it..."

"There are so many poor people in the world," he once told John Swenson. "It's like 80 percent of the world is poor, seen? And whenever inflation rises and the cost of living stepping up, people's wages are stationary and the shit-stem continues to be the same way. All the people get is promises from the politicians, saying what they will do 10 years later. Ten years accomplish and nothing happens, the same shit-stem goes on over and over again and the people remain the same way. That's the reason I sing this song, for the people, the poor people seen?"

Whilst the song he's written about the Stones ('That's What They Will Do') won't make the album, 'Guide Me (From My Friends)' proves an able replacement. It's a warning to beware of friends (brothers even) who'll come and sit round your table but "want to kill you like Cain and Abel..." According to the storyteller, these characters only hang around because they're looking for ways to "eliminate you". Peter's a generous soul and yet the expectations on him and every other successful Jamaican – especially those originally from the ghetto – are hard to bear at times. If he turns down people's pleas for help then he's got "a wicked heart", and yet he's nowhere near as wealthy as they imagine. He paints a picture of so-called friends approaching him with a smile, begging handouts whilst plotting to steal from him or kill him at the earliest opportunity, and it's chilling.

You'd be forgiven at this point for thinking the bombast heard on Peter's earlier records has been somehow muted, yet he's lost none of his talent for controversy. Herbie Miller says 'Oh Bumbo Klaat' had been originally intended for inclusion on 'Mystic Man', but that EMI got cold feet and relegated it to the flipside of 'Buk-In-Hamm Palace'. It'll come as no surprise to learn that 'Oh Bumbo Klaat' was banned in Jamaica, but this was nothing new to Peter of course. The chorus was (and still is) outrageous but after the initial shock came reasoning as Peter explained that due to a preponderance of lies, we've lost the true meaning of language and word, sound and power.

He told Roger Steffens that "one night an evil spirit held me down. I could not make one single sound. Jah told me, 'son, use the word' and now I'm free as a bird." He's talking about something that had happened when he was living in Trench Town, back in the sixties. Evil forces that only he could see had caused his mouth, hands and legs to stop functioning. He was conscious and could see, but was powerless to call out to friends and relatives sleeping in the same room.

"I could not tell a man nothing or ask a man to do anything to help me," he said. "I was on the brink of what you call death. I saw three ghosts or duppies, and they became terrified because they don't like to know that people are interfering in their business." Prior to the attack, Peter had been in hospital for three days. He'd been injured defending himself from a drunken man who kept hitting him with a stool and wouldn't stop. Peter went to punch him just as someone intervened, knocking him off balance and sending his fist crashing through a window, which lacerated his hand. One of Peter's companions then got hysterical after seeing two huge feet on the veranda of the room they were sharing, and this was just the beginning. Another friend had passed out on the table Peter used for pressing clothes, but then rolled onto the floor. When he came to, he swore something had pushed him through the window. Peter then saw a light enter the room and hover near the ceiling. He went to touch his friend to alert him but discovered that he couldn't move. Just as he wondered if he was paralysed, his feet began to swell up as if they were about to explode, then his tongue cleaved to the roof of his mouth rendering him speechless. He was fully conscious, but unable to respond in any way. He realised that he would have to "make some inner communication", and asked the Creator what he should do.

"The Spirit say, just say, 'Move yah bumboclaat!'" he exclaimed. "Me say, 'What?'" Even Peter was shocked, since the word "bumboclaat" is classed as foul or indecent language in Jamaica but the inner voice told him not to hesitate, and so Peter let loose one almighty "B-u-m-b-o-c-l-a-a-t-!" "It just fly out like a bomb!" he recalled. "Immediately every spell was released, I got up and say, "Bumboclaat. That's why these guys said this thing is indecent language. It's so they can release their vampires on you and if you don't have spiritual communication, then you go to heaven with your toes tied..." He remained convinced that such experiences were real and whilst shaken, felt grateful for the teaching.

Peter used several variations of "bumbaclaat", "bumboclaat" and "bloodclaat" according to mood. He'd change where to put the emphasis, and never once alluded to the usual meaning of these words. In fact "claat" means cloth in Jamaican patois and so "bloodclaat" is another word for sanitary towel – which is highly offensive to Rastafarians. Three years earlier, at Eppy's music festival in Trelawny, Peter had told Peter Simon that, "bumboclaat is one of Jamaica's passwords, one of the most highest potential of culture that relieve the spells of evil. I've been investigating this word so long to find out what these words mean and what they are for... Well, I was born and raised and grown up in colonialism and exploitation, and I heard that bumboclaat, Rassclaat, bloodclaat and every kind of claat you could think of is bad word and indecent language. They're banned here in Jamaica but why is it indecent? So I went on an investigation and found myself in some circumstances, held down by some spiritual vampires. My mouth couldn't move, my tongue couldn't shake, my hands couldn't move and the only thing that could make me move was by saying, 'Move your bumbaclaat!' and that set me free. Yes I and from that day on, I never stop say bumbaclaat."

"Peter was always cussing and using bad words and yet it never sounded rude," adds Robbie Shakespeare. "That was the way Peter Touch talked and how he was. He'd been singing that song before, from an earlier time and other people were against him doing it but we said, 'No man. Just go and do it.'"

"When I heard it through the studio monitors, I couldn't believe it!" says Nambo. "I said to myself, 'Oh, this has got to be something private. He's just going to play for himself,' but no chance. That was a seriously bold step, and even I felt bashful about it at first. A few people laughed their heads off, whereas others were a bit disturbed by it. Some said, 'Oh, that's just him,' y' know? To them, it just confirmed how crazy he was but I don't think so. I believe he was a thinker, and someone who believed in what he was talking about."

The last track they recorded was shared with Gwen Guthrie, and it's an unashamedly commercial slice of Jamaican lovers' rock. 'Nothing But Love' was written by Fred Harris and Ella Mitchell, and qualifies as Peter's most starry-eyed song ever. It's about two people who put love before all else, and yet Peter can't resist giving the song a personal, Jamaican twist. "You don't need expensive cars, you don't need no diamonds and pearls," he sings. "You don't need that *witchcraft world* to make your dreams come true."

Gwen was living in Jamaica at the time and they sang it live in the studio, which must have been a sight to behold. She's so soulful, but the six-foot-four Rastaman towering next to her can sing too, and who knows? They might have had a worldwide smash on their hands if 'Nothing But Love' had got a decent push, and the critics hadn't again denied Peter the right to explore different styles. In a bid to give it additional sheen and polish, Peter decided to use an American horn section. Arranger Clive Hunt duly contacted familiar names such as Lou Marini, Lew Soloff and Joe Faddis and invited them to A&R studios in Manhattan, where Peter would oversee the final mixes. He'd voiced 'Get Up Stand Up' there whilst touring behind *Catch A Fire* and so had positive memories of the place, although there'll be little to do compared to when he'd been finishing off the *Bush Doctor* and *Mystic Man* albums. The hardest task was deciding which tracks to use, since he had too many for a single LP. 'Peace Treaty' and 'Feel No

Way' almost made it but the rest will be discarded including 'Too Much Rats', 'Wicker Man', 'That's What They Will Do' and 'Cold Blood'.

On April 29, he performed at the Radio City Music Hall in New York City, safe in the knowledge that he had another top quality album ready for release. He then headed north, where he played a couple of rescheduled dates in Canada.

"Montreal 1981. Another Tosh concert and again I'm the co-promoter," reported Garry Steckles in *Caribbean Times*. "This time it's outdoors at the Place des Nations. Again we're driving from Dorval airport into Montreal and I've got the car radio tuned into a local Montreal station. I've been trying for weeks to get the city's radio station to plug the show and play some Tosh records and sure enough, the next thing we know a track from his last album – I think it was 'Crystal Ball' but wouldn't swear to it – is blaring out of the radio. Peter was like a kid on Christmas morning. His face lit up with excitement and unselfconsciously as always, he pointed to the radio and – in case anybody in the car hadn't realised – said 'Peter'. Later that night, quite by accident, he tuned into the Canadian Broadcasting Corporation's French language station and was equally astonished to find himself listening to an hour long special on reggae in which he knew all the music but couldn't make a word out of anything else.

"Everybody is in a pretty good mood and the following day after the soundcheck I'm driving Tosh and his manager Herbie Miller back to their hotel. I tell Peter I've been trying for years to get hold of a 45 pressing of 'Babylon Queendom' but couldn't find one. Any way you can get me a copy?' I ask. 'No problem,' replies Tosh. 'I'll make sure it's sent to you,' adds Miller. It never did arrive."

PART III

I AM THAT I AM

Chapter 23

Wanted, Dread And Alive

Bob Marley died on May 11, 1981, at the Cedars Of Lebanon hospital in Miami. He'd been in transit to Jamaica but couldn't hold onto life any longer since the cancer had spread throughout his entire body. Seaga's government awarded him a state funeral, which took place on Thursday May 21. Thousands of people filed past his body as it lay in state in the National Arena, and many thousands more lined the route to Nine Mile as the motorcade ferrying his body left Kingston for the hills where he'd been born 36 years earlier. The service itself was followed by a concert, backed by Marley's musicians. There were two notable absentees from the line-up – Peter and Bunny, who'd chosen to pay tribute to their fallen comrade privately, according to Rasta principles.

It's commonly believed that Peter didn't care about Bob's illness or subsequent passing, and that's why he didn't attend the funeral. This simply isn't true and some have wondered whether such thoughts were planted deliberately, to discredit him. This misconception is based upon what an Island representative told the makers of *Red X*, which remains the best documentary on Peter's troubled life. When she rang Peter with the news of Bob's passing, he'd apparently said that maybe now there'd be room for other reggae artists to gain recognition. He'll be proven wrong of course, but the fact remains that Marley wouldn't have been seen anywhere near Peter or Bunny's funerals either, should they have died before him. Rastafarians don't acknowledge death in any form, and have to cut off their locks if they attend funerals. "Let the dead bury the dead," as Peter sang all those years ago on 'Burial'.

In just a few weeks' time, he'll tell *Black Echoes'* Jon Futrell that, "My woman, whom I loved dearly and slept with for five years, died in a car accident. I was beside her and I did not go to her funeral. For spiritual reasons I go to no funeral so who is alive better stay alive and all my friends better stay alive because I won't go to their funeral either.

"It's against the Rastaman's philosophy," he asserted. "I don't care how much dreadlocks you see go to a funeral; dreadlocks and Rastafari don't interpret things the same way because they have spiritual differences."

Habte Selassie spoke to him soon after learning of Marley's worsening condition. "Peter was very shook up about it," he told CACE International in 1991. Esther Anderson also recalls a lengthy phone call with Peter after Bob died, in which he professed great sadness about what had happened. He ended their conversation by saying, "I have to go and grieve my brother now."

In a conversation with *Black Music's* Chris May, Peter said that when Bob died, his grief was "deep man, deeper than I can ever remember feeling, so deep I was angry, seen? Bob's death is a spiritual guidance to those who are left. Death is not pain. Rastas don't die. My greatest sympathy goes to Rita and his mother and his family. We grew together, sang together, lived together and ate together. But as it was prophesised, 'When two shall be together, one shall be taken away.' But I remember the road Bob and I travelled all those years."

Bunny will pay his respects to Bob on two albums, *Tribute* and *Sings The Wailers*, released on Island over the coming months, but nothing was heard from Peter, who also distanced himself from any wrangles over Bob's estate. "There was a time when we call a meeting to come together and make things happen but for some reason he didn't want it to be, just through some power struggle over finances," Family Man recalls. "That change up things a lot and then all kind of people come in to make the others turn confederate..."

Wayne Jobson, co-director of *Red X*, maintains that, "When your best friend and partner becomes one of the biggest stars in the world and you're still struggling like hell, it sets up that kind of jealousy and bitterness." Except Peter wasn't struggling or at least not yet, although his world was admittedly beginning to fray a little round the edges. Whilst in New York mixing *Wanted Dread & Alive* he met up with the Rolling Stones and even appeared in the video for 'Waiting On A Friend'. The rhythm track of that song dates back to the *Goats Head Soup* sessions, and was recorded in Kingston. It had taken Mick eight years to come up with some lyrics but 'Waiting On A Friend' will make a half-decent single, and then find its way onto the Stones' next album, *Tattoo You*. British filmmaker Michael Lindsay-Hogg directed the video, which will mark the Stones' debut on fledgling music channel MTV. It's a simple enough scenario. Peter and two other men are sat on the steps of 96-98 St. Mark's Place in Manhattan, which is the same building seen on the cover of Led Zeppelin's *Physical Graffiti*. The friend in question – Keith Richards – then joins them and squeezes himself in-between Peter and Mick, who's sat next to Peter by this stage. Keith's smoking a cigarette, and you can bet Peter didn't care for that.

It won't be all he takes exception to. Max Romeo, who lived in New York, was now an intimate of the Stones, suggesting that talk of him signing to their label wasn't so far-fetched after all. Keith had recently played guitar on four tracks from Romeo's latest album *Holding Out My Love To You*, which he'd co-produced with Geoffrey Chung. To add insult to injury, the album also featured several of Peter's musicians, including Sly and Robbie and Robbie Lyn.

"That album was supposed to be signed by the Stones and that's why Keith Richards played lead guitar on a couple of tracks from it," explains Max. "That was the idea but then I was told it wasn't going to happen because of Peter Tosh. I was offered a three-album deal and he heard about the first cheque and rebelled! His own contract was coming to an end and he said he didn't want to work with the company if they signed another reggae artist, so I got edited out of the whole thing. Around that same time he was supposed to work at the Capitol Theatre in Passaic, New Jersey and couldn't fill it... The promoter requested I come on the show and that's what helped to sell it in the end. Shortly afterwards Peter and his people promised me a tour which never materialised but we remained friends, and I never held it against him really. He was a fellow singer at the end of the day."

Soon, Peter will be reported as waving a cutlass around on stage and blaming the Stones for "fucking his career". He remained convinced they hadn't promoted him well enough but the possibility that his songs weren't likely to appeal to mainstream tastes, in comparison to Bob's, just didn't occur to him. Roger Steffens thinks that Peter put too much store in the Stones' ability to cross him over, and others are inclined to agree with him.

"Peter complained about lack of promotion, but wasn't writing hits," reflects Warren Smith. "It was Bob getting the hits. I would say that Peter was well promoted. I can remember working on radio promotions for him and the Rolling Stones had some really good people working with them. They had a strong network in place, which then seemed to turn its back on him. In my opinion, Peter made an unnecessarily big deal out of the whole thing, but then I guess some artists always want more..."

Habte Selassie says the realities of international music marketing eventually changed Peter. "He said he signed with Rolling Stones Records because he figured that Mick Jagger and the Rolling Stones, being recording artists themselves, would have some sort of understanding, some kind of compassion and some kind of sympathy with him; that some of the problems common to all artists would be worked out because this was a new company and again, it was being run by people who were in the business themselves, but he was to find out later that whether they're entertainers or not, the bottom line came down to how much money was being made and Peter ended up being totally dissatisfied with Rolling Stones Records."

"The Stones brought him to a much bigger level than where he was before," counters Eppy. "He went as far as they could take him because in all honesty, he wasn't a major talent. Most of the great songs were Bob or Bunny's, and Peter only had one or two of that same standard.

"I don't think he had much conception of what you needed to cross over. I think what happened was, he got into this brave new world. The Stones were bringing him to Studio 54 and what have you... I'm presuming he had future shock, if I can call it that. There was too much data coming in too quickly and he couldn't deal with it."

There are conflicting reports over what really happened to end Peter's relationship with the Rolling Stones, but sales figures for those first two albums hadn't been all that impressive and Peter's behaviour didn't help the situation any.

"I heard that Peter was over by Keith's house in Connecticut one time," says Warren, who was close to both parties. "He saw one of Keith's vintage guitars, took a liking to it and asked if he could play it. Keith agreed, Peter played it a while and then walked out with it. Keith didn't say anything, but he was really upset about it and that was the end. I mean to walk out with Keith's vintage guitar was really serious. Keith's not the kind of guy to make a scene but he couldn't forgive Peter after that. The fact is that Peter walked around as if everything was his in any case. He was just that kind of guy."

Herbie Miller has already been accused of helping himself to armfuls of jazz albums on trips to Eppy's office. The inference is that both he and Peter shared a sense of entitlement that had nothing to do with individual merit, but derived from some grievance they carried around with them.

"Peter was staying at my house in Ocho Rios," says Keith Richards. "I'd said to him, 'Of course you can use it – if you need to write some songs then sure, stay there a few months. I'd rather you use it and have friends staying there...'"

It's not a bad idea to have someone living in your house while you're away no matter where you live, especially in Jamaica where squatters were notorious for "capturing" vacant land and properties, and refusing to leave. Months later, when Richards returned to Jamaica, he says that Peter insisted on staying put.

"He knew I was coming to Jamaica and then he pulled this switch on me. He said he had a machine gun. I said, 'Well I'm at Mo' Bay and I'm going to be with you in about an hour and a half so you'd better figure out how to put the magazine in it. And by the time I got there the place was empty."

Legend has it that Peter trashed Richards' house before leaving. "He had like 10 people living there, and goats living in the house and walking all over the place," recalls Wayne Jobson in the documentary *Behind The Music*. "The house was in pretty bad shape, but he was just the sort of eccentric character that didn't care. In his own mind he seems to have thought that the Rolling Stones owed him millions of dollars, which was completely wrong. And because he believed that he thought, 'Well this is a nice place. I think I'll just capture the house.'"

Wayne will later revise his account, saying that Peter lived there alone and just went there occasionally "to write and cool out. I would always go and check him there because I knew him from the early days at 56 Hope Road, when the original Wailers were still together. I got on better with him than the others because Bunny was angry most of the time and Bob rarely smiled. With Peter, it was like hanging out with Eddie Murphy. It was just pure jokes and so I loved being around him because of that. He was the genius out of all of them but it was Jane Rose, Keith's personal assistant, who told me that Peter kept four goats in the house... I used to see one goat up there, living inside the house, but then one goat can eat up an entire house inside an hour and so what's the difference? I mean really..."

Wayne's right, and even one goat could cause a tremendous amount of damage inside the 40 minutes or so it would have taken Richards to drive from Montego Bay, but it still seems far-fetched for Peter to have been living in such conditions – not when visitors to his homes in Jamaica or New York have commented on how well-kept they were. Tosh's cousin Carlton frequently accompanied him to Richards' house and gives a very different account of what happened.

"At first, we just went there so Peter could get some peace and quiet. It started out like that but after he meet Melody now and invite her to Jamaica, he had his girlfriend in Kingston and so Melody would stay at the house in Ocho Rios. Let me tell you, there was never any whole bunch of people living there. It was just me, him and Melody, and this helper who used to work there, cleaning the place. They said there was a herd of goats running around the house but it was nothing like that – it was just the one little kid that used to go everywhere with Peter. He'd take it out in the car with him and always have it with him because what happened was, the goat's mother went missing and so Peter looked after the kid and raised it from a baby. He'd feed it from a bottle and when that kid see Peter, it would rise up on its two feet to greet him, thinking he was going to give it some milk. Peter loved that little goat, and it was clean too. There was no mess around the place. It's just that Peter love animals, because the man try and raise a mongoose as well and they're vicious man...

"We weren't at Keith Richards' house long. I'd say about a year, on and off, and we weren't there most of that time. It was just a place for hanging out, like at weekends. Peter had already bought a house at Sterling Castle in St. Andrew. That was his home, and he wasn't looking to take anybody else's. All these years I've been hearing how Keith Richards said Peter was waiting for him with an M-16 and all that crap but I know nothing about that. That's something I never saw or heard Peter talk about and I was with him from when we first start going there, until we stop. It's so sad that anybody would want to say that about Peter Tosh when the man never have nothing to do with guns at any time. Saying things like that is pure mischief and it travel so fast, but people should know the truth about what really happened, which is nothing..."

The tales surrounding this incident have now passed into reggae mythology, despite a distinct lack of evidence. With repeated telling they've helped further diminish Tosh's reputation over the years, which is something that also concerns Habte Selassie.

"There are people who've created an image of Peter Tosh that's very negative and they've succeeded in doing it rather well but then Peter's an easy victim, since he's never had anyone speaking in his defence – not even anyone from his own family. I asked him about the Rolling Stones once and he said that after signing with them he 'knows what a piece of shit feels like'. I also mentioned Mick Jagger and he said, 'Me nah join that', meaning that he wasn't about to bow down and worship this guy – that there were aspects to Jagger and the Rolling Stones he really didn't like. Peter has been maligned quite maliciously over this affair. My own feeling is that these people were afraid of him, because there was no sanitising Peter Tosh and they will have discovered that."

Don Williams begs to differ, and says Peter was really mean at times. "I saw that side of him a few times. He definitely had a very aggressive side to him," and Eppy agrees with him since he also witnessed "incidents of rage".

"There are so many kids from the ghetto who don't get a chance to improve themselves and wind up dead or living in jail because of that mentality," he says. "They're consumed by anger because of the way they were brought up. They have a chip on their shoulders and rather than working it out and learning about the world and doing something constructive, they fixate on the negative. I've seen that from so many reggae artists, and I could never get close to Peter because of it.

"He once showed me this gun he had... What happened was, Keith and Ronnie turned him onto hand weapons and he became obsessed with them. I heard that he was on a plane going back to Manley International Airport and he had a few guns on him. Jamaica's just like anywhere else. If you don't have a licence then you can't carry a gun, let alone bring any into the country but he'd figured that because he's the great Peter Tosh, he could just walk right through customs. As he approached the front of

315

the line he couldn't see any customs officers he knew and started to get worried. A second cousin had been on the plane with him and so Peter (allegedly) asked him to carry his bag and if anything happens, then he'll take care of his family and buy the guy a house. Well this cousin was found with the guns and Peter didn't buy him a house so he ends up getting shot. He was given an ultimatum when the guy came out of jail. The man wanted his house and Peter told him to go fuck himself basically."

There's no evidence to support this, and denials are plentiful. What's irrefutable is that Peter's character had hardened in certain respects. As preparations began for the next round of European dates, Sly and Robbie still felt aggrieved by his and Herbie Miller's refusal to let Black Uhuru open for them. An incident like that wasn't going to help morale any, and yet relations were cordial enough during the two weeks of rehearsals.

"That tour was completely different from the others," remembers Daryl Thompson. "We'd work out our cues, and how we were going to get out of a tune... There'd be specific lines we'd all play together, but everything else was just like jamming. We'd stop and discuss things occasionally but there wasn't a whole lot of talking going on. There's an old saying 'Don't leave the fight in the gym' and I guess that's what it felt like."

Just before the tour started, Peter put in an appearance on Jamaican station RJR. He and Gwen Guthrie's 'Nothing But Love' was already causing a stir, and *Wanted Dread & Alive* would be released the following week. The show started at ten in the evening and for the next two hours he and presenter Don Cooper will be sat in Studio 3, talking, playing music and taking phone calls from listeners. Peter has taken an acoustic guitar in the studio with him, and plays it quietly in the background. Cooper never refers to this or highlights Peter's proficiency on it, but elicits more from him than most other radio presenters.

Tosh opens by describing 1981 as the beginning of "a new musical era. Reggae is going to take over the world. It is going to dominate the musical scene internationally and universally. It's the beginning, because once upon a time you could never hear reggae on an international radio station, and especially if it is white-owned. Now you can hear reggae on any radio station and then once upon a time, it is not just any international artist who would sing reggae, seen? Now every artist would like to do at least one reggae song and get a full overstanding (understanding) of what reggae really is, and a full creative concept of it."

316

In response to being called "a controversial figure", he says he's no different from any other progressive person. "What I learn in school, I'm just practising," he retorts. "For example they say, 'Speak the truth, and the truth will set you free', so I just like to speak the truth. I'm just trying to be real, because I've been living in this world of fantasy and illusion, and there are so many things in this world they say go so but that don't go so, and I would like to know why."

During the course of their interview, Peter substitutes "kingdom" with "kingman" and "wisdom" with "wisman" – "because there is no dom". A caller then asks him where he gets the inspiration to write songs like 'Hammer' and 'Vampire', which deal with the supernatural. Peter first quotes Scripture, then says, "To protect yourself from death you have to be either physically or spiritually protected. That's not what I feel; it's what I see happening around me."

Many Jamaican country folks listening on their transistor radios would instinctively relate to what he's just said. Belief in the supernatural and the practise of obeah were (and still are) widespread in all parts of the island. Back in Trench Town, people would go and see an obeah man called Mr. Lawrence, who Bunny Wailer says dealt "with vampirism, astronomy and astrology and all kinds of demonology". People would pay him protection money or buy talismans – usually necklaces, worn out of sight – to ward off evil, but there was danger in such transactions since if he did you a favour or loaned you money and you were late repaying it, then all hell would break loose. Literally.

Obeah remains a taboo subject, and people are notoriously reluctant to discuss it. It's understandable therefore that Peter was far more forthcoming about the state of the local record industry, which he describes as "weak and fragile".

"It's not being handled in the same way music is handled, treated and respected in other places," he insists. "People don't know their constitutional rights in the musical fields of Jamaica and the few who *do* know, they hide it from those who don't. Many things were being hidden from me and I just take them for granted, like copyrights and mechanical rights... Once upon a time, those things just close over me like wet cement. I never know what it was 'til I investigate and discover it was my whole future...

"Then you have other things like the producers are not really producers, but are just hustlers who don't realise what music is. None of them can play a piano, organ or any instrument. I never see a producer who can play anything, or sit down in the control room and tell a bass man, 'I don't like that line there, so take out that and put in this'. Or tell the organ man, 'Don't shuffle there, shuffle here'. That's what a producer is and if you can't tell the musicians these things, then you have to get someone else to do the production. They only call themselves producers because they have money. They just sit down with them big, fat necks and look to get lucky and reap off someone's hit."

Another caller asks him what he is doing to help those artists who still don't know about their rights. "I help them by exposing verbally what I know to each and every individual within the field, whom I encircle daily, and sometimes I will talk to a couple of journalists so they can put it in their papers and the circulation goes around and people get to know," he replies. "I don't control the media, and I can't write a copyrights law book, yet I still let the youths know what is going on. I have all kinds of ideas within my mind but it's not time for them to manifest as yet."

"What are your personal plans?" asks Cooper. "What do you see in the future for yourself?"

"Well, I see progress in the future for I continual, and music reaching its highest level of performance and recognition," Peter responds. "I mean reggae music, seen? Reggae music being played in symphonic style, that all kinds of high guys in every different calibre can come and sit up in his three-piece suit and listen to it, seen? Because I don't see reggae as just a little drum and bass and five instruments; I see reggae played with many different instruments, covering the full 360 degrees of music."

The presenter says that some people in Jamaica think he's a millionaire. "Oh, goodness gracious. I have a million hairs, and I've come here to live for a million years," Peter says, laughing. "It runs like some form of joke, but what comes from out of these people's mouths is either prophecy or destruction, because people say certain things and they don't know. The only thing I feel bad about is that some people feel I am *really* a millionaire when I'm not. Because if I really were a millionaire, then I would do lots of things such as building schools where Rastas can go without creating a political environment, or all kinds of negative feelings. The little Rasta youths, they are so innocent. A Rasta child can go to school from about five years old and because he has dreadlocks, he's turned away from the school. It's degrading... If I had the opportunity or the money to make these things available, they are the things I would do. Like providing more transport, so people didn't have to stand up at the bus stop 15 hours to get to work and to be productive. Many things I could talk about, except I'm not a politician, I'm a musician."

"What would you do towards helping people repatriate?" Cooper asks.

"I wouldn't do anything about it, because repatriation is not my business," Peter snaps. "My business is to repatriate people's minds unto the consciousness of what Africa really is. That's the first repatriation. It's not getting into a boat and sailing to a place that I don't know about. That is ignorance and a form of complete destruction. First you have to repatriate the people's minds and let them know who they are, where they came from and where they're going."

The following day, Peter and Herbie leave for Brussels where the band, which now includes Gwen Guthrie on backing vocals, will join them later in the week.

"Jimmy Cliff is expected to make special guest appearances on two songs in Germany whilst Rico Rodriguez, a Jamaican trombonist living in Britain, will open the shows," a report in the *Gleaner* announced. "Linton Kwesi Johnson is expected to perform on the two shows in London. Tosh will return home for a three-week break before commencing the American leg of the tour on July 23."

The new album is released just as the festivities start. Although only 10 tracks remain from the sessions at Dynamic, *Wanted Dread & Alive* is still a major work, and it's noticeably more varied than his previous albums. Neville Garrick again designed the cover, which he styled after a wanted poster. He took a colour photo of Peter, changed it to black and white and then overlaid it with a mezzotint screen, so as to give it an old time feel like you'd see in a Western. On the back was a mock-up of a police arrest sheet and whilst the fingerprints are Neville's, Peter told him what to write in the spaces – e.g., Name: "Sgt. Lucifer." Offences: "Numerous offences." The graphics suit Peter's rebel image to perfection, and were mirrored by his quotes in the press release. "When you deal with the kind of music and songs and words I speak of and what I stand for, you are wanted," he explains, "and I will always be wanted until man is free."

There was even mention of the forthcoming tour in the *Wall Street Journal*, which alluded to the fact that at four months, it was the longest tour in reggae's history. It didn't start well however, after incidents of heavy-handed policing at the Stade Communal Festival in Brussels, where the *Wanted Dread & Alive* tour eventually got underway. A series of dates in Denmark, Sweden and Norway, where Peter premiered new songs like 'Coming In Hot', 'Rok With Me', 'Rastafari Is' and 'Cold Blood' went down well, as did half-a-dozen shows in Germany. On June 12 they returned to the Paradiso in Amsterdam, which had become a favourite destination of Peter's on these European jaunts. The following day he played at an anti-apartheid concert held in an Amsterdam skating rink. Further German dates followed, one of which went badly wrong for the Bush Doctor.

"We were in Germany and things reached a point where everyone decided to leave the group and it came as a shame really," explains Sly Dunbar. "Robbie and I were still expected to share a room and we were struggling to accept that."

"The musicians refused to play," Robbie Shakespeare concurs. "Peter start crying and I said, 'Peter. What instrument do you play?' He said, 'guitar'. I said, 'and you sing also, right?' He say yes so I tell him Sly and myself are with him and so the three of us go out on stage, playing and kicking up rumpus and getting the crowd behind us, then the rest of the musicians start walking on stage and joining in. That incident was all about money, and it reach that stage because Peter had people around him who were more interested in themselves than anyone from the band or even Peter himself. I was the one who always look out for the musicians and so if anyone had a complaint, they'd come to me with it. I used to tell the management, 'Please remember to give the musicians a little more money,' but they would just cuss me. They'd say, 'Start talking for yourself and stop talking for other people' but that's my nature, and I realise they weren't interested in treating us better. We were working like crazy, both on tour and in the studio, but every tour we went on, we'd be told it was for promotion. Nothing was getting better for the musicians. It probably was for them (meaning Peter and Herbie), but we didn't know anything about that. All we knew was that the crowds were getting bigger, and we were doing more shows each tour and yet the money would always stay the same.

"In the early days Peter used to trust me because he and I were really, really close. Other people began to interfere with that after a while, from I start demanding better treatment for the musicians. It's just that some of the hotels we used to stay in, they were really bad so we all wanted a change from that, as well as a better rate of pay..."

"We all knew the money we were getting wasn't good and there was friction with that," agrees Mikey Chung. "I was the first one to step away and say I was going to leave. I guess the others held back a little, just to see if things would improve but eventually everybody left. None of us were satisfied with the treatment we were getting after all the work we'd put into making those albums. I guess it was my fault because I hadn't specified what I wanted but I'm the type of person that if we're in a group and we're all together, then we're going to share what we make, whether it's said out loud or not. That never happened with Peter and I didn't feel as if I'd been properly compensated for the work I did."

As they crossed the border into Italy the atmosphere on the tour bus became increasingly toxic. Resentments no longer simmered under the surface but lay heavy in the air, waiting to erupt into trench warfare. Shows in Trento and Mira came and went without any further incidents, at least within the camp. It was now the third week of June, and the whole of Italy had been caught up in the drama of an 11-year-old boy who'd fallen into a well and then died several days later after a traumatic rescue attempt. Peter's party then arrived in Rome, and with a day's rest before the next gig.

"The stadium held about 100,000 people," recalls Winston Harriott. "I remember we went to see B.B. King and when we got there, there were only 15,000 people in this huge stadium, yet B.B. King was a legend. Peter used to call me "Stretch", and said, 'Bloodclaat Stretch, if B.B. King only get this many people, I wonder how many we're going to get tomorrow night?' We were talking like that, trying to make light of it but as we're driving to the stadium, it's packed to the rafters! Someone said the Pope had been there and only drawn 70,000 so Peter turned to me and said, 'Bloodclaat, I'm more popular than the Pope!' He was so thrilled by that, I tell you..."

"It was in Italy where he saved my life once," says Daryl Thompson. "The show was sold out. It was a big stadium and there were a lot of people outside, trying to get in. They had these very young Italian policemen on duty. They must have been in their very early twenties and they were all walking round with machine guns. The kids at the back were forcing down the gates to get in and the police got highly nervous about it. We were on stage playing when one or two of them let off some tear gas into the audience, which was a really stupid thing to do because if the wind changes, then you're in trouble and that's just what happened. The tear gas started blowing up on the stage and then hits me straight in the face, just as I was soloing. I'd never experienced anything like that before. My lungs felt like they were on fire and I could feel myself falling off the stage, which was about 25 feet high. I couldn't see or breathe and just as I was going over the side, Peter grabbed me by my collar and dragged me back. The next thing I know he's putting a wet towel over my face and over my eyes and when I'm able to see he's standing over me, making sure I'm OK. That was the kind of guy he was, because I could easily have fallen off the stage and broken my neck. He was great at improvising in situations like that. He'd know how to act in any given situation. He would never get angry or upset."

After Italy came France, where Francois Mitterand faced the first real test of his Presidency after Israel launched air strikes against an Iraqi nuclear reactor, purchased from France. Tensions were high, and armed security forces offered more than a visual deterrent.

"We risked our life on tour sometimes," the Tamlins' Carlton Smith told Roger Steffens. "One day we were in France, we went to the soundcheck and saw about 10 guys coming in from the roof wearing helmets and some bulletproof things, looking like spacemen. Nobody had told us what was going on. We then heard there'd been a bomb scare and they asked us to vacate the building, so we went back to the hotel. Despite the scare everybody was downstairs by eight o'clock to go and do the show. We went straight onstage and the show was wonderful."

Not for the first time, Peter headed for the UK after a successful appearance in Paris but the British media were poisonous as ever. A week before his return performance at the Rainbow Theatre, a review of 'Nothing But Love' in *NME* pointed out how "Tosh in the dictionary means 'rubbish', and there's an awful temptation to conclude that you can't fight city hall."

It claims the musicians knew no boundaries in taking liberties with the song, which the reviewer assumes is a Tosh original. "The drawback is that there ain't no tune to start with so everyone bounces about hoping to hit the same phrase twice and recognising it, establish a chorus," they wrote. "This never happens. The track is a shambles. Moral: Write things down first."

There's no name under these scurrilous remarks, although it could well be the work of Danny Baker – someone who will describe Peter as "the third best voice of a heavenly harmony trio", and a man whose talents amounted to "a Kalashnikov-shaped guitar, a decidedly scary personality and a degree of skill on the unicycle".

A month later and *NME* will run another feature on Peter under the heading of "Tosh, Pete!" Its anonymous, but clearly female journalist asks if he recorded 'Nothing But Love' in a bid to "put paid to his image of being tough on women".

"What me?" he answers with a laugh. "The Rastaman loves woman, seen? We know that woman is beautiful and woman has that tender touch so when anyone tells you that bullshit, tell them Peter *loves* woman, seen?"

The reporter "mumbles something about equality" and Tosh explodes. "What? How can a woman be equal to a man?" he exclaims. "Unless she can show me two balls, a woman cannot be equal my dear. The last time I saw the inequality of women was in America. There were some women libbers in New York trying to prove themselves equal to men so they went down to the wharf to get jobs and were given the task of moving 50 bags of flour. One of the women lift up the first bag and nearly went to the hospital. And that makes woman unequal to a man."

"And intellectually?" the woman ventures, just before Herbie Miller steps in and demands she asks something else. *Black Music*'s Chris May interviewed Peter prior to his London dates and reminds his readers that if people believed even half of what most rock journalists have written about Tosh they'd be excused for thinking he was "the most miserable, hate-filled mother on God's green earth". The truth, as May would soon discover, couldn't have been more different.

"Away from the camera and maybe away from hostile and racist interviewers – 'Who the hell does this uppity nigger think he is with all this nonsense about imperialism, colonialism and slavery?' – Peter presents a very different face, a warmly smiling face projecting a lot of love." May claims critical reaction to the new album "has, to put it mildly, been mixed and the duet with Gwen Guthrie, 'Nothing But Love', has been almost universally slagged".

"What I am trying to do..." begins Peter. "No, what I am *going* to do is bring the international audience to reggae and they can beat me or knock me down in their foolishness but I will not give up. The whole idea of that song with Gwen was to give the radio stations something they can safely play, 'cause they're normally frightened by reggae. And then when we have got that much airplay, they won't be able to deny us any more. The people will not allow them because despite all this knocking from the white rock press, there's a big audience for my music."

The only UK publications to consistently treat reggae (and most reggae artists) with respect were *Black Echoes* and *Black Music*. Otherwise, Peter had to run a gauntlet of uninformed journalists who probably preferred 2 Tone to reggae – the Specials having just released 'Ghost Town' – and whether intentionally or not, sought to emasculate him at every turn.

Steve Sutherland, writing in *Melody Maker*, described Tosh as being "very tall and very black. He speaks with an impressive, poetic, deep Jamaican accent and is very, very stoned. The reporter is a weed, pimply white, speaks with a high-pitched Wiltshire whine, and is woefully straight." It's Peter's tenth interview of the day in a small, featureless hotel room and he's on a hiding to nothing. Once again, he's taken to task for wanting to make his music more accessible.

"You have to make music on a commercial level so that you can get across to more people," he explains. "You don't just make music for yourself alone or for all the militant people but for everyone. Even the fool."

Sutherland decides that's as good a time as any "to take Tosh up on what he considers to be an alarming inconsistency in the musician's image – that the man most renowned as a militant Rastafarian, a self-proclaimed 'stepping razor' and the international Minister of Herb, should release a series of 'increasingly soppy, lightweight albums to satisfy a cliquey white audience'.

"Aren't you compromising yourself shamefully?" he asks.

"I wouldn't say compromise," Peter replies with amusement. "Just psychology." He points out that he's always incorporated other ingredients in his music yet takes care in using them with discretion, so they don't "dilute the potential or the roots" of his music. "Reggae music can go many places, seen? Reggae music can be played in jazz, reggae music can be played in funky and reggae can be played in country and western, because reggae music is the basis of *all* music."

After describing 'Nothing But Love' as "a schmaltzy ballad", Sutherland admits to feeling thwarted, like he's "the subject of someone else's silly game".

"Stevie Wonder has never written hit songs about Tosh like he did Bob Marley," he writes, in reference to 'Master Blaster'. "Tosh has never been courted by politicians or internationally acclaimed as a cultural giant like Marley but he has been clubbed unconscious by the Kingston police – that's the man's current career credibility. Wanted Dread & Alive."

When asked about the riots that had recently swept through Britain's inner cites, Peter reminds *Melody Maker* readers that, "It's not only black people who are burning up those places, white people are doing it too. It's not only black people who are suffering from inflation and lack of jobs and all those kind of things but white people too. Indians, Syrians and all kinds of people."

The writer then invites Tosh to admit if he's encouraged violence with his militant image. (Yes, you heard.)

"MILITANT?" roars Tosh, whose patience has finally snapped. "Me don't join the army. I'm a missionary, not military. When you're talking about the military, you're associating me with guns and missiles and all those kinds of things so you must say missionary. I deal with righteousness," he says, sucking every last syllable dry. "Yeah man, I think positive, go to bed positive and try to make 100 percent of my actions positive."

Sutherland may be at a loss when it comes to reggae, but he doesn't lack courage. "Has Bob Marley's death made you more aware or afraid of death?" he ventures.

"Afraid? You think many have never tried to assassinate me?" Peter snarls. "That does not make me fear. Many try to kill I many times spiritually and physically but that does not make me weak, it make me strong 'cause every blow I get and every blood I shed I get seven thousand powers."

By Sutherland's own admission, communication then broke down to "a forced, frustrated, almost comic politeness", so they "shook hands, smiled uneasily and parted". The journalist accuses Tosh of having "arrogantly shrouded his answers in mystic mumbo jumbo without the slightest inclination to sincere explanation". We also learn that "Tosh was amused by the writer's incomprehension". It's worth noting that few if any music-related questions were asked and since the writer demonstrated no understanding or appreciation of Peter's work, what did he expect?

Jon Futrell, writing in *Black Echoes*, encounters no such problems. The last time he'd spoken to Peter was December 1978, when Peter "was quick to take offence and often venomous in his replies". This time it was different. He calls Peter "a changed man. He's now more able to deal with issues that would have angered him enormously. He is more diplomatic and concerned with creating a good impression on the popular media and has tempered his aggression that once prompted observers to nickname him 'the lieutenant of reggae'."

He finds Peter dressed in a red tracksuit with matching hat, sprawled across a bed in his hotel room. They talk about music, and relations between the two men are warm and pleasant.

"Atlantic were not interested in reggae and so two of my albums, *Bush Doctor* and *Mystic Man*, went down the drain," Peter insists at one point. "They got no promotion in the United States so I withdrew my act and said I would not produce any more albums until someone else distributed them – someone who is interested, who knows my work and the business."

In a few hours' time Peter will be playing at the Rainbow Theatre in Finsbury Park – an area of North London that can draw on a large Caribbean population. Bob had played four nights there almost exactly four years ago. Peter played just two and whilst this rather grand-looking former cinema was full both nights, the audiences weren't all that responsive.

"We never liked playing reggae there because Londoners think they know it all," says Daryl Thompson. "When we played there sometimes it was like pulling teeth. The audience was very cold and would just stand there. The clapping was very mediocre and I guess it's because they're saturated with that kind of music so therefore the attitude is completely different to when you play other places..."

The last night, June 30, would mark the end of this current line-up of Word, Sound & Power after Sly and Robbie decide to quit the band. "There was some kind of bickering going on between Sly and Peter's manager, Herbie Miller," says Daryl. "Sly and Robbie had wanted Black Uhuru to open for Peter and our band to back both acts but Herbie Miller was against it for some reason. Maybe he thought it would affect Peter's show or something but that's when Sly, who never really talked all that much, told Herbie to be careful because this little band Black Uhuru were going to be really big. Herbie didn't like that and I could hear the bickering from the next room. By this time we were in London and I got a knock on my hotel room door, opened the door and it was Robbie Shakespeare. He normally wouldn't come in my room like that but he sat down on the bed and said that Peter was a guy who liked to sit down and fish, meaning that Peter was well off, and wanted to take things easy and just watch his bank account grow, but he and Sly couldn't afford to do that. They lived to work and so they were going to leave Peter. He said I had a choice – I could either stay with Peter, or I could go with them and help put the Black Uhuru thing together. I was nervous about this because I'd only been playing with Peter for two years and liked him quite a bit but Robbie said that he, Sly and Mikey Chung were all leaving. They'd already given me Black Uhuru's *Showcase* album by then and I really liked it... I also liked the idea of being part of something from the ground up, and building it from scratch so in the morning we were in Peter's band, and by that evening I was in Island studios with Chris Blackwell and Black Uhuru. There was no interruption whatsoever."

"Peter really didn't take it all that well," admits Sly. "They were saying they were going to give us more money but it wasn't only about money by then; it was to do with our creativeness because we had ideas as to how to take the music forwards and he wasn't interested in any of that.

"What happened was, after we'd gone to Nassau and worked with Grace Jones on tracks like 'Pull Up To The Bumper', we wanted to take Peter in a different direction – not for him to stop what he was doing, but to branch off just a little bit and do some different stuff. We gave him some ideas but he was just thinking of himself alone and this is where things started to fall apart.

"When we began touring with Peter in 1977 we used to drive around in a little station wagon," Sly recalls. "We were touring because we wanted to make music and it was good of Peter to expose us to the American public. By 1981, we wanted our own rooms and our per diem was almost nothing. We were carrying the brunt of the work so we told them that if they weren't going to change, we're going to leave. Other things happened too, like once on a show in Jamaica Peter was talking to the audience, we started to play behind him and he said, 'Hold on! Every bloodclaat time I start talking you want to play.' We were really surprised..."

"Peter got bigheaded, that's the only way I can describe it," says Bunny Lee. "He didn't like Sly & Robbie getting too popular, because it was all about him. One night he played at the Rainbow, I see what happen and say to him, 'Peter, they're your band and you can't handle them so.' Him no care, just like when people come to up him so he can sign autograph and he'd get very abusive."

"I think the superstar business started going to his head," agrees Robbie Shakespeare. "It wasn't like that at first, when the musicians were free to express themselves. We stayed friends and we used to see each other from time to time after that but we didn't go around him much really."

By the beginning of August, Peter's back in Jamaica. The US leg of the *Wanted Dread & Alive* tour was due to start in a few weeks, which left him just enough time to break in a new band. Replacing Sly and Robbie wouldn't be easy and yet Donald Kinsey told Roger Steffens the new line-up gelled from the start, much to Peter's relief.

"Fully, Santa, Stevie Golding, Robbie Lyn, Keith Sterling and the Tamlins... Man, that was the ultimate brother! When you look at those shows, you can see the confidence in Peter, knowing what he had behind him. He was able to truly express himself at that one point in his life."

Drummer Carlton "Santa" Davis shared Peter's Trench Town roots, and became a close personal friend. He'd learnt to play in church and military bands before joining the Graduates, who blended a little jazz, soul, and pop with their reggae. By the early seventies he was a member of Soul Syndicate, and would often see Peter at hangout spots in Kingston.

"Peter and I used to meet at a place on Oxford Road where Tommy Cowan had an office. All the musicians would meet there," he told Karie Russell of *Reggae Report*. "I always remember Bunny Wailer telling Peter that when he formed a band, then I was the right drummer for him. This eventually happened in 1981, with a US tour pending. Peter was in a spot, so he chose me and Fully. We had only five days to rehearse and learn a bunch of songs from the album *Wanted, Dread & Alive*."

George "Fully" Fullwood was the Soul Syndicate's bass player. His father had financed the band's start-up costs, and let them rehearse at the family home in Greenwich Farm. Soul Syndicate's reputation then soared once they'd begun recording with producers such as Bunny Lee, Phil Pratt and Niney The Observer, who used them on his apocryphal 'Blood And Fire'. Fully was living in California when he received a call from Herbie Miller, saying that Peter Tosh wanted him to come to Jamaica and join Word, Sound & Power.

"I asked what happened to Sly & Robbie and he said they quit," he told *Reggae Report*. "They wanted me and Santa, and I said, 'When do you want me to come?' The next day they had a ticket for me. I admired Peter very much. I never thought I would get the chance to work with him but

I ended up playing with him until the time of his death. I looked up to him as a role model in many ways. Peter never disrespected me and I respected him in a lot of different ways. I respected what he stood for as a black person, and the struggle of what he really fought for as far as human rights in this corrupt world was concerned. He wasn't the kind of person that wanted to see his black people go through the hardships of life, and that whole racist mentality. I respect him a lot for that and he was a very quiet person. You'd hardly see him talk. He respected his musicians and a lot of the things we discussed made sense to me. We were all involved when we were on tour. All I know is I appreciated him when he was around, what he was doing in terms of the music and what it stands for."

Stevie Golding was chosen to replace Mikey Chung on rhythm guitar. He'd played with Fabulous Five and the Dance Theatre Company of Jamaica before striking up a partnership with Donald Kinsey, who now took Daryl Thompson's place. Robbie Lyn and Keith Sterling stayed, whilst Constantine "Vision" Walker filled in for one of the Tamlins on backing vocals and percussion. Keen eyed readers will recall him singing with the Soulettes, and then standing in for Bob during the Wailers' final days at Studio One.

After less than a week of rehearsals, this new line-up made its debut in New York City on July 20, to an enthusiastic welcome. "His band with Fully and Santa was more cohesive and organic," states Warren Smith, who'd managed Soul Syndicate since 1975. "The music naturally sprang from them whereas with Sly & Robbie the music was sat down on its ass. The spontaneity wasn't there so much..."

It was Peter's first time at the Ritz, which was tucked away on 11th Street in the East Village. The place hadn't been open long but was already rivalling the Bottom Line as New York's favourite industry hangout. Two months earlier, John Lydon's group PiL had nearly started a riot there after taunting the hip clientele with a deliberately poor performance. Shows by Steel Pulse and Jimmy Cliff fared much better, with Keith Richards watching from the VIP section. It seems the Stones' appetite for reggae was unaffected by their recent experiences with Peter, who was interviewed by John Swenson for *High Times* in his Manhattan hotel room just before the show. After noting how "Tosh drinks brown banana porridge from a Thermos for his breakfast", Swenson describes the contents of Peter's bedside table – namely "a well thumbed Bible and two empty Johnny Walker bottles filled with a pastel liquid prescribed for Tosh by bush doctors". (And which had homemade labels bearing "intricate inscriptions with invocations to Jah".)

Swenson likes the new album and admires the scope of it. Peter tells him that, "Most people who listen to reggae don't know what reggae music is all about.

"Reggae is a spiritual music and you have to be spiritual to enter the garden of inspiration. Most people who hear reggae think that it should only be drum and bass and a guitar going chicka chicka and yet reggae music is one of the most symphonic music in the world. It takes many instruments but not everyone who makes reggae music is an architect. You have many shoemakers who try and build a house, but it is impossible. It is like an apple tree trying to be a mango, seen?"

It's a stance that's simple enough to understand from today's vantage point but few critics were that generous at the time, as we've already discovered. Swenson was, and Peter rises to the occasion by talking at length about his early musical experiences, and how that distinctive rhythm guitar style originated in attempts "to duplicate the sound of a machine gun", thereby confirming his admiration for Jimi Hendrix. As the mood deepens, Peter tells Swenson a little about the pressures brought to bear upon the Wailers – pressures that had resulted in Bob being shot, and himself being nearly beaten to death.

"I see it as being politically motivated," he confides. "There are always elements there to try and stop anything that is awakening to black people. If someone tries to give a message to black people, they always try to put obstacles in the way." After explaining how his work is the result of "divine inspiration", Peter makes a statement that speaks volumes – especially when dealing with a secular music industry.

"I don't look at myself as a singer," he begins. "I look at myself as a missionary who comes to preach, to teach and to awake the slumbering mentality of black people, because this is nothing new. From thousands of years ago there have been preachers who go around and preach and teach and tell the people of the true and the living, seen? And tell the people how to live. To teach the people what is right from wrong but whenever you start to deal with good, it becomes so political that bad gets jealous and tries to put obstacles in your way. They try *everything* to stop you."

Herein lies Peter's dilemma. He wants to raise people's consciousness and yet most rock fans resent any kind of authority and don't welcome

330

being lectured – not even by a Jamaican Rasta who smokes lots of ganja and hangs with the Rolling Stones. This mainly white, suburban, male teenage demographic may have bought *Bush Doctor* because of the Stones' involvement, but the majority had left *Mystic Man* well alone and won't be overly impressed by *Wanted Dread & Alive* either.

Dennis Hunt, writing for a Los Angeles broadsheet, notes that, "Tosh hasn't yet figured out how to make his material commercial whilst maintaining its integrity. His current album *Wanted Dread & Alive* is his biggest seller in America so far but has stalled near the bottom of the Top 100. His other albums have all flopped here. The problem with Tosh's music is that it's primarily a vehicle for his militant messages."

"Music is the fastest way of getting the message across to people," Peter counters. "If music can't accomplish the mission, what else will? And it's the only way I know."

After two concerts in Maryland, Peter and the band head south to New Orleans, and then Phoenix and Tucson – all on consecutive nights. They travel west on their rest day, in readiness for a sell-out performance at San Diego's California Theatre. (Because plenty of people were still buying tickets to see him perform, despite the negative press.) Two days later and Peter began a three-day residency at the Roxy on Sunset Strip, playing two shows a night between August 20 and 22. Los Angeles was as welcoming as ever and not only because of its audiences, but also thanks to Peter's circle of Jamaican brethren who live there, and old friends like Roger Steffens and Chuck Krall.

"Peter was arrogant on a certain level and I loved that," recalls Chuck. "He had a tremendous amount of self-respect and he was very respectful to others as well. Having said that, some of the people who interviewed him were intimidated by him and if they hadn't done their homework, that would infuriate him. I learnt by being around people like Peter that it's possible for people to educate themselves far more effectively than if they went to university. Peter had the opportunity to travel and meet with a lot of people and that really energised him. He was never impressed by people who had lots of education, if they didn't have much in the way of life experience.

"I found him very interesting. He was a sensitive, passionate man who kept abreast of what was going on because he'd read the newspapers in the morning and make it his business to find out what was happening in the city. Marley didn't like to mix with too many people, except maybe when he played football. Peter wasn't like that. He always kept in very good shape and rode his unicycle a lot but I never saw him doing sports or even watching them. In fact I never knew him to rise earlier than eleven-thirty, twelve o'clock in the morning..."

"Are there any final comments you want to make?" his old friend Roger Steffens asks him, during a televised interview for *LA Reggae*.

"Yes, every journalist come to me and want to say, 'Now that you're the new King of reggae...' Well I don't like to hear that," Peter replies. "I don't want anyone to tell me that, 'cause I am not new, seen? I am as old as the sun, from the earth as was, reincarnated millions of times and still doing the same work, musically. And I don't want to be looked upon as no superstar, and as no king. My music is just music. It's a message decorated with music for the awakening of people's consciousness onto certain levels of reality."

With no grievances or mutinies to deal with, Peter's feeling happier than for some time. The new band's bedded in well, and Peter likes how they play with more of a roots feel. He'll work his way up the West Coast, playing mainly university gigs for the next week or so. In Santa Barbara he performed at the County Bowl before visiting San Carlos, Berkeley, Rohnert Park and Portland. After a show at Seattle's Paramount Theatre on August 30 he'll finally get a few days off to rewind. It takes hard work and stamina to fulfil this kind of schedule, and Peter's nerves understandably began to fray on occasion.

"The Grateful Dead had parallel shows every night, in the same towns and cities, for the length of that entire tour," says Bob Andy. "I heard that Peter's management told him the guys from the Grateful Dead had been coming to the shows and how Jerry Garcia really wanted to meet him, but they stopped coming round because Peter was so aggressive towards them. Herbie Miller had begged him for a long time to see them but Peter refused, then one day they were together when Jerry Garcia called. Herbie said, 'Jerry Garcia is on the line. Have a word with him,' so Peter took the phone and said, 'So who is this? You're called Grateful Dead, right? Well you guys should be fucking lucky that you're alive' and just gave the phone back to Herbie! That's the kind of guy he was, but a lot of the time these guys stay so smoked up that paranoia was a part of it too. Peter was always fighting against the system or the 'shit-stem' as he called it and wouldn't miss an opportunity to show them how he felt. He was a rebel and he wasn't acting rationally most of the time. He was operating mainly from emotions and to some degree I think it was also a way of keeping in the news, and maintaining that outlaw status he had. He wasn't generally disrespectful to anyone though, or at least not to his peers..."

There'll be another two weeks of sitting on the tour bus, watching vast expanses of countryside roll past as they travel through Nebraska, Colorado, Missouri, Wisconsin and Minnesota on their way back to New York and another well-earned pit stop. This current US tour won't end until mid-October, by which time Peter will have played the Ritz (twice more) and all over New York State, including Syracuse, Rochester, Stony Brook, North Tonawanda and the Strand Theatre in Ithaca. Four Canadian dates – three of them at the O'Keefe Centre in Toronto – will finally bring Peter's Herculean labours to an end. He won't tour again until next August, and he'll have a new management team in place by then.

Ras Karbi believes that Peter thought Herbie Miller was profiting too much from their relationship and sought to change the situation. "I heard Peter confronted Herbie," he says. "There was a falling out between them after that tour." The relationship evidently went from bad to worse and the two were never reconciled.

"If Peter had got himself an experienced American manager with a few hit acts and some contacts already in place, then he might have been able to do more," says Warren Smith. "Unfortunately a lot of Jamaican artists don't see that and want a fellow Jamaican with them yet a manager's job is based on connections, and you don't learn that from newspapers or in school. You learn it through taking hard knocks from the business but I really don't think there'd been too much of that going on. That said, Herbie was as good a manager as ever came out of Jamaica in other respects."

Chapter 24

Mama Africa

The year before he died, Bob Marley had buried his differences with Danny Sims and asked for help with certain business matters. Peter did the same thing after sacking Herbie Miller and was immediately welcomed back into the fold, despite Sims already having Jimmy Cliff on his books. In the summer of 1981, Cliff and his tour manager – a former Jamaican dancer and singer named Copeland Forbes – had travelled to Cuba for the Varadero Music Festival where they'd met Nigerian singer Sonny Okosuns. Shortly afterwards Copeland began working with Peter, who told him of his longing to visit Africa and fascination with traditional healing. Although he looked healthy, Peter still suffered from severe headaches and other pains, and was convinced that an African bush doctor could help him. Copeland promptly got in touch with Okosuns, who invited him and Peter to come and stay with him in Lagos. This trip would prove a major turning point in the life of Peter Tosh, and give him a renewed sense of direction.

Sonny was a top-selling act in Africa, whose best known hits – including 'African Soldier', 'Papa's Land' and 'Fire In Soweto' – railed against South Africa's apartheid regime. He and Peter will discover they have much in common, and become firm friends. Both singers were around the same age; had grown up in a newly independent country and taught themselves to play a variety of instruments. They also shared many of the same foreign influences such as James Brown, Otis Redding, the Beatles and Elvis Presley, whose music had inspired them to make songs that reflected their own people's cultural needs. Sonny joined his first band in 1964. He then backed Sir Victor Uwaifo before forming Ozziddi, which is the Ibo expression for "There is a Message". Ozziddi's simmering stew of Nigerian highlife, Central African rumbas, Latin music, American funk and reggae was accompanied by lyrics calling for social change, just like the Rasta music of Jamaica. Whilst overshadowed by the larger-than-life presence of Fela Kuti, the music of Sonny Okosuns was no less influential in Nigeria itself, where Peter will land in the spring of 1982.

Lagos was Nigeria's capital back then, and the most populous city in West Africa. All the totems of Western affluence were there – from luxury cars, goods and properties, to a brand of political power that rode roughshod over the country's laws and served a wealthy elite. Despite attempts by President Shehu Shagari to implement badly needed reforms (his new government's slogan was "One Nation, One Destiny") poverty still prevailed, and Lagos teemed with thousands of slum dwellers with no access to running water, sanitation or electricity. It was a city well used to traffic gridlocks, soaring crime and armed robbery. The roads were in a perilous state, and unemployment was rife – especially among the younger generation, whose dreams of a better life often revolved around music, sport or cheating the system in whatever ways they could. The parallels with Jamaica, as Nigeria struggled to free itself from a colonial past, were all too evident. After Okosuns introduced him to Afro-beat, Peter immediately recognised similarities with reggae. This music was real. It was wrested from the city's heartbeat, and embodied the people's suffering.

"In Yoruba culture, music permeates every aspect of our lives," wrote Nigerian drummer Babatunde Olatunji, who played a major role in exposing the music of Africa to audiences in the US, and had met Peter in Kingston around the time of Bob Marley's funeral. "Where I come from, we say that rhythm is the soul of life. The whole universe revolves in rhythm. When we get out of rhythm, that's when we get into trouble... The drum, next to the human voice, is our most important, most sacred instrument."

The parallels with Rastafarians, who share much the same philosophy when it comes to the practice of nyahbinghi drumming, are obvious. Peter was inexorably drawn towards this cultural legacy emanating from Africa and couldn't wait to experience it first-hand. His mind raced with possibilities on the flight over there, although the trip wouldn't be without its difficulties. Almost 20 years earlier, Malcolm X had visited Nigeria and

335

was given the name "Omowale", meaning "the son (or child) who has returned". Others were not so fortunate, and audiences in Lagos were notorious for giving visiting musicians a hard time, whether black or white. A. B. Attah, writing in the *Lagos Evening Times* soon after Paul and Linda McCartney had gone there to record *Band On The Run*, warned of this in an article with the headline "Step Softly. This Town Is Jinxed".

"Step carefully, this town kills big stars," he'd cautioned. "Stars who were killed by Lagos include Mohammad Ali, Chubby Checker, Millie Small of 'My Boy Lollipop' fame (her uncle's juju wasn't strong enough to lick the jinx of Lagos), James Brown (Lagos jeered and called him 'Mr. Ugly'), Osibisa (who came to town as a group and left singly) and Ginger Baker."

Whilst he hadn't visited Lagos to perform, Peter was to discover the reality of this situation for himself after exploring the maze of streets surrounding Sonny Okosuns' house in Ogba.

"Adrian Boot, the best-known photographer of reggae musicians, came into frequent contact with Tosh, yet can only recall one mutually pleasant experience," recalls author Lloyd Bradley. "In Lagos, Nigeria, while attempting to photograph the seamier side of the city's life, Boot was led – via a series of increasingly shady contacts – to the inner sanctum of the local drug baron. There he was astounded to find Peter Tosh, who was having his Rasta ideology scornfully rejected by the assembled company."

"He was trying to preach roots and culture to them when all they were interested in was getting as many trappings of Western luxury as possible," confirms Boot. "They clearly had no respect for him and he felt very much out of his depth. It's the only time he's ever been pleased to see me!"

Sonny wanted to introduce Peter to Fela Kuti, whose music had long provided a voice for Nigeria's under-privileged, even at great personal risk to himself and his followers. Four years earlier he'd issued a song called 'Zombie', which humiliated the Nigerian security forces. In response soldiers had stormed his compound – known as "the Kalakuta Republic" – and burnt it to the ground, destroying priceless tapes and equipment. During the attack, soldiers had severely beaten Fela and members of his entourage and thrown his elderly mother from an upstairs window, causing her fatal injuries. No arrests were made, and the law courts determined that "unknown soldiers" had been responsible for carrying out the attacks. Fela, who was as fearlessly outspoken and confrontational as Peter, marched through the streets of Lagos after the verdict was announced and delivered his mother's coffin to the city's army barracks. He then married 27 of his backing singers and dancers in a group ceremony (ostensibly to protect them from further attacks) and in an act of defiance worthy of Peter himself, named his two latest recordings 'Coffin For Head Of State' and 'Unknown Soldier'.

Fela had decorated the walls of his nightclub in Lagos – called the Shrine – with photos of prominent black leaders such as Malcolm X, Patrice Lumumba and Kwame Nkrumah. He sold copies of their speeches from there, as well as books about black history. The Shrine also hosted workshops and theatrical productions promoting Black Nationalism. Sonny Okosuns knew that a summit meeting between Fela and Peter could prove important in some way, and yet he was left disappointed by his countryman's attitude.

"Peter's host Sonny Okosuns took him to Fela's house to introduce the two legends," explains Gbenga X-adebija, who is a prominent West African music critic. "When they arrived, Fela's household told Okosuns that Fela was upstairs in his bedroom with a woman – Fela was renowned for his rampant libido – and could not be disturbed. 'Well,' said Okosuns, 'Tell him I am here with Peter Tosh.'

"After much persuasion, an aide reluctantly went upstairs to speak with Fela who said he did not want to receive any visitors, whoever they may be. When the aide returned with the message, Okosuns was aghast. This was the great Peter Tosh! Because of his closeness to Fela, he went upstairs and banged on Fela's bedroom door. Fela was upset at being disturbed from his favourite pastime (apart from music that is) and wanted to know what Okosuns wanted. 'I have Peter Tosh downstairs,' Okosuns yelled through the door. Fela thought about this, then remarked humorously. 'So what? Peter Tosh? Is he carrying a torch? Go away and leave me alone.'"

Copeland Forbes tells of another incident that took place during their stay in Lagos, when Peter chased away some German construction workers who were laying pipes at a site owned by Western oil companies.

"He was very mad and upset, saying they are robbing the resources of the country so they should leave and not return. At the same time he was having these headaches, so we sought help from a bush doctor in the mountains of Benin, where he spent three weeks undergoing treatment."

Benin shares a border with Nigeria, and is a relatively straightforward drive from Lagos, heading west down the Lagos Badagry Expressway. It was in Marxist-Leninist hands when Peter went there, and most businesses and economic activities were under state control. The majority of people were French speaking and judging by the welcome afforded Pope John Paul II on his recent visit there, favoured Roman Catholicism over religions such as Islam and Vodun, which gave rise to voodoo. Followers of the Igbe religion consulted traditional healers known as "Igbedjobo" whilst animistic cults thrived in the mountainous region of Atakora, which is where Peter's entourage headed once it had crossed into Benin.

In many African countries, people believe the dead can interact with the living and those who intercede with the spirits are both honoured and feared. As Peter was quick to realise, the distinctions between these traditional healers and what Jamaicans call "obeah workers" are very slim. This was the moment Peter had been waiting for and you could almost reach out and touch the aura of expectancy as his vehicle entered the village. At least the surroundings were familiar. On either side of the road were shacks made of corrugated iron sheeting, and groups of youths stared balefully from the shadows. It was a scene he'd witnessed many times in rural Jamaica – the undernourished dogs stirring themselves from where they'd been sleeping in the shade, and the ceaseless comings and goings of goats, chickens, women and children. No one thought it strange that this tall Rastaman from Jamaica had come to see the local bush doctor. The villagers had grown accustomed to tales and manifestations of the unknown, and knew better than to ask questions since tribal medicine men are chosen by spirits, who enter their dreams and impart hidden knowledge. Interfering with their business could therefore have dire consequences and so most local people left them well alone, unless consulting them about something.

The man Sonny Okosuns had recommended employed similar methods to healers living in other parts of Africa – methods that can loosely be described as ritual magic, used in conjunction with herbal remedies. Such practices remain inseparable from everyday life in African villages and are deeply rooted in tradition. After seating himself opposite Peter, the old man took a handful of bones and in a low murmur, began singing incantations to the spirits. He then threw the bones in the air and studied the patterns they made on the floor without so much as a glance towards Peter, who was sat cross-legged opposite him. The man repeated this action several times until satisfied, and only then did he search Peter's face for clues as to his innermost secrets.

Peter wouldn't have been at liberty to divulge what was said, although it's not uncommon for bush doctors to recommend patients cover their heads, refrain from drinking alcohol and sleep with some specific object under their pillow. They may also be told not to speak with anyone for several days whilst following a prescribed course of action. In addition to his various other ailments, Peter had a peptic ulcer. The healer will have treated this with a concoction made from the leaves of four plants – the button weed, tamarind, banyan and goat weed – and insist that Peter drink it for a certain period. All we know for sure is that it was a momentous experience, and that memories of his visit to this remote village in the mountains of Benin will remain with Peter for the rest of his life.

On his return to Jamaica, Peter told local journalist Basil Wilson that visiting Africa was the greatest thing that had ever happened to him. "I was brought up in this Western hemisphere with this ignorance where Africa is concerned, but then I go to Africa and see how African culture is high, higher than anything you can think of. The culture of Africa is so high that nothing is impossible. That is how I see Africa. For the three weeks that I was there, the culture I saw was heavy, heavy – more heavy than magic."

He then stirred up controversy by declaring his wish to go and perform "in any part of Africa, including South Africa". Perhaps mindful of Jimmy Cliff's trip to Soweto, Peter said he was sceptical of the ANC's cultural boycott, which is based on the premise that artists who visit South Africa thereby automatically endorse the apartheid regime. Peter argued against this claiming that, "All this ignorance was created by the white man, who doesn't want black artists to go there and see what's happening.

"I am not going there to support apartheid – cramp, kill and paralyse apartheid!" he exclaimed. "But learn this. There is no more apartheid in South Africa than what is going on in Birmingham, Alabama or any other place where they're still lynching black people, and I want you to remember that. Every month the Ku Klux Klan marches and is engaged in all kinds of campaigns and parades and you know what the Ku Klux Klan is saying? 'Leave America and keep it white.'"

The intellectual merits of this stance were dubious, yet Peter believed that the messages in his music were of far greater relevance to the people of Africa than anywhere else. He raised the question that if he could perform in countries that supported the apartheid regime like England, Germany and America, then why shouldn't he go to South Africa? To his way of thinking there was only one place to be and that was at the heart of the struggle, urging his people to rise up and seize control of their own land

and assets. Peter's head was full of such romantic notions, yet those around him never doubted he meant every word.

The *Mama Africa* sessions began in June 1982, soon after he and Copeland had returned to Kingston. Danny Sims had succeeded in negotiating Peter a new record deal with EMI and once everything was in place, Chris Kimsey was commissioned to produce a follow-up album to *Wanted Dread & Alive*. This was a risky choice by Sims – not because of any technical shortcomings, but the fact that Kimsey had worked with the Rolling Stones on their last three albums.

"Because of my association with the Stones a lot of people assume that was the connection but it wasn't like that at all," he says. "I'm not even sure if Peter knew I'd worked with them. We never spoke about them, that's for sure."

Chris wasn't at all put off by Peter's reputation, or his break-up with the Stones. He'd known of similar situations where a relatively unknown artist – at least in mainstream terms – is championed by someone who's very successful or has a lot of money and then expects everything to happen for them, regardless of their own efforts, and assumed this was the case with Peter. Danny Sims had also commissioned him to work on albums by Jimmy Cliff and a local band called Native, and rented a large house in Ocho Rios for the duration of Chris' Jamaican adventure, which lasted several months. He shared this accommodation with another of Danny's clients, American soul singer Betty Wright, and guitarist Donald Kinsey who in addition to playing with Peter, had been asked to produce an album with Wright that in Kinsey's own words, "Would take her out of the 'Clean Up Woman' bag and get her into something more contemporary". The resulting album, *Wright Back At You*, was recorded whilst the singer was heavily pregnant and featured a track called 'Reggae The Night Away', which Donald had originally written for the Chosen Ones.

Chris Kimsey worked first with Jimmy Cliff, who'd jammed with Keith Richards and Ron Wood at the Hit Factory in New York only three months earlier and was never short of fresh ideas. Jimmy's album *Special* will result from his sessions with Chris, who had to complete a five hour round trip to Kingston most days – an experience he'll later describe as "mind-blowing", but at least the route was picturesque. En route to Kingston they'd drive under a canopy of arched trees called Fern Gully, then skirt Mount Diablo and follow the Rio Cobre River through Linstead and Bog Walk until the bright lights of Spanish Town loomed into view. From there it was but a short hop through Central Village and along the Spanish Town Road into Central Kingston.

"Jimmy's album was recorded at Channel One and the first time I went there they hid me under a blanket as we drove through Trench Town, because I was the only white person for miles around," says Kimsey, laughing. "For the first day or two I just sat on the couch in front of the console just listening and watching before being invited to actually do anything. After that we all got on really well although everything was so different – in fact it was quite a revelation. As a teenager I'd been a huge ska fan and I loved reggae music but then I realised why the drum sound was so kind of dark and special on some of those records. It's because they don't have any microphones! Also, the cymbal sound would bleed onto the tom toms which was really interesting but then when I worked with Peter we went to Dynamic, which was at the opposite end of the scale because they had a new MCI desk in there, and I'd brought a half-inch machine from Miami with me that we could mix down onto as well.

"I really enjoyed doing that album. Peter wasn't difficult to work with but he wasn't too friendly either. He'd come to the studio in the morning and play two or three songs to his rhythm section and then just disappear for the rest of the day. We never saw him after that, which was fine by me... He'd just run through the songs on an acoustic or electric guitar; we'd get the groove and map out how many verses and choruses there were and that was it. The next time we saw him he was ready to play guitar and sing on it. It was a very different relationship to the one I'd had with Jimmy Cliff but it worked really well and I think Peter quite enjoyed just being able to walk in and work quickly, knowing we would take care of things. When you've been in the studio that many years you don't particularly want to hang about. You just want to get the vibe down and get it done.

"We made a good team but Peter did have an image to look up to and he really did his damnedest to live up to it! In his situation, living in Jamaica, I guess you'd need to do that but he was also a very private person. It was all about music and work with him. My wife was there with me and I seem to remember he didn't like white women too much. I think a lot of it was bravado but Peter had this anarchic quality about him that was always there, bubbling under the surface. That's what made him such

341

a compelling artist but maybe it also prevented him from coming up with songs that would make him cross over, it's hard to tell..."

Chris says the new rhythm section "wasn't as slick as Sly & Robbie. There was something more organic about them. They were a bit more roots; not necessarily in reggae terms, but musically speaking."

It's Peter's road band essentially, and they *rock*. Santa played drums, whilst bass duties were shared between Fully Fullwood and Lebert "Gibby" Morrison, who toured with Jimmy Cliff. Steve Golding was on rhythm guitar, Donald Kinsey played lead whilst Keith Sterling and Robbie Lyn handled most of the keyboard parts except clavinet, which Peter played himself. Sticky and Scully, as was often the case, contributed percussion. There'll be marked differences between this album and the others. Peter's no longer concerned with trying to keep pace with America's top funk and soul bands, although certain tracks will be finely judged for rock radio in the US. His mission this time is to take roots rock reggae back to the dancehalls and not just those of Jamaica, but also Lagos, Zanzibar, Kinshasa, Sao Paulo and many other places besides. *Mama Africa* will be Peter's most danceable album yet, but with no quenching of that irascible spirit.

"Peter was full of conviction in what he was doing," says Santa. "Working with him gave me a lot of strength because he was very open and creative as regards music and whatever he did, you could *feel* it. It wasn't any ego trip or anything like that. He was aware of the situation that was going on around him, both in Jamaica and the world. He was very connected when it came to the suffering of the people and their rights. Everything was of the moment. He was spontaneous and allowed us musicians to do our own thing. He would come with a song and we'd just play it – it really wasn't anything more complicated than that, and there'd never be any arguments. He used to say that he was the general, and we were the foot soldiers..."

It was Steve Golding, Keith Sterling and Santa who worked out most of the arrangements. Copeland Forbes also contributed ideas on occasion. One of the first songs they recorded was 'Mama Africa' – an exhilarating hybrid of reggae and African funk that could have only been inspired by Sonny Osokuns and Peter's trip to Nigeria. There's unbridled joy in the melodies and rhythm, which is closer to Afro-beat than reggae, whilst the lyrics reflect Peter's excitement at having visited Africa for the first time and are voiced as direct testament, from a son to his mother. "I love you," he tells her at one point, and it's clearly no empty gesture.

"Peter was a great singer, and the vocal on 'Mama Africa' has so much soul and passion in it," says Chris Kimsey. "That's another thing with Peter, because he knew exactly what he wanted to do with his vocals. He knew precisely what he wanted to say and how he wanted to say it."

Peter is now an artist in full command of his craft, and *Mama Africa* will be the most perfectly realised of his albums to date. Listen to how he sings the second vocal lines and harmonies on 'Not Gonna Give It Up' in the same, deep baritone he used on early Wailers recordings. It's the hallmark of a master, whilst the song itself continues in the tradition of 'African' and 'Equal Rights', and fair takes the breath away. Peter casts himself in the role of a freedom fighter and announces that he'll keep battling for as long as it takes to rid the African continent of "bucky master" (meaning the colonialism.) "I've been up there and seen poverty beyond compare. And those slave drivers just don't care," he growls. It's doubtful that Bob Marley would have used a term like "bucky master", but then Peter Tosh had a lot more attitude.

'Glass House' was written about the failure of the Peace Treaty, and is couched in simple enough terms since "If you live in a glass house, then don't throw stones..." Peter's basically saying to the organisers of the peace treaty 'I told you so', and accuses them of failing the people. "You build your world on lies and illusion," he admonishes, amidst soaring harmonies by Pam Hall, her sister Audrey and their brother Raymond, who usually sang with Toots & the Maytals. Peter recorded two other new songs at these sessions, called 'Come Together' and 'Me No Go A Jail Fe Gang Jah', but wasn't happy with how they turned out – he'll return to them in future. His new band also recorded a cut of 'Reggae Mylitis' that was never issued, and may have just been intended as a rehearsal. Better by far was 'Feel No Way', with words intended to comfort the poorer classes since Peter promises that everyone must get their due reward, according to their works.

At another session in mid-June he recorded 'Where You Gonna Run' and a rip-roaring version of Chuck Berry's 'Johnny B. Goode' that'll deliver his second biggest-selling single after 'Don't Look Back' – more of which later. Donald Kinsey had written 'Where You Gonna Run' with his brother Ralph and it's a souped-up reggae/funk hybrid of such livewire vitality, you'd have a hard time explaining it as anything but a deliberate attempt to connect with African-American audiences, especially with Betty Wright singing her heart out in the chorus line. Rasping horns, Donald's biting guitar licks, a soulful harmonica and swaggering bass-line underpin Peter's conscious lyrics, whilst the opening and closing phrases are just a tiny bit reminiscent of 'I Shot The Sheriff'.

Santa, whose playing is superb on this track, told Roger Steffens, "It was a prophetical kind of thing. Peter show you that whatever you look for, you can't look for it outside yourself. You want the truth? You haffi check yourself."

Donald Kinsey also played a key role in masterminding Peter's take on 'Johnny B. Goode'. You'd expect this to sound like a rock record, yet nothing could be further from the truth. In fact it's far closer to what was being played in Kingston than Memphis or Chicago, and again we're reminded of how Peter is an artist at the peak of his powers – one capable of taking someone else's signature tune and doing something entirely different with it.

"I remember saying to him, 'You should do a cover of 'Johnny B. Goode' and he said, 'Me nah sing no white man's song,' so the next day I turned up with a picture of Chuck Berry, showed it to him and said, 'This is the man who wrote it.' That made all the difference," says Chris Kimsey, whose memories of the occasion are tinged with genuine affection. "The next thing I knew, he'd taken the original lyrics and totally adapted them until it was now *his* 'Johnny B. Goode'. In fact I think it's almost better than the original."

Donald Kinsey confirms that it was Chris who influenced Peter's decision to cover 'Johnny B Goode' but the guitarist's own contributions proved vital, as he explained to Leslie Singer. "When Chris first suggested it I had to just think for a minute. I said, 'Well a lot of rock'n'roll groups have done a version of "Johnny B. Goode", and they did it just like Chuck Berry had done. I didn't want Peter to do it like that, and so I sat down to work out an arrangement and then presented it to Peter, who didn't want to do it. For whatever reason, he wasn't into doing somebody else's song. He told me people were saying to him, 'You don't wanna do no bumboclaat rock'n'roll tune man,' and I said, 'But Peter, the tune is a real positive song if you check out the lyrics. It's just about a guy who plays guitar and wants to be a good musician so check it out.' (Peter will later tell Simon Hills that 'Johnny B Goode' "is for people with the ambition to learn to read and write and make a life for themselves...")

"I knew that if Peter Tosh did this tune it had to become his song so one night I just started working on it," he continues. "I had to beg them to let me record the track but once we laid it everybody said, 'Peter, the track hot!' He'd done most of the vocals for the album by then – everything but

'Johnny B. Goode', so I put a rough vocal on there to give him a guide, and I was there in the booth with him when he sang it."

Peter nailed the song in one take and you'd never imagine he'd once been so reluctant to sing it. Chuck Berry's original lyrics had been rewritten almost in their entirety and now suited Peter so well, it was hard to distinguish between art and his own life story as he told the story of a boy from the Jamaican countryside – "back in the woods, on top of a hill" – who carries his guitar in "a gunny sack" and practises playing it by the train tracks until stepping out as "the leader of a reggae band" and attracting people from far and wide.

"We had some fun times whilst we were making that album," reflects Chris Kimsey. "I remember there was this group of kids who were always hanging around outside the studio. I guess most of them were between 14 and 18 years old but they were fans of Peter's. They were never allowed in but they'd hang around the doors trying to see inside and one day we walked out after working on 'Johnny B. Goode' and this kid said, 'Peter, that's the best song you ever wrote!' Peter just looked at me and stared me down as if warning me not to say anything!

"That was the last recording session I think. We started mixing it after that and then I was supposed to fly back to New York City to master it. I was on my way to the airport with Danny Sims and by this time, unbeknown to me, there'd been a big falling out between Danny and some high-ranking Rastas who claimed to be Peter's representatives in Jamaica. We were pulled over at gunpoint and escorted to a makeshift courtroom in a school somewhere. It was the school holidays but we were taken to this little primary school and they were charging Danny with stealing from Jamaica's musical heritage and taking advantage of Peter Tosh. They thought he was cheating Peter which knowing Danny, he most likely was. But I was terrified. I wasn't that old at the time and to be pulled over by men brandishing M16 rifles, then herded into this dark little place...

"When we walked in I couldn't see anything for ganja smoke. I sat down listening to everything that was going on and then when it came to my turn to speak I said, 'Well if you don't let me go, the album will never come out and that means no-one will hear this great record and no-one will make any money from it.' That's when they let me go but they kept Danny, who must have talked his way out of it in the end. It was quite a chilling experience, I tell you."

Chapter 25

Youth Consciousness

Peter always denied that Danny was his manager, but there's little doubt that his one-time mentor played a senior role in management affairs.

"Danny managed Peter for a long time," says Janet Davidson. "He lived on the East side of Central Park at Fifth Avenue and 102nd Street in this huge six-bedroom apartment right in the middle of Manhattan. He was married to Beverly Johnson the supermodel and led a very rich lifestyle because he had a full staff, with a doorman, cook and everything. It was a beautiful apartment but Danny was rarely there, and Peter would usually stay with friends when we were in New York, until he bought somewhere of his own."

Beverley Johnson was America's top black model. She'd been the first African-American to appear on the cover of *Vogue*, and had tried her hand at acting and even singing after marrying Sims in 1977. Their marriage lasted only two years but around the time Danny was managing Peter they got back together and had a daughter called Anansa, who became the focus of a hard-fought custody battle.

Danny booked a series of US tour dates for Peter throughout August and September 1982. Jimmy Cliff, who'd just returned from Zambia, would join the line-up for some of them, and take turns to headline. Copeland Forbes was tour manager and Janet Davidson, a young, black British accountant from London, was hired to help him.

"I'd do all the co-ordination and setting up press interviews," she explains. "I quickly discovered that people were scared of Peter but he was

346

always extremely nice to me. It's not every time we'd take the tour bus because he and I would travel on ahead if he had interviews to do. Peter wasn't all that educated. He hadn't really finished school so I would go and represent him at the record company, or I'd step in if I thought someone was putting him in a difficult situation. They might say, 'Oh, we'd like him to read the Six O'Clock News' and I'd know that he either wouldn't be able to manage it or it would put him on the spot so I'd make excuses for him. There would be certain situations he just wasn't comfortable with."

Janet soon dismissed the myth that Peter was a wild man who smoked massive amounts of ganja and spouted hell and brimstone. Instead, she was struck by how considerate and professional he was, which is something I've heard time and again whilst interviewing Peter's women associates. Janet saw that he worked hard at being Peter Tosh, especially on stage.

"Peter always gave a strong performance no matter what. Every night we did the same show and we only changed it for the next tour, which would be based around the latest album. That's how we did it. It wasn't like he'd just get up there and sing whatever he felt like doing that night, or what people were requesting. Peter had a *show*, and it was well rehearsed. Nothing was left to chance. He'd even wear certain clothes or do things at the same point during each performance. We used to rehearse at SIR in New York. We'd be there for at least three weeks before a tour, starting each day at midday and then finishing at maybe eight, nine o'clock at night. It was all very professional and a lot of other reggae artists weren't like that."

Peter's new girlfriend, Marlene Brown, accompanied him on that 1982 US tour with Jimmy Cliff. She was just 20, and therefore 17 years younger than him. They also shared the same birthday, October 19 – a fact that Peter told everyone. Marlene's real name was Andrea. She'd swapped it for her middle name after leaving Gordon Town and starting college in Kingston. The symbolism was obvious. Marlene was preparing for a new life, and the day that Peter had charmed her with tales of visiting America, travelling free and staying in luxury hotels had been a lightning rod. For now she was out of her depth, but keen to see how things worked. Most onlookers recall a quiet, polite girl with dark, flashing eyes and a ready smile, who stayed close to Peter and said little. Melody Cunningham – his beloved "Riddim" – had been left back in Jamaica, where she was raising their daughter, Niambe and son, Jawara. Everyone in Peter's camp liked her, but no one dared to interfere as Marlene took over his affections.

The tour started in Detroit, and then headed northwards to Calgary where Peter told a local reporter he was cancelling four dates in Israel, scheduled for October. "There is no way I can sing and speak about equal rights and justice in a country that is supplying South Africa with the guns to suppress black people and continue the Apartheid," he said. When told he stood to lose more than $80,000 by cancelling the trip he replied, "When it comes to my message, money is secondary." He would have been the first reggae artist to perform in Israel, and the only one to have openly supported the Palestinians...

He'd incorporated a few new songs into his act for this current tour and Donald Kinsey must have smiled to himself at seeing the fervent reaction to 'Johnny B. Goode'. Even Peter was surprised at how well it was received. By the time he played two nights at the Hollywood Palladium in Los Angeles on August 13 and 14, he and the band were in great form. Reggae connoisseurs duly took note that this latest edition of Word, Sound & Power was anchored by the original Soul Syndicate pairing of Fully and Santa, who'd played on so many hits by the likes of Dennis Brown, Big Youth and John Holt back in Jamaica. The rest of the audience were just bowled over by how good they were.

Whilst they were in Los Angeles, a black journalist by the name of Dennis Hunt interviewed Peter for the *LA Times*, and asked him questions concerning his attitude towards African-Americans. Peter, not realising that Hunt will sensationalise his remarks, was less than complimentary. It still upset him that his audiences were predominantly white, and African-Americans generally had little regard for reggae – especially now that hip-hop had surfaced from the New York projects and gone mainstream. Everywhere they travelled that summer he'd hear the lines, "It's like a jungle sometimes, it makes me wonder how I keep from going under..." This was a record that Grandmaster Flash said was about, "Broken glass, pissing in the streets, being homeless, having your car towed and getting jacked by base-heads". The lyrics of 'The Message' were real enough, but reggae was now in danger of being sidelined by black America's latest musical thrill and Peter let his frustrations get the better of him during that interview with Hunt.

"Peter always had that militant edge and could be standoffish," says Warren Smith, who'd see Peter on trips to Los Angeles. "He had this frightening look and a way of talking that was very sharp and to the point.

He didn't mumble. He had a way of talking directly to people and was always holding court. He was a very interesting person to be around..."

Mervin Palmer had accompanied them to California. He was a friend of Marlene's, who persuaded Peter to let him paint the cover design for *Mama Africa*. "Peter gave me the song 'Mama Africa' to listen to so I could feel the vibes and come up with a design," says Mervin. "I listened to it every day for inspiration but Peter had some underdeveloped drawing talent as well. I was an art teacher at the Jamaica School of Art at the time, and could clearly see the hidden talent from a small sketch he did of a woman embracing Africa. It was just a line drawing in pencil to indicate a vague image that was in his mind. I then created this young, happy and beautiful African woman to represent Mama Africa and his queen Marlene Brown, who was a student at Camperdown High School when I used to teach there. She was a motivating factor and inspiration for the artwork I created. In fact it bears some resemblance to her...

"From there I visualised the whole concept and added symbols such as South Africa's mineral wealth, Ethiopia's shining star of spirituality, the big ganja spliff in Peter's mouth and the Rastafarian colours set against an African landscape. It was done in watercolours, on watercolour paper. I worked on it whilst I was travelling on the tour bus with Peter and Jimmy Cliff, and then I finished it whilst we were in Los Angeles, at a hotel in Hollywood."

Mervin remembers a heated argument between Peter and a representative from EMI over who should design the jacket. EMI wanted its art department to take care of it and Peter became furious. He even threatened to withdraw the album if he didn't get his own way. "Peter said if his artist isn't going to do it 'then there'll be no *bumboclaat* album'," he recalls, placing the emphasis in just the same way Peter did, in a slow drawl. "After he'd slammed down the phone he said, 'Ah wha' them tek this bomboclaat t'ing fah? Dis ah my album and ah me who decide who fi do the work, ta bumboclaat...'"

On August 19 the tour bus left for San Francisco, where Peter played to a full house at the Kibuki Theatre. Most of the dates on this tour would be well attended, with or without Jimmy Cliff. Two days later and the bus drew up outside Santa Cruz's Civic Auditorium with its arched granite pillars and Art Deco trimmings where Peter again showcased new songs like 'Not Gonna Give It Up' and a blistering 'Johnny B. Goode'. Shows in

Denver and Boulder preceded two nights at Kansas City's Uptown Theatre. He then appeared at Chicago's Park Way supported by local band Heavy Manners, named after the slogan used for Manley's last election campaign.

"Peter had a mesmerising quality to him that night," recalls lead singer Kate Fagan. "I thought he was really strong on stage and his show had a lot of energy. It was highly charged, because he stood up there and gave out a lot of intensity, especially on songs like 'Legalise It'. He was really trying to rally the audience with his lyrics and he liked preaching to people as well. He was a bit of a crusader, whereas Bob Marley would get into this happy kind of vibe sometimes with party tunes like 'Jammin''. Peter definitely wasn't about that because whenever he performed, he was so dominating..."

After a three-day break it was back on the bus for the journey to Cleveland, where he and Jimmy Cliff played the Front Row Theatre and then sold out the Metropolitan Centre in Boston before going their separate ways. Peter's next show was at a place he scornfully referred to as "a rum bar", i.e. Toad's Place in New Haven, Connecticut. He was much happier returning to New York, where he and Cliff were booked to appear at the Felt Forum – a 4,000 capacity hall in the same building as Madison Square Garden – on September 25.

Whilst they were in New York, a company called Avatar invited Donald Kinsey and Steve Golding to try out a couple of its guitars. Two brand-new instruments duly arrived at the sound check, and Donald couldn't have been happier since he'd recently had a couple of guitars stolen. He'll alternate the Avatar SG with a treasured Les Paul, and will also play Peter's yellow Gibson from time to time. Whilst he was friendly enough, Peter no longer fraternised with his musicians like he did before, although he and Donald were quite close.

"Peter would have a laugh with his musicians but it wasn't like he'd hang out with them," says Janet. "It was harder for him, having to entertain an audience night after night, so he'd be sat in a separate dressing-room, meditating or praying and reading his Bible. He was always practising his unicycle as well."

By the time he and Marlene's birthday came round, on October 19, they were back in Jamaica. His next performance won't be until the end of that month, on the 30th at the Sunrise Music Centre in Florida – a show that had originally been scheduled for October 8. Copeland Forbes made the introductions as usual, and ordered the 3,000 concertgoers to 'extinguish your cigarettes and light up your spliffs" before Peter took the stage in an African dashiki and red, gold and green headdress, and with a spliff clamped in his fingers.

"The band was hot all evening," wrote Roy and Janet Gold in *Reggae International*. "Santa on drums kept the heavy beat going and the two sets of keyboards gave the band a full sound. Peter played rhythm guitar during 'The Toughest', and then gave a short speech before launching into 'Johnny B. Goode'. The crowd was still standing when he went offstage and showed their appreciation with lighted matches held high."

In the aftermath of Bob Marley's passing, these shows with Jimmy Cliff represented a double helping of reggae royalty. Cliff was a star in his own right after hits like 'Many Rivers To Cross' and his lead role in *The Harder They Come*, which was now revered as a cult classic. Whilst he and Peter were friends, each provided the other with stiff competition. In early November, Peter played a four-day residency at the Roxy Theatre on Sunset Strip, playing two sets per night. It had been less than three months since he was last in Los Angeles but audiences there still wanted more. Peter met with Roger Steffens and Hank Holmes the day he opened at the Roxy, on November 5. The pair interviewed him for KCRW-FM in Santa Monica, and told him what Keith Richards said when asked if Peter was difficult to deal with. "If I want to handle Peter Tosh, I just grab him by his collar and he knows what I mean by that…"

Peter's response came back like lightning. "Keith Richards afraid of me like puss man," he sneered. "I don't know which collar he's going to grab me by. None that I don't have on."

So you are no longer involved with the Rolling Stones?

"No, because it has been un-progressive. It has been ten steps backwards in my life. It seems as if they couldn't have me make it, but is many things happen. I've written a song called 'Your Friends' which says, "They will come with great pretence to gain your confidence. They'll take you round the bend and fry you in the end…" I am always aware of what friends can do because the prefix 'fry', it means 'hot'. The suffix 'end' means 'eliminated' and so because of that, words should not be taken the way they are pronounced 'cause it is not what goes down that defiles, it is what comes *out*."

Roger, especially, delighted in Peter's unorthodox use of phrasing and his ingenuity in coming up with new words and phrases. Everything was questioned and disassembled in Peter's universe. He had a way of looking at things afresh, and this meant he could change them around whenever he wished. When Janet Davidson describes Peter as "child-like" this is what she's alluding to.

Accompanying all that fiery bluster was an innocence and naivety he'd somehow preserved despite the cruel realities of life in Trench Town, and those ferocious beatings by the police. Peter's love of toys and animals can be attributed to the same thing. Maybe this is what will make Marlene grow so protective of him, especially after seeing how he's treated by sections of the media.

"When you were here some months ago, you did an interview with the *Los Angeles Times*," a local radio presenter asks him.

"Yes, and I hear they wrote a whole heap of bullshit."

"There were a lot of criticisms…"

"Seen, and let me tell you something. That was the only black guy I talked to, seen? And when I talked to him, thinking he was a guy who was seeing what I was saying, I realise that he was whiter than the white guys that I spoke to, seen? Because he took what I said morally, and turned it around so that people could criticise, seen? And what I was saying was just spiritually awakening towards black people, seen? Because black people don't seem to realise that they are king and queen, prince and princesses, prophets and priests, seen? That's what black people are, and now they are the buzzards of the earth, seen?"

"We're interrupting Peter Tosh for a moment. We will not edit the interview, but we're sitting in the *Los Angeles Times* office with Dennis Hunt, who wrote the article."

"Dennis, you've heard what Peter Tosh has to say about your article. What is your response to this?"

"Well, first of all, I will stand by what I said in the article. Second of all, when I talked to Peter he made a distinction between blacks in this country and blacks in his own country. He's on record as saying some nasty things about blacks from this country that I did not agree with at all, and that's one thing we were clashing about when I talked to him. Looking back at the article, he was probably sorry he said some of the things, but he did say them. His feeling about blacks from this country, like I said, is not as high as it could be and that's what he and I were basically quarrelling about."

"During your interview, what kind of things did he say about blacks in this country that you can recall?"

"Well, the interview was so long ago that I can't recall lots of the details but there was a feeling from some of the things he said… Based upon some of the things I'd read in the past, I knew that he held those views and hadn't changed them either, so in the middle of the interview I started to get a little bothered by his attitude and there was some tension and friction. But as I said, and this happens with an awful lot of people, after you talk to them, they see the story in print and have negative feelings about what they say. They try and say that they didn't say it or accuse you of switching their words, but basically everything I quote him as saying, he actually said so I think his quarrel is nonsense really."

"You interviewed him approximately for an hour and a half. Was there any other angle or theme that you might have been able to write on?"

"Sure, I could have done a nice puff piece about his music and said he was a swell guy and makes nice music, but that's boring and that's what I always try and stay away from. I always look for what's interesting and what's different about somebody and this was the one aspect about Peter that was controversial, and that to me was more fascinating than… I mean people know all those other things so who cares? I'm more interested in what's controversial."

"So you stand by your story?"

"Oh definitely."

Peter is left mumbling how "the world is full of lies and hypocrisy" and accuses the paper of "promoting illusion". There seems little doubt that Hunt set out to make trouble for Peter, and yet he was given all the ammunition he needed.

After completing his stint at the Roxy, the battle-weary Tosh squeezed in a couple more US dates before returning home for the Jamaica World Music Festival – a three-day event due to be held in Montego Bay over Thanksgiving weekend. The festival was the brainchild of a Denver promoter named Barry Fey who promised to keep annual, open-air festivals there for three years running in return for the rights to develop a rocky spit of land adjacent to the Seawind Hotel. This is where he built the newly constructed Bob Marley Performing Arts Centre – home (between November 25 and 27) to the most impressive line-up of foreign talent yet assembled in Jamaica, when the Beach Boys, Grateful Dead, the Clash, Rick James and Aretha Franklin, as well as top reggae acts Peter Tosh, Jimmy Cliff and Black Uhuru played to 15,000 people. Peter headlined the final night but didn't take the stage until dawn, as Santa Davis recalled to Roger Steffens.

"That's the first time I'd experienced a sunrise show. It was like a mystic vibe. It's kind of hard to describe that feeling. I was elated... You got lifted, 'cause it was so different. Peter went on stage holding an Ethiopian crucifix... It was one of those rare, spiritual moments, so it was really magical in a way, like divine. In Jamaica, people always make it a point of duty to get up before the sun. They say that if you rise with the sun, then you get all that blessing from morning and so with the music and the sun rising it was like a blessing for everybody. Before Peter came on stage, everybody was in their sleeping bags but then the moment he started playing, people start waking up so it's like Christ coming out of the clouds or something, with all these people rising to meet him. It was *time!*"

Copeland Forbes says it was Peter's most disappointing show and for a team that prides itself on well-drilled perfection, that's easy enough to understand. Hatless for once, his dreadlocks flying free, Peter had taken the stage dressed in a white martial arts suit, with a scimitar at his waist and red, gold and green scarf around his neck. Holding the Ethiopian cross in his right hand as if blessing the congregation, he sang two bars of 'Steppin' Razor' and then everything shut down except for the feed from his new radio microphone. "When this power come, all power cut!" he roared. "Look at how many heathens play the music and nothing happen but as the most progressive come, something must bumbaclaat happen!" He'd now drawn his scimitar and was slashing the air with it in frustration. Two minutes later he turned towards the wings and yelled, "Come out here and do bumboclaat something. The people are out there waiting for the music. What the bumboclaat yuh take this thing for?" There's a temporary respite as he launches a wind-up bird into the sky, and then the power returns. Several songs later, after he's eased into 'Rastafari Is' and begun chanting in Amharic, Peter's frustrations again get the better of him. It's a rowdy crowd, even though some of them have been on their feet all night, and Peter's haranguing them. "Years we've been living this illusion of Jesus die and go to heaven, because that don't exist," he tells them, in-between warnings about false Rastas and "wolves in sheep's clothing". He then orders the crowd to be quiet and stop acting like they're on coke, which meets with a predictably frosty reaction.

Peter will later give an emotive interview to Sharon Smithline, in which he refers to the Jamaica World Music Festival as "pure madness".

"It was pure fuckery because first of all, plenty of the artists that come here is useless. It's a good thing myself and a few others were there otherwise there would have been no reggae, seen? Many of the artists they brought here, nobody don't want to hear them. Who wants to hear the Grateful *bombaclaat* Dead?"

Jimmy Cliff disagreed, and told the *Daily Gleaner* it was "a good achievement".

"I was satisfied with the organisation and think it was good for the image of the country," he said. "It was a good lesson in how to run a show professionally. We have brought the music to a stage where it can attract people like these (meaning the promoters) and what we need to do now is to introduce their methods into our own productions."

The Gleaner announces that "He, Peter Tosh and Bunny Livingston have decided to promote a big show scheduled for Christmas Day at the National Stadium named 'Youth Consciousness' at which they will be the featured performers." Jimmy says they learnt valuable lessons performing at the World Music Festival and this can help them when staging similar events. He also warned there was a need for first class equipment, which is not readily available on the island. "Technology is always a problem," he said. "This being a technological age, we have to learn to live with the times."

Tickets for the Youth Consciousness Reggae Festival went on sale the week before Christmas. There were now a dozen names on the bill and with Bunny as the headliner, even though he hadn't performed in public since the Wailers opened for Stevie Wonder at the Dream Concert, seven years ago. The success of *Blackheart Man* had fuelled demands for him to play live and Bunny will provide the Festival with its biggest attraction.

Sharp-eyed readers will remember the first two Youth Consciousness concerts had been disappointments, and Peter was determined not to repeat the same mistakes. This one will be far better organised, and it'll also give Peter the opportunity to put the World Music Festival experience behind him. Preparations were going well until Robbie Lyn – last seen sporting a thin tie with keyboard motif at that show – left the band at short notice. Robbie usually played organ and clavinet, whilst Keith Sterling alternated between a Fender Rhodes and synthesizer. Since Keith couldn't play all the keyboard parts Peter decided to draft songs with less complex arrangements into his set such as 'Ketchy Shuby', 'Can't Blame The Youth' and 'Brand New Second Hand'. He was still conducting rehearsals when talking to New York reporter Sharon Smithline, who described Youth Consciousness as "a concept that will help youths to follow the right path. In this crazy world there are very few people that a youth could emulate. Most adults do not treat the youth with any respect. They are like second-class citizens. They are the future generation, but how can they grow into progressive adults if they are not treated the right way? The people behind Youth Consciousness want to lead the youths in the right direction with things like the Wailers' talent centre for amateur groups and tent concerts around the island."

Sharon interviewed Peter on Christmas Eve, 24 hours before the Festival was due to start. 'Peace Treaty' b/w 'Glass House' had just been released on 12″ single, but the *Mama Africa* album wasn't due for another month. Asked how the Youth Consciousness concept came about, Peter admits the idea wasn't new, but explains that he hadn't been able to accomplish his mission before now "due to unfavourable financial conditions". He talks about the need for determination, "knowing that youths of today born and raised in poverty and ignorance; lost in fantasy and seeking to find reality, won't get no direction in life. I and I who were approximately a victim of the same shit-stem said there has to be someone, some way, somehow to do something to alleviate that degrading way of life which was not meant to be, so that's what we are doing."

The National Stadium will be half-empty due to a combination of wet weather – it hadn't rained for months before the day of the concert – and competition from the Drifters and Stylistics, who toured Jamaica over Christmas. A lot of people couldn't afford tickets for both, yet it's the Youth Consciousness Festival that'll grab the headlines. Penny Slinger, writing in *Everybody's International*, describes it as "an extraordinary event" and "a landmark in the history of reggae music. More than just a concert, it was a vigil, an adventure, a celebration and a revelation.

"Night seemed to have fallen early," she reports. "Dark clouds covered the Stadium like a canopy. The audience was seated by 6 p.m. and after two hours of warding off intermittent rain, MC Bagga Brown introduced Nadine Sutherland with the words, 'And a little child shall lead them, a conscious youth who has sung her way into the hearts of everyone.'"

Judy Mowatt came on next wearing a long satin dress, her hair knotted at the sides. Bob's former backing singer was described as "exhibiting self-

356

possessed confidence, dignity and resolve". Her set revolved around songs she'd written about the empowerment of women, interspersed with one or two Wailers hits. The crowd was still lustily belting out 'One Love' as she left the stage.

"What followed was a real surprise," recalls Sharon Smithline. "Bagga asked the crowd if there was 'anyone here from Chancery Lane, downtown Kingston?' Gregory Isaacs then strode onto the stage to an enthusiastic welcome. He'd returned to Jamaica from tour especially for the occasion and was backed by the Roots Radics, the hottest young band on the island. Gregory had the crowd rocking in their seats and singing along to hits such as 'Tune In', 'Top Ten', 'Oh What A Feeling', 'Mr. Brown', 'Soon Forward' and 'Front Door'. The biggest applause was for 'Night Nurse', which had them whooping for joy."

After a short intermission, Marcia Griffiths reminded the audience that artists like her weren't just there to entertain, "but to uplift each and every one of our souls". This was just before she dedicated a song to "the sisters who are being oppressed by some of these brothers". As several males shifted a little uneasily in their seats, she broke the spell with 'The Way I Feel About You', then sang an extract from *West Side Story* before halting at the line "death won't part us now" and announcing that "Bob Marley is right here with us this evening".

Marley may have been there in spirit, but it was Peter Tosh who "entered the stage wearing a long robe emblazoned with golden sun-like motifs.

"Hailed as 'the intellectual diplomat and original Wailer, the Mystic Man,' he was really in top form," purred Smithline. "I haven't seen or heard Peter so warm, mellow and outreaching in a long time. He seemed larger than life and unflinchingly braved the pouring rain. Finding strength in adversity, this musical warrior rose to the situation and had the crowd behind him all the way. After premiering 'Not Gonna Give It Up' he then went into a rap, saying, 'This moment is an event that never happened in 400 years. We in this generation must be proud and glad, especially we who are here. This thing that is happening right now, do you know what it is? Illegal. Consciousness is illegal in a world of fantasy and illusion.' He went on to say that people could have the highest educational achievement and still be lost in darkest fantasy. He spoke articulately and with a sense of humour, often poking fun at himself. It was a pleasure to hear him talk and be appreciated, rather than alienating his audience as I saw recently in New York. He was never abusive, dedicating himself to the spirit of the occasion and mentioning that August 23 was Peter Tosh Day in the Bedford-Stuyvesant area of Brooklyn, New York. As he moved around the stage he played the guitar, shook his locks, toked on his spliff and generally sent out good, positive vibes. He sounded great; seemed to be enjoying himself and singing from his heart."

It's certainly one of his better performances. The band's so tight, despite those last-minute changes and it's amusing to watch Donald and Fully moving in tandem, as if part of a sixties soul revue. Peter is magisterial throughout and remains unconcerned by the weather until the stage starts to get slippery and stagehands hurriedly throw polythene sheeting over the equipment. Keith Sterling, who's already under pressure, has to play from under a man-sized, see-through bubble wrap for the next few numbers as Peter continues with his gawky crane impersonation, oblivious to everything except the music. 'Rastafari Is' features a beautiful solo by Donald. Peter plays conga drums on that one and then straps on his Gibson for 'The Toughest'. It's rock'n'roll Jamaica style – an impression reinforced when he runs on the spot during 'Johnny B. Goode' and declares that he's "the most controversial man on Earth". He's got the vibes now and tells everyone in the auditorium he loves them – a real rarity – before arguing with a heckler and likening himself to Christ after the crowd voted for Barabbas to escape crucifixion. It's the kind of spurious comment John Lennon might have made but since no one from the media appeared to notice, Peter gets away with it.

Following him wouldn't be easy, so the stage managers opted for a change of pace instead. Jamaican dub poet Oku Onuora, recounting his experiences in jail, read from his book *Reflections In Red* and issued warnings about nuclear armament. "Learn or burn!" he shouted, raising his fist heavenwards. Jimmy Cliff, dressed in a colourful robe, came on next and gave another galvanised performance. After crisscrossing America for the last three months he and Peter were in imperious form. Jimmy had chosen his set list to reflect the occasion and songs like 'You Can Get It If You Really Want It', 'Roots Radical' and 'Treat The Youth Right' carried such resonance.

A short time later Bunny Wailer, whom Smithline describes "as the most mystical man in the universe" arrived on stage amidst clouds of smoke, like a magician. Hundreds of firecrackers had gone off as he'd walked on stage, adding to the excitement. The rain had now stopped and the sky was completely clear. After praising Jah for performing miracles Bunny then complimented the audience on having "fire in their souls" before delivering a three-hour masterclass composed of hits like 'Blackheart Man', 'Armageddon', 'Dreamland' and 'Battering Down Sentence'. Those who doubted Bunny's ability as a live performer were left speechless. It was a landmark appearance and crowned by him, Peter and Jimmy singing 'Get Up Stand Up' for an encore, and then inviting Judy Mowatt to join them for a farewell 'No Woman No Cry'.

The show finished at 8 a.m., and yet still people were reluctant to leave. They'd shared in something special and whilst all the performances were good, Bunny's had been a revelation. Backstage, the artists knew the takings wouldn't be sufficient to fund everything they'd talked about, but they agreed that the concert had been a success overall. They'd tried their best, and there was no shame in having fallen victim to the weather.

A review in the *Daily Gleaner* praised the Festival, but neglected to mention the reasons for staging it. Bunny is naturally singled out for special mention, closely followed by his friend of 20 years. "Peter Tosh disappointed his critics who expected another round of expletives and gave a truly professional and decent performance before an average sized crowd at the Youth Consciousness Reggae Festival, at the National Stadium on Saturday. Tosh who has earned notoriety for colouring his performances with "indecent language" – the latest case being during his performance at the recent Jamaica World Music Festival in Montego Bay – told the crowd that although some people expected him to behave that way, he would not as he was really an 'international diplomat'."

It ends by saying Peter "literally had the crowd eating out of his hands by the time he left the stage".

Chapter 26

Midnight Dread

February and March are summer months in Australia, and reggaemylitis was sweeping the country in the wake of Toots & the Maytals' recent visit. Peter Tosh, who was interviewed for the *Sydney Morning Herald* prior to leaving Jamaica, would be the next major reggae star to tour there. Journalist Rosalind Reines had seen him perform in London and peppers her prose with tales of unicycles and wraparound welders' goggles, and of how Peter took to the stage during a fireworks display... "Who knows what he'll get up to when he hits Sydney on March 10," she gushes, before quizzing him about the forthcoming album.

"You'll have to hear it for yourself," he snaps.

On arriving in Sydney he was escorted to the Sebel Townhouse Hotel – a European style hotel popular with celebrities, overlooking Elizabeth Bay. Janet Davidson, who was on her first overseas tour with Peter, says he was well received everywhere he went, but that he often got annoyed at being asked about Bob Marley. "Death becomes so natural that people come to believe they must die, but there are angels living on earth who defy death," was his most cryptic answer. "And are you an angel?" the journalist asked. "Of course I am, because only angels can go through what I've been through and not die in the process."

That first concert was widely praised. Reines reported how "Tosh has followed in the footsteps of Bob Marley to give Sydney a truly inspirational reggae show. It was a concert that built up in momentum like slow rolling thunder, and from the moment the reggae star first appeared on stage. For five minutes the Hordern Pavilion was in total darkness and then to the strains of 'Hallelujah', the reggae maestro entered disguised as an Arab, or perhaps he was supposed to be one of the three Wise Men... He then told the audience 'You have never heard this music before, because I in person am the only one in the world who can represent it'."

This is a staggering conceit considering that Toots & the Maytals had played there just weeks earlier and were every bit as authentic as Peter Tosh, who admittedly never sought to be liked by his audiences, yet demanded their respect because of the truth in his songs. Reines called this show "another highlight in an extraordinary career", yet missed the irony in his introduction of 'Johnny B. Goode'. "This is music from the beginning of time," he announced, "not some little song from yesterday."

Aboriginal band No Fixed Address supported him on the first three dates, including that opening show in Sydney. Their pioneering fusion of rock, reggae and indigenous music is best defined by 'We Have Survived', which remains an anthem of the Aboriginal land rights movement. "You can't change the rhythm of my soul," it begins. "You can't tell me what to do. You can't break my bones by putting me down, or by taking the things that belong to me... Cos why? We have survived the white man's way, and the horror and the torment of it all. We have survived the white man's way and you know, you can't change that."

Drummer Bart Willoughby had formed the group five years earlier. He'd been separated from his family as a child after the government conducted nuclear tests in their home territory. The authorities sent him to an Aboriginal mission thousands of miles away where he says the climate was "1,000 degrees in the shade", and the inmates were regularly beaten and humiliated.

"What Peter Tosh taught me was not to let the pain destroy you," he says. "He taught me that you have to live with it, learn to understand it and then to use it in making beautiful music. One you're in harmony with it then you can explain it to others and become a philosopher, which is someone who knows the truth. The rest of the world wasn't going to teach me something like that. The system here in Australia doesn't want traditional people to know anything about themselves or their own history, so it made a big difference to me when Peter Tosh popped up. That's when I started getting curious. A lot of singers are going to say that 'songs do not change the universe', but that's not true. That's something else that Peter Tosh taught me, because songs *can* change the world. They can change individuals, who then change the world around them. The man was so politically aware, and that's where I got the teaching from – from singers like him and Bob Marley, who show you how to get to a point where there's no turning back..."

No Fixed Address opened for Peter at the Myer Music Bowl in Melbourne on March 14, and then Adelaide's Thebarton Theatre four days later. Bart didn't spend a lot of time hanging out with him, yet still got a sense of where Peter was coming from.

"I felt like I'd met him already, because he reminded me of people I'd known in the boys' home. I'd just started on my music adventure back then, and I was still learning how to be a performer. What Peter Tosh had, coming from the kind of background he did and making all that powerful music, that's what I wanted. I felt we were the same. I wasn't taken away from Africa and forced into slavery like the Jamaicans were but it felt like that, even though I was living in my own country. And that's another thing, because our land and our culture is very old. It stretches back many thousands of years and I think that's what Peter loved about Australia. He saw that our music came from a similar cultural imagination as his own, and it had a tradition. Everybody can see it in you, and hear it in what you're singing about. That's what's different about artists like us. We sing for the people."

Shows in Perth – at the Entertainment Centre on March 21 – and Brisbane's Festival Hall followed. Peter then travelled to Australia's Gold Coast for a date at the Play Room on March 25 before heading for Canberra and Newcastle, where he finished the tour with a near capacity show at the Civic Theatre three days later. Attendances had been good from the start, aided by a television documentary called *Peter Tosh On Tour*. Peter also filmed the video for 'Johnny B. Goode' whilst he was in Australia. Director Michael C. Collins had flown out from Los Angeles and driven three days through the outback to meet with Peter.

"It was in the middle of nowhere, at a remote hotel. Initially he wouldn't look at me," Collins will later tell Roger Steffens. "He just stood in the corner with his dark glasses on whilst Donald Kinsey, his guitarist, did the talking. I explained my concept – that 'Johnny B. Goode' is a story about a young boy striving for success. That's how I came up with the image of the boy racing the train in the video. I said I'd had a dream the night before in which I saw Peter as a white ibis flying over the ocean. Hearing this Tosh suddenly stirred, announcing in portentous tones, 'The Mystic Man told me I was a white bird flying over the ocean!'"

Collins had his total co-operation from that moment onwards and says Peter did everything asked of him, including lying on his back by the edge of the ocean.

The resulting video will convey both message and mood, and whilst the Australian landscape is hardly the rural Jamaica portrayed in Peter's lyrics, it's beautifully filmed. 'Johnny B. Goode' will be among the first set of videos by black artists to get regular exposure on MTV, and proved that Peter didn't need the Rolling Stones to compete at the highest level. Unfortunately he missed out on a visit to an Aboriginal settlement because of his filming commitments, and was then dismayed by what he heard of the trip.

"We went without him and they all came to meet us but what we saw, it hurt us real bad," says his cousin Carlton. "The level of drinking really surprised us because I remember this big bottle of beer cost next to nothing – maybe about a shilling and so they all drank hard. The alcohol abuse was something else. It's like the people's spirit get broken, like a bad heart."

In telling *Black Echoes'* Mark Kamba of the Aborigines' social problems, Peter claims, "It's all part of the white man's scheme to really wipe them out in this time." The pair met at a flat in Earl's Court, since Tosh had flown straight to London after leaving Australia. Kamba arrived to find him deciding on the album credits for *Mama Africa*, and notes how there was "an aura of discipline" in the place.

"An audience with Peter Tosh means at least partial submission to his rigorous standards, as no cigarette smoking will be tolerated," he writes. "In the kitchen is a stack of empty mineral water bottles and from time to time, Peter reaches for one of a variety of health drinks containing everything good for your body, from iron extract to ginseng. On the floor under the table are two fermenting root mixtures from yard. Strong stuff, strong enough to send a cork flying through the air like a high velocity bullet. BOOM!! Very conspicuous in the front room is the infamous unicycle. Peter really is at the peak of his fitness, both physically and mentally, Jah know."

Kamba mentions how Peter's latest single, 'Johnny B. Goode', seems at odds with his philosophy of music being "a schoolroom", and intended "to teach the youths what is hidden from them".

"Commercialism," Peter replies. "That is a tune that will get radio play and sell and make money. I man have to make money."

He's then goaded into defending himself from accusations that he's sold out. "Can I go where I want to go without money?" he yells, springing to his feet. "Can I dress good without money? Can I buy a house without money? Can I cut an LP without money? Can I buy studio time without money? I want *my* money, billions and trillions. Let me tell you something. When some white journalist asks me some primitive question about what I want money for and what am I going to do with it, it's like the old times when a man catch you with $25 and it was like, 'Where you get so much money nigger? You must have stolen it.' It's like he's supposed to have money and me nah have none. You want to see me give away money I don't even have... Every day in Kingston, man stop me from when they see my briefcase and say, 'Peter, gimme a five dollar Rasta.' Me is no superstar, no matter what them little men out there might want to tell you..."

Lloyd Bradley, writing for *NME*, fared even worse and in his own words, had to "pack up and flee" after Peter gave him short shrift. The only surprise is that Bradley lasted as long as he did after calling 'Nothing But Love' "an amateurish soul record" and stating that Tosh left the Wailers "just as they were hitting the big time. "There is something disconcerting about sitting with a man who, when he bothers to listen to you, is hell bent on intimidating you," he writes, before opining that 'Johnny B. Goode' is "nowhere near as good" as Musical Youth's 'Pass The Dutchie'. Granted, it didn't sell as many copies, yet 'Johnny B. Goode' did reasonably well after entering the UK charts on April 2, 1983 and staying there five weeks, peaking at number 48. If *Top Of The Pops* had wanted him on the show it would have been during that first week and yet there's no record of him ever appearing, despite taping something in readiness.

"We actually did a session with him for *Top Of The Pops* – not on the television, because we just recorded it in the studio," says Tony "Gad" Robinson, bass player with Aswad, who backed him that day. "Because of the Musicians Union, you weren't allowed to use the records when you played on *Top Of The Pops*. You had to keep the musicians here in England in work so when Peter Tosh had a hit with 'Johnny B. Goode', he came in the studio with us and we did the recording for *Top Of The*

Pops. At first, he said the track was a bit slow. He said, 'Listen, you can make it one fast quicker. Just one fast.' We all just looked at him with blank faces, thinking, 'What's he talking about?' He said it as he was heading for the door and we just didn't get it at first. We just thought, 'Say what?' Then the penny dropped and we laughed, because only a yardman could say it like that. It was just so off-the-cuff – not *too* fast, but *one* fast. It was perfect, and he really couldn't have said it any better."

Peter knew that 'Johnny B. Goode' wasn't right for the Caribbean market and so released 'Glass House' instead, which had already made waves on 12″. Now available as an Intel Diplo 7″, it had entered the JBC Top 20 soon after his return home and earned him a slot on local weekly television show *Where It's At*, where he shared a bill with Judy Mowatt and Native – a band from the north coast managed by Danny Sims, and featuring the brothers Wayne and Brian Jobson. Peter welcomed JBC's support since he faced stiff competition in Jamaica. Bob Marley's 'Buffalo Soldiers' sat at number one, but was already under pressure from Dennis Brown's 'Revolution', Sly & Robbie's 'Unmetered Taxi' and Gregory Isaacs' 'Night Nurse'.

In May, Island released the first posthumous Bob Marley album, *Confrontation*, just as Peter's *Mama Africa* hit the stores. This was an ill-timed move, and would inevitably lead to further comparisons between the two. Even the sleeve designs were similar. Both traded on mythology and featured illustrations, rather than photographs. Marley is depicted as St. George slaying the dragon, whilst Mervin Palmer's watercolour is, as he describes, of Peter with his arms around a map of Africa that doubles as a regal looking black woman – one who definitely resembles Marlene. This latest album has just nine tracks and three of them – 'Peace Treaty', 'Maga Dog' and 'Stop That Train' – are from the *Wanted Dread & Alive* sessions. The latter two are re-recordings of old songs and yet there's undeniable cohesion to *Mama Africa*, which some regard as Peter's best-ever album. The title track is so joyful, despite its anti-colonial sentiments, whilst 'Not Gonna Give It Up' wouldn't have sounded at all out of place on *Equal Rights*. It would also take serious prejudice to dismiss 'Johnny B. Goode' and 'Where You Gonna Run', except it never paid to overestimate rock critics.

Lloyd Hollet called the album "Tosh dross" and gave it two stars. He then accused Peter of having built "a surprisingly long-lasting career out of co-writer credits for 'Get Up Stand Up' and a blustering ego. For all his protestations to the contrary, his music has long lacked any sort of substantial message, being built instead on a limited string of philosophical and verbal clichés."

What arrogance! And there's more... The title track is said to be the sort of "slick rock and reggae that pleases precious few serious followers of either style" and "does nothing to reverse the slide into predictable mediocrity. OK, it might succeed in getting radio-play where most other reggae doesn't, but who listens to radio any more anyway?"

Thankfully plenty of New Yorkers did, and the hippest among them tuned into radio station WBAI, which still broadcasts from an address on Wall Street. A genial Rastaman named Habte Selassie hosted a late night show called *Labrish*, which is the Jamaican term for "gossip". Peter will make several appearances on this programme over the next few months, starting in May 1983. One of his first tasks was to voice a radio announcement: "Hello there, this is Peter Tosh reminding you that if you're down and out and in frustration and suffering from financial inflation, just switch your station to WBAI and it'll keep you high."

After such ringing endorsement he then answers questions about the new album. "It's a long time *Mama Africa* has been crying out inside of me," he begins. "During that period of time, when my heart was crying out loudly towards Africa, I scientifically and automatically find myself in Africa, and that is what helped to motivate that song. I found myself standing on the soils of Africa, walking through the atmospheres of Africa, feeling the sunshine of Africa and meeting the people of Africa, and feeling the whole spiritual vibration, the cultural vibration of Africa. I don't know how many songs that must have motivated. I went there for the first time about a year ago, could be less, and I am hoping to go back there right now."

"But why the long wait for the album?" asks Habte, who's a fellow member of the Ethiopian Orthodox Church.

"Good things come to those who wait," Peter replies. "Look how long you wait for Jesus and He don't come yet."

A representative of the African National Congress joins them at one point, and reiterates that artists should refrain from any cultural collaboration or co-operation with South Africa. Habte asks Peter for his reaction and gets a typically forthright response.

"It is my pleasure to go to South Africa and to sing for people who are oppressed by the shit-stem, because they are my people, seen? The music that I sing is designed to relieve the pressures of the mind and so it would be my greatest pleasure to play there, but at the same time there are organisations that would have branded me as being... I don't know the names they would call me, whether an illegal or illegitimate, but they would have some form of name where I would be branded for life and I can't afford that, because I know my hopes and my aspirations and intentions and determinations.

"When it comes to America, the Ku Klux Klan is legal, seen? And there are many organisations like that which say, 'keep America white'. And if you go to England it's the same thing, or to Germany... Everywhere you go it is the same thing. It may look a little prettier, but the discriminations are there, seen? And the racial injustices within the regimes are there, and yet still I go and play in these places. These guys go to South Africa every weekend and yet still a guy can tell me I cannot go to South Africa to play for *my* people."

A few months earlier, after Sharon Smithline had pointed out he could always go as an honorary white, he said he'd been offered "that bullshit title" already and would rather visit as an honorary black.

"What am I gonna do? Leave my black skin here? Can you imagine going to your own black country and you cannot be accepted there because of mercenaries who say that South Africa is white? The reason why I sang a song called 'Fight Against Apartheid' is because I was watching the news and they were showing what was going on in South Africa. I saw four little black children coming from school, and a Jeep passing by. When the Jeep slowed the youths held up their hands and said, 'Power'. And one of the guys in the Jeep shot down the four youths and just drove slowly on. That brought tears from my ankle, so you can imagine if I was actually there?"

The last hour of Habte's show consists of a phone-in and whilst Peter refuses to answer questions about Mick Jagger, he's generally good-natured. To a surfer who can scarcely believe his luck at speaking with Peter Tosh he says, "Go with a waterproof walk man." Another caller then asks him what he thinks of Yellowman, who's now a major star in Jamaica. "Yellowman?" Peter responds. "He's yellow, and very yellow too."

Dancehall music had taken over in Jamaica thanks to a new generation of acts who'd made their reputations on local sound systems. It wasn't so much their lack of craft Peter disapproved of, but the "slack" or bawdy lyrics that MCs like Yellowman specialised in. These youngsters hadn't

367

been raised on the same diet of Rastafari and Black Nationalism that artists like Peter had, and so their ambitions were a lot less altruistic. The reason they were so popular in Jamaica is because they sang about everyday life – warts and all – for the poorer classes. They weren't preaching religion to them or berating them. Also most of these singers were still living in ghetto communities, whereas many of the more successful roots artists had moved uptown or left Jamaica altogether.

Peter was in danger of being mistaken for one of them. After a lengthy search, he'd bought an apartment at 382 Central Park West on 97th Street, just five minutes from Central Park. At first sight, it was an unlikely resting place for a Jamaican legend. Central Park West is a large, imposing apartment block made of red brick. The well-kept gardens are populated by shrubs and flowers, and crowned by a Japanese maple. Yew hedges run along the perimeter whilst inside the spacious lobby is a concierge's desk, offering an uninterrupted view of who's coming in and out. Only a handful of the flats have balconies but there's spacious car parking at the back, next to the residents' play and recreation areas. Peter's done well for himself. He's now living in a decent Manhattan location, close to his favourite health food shops and restaurants, and that's handy enough for studios, venues and rehearsal facilities although his "L" shaped studio flat is far from ostentatious. Friends recall seeing a large portrait of Haile Selassie I on the wall and various musical instruments strewn about the place, awaiting their owner's touch. Peter also owned a statuette of the Madonna, which surprised Habte Selassie, who visited him there several times.

Peter joined him in the WBAI studios again on June 1 and gave the most in-depth interview of his entire career. The difference is down to respect – respect for Peter's Rasta faith and also his art. He talks about the piano lessons he had as a child and after claiming that reading and writing music are "the greatest things", intimates that the music he's making now "is limited".

"I just play by ear now. I feel out the chords and make lots of mistakes on the keyboard. I don't play it like I did when I was 13. That was the music I loved but I know that one day very soon, when I clean out myself physically and make myself whole again... Because I've been going through so much aggravation, humiliation and police brutality, but it's not lost so it cannot be found. It's just lost inside of me and the time will come very soon when I find that spot where the music lies and then it will be incredible, seen?"

He sheds light on how he writes songs, whether by playing around on the keyboard and guitar, or creating lyrics from something he's overheard. "I don't have to sit down and do any specific thing for me to motivate the creation of a song," he tells Habte. "It's a thing that just flows and any time I sit down, the first thing that comes out of my mind is music."

He then explains his approach to recording, as outlined in previous chapters except with one important addition. "After those foundations have been laid down, you call the musicians to the studio, play them the tape, get them to listen and then it is very easy for them to know what to play, seen? Except there are some internal sounds that are impossible to hear, and you have to *feel* them. And it's not everyone who makes the music can feel it."

Habte signs off by thanking Peter for his time and the appreciation's clearly mutual. "These kinds of interview are very important because people need the facts," his guest counters. "There is too much fiction, too much propaganda and too much public mischief, y' no see?"

Peter's referring to Timothy White's recent book *Catch A Fire: The Life Of Bob Marley*, which continued to receive a great deal of publicity. In a lengthy article for US publication *Trouser Press* headed "Tough Tosh", Peter is quoted as saying, "I just *heard* about the biography, but these guys want to promote Bob Marley even more than Emperor Haile Selassie I and that's why Bob Marley is where he is today, seen?"

"Before our meeting, everyone I'd spoken to shared a vague sense of discomfort about Peter Tosh," writes John Walker. "He was too full of himself, and a tough nut to crack. Even the publicist who arranged the interview gave me a mildly distracted pep talk about how Peter may come over as a little spacey, but he's really a lovely fellow. The thing is, for every minute you spend with the Steppin' Razor you get two with Ward Cleaver in dreadlocks."

Ward Cleaver was a character in the American television series *Leave It To Beaver*, who ends each episode dispensing moral instruction to his sons. A movie version was screened in 1983. The comparison would be lost on Peter, who noting the Michelob beer in Walker's hand, says, "You cannot understand Rastafari and drink beer. I live higher spiritually than you." No wonder Walker writes that, "Nine out of ten people would call Peter Tosh arrogant." Tosh himself admits that, "Most people don't want to deal with me because they say I'm hostile. Some people say I'm arrogant.

Them have all different names to class me as and most people who hear these things are in fear to even talk to me so with that, I get around." Cryptically, he claims to know psychology and to have learnt how to be "absent in my presence".

Walker must have winced when Peter says he was Bob Marley's teacher, and is rewarded by a veritable tirade. "Eighty percent of the songs Bob Marley wrote were co-written by me and never credited. And not only co-written, but musically architected by me because I *am* the music, and I *was* the music. When I first met Bob Marley he played no instrument, so he did not know how to design a song. He could only sing out of his mouth, but the world don't want to accept that shit, seen? They want to keep me in the back and keep Bunny Wailer in the back like we were doing *nothing*, and were just two baggages. *That's why I have to write my book!* And when my book is written, then they will know."

Peter is still smarting over Marley's betrayal after colluding with Chris Blackwell and renaming his backing band the Wailers, thus relegating the group he shared with Peter and Bunny to a virtual afterthought.

"It's like he wasn't concerned about that. Maybe that was his *intention* because nothing was said after he saw what was done, seen? I wouldn't know if he *helped* them to create it, but he accepted the fact that they divided us. He said nothing about it, so silence is *consent*."

Walker then raises the subject of the Rolling Stones, whom Peter accuses of "inhumane treatment". He says that if he hadn't have been prepared for their treachery he would have been left "exhausted and frustrated", and feels the records he made for them were "wilfully or accidentally under-promoted and incorrectly marketed".

"When him and Keith Richards got into it and they decided they weren't going to deal with Peter any more EMI took him over because remember, he started living in Keith Richards' house, he wouldn't move out and then the police got involved, but it was all to do with money because he claimed they'd robbed him," says Janet Davidson. "There was no proof of that but the thing is, record companies make more money than the artists and that's what happens. The Stones spent a lot of money on Peter. He opened up for them for nothing during that tour in the States and it was a great opportunity for him. It introduced him to a lot more people but he never really understood how it could open doors for him. He never appreciated it, and he acted like *he* was the one doing Mick

Jagger a favour. That's how Peter was. He was arrogant but he honestly believed it. Also, EMI wouldn't have taken him on if they hadn't believed he'd do well, and he did have some excellent people around him like Bert Cordell, who was his business manager in the States, and this lawyer from Texas who was really, really good. Everybody involved with him was very professional..."

Peter's interview with Walker was cut short so he could appear on local NBC-TV News. *Live At Five* presenter Sue Simmons is African-American but in Walker's words, "Isn't about to ditch her plum co-anchor spot for repatriation". Peter sits on a couch wearing impenetrable shades and picks out flamenco-style runs on his guitar whilst she shows a clip of 'Johnny B. Goode'. He looks bored. After calling Simmons "my dear" in a patronising tone of voice he then sounds off about the "shit-stem", whereupon she hastily concludes their interview.

Was Peter Tosh his own worst enemy? Possibly, but at least he wasn't two-faced, even if he did lack manners at times. His behaviour is now increasingly marked by anger and impatience. He could well have been in a lot of discomfort – not only from frequent headaches, but also his ulcer and other physical aches and pains which never seemed to go away, no matter what remedies he tried. He was also suffering from exhaustion and yet had a lengthy tour to complete, beginning on July 6 at New York's Pier 84. A group of indignant people tried to get in without paying, and so the gate was slammed shut in a panic. This meant that ticket holders couldn't get in either and so mayhem ensued before it was opened once more. Four days later and he was back in New Haven, Connecticut – not to play Toad's Place this time, but the Agora Ballroom. He then travelled to Pittsburgh where he played at the Stanley Theatre on July 12. This was the same venue where Bob had given his last-ever performance and the atmosphere was predictably muted that night – not during the actual gig, but among the musicians. After a first appearance at the University of Vermont, Chicago then welcomed them with open arms. The Aragon Ballroom was full to overflowing that warm summer's night on July 15, after 4,500 revellers had crowded onto the 'L' train heading for the Uptown district. It was a fabulous venue, designed to look like the courtyard of a Moorish castle. To reach the dance floor, customers had to mount a thickly carpeted grand staircase flanked by large plaster dragons. Once inside, their eyes were inexorably drawn towards the ceiling, where twinkling lights and painted

371

palm trees gave the impression of being under a Spanish sky. The key word was elegance, and Heavy Manners were again the support act.

"We were playing in our hometown and had a pretty good following," says lead singer Kate Fagan. "I remember seeing Peter watching us from the side of the stage. We'd played with him a year or two earlier and I think he really liked us. He seemed to enjoy the atmosphere around the dressing room and he had good feelings for Chicago as well, because it's such a political city. We were the top band in that scene, and relieved that Peter Tosh really liked the idea of mixing punk and reggae with politics. That was something dear to his heart and I think that's why he felt this kinship with us. We were tenacious and scrappy in some ways, and he was living that. I remember this feeling that we were just waiting to be discovered. We'd been working up to that in all honesty. We wanted to record an album and had half a dozen or so songs ready but we needed an outside producer, and reckoned Peter could give us an interesting sound and also give us some credibility as a band, since he was so established in reggae and on the international scene. We were managed by this attorney from Chicago called Linda Mensch at the time. Peter had told his record company he liked us so Linda made an approach, firstly to EMI and then Peter himself about coming to Chicago and producing us."

Linda Mensch was (and still is) a top entertainment lawyer based in Chicago. She confirms that Heavy Manners were a top draw in and around Chicago, but needed the help of a major label to progress.

"It was a real frustration for me. I had the ears of people working at major labels because I was also representing the Ohio Players who were very successful, and Cheap Trick who were selling millions of records... I had a sense of what was going to be a hit and yet nothing was happening for Heavy Manners. That's how Peter got to be involved because I finally said, 'Let's hire a producer'. We'd been thinking of who we could bring in that could take them to the next level. We knew that a pop producer wasn't going to be the right thing for them and there was a movement at the time for white reggae bands."

It'll take a couple of months for the arrangements to be made, but Peter agreed to return to Chicago later in the year and produce Heavy Manners' debut album. Whilst he ran his own label and also his own sessions, it would be stretching the point to call him a producer. He may have been swayed by Bunny's success with Marcia Griffiths, since their latest release

'Electric Boogie' had already sparked a dance craze and was a massive hit in the Caribbean and elsewhere. It would be something for Peter to think about as the *Mama Africa* tour continued to Minneapolis and then Texas, where dates in Austin and Houston awaited.

Even as Peter continued to be derided by (mainly) white critics, the black community hailed him as a powerful spokesman for their concerns. This wasn't widely reported at the time and yet Peter understandably felt very proud whenever such recognition came his way. On July 29, shortly before playing at the Agora Ballroom in Atlanta, Mayor Maynard Jackson presented him with the keys to the city at a ceremony attended by several hundred people including local media figures. Why is it that such honours were rarely reported by rock journalists, who preferred to disparage him at every opportunity? Was there a hidden racist agenda behind their actions, or were they just poorly informed? The instant access to news afforded by the Internet was still a long way off but you still can't help feeling that where Peter Tosh was concerned, the script was already written. Two days later he was in Washington, at the Constitution Hall. This was the same venue where, ten years earlier, riots had broken out after Sly & The Family Stone had threatened to cancel. The Daughters of the American Revolution, who owned the place, had reacted by banning all rock concerts for months yet Peter's visit went ahead without complaint, despite his usual antics with a spliff and some choice remarks about "the shit-stem".

On August 2 and 3, the Police headlined two shows at the Montreal Forum. They were now one of the biggest bands in the world, and regularly performed to stadium-sized audiences. As they prepared to play at the Forum, expectation was at fever pitch. In Andy Summers' own words, the desire "to be near us or see us spreads like an epidemic. Emotions run high and male and female fans alike dissolve into tears when and if they get anywhere near us. We have become the locus of a huge projection, the recipients of a collective fantasy. The only comparison we can imagine at this point is the Beatles."

MTV, still only in its second year, had been promoting them all summer long. Their latest single, 'Every Breath You Take', had sat atop the *Billboard* charts for two months and the *Synchronicity* album was outselling even Michael Jackson. They'd come a long way since supporting Peter at the Pink Pop Festival in Holland, when they'd cowered in the corner of the dressing room and were too shy to speak with him or the other musicians.

The tables had now been turned, and Peter wasn't enjoying the experience all that much.

"Peter's career has slowed down a little but with the death of Bob Marley and Bunny Wailer's consistent refusal to tour, he's still the biggest reggae star in the world," reported Garry Steckles of the *Caribbean Times*. "He's booked as part of a massive package coming into the Olympic Stadium along with Stevie Ray Vaughan, Talking Heads and the Police. Peter thinks he should be given second place on the billing, appearing just before the Police and is far from amused when he finds out he's got to go on before Talking Heads. He sulks in the afternoon and there's no sign of him when Word, Sound & Power take the stage. They go into their opening number and play, and play, and play... 'Where's Peter?' everyone keeps asking. The crowd, something like 50,000 strong, is getting restless. I'm at the rear of the massive stage, right in the middle of the cavernous stadium and after what seems like an eternity we spot a stretch limousine emerge from one of the tunnels at the back of the playing field. It heads to the side of the stage and Tosh, spliff in hand, emerges a little unsteadily. He looks around and starts to walk away from the stage. Yells of 'Peter! Peter!' don't get his attention and roadies are dispatched to steer him back towards the stage. The concert wasn't one of his best. It was the last time I saw Peter alive..."

During an appearance on Canadian television, he told presenter Laurie Brown that he sees himself "as a preacher, a teacher", and says reggae has the greatest potential of any genre, but suffers from having been branded political. He's wearing a T-shirt with "TRULY" written across it and has an electronic keyboard on his lap. Brown asks him, "If someone was to say to you, 'Peter Tosh, tomorrow you will be a dead man...'"

"If a guy tell me that tomorrow, *he* will be going in the coffin and not me," snaps Peter. "Because that is one of the secrets of life – to know how to live, and how to counteract the negative forces of death. Many people search, but their search takes them to the grave. My search takes me to life and there is no man on earth that can threaten me and create any amount of fear inside of me because my search teaches me to kill death, to frustrate frustration, to mad madness and to assassinate the assassinator. Spiritually, not physically and without a hand move or my eyes squint – only with the meditation of the mind."

Ann Arbor, Michigan and Cleveland come and go before a show at the Hollywood Palladium, shared with Jimmy Cliff. After journeying up the

Peter first began learning martial arts as a teenager, and would regularly incorporate karate moves into his stage act.

Peter with his M16 guitar, 1983. PIERRE TERRASON/DALLE/ICONICPIX

A reflective Mystic Man, with ganja pipe. PICTORIAL PRESS/ALAMY

Peter demonstrating support for the Palestinian cause – an act that would bring recriminations in its wake – not least when he appeared at the No Nukes Concert at Madison Square Garden in New York. RICHARD E. AARON/REDFERNS

Peter performing in Brooklyn. CHUCK PULIN

Relaxing with friends in New York. ADRIAN BOOT/URBANIMAGE.TV

The Bush Doctor in familiar pose, performing with a spliff in his mouth. ADRIAN BOOT/URBANIMAGE.TV

Lee Jaffe and Peter, 1976. LEE JAFFE

Peter and Rasta brethren, with chalice. FIKISHA CUMBO

Peter's funeral, National Arena, Kingston, 1987. JOHNNIE BLACK/URBANIMAGE.TV

Andrew Tosh, in concert at Wetlands, NYC 1990. STEVE EICHNER/WIREIMAGE

Above and below: Scenes from Peter's mausoleum in Belmont, Westmoreland. KEVIN CUMMINS/GETTY IMAGES

A reminder of how Babylon system continues to enslave us. PETER MAZEL/SUNSHINE/RETNA PICTURES

West coast to Seattle, he then returns to California on August 17 and joins Doug Wendt on San Francisco radio programme *Midnight Dread*. Doug tells him he's never yet received promo copies of Peter's records from Columbia, Rolling Stones Records or EMI despite being one of the few DJs in America to host a commercial reggae show. He also mentions how these major labels will spend $20,000 on an ad in *Playboy* magazine, whilst ignoring the network of grassroots press and radio people.

"Yeah, I know the shituation," says Peter wearily. "I am tired of that but this is the last year of me being treated that way, seen? And it's a pity that the few fans I have here in the western hemisphere won't be seeing me no bombaclaat more because I am tired of being abused, seen?"

This is the first indication that Peter's planning on retiring from touring for a while. He's then asked about 'Steppin' Razor', which had been credited to Peter but was now being contested by Joe Higgs, who said no one over six feet tall could have written it.

"I never take the credit for it," Peter assures him, "but as I told Joe's lawyer when he wrote me and told me about that, no man under six foot short could administer that song either 'cause until it was done by me, Joe would not be tough enough to identify himself with that song."

Peter handed the publishing of 'Steppin' Razor' back to Joe Higgs without a murmur. He liked and respected Joe, and hadn't deliberately falsified the credits – it had been someone from the record company who'd assumed that Peter had written the song. Whilst still in California, he heard how JLP supporters had stoned dub poet Michael Smith to death after he'd argued with a government minister at a political rally in Kingston. This killing offered further proof of how dangerous it can be to speak out and criticise the authorities in Jamaica. Peter knew this from personal experience of course, but had felt the shock waves all the way from Berkeley, where he and Dennis Brown played the Community Theatre on August 19. He'd visited Berkeley station KALX-FM that same afternoon and told presenter Mel Cheplowitz that the music industry didn't respect reggae "because it's Rasta music, and they're trying to corroborate it with smoking ganja and make it look like it is illegal, dangerous and the most deadly element that ever exist. If a man commit murder, he would get away but if you smoke herb, you will be sent to hell for 400 years."

"What is public opinion like in Jamaica regarding the legalisation of marijuana?" he's asked.

"The public have no opinion," he sneers. "They see so many things to say but they're not saying and then when I say now, they say I say too much, seen?"

He then announces that, "this is my final extensive tour because there's much more work to be done and lots of artists to be produced that have never been heard yet." There's no mention of Heavy Manners, only a 17-year-old singer he'd recently met in New York called "Philip Wonder" (who subsequently disappeared without trace).

On Sunday August 21, he headlined the First Annual Santa Barbara Reggae Sunsplash at the County Bowl. Dennis Brown again shared the bill. Three days later Peter made the front cover of the *Santa Barbara News & Review*, next to the headline "The Rasta Wisdom Of Peter Tosh".

Interviewer Wayne Newton asks him if he's been making money and "if so, what are you doing with it?"

"That is your assumption and I cannot bother to think about it," retorts Peter. "What I make is just hand to mouth and to keep myself alive."

Newton then asks him, "Why did you become a musician?'

"I didn't become a musician," he replies. "I was *born* a musician."

So far so good, but when Newton broaches the subject of Jack Anderson, Peter doesn't even let him finish his sentence. "Jack Anderson is full of shit!" he cries. "He's a vampire!!" Earlier in the year, Jack Anderson had warned readers of the *Washington Post* and *Philadelphia Daily News* that "terrorism experts believe that racist Marxist-tinged criminal elements of the Rastafarian cult, already armed to the teeth, will begin striking at American political targets in the next few years."

Hollywood will later reinforce such views with the film *Marked For Death* which sociologist Randal L. Hepner says "presented Rastafari as a crazed and murderous black magic-like cult controlling illicit crack and cocaine distribution". Hepner has also documented how US prison authorities "treated Rastas as drug-crazed cultists. All were forced to undergo a humiliating shave and haircut, which typically resulted in physical confrontations and long periods in solitary confinement. No provision was made for their dietary needs, and nor did they have access to any cultural programmes. By the mid-eighties, more than 2,000 Rastafarians were behind bars in New York's state correctional facilities and scores more languished in state and federal prisons around the country." By way of conclusion, he urged researchers to "look through and beyond reggae to the wellsprings of creativity contained within the Rastafarian movement in its confrontation with the modern world."

Hepner's was the rare voice of reason, since many thought differently. Three years earlier, *60 Minutes*' Dan Rather had portrayed Rastafari as a multi-national drug smuggling corporation that used religious beliefs to conceal its illicit narcotics-importing activity – a view also shared by the New York City Police Department, which issued a confidential report headed Rasta Crime which states, "Many of the Rastas in this country tend to stray from their (religious) tenets and engage in criminal activity, using their religious doctrines as a cover for their criminal activities." It goes on to suggest Rastafarians have "a propensity for violence" that's related to "heavy ingestion of marijuana", and claims the movement has been infiltrated by "Marxist groups, revolutionary Cuban terrorists and violent, pro-People's National Party forces. Cult members were being sent to Havana for extensive training in guerrilla warfare and graduating above the level of street crimes." It then laments how "the absence of available Federal funds and limited manpower restricts efforts to wage a full-scale campaign against the Rastafarians." Finally, law enforcement officers were warned that, "Most of the Rastafarians are armed and will kill to avoid detection or apprehension. They believe in reincarnation and do not fear death. They pose a definite threat to any police officer they come in contact with."

Chapter 27

Heavy Manners

Even as his faith was being laid to waste, Peter prepared to play one of the more important shows of his career, at the Greek Theatre in Los Angeles. Dennis Brown opened for him, backed by We The People and the same brass section that had played on *Wanted Dread & Alive*. Following Brown always seemed to bring out the best in Peter, whose performance will result in an album and film called *Captured Live*.

"One of the reasons that album is so hot is because Copeland Forbes told us that EMI were going to drop us if we didn't kick ass!" says Brown's guitarist Andy Bassford. "Dean Fraser goaded us and we blew the roof off, which is why the Greek Theatre doesn't have one today! (It's an open-air venue.) Nobody liked following We The People anyway and so Word, Sound & Power really had to throw it down when the tapes started rolling, which is what they did. Peter Tosh had a great band and it was good fun touring with them. He used to come out and watch us from the side of the stage a lot, before getting ready for his own show."

Michael C. Collins was again hired as film director. He told Roger Steffens that he saw Peter as an evangelist for Rasta. "His songs tell his life story, revealing how he sighted Rasta. I saw him as a figure in a tent show and that's how I wanted to put him across. That's why much of what we shot was looking up at him. He was truly larger than life.

"I wanted to use smoke but the Greek objected to that so we put sticks of incense all around the back of the stage, which we had to keep lit throughout the show. My concept was that the film should have no dissolves. I wanted you to go into his world and become part of the music, with a jazzy structure to the filming so I hired the very best cameramen in Hollywood, people you didn't need to give constant directions to."

Dayton "Bones" Howe, whose credits included Elvis Presley's 1968 NBC-TV Special, supervised the live recording. In a few years' time he'll become Vice-President of Columbia Pictures, which goes to show the level of expertise involved in the making of this project. Front-row seats at the Greek that hot summer night on August 23 cost $13.95 – those at the back were five dollars cheaper – and will be worth every cent. Dennis Brown was hailed as the reggae Crown Prince, and many of his songs had been massive hits in Jamaica. The crowd loved him, but it was then time for a different kind of reggae experience. Out of the darkness came a spotlight on the drums, and the sound of a heartbeat. It was as if Santa's kit was breathing, like a living organism. After an opening 'Creation', Peter walked on stage dressed in full-length yellow robes and Arab headdress, gripping an Ethiopian cross in his right hand. At times like this, Peter Tosh looks majestic, and yet he's funny with it. Note how he lists countries like "Germs–many" and "Taitwo" (instead of Taiwan) on 'African'. Whatever the nature of his inner struggles, he's still a compelling figure. The crowd cheers when he flashes his dreadlocks, just before a sonorous organ introduces 'Rastafari Is'. Michael C. Collins' vision of Peter as a preacher suddenly lurches into focus except rather than whipping up his congregation, this one's busily reaching into the folds of his robes and fishing out a spliff large as a carrot, which he then lights up on stage. It's an act that still seems daring, especially with the cameras rolling.

The music's really grooving now. Donald Kinsey isn't such a showman as Daryl Thompson was, but he's burning on songs like 'Rastafari Is', 'Where You Gonna Run' and 'Johnny B. Goode'. The music takes on a reverential hue during the former as Peter and Vision sit side-by-side, playing conga drums painted red, green and gold. There's a message for "baldheads" to respect the Rastaman on 'Glass House', which may be in response to Jack Anderson although Peter's not leaving it there, since this triggers one of his impromptu rants. After complaining that reggae is being starved of promotion – a situation he says embarrasses him – he then warns the audience they are headed for World War Three. "*You*, not *we* because the Rastaman has been fighting the first, second and third world wars from before they ever started."

This speech will be missing from the *Captured Live* film, as will 'Legalise It', 'Bush Doctor', 'Don't Look Back', 'Buk-In-Hamm Palace' and 'Mama Africa'. There were time restrictions to consider, but omitting Tosh's finest herb anthems and also two of his best fusion tracks must have been a hard call to make.

Eric Olsen interviewed Peter on August 24, and titled his article 'The Shit-stem'. "I met with Tosh the day after a magnificent performance at the Greek Theatre in Los Angeles. As I approached Tosh's Hollywood hotel room, incense billowed out from under the door. As the photographer and I entered the room, several members of Tosh's entourage lolled about, Jamaican-style. Tosh was renowned for giving writers - especially white writers - a hard time.

"Tosh stretched to his full 6′ 4″ height and shook his Medusa tangle of dreads, then composed himself into an alarmingly compact coil on the couch. I was seated across from Tosh, sensing that all of this was aimed at maximum intimidation. Tosh wore a preternaturally white T-shirt and sweats. He corralled his dreads under a Jamaican-style cap, put on his shades, lit five more sticks of incense and signalled his willingness to be addressed.

Why did you leave the Wailers?

"I never left myself, mon. It was belittling my integrity. I taught Bob Marley. How can you compare the teacher with the taught? I and I and the devil are at war. The devil make Marley leader of the band. I had no desire follow the path of destruction."

Are you saying that Bob Marley is a devil?

"Bob Marley is dead mon."

During the conversation, Tosh carefully cleaned, pruned and rolled a spliff the size of a banana. He lit it, blew a volcanic stream of smoke at the ceiling and smiled.

How do you like having a hit single? (He's referring to 'Johnny B. Goode'.)

"What hit single?" Peter testily replies. "A black man sells 50,000 copies and he's got a hit. The white man sells four million, and he has a hit. The ministers of the shit-stem seek to kill me spiritually, verbally and physically, so that I might be crucified like Christ and all true Christians. The shit-stem is white and black, Christian and Jew. It's a conspiracy, yah mon. It will be in my book, *Red X*. They know who they are."

Does it bother you that the majority of your American audience is white?

"Every time, mon! It is 99.9%! It is again a conspiracy to demote I. Don't feel no way. My counteraction will be lightning and earthquake."

What is your goal?

"To promote equal rights and justice for every man."

Do you offer any advice?

"Buy more reggae records. Stop smoking cigarettes and start smoking ganja. If you live the reggae beat, you will not perish from it."

"I felt my consciousness drifting to another planet," writes Olsen, who'll soon stop trying to make sense of it all. "A contact high in such an environment could only have been avoided by cessation of respiration. The incense and ganja had long since thickened the room into a Martian swirl. The smoke seemed to develop a life of its own, obscuring all of the physical Tosh save for his sunglasses. Tosh progressively resembled a Rasta Cheshire cat."

The publicity for the Greek Theatre show had promised that, "Peter Tosh could, if he so chose, claim the throne of reggae music left vacant since the passing of Bob Marley." This is probably optimistic given the level of attrition coming his way, and also his own increasingly erratic behaviour. It insinuates that he hasn't really been trying whereas Peter – not for the first time – sees himself as the victim of prejudice and conspiracy. He's especially upset over Timothy White's book *Catch A Fire* and after admitting that he didn't "know specifically what this guy wrote", dismissed it as "lies, public mischief, propaganda and defamation of my character".

"Him gonna have to pay me for that," he told Sharon Smithline. "I didn't give him permission to put anything in a book. I'm writing my own book, the whole truth about my life and when a guy like this writes these things it makes me want to go to his office, pick up one of his chairs and empty it in his head because any guy who writes these things about me, especially a white man, is trying to defame my black character.

"What they want to do is whiten reggae because all music in America started with the black man and if you check it, it's the white man who controls everything. It's the white man who says it's him who makes rock'n'roll, it's the white man who makes the blues and it's him who makes jazz. It's him who makes everything. The black man didn't do anything. Well he didn't make reggae because until now they don't know the beat of reggae. They have many groups trying to play reggae but there are things inside of reggae they cannot hear. It's so spiritual that it cannot be heard. It cannot be identified. You have to feel that thing and it cannot be written and that is why no musician, I don't care how professional he is, even if he is a professor in music, he cannot write reggae music because it has hypnotic power. It's not a music that comes today and dies tomorrow like this funky, get down and shake your booty kind of thing. Reggae music is a spiritual music and I will not sit down and have a little white guy writing all this whole heap of shit about musicians who play reggae or reggae music itself…"

Peter repeats these claims to Roger Steffens, saying that such people "haven't got the guts enough to sit down and truthfully reason with me, and to know the facts of my life, seen? Well, I am going to write some of the facts of my life because all the facts of my life cannot be written in one book. That would be an encyclopaedia, seen? But chapter one is in function right now. First Peter, chapter one."

He's made a start on his autobiography by recording his thoughts and recollections on cassettes late at night when he's alone. Extracts from these tapes will later surface in a documentary made after his death called *Stepping Razor: Red X*. They portray a man confronting his destiny, or at least seeking to understand it. Reappraisal isn't an option, although reconciliation is. During that same interview with Roger Steffens, Peter confirms that he and Bunny plan to reform the Wailers with Vision and Junior Braithwaite, although the latter has yet to confirm whether he'll be participating or not.

"What happens to the Wailers Band?" asks Roger, not unreasonably.

"The who?"

The band with Carly and Tyrone…

"What the bombaclaat you talk 'bout? Their name isn't Wailers. Are you telling me that Carly and Tyrone can sing? Well, these are things that the world still doesn't understand. There have been no other Wailers but I, seen? There are lots of impostors in this earth, and to every first there will always come a second, seen? To every reality there always comes a fantasy, seen? And the fantasy want to come and live the life of the reality and to say that, 'I am he,' but that can't work because to be a Wailer, you have to cry, seen? Because that's what it means to go through troubles and temptation, seen? Humiliations and aggravation, police brutality and how many of them go through that? How many of them have been to jail, how many of them have been humiliated and how many of them ever been executed, seen? So a man can't come claim that just because he was playing with Bob Marley, because Bob Marley wasn't the Wailers either, seen? Bob Marley was Bob Marley, seen? And that's how he wanted it to be, because it was the Wailers before the segregation came with Chris Whiteworst in London 1973, and he was the one who agreed or stimulated this idea of Bob Marley and the Wailers."

Intrepid as ever, Steffens pulls out a handful of early Wail 'N Soul 'M releases which predate any involvement with Blackwell and that are clearly labelled "Bob Marley and the Wailing Wailers."

"Well, that's where it started," says Peter.

"Even some of Lee Perry's sessions were marked "Bob Marley and the Wailers," Roger added helpfully, at which point the conversation came to a close.

The Tosh entourage was still camped in Los Angeles' Franklyn Plaza Hotel when Copeland Forbes got a call to say there was a fan in reception with a special gift for Peter. Copeland went downstairs to see him and "in his hand he clutched this guitar which was in the shape of an M-16 rifle. It was a customised Fender Stratocaster. He told me that because Peter was a freedom fighter and his music was a weapon to free Africans and to trample down apartheid, he'd personally built this guitar for him." Copeland took the fan up to Peter's room, as he knew Peter would be pleased to see him.

"The moment we walked into Peter's room and he saw the instrument his expression to me was, 'Wait. A where yuh get that bombaclaat from?' Peter called for Donald Kinsey to come and take a look. Kinsey took it from Peter and started playing it. He remarked that it was a great piece of work, well crafted, and proceeded to make a few adjustments to the fret board and the strings."

At first the fan refused to take any money for it. All he wanted was an autograph, and Copeland had to virtually force him to take some money. In an interview with *Music Times*, Peter will claim the guitar was made for him by one of his "white, musical terrorist friends". It was actually built by Bruno Coon, a veteran of southern California bands Rebel Rockers and Talk Back. Bruno will later write to Roger Steffens informing him that, "I built it, that makes me 'his white terrorist friend from the US' – a title I would never have made up for myself. I used to play the thing for a while but it seemed to scare people a bit too much. Eric from the Rebel Rockers introduced me to Third World's Cat Coore who was intrigued, but in turn introduced me to Peter who loved it and bought it on sight. I'll never forget him "coming in hot" playing that thing with the crowd cheering – context is crucial."

The following day Peter played it for the first time at a show in San Diego. He then took off for Maui before returning to the mainland for shows in Oakland and Florida. From there it was straight up the East Coast to New York and an appearance on *Late Night With David Letterman*, filmed at NBC's Studio 6A in the Rockefeller Plaza and broadcast on Thursday September 1. Letterman's show ran from Monday to Thursday and was especially popular with beery young males, which makes Peter's choice of outfit intriguing to say the least. That's because he was dressed in a white, Greek-style tunic decorated with religious iconography that may have just worked had he flashed a smile and not worn shades, but ended up making him look ridiculous. At first glance, he could have been wearing a short dress and nightcap. He even uncharacteristically fluffed a couple of lines whilst singing 'Where You Gonna Run'. What a contrast to his last appearance on *Letterman* four years earlier, when he'd treated mainstream America to fiery renditions of 'Steppin' Razor' and 'Equal Rights'. Fellow guest George Hamid did a sketch called Men And Their Vegetables, with Peter watching from the sidelines. That should give you some idea of the show's remit, except Letterman enjoyed impressive viewing figures. Peter could have made a real impact and he blew it, because here was the heir to Bob Marley's throne and he's kitted out like a rogue Rabbi holidaying in the Caribbean. Also, where was the M-16 guitar? Peter had a reputation to uphold. He was supposed to be reggae music's rebel incarnate but failed to capitalise on it, just as with some of the other opportunities that came his way.

"Had Peter been a bit more accommodating then we could have gone far but there were certain things he simply wouldn't do," says Janet Davidson. "He could have been rich but if it meant going against his principles, there was no chance of that happening. They wanted him to film commercials but he refused to do them. I remember he got offered a lot of money by Bud-Lite beer but he wouldn't even consider it. All he had to say was 'This bud's for you' but it made no difference. It was just a slogan but he didn't care. He was offered soda pop commercials too but turned them down because he drank this stuff called "roots" which had all kinds of things in it, like pimento, ganja, this leaf and that leaf... They bury it and let it ferment for years and years. It's really bitter, but he always had a bottle of that on him and wouldn't endorse anything else. Those things limited him a lot, and his career could have been a lot more lucrative than it was."

Needless to say, there was no chance of sponsorship from the world of marijuana growers, natural health foods and Rasta clothing companies back in 1983. Peter's "revenue streams" – don't you just hate that term? – will therefore be confined to record and publishing deals, and concert fees. In a world that still feeds on mythology, Peter Tosh refused to play the game or to sell out, which is exactly what his critics regularly accused him of.

He and Donald Kinsey travelled to Chicago the day after filming *Late Night With David Letterman*, where they'll produce four tracks with Heavy Manners. He was there over the Labour Day holiday weekend, September 3-5.

"We flew him in and the whole kind of circus that goes with having someone like that with you started straightaway," says Kate Fagan. "He had a couple of requirements. One of them was that he had to be driven around. We had to personally take care of him like that and also supply him with pot. That was just hilarious because one of the guys in our band was real vain about being a connoisseur when it came to such things. He had this exotic herb that he kept in a safety deposit box. It was expensive stuff, and so he was exuberant at the idea of impressing Peter. The first day we picked him up he presented Peter with this stuff... It was Thai stick, which was wonderful for that time. He couldn't wait for Peter to acknowledge how exceptional it was but Peter takes it, rolls it into one joint – all of it in the one spliff – smokes it all by himself and then the next day he came back and wanted more! We'd all chipped in to pay for the herb and were amazed he'd smoked it so fast. This band member, he almost turned white!

"Peter was with us a week and he'd arrived with his personal chef, who had to come with him as well. He called this cook his bush doctor and the whole time we were in the studio there was this fish fry going on – not out in the corridor, but in the actual control room! I'll never forget that. For the rest of that week, everything reeked of fish but after all the performance in cooking them, making trips to certain stores looking for special ingredients like spices and all of that, he'd then eat the fish heads as well. I couldn't believe it..."

Kate trained as an actor in London, which is where she'd discovered reggae. She then spent time in New York just as the Ramones, Patti Smith, Blondie and Television made their breakthrough. Once back in Chicago, she fronted the punk bands Banned and B B Spin before forming Heavy Manners with bass player Jimmy Robinson. Right from the start, they were different from most other local bands since Heavy Manners' main influences were punk and reggae, rather than rock and blues. Not only that, but several of the band members also shared a strong interest in politics.

"My dad was involved with the Equal Opportunities Commission in Washington and my African-American stepmother was Head of the FBA (Federal Bar Association), so I was brought up with all that," says Kate. "I was the organiser for Rock Against Racism here in Chicago and Frankie Hill, his father was a Jewish cantor who was very involved with Civil Rights issues as well. We were both brought up in somewhat radicalised households."

Frankie was the band's business manager, as well as their sax player. The other members were Mitch Kohlhaged (guitar), Shel Lustig (drums) and Kevin Smith, who doubled on alto sax and keyboards. Frankie would liaise between the band and their agent, local entertainment attorney Linda Mensch, who'd arranged Peter's visit and booked studio time at Chicago Recording Company. Linda would call round there after office hours to see how they were getting on and says that Peter "really wasn't all that verbal. You could only tell whether he liked something or not by studying his facial expressions. He was very quiet as I recall and seemed very spiritual – not as a proselytiser, but more like a yogi. I don't remember him making any speeches or anything like that. He would just communicate with the musicians mainly."

"Peter had a couple of people he wanted to bring in on the sessions," adds Kate. "One of them was Donald Kinsey and the other was Dennis Thompson, who used to do the live sound for Bob Marley. We didn't know either of them at the time but Peter put together this production team as it were, we went into the studio and he chose four songs. 'Say It!' was the first and that really surprised me because it's a typical woman's song. It's so personal, and kind of emotional as well. By this point I'd already spent time in Jamaica and had delved into the culture to an extent. I knew about Bob Marley and Rastafarianism but as a female I was also tuned in to wearing no make-up and being natural, but then Peter walked in looking like a gangster! He had this guitar case shaped like a Tommy gun and showed up with this Vegas showgirl type of character who looked just like a drag queen. I couldn't believe what I was seeing at first. She had these long, gold fingernails that had designs painted on them and a full-length, shiny raincoat but there I was, wearing jeans and a T-shirt..."

Donald Kinsey is credited as co-producer and plays lead on 'Say It!' – a reggae/rock passion play also known as 'Under A Mad Moon'. Kate's often been compared to Debbie Harry and 'Say It!' could easily pass for a Blondie track. It's certainly catchy enough, and ideally suited to FM airplay. Kate says that Peter really liked rock music, which none of the band had expected, and that it was his idea to do a dub version.

"He said he wanted to do a dub mix, and he and Dennis really got into that but it wasn't like he was coming up with ideas all the time. He wasn't like the fifth Beatle but he had this charismatic presence and he'd come in and then maybe suggest we did something slower, or change up the bass and guitar. He was more into the vibes of the tracks than the actual compositions and whilst he sang a little, he didn't play any instruments. He worked with the engineer a lot. He had a close relationship with Dennis Thompson so I'd say that was his main contribution but it was quite an atmosphere in there thanks to the fish fry and the ganja!"

'Waiting For You' sounds just like early Steel Pulse, but is let down by rather naïve lyrics. It's the most unlikely tribute to Peter Tosh, even if it does list a few of his songs. Kate wrote it in Peter's honour, although Frankie worked out the arrangements.

"Frankie did the music but hadn't really got any lyrics and so he asked me if I would write a song about Peter," she says. "The only line I had was, 'I was walking down the road in Kingston...' I had this vision of being in Jamaica but then I came up with all this other stuff, and mixed it in with this Earth mother type of thing. I was amazed when he sang backing vocals on it. That was so cool..."

Unsurprisingly, Peter passed on the jaunty homosexual murder ballad 'Old Man Bates' (yes, truly) but listen to the opening bars of 'Heart Of Steel' and you'll realise what had first attracted Peter to this band, since they share the same kind of infectious punk/reggae beat that groups like the Specials had made their own over in England. Punctuated by horns and snappy choruses, it's certainly feisty but there's something unconvincing about Heavy Manners. The music coming from Britain's rundown inner cities has a lot more grit to it, and their US counterparts sound studied or even corny by comparison, as heard on the Latin style romance 'Tell Me'. Heavy Manners were an accomplished band who looked and sounded good, yet they were definitely in need of an outside producer. Unfortunately Peter wasn't up to the task of helping them find the right songs or bringing out the best in them. Either he lacked the necessary skills (which is why he'd taken Donald Kinsey along with him), or maybe he just didn't feel what they were doing.

"He was a strange guy, no doubt about it," observes Kate. "I hadn't been around too many Rastafarians before that. To be honest, I got the impression that he was angry or bitter about something. We were a band who had our act together, and we felt ready at all levels but we thought he would have liked to have been able to pick and choose a little more once he'd got into a position to do something like that. He'd never shown any sign of resentment towards us, but the feeling I got from conversing with him was that he felt he should have been a bigger star and involved in bigger things maybe."

At the Greek he'd haughtily announced that, "I cannot afford to have myself wasted in these places" which suggests he wasn't exactly happy with things as they were. The man who set out to change the world is feeling tired and frustrated, and there's another European tour due to start soon. Linda Mensch confirms that Peter's team didn't help with finding Heavy Manners a deal, and says she shopped the tracks extensively without attracting too much interest.

"I must have contacted every A&R in the country. Ironically, the consensus was that Kate didn't have the vocal chops to be that special lead singer they were looking for. People didn't think the tonality of her vocals was right for that time. That was the ultimate verdict. It wasn't the songs, because she had everything else going for her. They just felt her vocals weren't happening but I doubt that would have been the case two or three years earlier. It was pretty frustrating but our planning wasn't right and that's the story of the music business. It's all about timing and perseverance, because the talent was there."

Heavy Manners never quite managed to transcend regional success, and Frankie Hill eventually issued the tracks on his own label. The band subsequently reformed, and continues to be a popular draw around Chicago. Whilst Peter had declared an interest in producing other acts –

Philip Wonder for instance – he doesn't appear to have had an agenda or major label backing. Some suggest that Marlene – who wasn't the "Vegas showgirl" with painted fingernails by the way – had put him up to it after taking note of Bunny's success and pushed Peter into doing something similar. The thought of this imposing Rasta warrior being harried by a woman 17 years his junior is a disturbing one, and yet shouldn't be discounted. Whatever the truth of this, his interest in Heavy Manners will barely last the plane journey back to New York.

During another appearance on Habte Selassie's late night radio show the following weekend, he didn't even mention them. Maybe he was too focused on headlining the Summer Concert at West Side Highway and 43rd Street in a few days' time, or distracted by an old knee injury dating from 20 years ago, when he'd been thrown from the back of a speeding Kingston bus. He'd tried to land on his feet but jarred his knee, which then swelled to the size of a watermelon. He didn't get any proper medical attention at the time – "just some hot water and wintergreen" – and despite the recurring pain, still won't let the doctors "cut it". When Habte later visits him at the apartment in Central Park West, Peter tells him he's discovered some isometric exercises that are helping the situation. He'd been taken to the Wise Fools nightclub whilst in Chicago and informs Habte that he hates such places, which he says are for people "drinking alcohol and getting low", i.e., high. "They tend to see me double," he said.

His daily herb intake was still colossal by most people's standards and no matter how holy a sacrament he believed it to be, smoking such vast quantities of high-grade marijuana must have had some kind of adverse affect on him, not least worsening paranoia. He kept glancing towards the kitchen during their interview – a room shrouded in darkness and that had just the one door, which was open. When asked why he kept looking in that direction, he said he needed to see if anything was coming out of there. Peter's having visions – something that's later confirmed by Wayne Jobson who said, "You'd be talking to him and then all of a sudden he'd say, 'Look out!' and he'd see a vampire coming through the wall."

The next leg of his *Mama Africa* tour started during mid-September with shows in the Spanish cities of Pontevedra and San Sebastian. His cousin Carlton accompanied him on the trip, and says they nearly missed the first concert due to immigration problems.

"I remember we leave Kingston and then when we arrive at the airport, Peter realised that he didn't have a US visa. We were supposed to catch a plane from Miami heading to Spain so Copeland said he thought it might be OK because we could get an escort to take Peter from one terminal to another. One time they used to do that but on this particular occasion, a man decided they weren't going to allow that. What happen now, when we were in the line waiting for immigration, Copeland asked Peter if he had any herb on him. Peter says, 'Yeah man.' He had some squeezed in his fist, which was jammed in his pocket. We didn't know what was going to happen, whether we were going to be searched or what so I decide to take it from him and there was a bathroom nearby, so we just go in there and I take it from him and push it in my back pocket. Copeland asked for an escort but they turn him down and say that Peter has to go back to Jamaica. They try and give him a hard time, even though he wasn't really entering America but just wanting to pass through. Copeland decide, 'OK. Go back to Jamaica, catch a plane from there to Canada and then we can leave from there to Spain. That work out good but then over the Atlantic we hit a storm and the plane start to get a beating. We can hear all these noises, like cracking and the plane starts nose-diving... Vision, he was coming from the bathroom and every time he tried to stand up, the turbulence was so bad he kept falling down. He had to crawl on his hands and knees until he reach his seat. We're there now, waiting on Peter to come and Peter run into a roadblock in Canada. They find his M16 guitar and they try to give him problems and he almost missed his flight. He got through it in the end, but it was never too easy..."

On September 30 he played at the Ahoy Sports Palace in Rotterdam and indulges in pure theatre after strapping on his M-16 guitar and firing it into the crowd.

"His stagecraft noticeably lifted a notch from the time he received it," commented Milton Wray. "During his performances, the M16 guitar was reserved for specific songs – songs which spewed verbal bullets of damnation on the world's oppressors. His audiences looked forward to the times he would go for the rifle-like instrument. It seemed to transform him, giving him invincible power to trample the enemy of injustice his music opposed..."

Apart from the guitar posturing, it's the same show as premiered at the Greek Theatre. The rhythm section is again superb, and the music visibly lifts Peter's spirits. He's now working the stage with confidence, and mixing up kung fu moves with robotic dancing yet pays precious little attention to the audience. As he fingers the M-16 guitar during 'Bush Doctor' and surveys the ranks of mainly white youngsters, Peter's face looks suddenly drawn. He's either bone-tired or very stoned and quite possibly both, but it's a telling moment. Several French dates will follow beginning on October 4 at the Hippodrome de Pantin in Paris, where Carlton Tosh says they could hardly breathe because of the amount of tobacco smoke in the air.

"Peter told them they must stop smoking and light up their spliffs instead, otherwise he wasn't going to stay in there. People were drinking and not really listening so he just walked off the stage and told the promoter he wasn't coming back on until people showed more respect. That's how he was and he meant it, because he wasn't going to stick around. Peter wasn't into any corruption. He was just into what Rasta people did and nothing bad, no way!"

No sooner had they crossed the border into Germany than his M-16 guitar went missing. Charlie Comer told Fikisha Cumbo that German customs would not allow the guitar into the country and Peter had argued with them saying, 'Why pick on me? You want to play it? Does it look like a gun? Do you think it fires bullets?'

"I had him stopped because I phoned every wire service and every television station in the world, telling them to be there," says Comer, who insinuates it was a publicity stunt. In fact the airline admitted liability and since Peter was upset, Copeland Forbes had called Charlie in New York, who alerted *Der Spiegel* about the guitar and its famous owner. Shortly afterwards the guitar was found, and returned to Peter. It turns out that German customs officials had impounded the guitar as they suspected it might be a real weapon. It wasn't until after reading the article in *Der Spiegel* that they conceded it might be a genuine musical instrument.

"It was on that same German tour that the high command of German police paid Tosh a visit to warn him not to perform any song espousing the virtues of marijuana," says Copeland. "Being the strong-willed person he was, Tosh was hell bent on ignoring the warning, but the members of his entourage eventually managed to change his mind. Though he had to omit some songs, he did fairly well on the tour."

There was barely pause for breath as they played a string of one-nighters, beginning at the Messehalle in Sindelfingen on October 11. Shows in

Offenbach, Mannheim, Hannover and Hamburg followed before he arrived in Berlin on the 16th and was interviewed by Ulli Gueldner, who asked him why he'd declined to appear at Reggae Sunsplash. Peter replied that when he performs "It must be for cultural reasons, not just for entertainment, come drink rum and champagne and get happy and all them kinds of madness". He says that's why he and Bunny had come up with the idea of Youth Consciousness, beginning with that 1981 show in Kingston. "It was for the people of Jamaica, directly," he told Ulli, who says that people claim Peter had priced himself out of appearing at Sunsplash.

"The ministers of propaganda always say these bullshit. They say I want a huge amount of money? If they're saying I want a huge amount of money, did they say how much?" Peter asks him.

The rumours say US $14,000...

"Well, if they pay me $14,000 then they're not paying me enough because they had to pay me four times that when they had the World Festival in Jamaica, seen? It's just propaganda, but I deserve that because if those same people bring any foreign artists from anywhere in the world, they pay them $100,000, seen? And those artists can't even play reggae. Reggae Sunsplash is just a t'ing for guys to make money and get rich and go sit down the next day in the Sheraton Hotel and drink champagne and laugh at the singers, and me nah into that no more, seen? Because if guys are going to get rich off a my talent, then pay me what I deserve."

Talk like this made his occasional lapses into bad taste all the more difficult to understand. Tosh made a number of appearances on European television during the *Mama Africa* tour and none showed him in a particularly good light. One found him miming *Mama Africa* in front of fake flames, a giant African mask and the kind of graphics you'd see on a box of cut-price washing powder. You want to avert your eyes as he breaks into an ungainly dance, his Rasta coloured hooped socks making him look like some exotic species of stick insect. Whilst in Italy, he'd mimed 'Johnny B. Goode' dressed in a long white robe and surrounded by dancers who must have been bussed in from a local model agency. Then there was the German station who got him to mime 'Johnny B. Goode' (badly, since he can hardly be bothered) whilst wearing a red and yellow woolly hat with earflaps and the word "MAGIC" emblazoned across the front. The set's made to look like Skid Row as drunks slouch around him, clutching bottles and acting drunk. It's frankly embarrassing, and a far cry from the visionary art direction and slick production values that graced Collins' original film version.

Ulli Gueldner mentions none of this, although he does raise the subject of *Newsweek*, which had recently printed an article entitled 'The Third World Goes Pop', highlighting the music of Jamaica, Brazil and Nigeria. Bunny Wailer was described as "the man after Marley" whereas Peter – who saw the article but declined to read it – was omitted altogether.

"The people from the press are always depressing me every time, and I am sick and tired of their bullshit," he told Gueldner. "What they are trying to do is create conflict within the consciousness of our livity, seen? They are trying to divide us and make it look like we are rivals and that we're not on the same mission but we know those devils. They have been there for a long time, and it is very sad for them to know that they cannot make Bunny into what they want. They could Bob Marley, but not Bunny or Peter, seen? And that's the reason why we are here..."

On a lighter note he announces that he's learning to play the didgeridoo – the world's oldest wind instrument of which it's been said that, "If the earth had a voice, then it would be the sound of the didgeridoo." He'd brought one back from Australia and was fascinated by its eerie, otherworldly tone. After concerts in Dusseldorf and Munich he then celebrated his 39th birthday by heading for the airport and flying to London in readiness for an appearance at the Dominion Theatre on October 23. This show was recorded by the BBC and later broadcast on college radio in the US. Highlights include a slowed down 'Can't Blame The Youth' and Donald Kinsey's Hendrix-like, sobbing wails midway through 'Coming In Hot'. A couple of minutes later the band swerves into some heavyweight dub, as if they'd just swaggered out of Channel One. Kinsey again excels on 'Where You Gonna Run'. His playing energises the crowd as well as Peter, whose vocals have a little more edge to them than usual. This is London remember, and his sternest critics lay in waiting. As heard on the live recording, the crowd are enthusiastic and after calling for an encore, were treated to a flawless 'Mama Africa' yet according to Lloyd Bradley, Peter's last London appearance "was a tragic affair".

He writes: "Decades of ganja consumption, a recently acquired and copious cocaine habit, the after-effects of his treatment from the police and years of bitterness about his modest international standing all conspired to produce a series of explosive interviews and a stage show that presented him as – to put it mildly – a few bricks short of the load." Bradley, who is black, assured *NME* readers that the most memorable part of the concert was Peter "spending a good 20 minutes informing the audience their tiny minds couldn't possibly comprehend the magnitude of his performance".

Speaking more generally, Bradley claims that Peter "roundly intimidated members of the music press – methods included verbal abuse, ignoring them for up to half an hour, not allowing them to use tape recorders, forbidding photographers to take more than one picture and demonstrating his kung fu prowess by, without warning, lashing out with kicks and punches mere inches from the journalist's face. (And I bet Peter wishes he could give him a good kicking even now.)

"Peter Tosh was not an easy person to like," he continues. "He went out of his way not to be. It was actually impossible to find anyone who had met him and didn't have a vested interest, to say something nice about him."

Bradley accuses Tosh of having "an open dislike of white people", of being violent and having signed with EMI because "they offered the largest advance". He describes the *Mama Africa* album as "patchy", and derides the "lame reggae arrangement" of 'Johnny B. Goode'. He then points out that, "Tosh's commitment to roots reggae was questioned in both critical and artistic circles."

In fact there's no evidence of Peter ever having used cocaine, not even when a close associate of the Rolling Stones. It's well known that Peter just smoked herb, and we can only assume that such remarks say more about the writer than anything else. Peter's problem, if we can call it that, is that he was outspoken and didn't suffer fools gladly. This made him unpopular with people trying to belittle him, or who'd made up their minds about him before even meeting him. So was Peter arrogant?

"No," says Santa Davis. "He was just a soldier who talked for his rights and who'd experienced a lot of tribulation. He cursed bad words and people – especially the police – didn't like him. Even on tours, people would say, 'Yeah, Peter is nice, but why is he so harsh?' They didn't understand it was because he lived what he believed and when he left the stage, he just didn't forget all he said, it was something he genuinely felt. He was fighting the injustice and cruelty of the "shit-stem", as he would call it. He was a freedom fighter and they always get rid of them when they become too militant, but Peter was also free hearted. He loved people. He was humorous and would run his jokes, but on stage he was different... He was militant with a purpose to destroy the wicked system that oppresses earth. He was the first man I know that sang against apartheid and opened the eyes of the whole world against the wicked system of oppression. Peter was a good person, but he was also the victim of circumstance, Jah know."

"Backstage was a nightmare," remembers film director Howard Johnson, who was at the Dominion that night. "There was always so much shouting. You'd hear the same kind of mad dialogue, and from the same kind of characters. All of them would be there boosting him up and massaging his ego, calling him 'boss' or whatever. They'd do it to gain money and recognition from him and other impressionable people who'd see them hanging around him. It was like a circus, but then after a while all of them were blown away by this woman who took over his head, and Peter would lose the influence he once had."

The schisms within his personality would deepen rapidly from now on. The next day journalist Simon Hills found him "sitting in a London hotel suite, strumming a guitar, smoking ganja and watching *Play School*". He's so engrossed in the programme (which is aimed at pre-school toddlers) that he forgets Hills is there, except this isn't as out-of-character as it may seem.

"No, because we'd get to a new place and the first thing he'd do is go off and find a toy store because Peter loved toys," says Janet Davidson. "He'd buy robots and remote control cars that he'd race up and down the hallways, or Stretch Armstrong figures... Whatever new toys were out on the market for boys, that's what he'd go for. He'd say that the only toys he had as a child was two juice boxes, and he'd never forgotten that."

Colin Irwin, who interviewed Peter for *Black Echoes*, experienced yet another side to him after noting how Peter "gazes furtively out from behind his acoustic guitar and his regulation Rasta hat with epic coolness, the faintest glimmer of amusement about him. It's a look that says he's playing games – the record industry's *own* games – and winning so easily somebody should call 'no contest'."

Irwin talks about Tosh's undeniable charisma, but admits that he makes "outrageous statements, long speeches about imperialism and herb, and curt dismissals of Bob Marley, whom he dismisses as his student". He also claims that his new album is likely to "completely alienate the reggae purists already disenchanted with much of his recent work".

"The world will acknowledge me man," Peter insists. "The reason why the world won't acknowledge me is that I am different from Bob Marley – totally different. For commercial reasons the world will accept Bob more than me, because he was more commercial than I am. He was singing commercial songs acceptable in a commercial world but I sing songs of *protest*."

By the time he's flogged in the media like some unruly slave, Peter will be in New York where the main topic of conversation was America's invasion of Grenada. In the aftermath of Maurice Bishop's assassination, "Operation Urgent Fury" had sought to end Soviet and Cuban influence on the island. The UN called America's response "a flagrant violation of international law", but the motion to pass a resolution was vetoed by... the US. Peter had been to Grenada with Michael Manley, and met Bishop personally. He knew him as a socialist who posed no threat to democracy, and felt very angry about what happened in the tiny Caribbean nation.

To try and take his mind off it, Charlie Comer took him to see Judy Mowatt's first-ever solo performance in New York, at the First City Cabaret Club in Manhattan. Comer recalled how Peter got on his unicycle and pedalled all the way to the health food store on 57th Street prior to the show, just to burn off some of his agitation. Judy was advertised as "the High Priestess of Reggae" that night. Towards the end of her set, when she announced "brother Peter", his appearance raised a huge cheer and yet his singing was a little ragged at first. He didn't properly get into his stride until the verse, "Let's get together and fight this holy battle..." After Judy asks members of the audience to hold hands with each other, he then addresses them with a message of his own. "Hear what me nah like now," he says. "Me don't like for people to listen to reggae and sit down like they're crippled. I want everybody to get up, up, up, up..."

He's admonishing them as usual, but that's Peter Tosh for you. On Saturday December 3 Habte Selassie hosted a special edition of *Labrish* called 'A Look At The Enigmatic And Controversial Peter Tosh', which included some useful insights into the man's character. Habte began by stating the obvious, and informing listeners that Peter was "very controversial".

"Tosh is one of the few highly articulate individuals within the music that you can pose a question to and get a response whether you like the answer or not. He has perennially been in trouble with the powers that be in Jamaica because of his forthrightness, because he's outspoken and he's not afraid to say what he means and mean what he says. Because of that he's been brutalised on several occasions by the police.

"Tosh has a personality quite different from most others and particularly reggae artists. He's very, very strong. He once said that if he weren't a musician, then he would be fighting for the liberation of Africa. I've met him on several occasions, basically to interview him and he's always pleasant. He has a front. I guess that's because artists like him are dealing with so many different people they have to feel people out and in a sense learn who they can and can't trust but after you get through the test, you find that Peter Tosh is one of the most pleasant individuals you can find. Like I said before, he's very articulate and intelligent and again, he's not afraid of making mistakes. He will say things and may have to come back later and change what he said, or a decision... For example, he was making plans to go and do some shows in Israel and after the situation was explained to him he cancelled them, saying it was not fitting for Peter Tosh to go there when Israel was supplying arms that are killing black people. He's an individual of conviction and someone we can emulate in many, many respects."

Habte goes on to say that Peter "has done his finest work with *Mama Africa* since *Equal Rights*.

"It's as if Tosh has regained some sort of artistic direction. He has not only improved himself in terms of recording, but in terms of what he's doing on stage. He's beginning to recognise Peter Tosh the artist and because of that, I think his impact will be even more profound in future and I can hardly wait to see and hear what his next album will be like, because he has gone through some very serious and important changes..."

Chapter 28

Swaziland

Peter felt the elation of being back in Africa from the minute he stepped out of the plane and into that wall of searing heat. Africa wasn't all that unlike Jamaica in some respects, but this was the land of his forefathers. It's where the ancients of his bloodline were buried, which meant he had a direct and living connection to the ground he was standing on. The realisation had been there since the days he first visited the Rasta camps in Back O'Wall except it now hit him with such force; it brought him to his knees. Peter lowered his head and kissed the tarmac – an act that loosened the seal and released his unchained self, who'd lived here in the days before slavery. In this state of mind anything is possible, and that's what it felt like as he brushed himself off and made his way into customs.

He and his party were in Zimbabwe and on their way to play two concerts in neighbouring Swaziland, due to take place over the coming weekend. There's a heightened sense of anticipation among the group – which includes Marlene, Copeland Forbes, Janet Davidson, Peter's cook and cousin Carlton – especially once Peter receives an invite to meet Prime Minister Robert Mugabe.

Three years earlier, Mugabe and members of his rebel army had stood in Harare's National Stadium, watching on proudly as the Union Jack was lowered and the new Zimbabwe flag hoisted in its place. Bob Marley had performed that night and now Peter Tosh was sat with Mugabe at a dining-room table in the Presidential Palace, talking of world affairs and no doubt still feeling the effects of the country's finest herb – a strain so potent, the rebel soldiers believed it made them invisible. Others claimed it made them bulletproof, or gave them powers to transform themselves into animals or spirits, yet the pair of them are said to have had a decent conversation nevertheless. South Africa had been trying to destabilise Zimbabwe since Independence, and there had been a number of assassination attempts on Mugabe's life after he'd enlisted help from North Korea. Michael Manley had faced similar challenges after befriending Fidel Castro, which is something Peter no doubt mentioned.

A year earlier, the South African Defence Force had raided Lesotho and massacred more than 40 people, mostly ANC members and their families. They were murdered after their homes had been designated terrorist strongholds. Nowhere was safe as South Africa's death squads continued to make excursions into neighbouring states, including Zimbabwe and Swaziland. A battle was taking place for the soul of Africa – and also to safeguard majority white control – yet the groundswell of resistance continued to gain momentum. The first Nelson Mandela birthday party celebration had taken place earlier in the year, after ANC President Oliver Tambo had initiated moves to promote Mandela internationally as the central figure in black South Africa's liberation struggle. Soon, exiled political activists would come under threat, whilst in South Africa itself many were now detained under house arrest. People were living in fear and the atmosphere was tense, but the picture wasn't quite so black and white as it was painted.

The outside world knew little of the Zimbabwean government's ruthless suppression of opposition groups at this stage, and we can be sure the subject never arose as Peter and Robert Mugabe held their informal talks. Instead, the focus would be on nation building and promoting solidarity between black people worldwide – also the situation in Swaziland, where Peter is expected in a day or two. Mugabe will become a hate figure to Westerners but he was a major figurehead back in 1983, at a time when Nelson Mandela still languished in jail, and was being reviled as a terrorist by Margaret Thatcher and Ronald Reagan. Donald Kinsey has spoken of how motivated Peter was at this juncture, and being afforded hospitality by an African head of state will have done wonders for his confidence and self-esteem. In Africa, the doubts that assailed him could be dispelled more easily, at least for the time being, and he felt a mix of pride and expectancy whilst flying over the border into Swaziland, where he'll headline two shows that coming weekend, on December 17 and 18. As they land at Matsapa airport he looked out the window and saw thousands of people on the tarmac and neighbouring rooftops. Carlton says that coming to Swaziland had been a compromise, and yet such a welcome made it all worthwhile.

"Peter was offered a lot of money to go to South Africa but said the only way he would go there is if he went to where the poor people were, and where there was no regime. That's how we end up in Swaziland. They charter this small plane to take us over there and when we land, we saw all these trees full of people. There were so many of them it looked like leaves! They'd all come out to see Peter. He got good greetings there, I tell you. We were so delighted by it."

South African publication *Drum*, under the heading "Swaziland Ablaze", opened its coverage that weekend by stating, "It was like the coming of the Messiah to Africa when Peter Tosh the reggae maestro and acclaimed Prophet of the Rastafari religion landed at the tiny Swaziland airport on Thursday. The streets, shops and other places of note were swarming with the bright and familiar red, green and yellow colours splashed on T-shirts, caps, badges and scarves. For the thousands of Rastafarians who thronged Swaziland it was a unique phenomenon – their dreadlocked leader, king and prophet had come. Jah's children had, after 400 years, found one another."

"Like a demi-god, Peter Tosh breezed into Swaziland in a cloud of ganja fumes," trumpeted another. "With dreadlocks swinging, he walked tall and proud, radiating an air he was feeling bigger than the Swazi mountains."

Throngs of people gathered around him once he'd stepped from the plane, including high-ranking Swazi government officials who'll be tested from almost the first minute he arrives. After being hurried through customs he was ushered into the VIP lounge, which had been specially reserved for him.

"He was soon rolling a cigarette of ganja," said an eyewitness. "Somebody shouted, 'Hey Tosh, have you got permission to smoke that here?' He replied, 'I *am* permission,' and with that he lit up and smoked. Peter Tosh is a chain-smoker and his ganja has only two places. It is either between his fingers or between his lips."

Before agreeing to do the shows Peter had insisted he be freely allowed to smoke herb, or "dagga" as it's known locally, during his visit. He'd also issued instructions that cigarettes should not be smoked in his presence. In Swaziland the King makes the rules although King Sobhuza II had died a year earlier and his heir had yet to be crowned. Peter's dictates therefore couldn't have been timelier. The fact that most of the country's million or so inhabitants spoke English was another advantage, as this made communication easier. Unfortunately December marks the start of the rainy season when the climate can get oppressively hot and humid, which it was during the press conference.

"After letting the press roast in a hot, small, stuffy and packed room for an hour – ganja smoke infiltrating the room from a side door – Peter Tosh emerged from behind a cloud of fumes," reported *Drum*. "He walked in like a Rasta warlord, dreadlocks swinging from shoulder to shoulder, his guitar dangling in one hand. He took his place, took a puff on his "J" and started twanging his guitar as if he were sitting alone under a Jamaican palm tree."

He's described as "witty and philosophical. His ready-made answers are sharp and brief. Sometimes, he answers questions with other questions or in parables but his pompous air makes it difficult for one to separate the real Peter McIntosh from the public Peter Tosh."

Peter told the conference that, "Rasta music started in Africa. When the slave-masters stole us from our motherland, they took us with reggae in our hearts. That is why I believe that the future of reggae is in Africa, where it originated from." He goes on to say that, "Peter Tosh is my slave name. It was given to me without permission. Please note that the name Peter Tosh is just a handle. It does not define me."

He also claimed to have been taken away from Africa "a warrior... and I'm still a warrior", he assured them. "My hopes and aspirations give me the determination to fight on, and not to let people tell me what to do because I know what to do, seen? I'm a man of my own spirits, seen? I rule my destiny, and I've discovered that within myself. It gives me the impetus and the urges and energy to do this, through the powers of Jah."

The attention then moved to his ANC T-shirt. A Swazi government official wanted to know what it stood for. "You shouldn't be asking me that," chided Peter. "You don't know? That is very embarrassing for me. All Africans should know what the ANC means. It means African National Congress."

Asked if he sympathised with the ANC, he says he wasn't there to show sympathy, but to waken the slumbering mentality of people with his music. This doesn't mean he's against other anti-apartheid organisations – only that he "couldn't wear four T-shirts at the same time".

Such humour was rare since he lost no time in attacking the local authorities, calling them "the same governments of colonialism that were there 400 years ago and it has never changed. And it's white democracy, but I and I don't stand for that."

That must have caused a few flustered expressions among the dignitaries present. Soon afterwards, he confirms that he was offered "hundreds of thousands of dollars" to perform in South Africa "but even when I'm broke, I still don't go". After assuming the majority of them are black, he's pleased to hear that thousands of South Africans are expected to come and see him. Swaziland shares three of its borders with South Africa, and the promoters are from there also. The day after his arrival, *The Times Of Swaziland* printed an article headed "Tosh Fever Hits Town" which began, "Today, a stampede on the border gates is expected with people off work for the weekend. All hotels in Mbabane, Ezulwini and Manzini are fully booked, and scores of people have been turned away. Some people are sleeping in their cars or in tents."

Local businessmen said they hadn't been so busy for years, and with tickets on sale at Holiday Inns and the Royal Swazi Spa – as well as outlets in Johannesburg and Durban – large numbers of tourists were expected to be in attendance. The advertisements in Saturday's papers screamed "Tosh Has Arrived!" but there was another reason why there were a lot of visitors in town that weekend. The two concerts would be curtain raisers for an annual, three-week period of festivities called N'cwala or "Festival Of The Fruits". Because of this, there was already a carnival atmosphere in Lobamba, where the 20,000 capacity Somlolo Stadium awaited Peter Tosh's first-ever concert in Africa. Lobamba is Swaziland's administrative capital and less than half an hour's drive from Mbabane, where Peter and his retinue were based. Reggae was popular throughout Southern Africa although it was mostly circulated on pirated cassettes, rather than official releases. Peter, together with other Jamaican artists, may not have been selling too many records in Africa yet he was revered there after tracks like 'Equal Rights', 'African' and 'Get Up Stand Up' had sealed his reputation as a musical revolutionary, and he'd then returned their love on the jubilant *Mama Africa*, which could be heard pouring from speaker boxes all over the city. Every time Peter left the hotel he was mobbed by people eager to see him and hear him talk, and who'd then try and follow him everywhere he went.

"Man I tell you, it was something else because what happened was, I was driving Peter's car and they put this special licence plate on the car saying 'PETER TOSH' so everywhere the car go, whether Peter is in it or not, the crowds would be unbelievable!" says Carlton. "I remember one day Marlene and I go to a store and when they realise we were in there we couldn't get out, there were so many people crowded around us."

Each concert would last three hours and start at noon. Brenda Fassie, Babsy Mlangeni, Carlos Djedje and Dread Warriors were among the support acts. The first show was the largest reggae concert ever held in Southern Africa – providing, that is, you don't count Bob Marley's appearance at Zimbabwe's Independence ceremony. Never before had so many people (illegally) crossed the South African border into Swaziland. Thousands didn't have tickets and some had travelled for days to get there, even crawling flat on their bellies through the bush to avoid capture. History was in the making. The great Peter Tosh was about to perform on African soil for the first time, and it was a landmark occasion no one wanted to miss. His entourage had a police escort with sirens blaring on its way to the stadium, where the atmosphere became even more charged once people realised he'd arrived. Security was tight, as Carlton Tosh would soon discover.

"When we got to the show I had some free passes on me and so I went outside to give them away. I see these nice young people who didn't have any money to go in so I give them the passes and we're walking into the stadium when the police decide they're going to search me. I have all the credentials so I don't know why they tried to do that, but I say for them to go ahead because I knew I was clean. Except guess what? I'd forgotten I had a nice piece of Jamaican herbs hidden in a film canister. I'd just forgotten all about it, otherwise I wouldn't have given them such easy access when they searched me but I honestly believed that I was clean! They start looking through all my things, opening up these film canisters and that's when they found the one rammed with herb. The guy told me to stay right there and said the minimum sentence for something like that was 10 years' imprisonment. The show start and Peter was on stage, the news go around they'd got me and so Peter just stop the show and come off the stage. He sent Copeland to go and find me. Meanwhile I'd told the guy the herb belonged to Peter, and that he had permission to smoke it when he was in Swaziland. Copeland come and get me, they release me but then Peter started into a speech and when he was done with them their ears were *weak*!"

Bona magazine began its review by noting how the crowd had arrived "by air and by roads – in old vans and flashy cars. When all the hotels were full, many people slept in cars and buses – just so that they would see reggae superstar Peter Tosh in person.

"After he'd played only two songs at that first concert, a storm started and rain came pouring down – but the crowd only got more excited, and screamed and danced to the rhythm of Tosh's music. Peter Tosh carried on playing in spite of the rain, occasionally taking puffs from his dagga pipe between songs."

"The heavens wept to this rapturous reunion, bringing torrential rain and lightning as this son of the soil embraced Africa with an affectionate tune, 'Mama Africa'," confirmed Drum. "The harder it rained, the harder Tosh sang as the lightning seemed to symbolise applause from the ethereal vaults of heaven.

"'You see,' declared Tosh loudly, 'the rain and the lightning are my security. I am home. Jah Rastafari!' Like a true saviour, Tosh wore an embroidered cassock and carried an ornamental wooden staff that he repeatedly pointed towards the clouds. There was no failing to catch the whiff of ganja smoke as the King of Reggae openly smoked his 'joints' in defiance of the kingdom's anti dagga smoking legislation. Throughout the week police had issued stern warnings to the public against dagga smoking. But as Tosh puffed on his pipe the several hundred policemen found they had several thousands of people to control, and the clouds of smoke went ignored.

"Peter then took up his M–16 guitar for 'Fight Against Apartheid' and the crowd went crazy. People kept shouting 'Freedom! Freedom! Freedom!' The sight of the guitar, shaped just like a real weapon, caused temporary panic among the security forces. It was still raining heavily but Tosh's music sent everybody ablaze in dance. The King himself was an energetic stage performer, hop skipping from one side of the stage to the other, leaping in the air and bending double... For the 12,000 who came from as far afield as Kenya, Malawi, Zimbabwe, Lesotho, Botswana, Tanzania and South Africa, it was one hell of a memorable weekend."

"People said that no rain had fallen for like 10 years before that night, but that's the kind of stuff the man carry with him, everywhere he goes," says Carlton. "That first night the stadium was full. It was packed out, but the second night it was only like half or maybe three-quarters' full. We were told there were more people outside the stadium than inside because those people used to get like nine dollars a week, yet the ticket was 12 dollars to go in so can you imagine a guy getting nine dollars a week and he has to buy a ticket costing a third as much again? It was hard for them and so Peter stopped the band, then called the promoters on stage and ordered them to open the gates. 'Do you want to cause a riot here?' he ask them, 'because me nah play another bombaclaat note 'til you let the people in.' The promoter, he didn't want to do it and so the show stop again until he do what Peter said, because they'd made back their money by then in any case. And when those Africans burst into that place man, they start hollering and jumping around, I tell you!"

Referring to the small crowd on the second day, Tosh told a reporter from *Bona* that, "It is sad to see how colonialism has left Africa poor. In Germany, over 75,000 people came to see my show and it was the same in Italy, but in the land of my birth (meaning Africa, not Jamaica) only a few thousand turn up."

This was due to overpricing, and no other reason. The promoters had targeted wealthier visitors from across the border, rather than local people who struggled to make ends meet and were forced to look on as Swaziland's royal family commandeered the country's coffers and enjoyed every advantage, including shopping extravaganzas abroad. It's not clear whether Peter understood the reality of this situation before going to Swaziland. Judging by his dismissive attitude towards local dignitaries we can assume that he did (especially after talking with Robert Mugabe), but it was the events surrounding that second show that had brought it all home to him. Such realisations will take away some of the euphoria Peter felt on performing there, as would the front page of Monday's *Times Of Swaziland* which declared "Show Ends In Terror", and told of a horrific car crash that claimed the life of football player Alfred Sibisi. Africa wasn't the Promised Land after all. Not politically at least, although it still held secrets Peter wished to unlock, and which might bring relief from his various ailments.

"Peter rarely saw doctors or took proper medicine," says Janet Davidson. "He'd had lots of car accidents in Jamaica and still suffered from some of those injuries. Somewhere along the way he'd hurt his coccyx, which meant he couldn't walk properly. We had a chiropractor on tour with us for quite a while because he was in a lot of pain, and he suffered from migraines as well."

Both she and Santa recall Peter visiting a bush doctor in Swaziland – a local healer who was 78 years old but looked many years younger, "almost like a child". A second man who read bones sat in another room with Peter, who threw his bones in the air and then watched as they landed face downwards, which is considered unlucky. The man saw he had a lot of problems, both financial and otherwise, but told him the main problem was in his home. Santa took this to mean Marlene, whom Peter had described as "just a friend" to inquisitive news reporters. The elder man, who steadfastly refused to acknowledge Marlene despite the fact that she was sat in the same room, said he would make something for Peter to wear that would protect him from gunshot and accidents. When they returned to collect it this object was quite small, shaped a bit like Africa, and made of some natural substance. It was to be worn like a pendant and Peter immediately put it round his neck, saying it was something he'd wanted for a long time. The bush doctor said not to take it off for any reason or let anyone else wear it, otherwise the spell would be broken and the amulet would lose its power.

Rumour has it that Peter put it on, stood in the Christ position and the bush doctor fired a shot at him, which only grazed him. At 78 maybe his eyesight wasn't so good, but it's an interesting story nevertheless.

Marlene will later claim that she and Peter got married in Africa although Janet Davidson disputes this, and no paperwork has ever surfaced to corroborate it. Marlene was still only 21 and kept having miscarriages, which couldn't have helped her mental state. Like Peter, she was inclined to mask her insecurities with bluster and even aggression at times. Peter told one insider that he was planning to leave her, as she'd become increasingly irrational yet their relationship would deepen in future, rather than deteriorate.

After their return to Jamaica, Copeland was visiting their house when he saw Marlene wearing the pendant the bush doctor had made. He immediately went outside to tell Peter, who rushed back in the house and snatched it from her neck. The most important souvenir from his African trip – one that might hold the key to his innermost fears – was now useless, and darkness began to draw near.

Chapter 29

No Nuclear War

Even as Peter was winging his way back to Jamaica, the British press was ridiculing him again. In its December 24 issue, *Melody Maker* printed a picture of Peter under the heading of "Fruitcake Of The Year".

"Uni-cyclist, witch doctor, personal confidant to Jah, 'erb missionary and the self-styled future of the world, Peter Tosh certainly seems to have more loose screws than most." He's then derided for expounding "loudly voiced theories about his own immortality" and having the nerve to discredit Bob Marley – described by *Melody Maker* as Peter's mentor – after telling a journalist that "if a student die, the teacher is still here".

He's in good company at least, since Marvin Gaye and Michael Jackson are listed among the runners-ups. The fact that Peter really did teach Marley how to play guitar isn't allowed to interfere with another typically scurrilous jibe from the Brits, who'd seized upon his frustrations and were revelling in them. On December 31, as one of the most successful years of his career drew to an end, Peter headlined Reggae Super Jam. This was the name given to three nights of concerts at the National Arena in Kingston starting December 28, when Beres Hammond, Steel Pulse and Dennis Brown shared the bill. Black Uhuru headlined the following night and then it was Peter's turn, with Gregory Isaacs and the Skatalites in support.

"Tosh reserved some of his best performances for home," says Copeland Forbes. "One standout gig was his appearance at the Kingsley Cooper promoted Reggae Super Jam in 1983, at the National Arena. I remember that the many people who had come expecting Tosh's usual spiel of expletives were disappointed, as he delivered a professional, uniformed show."

It was a full house that night, with both downstairs and cheaper balcony seats having sold out. If Peter really is a fruitcake or lacks authenticity then Jamaican audiences – who are the most discriminating reggae fans on Earth, bar none – clearly hadn't noticed. He looks a little tired as he walks on stage to a tumultuous welcome, dressed in a long black robe and Rasta scarf; his dreadlocks tucked inside a black beret that remains a potent symbol of Black Nationalism. At first sight, the pendants bunched around his neck could be mistaken for hip-hop style excess, except he's wearing some of them because of their healing properties, and not in a bid to impress. Peter is still the "Mystic Man" and it's far from being an act, despite his theatrical use of an Ethiopian cross and wooden staff during the first few songs. His stage persona isn't contrived, and never really was. It just amplified what's real about him and this crowd knew that. He'll reciprocate by singing a few old favourites like 'Can't Blame The Youth', 'Burial', 'Legalise It' and 'Hammer', complete with newly worked, gospel-fired intro.

Copeland's right and it's a great show. Songs such as 'Wanted Dread & Alive' and 'Not Gonna Give It Up' reaffirm his role of reggae outlaw – a holy warrior who's unjustly persecuted for speaking the truth and yet never resorts to self-pity. It's a persona he's made his own over the years and on nights like this, armed only with religious certitude and an arsenal of rebel anthems, Peter remains a truly compelling figure. When he tells you victory is within reach you believe him, whilst 'Rastafari Is' gains in spiritual power every time he performs it. Keith Sterling stands at his keyboard, playing as if in a trance during the lengthy instrumental passage as Peter and Vision trade counterpoint rhythms on conga drums. The spell's finally broken when Peter suddenly yells "Jah, Rastafari!" and starts chanting Scripture. He then turns freedom fighter on 'Fight Apartheid' after strapping on his M-16 guitar. This isn't one of those concerts where he walks a tightrope and you begin to fear for his safety. The sense that anything could happen only surfaces near the end when he stands centre stage – showily lights his spliff, tilts back his head and almost disappears in a cloud of smoke. Because of everything that's occurred between him and the police over the years it's still a daring act, and the crowd immediately acknowledge it as such. This is the National Arena after all, and not a festival stage safely tucked away in some tourist location. Suitably refreshed,

Peter then urges them to their feet, just as the band launch into 'Get Up Stand Up'.

When he's not singing Peter loses himself in that stiff-legged, angular dance of his – the one that makes him look like a cross between Charlie Chaplin and Bruce Lee, yet is also transcendental. Like all major artists – Bob Marley, Jimi Hendrix and James Brown included – Peter Tosh often performed as if under a spell, as he did on that New Year's Eve show. After the twin triumphs of 'Bush Doctor' and 'Johnny B. Goode' – on which Donald Kinsey is outstanding – 'Legalise It' segues into a cover of Blue Mitchell's 'Who Dun It' by which time Peter's seated by the drum riser, rolling another huge spliff. Soon he's back on his feet, encouraging the audience to sing along as he returns to 'Legalise It'. Five minutes later and he's still ad-libbing as he walks off stage. "Keep on keeping on," he repeats over and over, as the band head for the climax. Soon, his voice trails off into silence. Peter Tosh has just performed his last-ever full-length show, and there wasn't a soul in the National Arena who knew it.

In a couple of weeks' time, the *Daily Gleaner* will be hailing Dennis Brown as "Reggae's Crown Prince", who's said to "stand only below Peter Tosh for acclaim in the Rockers Awards". The Second Annual Rockers Awards were held in Kingston's National Arena on Saturday, January 28. Neville Willoughby was MC and Peter was expected to perform since he'd been nominated in several different categories, more than any other artist. He won all the top awards that night – Reggae Personality, Reggae Ambassador, Best Reggae 45 (International) and Best Reggae Album – and made a brief, but blistering appearance backed by a band that had been hired to play behind the 20 or so nominees.

"I actually played with Peter at his last public appearance," says Andy Bassford, who was guitarist with Lloyd Parkes & We The People. "There was this show called the Rockers Awards and Peter was on it that year because he had the album with 'Johnny B. Goode' on it. He'd seen me play already, when Dennis Brown had opened for him on the *Mama Africa* tour. Fast forward to 1984 and he's at this show after getting nominated for some awards and so we rehearsed two songs by him but none of the nominees came to the rehearsals, because nobody was supposed to know who they were. We go to the gig and he does 'Where You Gonna Run', then closes with 'Johnny B. Goode'. And of course both those songs have great guitar parts and especially 'Johnny B. Goode' so here I am playing with Peter Tosh who I've never even spoken to... I'm thinking, 'I'll never get to do this again. This is like the coolest thing ever. I'm about to play 'Johnny B. Goode' with Peter Tosh and it'll never get better than this...' It came to the solo and I'm wailing away, then we get to the outro and I'm *really* wailing away. I'm really trying to make an impression and then as I'm walking off, J. C. Lodge and her husband were standing there... They'd been stood watching in the wings and said when Peter Tosh came off stage he looked back at me wailing away, then turned to them and said, 'The white man, he respect I.' They were in hysterics about it but I thought it was just the best compliment ever."

It will be the last time Peter Tosh sings in front of an audience, and he hadn't enjoyed the experience all that much. J. C. Lodge remembers him shouting, 'Take the bloodclaat lights out of my eyes!' at one point. He may have had another of those blinding headaches that gripped his head like a vice and made his senses reel – something that was happening with increasing frequency. At such times he felt possessed, and would then be left feeling emptied out and exhausted when the pain subsided. The tragedy is that as Peter combated fatigue, a raft of medical complaints and his own inner demons, his profile had rarely been higher. He was voted Top International Reggae Entertainer at the Third Annual International Reggae Music Awards in Chicago around this same time, although he failed to show up for the ceremony, despite having been invited.

He may have been too busy recording, after booking a session at Dynamic back in early March. Donald Kinsey had already returned to the US and so Peter invited Tyrone Downie to augment the band, and contribute keyboard flourishes that'll bring the sound closer to what's happening on the international market. Only one song, a reggae gospel tune called 'Testify', will result from this session. It's a continuation of the Wailers' 'Thank You Lord' in a way except we're not talking shiny-eyed exuberance here, but the proud voice of experience. There's a Rasta hymn on all of Peter's albums and this one – set to a skipping reggae beat and brimming with melody – is a gem. His singing is superb, whilst the joy in his voice denotes a measure of optimism. "I've got to testify what Jah has done for I. When I'm down he picks me up. When I'm empty he fills my cup. When obstacles are in my way, He removes them for me..."

He won't return to the studio for almost a year. To quote Marlene, "The man had been out there for 20 years without any rest and with a

410

nasty stomach ulcer when I first met him. The man needed rest. The man needed some time for himself." Peter's erratic behaviour is now beginning to worry close friends and family, the majority of whom think Marlene's influence is to blame. Mervin Palmer, who designed the *Mama Africa* sleeve, had already witnessed this different side to Peter's character.

"My relationship with him ended when the tour finished in California. I went back to Jamaica because I had lost my camera bag with my passport, camera and other important papers in it. This meant I couldn't travel with the group to their next destination overseas.

"Peter Tosh's manager Copeland Forbes gave me some money to give to Dynamic recording studio but when I got to Jamaica I held onto it as my payment for designing the *Mama Africa* album cover, a T-shirt, tour jacket and huge backdrop. Peter's manager felt the $4,000 I charged was unreasonable so that caused a stalemate between us, but I felt this was the only way I would have received payment for my work so I took it and they weren't prepared to bargain. Peter was not amused. In fact he was really mad. While on tour he called me and said, 'Hey Mervin. What kind of bumboclaat yuh a deal with?' He then threatened me and put the phone down.

"After the tour ended and Peter came back to Jamaica I was in my studio when his gold Volvo drove up in front and he came out shouting, 'Hey bumboclaat Mervin. Wha' ah g'wan? Me and you have nuff more work to do!' We talked for a while as if nothing had happened but the truth is, he felt I'd been influenced by Evon Gordon to take the money and so he was more mad at him, despite the fact that Evon had nothing to do with it."

Mervin closed up his studio and migrated to the US soon after this incident. He now owns a media company in Ghana and describes Peter as "A very kind, disciplined, warm and loving person who was truly committed to the liberation of his people.

"I personally feel that he got distracted spiritually and lost his focus. Peter was open to a lot of negative influences that resulted in bad experiences up until the time he met his tragic death. So many of our musicians fall prey to this same negative force after they've reached a high point in their careers. A lot of bad things happened before he died and this clearly showed he was under spiritual attack."

Tosh's eccentricities now took on a slightly different form, and were described by one insider as "teetering on the brink of madness". Peter had changed, and even close associates began to tread warily in his presence.

Soon after speaking with Mervin that day he'd taken a machete to Evon Gordon, wounding him so badly he required weeks of hospital treatment. Copeland Forbes also narrowly escaped Peter's wrath.

"For days he walked around with a machete looking for me, because he'd heard that I'd gone into his chest and had stolen money. But it was the strangest thing, because I never knew him to own a chest. It was around that same period that Tosh disowned his sons, accusing them of making overtures to Marlene. It wasn't the same Peter Tosh. He was doing some strange things. He drove fear into everyone around him. It was a dark period for the singer. He was apparently experiencing some kind of mental trauma and had constant headaches."

Copeland had helped Peter and Marlene find their present address, which was a large, detached house at 5 Plymouth Avenue, in an area of uptown Kingston known as the Barbican. It was a fitting abode for a major reggae star with its marble floors and bathrooms, and yet the house remained empty for a while.

"I just didn't like the feel of the place to be honest," says Janet Davidson. "Copeland didn't think Peter should have bought it but Marlene wanted it and then they used to kill goats there. There was all kinds of stuff going on..."

Peter was heard to remark that 49 "duppies" or ghosts had been living at the house when they bought it. It's now apparent that Marlene was either practising obeah, or using it to gain control of him and his affairs. One female acquaintance, after seeing Marlene add something to Peter's food, was told, "We have to control our men." Soon, a New York law firm called Padell, Nadell, Fine & Weinberger will issue a statement on behalf of Intel Diplo Enterprises Inc headed "Peter Tosh Under New Management".

"Reggae superstar Peter Tosh, who recently completed a nine-month world tour, is under new management. He has terminated his management of Copeland Forbes and Janet Davidson. His new manager is Pauline Morris. Forbes was fired due to poor management, immoral acts and lack of respect. Just a few weeks ago, Tosh won four Rockers Magazine Awards in Jamaica for Reggae Personality Of The Year, Reggae Ambassador Of The Year, Reggae Single Of The Year (International) for 'Johnny B. Goode' and Reggae Album Of The Year (International) for *Mama Africa*. He is in the process of completing an album with Bunny Wailer and will soon start recording a follow-up album to *Mama Africa* for EMI."

Copeland must have been doing something right to help Peter achieve such success, and will remain a well-respected figurehead within the reggae industry. Janet Davidson points out, "It didn't say Copeland stole anything. They couldn't accuse him of anything, because nothing could be proved. It was done just so Marlene could get control of Peter. That's what happens when you allow your wife or partner to get involved in business."

Peter's cousin Pauline was still living in New York, and assisted him and Marlene with certain business deals. According to Roger Steffens: "From then on, their mystical connection began to grow. Peter would seemingly reach Pauline through her dreams, often appearing in them to tell her he was coming to town. On the days following these visions, Peter would arrive in Manhattan and call her, saying, 'So wha' 'appen Pauline? You dream anything about me lately?'"

"I started to look after Intel-Diplo when Peter was still alive," says Pauline. "I pretty much manage that label and control all the masters. At least Peter was wise enough to make that decision in spite of what was going on back then, because there were certain people involved in his life who really shouldn't have been. I want to make it clear that I'm talking about Marlene Brown because Peter pretty much got rid of everyone in his life after being with her. He got rid of his family, friends and musicians... Let me tell you something – this woman didn't even know who Peter was or what kind of person she had in her possession. She just didn't understand him or what he stood for. He was in a fog really. It was totally sad."

Peter was advertised as headlining the World Cultural Music Festival at the Hollywood Bowl in Los Angeles on August 19, 1984. He was to have shared a bill with Fela Kuti and calypso king Mighty Sparrow but then Fela was jailed in Nigeria – on trumped up currency charges – and the show was cancelled. Donald Kinsey has reason to remember events surrounding this show more than most, since it signalled the end of his friendship with the Bush Doctor.

"People feared Peter. He really was a mystic man. You never knew what might be on Peter's mind," he told Lesli Singer, who then asked him whether Tosh was into obeah.

"I think Peter knew about that, but I don't think he was into it. I think he needed to know about it to protect himself from it but in the end it got to him really. I had seen such a drastic change in Peter. It hurt me from the bottom of my heart. It got bad after the *Mama Africa* tour. During that time something strange started coming over him. His closest friends became the most distant people in his life. People who really cared about him were so far away from him.

"He was supposed to be doing a show in LA so he called me and at five in the morning I'm packed and ready to catch the limousine when the phone rings and it's this agent calling me from New York to tell me the show's been cancelled. Three weeks later, he calls me again to reschedule it but I had a terrible toothache so I said, 'Man, I got to get this tooth fixed so why don't you advance me $500 so I can get some things taken care of?' The guy tells me he needs to ring Peter and tell him but then Peter's girlfriend, who was taking care of his business, starts cussing me out. After that Peter gets on the phone and says, 'Donald man. You think you're the only man wanna play guitar for the I? You're not gonna stop this music.' I said to myself, 'Man, what's happened to my brother?' That was the last time I spoke to Peter Tosh..."

Donald compares the last phase of Peter's life to "the things you read about but never see" and points the finger directly at Marlene.

"I saw Peter helpless," he told Roger Steffens. "I couldn't believe what I was seeing right before me, after working so hard to get there and then see this going on. She was strong, strong and put some stuff on Peter. She almost had him in the zombie stage. The things that she was saying in front of people, she knew that she had him in the palm of her hand. She'd tell people, 'If you mess with me, I'll have Peter do this or that.' She busted the windows out of his car, and people came and raided all of his trees...

"When I first met Peter he was a health freak who drank juices and fresh this and that. Hey she got him, man. Peter's son told Copeland she had him take her out in the country where she picked up so many things of blood. It was obeah, without a doubt. She was walking around the house wearing a sweatshirt with "voodoo" written on it during rehearsals. She was showing it right there, putting it in your face and I started thinking about all those old superstitions because that's where she was coming from. Peter was trying to keep up some kind of shield. He must have felt something coming, to want to put up a defence like that. I guess he felt that sooner or later it would break him down and once she got him like that, it was all over. She drove everyone away from him because that wasn't Peter. He was sick and she'd got him in some kind of way. She had enough time to do what she had to do and I never saw a guy so strong in so many ways come down like that, by a woman. She wasn't a loving person..."

"This mad girl who come into Peter's life, Marlene Brown, she's the one who throw off the good vibes," reflects Carlton Tosh. "Because when your spirit gets tampered with, then anything can happen to you because you can't hold that focus any more or concentrate on anything. It's like there's something interfering with you and messing up your wavelength. It's like a disease. It can easily crawl in on you if you let it get its way.

"What really happened was, Peter really love this girl and when he first meet her, she was so humble, believe me. Even I find it unbelievable that someone who started out so humble could change in the way she did. She was a very nice girl, I swear to you. Maybe she was just working in herself because she then turned into something else entirely. She was acting crazy and after a while, Peter thought she was mad. Peter wanted to help her. He didn't want to leave her like that and that's what happened because then she started to move in on a different level, acting up and all that... It was so crazy man but she wasn't really his manager. She just take that title for herself; like when she say that she's his queen and all that. That came from when we were in Africa, and Peter see all these albums and singles from EMI that he didn't know about. He get suspicious of what they'd been doing and that's why *No Nuclear War* was delayed for so long, because he wanted to clear these things up before doing anything else for them. The man had to go through all kinds of stuff, I tell you..."

Whilst they'd been in Swaziland, fans had asked Peter to sign copies of albums and singles they'd bought locally and that's how he discovered EMI was distributing his records in South Africa. "Except I don't think they'd been pressed there," says Janet Davidson. "I think they were imported. "The thing is, Peter didn't understand the business side of it and neither did I at the time. Peter always had top Jewish lawyers though. They were the people who controlled the business and if you wanted to get anywhere, you needed someone who could enter that world and meet up with them at bar mitzvahs and in the synagogues, because that's where most of the deals were done. That's how it was before Marlene took over, and then it all started to go downhill from there..."

Janet stopped working for Peter in 1984 and says it was because of Marlene, who'd assumed control of his career despite lacking the requisite skills.

"I genuinely believe that if it hadn't have been for her, he would still be alive. She was rude to people; she used to box people down. She did all kinds of things. It's like she turned mad. She thought she was a queen and she got real nasty. She gained control of Peter, but then didn't know what to do with him. For some reason he was captivated by her and it got very, very embarrassing. She wanted to get involved in the business side of things but since she was a child who'd never been in the industry at all I just left them to it."

"Women were his weakness," admits Ras Karbi. "I visited his house in Kingston around that time to talk to him about doing a show in Negril and he said I would have to talk to Marlene, because she was the one who was in charge of everything. She said Peter wasn't doing any shows and they were just concentrating on making an album but Marlene messed everything up once Peter started dealing with her. I was shocked that he allowed it to happen like that."

Back in April, Marvin Gaye had been shot dead by his father. Marvin had married a girl 17 years his junior who insiders said had control over him before his death. The parallels with Peter's situation were self-evident, even as his career began to suffer. He was at war with his record company after accusing them of contractual breaches and whilst it's unclear that he'd legally forbidden them to manufacture or sell his records in South Africa, there *is* evidence that EMI did so. A double album with gatefold sleeve entitled *I Am That I Am* reprised choice tracks from *Bush Doctor*, *Mystic Man* and *Wanted Dread & Alive*, and will later be repackaged as *Revival*. Each of these albums carry the disclosure "marketed and distributed by EMI Music South Africa (PTY) Ltd". The liner notes of *Revival* include the following quote, which made interesting reading.

"When you deal with the kind of music and songs and words I speak and what I stand for, you are wanted but they cannot make it too obvious because they know that what I am dealing with is truth and rights. Because of what I speak about, I know that I am wanted and I will always be wanted until man is free..."

Even the times were against him. Musical tastes had changed, and the idealism that had informed so much of sixties and seventies music been swept away by a hedonism that allowed precious little room for Old Testament style proselytising. 1984 was the year of Madonna's breakthrough and Prince – whom Bob had once slighted by refusing to shake his hand – was the reigning dandy on the scene, pushing at the boundaries of funk in eyeliner, lace and G-strings. To quote Gerri Hirshey, "America – and

MTV's growing audience – felt the full flowering of makeover madness. Anti-fashion became fashionable; genders were bent, trash beatified, *Doonesbury* yuppified and punk tamed for shopping mall sensibilities. Boy George and Annie Lennox raided each other's closets and shared a *Newsweek* cover, complete with a photo documentary of George's beauty tips."

Thankfully, that wasn't the whole story – not in a year when Desmond Tutu won the Nobel Peace Prize and thousands of demonstrators picketed the South African Embassy in Washington – an action that will jump-start the US anti-apartheid movement. An artist like Peter Tosh should have been out there on the frontline, getting his message across. Instead he'd become a virtual recluse, when not venting a now familiar litany of frustrations.

A US publication called *Reggae Review* was launched in November, and featured Peter on its front cover. Inside, he unleashed another stinging diatribe in Timothy White's direction. After calling White "a preposterous liar", Peter threatens to take him to court and suggests he prepares to hand over "150 million dollars".

"I'm sick and tired of people asking me about what is written here," he says at one point, which begs the question 'why hasn't he read the book himself?'

He finally went back in the studio during the summer of 1985. With no income from touring, Tosh had found it difficult to pay for studio time and also his musicians, although everyone except Donald Kinsey made themselves available once he was ready. This time he'll record at Music Mountain – a 24-track facility owned by producer/arranger Chris Stanley, who worked to the highest international standards. His studio in Stony Hill had already begun to attract Jamaica's leading talents and Peter was keen to try it out, especially after convincing familiar faces like Dennis Thompson and Tyrone Downie to get involved. The sessions will be spread out over a two-month period and yield multiple takes of most tracks – not because he was writing songs in the studio like the Rolling Stones used to do, but improving upon them to get the best possible results.

Santa will tell Roger Steffens that it took some time to get this next album finished, because of the ongoing dispute with EMI. "It took a little time for Peter to put each song together because at the same time he was going back and forth to New York for a court case, so every time he would go and come back with some money, he would go in the studio. Sly and Robbie had done a lot of those tracks from before and then I went and did drum overdubs on them. I just fine-tuned them. He wanted to change the drum sound so I would say the album took a year, two years to actually complete because there were so many other things going on."

The first session took place right at the beginning of June, when they recorded 'Jah Love' and 'Guava' – songs that still haven't officially seen the light of day. Peter was probably just getting the feel of the studio, and allowing time for the musicians to gel. Another on June 4 yielded early versions of 'No Nuclear War' and 'Fight Apartheid', which he then revisited the following day. According to Santa, he, Peter and Vision Walker had first worked on the song 'No Nuclear War' in the basement of Peter's house, where they'd rehearse from time to time. It was Vision who'd come up with the bass line, after Peter had sketched out his apocalyptic warning.

"Peter was aware of the fact that if a nuclear bomb go off, then the whole world a go feel it," says Santa. "So that was his cry to the system. It was just a cry from him saying, 'We don't want no nuclear war, 'cause with nuclear war we won't get far.' It'll just end everything."

'No Nuclear War' is a masterpiece – a song of triumph delivered amidst the threat of annihilation, and voiced with imperious authority. Over the next few weeks he'll hone 'No Nuclear War' into one of reggae music's greatest-ever protest songs, especially after adding gospel style harmonies that resemble siren calls, warning of danger ahead...

"Peter used to read a lot you know. He read intellectual stuff that deal with things of the earth and world issues," says Santa. "Him was really into that. I think most of his songs were based on stuff that he read and really see, because he used to watch the news and would comment on certain things. Of course Peter did watch some cartoons and whatever, 'cause Peter was a real human being too. He wasn't just a serious man who screwed up his face all the while. No, he used to laugh too..."

David Hinds, lead singer with British reggae band Steel Pulse, can attest to that. He visited Peter at 5 Plymouth Avenue during these sessions, and found him in remarkably good spirits. "The thing with Peter, he was very eccentric but he didn't act as if he was a superstar, or see himself as being better than anyone else. He knew we were up-and-coming and yet still took the time to hang out with us and talk. One of the last times I saw him was at his house in the Barbican. We sat and chatted and he was a bit of a comedian as well to be honest with you. His lyrics were so serious and potent, yet he made fun of the beatings he'd had because I remember him saying how the last time they tried to kill him, he'd had to play dead. He also made this comment about how a man tried to shoot him from a distance of about three and a half feet once, but missed. I think he saw himself as omnipotent in a way. The strange thing is, we were taking pictures of him and after a while he said to stop, which we did. He said the last set of people he told to stop taking photos didn't listen to him and when they developed them, he wasn't in the pictures! Those were the kinds of things he used to say. He literally believed that he was the mystic man and looking back, I think I believed it too."

During that June 4 session he also voiced two cuts of 'Babylon Queendom', but wasn't happy with either of them. As he always did when working on a new album, Peter re-recorded certain songs – not because he'd run out of ideas, but in a bid to develop them further. He'd first recorded 'Vampire' during the *Equal Rights* sessions, but that version had only been issued on 7", for the grass-roots market. The opening howl remains, and so too the biting commentary that prompted Santa to call it "a song about the whole shit-stem and people in general who are just evil". Despite 20 years of independence, Jamaica's government apparatus still operated along colonial lines. Peter calls the island's politicians "old vampires, sucking the blood of the nation" who want to "drink up the old wine, leaving no room for the new wine", meaning a change of approach and ideally, the introduction of social reforms designed to help Jamaica's poor. "You fight against democracy, fight against integrity, fight against everything good for the younger generation," he tells them, whilst warning his listeners that, "vampires don't like to see you prosper. They only like to see you suffer."

Despite the seriousness of its lyric, you can dance to 'Vampire'. Some of the rhythms Peter was recording at Music Mountain were easily a match for those heard in the Jamaican charts behind the likes of Gregory Isaacs, Dennis Brown and Half Pint. Whilst he always sought to introduce a level of sophistication to his music, Peter still wanted it to reflect current trends in Jamaica to a certain extent. Talking of sophistication, Nambo Robinson recalls seeing him with a violin at Music Mountain one day.

"That really took me off guard. He was actually sitting there, playing a violin! I can't remember whether he used it on the actual session or not but he was the kind of person that once he'd decided he was going to teach himself something, then he'd do it. He wasn't afraid to take up a challenge, but I mean that was quite a vision..."

On June 10 he voiced definitive cuts of 'Nah Go A Jail (Fe Ganja)' and 'Fight Apartheid'. He'd previewed the latter on stage once or twice and it's another of his classic protest songs – resolute in its integrity, and perfectly timed as world opinion continued to exert pressure on South Africa. Peter declares the apartheid regime illegal, and accuses its leaders of robbing *his* resources. "You've built no schools for my children," he scolds. "All you build is prisons, and set up your army camp. So come out of me land."

"A lot of people weren't brave enough to sing certain songs," says Santa. "People a more say, 'Boy, I want to keep out of that kind of thing,' because after a while you get branded but Peter have no care about that. He just say people have to hear these things and somebody have to stand up, so that's why he write the song."

No Peter Tosh album is complete without a ganja anthem and there's a celebratory air to 'Nah Go A Jail (Fe Ganja)' that makes it a good deal more playful than predecessors such as 'Bush Doctor' and even 'Legalise It'. There must have been a smile on Peter's face when he sang, "You see this spliff, I just got it from my officer, and this little piece of sensimelia, I just got it from a minister. He's my friend!" He's being amusing yet there's also an edge to his lyrics, as you'd expect from someone having suffered at the hands of the police.

"Him just get tired of the fact that him can't smoke his herb in peace," Santa explains. "Him said he would write a song like that and at first we think, 'Boy Peter, that song there is kind of harsh...' I mean you never really go up against Peter because if he's going to do something, him just going to do it. And there was no opposition because we understood exactly his feelings towards all of this. Any song Peter sing was for a reason and him suffer the wrath of smoking weed, because the man them nearly kill him just for a little spliff."

Five days later, on June 15, he finishes 'In My Song' – a reggae hymn built on spiritual certainty, but that hints at personal vulnerability. As well as identifying the source of Peter's inspiration it also tells us something of the process, as heard in the lines "Jah is the melody. In my song he is the symphony. In my song he's the sweet inspiration. It's called perfect meditation. When I'm feeling down, nowhere to go, I go inside myself, put on a show."

This is already a better album than *Mama Africa*. Peter's moved with the times and his music has continued to evolve, despite the upheavals happening in his life. His newer material has continued to benefit from a broad worldview and yet he's never afraid to commit, either politically or personally. After further attempts at 'Jah Man' on June 16, he then takes a two-day break and nails 'Lesson In My Life' – a song that had languished in the vaults ever since being rejected for the *Bush Doctor* album, but that now gives him an opportunity to reaffirm what he's all about. "I'm an upful man and I love upful people," he sings, in a voice that conveys just a hint of weariness. "I'm a progressive man, and I love progressive people. I'm an intelligent man, and I love intelligent people. I'm a truthful man, and I love truthful people. I'm an honest man and I love honest people..."

It's a successor to *Mystic Man*, but with a sting in its tail.

"Always be careful of my friends," he warns. "Money can make friendship end. It makes friendship end..."

Santa says the song gave him an eerie feeling from when he first heard it.

"Every time I hear him singing it, it's like something out of this world – something you hear and can't explain the feeling it gives you. I was getting little visions here and there, like some weird stuff that never really compute... I saw things coming and start to vision things. It was like those were the last words he was putting out. I think he knew that it would only be a matter of time..."

This new version is more regal than the one cut during the *Bush Doctor* sessions, featuring John Sebastian's harmonica. It's statesmanlike, and borne on a tide of heavenly harmonies. The combined voices of Nadine Sutherland, Pam Hall and J. C. Lodge – also Cynthia Schloss – are a wonder to behold. Throughout the next decade they'll record with a multitude of top singers, including Dennis Brown, Maxi Priest and Shabba Ranks. Nadine had been around the Wailers' clan since winning a Tastees' talent show more than a year earlier. First prize was a recording date at Tuff Gong, where she'd voiced her debut single, 'Starvation On The Land'.

"My father was a taxi driver and Peter did the right thing because he came up to the house to ask his permission if I could sing for him. I remember him telling my father what time he should drop me off at the studio and then promising to see that I got back home safely, which he did. He really went out of his way for me, and acted so gentlemanly. I was only 16 at the time and still at high school, because I was wearing my uniform at that first session! I was terrified, because I'd never sung background vocals before. I sang harmony naturally, as most country girls did, and I'd listened to the I Threes but I went into that session and here's Peter Tosh smiling at me... I'd felt totally intimidated before arriving. I was expected to sing with Pam Hall and J. C, who'd sang on some major albums so I was like wide-eyed... I had the highest parts on 'No Nuclear War' but Peter would sing them to me line by line, so I could follow him. I felt so honoured to be singing with a legend like him at such a tender age but I made a lot of mistakes initially, and he'd go through it with me gently each time. He was so nurturing towards me. I was a young person who didn't know the ropes and I tell you, he never took advantage of me once. People make out that Peter was this ogre who was always angry, like some raving firebrand who goes around fighting with police, but the Peter Tosh I knew wasn't like that. I guess it's not every day a knight wears his armour, but there were so many sides to this man.

"He wasn't like this person walking round kicking ass, even though he was an established reggae star. He was softly spoken and considerate towards other people. He conducted himself in a professional manner, and he treated everybody like they were co-workers. There were no displays of ego or arrogance; nothing like that. He was caring and extremely polite, and everyone seemed to get along with him just fine. He was clearly enjoying his time working on that album, giving directions and being totally immersed in it. That's what I saw. I also remember how much he trusted Marlene at those sessions and opened up his heart to her, because I recall seeing her wait on him, and bringing him coconut water. She really did care for him and I saw him as this man who wanted to have a queen and to share love with someone he trusted."

On June 21, he had three more attempts at 'Babylon Queendom'. It'll be a couple more weeks before he changes the title to 'Mystery Babylon' and feels satisfied. By then he will have finished 'Come Together', which isn't the Beatles' song, but could have easily been written around the time of 'All We Need Is Love' since the sentiments are much the same. "Where do we go from here? Is it here, there or nowhere?" he asks. The answer is simple, and so is the message. We need more unity, and we've got to learn to love and respect one another. That's it, except he can't resist stirring a little kung fu into the mix as well. "One eye can't see, one ear don't hear," he sings, mischievously. "One hand can't clap, one foot don't run..."

The harmonies are again outstanding. J. C. Lodge, who'd opened her account with a cover of Charlie Pride's 'Someone Loves You Honey' for Joe Gibbs, says the arrangements were largely due to Peter.

"Most of the time the producers would let us do our own thing and we'd prefer that, because then we could be more creative. Pam and I would both make suggestions and normally the artists or producers would just go along with it. It wasn't very often that we'd arrive at the studio and find that our parts had been worked out for us beforehand. That's because Peter had a very clear idea of how he wanted it to sound and I respected him as an artist, definitely. He wanted a full sound when it came to the harmonies, and I thought that project went very well although I was a bit wary of him at first. He seemed a bit taciturn and I didn't want to step on his toes. The way he spoke was very direct and he didn't make any effort to be polite. I think he was pleased with what we did though, otherwise he would have certainly let us know about it! I remember he seemed very intent on rolling up his spliffs whilst we were there at the studio, and I liked the way he'd eat out of this calabash he had. He was a real character."

Three days after the last *No Nuclear War* session, Mick Jagger made his debut as a solo artist at Live Aid, singing with Tina Turner. Bob Dylan followed him, accompanied by Keith Richards and Ron Wood, who sounded as ragged as they looked. If Peter was watching, we can only imagine the cursing that ensued... Six months later and reggae singer Patrick Alley will sue Jagger for plagiarism, although a New York judge will eventually rule in Mick's favour. "My reputation is cleared," he'll announce. "If you're well known, people stand up and take shots at you."

No Nuclear War still won't be released by then, despite having been mixed and mastered.

"From what I heard, there were a lot of hold-ups that prevented the album coming out on time," says Nadine Sutherland. "As an artist myself, I can understand that level of frustration because I've been through it several times. You have an album finished, but the record company are holding it back. I think that will really affect Peter later on, but whilst we were making that album he was totally enjoying his art and there was real legitimacy to what he was singing about as well. He was no run-of-the-mill kind of performer. He basically was in the same league as Bob Marley, because the album I sang on was a work of genius and there's real depth to what he did. It was an assertion, and he'd obviously read a lot about world affairs and African history. You can tell because of the beauty of his poetry and the intelligence of his lyrics. He had a level of wry humour too, and that led him to use Jamaican bad words sometimes... I mean can you imagine hearing that song 'Oh Bumbo Klaat' all those years ago? I would be holding my belly with laughter at things like that. That song wasn't played in my house and it would be barred from every jukebox on the island but some sound systems would play it over and over again. People would be singing it with tears of laughter running down their faces..."

J. C. Lodge confirms that recording *No Nuclear War* took so long because Peter was funding it himself and may have had problems coming up with the money.

"I know that he had difficulty paying us, because after we'd finished he told us to go and check him at his yard. I didn't like the sound of that and wasn't used to it, because the money would usually be there ready for us whenever we finished working. We went to his house and Marlene said Peter would deal with it but then Peter turned round to us and said, 'Bwoy, me don't know what we haffi do because all I have is a little ganja money and that can't work...' I thought to myself, 'No, he's not saying this. Don't tell me this is going to become a problem,' but it was Marlene who sorted it out in the end. She took some money out of a safe they had at a house and gave it to me but I wasn't too impressed. She was supposed to be managing him but it didn't seem very professional because he was still very vocal in the dealings. And it was him who'd said we should go up there and see him. He didn't say, 'Well Marlene will take care of you.' I did get paid most of what they owed though, and so can't complain..."

Chapter 30

Vampire

In the latter part of 1985, Peter and Bunny Wailer had unfinished business to attend to. They wanted to show the world that the Wailers wasn't a rhythm section featuring the Barrett brothers, but a vocal group – one that sprang from the tenement yards of Trench Town, and had endured years of adversity before signing to Island Records and making *Catch A Fire*. With this aim in mind, they decided to reform the original line-up as far as possible and make an album using some of Bob's unreleased vocals. Vision Walker and Junior Braithwaite, who'd sung with the Wailers in the past, were then added to the line-up. Junior's lead on 'It Hurts To Be Alone' had been a smash hit over Christmas 1964, crowning an unbelievable six months that had started with their debut 'Simmer Down'. Coxsone had considered him a better lead singer than Bob at the time and whilst he'd done little since then, Junior had impeccable credentials. He'd come back from America especially for this project whilst Vision had toured and recorded with Peter for years, and was Rita Marley's cousin. He'd sung with her in the Soulettes before briefly replacing Bob in the Wailers. It's his harmonies decorating Peter's earliest versions of 'The Toughest', 'Can't You See' and 'Treat Me Good', as well as Wailers hits like 'Let Him Go', 'Dancing Shoes' and 'I Stand Predominant'.

On paper at least, the new-look Wailers were world-beaters, and given Peter and Bunny's international standing there was no reason why they couldn't make an album of outstanding material. Their first act was to strip the rhythms from a handful of old recordings – most of them Wailers self-productions voiced circa 1971 – and take them to Channel One where Sly & Robbie rebuilt them from scratch, using Bob's vocals as a guideline. Afterwards, they'll book sessions at Music Mountain and begin work on an album called *Never Ending Wailers*. The lead single, credited to the Original Wailers and released in December, was 'Music Lesson' – a song reaffirming reggae music's ability to educate as well as entertain, and questioning why the likes of Marco Polo are mentioned in Jamaican school history books and not famous African figureheads. It's a salutary message, covering similar ground Peter had explored in 'Here Comes The Judge'. Bob's voice is quite distinct, and it's a joy hearing the five of them sing in combination. On the flipside was 'Nice Time', or rather an updated version led by Bunny. Bob doesn't feature so prominently on that one, but it's a beautiful production nevertheless – one that serves to underline what a loss Junior Braithwaite's absence from the music had been.

Alas, the response was muted to say the least. Reggae music had undergone a massive upheaval in the past six months, after singer Wayne Smith had jumped aboard one of Prince Jammy's computerised rhythms and turned the industry upside-down with a catchy herb ditty called 'Under Mi Sleng-Teng'. Jamaica's digital revolution was now in full swing and a flood of other tracks using computerised rhythms quickly swept all before them, rendering old style recordings virtually redundant. Not even a Wailers reunion and hearing Bob Marley sing from beyond the grave in such mesmerising fashion could stem the tide. Those exquisite reconstructions of 'I'm Still Waiting', 'How Many Times', 'It Hurts To Be Alone' and 'Hammer' would have caused a sensation just a year earlier but then timing is everything in the music business, and so it proved.

"That one never pass through the iron gate at all," commented Family Man, without so much as a hint of satisfaction. This – coupled with various administration difficulties – is probably why the album won't surface for another eight years, adding to the storehouse of unreleased Wailers material.

Bunny drove the project, and was responsible for the majority of production and writing credits. A short film made of the group in the studio shows what a dominant force he was. At the start of it, the four Original Wailers are sat in the voicing room, rolling spliffs from stalks of fresh sensimelia. Peter has a flask at his feet and is wearing a garish, short-sleeved T-shirt with a rainbow design on it. He has a different look about him. It's as if he's not quite there, although this could have something to do with the herb he's smoking. After a while, the quartet gets to its feet and sways in unison whilst crooning, "We'll be working, together again…" They're highly charged, and so is the music. Each member sings a few solo lines and Peter's are especially poignant, bearing in mind what lies ahead. "Who will be the survivors?' he asks. "Only Jah Jah knows. Moving on in unity, and doing the best we can."

'Together Again' was one of a handful of songs that Bunny had written especially for these sessions. 'Dutch Pot', 'Rescue Me' and 'Coolie Plum' were among the others, and the lyrics of 'Coolie Plum' speak volumes. "Were you there in Trench Town when the Wailers came together, under that coolie plum tree? We used to sing songs of freedom, sing songs of joy…"

Peter hardly figures on that track, and wasn't there for all of the sessions. His son Andrew, who'd recently made his recording debut for Neville Lee, helped out on 'Music Lesson' but the atmosphere was far from being convivial. Peter's clearly uncomfortable at being filmed and bolts from the studio at the earliest opportunity. Nambo Robinson remembers visiting Music Mountain around this time, and getting a surprise as he walked through the door.

"I went there to do a session one night and there was this poster of Bob Marley on the wall as you went in the control booth that we all liked. Everyone respected Bob but someone had gouged the eyes out of the poster and I said, 'Who the hell did that?' Because nobody could understand why anyone would want to do something like that. The owner of the studio was complaining that Peter had just come in there and gouged the eyes out of the poster in a fit of rage. This had happened the day before we got there."

A friend of Peter's called Michael Robinson visited him at home during this same time frame and saw a painting of a white Jesus hanging on the wall, pockmarked with tiny holes. He was stood there looking at it when a dart whistled past his head and stuck in Jesus' face. Peter was using it as target practice! Things were clearly getting on top of him, and no wonder. At 40 years of age he'd mastered his craft and yet was constantly beset by troubles, including plenty of his own making. He'll play no role in either finishing or helping to publicise the Wailers' album and in the meantime *No Nuclear War* remained largely unheard, despite being the most accomplished album of his career in many ways. The finished version will have just eight tracks on it and contain no love songs or fusions with other musical styles. It's a straightforward, but highly polished reggae collection and in Donald Kinsey's absence, lead guitar pyrotechnics are kept to a minimum. Tyrone Downie's keyboards aside, it's the actual production – credited to "Peter Tosh and Marlene Brown" – that gifts this album its modernity, and tracks like 'No Nuclear War', 'Fight Apartheid', 'Nah Go A Jail' and 'Come Together' affirm Peter's role as Jamaica's most outspoken and revolutionary singer.

He'd written the title track more than a year ago and yet global fears surrounding nuclear energy had increased massively since then. In April 1986, explosions at the Chernobyl nuclear power plant in Ukraine had released large quantities of radioactive contamination into the atmosphere, which had then spread over much of Western USSR and Europe. It was the worst nuclear power plant accident in history and 500,000 workers were still working flat out to avert an even greater disaster. Peter's warning couldn't have been timelier, and he'd wanted the cover art to reflect this. Neville Garrick, who'd designed *Wanted Dread & Alive* and the majority of Bob Marley's album sleeves, was entrusted to depict Peter's vision, and told Roger Steffens how it happened.

"He basically came and said he wanted to be standing on the two missiles of Russia and America, in front of a mushroom cloud. The gas mask on his face would give it a kind of death look but he also wanted to be flashing lightning out of his hands towards the missiles. On my original painting Peter had no shirt but his woman said he couldn't go to war without armour plate. I said, 'If you were flashing lightning from your hands, you wouldn't need no shirt,' so I painted on a metallic armour-like shirt. The gas mask was also his conception. He always had a gas mask with him at his house. I used a picture I took of him wearing it on the back cover, solarised, like the x-ray of an atom bomb blast."

Certain Amharic words appear in the design. Those on his arm bracelets mean "Word, Sound And Power" whilst the ones on his chest read "Head Creator", which is the title of Emperor Haile Selassie I. It's Peter's most striking album cover yet, but will be shelved until EMI formalises an official release schedule. In May 1986 the label and Peter were still at loggerheads, but agreed to a press conference so he could preview tracks from the album and announce any future plans. This will be held in the courtyard of SIR studios in Manhattan, where Peter had rehearsed for the majority of his tours since 1978.

"When EMI was getting ready to release *No Nuclear War*, it set up a press conference for Peter in this really nice place," says Winston Harriott. "It was part of a major press campaign and journalists arrived from all around the world, because there was a lot of attention on him. I was with Peter and Marlene in the car and as we arrived, Marlene said she was going to have a look inside before Peter made his entrance. We said, 'cool', and drove round the block. When we get back now she said we're not going in there. I jumped out to see what the problem was and saw the place was full. The guy from *Rolling Stone* magazine was there, and Earl Chin from *Rockers* TV... People from EMI were there too. Everybody was sat there smiling, looking forward to seeing Peter but Marlene said there were too many white people in there and I couldn't believe it!

"I watched the whole thing come down and you have to blame Peter because he allowed it to happen, but that Marlene Brown was such a bad influence on him, believe me. She was an obeah woman and she just locked him away. She destroyed him and also other people too, like Free I. People got really disturbed about what was happening to him."

Eventually they go in and Peter takes his seat at a table decorated with flowers and a toy lion. Marlene's introduced as his manager and is dressed all in white, with her hair wrapped in a white turban. It's an outfit that some people might associate with obeah, especially in rural Jamaica. The gathering has already been played a selection of tracks from the album, which solicited definite signs of approval. Peter then signals that he's ready to start answering questions. "We can go into it, y'know?" he chides. "I'm alert." A woman from *Reggae Times* opens by asking him whether it's true that he's considered visiting South Africa, despite the cultural boycott. This has Peter muttering about "journalistic propaganda", and how words "that are not even spoken" can be turned around... Roberto from Los Angeles then talks about protest songs but Peter corrects him, and says he prefers to calls them "manifestations of prophecy".

"These things were prophesised thousands of years ago. There is nothing new under the sun. It is only man who's trying to change the time by pushing the clock forwards or backwards one hour, but that doesn't make the time change. What is taking place *has* to take place, and nothing has changed."

"Why have you been quiet?" asks someone else, more pertinently. "Have you been meditating in a different vein, or been working on music still? Where is your head at right now?"

"My head is always on my shoulders my dear, and I always try and keep it there because I see guys walking on their heads in these days and their toes dangling in the air, seen? Well people can try experimenting, but I am not. I've been here for thousands of years and I'll be always here but there have been many detrimental things taking place in my business. Damagers who they call managers have been trying to destroy me physically, mentally and in every form, so what I've been doing is trying to reorganise myself and get myself back together again, because I see where many entertainers come and go down. I'm not an entertainer, I'm a preacher and preachers don't preach every day so these are the reasons why you will see me when it's necessary."

Over the course of the next 40 minutes or so we learn that *No Nuclear War* is likely to be distributed by EMI America, but no tour dates have been finalised as yet and especially not in Europe, where he says "detrimental things" are taking place.

"There are all kinds of dangerous gases there. It's only a pity I didn't bring the album cover to show you. On it I am wearing a gas mask, so this was to tell you that I know what was and will be coming, seen? But my gas mask is spiritual. I would only wear it physically over my eyes and nose because in these times, man will be invincible. Don't look at your television and think it is only Incredible Hulk and all these dangerous looking guys. These things going to be for real because what the devil is designing, man has to be spiritually invincible to avoid these things, to eat of deadly food and not poison, seen? So we're living to live and pertaining to a tour in Europe right now, I have to be observing. There are gases in Poland and I am planning to go to all these Scandinavian countries where the food is dangerous, seen? The water there is dangerous, the air is dangerous and I have to use all these things so I am observing and America may get me this time."

Who's your US booking agent?

"I definitely don't have no booking agency because every day people call me at my house. I am my own booking agency. Just name a number and I'll be available. Every day thousands of people call me."

What's the release date on the album?

"Well we don't prescribe that as yet because I'm still waiting to get the jacket. The jacket is finished but I'm supposed to get it tomorrow. I'm hoping for the album to be released within the next four weeks because as I said there is a meltdown in Russia and that is a very serious thing."

There's plenty of talk about herb as you'd expect, which he says has "spiritual, botanical allegiance".

"It's anti-fungus, anti-virus and anti-hypnosis. Jah created it for the motivation of the mind of man, to relax the mind of man, and to cleanse and purify the blood. It's a long time they've been researching, and they have cancer patients using herb now so let's not play games. The games are over. I went to England from 1973 and they've been planting hundreds of acres of herbs there for medicinal purpose, seen? And experimenting with it and saying it's for mad people. Yet as a youth growing up I was told that if you use this thing they classify as drugs, it's detrimental and it's so deadly, yet I am still not dead. But this cocaine business that's going on out there, it's an intentional campaign and the reason why so many people get caught up in these things is because they want to be someone else, and as long as you want to be someone else, then you won't have two feet to stand up on. You will be led away by devils, because devils come in many different guises, also in your friends."

Someone asks him about import copies of a video called *Live At Greek Theatre* that's recently turned up in reggae specialist outlets. This is the film of Peter's performance in Los Angeles from autumn 1983, directed by Michael. C. Collins. Hendring will soon issue it under the title of *Downpressor Man*, prompting one reviewer to describe Peter as "an articulate, self-assured performer who was gearing up for more substantial recognition", but who then dismisses 'Johnny B. Goode' as "a concession to Whitey". Oh well, you can't win them all... EMI has already released the soundtrack on LP as *Captured Alive*, but Peter is clearly unhappy with this situation.

"When I ask EMI why the live album is not available, they told me they released 40,000 and it sold off in one day, seen? And no more was put out from that time. These are the things I bombaclaat talk about and when I get so fucking upset I don't bother talk English bombaclaat grammar any more 'cause them things get me very bombaclaat upset, seen? And all because I am not singing 'darling I bloodclaat love you and come shake my Rass and I'll come swim the ocean and climb the mountain', seen? And that's not going to change me, seen? Because I am going to kill the fuckery out there and people are going to demand the truth. People are sick and tired of hearing bombaclaat 'get down, shake your fucking booty' and 'darling I bloodclaat love you', seen? You turn on the radio 24 hours a day and all you hear is 'darling I love you'. A man wouldn't sing to the Almighty; he'd rather sing to a woman than the Creator who create the sun, the moon and the bombaclaat stars. I'm sick and tired of hearing that bombaclaat, seen?"

His outburst gets a round of applause, which means those present either agree with him, or appreciate how he's unafraid to speak his mind. Peter may not always make sense but he's never shrunk from saying what's on his mind, even after venturing out on a limb. The media people attending that press conference fully expected to see *No Nuclear War* released within a month or so. In fact it won't appear in the shops for well over another year after his dispute with EMI rumbles on, fuelled by Marlene's interventions.

"I was up at the house one day when Peter played *No Nuclear War* to me and it blew me away," says Ras Karbi. "He sounded so strong vocally and although his message was anti-establishment, he was saying all the right things. It was perfect. I listened to the whole album and thought it was great but then that girl Marlene shake everything up because I heard she went to EMI and took out Peter's file. She demanded it and walked out with it. She broke the whole thing up and they never got the money they were looking for. Nobody liked that girl. She had no business knowledge and she didn't know the ethics of how to behave around the music business. She just saw the power she could have and she had Peter sat right there, saying nothing, and yet he was one of our most important artists."

Time was catching up with Peter Tosh, even as Bob Marley began to define reggae music to the world at large. Eighteen months earlier, Island had released a greatest hits compilation of his called *Legend* that was already well on its way towards becoming the biggest-selling reggae album of all time. Bunny too was on a high, and will soon return to the stage. This happened during the summer of 1986. His first appearance since the Youth Consciousness show will be at the Long Beach University in California on July 12, followed by a night at Madison Square Garden in New York on July 16. He'll then return to the West Coast for shows at the Greek Theatre in Los Angeles during November. Peter could have shared in his triumph but Marlene again interfered, causing Carlton Tosh to despair of her continuing influence in Peter's affairs.

"She was feeding him with all kinds of crazy stuff. That time Bunny Wailer performed at Madison Square Garden, he wanted Peter to come on the show with him. Peter agreed, but then all of a sudden he didn't agree any more because this girl start to push things in his head by saying things like, 'Oh, Bunny Wailer wants you to open for *him*?' But it was Bunny Wailer's show, and so why should Peter be the headliner? She tried to make such a big thing out of it but that's what she was like because if anyone drew close to Peter, including Bunny, then she'd try and get them out of his life. That was her motivation and though the girl was so crazy, everybody just have to ease off. She was something else man, I tell you. She get right into the man's life, but she wasn't good for him."

Bunny once said Peter "went through hell' and that after 20 years' friendship, he no longer recognised him.

"I don't know what got into Peter that he would have said those things, even about me. Peter was taken over by some force that would have destroyed us all, and it destroyed Peter without him even knowing it. That was the kind of element that took Peter over, I'm telling you that, because Peter was no longer himself by then. When I saw Peter in the last stages before he leave, that wasn't Peter. Something had taken over Peter totally. *Totally.* When I look into his face, that wasn't Peter, it was a stranger. I was trying to figure out, 'who the fuck is this guy?' He didn't look like someone I remembered, or was even familiar with. It was as if a total stranger controlled him, because Peter deal with me like he never even know me. Peter actually said to me that he's no Wailer. 'The Wailers are dead!' he said. He told me that right to my face. Imagine Peter saying that! 'Once a Wailer, always a Wailer', that was our motto and even Bob never use that on us, right through our being together…"

"Peter was an inspiring person to me spiritually, but somewhere along the line he got broken down," Santa told Karie Russell. "Someone or something came in and stole the 'mystic'. I knew Peter to be a very strong-willed person who meant well for the people, no matter their colour, class or creed but I guess even wise men get led astray sometimes. Peter lost all those mystic vibes and all kinds of evil elements started to surround him."

"He dropped his guard and became blind," says Pauline Morrison. "I pitied him. We all did. The entire family knew it and we all pitied him."

"Peter couldn't see that Marlene was an evil person," confirms Ras Karbi. "He was totally blinded by her. I remember she had this obeah man living at the house with them. He was a very black-skinned man and that's how Peter introduced him to me once, as his obeah man. I was shocked when he said that. I started picking up on what was happening and stopped going there after that, but that girl would disrespect anybody. She said that Andrew Tosh tried to rape her and so Peter beat the shit out of him with a machete – chopped him all around the head right in front of the police station at Savanna La Mar. There was this other guy who was an old flame of Marlene's. He was a photographer who went to prison and when he came back out Marlene told Peter he'd tried to rape her, and so Peter beat the shit out of that guy also. He hit him up real bad, but he and Marlene was a bad combination for sure. They say demons attract demons and maybe it's true because they believed in vampires and all that kind of stuff, but then once you let that type of thing into your life it can take over..."

Mortimo Planno will later inform the makers of *Stepping Razor: Red X* that, "If you fear duppy, you draw the duppy to you." Peter has certainly been fearful of them in the past, but told his chiropractor that he was protected from duppies and vampires because he "knew about obeah".

He'd been exposed to such things during his childhood in Westmoreland, where children played African-derived ring games and gazed in wonder as villagers made "moonshine babies". These were made from placing little pieces of broken crockery and decorative stones around the outline of someone lying on their back, under a moonlit night. The villagers would then hold hands and sing and dance around the shape until the spirits departed from them, usually around dawn. Herbie Miller spoke to Peter at length about his upbringing in Westmoreland, and has a clearer insight into it than most.

"It was there he paid attention to Friday and Saturday evening drum and clap hand street-side and market-gate religious meetings, and he was aware of healing rituals practised in the shadows of balm yards. Creolised versions of revivalism, Pocomania, myal, obeah and other African-derived worship, spirit possession, healing and malevolent mores all played a role in Tosh's personal and artistic development."

Obeah, as distinct from natural healing, is where Rastafari parts company with African religion. Rastafarians view controlling dark forces as the Devil's work, and generally leave well alone. Peter was raised in the Pentecostal faith and knew about possession and trance states, which are also key elements of revival cults like kumina, whose members believe ancestral spirits see and know of earthly things, and will protect and guide you if they're treated well. Treat them badly however, and the consequences don't bear thinking about. Deep in the Jamaican countryside, it's easy to believe the dead are all around us and can take control of a living human being. The villagers have all seen people they know jerk as if struck by lightning and then dance with abandon as drums pound out an incessant beat and drive away their fears like they never existed.

Peter was fascinated by these fragments of a distant African past and learnt all he could about them. He knew the Christian church had tried to instil fear into slaves by branding these ancient rituals "pagan", and saying they were inspired by the Devil. Maybe that's what had made him take the risk in plunging even deeper into such practices and crossing the line into obeah. Was it the impulse to draw ever closer to his African roots and thereby discover his true self that had led him to get involved with the supernatural? Or was it the wiles of a woman skilled in obeah's dark arts? He still suffered from crippling migraines and his search for a cure was now desperate, although his faith in natural healing never wavered. The bush doctors he'd sought out in Jamaican country parishes and remote parts of Benin and Swaziland represented the only tradition he truly respected, and he wasn't going to give it up anytime soon.

"Peter swore by the bush medicines and was quick to offer anyone showing the slightest sign of poor physical condition or spiritual need a dose from one of his phials," says Herbie Miller. "He talked about bushes that certain rebellious slaves would rub over bodies to make them invisible and of powders that made them immune to bullets. It was his belief that African-derived sciences and folk potions could be used for good (protection, healing and good luck charms) and evil – inflicting "blows" on one's foes, causing destruction, illness and even death. Peter's developed knowledge of the spirit world must not be overlooked and nor should it be taken lightly."

Herbie recalls him telling the story of a woman whose sore foot continued to trouble her, despite regular medical treatment. Finally a "bush doctor" cured her with herbal medicine and extracted "a fat worm covered with hair" from her foot. That's the thing with Peter. The boundaries keep blurring between something very ancient and of the earth, which is essentially benign, and then a realm of darkness populated by ghosts and vampires. Friends say he used to dream about vampires standing over him, watching his life force drain away.

"We're living in a world of vampires," he once told a journalist who'd asked about the inspiration behind 'Vampire'.

"It's no joke, even though people may pretend and not accept the fact that it exists. Every day you see it on television. It's no fantasy because to every fantasy there is a reality and don't forget that."

According to Konstantinos, author of *Vampires: The Occult Truth*, psychic vampires are most dangerous. These can attack day or night, and feed on their victims' life force – that river of energy that determines all of our actions and even our thoughts. Everything in fact, that makes us the person we are.

"The basic element of the attack should be familiar by now. Sometime during the middle of the night, a sense of dread is felt. The victim of the experience finds it difficult to move and notices that something is either already in the room, or is approaching. Either way within a few seconds of waking, the entity either becomes visible as a dark shape (sometimes with eyes), or is just sensed by the victim. The entity is then seen or felt to approach the bed where it sometimes comes next to the victim or actually moves on top of them. The victim usually begins to feel a weight pressing down on their chest, and notes other visual and audible sensations. The dark entity may take on some shape, or be surrounded by a coloured light..."

It's the victim's sensitivity that determines how much of the vampire is seen, and also the level of dread they experience. People who see vampires most clearly always feel the most terror, and "whatever force is responsible for the paralysis, it occurs in every attack and makes the victim an easy target". The victims wake up feeling tired, and some complain of their heads "swelling and thundering from some kind of weird vibration".

If Peter had turned to Marlene for protection from psychic vampires then something had gone wrong and she'd failed to protect him. Either she'd gone into it over her head and made things worse, or deliberately set out to take control of him. When he was a teenager and living with his uncle in Trench Town, he'd fended off an attack by yelling the word "B-U-M-B-O-C-L-A-A-T!!" at the top of his lungs. These days nothing was quite that simple, and the sense of foreboding was now palpable.

Dennis Lobban, better known as "Leppo", was one of the few people who still visited Peter at the house. He was from Trench Town, and would also frequent Ford Penn Lane off the Barbican Road, not far from where Peter and Marlene lived. Thirteen years beforehand he'd been jailed for multiple offences, including aggravated robbery and wounding with intent. He'd been released only recently and had already begged handouts from several other well-known entertainers before latching onto Peter. First he asked him for a bed. Marlene had wanted to give him a spare bed from the music room but Peter said, "No, this man has been in prison. Let's buy him a new one." Leppo would go and see them every two or three weeks after that, asking for money. He wasn't a friend, despite Peter feeling a degree of sympathy for him, but the very definition of a "maga dog". That's because he probably harboured resentment towards Peter, even whilst taking his money. He'll certainly have cause to resent Marlene in due course, and kept a close eye on the couple's comings and goings in the meantime.

It's September 8, 1986, and Amy Wachtel is playing excerpts from one of Peter's concerts on station WBAU-FM in New Garden City. The tracks were recorded at London's Dominion Theatre in 1983 and first aired in the US as part of a College Rock Concert series, with each instalment being sponsored by a local business. *Omni* magazine, "where art and science becomes one", sponsored Peter's slot. Amy ends her show by telling listeners that *Mama Africa* "is widely regarded as Peter's best work yet" but can offer no up-to-date information regarding his latest projects or forthcoming tours. In fact he was staying low profile while seesawing between Jamaica and New York, where his lawyers were still attempting to unravel the legal dispute with EMI. The *No Nuclear War* album had long been ready for release, and yet a breakthrough seemed as far away as ever.

"Peter used to call me up sometimes when he was in New York and get me to drive him around," says Winston Harriott. "One day he asked to go to this bank in Manhattan so we went in, he pulled out his chequebook and then discovered that Marlene had drawn out some money using his name. She'd learnt how to forge his signature and write 'Peter Tosh' because I remember him saying, 'look at that bloodclaat...' That woman got away with a lot of things, I tell you."

If Marlene was acting as Peter's accountant then she'd have access to his banking arrangements, but forgery is a different matter. Writing in the *Jamaica Observer*, Basil Walters made the following observation.

"Marlene boasts about her getting the best recording deals for Tosh. She spoke with pride of how she, through the courts in New York, got EMI to double their payments of advance money as well to pay up unpaid royalties to Peter.

"Managing Peter Tosh was more than I had bargained for," she said. "I did all his secretarial work. I did his accounting, bookkeeping and his negotiations. I helped to keep his musicians organised. I help to keep Tosh comfortable in the studio. When I started, Tosh was hardly getting any royalties from record companies. He barely saw anything from his publishing even though he wrote most of his music so I decided to correct this by meeting directly with the Presidents and Vice-Presidents of record companies."

In reality it could have been a change of lawyers that eased the deadlock, as intimated in an interview Peter gave to *Music Times*. When the journalist asked why there'd been a four-year wait since his last album, Peter replied that *Mama Africa* had sold over a million copies, and "it seems as if a million dollars is too much to give a little dirty Rasta as we.

"It's the general black/white discrimination man. EMI violate my contract about 75 times. I've just fired nine lawyers in New York and hired one in Kansas City because I came to realise the lawyers in New York are a set of clans, and crooks... They treat West Indian people like we're idiots and don't like it when you are intelligent, and know what you want.

"CBS Records also owe me $49 million since 1976 until now. Everyone owes I," he laments. "I am broke. They are holding up progress because the world needs to get *No Nuclear War*. It's anti-nuclear, anti-apartheid, anti-vampirism and anti-drugs, because I don't take cocaine and that shit, which is made intentionally. It's like some guy went into a laboratory and say, 'Let's make a drug that can turn those niggers into a monkey', but you know what is a pity? That so many of you are easy victims of the shit-system."

In that same interview, he claims to have received an award from the University of Houston "for my knowledge and study of herbs, because that is not a drug. Cocaine and heroin are drugs," he says, before pointing out rather ominously that marijuana "is being used to cure madness, and I love to be mad for the cure it gives."

Kevin J. Aylmer interviewed him for *Reggae Report* on November 25, at the apartment in Central Park West. Peter sat strumming his Ovation guitar and is described as "dramatically disarming in person. Charming, polite, ever-conscious, Tosh is not only a musician and mystic man, he is a consummate teacher, a wordsmith dispensing knowledge, sharing insights and reinventing language with an aplomb that would make even George Orwell envious."

He's said to talk in a voice "dark and rich like molasses, resonant in irony and sadness, alleviated by sudden shafts of wit or penetrating melody". Aylmer says when "visiting a fashionable sushi restaurant on New York's Upper East Side, Peter found the slow service irritating. Eventually he decided that some herbal meditation might be in order. After one of those minimalist appetisers consisting of exorbitantly priced, hand-carved cucumbers, a rather long wait ensued. Nonchalantly, Peter prepared to light up a spliff as Marlene and fellow guests sat back, much amused, awaiting the fireworks. As the receptionist, maitre d' and serving staff looked on, their faces frozen in disbelieving horror, Peter proceeded to lecture diners. Waving the smoking, croissant-sized spliff magisterially, Peter would inhale deeply, exhale and announce in ever-rising tones. 'I'm a Rastaman. These are herbs. A Rastaman must smoke herbs!'

"Nervous chatter about the room, an occasional cough or grimace, arrogant verbal reminders of non-smoking decorum – all left Peter nonplussed. When finally confronted by an unctuous, trembling manager, Peter diplomatically complied with his request, having left not only an indelible impression, but the unmistakable fragrance of sensi amidst the sushi."

It's revealing how his companions get a kick out of his behaviour, instead of trying to modify it. 'Are these people any good for him?' we ask ourselves.

Shortly before his death, John Lennon had told *Newsweek* "the king is always killed by his courtiers. The king is overfed, overdrugged, overindulged – anything to keep the king on his throne. Most people in that position never wake up. They either die mentally, physically or both."

Flash forward to April 17, 1987 and Wailers drummer Carlton Barrett is having similar trouble. That morning Carly backed his Mercedes out of the driveway and left home in search of fried chicken for his wife, Albertine. It was Good Friday, and so the only places open were roadside stalls. The Wailers band had started to tour and record more frequently of late. They'd had to. The Marley Estate wasn't paying them any longer and only a few months back, his brother Family Man had been evicted from 56 Hope Road – a place they'd dreamt of owning and converting into a studio from the first time they'd gone there to rehearse with Bob, Bunny and Peter back in 1973. Those were happier times. Singers and musicians alike had shared the same vision, and were determined to work hard in making it a reality. They'd dreamt of Rastafari, set to a reggae heartbeat, sweeping the world and righting every wrong. No one had foreseen that the closer they'd come to realising such ambitions, the more their personal lives would be left shattered.

Carly hadn't been in good health of late. His weight kept fluctuating alarmingly, and he was always suffering from stomach pains. Every so often he'd forget where he was or what he was doing and wander around aimlessly, looking absent and distressed. It was as if he'd been drugged, even though he hadn't taken anything. One time he abandoned his car and started walking down the road in just his underwear, taking no notice of the jeers and catcalls from passing motorists. On another occasion, whilst touring in the US, he disappeared for two days and was eventually found walking barefoot in the snow, his feet covered in blisters. Family Man remembers his brother sometimes having "the force of three men" and then being rushed to hospital, where they'd give him "the liquid cosh". Something was definitely wrong with him and yet doctors hadn't been able to make a diagnosis. They'd been puzzled, and so had his family.

Carly felt a little better as he drove back home that day. The chicken was still warm, and wrapped in paper on the passenger seat. He hadn't expected to be gone long, and had left the gates open. When he reached the house he saw they'd been closed, and so had to park outside whilst he went to open them. As he stepped out of the car a lone gunman walked swiftly up to him and shot him twice in the head, killing him instantly.

His murder left Jamaica's tightly knit music fraternity stunned. The Wailers' drummer was well liked and had no enemies anyone knew about, nor did he have connections to Kingston's criminal underbelly. As is often the case, the danger had come from within. His wife and her lover, taxi driver Glenroy Carter, were later charged with plotting his death and commissioning a man named Andrew Neil to carry out the shooting. Family Man alleges that Albertine had wanted Carly to take out various insurance policies before his death. And he's adamant that his brother's medical problems stemmed from her attempts to either poison him, or bring misfortune upon him in some other way.

"After his wife go to jail I stop by the house to tell whoever's there that I am Carly's brother and to ask them if they have keys to his room, but it's like nobody want to say anything. I walk into the kitchen and I see a whole bunch of keys and so I go to his room, open the door and when I click the light on, I see a doll sat in a rocking chair with all pins sticking out of it, like some voodoo business. I see another doll with pins in it on the bed, candles, incense and more pins lying about... It was pure obeah in there, and so I build a fire out back and burn the whole lot of it."

Darkness had begun to close in on members of the Wailers' inner circle, but Peter's mood was lifted by news that his stalemate with EMI may soon be over. *Music Connection* reported that the company had admitted breach of contract after releasing his music in South Africa and would have to pay him $250,000, as well as allowing him access to its books. This cleared the way for *No Nuclear War* to be released at last. Advance copies will soon make their way to the UK, in readiness for a September 10 release date. *NME* printed a review under the heading "Shopping List Of Evils". It's accompanied by a photo of Peter sat facing the camera with a violin balanced on his knees. He's holding a bow in one hand and looking rather sad. It had been taken at Music Mountain during the *No Nuclear War* sessions, more than two years earlier. Peter is about to discover that little has changed in the meantime.

"Unlike Bunny Wailer, Peter Tosh has never found a useful role for himself, post-Wailers, post Marley," writes Mark Sinker. "He seemed stuck on an overheated reggae-rock-rebel posturing and his talent taken for granted, put on one side, wasted. Every record he made may have spelt the start of some new direction in itself, but added up they were just a frustrating handful of starts and never followed through."

After describing *No Nuclear War* as "another of those" he says, "It's reasonably coherent, but it certainly isn't strong enough to make it as any kind of Last Testament." He waffles on about it having "a rich, fat sound" that "overwhelms itself", and then criticises Tosh's lyrics. "It's not that his integrity's in question so much as his ability to personalise a standard sentiment. What's the point of writing a song if it's just going to add up to one more vote for or against some shopping list of evils? It isn't until 'Vampire' that he finds some obsession bent enough to gain strength to justify its existence. It's cartoon emotion, but it casts some kind of light on his whole project, warps it away from dulled recycling of A Plain Man's Politics." In summing up he calls *No Nuclear War* "a shadowed, distended collection".

Chapter 31

Why Must I Cry?

Peter and Marlene were in New York during early September. One day the phone rang at their apartment. It was guitarist Daryl Thompson.

"I hadn't spoken to him in years but I was in New York and something just told me to ring him. I had his number, gave him a call and he said he was glad to hear from me because he was having a meeting with his management and they were getting ready to go on tour. He asked me if I wanted to tour with him and I said yes, because I wasn't playing with Black Uhuru at the time. From what I remember, the tour was supposed to start in November and the first gig was at Madison Square Garden."

Peter had already asked Fully and Santa to come and rehearse in readiness for a tour, and intimated that Al Anderson might join them as well. After nearly four years away, he knew he'd have to come out with all guns blazing. This time he was going to carry a horns section, and also a trio of female backing singers. Nadine Sutherland says that as *No Nuclear War* was about to be released she'd "left high school, been to college and was trying to see a way forward in the music business.

"I guess Peter had been struggling with all of the politics involved but I spoke to him and he was planning to take myself, Pam Hall and J. C. Lodge on tour with him as his backing singers. I wasn't really doing much else at that point and so the idea of touring the world with Peter Tosh was the most exciting thing..."

"I was supposed to go up to his house to see him but my car broke down and I couldn't make it," remembers Pam Hall. "He'd said to collect copies of the album and normally when you go up to Peter's you wouldn't just say, 'Give me the album' and then leave, because he'd expect you to stay and reason with him for quite a while. He really liked my son, who was a little busybody and always rushing around. Peter never seemed to mind though. He'd say, 'bring him up man', so I'd go up to the house and I remember him giving my son these African carvings in green stone. He was a very loving man. I guess there was a side of him that could be quite aggressive, but I never saw it. I saw him as a nice, gentle, humorous person – someone who was very creative. Peter always was more of a home-loving roots man. He preferred to chop a coconut, drink up some juice and reason with his friends really..."

"I'd meet at the market in Crossroads," says Nambo Robinson, trombonist with Rass Brass. "I got the impression he liked to cook because quite a few times I'd see him shopping for fruit and vegetables, but whenever I'd see him he was always talking about music and where he wanted to take it. He was a visionary like that but then just before his death, he asked us to go on tour with him. I'd never seen him use horns on stage before. He was working towards it though because he'd already mentioned it to us and that would have been so special..."

Peter and Marlene arrived back in Kingston on Sunday September 6. The following Wednesday they received a visit from Leppo. He and Marlene had fallen out a while back after he'd interfered in an incident involving her brother Dennis, who'd crashed Peter's Volvo whilst they were away and then tried to shift the blame. Peter hadn't authorised her brother to drive the car, and was very upset when it had to be written off. It was Leppo who told him what had happened, which had angered Marlene and turned her against him, although she'll later deny this.

"It was a lie Lobban told about my brother, and that lie upset Peter and myself because Lobban eats at our house. The bed he sleeps on, we'd bought it for him but I did not get upset about this. He visited the house two months after the incident and I fed him same way. I am not in the habit of abusing Peter Tosh's visitors. I am not in the habit of disciplining them when they get out of line."

According to Wayne Jobson, when Leppo asked Peter for money on that Wednesday he'd been confronted by Marlene, who called him a "batty

443

man" or homosexual. Leppo had been in prison and so this remark may well have hit the mark, causing him considerable shame. Peter apparently just looked down at the floor and said nothing. Leppo accused Marlene of stopping Peter from "coming to Jungle" – meaning Trench Town – and treating his friends but the truth was, Peter didn't have a great deal of money. Carlton Tosh remembers the situation only too well but says that whatever Peter had, he would share.

"Anywhere he is, there's a lot of crowd because they always like to hear him talk and plenty man go up to him and beg him some money. Peter would say 'all right' and then when the time's right, he'll discreetly give it to them or he might say, 'Come check me up at the yard'. That means go to his home and collect it. When this guy Leppo come out of jail now, he try to get money from a whole lot of artists. He go around and beg from them, and Peter invite him up to the house. Peter might not even remember this guy but he'll make out like he knows him. That was how he was. He bought him a bed and made sure that he had food and clothes. He did whatever he can for this little guy and yet he don't owe him nothing. That's just the type of guy he was. If a man say he want to start a little business selling dumpling and needs a hand cart, Peter would ask him how much a hand cart costs and give him the money. It wasn't like Peter was wealthy or anything like that. He hardly had any money. It was his ambition that made people think he was well off but that's how that guy came to visit Peter's house, and then some other guys use him. Peter didn't do anything to anybody, and we need people to know this."

What Carlton calls "ambition" was often mistaken for arrogance and with good reason. Peter had been a guest on Barry "G" Gordon's radio show before leaving for New York and with his usual rancour, had reiterated how EMI owed him millions of dollars in unpaid royalties – money that he was determined to recover. It's one thing saying something like that to foreign journalists, but quite another to broadcast it over the Jamaican airwaves, as Wayne Jobson explains.

"Peter went on Barry G's show and told everyone how EMI owed him millions of dollars and he's going to the States to get it. And he comes back with a briefcase and word spread around the ghetto, 'Peter come back with a briefcase, there must be $50,000 in it, let's go and get it.'"

Bearing this in mind, it's a wonder that Leppo left it as late as Wednesday before going to see Peter for money. He was nursing serious grievances after being humiliated by Marlene that day, and already plotting revenge.

"People like him, they think you is a big star and you're supposed to have a lot of money," says reggae artist Big Youth, "but every heart knows their own sorrow, and they don't know when we're hungry. Them just say we're big, and when you can't do things fi them, they act like them don't have sense and move against you – all because you don't do what they think you're supposed to do for them. Because some of our people are really in need, and they'll set your own people against you to kill you."

Rumours have circulated for years that Peter had got caught with a gun back in the early seventies during a police roadblock, and that Leppo took the rap for him. The deal was that Leppo would serve the jail term, in exchange for Peter buying him a house and looking after his family whilst he was inside. It's said that Peter then failed to keep his end of the bargain but his cousin Carlton denies this.

"Bullshit they're talking! And they know that it's bullshit too. This guy Leppo, the time he's supposed to get arrested and spend all that time in jail is during Gun Court, right? Too much gun violence is going on and yet in Jamaica if the police find one gun in your car, your home or wherever, trust me if the cops don't kill you, they're locking up *everyone*. If you're caught up in that situation, even if it's not your gun, then you're going to jail until it's time to go to court in front of the judge, and it's them decide who they're going to let go and who they're going to keep. We know already how much the cops hate Peter and so if they find a gun in his car and somebody else take the rap for it, they would have taken him in as well. Nothing is more certain than that, trust me.

"The one time I see Peter with a gun, other than a spear gun he use to catch fish, we were in Miami and we have this friend who have a big property, like some farm land and we all go out with the guy when he was hunting. Peter pick up the gun and act like he's about to shoot at some bird, but that's all. He never even fire it, and I never see him with a gun apart from that. He was too conscious of the wickedness people do with guns, and how they destroy people's lives. Peter wasn't into that, and that's why I say these people are talking a whole lot of lies."

Flo O'Connell, who was head of the Jamaica Human Rights Commission, has verified there was no official record of Peter Tosh having been arrested in a roadblock. There is also no evidence of Peter or any of his relatives trying to smuggle handguns into the country, as Michael "Eppy" Epstein has alleged.

"I don't know what the misunderstanding was between them, but there was definitely something that went down between that guy and Peter," says Bob Andy. "Peter had become very abusive by then. There was a guy, a Rastafarian who'd been his chef for years, and Peter just held him down and trimmed the guy's hair off and that of his child as well. I hear the guy went back to Ocho Rios shouting, 'Peter Tosh, you're gonna be dead!' That's the kind of thing Jamaicans will say to each other anyway but there was definitely a connection between Dennis Lobban and Peter."

The most disturbing element of this story is that Peter is supposed to have videotaped it, which suggests he got pleasure from it. He told a mutual friend that he'd disciplined the man according to Rastafarian principles, except this was a long way removed from what Peter had been taught in the Rasta camps because whatever happened to love, peace and harmony? And wasn't judgment usually left to the Almighty? According to the authors of *Reggae Routes*, Peter "would disrespect people undeserving of such treatment and use profanities anytime and anywhere, cursing stewardesses, policemen, hotel workers, waiters, even record company executives – one reason, allegedly, for CBS' failure to renew his contract in the eighties. Tosh began alienating even close, lifelong friends. And the cause of his altercations with his Matthews Lane brethren often seemed to be his lady Marlene."

There's another rumour that suggests one of his friends in New York – an expatriate Jamaican, and a former singer and producer – had made a lot of money selling herb, and Peter had become involved in his operation. Some say he'd taken a large sum back to Jamaica with him that he was supposed to pass on to someone, possibly in exchange for a percentage. According to inside sources this money never reached the person it was supposed to, and so the dealer sent word to Peter that he'd be assassinated unless the money was repaid. Marlene admitted they were warned that a contract had been taken out on Peter (without saying why), but said he hadn't taken them seriously, saying, "Rastaman can't dead."

"Peter, he was a mystic man, and he never believe that could happen," says cousin Carlton. "He always think your gun must stick or something would happen to prevent that from taking place. Even if a man planned it, Peter believed something would happen to them along the way."

Friday September 11 was Ethiopian New Year's Day and therefore an auspicious day for Peter, who still belonged to the Ethiopian Orthodox Church. US President Ronald Reagan had declared it "Emergency

Number Day" in recognition of emergency service workers and the success of the 911 call system. Americans were asked "to observe this day with appropriate ceremonies and activities", although most settled for an office party or "thank you" to local fire fighters and paramedics. Over in Miami, Pope John Paul II announced his arrival in the US by stating "I come as a pilgrim in the cause of justice and peace and human solidarity, striving to build up the one human family." Contrary to lurid tales of "heavy winds, torrential rains and lightning and thunder that forced him to abandon a public Mass for the first time in history," it was a gloriously sunny day in Florida. The only storm clouds were those gathering around Peter Tosh, who was sat at home enjoying a midday spliff with Marlene and Michael Robinson. The latter made hats and various other craft items, but didn't work for Peter as reported elsewhere.

Late in the afternoon on that same Friday, a man in his early twenties called Steve Russell was at the offices of Hermes Engineering at 691 Spanish Town Road, Kingston where he'd been employed as a driver since June of that year. He drove a white Volkswagen mini-bus, registration plate 6376 AF, which he was allowed to use in his free time. Russell was already thinking of the weekend ahead when according to a police affidavit, the firm's watchman's son – who everyone knew as "Watchie Son" – came and spoke to him.

"Watchie Son asked me if I was going downtown and I told him yes. When I was ready he came in the van I was driving, along with several other workers. On reaching Three Miles most of the workers came out of the van leaving Watchie Son and maybe one other. I drove along Spanish Town Road and the other worker came off at Denham Town. Watchie Son and I then drive to Bond Street where I stopped at my mother-in-law's house. I spent about 10 minutes there whilst Watchie Son waited for me. When I returned to the van I asked Watchie Son where he was going and he said he was going up to Half Way Tree. I told him that's where I was going to pick up my wife and he asked me to drop him there.

"On my way, Watchie Son asked me to drive by Oxford Street and Spanish Town Road where he went to check his friends. After we drive there I stopped and Watchie Son come off the van and go over to the fish place."

According to Steve Russell, Watchie Son spent 15 minutes in this fish restaurant before returning to the van with some friends, who wanted a lift to Half Way Tree. Russell agreed to take them, but he and Watchie

Son first drove to a supermarket at Wildman Street and East Queen Street, where Russell tried to cash a cheque. The cashier didn't have enough money in the till and so they returned to Oxford Street to pick up Watchie Son's friends, who then climbed in the van – two in the back and one in the front. According to Russell, Watchie Son didn't come with them, but stayed at the restaurant.

"On reaching Crossroads the man who was in front with me asked if I was going to drive up Half Way Tree. I told him yes, and he asked me whether I could drive up Old Hope Road, as it was not far from where he was going. I drove up Old Hope Road and on reaching Barbican Road, drove through the stop light and continued as the man directed. On reaching the gas station at the foot of Jack's Hill I stopped, as the man beside me said I should go no further. The two men in the back came out and started to walk along Barbican Road. The man beside me hesitated to come out. He said he would give me money for gas. I told him gas was not my problem but that I was late meeting my wife. The two other men then returned to the van and one of them said, 'The place too far man. Mek the man drop we and we done man.' The man beside me took out $40 and handed it to me but I told him I didn't want the money. He then said, 'Just drop we up ah the road man, because them men deh nuh nice.' One of the men in the back directed me to drive towards Mathilda's Corner and on reaching a turning on the left near to the Pines, I was told to drive along that road. After going so far the van had difficulty in climbing the hill, so I stopped and try to turn it around. Two of the men then came out of the van, leaving the man in front beside me. I was about to drive down the road when he told me to park beside a gate on the right. The two who'd come out of the van went into the yard next where I'd parked. Then the man who was beside me came out of the van and went into the same gate where the other men had gone."

Leppo was one of the three men who'd just entered Peter's yard that night. More than two hours had passed since the van had left Hermes Engineering. None of the men wore masks or bothered to conceal their identities in any way. Leppo had probably expected Peter and Marlene to be alone and yet they had three friends with them – Michael Robinson was still there, and he'd since been joined by Santa Davis and Wilton "Doc" Brown, who owned a grocery store in Seaview Gardens. The group were watching television and sampling Doc's latest "front-end lifter" – an especially potent herbal brew – when they heard the doorbell at around

7.30pm. Peter's house had two storeys and there's only one entrance from downstairs to the upstairs living room, where the television was. Marlene sent Robinson downstairs to answer the door and Leppo was standing there, wearing a mustard-coloured striped shirt and grim expression. Next to him was a tall, slim man who Robinson hadn't seen before. By the time he motioned for them to come upstairs, a third man, shorter and with a lighter complexion, had stepped from out of the shadows. There was a light on the downstairs wall and the outside of the house was illuminated by a streetlight, yet Robinson hadn't noticed this other person until then.

"On reaching the door by the reception area all three men pulled guns from their waists and the shorter man said to me, 'Me nuh want yuh to mek any noise.' Lobban asked if Peter was there. I nodded and we then headed upstairs. The tall one first, then the short one and Lobban behind."

Marlene saw tears in Robinson's eyes as he came back into view.

"When I see Leppo I never think it was nothing, because I know it is Peter's friend. Then I see Leppo with a gun, a silver gun that just glisten, the way the gun pretty. I say my vision come true and when I look, I see these two other guys come in with two black guns. And the two of them stick us up, then I say to myself 'Free I and Joy on their way' so I start thinking what to do, because Free I just call and say, 'Marlene, seven-thirty.'"

After entering the living room, the men told everyone to lie face down on the floor. Marlene says the first thing they said was, "Peter, yuh nuh badda say nothing because yuh dead tonight." When she told them there was no money in the house Leppo replied, "Shut up your mouth Marlene, as you is the cause of this, because it is you who obeah the dread and why ghetto man can't get money."

Marlene will later testify that Robinson returned "with three men at gunpoint. The men had their guns pointing at Michael Robinson. I recognised one of the men as Dennis Lobban. I had known him for seven months. He came to visit Peter Tosh." The men told them to "belly it", meaning get on the floor. "Leppo then started to ask us for money. He said, 'Me want all the money, me hear say unno just come from foreign and me want all the US dollars.' Peter said, 'I don't have any money.' One of the others said, 'Yuh nuh say anything tonight because yuh a go dead. We come to kill yuh.' The other man started to search the house. He returned without finding anything. He said to me, 'You a Peter manager and accountant. Ah yuh have all the money a hide and yuh gwine dead tonight.' He started

449

kicking and gun butting me. I told him I did not have any money. Leppo then started cursing me and said, 'Is you why Peter won't give us any bumbo Rassclaat money. A yuh mek Peter nuh work for three years and nuh have any money to mind us. Peter give you Rassclaat power to rule, and me just want to kick Peter in his bumboclaat.' That's when I heard a knocking at the gate. All three men enquired who it was. I told them it was Free I and his wife, our friends. I shouted to Free I, 'Don't come in', and the tall skinny one said, 'If yuh don't shut your mouth gal, I gwine shot you in the bumboclaat mouth.' This same man then ran downstairs..."

Free I was a local DJ who'd known Peter for years, from Studio One days. He'd recorded there under his given name of Jeff Dixon and even cut a tune with Marcia Griffiths. He and Peter were rumoured to be hatching plans to buy radio station JBC, which was up for sale. The two friends would then re-launch it along Rastafarian lines – a move that was sure to start alarm bells ringing in government circles. Free I and his wife, Joy, arrived around 7.30 p.m. As they pulled up outside both noticed a Jeep parked on the soft shoulder outside of Peter's house, which turned out to be Santa's. Across the road was a white VW van. When Free I knocked at the gate there was no response at first. They then heard shouting but couldn't make out what was being said. "It was a female voice that was shouting," says Joy. "My husband knocked again, and a man we didn't know came down and spoke to us."

She followed Free I inside the house. When they reached the second set of steps, she felt something in her right side and quickly realised it was a gun. The man told her to hand over the chain she had round her neck. On going into the room, she saw people lying on the floor. She recognised two of them as being Peter and Marlene, but didn't recognise the others. Two men with guns were standing over them. As she entered, Marlene had pleaded with the men not to hurt her. Both were ordered to shut up and lie face down on the floor. Meanwhile, Free I was being searched near the doorway. "The man pulled out my husband's trouser pockets and took a plastic envelope which had money in it and took his watch. The three men were arguing with Peter Tosh and Marlene Brown over money. I did not recognise any of them. I had never seen these men before."

As Joy had attempted to look over at her husband, she was struck on her right cheek by a gun butt, which sent her sprawling to the floor.

"I was still on the floor," says Marlene, "and told them not to hurt my sister... I said for Joy to come over to where I was, and sit on the floor besides me. One of the men spoke to Free I and said to go down on the floor. Free I continued to stand up. I told him it was something real, and that he should go down. 'Don't let them hurt you,' I said, but Free I still wouldn't go down. He was then forced to the floor. Leppo started to curse me again and said I mek Peter nuh want to give them any money. 'Yuh think me don't know gal, 'bout him give you power.' Leppo turned to the other two gunmen and said, 'Unno don't bother give Peter any chance because Peter is a karate expert and him kick off all ah we head.' I was wearing a gold chain around my neck with a round gold pendant. The short man took this from my neck. I had on a gold ring with a big diamond on top and he asked me for it so I took it off and gave it to him. The tall slim man took off Peter's two gold rope chains and his watch. I saw Leppo take off Doc's chain and bracelet and rob him of his money. The short red man went back to the bedroom and returned with a machete that Peter kept under his bed as a protection. He went over to Peter and said, 'Me gwine chop off yuh head and yuh not gwine mek any sound when I do it.' At this time Peter was lying on his belly on the floor. I was lying beside Peter. I jumped up and said, 'Yuh can't chop off my man's head.' He asked who could stop me. I said, 'In the name of Jah, yuh can't chop off Peter's head.' He said he'd chop off my head instead. He had the machete in his right hand and the gun in his left hand. He started to beat me with the machete and started kicking me to the ground."

Joy Dixon heard Peter send for suitcases, which were searched. There was no money in any of them and the men had become irate. It was at that point the man holding the machete had wanted to chop Peter's head off. After Marlene protested, Joy heard one of the men saying how she was the problem and that Peter should get rid of her.

"Marlene Brown kept arguing with them. I heard Peter telling the men they could search the house from top to bottom and take anything of value as he had no US dollars. I remember hearing Marlene telling one of the men that they'd already told his brother Handsome they had no money and they should check him back on the Monday."

Michael Robinson remembers the man threatening to cut off Peter's head, and says that Leppo was insistent the money must be hidden somewhere.

"Peter said there was no money in the house as he had forgotten to go to the bank earlier that day. Leppo then said, 'Where is the chest yuh have in the house?' Peter said, 'What kind of chest unno talk 'bout Leppo?

Me nuh have any money in the house.' I then heard one of the gunmen say, 'Star, how yuh just a argue with them, so mek we do what we come here to do nuh.' That's when I heard the first shot fired. There was a split second's silence, then I heard two more..."

Joy Dixon recalls one of the men saying that since they hadn't got what they came for, they may as well "kill the whole bombaclaat lot of them and leave". She heard a shot fired just after the suitcases had been searched. "After the words were spoken I heard a barrage of shots. I got a shot in my mouth and my right leg. I felt my mouth burning me. There was a small pet dog in the house that ran behind the bar and I pulled myself on my stomach behind it..."

At that precise moment Santa smelt blood and "had a sensation of death". They shot at Marlene, who was hit but played dead. The shot that grazed her scalp then struck Joy in the mouth.

"All three men started to shoot up the room," says Marlene whose quotes – like those of the other survivors – are taken from official court transcripts. "We were all lying in the room in a semi-circle. I heard about 25 shots but I was still conscious. Everybody remained still and the men left the room. I remained in the same position until I heard a vehicle start up and drive away. I jumped up and turned on the light in the drawing room area. The television light was still on. Joy Dixon got up. I went over to Peter and I noticed he was bleeding from his head top. He was lying in a pool of blood and breathing heavily. I spoke to him but he didn't answer. He was sucking up his own blood, so I pushed out the blood and cleaned up his face. I went over to Doc and shook him but there was no movement from him. I went over to Free I and noticed that he was still breathing. I went over to Michael Robinson and when I spoke to him, he answered. I noticed he was bleeding profusely from his head. I noticed that Santa was not in the room when I got up. I could not find him. I went downstairs to seek for help. Reaching the gate I saw Santa standing in the middle of the road but Santa refused to assist me. I pleaded with him and he said he was not helping any of us. He said, 'Me get shot too, and a go hospital left unno.' I saw some vehicles coming down Plymouth Avenue, waved them down and two of them stopped. Three men came to my assistance and went upstairs with me. I spoke to them and they carried Peter downstairs. Peter was placed in one of the cars and I went in the car with him. I placed Peter's head in my lap. Michael Robinson came in the same car and we were taken to University Hospital. About 20 minutes after arriving at the hospital, Peter Tosh died. I was admitted to hospital, as was Michael Robinson. I remained in hospital for three days."

After Marlene had gone downstairs, Joy went over to her husband who was lying in a pool of blood with an orange substance coming from his mouth. It sounded like he was snoring. After a while the police arrived and took them both to hospital. While she was treated for her injuries, Free I was rushed into intensive care but would never regain consciousness. Michael Robinson had been shot in the back of his head and left leg, whilst Santa had a bullet lodged between his heart and lungs. After making sure the killers had left, he got in his Jeep and drove to the hospital, where he passed out in the arms of a porter. He'd lost a lot of blood and would still be in hospital five days later. Wilton "Doc" Brown was pronounced dead on arrival at the hospital. Detective Corporal Kirk Whyte had found him lying motionless amidst all the carnage, and said the house looked as if it had been ransacked.

"On entering the premises I observed bloodstains leading from the yard to the ground floor of the house. This continued along the stairway to the upper floor of the house to the living room area. I observed several pools of blood. I saw the body of Wilton Brown lying face down in a pool of blood. I noticed blood on his head. The body was photographed and later removed by Madden Funeral Supplies."

People who weren't there have claimed that Marlene was wearing the amulet Peter had been given in Swaziland and that's why she'd escaped death on the night he was killed. No wonder that Basil Walters, writing in the *Jamaica Observer*, said that "more disparaging remarks have been made about her than any other woman who has ever had a love affair with a Jamaican artist. Her name will probably go down in history as the contentious virago, low-class rebel queen of the late international reggae star Peter Tosh.

"Many condemned the relationship and rued the day she was born because for them, she was the root cause of Tosh's demise. Frankly speaking, one could argue that her characteristics reflect those of Tosh's. After all, they shared the same birth date and almost died together."

Marlene expresses disappointment with Peter, who she says did nothing to protect her when the gunmen struck and abused her.

"Knowing Peter, knowing his style, his personality and temperament, wouldn't you say it was a little strange for Peter to remain calm during this time?" asks Walters.

"I'm still astonished," she replied. "I'm still astonished and shocked and disappointed with Peter. Me say no lamb to no slaughter, that is my philosophy man, death before dishonour. If we had even all fought for our lives that night, he would have still been here today. I fought for my life and God give me my life with two holes in my head from shots."

Walters asks if it's true that Peter attempted some karate kicks.

"No, nobody did anything. None of the five men did anything; nobody lift a hand or a foot and everybody took their beating. I fought for my life and Tosh's also. I remember I had to fight for Peter. One of the boys was going to chop off Peter's head with Peter's own billie (cutlass) and is me jump up and start fight the bwoy off Tosh. Him kick me down to the ground and all the time he kick and kick me, Peter never put a hand and say, 'Don't kick my woman so.' None of the four men tried to defend me like I was defending them the whole night. That's why I was shot in my head, because I wouldn't let the boy behead Tosh."

Maybe Peter had remained lying face down on the floor because he was injured. Joy Dixon says his head was bleeding when she and Free I first walked into the room. This would suggest he'd been pistol-whipped and was unable to respond. The autopsy will also reveal evidence of a nasty head injury, separate from any bullet wounds. Marlene told Walters that when they got to the hospital, the staff left him unattended for what seemed like a very long time. Her inference is that if Peter hadn't have been in dreadlocks, they would have probably seen to him quicker and he might have been saved.

"If that had been the Prime Minister with the exact same injury, he would have lived because they would have rushed him straight in. He would have been treated right away and they would have done everything to keep him alive but nobody was doing anything for him and after some time arguing, an Indian doctor came who didn't know it was Peter; put his finger in Peter's head where the bullet holes were and pushed it far down inside, like he was pushing the bullets in further. I was wondering what he was doing because he didn't have gloves on or anything, and then he left. And Peter died right after."

Steve Russell will later tell Detective Assistant Superintendent Donald Brown of Kingston's homicide division that after he heard gunshots coming from the house, he started up the van and was about to drive off when one of the three men jumped in the front seat.

"I continued driving and by the time I reached the bottom of the road I see the two other men had climbed in the back of the van. I drive back to Barbican Road and continued down Hope Road. When I reached the stop light at King's House one of the men in the back came and sat in the seat behind me. He had a gun in his hand and said I should turn along Lady Musgrave Road. He said to me, 'You don't see anything and you don't hear anything.' He appeared very nervous. They directed me and I drove back to Crossroads where I saw a police roadblock at Brentford Road and Retirement Road. I became afraid and let go of the steering wheel. The man who was sat beside me then took out a 9mm and pointed it into my side. He said I should take it easy. I drove through the roadblock and the police did not stop me. I then drove to Slipe Pen Road where they told me to turn around, and the three men jumped out of the van at Drummond Street and went towards Kingston Public Hospital. I then drove straight to Trench Town police station in search of Detective Corporal Leonard Austin but didn't see him."

Russell said he went straight home after this, and it wasn't until he saw the news on television that he realised Peter Tosh lived at the same address where they'd been parked. "I was very frightened and I walked over to Detective Austin's house at Coreville Gardens but he was not at home." He was told Austin would be home the day after next so on that Sunday morning he walked over to Austin's home along with his wife and two children. He told Austin what had happened, and was cursed out. Austin said he'd been stupid to let the gunmen use him but didn't give him any definite advice. Some time later, in mid-October, Russell will consult lawyer Lawton Heywood, who remained unconvinced his story was connected with Peter's death.

"He said that I should try and find an obeah woman and get a bath," said Russell. "I later went and told my pastor's wife, Mrs Reynolds, about the matter and she prayed for me. Sometime later I saw a photograph of a man in the *Star* who I recognised as one of the men I drove to Peter Tosh's house. He'd been sat in the back. He was the man I saw with the gun when they were coming from the house. The name below the photograph was Dennis Lobban, otherwise known as 'Leppo'."

Russell will eventually be acquitted of all charges although the testimony of Patrick O'Connor, managing director of Hermes Engineering, may serve to introduce a note of caution. O'Connor sacked Russell in October, after he'd disappeared for nearly a week with no explanation.

"He was not a good worker. When he went on errands that would normally take an hour and a half, he would be out for nearly half a day at a time. During the period he worked for me, he was robbed twice whilst in charge of the pay roll. I have been manager of Hermes Engineering for about 11 years and these were the only two robberies I know of in the history of the company. At one of them, members of staff were locked in the vault and the money taken from Vincent Ellis, our company watchman, whilst he sat in the pick-up driven by Russell."

By the time he gave evidence, O'Connor hadn't seen anything of Ellis' son Honey, aka "Watchie Son", since the day of Peter's murder. That was a month before, by which time Marlene, Joy Dixon, Santa and Michael Robinson were over the worst of their injuries. After spending three days in hospital, Robinson told court officials that he'd seen Leppo at 5 Plymouth Avenue at least five times before the night of the shooting, and that whilst he hadn't seen the other two men before, he'd be able to identify them if he ever saw them again. This was unlikely, since according to Wayne Jobson, "the other two gunmen were Yami Yow, a big tall guy who allegedly supplied the arms, and was then shot whilst riding his motorcycle the very next day. Some say he had been contracted in New York to come down and kill Peter. The other was said to be a serial killer from New York but there are so many stories going around we don't know for sure. I heard about a barkeeper who claimed that Leppo was with him at the time of the killing. It was said this man's nephew was one of the killers, so he was trying to cover up for him. A couple of months later, this same nephew got killed in a police shootout in Spanish Town..."

If it was a deliberate hit, then it's possible the people behind it had the murderers killed to cover their tracks. In a place like Jamaica that wouldn't have cost much although this doesn't explain why Leppo was spared, unless they'd just used him to gain access to Peter and then left him to take the rap. So who was to blame for Peter's murder? And why kill a singer whose name and reputation far exceeded the state of their bank balance?

Peter Tosh wouldn't have been the first reggae artist to raise extra cash by "juggling herb" and as a well-known connoisseur, must have known every ganja farmer in Jamaica. Peter also had strong connections with expatriate Jamaican communities in New York, which had been swelled by gang members of both sides after the 1980 election. Whereas Kingston's area leaders had once been dependant on political handlers for weapons, the lucrative drugs trade now enabled them to finance their own activities. Some joined forces with Colombian cartels, especially after Reagan's ill-conceived "war on drugs" began to make life difficult for Jamaican growers, thereby clearing a path for cocaine traffickers. If he were involved in ganja smuggling, Peter certainly wouldn't have considered this to be immoral or even illegal. The big question is whether he would cheat on his associates, because why else would New York hit men have come after him? Did he get too greedy? Or had he overreached himself? Peter had a dozen or so children to support by almost the same number of mothers, and properties to maintain in Jamaica and the US. He also faced expensive legal bills resulting from his dispute with EMI. Eighteen months earlier he'd struggled to pay musicians and studio costs, and whilst he'd installed Marlene as his manager and accountant, she was hardly equipped for the task. When you examine the different theories as to what got him killed, there are two possible explanations that make most sense. One is that he borrowed from underworld associates against money he'd hoped to get from EMI, and then found he couldn't repay it. Peter may not have intended to keep the money but then might have run out of time, at which point he – or possibly even Marlene – had become abusive and therefore angered some very dangerous people. The other likely scenario is saddest of all, since it might have been Peter's own big mouth that brought about his downfall after he'd bragged of going to collect millions of dollars from his record company. Most people would have dismissed these claims as mere bluster but not necessarily a hardened criminal like Leppo, who'd spent half his life in a prison cell and the other half begging from Jamaica's rich and famous – especially those who'd come from poor ghetto communities and therefore had a certain amount of sympathy for people like himself. In addition to being semi-illiterate he hated Marlene, and probably viewed Peter with scorn for having allowed himself to be controlled by a woman.

"Jamaica has continued to be a breeding ground for very serious murderers," noted author Ras Cardo. "I mean people who will kill you for the slightest nonsense. It may be the clothes you wear, the beliefs you share, the music you make, the love you give to others or the success you have or don't have. If your future is looking bright, watch out or you may die tonight..."

"When you look at it and analyse the whole situation it could have been a hit as well because Peter was a very radical man and wanted to change things," observes Dennis Alcapone. "Peter wanted to be his own government and the amount of persons they hurt that night, it could have been a hit – and with Peter and Free I as the main targets. It had the feel of an assassination, because Peter was planning to set up a radio station with Free I, and that's what the meeting was about. The thing is, we don't know what transpired whilst Peter was away in America and what could have made these people mobilise against him. What makes it more suspicious is that they got Free I as well, so it's like they get two birds with one stone. A lot of different stories come out, but I don't think Jamaica would have been ready for what he and Free I had planned to do, because Peter's vision was for a radio station that challenged the government, and they didn't want another media to spring up and influence people. They wanted to be in charge of whatever information was given out to the people. They wanted strict control, and they didn't want people to be educated. They wanted the ghetto people to stay ignorant. It's the 'shit-stem', as Peter would say..."

Ras Karbi doubts the sale would have gone through in any case whilst Carlton Tosh insists, "Whoever say these things, they do it to try and throw people off. They divert people from their cause and up until now, no one gets the truth. Peter lose his life and yet nobody know why to this day."

The notion that Peter and Free I were murdered because of wanting to educate and inspire Jamaica's black underclass is one that fuels Tosh's reputation as a reggae Che Guevara, but why should the government go to all the trouble of having them killed – even importing gunmen from as far as away as New York – when they could have easily made sure JBC was sold to someone else? Such shady manoeuvrings happen in governments and local councils the world over, and carry far less risk than a covert assassination.

Andrew Tosh was at a popular dancehall spot in Central Kingston the night Peter was murdered. "I felt my father's spirit come right there at Skateland where I was, and the spirit said leave that place right now." As the first news reports began to filter through, the general feeling was one of shock. More than 100 people gathered at the University Hospital up at Mona after the news broke and milled around outside the entrance, not quite knowing what to do. Some assumed the police had killed him – others that he'd died in a failed robbery attempt. The day after his death, a Jamaican radio station replayed an interview with him "in which he lamented the role of money in society and concluded it caused more harm than good". *Rolling Stone*'s Michael Goldberg hinted darkly that, "whilst robbery has been suggested as the primary motive in the shooting, another theory is that the murder was an act of retribution stemming from a disagreement with Marlene Brown, who one source claims had enemies in Kingston".

Former Prime Minister Michael Manley extolled his old friend as someone who "gave to Jamaica and the world an unforgettable library of musical works which will be played and sung by many generations of people". Prime Minister Edward Seaga extended his condolences to Peter Tosh's family and friends, whilst independent radio stations around the world broadcast tributes and hosted phone-ins, thereby allowing fans to express their feelings. Alas, (and again according to *Rolling Stone*), "commercial radio was almost silent in its recognition of the tragic passing of a musical giant".

Roger Steffens told one US publication: "Peter Tosh aroused controversy and left no one indifferent. He was the biggest living star reggae had, even though he had been inactive since 1983. His death is another major blow to the music and indicates how frightened the Jamaican power structure is of the musicians – the only people left on the island who tell the truth."

Tosh, who once said, "Death and I do not associate", wouldn't be universally mourned to the same extent that Bob Marley was. There was only room for one reggae legend although his passing did elicit the following remarks from Keith Richards.

"I was shocked it didn't happen a lot sooner. He threatened to do the same thing to me. I let him use my house years and years ago and suddenly he thought it was his. I got in touch with him and said, 'I'm coming down to the house, I need it for myself,' and he said, 'If you come anywhere near here I'll shoot you...' He was always gonna shoot people. In a way I liked him very much, I found him very interesting, but that part overtook him and he was executed."

Mick Jagger, whose second solo album, *Primitive Cool*, was released on the same day Tosh was murdered, declined to comment. Years later, when Richards publishes his autobiography, Peter won't feature in it – not even one word. It was almost 10 years since he and Ron Wood had first seen Peter play at the Island Music Festival in Trelawny and now their best-known signing lay dead on a mortuary slab, waiting for medical practitioner Patricia Ann Sinclair to perform a post-mortem examination, which took place on September 16.

"On external examination there was a 1cm circular entrance gunshot wound on top of the left side of the head. It was located approximately 10cm behind the forehead and 10.5 above the left ear. His brain could be seen through the defect and no powder marks around the wound were noted. There were two bruises on the forehead, one measuring 1.5cm located above the right eyebrow and one measuring 0.8cm about the left eyebrow. Blood was seen in both nostrils, in the mouth and the left ear. There was a 3 by 3cm entrance gunshot wound on the top of the skull on the left side and fractures extended from it forwards in the skull for 12cm, and backwards for 16cm. A copper coloured bullet was recovered at the site where it had not exited from the skull and there was extensive haemorrhage under the coverings of the brain on the left side. The brain was very swollen and contusions were present. In my opinion, the cause of death was due to gunshot wound to the head with extensive skull fractures and laceration to the brain."

Free I died on the same day, and Sinclair's colleague Maureen Martin performed a post-mortem examination approximately 40 minutes later.

"On external examination of the body there was a 5cm diameter gunshot entry wound in his scalp in the left occipital region. In my opinion the cause of death was due to severe brain damage due to a gunshot wound to the head."

The bullet had passed right through Free I's head, and then ricocheted back into his brain where it remained lodged. Recovery had never been an option. A day later it was announced that two men had been detained in connection with the murders, but their identities were being withheld. Police also issued a warrant for a third suspect, who they named as Dennis "Leppo" Lobban of Ninth Street, Kingston 12. He was described as 33 years old, 5′ 8″, and "scarred on the left forearm and left cheek". A police spokesman said he was to be considered armed and dangerous, and should be approached with caution.

Fearing for his safety, Leppo gave himself up the following day at the offices of the Jamaica Human Rights Council in Kingston. He assured police that he'd been with George Brown at a bar in Jones Town on the night of the murders but was duly charged with three counts of murder, robbery with aggravation, illegal possession of a firearm, and four counts of shooting with intent. Leppo was found to have eight previous convictions stretching back to 1971. These included vagrancy, robbery with aggravation, assault with intent to rob, and wounding with intent. On his last visit to court in July 1974 he'd been sentenced to 25 years hard labour, although he'd only served 12 years and five months of this sentence before being paroled in the autumn of 1986.

As the date of Peter's funeral approached, Kingston police couldn't establish a clear motive for the killings but were working on the premise "that it was the result of a feud between some of the victims and the gunmen". The circumstances surrounding Peter's burial arrangements had already proven farcical after Marlene, Peter's mother and his estranged father, James McIntosh, all claimed rights to the body. In the meantime another man called Alfred McIntosh appeared on the scene alleging he was Peter's real father, despite his mother saying that she'd never clapped eyes on him before!

"Marlene had cut Peter off from his mother before his death," explains Wayne Jobson, "then when Peter died, Marlene wanted control of everything so she found this old, drunken guy in Savanna-La-Mar named Alfred McIntosh. The thing is he was little and short, so he could never be Peter's father. He'd just go up to people and say for them to buy him a drink because Peter is his son. People would feel sorry for him but Marlene went and found the guy and made friends with him, thinking that a common-law wife and father would have more power than just the mother. Peter's real father was a mechanic who lived in Falmouth but only Peter's mother knew who he was, and she hadn't seen him in 30 years. After a while she sent someone to go and get him and when the man find out that the singer Peter Tosh who'd just died was his son he nearly faint! That's because he'd only seen him once, when Peter was a child but he was told he had to go to Kingston and give evidence; the government interviewed him and the mother and that's how it got sorted out."

A court eventually granted Alvera custody of her son's body, which Fikisha Cumbo says was subject to yet further indignity.

"Marlene sent the clothes that Peter was killed in and told them to bury him in those clothes. That's the kind of woman she was. She also told Peter's mother that she would die in three days' time but Mrs. Coke was a real diehard Christian and so she just brushed it off..."

A thanksgiving service was finally arranged for Saturday September 26 at the National Arena, where Peter lay in state from noon until four in the afternoon. Sections of Jamaican society had disagreed with the decision

461

to give Peter Tosh a state funeral, but there were still long queues of people wanting to pay their last respects. Once inside, they were greeted by a Rasta warrior's final resting place. Red, green and gold flags were draped over the dais bearing his casket, and portraits of Marcus Garvey and Emperor Haile Selassie I served as backdrops, together with a large painting of the African continent. Ceil Tulloch, author of *Remembering Peter Tosh*, gave the following eyewitness account.

"Throughout the funeral service, there were readings from the Scriptures, prayers offered, singing, and music (including Tosh's own beautiful composition 'Creation'). Acclaimed Jamaican saxophonist Dean Fraser performed a stirring rendition of Jimmy Cliff's ballad 'Many Rivers To Cross'. Four members of the Ethiopian Orthodox Tewahedo Church's clergy officiated at the service. At predetermined intervals throughout Tosh's service, the four priests circled and blessed the casket. The solemn procession is led by the cleric carrying a cross, while the archdeacon, who at precise moments swings the censure, brings up the rear. Celebrated musicologist, media personality and author Dermot Hussey delivered the eulogy."

Prime Minister Edward Seaga called him "a musical giant" whilst Michael Manley, eloquent as ever, praised Tosh as a musician saying, "There was an integrity to his anger about injustice. I think that no matter how famous he became and no matter what he earned, what burned within him was this indignation about what is wrong."

People say the Reverend Kes Estafanus of the Ethiopian Orthodox Church was asked to officiate at the ceremony but that he'd refused. Carol Amaruso, writing for gospelreggae.com, states that, "Tosh too, was buried by them, apparently at his family's insistence but since he had 'cursed and cursed and cursed the church', the Archbishop neither presided over nor attended the rites." Others claim he didn't officiate at Peter's funeral because the singer had vociferously championed herb and the Church was opposed to it.

There was often a tragicomic side to Peter, and his funeral would prove no exception. At one point the proceedings were interrupted by a young man holding a large banner with the word "FREEDOM" painted on it in large red letters. In the corners of the banner were the three colours of Garvey's organisation – red, green and black. After parading back and forth and making his protest known for several minutes, he was finally escorted out. Peter might have recognised a little of himself in this youth but revolutionary ardour then turned to complete farce when an older man carrying a staff and wearing a white cap mounted the platform and stood over the coffin, yelling for Peter to "Arise and open the casket!" You couldn't hear a pin drop for several seconds, until those stood around watching recovered their composure. Peter was no Lazarus so the interloper turned his attention to Edward Seaga, who'd left the building, and ordered *him* to open the casket. People started laughing and so the man drew his last card. "Mr. Prime Minister," he asked, "why did you kill Peter?"

Controversy had followed Peter Tosh into the grave and it wouldn't end there, not even after Sly Dunbar, Robbie Lyn and two of Peter's sons – Andrew and Horace (also known as "Dave Tosh") – had shouldered his coffin and placed it in the hearse that would ferry Peter's body to Westmoreland. Alvera had planned to bury him in the family plot at Belmont, close to where she lived. The proceedings then degenerated into a shambles after James McIntosh, who hadn't even met his son until Peter was almost grown, made an official complaint on the grounds that Alvera had kept pigs on this same stretch of land. He insisted this would have offended Peter, and that no Rastafarian could have tolerated such a thing. His mother later admitted to keeping pigs in "the near vicinity", but insisted they'd been housed some distance away. Peter was thus laid to rest amidst circumstances that were curious at best, but also deeply tragic.

Bunny Wailer didn't attend the funeral, and Peter wouldn't have had it any other way. He'd recently had problems of his own after recording a rookie MC called Johnny Scar. Bunny was about to release a song by him – written about Zimbabwe – when someone told the youngster it had already sold two million copies in Africa. Scar believed them and aggressively demanded money from Bunny, who gave him the metal stamper used to press records and said never to bother him again. It was only later that he discovered Scar's real name was Lobban, and that Leppo was his brother. There were whispers in Trench Town that Scar may have been outside Peter's house on the night of his murder, but hadn't ventured any further. Kingston's ghettos were full of dark imaginings, especially after stock markets around the world crashed on what would have been Peter's 43rd birthday, October 19, 1987. The news reports called it "Black Monday" as the Dow Jones index fell to its lowest level since the Great Depression of 1929. It was "the day the dollar died", and Rastafarians weren't the only ones talking in hushed tones of ancient prophecies.

Both Leppo and Steve Russell were accused of murder at a preliminary examination held in the Gun Court on November 18. Their trial will keep being deferred until the summer of 1988, when the rumours started up again regarding the reasons for Tosh's murder. National Security Minister Errol Anderson had said there could be a connection between Tosh's murder and guns involved in drugs trafficking. The *LA Times* reported how "the most bizarre theory came from bookkeeper Marlene Brown, who told the wire service that Satan killed Tosh because she and Tosh were going to conceive a baby that would be a 'powerful boy with a Star of David on his forehead'."

Leppo's trial was initially scheduled for April 19 but the defence experienced difficulty in preparing witness statements, and was duly granted more time. A new trial date of June 13 was set in the Home Circuit Court where Lobban – now described as a "dub poet and haggler" – was jointly charged with 26-year-old Steve Russell. He was later freed after the judge upheld a no case submission made by his lawyers.

Eleven people testified during the five-day hearings. The judge had denied press permission to report the trial and whilst Lobban's lawyer made several complaints about alleged breaches involving the media, he was referred to the Director of Public Prosecutions on each occasion. On June 17, the jury reached their verdict in record time, after taking just six minutes to find Lobban guilty. Mr. Justice Patterson sentenced him to hang and informed the court, "I would have arrived at the same verdict. I have no doubt in my mind that he went there that night and killed Tosh and the others. It was just by chance that the other four survived or we would have had seven people lying dead."

Wayne Jobson says that when Leppo went to court and Michael Robinson and Marlene walked in, "his eyes got wide-wide".

"He freaked out that they were still alive. He thought they'd been killed. I don't know whether he'd been denied access to newspapers in prison or what, but he really thought that all these people were dead so when he went to court, he thought he was going to get off. He told everyone that he'd had nothing to do with it, and there were no witnesses. He knew that he'd shot so many bullets into these people's heads that all of them *must* be dead."

Leppo had maintained his innocence throughout the trial but was taken to Spanish Town prison after being sentenced and left to await his fate on death row. He'll later appeal to the Privy Court in London and get his sentence commuted to life imprisonment. The other two killers were never identified, but were almost certainly shot and murdered by unknown assailants.

In March 1989, Leppo wrote to Flo O'Connor, co-ordinator for the Jamaica Human Rights Council, and thanked her for shedding light on his case in a recent radio debate. He signed himself "Parolee Dennis Anthony Lobban, aged 35, born January 16, 1955. Dub poet" and said her arguments were "meticulous. I am glad you have learnt about their corruption". He goes on to warn her "that the stand you take against injustice, it's a serious stand and you must always beware of sinister elements. I understand that your house was burnt down and although I am in this predicament I would not like to hear nothing wrong with you."

He calls her "a mother of sympathy" and goes on to say, "The rope is around my neck psychologically in which I am now looking to face the gallows without the clemency of society. The weight is heavy and it's a hard road to travel but I believe in the Almighty that He will guide I unto victory." In the same envelope were two books of poetry – one called *From Prison*, and the other *Disenfranchised Inmates*. "I would love the next generation to get those two books of poems," he tells her. He ends his letter by saying that he was tried by the media before his trial, and quotes from one of his poems called 'Justice'.

"Justice, where are you? Because I am poor, I am locked behind the door. I cannot take it no more. I need my freedom some more…"

The Court of Appeal will uphold his murder conviction. In the wake of this decision, on May 22, Leppo again wrote to the Jamaica Human Rights Council's Flo O'Connor.

"I was charged for the murder of Peter Tosh, international reggae singer and others in which I have no knowledge about it whatsoever. I was tried and sentenced to hang on the 17th of June 1988, in the Kingston House Circular Court which I then appealed and lost…" He accuses the media and judiciary society of prejudice and complains that Steve Russell could have identified him from the photograph in the *Star* newspaper. On the same day, Leppo also wrote to his solicitors and barrister-at-law, Dr. Peter Jackson, pleading for their "physical and moral assistance to the highest of your abilities.

"I don't want to waste my precious time on this place. I have seen inmates here for five, 10, 15 years awaiting the Privy Council in England

and up until now they haven't heard anything about their cases. Please don't let me be a wastage on death row. I have my loving family and my children to support. I am the first child for my parents in which I am the breadwinner. My mother and father are sickly at this time. My mother has trouble with arthritis and can hardly move, whilst my father has trouble with abdominal pain."

The Privy Council in London is the final court of appeal for 16 Commonwealth countries and hears about 60 appeals a year. On April 7, 1995 the Council threw out Leppo's final appeal, calling him "Jamaica's most notorious death row prisoner". The committee acknowledged there had been material irregularities in his trial including a prosecution cross-examination of him on hearsay evidence, which they deemed inadmissible. The judges said this was a serious departure from a well-established rule, but "the prosecution case was based on strong recognition evidence from two witnesses".

Explaining why his sentence had been commuted to life imprisonment the British law lords said that conditions in Kingston's General Penitentiary were so bad, it would be inhuman to hang any prisoner who had spent more than five years in there on death row. Leppo had been kept in isolation for fear of other prisoners killing him and when Wayne Jobson went to visit him during the making of *Stepping Razor: Red X*, he was shocked to see that he looked just like a vampire, with two protruding canine teeth. "He looked just like Satan," says Jobson.

Dennis "Leppo" Lobban has now served nearly 25 years in prison and continues to proclaim his innocence, saying that Peter Tosh was his friend.

Chapter 32

The Legacy

Six months after Peter's death, *No Nuclear War* won Best Reggae Album at the 30th Grammy Awards, held at Radio City Hall in New York. It was a timely reminder of what he'd stood for, as well as his musical achievements. Greenpeace was moved to announce, "Any artist that would title a song 'No Nuclear War' is truly an activist," and then praised him for "using his music to deliver such a strong, clear and important message".

The legend of Peter Tosh should have gone into overdrive at this point and on the surface at least, there was never any reason why he shouldn't have become another cultural icon like Bob Marley. They were two sides of the same coin after all, except Peter was a lot more rebellious and outspoken. Imagine if he'd sung rock'n'roll instead of reggae, because Tosh possessed all the essential ingredients for rock immortality. He was the archetypal outlaw, fighting against the system and who never stopped defending the poor. The Rolling Stones couldn't handle him, and he courted controversy at every turn before withdrawing amidst claims that he'd gone mad and was seeing vampires. He then returned with one of the best albums of his career, only to be gunned down and murdered in mysterious circumstances. Not even a Hollywood scriptwriter would have dared write his story, yet where were the sustained and well-co-ordinated campaigns aimed at keeping his memory alive? Columbia and EMI own most of his classic material and yet have always acted independently of each other. This meant there'd be no definitive compilation like Marley's *Legend*, and no single, guiding influence like Chris Blackwell, who first prepared the ground for Marley's canonisation and then constructed a mythology around him until the name "Bob Marley" became synonymous with the entire reggae genre. We can only imagine what would have happened had a major company got behind Peter Tosh and actively promoted him to the same degree. The differences between him and Marley would have certainly led to a wealth of interesting possibilities. Neville Garrick called Peter "a musical freedom fighter", and says he represented the Wailers' "most militant and defiant side".

"Each man had his own qualities. Peter's spirit was always very black consciousness and Afro-centric, even in his way of dealing with the mystic man, the black arts. As a revolutionary voice that spoke for the African, he summed it all up in that song, 'No matter where you come from, as long as you're a black man, you're an African.' Peter was the call-to-arms type of lyricist. If Peter had been in the Black Panthers he would have been Minister of Offense."

Jamaican historian Dermot Hussey saw him as "an African knight who came to do war with his words and his band" whilst Professor Rex Nettleford described Tosh as "a poet of the utterance".

"Prophets of the people if you like, who had a deep insight into the reality of contemporary Jamaica and who spoke out against the endemic injustice and lopsidedness of a society that has yet to liberate itself totally from colonialism and slavery. He was a latter-day Maroon who conducted resistance against an unjust society under the cover of art and music. It was as if he was forcing it into decency and a particular form of sanity."

"He believed every word he sang," said Jimmy Cliff. "He didn't just make up some words. He believed in everything that he did. He was a protest singer and he absolutely believed the system was corrupt. He was fighting against this, but underneath that he was a warm and gentle, kind person."

"The life of Peter Tosh was one of constant harassment from Babylon and as a prophet, he was not truly accepted in his own land," notes Ras Cardo. "Peter was targeted and persecuted constantly in his life. He was a very kind, caring, compassionate and no nonsense person who despised injustice with a passion. He despised the conditions of poverty and was not going to stop singing about it, so it cost him his life...

"Peter was hurt by a lot of things around him – the broken promises of government, and the betrayal of those he thought he could trust. Bob

Marley also fell prey to this deception because at the time he was too anxious about getting his message to the world. Those around him did not really give a damn about his protection. They were able to get close to him and destroy him. These same enemies divided and separated Peter and Bunny from him and discredited and tortured Peter in ways too numerous to mention. They made Peter's life a living hell because he would not give in to their demands. They made the world believe that Bob and Peter hated each other – NOT TRUE!

"Peter was then killed by these same heathens that Bob sing about. Today these same traitors and murderers walk around freely while their offspring benefit from the fruits of these slain legends. Let me say without a doubt and with knowledge of certain truths that the deaths of Bob Marley, Peter Tosh and others were not accidents, but were deliberate and intentional acts by those who wanted to silence them and to control reggae, reggae music and the monetary profits from reggae artists by leaving them dead and their children to suffer."

On the first anniversary of Peter's death, the heavens opened and Hurricane Gilbert ripped through Jamaica, devastating the island and leaving thousands homeless. Some were tempted at this juncture to evoke visions of Peter as the Mystic Man, who'd used thunder and lightning on his records and given some of his best performances when singing in adverse weather conditions. The fact is that many Jamaicans were now in urgent need of basic provisions, and had no time for fantasists. 'Peter Tosh: The Last Concert. Live At Reggae Super Jam' premiered at the La Roose Restaurant and Entertainment Complex in Port Henderson soon after tragedy struck, with all proceeds going to the Hurricane relief fund. Just over a year later, Wayne Jobson's band Native played at a show in San Diego held to commemorate Tosh's 45th birthday. That's when Wayne had the idea of making a film about Peter – one that focussed on his murder, and events leading up to that fateful evening in September 1987. In an interview with Roger Steffens for *The Beat*, he told of how the project came about.

"The Tosh Estate was in total chaos because like Bob, Peter didn't leave a will and he was never legally married. The Jamaican government had all the access to the money but there were no proper lawyers collecting it, no managers, nothing, so everything was insane. Then I learned that a lawyer named Michael Lorne was in charge, which was very interesting because he and I had gone to law school together and lived together in Barbados, so I got the rights for the film from him.

"I'd already met the Canadian actor and director Nicholas Campbell at a Junior Marvin show in Ocho Rios. In the beginning, I had the idea that it was going to be such an incredible story. I just wanted to show the power of the man and his music, so Nicholas and I went down to Jamaica to start researching. Dermot Hussey took us to meet Marlene at the house and she gave us a great deal of help. Peter's mother too, gave us her whole story."

It was Marlene who loaned them the "Red X tapes" – two and a half hours of recordings Peter had made during the *Mama Africa* tour, after his animosity towards Marley biographer Timothy White had compelled him to write his own book, and he'd started to verbally jot down recollections into a cassette recorder. Another two and a half hours' worth of tapes had been destroyed by one of his children but Peter's account is riven with such stark honesty, it's no wonder that Jobson's team made it the centrepiece of their film. Peter thus became the narrator of his own story and his testimony – together with those of Michael Robinson, Joy Dixon and others – invests *Stepping Razor: Red X* with remarkable power and intensity.

Wayne is both Jamaican and a musician. His cousins Dickie and Diane Jobson had both worked for Chris Blackwell and were close associates of Bob Marley. Such credentials afforded Wayne a greater degree of access than most, although he still encountered his share of difficulties.

"The first day we went to interview people in Trench Town it was really rough. The headline in the paper that day said, 'Six Dead in Western Kingston Violence'. I had a crew of five white Canadians who freaked out and didn't want to go so we went to Admiral Town police station and hired three cops with M-16s for protection, which I now realise was a terrible mistake because a Trench Town don named Massive came up to the windows, pushed the cops' guns out of the way and said, 'Move now!' and asked $1,000 an hour for us to shoot there."

Wayne got him down to $250 and went back the next day without a police escort. Local residents showed them the house on West Road where Peter had stayed with his uncle and the singer's battered acoustic guitar was still there, propped in a corner of the room. The following day Jobson hired a helicopter for half an hour, went up in it just as the sun was rising and circled Trench Town, filming all the while. When they went back there that evening Massive said they'd only been spared being shot down because it was a tourist helicopter! Wayne had initially approached the Jamaica Defence Force about hiring one of theirs, but found it too expensive. If he'd succeeded, there's no telling what might have happened. Filming in Jamaica wasn't easy at the best of times, and danger was never far away. One day several mean-looking dreadlocks came to their office and threatened them, saying no white people were supposed to make a film about Peter Tosh and they'd come to put a stop to it. Luckily, director Nicholas Campbell managed to talk them round and even persuaded one of them to play Peter in some of the reconstruction scenes. These remain compelling, no matter how many times you see them. To date, *Stepping Razor: Red X* is still the best Peter Tosh documentary on the market, and it's the only one to feature Peter's killer, who was interviewed in his cell.

Dennis "Leppo" Lobban will later write to Tom Marshall of MTV Networks expressing disappointment at being portrayed as a killer in the film, and not having received any royalties. He'll also accuse MTV of having approached him in the guise of lawyers "when they clearly weren't legal representatives of any kind". This refers to when Wayne Jobson had visited him and claimed to be an attorney, at Leppo's own suggestion. It had been this deception that had made their interview possible. Despite this, Lobban declared himself willing to co-operate with MTV in future, and demanded $2 million for his involvement in a follow-up documentary. He also suggested they bring "half a dozen footballs and bone dice for the inmates" and a twin cassette player for himself, in addition to JA $50,000 that he wished to distribute among his fellow prisoners, who were "without anyone to visit them or even carry soap particles to give them". He signed off with, "Jah guide, Death Row inmate Dennis Lobban, Jah Leppo Lion. One love, one heart, no hatred."

Stepping Razor: Red X first appeared in cinemas during the summer of 1993. Its release coincided with an article on Marlene Brown, written by Basil Walters for the *Jamaica Observer*. Marlene's quoted as saying that she's about to become a record producer, and start her own label.

"Over the years I have been observing what has been happening to reggae music in Jamaica and it's a damn shame. I think it is my duty to stand up for this music. I am now forming a company that will be producing young, cultural artists. Reggae music has been derailed, and I think it's about time artistes, musicians, fans and producers like myself put it back on track."

The name of her company was to be Mabrak Promotion – "mabrak" meaning thunder and lightning. The launch date would be September 11 1993, which was the sixth anniversary of Tosh's murder.

"Marlene boasts about her getting the best recording deals for Tosh," wrote Walters. "She spoke with pride of how she, through the courts in New York, got EMI to double their payments of advance money as well as pay up unpaid royalties to Peter."

Marlene was still living at 5 Plymouth Avenue although the family had already decided to sell the property and there'll be nothing she can do about it. She and Peter hadn't married, nor did they have any children. Walters' article refers to four miscarriages – two of them having resulted from "fighting", which is rather worrying. Marlene therefore had no claim to Peter's estate, despite having been his common-law wife for five years.

Needless to say, the studio and record label never materialised, and Marlene will sadly fall upon hard times after being evicted from the home she shared with Tosh who she calls her "first man" and her "idol". It'll be left to the record companies and a handful of lawyers to keep Peter's legacy alive, aided by experts like Roger Steffens and Herbie Miller. There'll be no posthumous hit singles or lucrative advertising tie-ins, and mainstream radio play will be negligible. Paul Khouri believes this has more to do with Peter's music than any lack of corporate push.

"Peter Tosh was more revolutionary in his mentality than Bob. Revolutionary comes in many different formulas but he wasn't the storyteller that Bob was. Bob looked at things, saw things and because he had that deep love and affection for people, he wrote the stories that touched their hearts. It wasn't cool to be soft hearted, but that's how he was. He didn't write songs with anger, but love. It was almost a teaching instead of being judgmental, because he wasn't a prejudiced person. He never had a prejudiced bone in his body but Peter didn't have the social skills or the sensitivity to write those kinds of songs. His background and his upbringing were different."

The upbeat melodies of songs like 'Jammin'', 'Could You Be Loved', 'Is This Love' and 'Three Little Birds' have ensured they've become staples of daytime radio the world over, underlining Marley's status as King Of Reggae. None of Peter's songs have achieved anything like the same degree of popularity but then hardly any were reissued outside of Jamaica, and major label promotion has been non-existent. It's only fellow reggae singers who'll keep his music alive on the grassroots scene – most notably Luciano, who hit with 'Legalise It' back in 2001 and then Bushman, whose tribute album *Bushman Sings The Bush Doctor* appeared a decade or so later. Peter's son Andrew Tosh, who recorded his debut album for Niney The Observer back in 1987, has also continued to highlight his father's work over the years. Andrew looks and sounds just like his father – especially when covering his songs – and even rides a unicycle. In more recent times we've also seen the emergence of Melody Cunningham's son Jawara, a rapper who records under the name "Tosh 1". Yet the fact remains that none of Tosh's progeny have attained the same heights as Stephen, Damian, Ziggy, Ky-mani and Julian Marley, whose songs have equalled those of their father at times. Arguably, the most fitting testament to Peter can be heard on albums by South African reggae star Lucky Dube, who had a similar vocal style and faced considerable police harassment after growing dreadlocks and writing songs that opposed the apartheid regime. Dube would earn an international reputation – even performing at Jamaica's Reggae Sunsplash – before being gunned down in a failed carjacking during October 2007.

These days, thanks to Google and YouTube, the work of any musician has never been so accessible. That's a fairly recent development of course, since fans of Peter Tosh had little to cheer for lengthy periods of time before the Internet came along. That inspired series of solo albums he recorded between 1976-1987 will stay in print at least. These will regularly get updated as formats change – some of them as deluxe editions – whilst companies such as Trojan and Heartbeat will reissue the majority of his early vocal and instrumental tracks. Even that fiery performance at the One Love Peace Concert surfaced eventually whilst *Honorary Citizen* and *The Ultimate Experience* remain the monarchs of all Tosh compilations, and contain plenty of rare and previously unreleased material.

As I write, there are still no books, biopics, clothing lines or sponsorship deals in the name of Peter Tosh. His legacy remains a sleeping giant – something Bunny Wailer attributes to "some little domesticated stuff that Peter got mixed up in.

"That kind of broke down the respect within a sense, but Peter Tosh being the artist he was and still is, we know that his works and his words live on. As an individual, Peter Tosh might have done some things that turned off people but as far as his works are concerned, that's unquestionably something we have to admire, cherish and respect and to uphold because if we don't, we're going to feel the after-effects of not having done so."

Bunny has supported attempts to preserve Peter's legacy by occasionally appearing at annual tribute shows hosted by Westmoreland promoter Worrell King. These free events were held at Independence Park in Savanna-La-Mar, from 1991 onwards. Stalls and sideshows would keep the crowd entertained until darkness fell, and singers like Luciano, Bushman and Everton Blender took the stage. Such tributes were timed to coincide with Peter's birthday, rather than the day of his murder. 1991 was also the year Pauline Morrison visited Belmont and first spoke of building a proper memorial to her cousin. Pauline hadn't been able to attend Peter's funeral, and was disappointed with what she'd seen on that initial visit to Westmoreland. Five years later, in April 1996, she'll tell *Rastamon Times* that the "humble tomb, although crafted with love and reverence, did not befit a man of Tosh's international stature and musical legacy". She'd been sat on her aunt's veranda when the idea came to her to turn the property into a memorial with a museum, library, gift shop, recreation area and even a medical facility. No sooner had she arranged to meet with a local architect than Peter appeared to her in a vision and requested they install a duck pond behind their cousin Prince's shop, which was just a few hundred yards away. Alvera told Pauline the previous owner had kept ducks on that very spot, but at a time before Peter was even born. Soon, Pauline will rent an office in Lower Manhattan and start a company called Tosh Is Within Inc, aimed at "getting Peter's music heard by as many people as possible".

She also launched the Peter Tosh Foundation – a non-profit organisation that was intended to oversee the building and maintenance of the memorial park. After getting planning permission from the Jamaican government and funding the initial work from her own pocket, Pauline broke the ground at a ceremony held on February 4, 1995. "My greatest hope for the park is to be able to maintain it for many years to come, even after my passing," she said. "For people to be educated from it and for people to understand who Peter really was and what Peter really stood for."

Nothing much happened for several years afterwards, thanks to a combination of lack of funds and family disunity. In June 1999, another member of the Wailers' circle was shot and killed in Kingston. This time it was Junior Braithwaite, who'd faded back into obscurity since contributing to *The Never Ending Wailers*, but had stayed friends with Bunny. News of his death arrived as the latter and representatives of Peter's Estate did battle in the law courts with Island Logic Ltd and the Marley Estate over unpaid royalties relating to Tuff Gong. According to Bunny, Tuff Gong was the label he, Peter Tosh and Bob Marley formed back in 1971, after disentangling themselves from Lee Perry.

"It was originally registered here in Jamaica in the names of Bob Marley, Peter Tosh and Bunny Wailer as the three shareholders of the company," he told Roger Steffens. "Tuff Gong Records is the mother company, whilst Tuff Gong Music is the child company." The latter refers to the label controlled by the Marley Estate, which issues family product in Jamaica and overseas. Bunny had challenged their continuing use of the Tuff Gong name, logo and early recordings, which then led to the Bob Marley Foundation, Tuff Gong International and Fifty-Six Hope Road Music Ltd launching a petition in 1996, asking the courts to decide who were the rightful owners. Legal action commenced in both Jamaica and the UK, and resulted in a final settlement on June 28 of that year. Bunny and the Peter Tosh Estate were given six months to file certain documents, but didn't comply. It was therefore considered "just and equitable" that the original company be wound up. Jamaica's Supreme Court duly gave the order to do so on Thursday September 28, 2000. Yet another landmark in the Wailers' story had come to an end, although at least it involved financial benefits this time. Under the terms of the settlement (which had been made out of court), about $2 million would be paid to Bunny and the Peter Tosh Estate, in lieu of backdated royalties. The end of this dispute was described by lawyer Kendall Minter as "a healing and re-allegiance between the Marley, Tosh, and Wailer families, who will now be able to act in unison in promoting certain products and to help stamp out the piracy of these products."

Bunny will embark on a number of joint ventures with members of the Marley clan thereafter, including recordings and tours. Harmony was in the air and after a meeting held at Peter's grave in Belmont during October 2001, the Tosh family made the decision to resurrect the Intel Diplo label and launch a Peter Tosh Foundation. A month or so earlier, the 14th anniversary of Peter's murder had been totally overshadowed by the terrorist attacks on America, and "9/11" will forever have a different meaning. It was time to get serious and after that injection of cash into the estate's coffers, the possibilities were looking good.

Two years hence and there'll have been few improvements. Pauline Morrison's vision still hadn't become a reality, and major improvements to the burial site remained a pipedream. Promoter Worrell King kept busy though and in October 2003, his annual Tosh tribute was held outside of Jamaica for the very first time. 'Tribute to Peter Tosh 2003' now lasted a whole week, beginning with a Tosh Birthday Party at a hotel owned by Chris Blackwell in Miami Beach. Over the next few days Florida International University hosted a Tosh Film Festival and Peter Tosh Symposium before the festivities reached their climax with a concert held at the Bayfront Park Amphitheatre headlined by Lucky Dube. King invited a panel of intellectuals and former Tosh associates to appear at the Symposium, including Dr. Omar Davies, Jamaica's Minister of Finance; University of the West Indies lecturer Dr. Clinton Hutton and Tosh's former manager Copeland Forbes. This was the beginning of a serious attempt to shed light on Peter's political and intellectual ambitions, in addition to honouring his musical contributions.

Earlier that same year, the *Jamaica Observer* had reported that promoter Mike Malott planned to produce a Peter Tosh tribute album featuring some well-known names from the rock and pop fields.

"Malott hopes the project would generate revenue to help repair and restore the mausoleum. The mausoleum's cinder-block walls are partially erected but were vandalised, and several items including Tosh's own grave marker had been stolen. If restored and developed, the museum could be a major pull for visitors, enhancing tourism on the island's south coast.

"According to Dave Tosh, son of Peter Tosh, 'Tourists come by the bus load. We get a lot of European visitors. They want the history and they also like the tranquillity of the area,' he said, indicating that much more needs to be done to promote his father's birthplace and burial site. 'We are hoping to complete the museum for his 60th birthday, October 2004, and that is my aim and ambition right now.'"

Two years later and Herbie Miller, writing in the *Jamaica Observer*, will lament how little had been done to preserve and enrich Peter's legacy. "For someone second only to Marley, who has spread Jamaica's cultural image across continents and to millions of people, he has been severely snubbed by the local arts and heritage organisations, cultural czars in government, the media and as a result, the Jamaican music loving public. Perhaps the submerged artistry of Peter Tosh is because he was a revolutionary in fact and not just a rebel.

"He was, and continues to be viewed in many circles as a somewhat cantankerous individual who existed in the shadow of his former group member and brother Bob Marley. Yet, in my mind, Peter Tosh was not only a most complex human being, but also was one of his era's most politically aware, incisive, musically engaging, and truly entertaining performers.

"For me, he remains one of the most important, insightful and committed twentieth century political musicians and activists I have observed. His pragmatic observation of local and world politics influenced his compositions. Tosh was a musician whose best socio-political works parallel that of anyone working in that style. That is, everyone from Robeson to Marley."

A skirmish over Peter's M-16 guitar, which Marlene Brown had tried to sell on eBay, then demonstrated some welcome family unity in safeguarding one of Peter's best-known artefacts. The guitar was subsequently withdrawn from auction after complaints from various interested parties, including Copeland Forbes and Peter's youngest son Jawara. Marlene said the guitar had been locked away in a closet in the United States for the past 19 years, and that she'd been trying to raise funds for an orphanage and old people's home in Jamaica. The following year marked the twentieth anniversary of Peter's passing, and the *Daily Gleaner* had good news to report for a change.

"With the legal battles over his estate settled and his family committed to preserving his rich cultural legacy, the quiet fishing town of Belmont, in Westmoreland, seems set to finally get the promised monument in honour of their most revered son Peter Tosh.

"'As a family, we have always recognised the greatness of my father and have never lost sight of our obligation to preserve his memory,' said Dave Tosh. 'We are now ready to turn our attention to finishing the theme park in his honour.'

"The theme park, under construction at Tosh's family home in Belmont, had its groundbreaking back in February 1995. It has seen very little development since and in fact except for the completion of the mausoleum, which holds the singer's mortal remains, the project has been in limbo.

"On completion the theme park will feature a museum of Tosh's work, a library, recreational area, a gift shop for local craft and a mini-medical facility. It is expected to project the spiritual, cultural, social and musical ideals that Tosh stood for. While Tosh, who was murdered by an old associate in 1987, has never gotten official recognition, his memory has never been allowed to fade, especially by businessman/promoter Worrell King. With the blessing of Tosh's mother, Mrs. Alvera Coke, King has almost single-handedly been trying to preserve the singer's memory through the staging of the annual Tribute to Peter Tosh. 'Peter has been an inspiration to all the lovers of conscious uplifting music,' said King, who's an uncompromising advocate of "clean music". 'As a fellow son of Westmoreland and one who identifies with Tosh's music, I feel obliged in playing my part in highlighting the things he stood for.'

"The week of celebration, designed to showcase Tosh's life and work, will include a night of drumming on October 19 (his birthday) in Belmont; a symposium on October 13 at the University of the West Indies and the 'Tribute to Peter Tosh Concert' on Saturday October 20. 'We have a lot of respect for what Mr. King has been doing to keep my father's memory alive,' said Dave Tosh, who came aboard as a part of the promotion team last year. 'Be it the theme park or tribute show, we will always be showing respect to my father.'

"The line-up for the tribute, which is slated for the newly refurbished Central Park in Negril, will be headlined by Tosh's musical son Andrew, along with fellow reggae stars Michael Rose, Everton Blender and Edi Fitzroy."

Dr. Clinton Hutton, speaking to the *Jamaica Observer*, said that speakers at the Peter Tosh Symposium would be "taking the opportunity to look back at the last 20 years to assess how we as a nation have looked at the work and life of one of our best finds. We are also looking specifically at the treatment of Tosh by the academia and the music community. In addition, a book on Peter Tosh is in the works, with the hope that it will come out before his 64th birthday next year." Hutton promised this would be a collection of views on Tosh by different people, among them Omar Davies, Dr. Michael Witter, Professor Barry Chevannes, Copeland Forbes and Herbie Miller. Whilst this book still hasn't appeared at the time of writing, it's part of a trend to reappraise Tosh's worth as both singer and activist. *Rolling Stone* magazine described him "as reggae's Malcolm X" whilst Matt Cibula compared him to John Lennon for his cynicism and artful use of wordplay, except "Lennon's weak and passive Monty Pythonisms pales beside Tosh's holy wrath".

After noting how Peter's voice "was stilled when it had so much more to say", Stan Evan Smith said he "remains for many, a salutary, misunderstood, controversial and complex figure. A controversial figure because of his political radicalism and his unceasing championship of equal rights and social justice and the legalisation of marijuana, Tosh's talent, greatness and musical achievement go largely unheralded and his music has not yet received the acclaim it so richly deserves. Why is he not celebrated and honoured in Jamaica?"

Carol Cooper, writing in the *Village Voice*, thought it had something to do with how "critics raved about the imagery and spectacle of Rastafarian music without ever touching on the heart of the message". In her view, this accounted for Tosh not being asked serious questions, and explains why (presumably foreign) journalists rarely probed beyond his public persona to find out who he was and what he was trying to accomplish. The problem with this theory is that it brings Tosh's role as communicator into sharper focus and implies that he failed in getting his true objectives across, either in person or within the scope of his music. Stan Evan Smith thinks it may have more to do with the obstacles faced by those black artists who are insistent in remaining true to themselves and their racial identities.

"The black artist, whose work must, like all true artists, reflect his life experiences, is instead forced into the false option of being just an artist. In a racially discriminatory society where black skin proved to be an impediment to civil and social equality and claims to black individuality were ignored... Where indigenous language and culture was marginalised and suppressed, this creates an 'urge towards whiteness'. Peter Tosh was forced to work against bruising criticism and misunderstanding from his own people. This is the mountain that Tosh, as a true artist, had to climb."

Tosh's anti-establishment stance, his outspoken views on marijuana, alienating behaviour and affinity for curse words were hardly likely to endear him to the Jamaican authorities, or the island's middle class. Recommending him for any kind of official recognition would send out the wrong message, and this same mindset wasn't going to change in a hurry. More than 30 years after the One Love Peace Concert, artists were still being arrested in Jamaica for using profane language, and the conditions that Peter Tosh railed against during his lifetime remain intact, as levels of social inequality, crime and poverty in Jamaica and elsewhere continue to rise. Alas, the messages in his songs haven't been heeded by anyone in a position to actually do anything about them. The days when artists like him could sit and reason with the Prime Minister are long gone, and you'd be forgiven for thinking his music just preached to the converted until discovering that the US Library Of Congress had chosen the Wailers' *Burnin'* album "for perpetual preservation" in December 2007.

"Each year the United States Library of Congress selects a small number of audio recordings to preserve for all time in the National Recording Registry, based on their historical, artistic or cultural importance..."

Rita Marley said the album was "the work of prophets" but there was no word from the Peter Tosh Estate, which had lacked an articulate spokesperson ever since Pauline Morrison bowed from sight a few years earlier, citing family differences. An event like that should have prompted an official response but there was still no organisation in place, and no one willing to take on that kind of function. Even worse news came the following year, when Yardflex published an article headed "Peter Tosh traditional tribute quiet in Jamaica this year.

"For the first time in 16 years the birth of this legend of reggae music went without the regular celebration that ordinarily takes place at Independence Park, Savanna-la-mar, Westmoreland. Worrell King, who has been organising the free tribute from its inception, said the cancellation came as a result of insufficient co-operation from members of Peter Tosh's family who would not endorse this year's celebration. It has always been that King would receive a verbal endorsement, but this year none was forthcoming from the Tosh family who wanted to host the birthday tribute in Belmont. Unfortunately the police turned down the application to host the show there, since the space would have been inadequate for the expected crowd. King lamented, 'For over 16 years we did not exploit Peter Tosh in any way, shape or form. Instead we always highlighted him. For the first time, this year is proof that Peter Tosh really died.'"

It's easy to overstate the importance of the Internet in determining how well a person is remembered, but Peter Tosh is a supreme example of how popular opinion can outweigh years of largely unfavourable press and neglect of all kinds. Since file sharing began in earnest, fans have continued to post, repost and trawl through a vast archive of documentary material featuring songs, videos, live performances, photographs, interviews, foreign documentaries, excerpts from television shows and every other form of memorabilia you can think of. There are now endless blogs and websites devoted to him, and we can download virtually everything he ever recorded within minutes. It's been Peter's own charisma and the power of his music that's won him such a huge global following, and not astute marketing by his record companies or the concerted efforts of his family. His fans have spoken and it's now surely time for someone to take matters in hand, and give proper shape to how Peter Tosh is remembered in future. A law firm in Los Angeles currently administers his estate and whilst a lot remains to be done, there are signs of a cohesive structure at last. Shortly before this book went to print, they invited enquiries from parties interested in becoming political advocacy partners.

"Partnering with Greenpeace, Amnesty International and other advocacy organisations, Tosh's music will be used as a rallying cry for activists in campaigns from Greenpeace International, Students for a Sensible Drug Policy and the Marijuana Policy Project. The campaign will spotlight Legacy Edition reissues of Tosh's albums *Legalise It* and *Equal Rights*, with Amnesty International offering downloads of the Tosh classic 'Get Up Stand Up' to anyone getting involved in the case of Mexican journalist Lydia Cacho, who received death threats following her expose of a child pornography ring."

"As we face the new century there is no better message than 'Get Up Stand Up,'" said Martin Lloyd, marketing communications manager for Greenpeace International. "Peter Tosh's music has inspired activists around the world not to give up the fight for a green and peaceful future."

Karen Scott, manager of music relations for Amnesty International, said 'Get Up Stand Up' was regularly played at various Amnesty International music events and tours, and "continues to be a musical call to action for people worldwide to fight for dignity and freedom. Peter Tosh was a true pioneer and, like Amnesty International's activists, his music and legacy march on and continue to demand human rights and justice."

The Steppin' Razor's reputation is undergoing a major overhaul but then singers like him, who stand up to authority and are unafraid of telling a few home truths – especially about racism, colonialism and the rights of poor people – seem a lot less dangerous from a distance of 30 years or more. Whilst the causes of his grievances remain, even the Jamaican government felt assured enough to pay tribute eventually. In August 2012, amidst her country's 50th anniversary celebrations, Prime Minister Portia Simpson Miller recommended Peter receive the Order Of Merit "for his seminal contribution to the evolution of Jamaican popular music". The O.M is Jamaica's third highest honour, and he and Bob Marley are the only two reggae artists to have ever received this distinction. Whisper it quietly, but after awarding Peter Tosh his place in the pantheon of reggae greats – and by government appointment no less – Jamaica too, may finally be coming of age.

Index

483

Collins, Michael C 362–363, 378–379, 431
Cordell, Denny 108, 127, 136
Cowan, Tommy 139–142

Davidson, Janet 346–347, 350, 352, 360,
    398, 405–406, 412–413, 415–416
Davis, Carlton "Santa" 139, 159, 328, 342,
    344, 354, 394, 406, 417, 420, 448, 452,
    456
Dillon, Leonard "Sparrow" 38, 103
Dixon, "Free I" 450, 452–454, 460
Dixon, Joy 451–454, 456, 470
Dodd, Clement "Coxsone" 30–31, 33–34,
    36–38, 40–43, 45–52, 84, 96, 118, 129,
    248
Downie, Tyrone 125, 132, 159, 163, 410,
    417
Dunbar, Sly 162, 165, 170, 174, 194, 200,
    202–203, 209–210, 215–216, 235,
    243–244, 246, 248, 252, 266, 271, 277,
    320, 326–327, 463
Dylan, Bob 49, 114, 144, 157, 174, 225

Epstein, Michael "Eppy" 182, 188, 190, 218,
    241, 255, 258, 312–313, 445–446

Fagan, Kate 350, 372, 385–387
Forbes, Copeland 334, 337, 340, 346, 354,
    398, 403, 406, 408, 411–413
Forde, Brinsley 97–98
Fullwood, George "Fully" 328, 342, 350

Gale, Eric 132
Galuten, Albhy 134–135
Gaye, Marvin 123–124, 169, 280, 407, 416
Gibbs, Joe 52, 89–92, 203, 423
Golding, Steve 329, 342, 350
Green, Cherry 40
Griffiths, Marcia 124, 239, 357, 372
Guthrie, Gwen 211, 243, 254, 279, 304,
    319, 323–324

Hall, Pam 421, 443
Harvey, Bernard "Touter" 100, 212
Heavy Manners 350, 372, 376, 387–388
Higgs, Joe 20, 24, 28–29, 34–35, 40, 56,
    113, 115–117, 141, 174, 375
Hinds, David 418–419
Hinze, Chris 285–286

Jacksons, The 129–130, 142
Jaffe, Lee 101, 107, 113, 125–127, 130, 134,
    137–139, 144, 150, 152–154, 156–159,
    162–164, 205
Jagger, Mick 48, 110, 128, 190, 192,
    197–199, 204, 206, 208–215, 217, 219,
    221–223, 231–232, 234, 236, 241–242,
    252, 255, 258–259, 262–263, 272–273,
    282, 290–291, 293, 297, 311–312, 315,
    367, 423, 459
Jenkins, Arthur 59, 61, 72–73

Karbi, Ras 150, 166, 270, 333, 416, 432–
    434
Kelso, Beverley 25, 31–34, 36–40, 44–45,
    68, 87
Khouri, Paul 60, 472
Kimsey, Chris 249, 340–341, 343–345
Kinsey, Donald 139, 156–157, 167–168,
    206, 210, 215, 217–218, 223, 261–262,
    280, 328–329, 340, 342–344, 348, 350,
    358, 362, 379, 383, 385–388, 393, 409,
    413–414, 417,
Kong, Leslie 28, 79–81, 248
Kurfirst, Gary 139, 154, 156
Kuti, Fela 336–337, 413

Lee, Bunny "Striker" 28, 52, 76, 78, 83, 91,
    180, 229, 327
Lewis, Roger 100
Lindo, Earl "Wya" 89, 108, 163, 165, 175
Lobban, Dennis "Leppo" 436–437, 443–445,
    448–451, 455, 457, 460, 464–466, 471
Locksley, Gichie 97–98
Lodge, J. C 410, 421, 423–424
Lyn, Robbie 190–191, 200, 228, 232, 237,
    311, 342, 463

McDonald, Larry 205, 281
McGrath, Earl 188, 197, 204, 214, 233, 240,
    297
McLagan, Ian 212, 214
Mahal, Taj 126, 156
Manley, Michael 69–70, 94–95, 123, 126,
    142–143, 152–153, 161–162, 168, 176,
    192–193, 201, 287, 289, 295–296, 396,
    459
Marley, Bob 27–32, 34, 37–40, 42–46, 49,
    51–52, 55–56, 58, 60, 63, 68, 71, 78–
    81, 86–88, 93–96, 102, 109, 111, 113–
    114, 116, 118–119, 123–125, 128–129,